D1395437

# ADOLESCENT DEVELOPMENT AND ADJUSTMENT

**SECOND EDITION**

Lester D. Crow, Ph.D.
*Brooklyn College*

Alice Crow, Ph.D.
*Formerly, Brooklyn College*

## McGraw-Hill Book Company
*New York*
*St. Louis*
*San Francisco*
*Toronto*
*London*

# ADOLESCENT DEVELOPMENT AND ADJUSTMENT

# Preface

Adolescence is an important period in the life of an individual. Regardless of the country of his origin, the adolescent undergoes basic changes during this stage of his growth and development. Moreover, his life adjustment is much affected by the cultural and environmental factors that constantly influence him. He is commanding increasing attention from all adults who are concerned with his personal and social welfare. Since the publication, about a decade ago, of *Adolescent Development and Adjustment,* considerable progress has been made in the study of the behavior and problems of present-day teen-agers. The authors' purpose in this second edition is to incorporate into the material some of the significant findings of recent research in the field.

In this edition, much attention is given to the impact on the developing individual of his widening experiences in a rapidly changing world. Living conditions are becoming so complex that a maturing young person needs to gain increasing power of adaptation in order to meet new situations. However, since adolescent behavior continues to have its roots in childhood growth patterns and to affect later experience, no attempt is made to present a sharp demarcation between childhood and adolescence or between adolescence and adulthood.

The emphasis throughout the second edition is on the positive approach. Suggestions are offered to students, teachers, and other adults who are interested in helping adolescents develop their potentialities for wholesome living. The discussion centers around what can be expected of the normal adolescent in his growth, development, and education; yet deviations among them also receive attention.

Parts I and II are devoted to a consideration of the significance of the biological and cultural bases of adolescent behavior tendencies, the techniques used to study adolescent behavior, the sequential patterning of physical and physiological growth, maturing mental abilities, changing emotional patterns, and personal and social aspects of personality development.

Various inherent and environmental factors that serve as motivators of adolescent attitudes and behavior, including those of the developing sex urge, adolescent deviations, conflicts, and behavior disorders, are given consideration in Part III. An exploration of the present problem of delinquent behavior and a comparison with problems of ten and twenty years ago are included. This part concludes with a discussion of the adolescent's personal, religious, and moral values.

Part IV deals with the problems that adolescents meet in their family, school, vocational, and social living. Even though few adolescents experience major crises in these areas, many of them encounter numerous minor thwartings, frustrations, or conflicts. The authors have drawn heavily on current research in attempting to clarify the more common problems of adolescents.

Special exercises are included in the Questions and Problems for Discussion found at the end of each chapter. These special exercises are intended to give the student firsthand experience in working with and studying adolescents at different stages in their development.

The authors wish to take this opportunity to thank all who have given permission for the use of their material in this book.

LESTER D. CROW
ALICE CROW

# Contents

## Part One. Adolescent Experiences

## Part Two. Adolescent Development

## Part Three. Adolescent Behavior Motivations

# List of Figures

# List of Tables

# Part 1

## ADOLESCENT EXPERIENCES

# Chapter One
## Significance
## of Adolescence

Young people between the ages of 12 and 20 constitute more than one-sixth of the world population. Increasing birth rates indicate that this proportion will continue to grow larger. Every adolescent should be given an opportunity to develop wholesome, personally satisfying, and socially acceptable physical and mental status and emotional and social adjustment. Adolescent development and adjustment are matters of serious concern not only to parents but also to school people and other adults who are interested in the welfare of young people as well as in the progress of society. Youth represents the energy of the present and the hope of the future. It is imperative, therefore, that parents and educators gain as much understanding as possible concerning the various characteristics, needs, interests, and growth potentialities of maturing adolescents.

## Characteristics of the Adolescent Period

The first six years of a child's life are considered by psychologists to constitute the period during which are formed the basic attitudes, habits, and controls of self that are likely to help or hinder the youngster's future development and adjustment. From the early years of childhood, growth and maturation can be expected to follow a relatively general and continuous pattern. At the same time, individual variations occur as a result of differences in inherited potential and environmental stimulation. Physiological and environmental changes that are experienced during the later years of childhood may represent a series of climactic conditions that would seem to interfere with growth continuity and bring about a kind of "rebirth," characterized by new impulses and urges, interests and attitudes, and ambitions and behavior patterns. The validity of this concept of adolescence can be tested by a study of adolescent characteristics in comparison with those of childhood and adulthood.

### The Adolescent Age

The term *adolescence* is derived from the Latin verb *adolescere* which means "to grow up." The period of transition from childhood to adulthood or from dependence on adult direction and protection to self-direction and self-determination is referred to variously as adolescence, adolescent age, or adolescent period of development.

The length of time generally recognized as a transition from childhood to adulthood varies with differing cultures. In modern Western societies adolescence includes the years approximately from age 12 to 19 or older. This period sometimes is called the teen-age years. Preadolescence refers to those years of late childhood when definite physiological changes are taking place which, during the early years of adolescence, or the *pubertal* stage, bring about the development of sexual maturation. The age at which sexual maturity is achieved varies with the individual, however. Among girls, pubertal changes may begin as early as age 10, or be delayed until age 15 or later. Boys tend to develop sexually later than girls; hence sexual maturity among males usually does not occur before age 11, and may be delayed until age 16.

Mental maturity is reached during adolescence. The age at which an individual becomes emotionally and socially mature varies. In some cases emotional control and social adaptability are evidenced during the early adolescent years; relatively few individuals give little evidence of maturity in these developmental aspects during all or much of their adult life. Reaching the age 18 to 21 usually gives the citizen of a democracy the right to vote. Society then accepts him as an adult, even though he may be emotionally and socially immature.

## Theories of Adolescence

During the present century there has been evidenced a tremendous interest in the adolescent period of development. Many varying theories have been promulgated concerning adolescence.[1] G. Stanley Hall, often referred to as the father of adolescent psychology, based his conclusions concerning this period of development on his theory of recapitulation, according to which the individual passes through those stages that are characteristic of the history of mankind. He regarded adolescence as a period of "storm and stress." He emphasized the importance of the developmental process and underplayed the effect of environmental influences on the developing individual.

Hall's work did initiate further study of adolescence, but later theorists disagreed with him and among themselves concerning the meaning and characteristics of adolescence. Yet certain aspects of individual development are generally accepted. Muuss lists these as follows:

[1] For a review of some of the major theories, consult Rolf E. Muuss, *Theories of Adolescence,* Random House, Inc., New York, 1962.

The most widely accepted assumption is that childhood, adolescence, and adulthood are three periods which can be recognized psychologically and sociologically, and even physiologically. It is also accepted that there are individual as well as cultural differences in the length of adolescence and the age at onset and end. The earlier maturing of girls is generally recognized. The physiological changes of pubescence are frequently used to determine the beginning, while sociological criteria, namely adult status, duties, and privileges, as well as marriage, end of education, and economic independence are most frequently cited for the end of that period. Termination of adolescence depends primarily on the requirements and conditions of the culture. It occurs earlier in primitive cultures and later in more civilized ones.[2]

## Differences among Adolescents

Friedenberg describes adolescence thus:

Adolescence is the period during which a young person learns who he is, and what he really feels. It is a time in which he differentiates himself from the culture; though on the culture's terms. It is the age at which, by becoming a person in his own right, he becomes capable of deeply felt relationships to other individuals, perceived clearly as such.[3]

We know, however, that no two individuals are exactly alike in any phase of their total personality. At no age period are these differences more apparent than during adolescent years. Personal, social, and economic factors are powerful molders of adolescent attitudes. Concerning the bases of differences among adolescents Hemming says:

A great body of research has served to establish the wide range of human variability. Children differ from one another in attributes, potentialities, and pace of development; there is only a particular individual passing through the years of adolescence under the formative impact of the particular culture in which he happens to be living.[4]

What, then, are some of the ways in which young people differ from one another? Let us imagine that a cross-sectional procession of youth is passing before us as we watch them march along. What are they like? Some are tall and some are short. Some are stout and some are slender.

[2] Ibid., p. 163.

[3] Edgar Z. Friedenberg, The Vanishing Adolescent, reprinted by permission of the Beacon Press, copyright © 1959, Edgar Z. Friedenberg, p. 9.

[4] James Hemming, Problems of Adolescent Girls, William Heinemann, Ltd., London, 1960, pp. 8–9.

Some are graceful and some are awkward. Some are well dressed and well groomed, and some are slovenly and unattractive in appearance. Some are strong and healthy, and some are weak and puny. Some seem to be mature beyond their age and others are still children. There are those among them who swing along in the full glory of adolescent strength and beauty, with chins up and dreams of conquest in their eyes. Others, with timid feet and bowed heads, appear to have difficulty in keeping up with the procession. A few others lag behind, as if hesitant to join the procession, as if bewildered and fearful of what is ahead.

These young people represent differing degrees of economic security or insecurity. They are the products of many national, cultural, and religious backgrounds. As they move along we realize that they already have experienced varying degrees of success or failure. They possess great potentialities for good or evil. Unless their ardor has been dampened by unfortunate childhood experiences, they are equipped with boundless energy and enthusiasm, are looking to us for help in achieving the ideals and ambitions toward which they are striving. Teen-agers are sensitive to any actual or imagined characteristics that would seem to set them apart from their age peers. They are especially responsive to apparent lack or inferiority in any area of personal or social status that is governed by adolescent standards of acceptability.

Some observable differences among adolescents may be extremely important to young people during their growing-up years, but lose their significance by the time adult status is achieved. Other adolescent characteristics exercise an influence upon the total life patterns of those who possess them. Consequently, whether adolescents will be fitted to meet adult responsibilities successfully and to experience good personal and social adjustments depends in part upon the kind of guidance they receive during the preadult period and the kinds of adult behavior examples to which they are exposed. The future is theirs. What they will make of that future is society's responsibility as well as theirs.

## Adolescent "Problem" Areas

Since the teen years represent a period in an individual's life of finding himself as a person, there is likely to be more or less struggle within the maturing adolescent as he attempts to determine his rights and responsibilities in his relationships with adults and within his peer groups. Adolescence is not necessarily, as was believed at one time, a period of constant stress and strain. Some young people are helped to experience a gradual, relatively peaceful, and successful continuum of development from early childhood to adulthood. There are conditions and situations in the lives of most teen-agers, however, when the apparent thwarting of strong urges, impulses, or ambitions may stimulate the arousal of severe emotional disturbance.

## Problems at Different Age Periods

We have stressed the fact that adolescent growth and maturation constitute a continuing process. Yet for the purpose of study we can assume that within the total growing-up process there are several stages, each of which represents a cumulative amount and kind of change that differentiate it from the stages that have preceded it and that can be expected to follow it. For example, it would be difficult, if not impossible, to determine the exact amount of maturation that has taken place in any young person during a week, a month, or even a year, except for such phases of development as weight, height, and body proportions; it usually is possible, however, to recognize changes in attitudes, skill performance, and behavior patterns if we make a comparative study of a relatively average young person (there is no "normal" child or adolescent) at the ages of 8, 11, 14, and 17. For convenience we can term these ages as representative of childhood, preadolescence, early adolescence, and later adolescence, respectively.

Recognizing the fact that these developmental stages apply to large unselected groups rather than to particular individuals, we discover that general as well as specific problems of adjustment are peculiarly characteristic of each stage of the developmental process. Some adjustment trends, however, may be pervasive from preadolescence through later adolescence. Whether certain tendencies persist depends in part upon the kind and extent of preparation the young adolescent has received during childhood for the physical, emotional, and social changes which he will soon begin to experience.

## Problems Associated with Sexual Maturing

The physical and psychological accompaniments of achieving sexual maturity provide the background for many of the problem situations encountered by preadolescents and young adolescents who have not been prepared by intelligent and tactful adults for the onset of pubescence. It is normal for the child to be interested in his body functions, the meaning of marriage, the process of birth, and other matters dealing with sex. His curiosity is intensified to the extent that he comes to recognize the fact that he is not supposed to think or talk about such things. The information or misinformation that he acquires from other young people may result in the development of attitudes of fear or disgust, or may stimulate the urge to experiment, alone or with other children, in fumbling and unsatisfying sexual behavior. Moreover, the unprepared adolescent may suffer extreme embarrassment or anxiety that is caused by changes in body contour, unaccustomed aches and pains that are passed over lightly by his parents as "growing pains," and newly experienced urges and impulses, especially in relation to members of the opposite sex. The boy's first erection and discharge of semen, or the girl's first menstrual flow, may become emotionally charged incidents in the young person's life.

## Problems Associated with Changing Attitudes

Regardless of whether a young person is helped to accept and to adjust satisfactorily to his changing physical and physiological status, he is likely to encounter problem situations that are rooted in his increasing awareness of himself as a person in his own right rather than as merely the child of his parents. With self-awareness comes the struggle for self-realization. He begins to want to make his own decisions and to experience freedom of action. He no longer regards himself as a child; he demands independence, but often discovers that he is not yet ready to manage his own affairs. He needs adult help in solving his many emotional, social, and other adjustment problems; yet he may resent adult assistance when it is offered him. The many and different areas of adolescent problems are treated in detail throughout this book in terms of their specific applications. Two such studies are presented here.

Luella Cole and Irma N. Hall [5] have grouped adolescent goals with their accompanying problems into nine categories: general emotional maturity, establishment of heterosexual interests, general social maturity, emancipation from home control, intellectual maturity, selection of an occupation, uses of leisure time, philosophy of life, and identification of self. Cole further indicates in table form the various kinds of transitions that can be, are, or fail to be effected during the years between childhood and adolescence (see Table 1).

Hemming [6] based his study of the problems of adolescent girls on the contents of letters submitted by 3,259 girls to a weekly British periodical from April, 1953, to March 31, 1955. Since some of the writers included more than one "worry" in their letters, the total number of problems

[5] Luella Cole and Irma N. Hall, *Psychology of Adolescence*, 6th ed., Holt, Rinehart and Winston, Inc., New York, 1964, pp. 6–7.
[6] Hemming, *op. cit.*, pp. 15–17, 32–35, 38–50.

*Table 1.* Goals of the Adolescent Period

| FROM | TOWARD |
|---|---|
| **General Emotional Maturity** | |
| 1. Destructive expressions of emotion | 1. Harmless or constructive expressions |
| 2. Subjective interpretation of situations | 2. Objective interpretations of situations |
| 3. Childish fears and motives | 3. Adult stimuli to emotions |
| 4. Habits of escaping from conflicts | 4. Habits of facing and solving conflicts |
| **Establishment of Heterosexual Interests** | |
| 1. Exclusive interest in members of same sex | 1. Normal interest in members of opposite sex |
| 2. Experience with many possible mates | 2. Selection of one mate |
| 3. Acute awareness of sexual development | 3. Casual acceptance of sexual maturity |
| **General Social Maturity** | |
| 1. Feelings of uncertainty of acceptance by peers | 1. Feelings of secure acceptance by peers |
| 2. Social awkwardness | 2. Social poise |
| 3. Social intolerance | 3. Social tolerance |
| 4. Slavish imitation of peers | 4. Freedom from slavish imitation |
| **Emancipation from Home Control** | |
| 1. Close parental control | 1. Self-control |
| 2. Reliance upon parents for security | 2. Reliance upon self for security |
| 3. Identification with parents as models | 3. Attitude toward parents as friends |
| **Intellectual Maturity** | |
| 1. Blind acceptance of truth on the basis of authority | 1. Demand for evidence before acceptance |
| 2. Desire for facts | 2. Desire for explanations of facts |
| 3. Many temporary interests | 3. Few, stable interests |
| **Selection of an Occupation** | |
| 1. Interest in glamorous occupations | 1. Interest in practicable occupations |
| 2. Interest in many occupations | 2. Interest in one occupation |
| 3. Overestimation or underestimation of one's own abilities | 3. Reasonably accurate estimate of one's own abilities |
| 4. Irrelevance of interests to abilities | 4. Reconciliation of interests and abilities |
| **Uses of Leisure** | |
| 1. Interest in vigorous, unorganized games | 1. Interest in team games and intellectual contests |
| 2. Interest in individual prowess | 2. Interest in success of team |
| 3. Participation in games | 3. Spectator interest in games |
| 4. Interest in many hobbies | 4. Interest in one or two hobbies |
| 5. Membership in many clubs | 5. Membership in few clubs |
| **Philosophy of Life** | |
| 1. Indifference toward general principles | 1. Interest in and understanding of general principles |
| 2. Behavior dependent upon specific, learned habits | 2. Behavior guided by moral principles |
| 3. Behavior based upon gaining pleasure and avoiding pain | 3. Behavior based upon conscience and duty |

*Table 1.* Goals of the Adolescent Period (*Continued*)

FROM                                          TOWARD

Identification of Self

1. Little or no perception of self

2. Little idea of other people's perception of self

3. Identification of self with impossible goals

1. Moderately accurate perception of self

2. Good idea of other people's perception of self

3. Identification of self with possible goals

SOURCE: Luella Cole and Irma N. Hall, *Psychology of Adolescence*, 6th ed., Holt, Rinehart and Winston, Inc., New York, 1964, pp. 6–7.

classified was 3,738. These were reported by girls presumably over 10 years of age. The four main categories are presented in Table 2.

*Table 2.* Number and Proportions of Problems in the Main Categories: Friendship, Home, School, and Personal*

| MAIN CATEGORY | NUMBER | PERCENTAGES | RANK ORDER |
|---|---|---|---|
| Friendship........... | 1,351 | 36.1 | 1 |
| Home............... | 817 | 21.9 | 3 |
| School.............. | 443 | 11.9 | 4 |
| Personal............ | 1,127 | 30.1 | 2 |
| Total............. | 3,738 | 100.0 | |

* Because of the organization of the periodical, vocational problems, except as related to parent-adolescent conflict, are not included.

SOURCE: James Hemming, *Problems of Adolescent Girls*, William Heinemann, Ltd., London, 1960, p. 33.

The four main categories of problems were further classified into 22 subcategories and 227 sub-subcategories. The 22 subcategories are presented in Table 3.

For an adolescent to realize successfully all the objectives included in these and similar studies would involve the experiencing of many complex situations and conditions including numerous subtle elements of influence. Hence few, if any, adolescents can be expected to achieve complete maturity in every area of adjustment. Many young people manage to make good beginnings in all areas, however. Strong feelings of frustration and consequent adolescent conflict are likely to result when or if a young person is impelled to solve one or more problem situations associated with the gaining of adult status, but lacks the ability or opportunity to achieve his goal.

Vital statistics for the adolescent period indicate that the death rate during the later half of the period is very much higher than for the earlier years. Among the more significant causes of adolescent deaths can be

*Table 3.* Number and Proportions of Problems in Twenty-two Subcategories

| SUBCATEGORY | NUMBER | PER- CENTAGES | RANK ORDER |
|---|---|---|---|
| Friendship (girl-girl)..................... | 615 | 16.5 | 1 |
| Friendship (girl-boy)..................... | 494 | 13.2 | 2 |
| Crushes on older girls or adults............ | 242 | 6.5 | 4 |
| Difficulties with both parents.............. | 176 | 4.7 | 8 |
| Difficulties with mother................... | 173 | 4.6 | 9 |
| Difficulties with father................... | 74 | 2.0 | 18 |
| Difficulties with sister(s)................. | 108 | 2.8 | 13 |
| Difficulties with brother(s)................ | 103 | 2.7 | 14 |
| Difficulties with both siblings............. | 12 | 0.3 | 22 |
| Disagreement about bedtime............... | 45 | 1.2 | 20 |
| Other family problems.................... | 126 | 3.4 | 10 |
| Difficulties with authority at school........ | 109 | 2.9 | 12 |
| Difficulties with a particular subject at school. | 93 | 2.5 | 15 |
| Anxiety about school failure............... | 89 | 2.4 | 16 |
| Difficult contemporaries at school.......... | 50 | 1.3 | 19 |
| Problems of leadership.................... | 25 | 0.7 | 21 |
| Miscellaneous school problems............. | 77 | 2.1 | 17 |
| Anxieties about personal deportment........ | 367 | 9.8 | 3 |
| Anxiety about physical characteristics....... | 237 | 6.3 | 5 |
| Fears (other than examination fears)........ | 197 | 5.3 | 7 |
| Problems of dress and appearance........... | 126 | 3.4 | 10 |
| Other personal difficulties................. | 200 | 5.4 | 6 |
| Total................................. | 3,738 | 100.0 | |

SOURCE: James Hemming, *Problems of Adolescent Girls,* William Heinemann, Ltd., London, 1960, p. 34.

included accidents, heart diseases, tuberculosis, appendicitis, and pneumonia-influenza. The fast pace at which some adolescents live, carelessness concerning health status, and low physical resistance brought about by too great or unwise activity and emotional involvement represent some of the factors of youthful mortality rates.

## Effect of Environmental Conditions

As we consider adolescent problems of adjustment we should remember that we are living in a so-called "problem age." In sophisticated societies, newspapers, news reports over radio and television, lectures, books, and general group conversation constantly stress the political, social, and personal problems that are being experienced by individuals, groups, nations, and groups of nations. Emphasis usually is placed upon those problem areas that seem to elude solution, that involve the problem sufferers in legal action of one kind or another, or that would appear to be a threat to the welfare and security of society. Destructive factors in the lives of the citizenry provide more thrilling tidbits for popular consumption than do the many fine, constructive ideals, attitudes, and activities that are characteristic of the great majority of individuals. There probably are few adults who do not engage in problem solving in one or more areas of their life activities. By the great majority, however, difficulties of adjustment are taken in their stride; they are met and resolved more or less satisfactorily without making newspaper headlines.

The adjustment difficulties of teen-agers may differ little in seriousness from those suffered by adults, in spite of the fact that adolescent problems may seem to the adult to be of minor significance in comparison with those frustration situations to which he is exposed. Furthermore, many mature persons, as they review their adolescent days in retrospect, are amused by the conditions and situations that had seemed tragic to them during their growing-up years.

Adolescents suffer feelings of frustration, thwarting, and conflict in their struggle for status. These youth are still dependent upon their parents, yet they have the natural urge to be independent. Young people experience a wide gap between their desires and ambitions to become adults and their ability and readiness to make these yearnings realities. They are passing through a new phase of physical development and interpersonal relationships, and in this new state they make errors in judgment and experience embarrassing conditions that lead to thwarting and conflict. They have trouble in developing emotional control, self-discipline, and independence of action. Moreover, adolescents tend to dramatize themselves and their relationships with others. They must be helped to acquire some objectivity in self-understanding. Otherwise, they will find that their day-by-day attempts at self-assertion may be highly unrealistic. They will experience at one moment intense elation, at the next moment deep despair. An adolescent bewilders the elders who seek to understand him, so quickly does he pass from one emotional state to the next.

## Adult Attitudes toward Adolescent Problems

If the developmental progress is to be socially acceptable and effective, a young person's transition from childhood to adult status must proceed gradually under the guidance of self-disciplined adults. Too much and too suddenly gained liberty leads to adolescent confusion; the boy or girl may become the prey of destructive influences. Adult overprotection or domination may arouse in the teen-ager strong feelings of resentment, or it may result in retarded personal and social development. Also, adolescent confusion and conflict can be intensified as young people are exposed to contradictions between what adults say should be done and what they do. According to Bauer,

We advocate respect for authority while we disparage the public officials we helped to elect. We tell the adolescent he must respect the law while we bribe policemen. We tell him to be decent and honest and, above all, upright while we cheat on our income tax. We try to teach him the value of money while plunging ourselves more heavily into debt. We deny him an advance on next week's allowance while we use carte-blanche and apply for ready credit. We insist that he obtain the best education possible and we cooperate by voting down school budgets. We tell him about the dignity of an honest day's work and formulate plans for the twenty-hour week. We stress the importance of scientific and academic achievement while we make millionaires of our entertainers and paupers of our professors and arrange things in such a way that many teachers need outside employment to survive.[7]

## Need of Adult Insight

Many parents, with the assistance of other adults, can and do help young people achieve a desirable balance of security and individual freedom. Perhaps never in history have adults evidenced a greater interest in adolescent psychology and mental hygiene than is now apparent. There is danger, however, that with this increased concern for the welfare of young people there may develop an undue emphasis upon failure rather than upon success in achieving adolescent adjustment.

"What is wrong with our boys and girls?" "Young people have no respect for authority." "I have no control over my child; he will not listen to anything I say." "Juvenile delinquency is increasing daily." These and similar criticisms of young people have become the theme of newspaper and magazine articles and are a popular subject for general conversation. Many groups have been organized to help adolescents solve their problems of adjustment in our present culture. At first these groups limited their discussion to a survey of the known delinquencies. They admitted the existence of a youth problem but found it difficult to discover the causes and to agree upon the treatment of specific individuals. Gradually, however, they have been able to analyze some of the more potent factors of teen-age disturbance and are beginning to set up certain basic principles for the guidance of adolescent boys and girls toward desirable behavior controls.

[7] Francis C. Bauer, "Problems of Dependence and Independence," in William C. Bier, S.J. (ed.), *The Adolescent: His Search for Understanding*, Fordham University Press, New York, 1963, p. 148.

Such preventive measures constitute the fundamental means of assuring for young people the opportunity to develop good mental and emotional health, especially if they are begun in early childhood. At the same time, however, curative measures must be undertaken to recondition those adolescents who are evincing symptoms of asocial attitudes and behavior or who are beginning to break under the strains of achieving satisfactory adjustment.

## The Mental Health Approach

Mental health principles emphasize the value of preventing the development of unwholesome attitudes and behavior, and of preserving desirable habit patterns, as well as of curing observable evidence of inner conflict and maladjustment. Prevention of mental disorder and preservation of emotional stability are socially and economically satisfying both to the individual and to the group. Even though therapeutic procedures may be costly and difficult to apply, they are needed to rehabilitate those young people who, through society's indifference or neglect, have become maladjusted or nonconforming members of their groups.

Many young people are confronted by relatively serious problems connected with their homelife, their school experiences, their work activities, and their social relationships. The factors most commonly cited as those which are likely to predispose toward adolescent maladjustment include the following: economic instability, parental discord, inadequacy of school offerings, lack of understanding of adolescent psychology on the part of parents and school faculties, unwholesome neighborhood or community conditions, inadequate recreational facilities, unpreparedness for vocational activities, and unintelligent job placement.

A study of individual maladjustment indicates that no one of these factors, in and of itself, is necessarily a cause of asocial behavior. Sometimes the difficulty must be sought in a subtle blending of causes or in the interrelation that exists between the inherent nature of the individual and external factors. To one young person an economically underprivileged home may offer a challenge which will encourage him to develop within himself the power to improve these conditions. Another adolescent in a similar situation may become so discouraged by the apparent lack of opportunity to improve himself or his conditions that he will allow himself to be influenced toward undesirable ways of satisfying his natural longing for the comforts of life which are enjoyed by other young people.

The remaining chapters of this book are devoted to a detailed consideration of the many facets of adolescent experiences that have been indicated briefly in this chapter. Individuals may differ from what might be regarded as a more or less general pattern of development and adjustment. Some of those differences will be highlighted by means of examples of various deviations among young people.

## Questions and Problems for Discussion

1. Explain why the satisfaction of personal wants is important to the adolescent. Explain how both his needs and his wants can be satisfied without disturbance to himself and to others.
2. Indicate ways in which the factors that influence the adolescent often cause his life values to differ from those of his parents.
3. Present suggestions concerning the kind of education that might help adults better to prepare young people for entrance into adolescence.
4. Indicate at least three things that adults might do differently that would be of great help to maturing teen-agers.
5. Give reasons why there are many nonconforming adolescents today in light of the attention directed toward the solutions of their problems.
6. *Special Exercises:*
   a. Observe four children—two boys and two girls—between 5 and 8 years of age. Note especially (1) their general behavior, (2) their motives, (3) their attitudes toward their friends, (4) their attitudes toward their elders, including their parents and teachers. Record your observations.
   b. Observe four adolescents—two boys and two girls—between 12 and 16 years of age. Note especially (1) their general behavior, (2) their motives, (3) their attitudes toward their peers, (4) their attitudes toward their elders, including their parents and teachers. Record your observations.
   c. Compare your findings. Interpret the reasons for any differences noted between the two age groups.

## Selected References

Bernard, H. W.: *Adolescent Development in American Culture,* Harcourt, Brace & World, Inc., New York, 1957.

Cole, Luella, and Irma N. Hall: *Psychology of Adolescence,* 6th ed., Holt, Rinehart and Winston, Inc., New York, 1964.

Bier, William C., S.J. (ed.): *The Adolescent: His Search for Understanding,* Fordham University Press, New York, 1963.

Blos, P.: *On Adolescence,* The Free Press of Glencoe, New York, 1962.

Crow, Lester D., and Alice Crow *Readings in Child and Adolescent Psychology,* David McKay Company, Inc., New York, 1961.

Friedenberg, Edgar: *The Vanishing Adolescent,* Dell Publishing Co., Inc., New York, 1962.

Grinder, R. E.: *Studies in Adolescence: A Book of Readings,* The Macmillan Company, New York, 1963.

Horrocks, J. E.: *The Psychology of Adolescence,* 2d ed., Houghton Mifflin Company, Boston, 1962.

Hurlock, Elizabeth B.: *Adolescent*

*Development,* 3d ed., McGraw-Hill Book Company, New York, 1956.

Jersild, A. J.: *The Psychology of Adolescence,* 2d ed., The Macmillan Company, New York, 1963.

Kiell, N.: *Adolescent through Fiction,* International Universities Press, Inc., New York, 1960.

Kuhlen, R. G., and G. G. Thompson: *Psychological Studies of Human Development,* 2d ed., Appleton-Century-Crofts, Inc., New York, 1963.

Lorand, A. S., and H. I. Schneer ('eds.): *Adolescents,* Harper & Row, Publishers, Incorporated, New York, 1961.

McCandless, B. R.: *Children and Adolescents: Behavior and Development,* Holt, Rinehart and Winston, Inc., New York, 1961.

Malm, M., and O. G. Jamison: *Adolescence,* McGraw-Hill Book Company, New York, 1952.

Mohr, G. J., and Marian A. Despres: *The Stormy Decade: Adolescence,* Random House, Inc., New York, 1958.

Muuss, Rolf E.: *Theories of Adolescence,* Random House, Inc., New York, 1962.

National Society for the Study of Education, Forty-third Yearbook, part I, *Adolescence,* The University of Chicago Press, Chicago, 1944.

Remmers, H. H., and D. H. Radler: *American Teenager,* The Bobbs-Merrill Company, Inc., Indianapolis, 1957.

Rogers, Dorothy: *The Psychology of Adolescence,* Appleton-Century-Crofts, Inc., New York, 1962.

Schneiders, A. A.: *Personality Development and Adjustment in Adolescence,* The Bruce Publishing Company, Milwaukee, 1960.

Seidman, J.: *The Adolescent: A Book of Readings,* rev. ed., Holt, Rinehart and Winston, Inc., New York, 1960.

Stone, L. J., and J. Church: *Childhood and Adolescence,* Random House, Inc., New York, 1959.

Slaton, T. F.: *Dynamics of Adolescent Adjustment,* The Macmillan Company, New York, 1963.

# Chapter Two

## Biological and Cultural Heritage

From prehistoric times to the present, growth and maturation probably have followed relatively similar sequences. Physical, physiological, mental, and emotional potentialities have been and still are biologically inherited by way of family lines. The developmental and adjustive patterns of inherited potential, however, are rooted in the kind and amount of environmental stimulation that are experienced by a young person during his maturing years. The controversy among biologists, psychologists, and sociologists concerning the relative significance, in the life of a human being, of nature and nurture is significant in that it indicates the recognition given thereby to the fact that growing up is a complex process. Many factors, both within and outside an individual, are responsible for his ultimate adjustment in and to his group or groups.

## Factors of Adolescent Development

It was suggested earlier that there probably is no such human being as a "normal" child, adolescent, or adult. Studies of adolescent developmental patterns present evidence of the fact that general physical, mental, and emotional differences are characteristic of different age levels. For any individual, processes of growth and maturation tend to be relatively continuous from conception onward during the formative years. Developing attitudes and behavior patterns, however, are the resultants of multitudinous interactions that take place between a person's biologically inherited potentials and those situations, conditions, and individuals or groups of individuals that constitute his social heritage.

### Inherited Factors Influencing Development

Regardless of the societal group into which a child is born and in which he develops, he possesses at birth certain so-called "native characteristics" that identify him as a member of his particular family. The newborn infant is not only the child of his parents; he may be also the recipient of characteristics that are peculiar to the family line of either or both of his parents. Physically, mentally, and emotionally the growing boy or girl shows evidences of differences from, as well as likenesses to, his parents and his other immediate relatives. One need only observe the physical appearance, the exhibited degree of mental alertness, and the temperamental reactions of siblings, to recognize the potency of various factors of inheritance. It is not unusual for young parents to become extremely distressed by the fact that their second baby is very different in appearance and behavior from their first child during his babyhood.

Relatives and friends attempt to discover which parent the child "favors." Too often parents expect their children to mirror parental characteristics, especially if the possession of these qualities has been basic to parental success and good adjustment. A parent may refuse to admit that his child is different in some ways from himself. Consequently, the adult tries to mold the child according to his own personality pattern. If the parent is not successful in achieving his goal, he is likely to explain his failure in terms of situational influences associated with the attitudes and behavior of the other parent, with the educational system, or with general social deterioration. A parent of this kind may not or will not admit that his child is an individual.

Genetically induced differences and likenesses in physical appearance usually can be recognized early in the life of a child. Height, body contours, hair, skin, and eye coloring, and other physical characteristics may or may not be similar to those of either parent. Some family tendencies may begin to show themselves during childhood. Certain specific biologically inherited personality traits may not be evidenced in the attitudes and behavior of the individual until the later years of childhood or during adolescence, however. As these potentialities develop, parents sometimes come to believe that they do not know their own children. For example, Mary Cole began to teach at the age of 17. She had been bright as a child and a young adolescent, but extremely docile and submissive in her home and peer relations. One day Mary's mother visited her daughter at school while the girl's class was in session. The woman sat at the back of the room and watched her daughter's behavior in relation to her forty pupils. This parent, accustomed to regarding Mary as a dependent, retiring, and rather serious young person, received a tremendous shock. Surely this mature, completely poised, and humorous young woman could not be her "little child." Mary possessed the capacity for independent self-direction, but during her younger days she had not been stimulated to display it except in connection with her studies. The girl herself had not recognized her own powers until, as a teacher, she was challenged to use them.

## Environmental Factors Influencing Development

The preceding discussion concerning biological inheritance might lead the reader to conclude that the authors are hereditarians in that they seem to have placed much emphasis upon the significance of native endowment. Important as the natural potentialities of an individual are, they cannot be developed in a vacuum. Every newborn baby can be expected to grow and mature, yet the kind of adult that he will eventually become is dependent upon the kind and amount of environmental stimulation to which he is exposed during his developing years. Both biological inheritance and social heritage are effectors of accelerated, average, or retarded development. From the beginning of life, the growing and maturing young person is stimulated to respond to physical conditions and social custom in one way rather than in another way. He is motivated constantly to meet his physical, mental, emotional, and social needs, wants, urges, and ambitions according to socially acceptable standards. A young person's inherited potentialities are basic to his achieved degree of ease and success of adaptation to the societal mores and customs by which he is surrounded. At the same time, his development or learning is limited in terms of the opportunities that are available to him during the crucial years of childhood and adolescence.

## Adolescent Status in Primitive Cultures

Since prehistoric days the role of an adolescent in his society has varied with the cultural concept of what constitutes change from childhood to adulthood, as well as how a young person should be prepared to assume adult responsibilities. Adolescence as a developmental period that may last from six to eight years or longer is peculiar to our present cultural pattern. Among primitive peoples an immediate transition from childhood to adulthood was considered to take place during puberty or the period of sexual maturation. Hence, although the adolescent period might be brief, it was regarded as a crucial point. The attaining of sexual maturity usually was the criterion according to which all forms of adolescent development were measured.

## Pubertal Rites

During the pubertal period, formal and rigid pubic rites or ceremonies were conducted by the elders of sexually maturing boys and girls. For several weeks or months a young person was subjected to various "tests" to determine fitness for the assumption of adult status. The advent of sexual maturity meant that the relatively unrestrained activities of childhood were supposed to be supplanted by controlled behavior and active participation in adult affairs.

## The Boy's Preparation for Adulthood

The boy was tested for strength, physical endurance, courage, and ability to endure physical pain. He was tortured in many ways: he was usually isolated from other members of the tribe; he was forced to endure exposure, hunger, thirst, and extreme heat; he was circumcised; he was subjected to physical pain through body laceration, tattooing, knocking out of teeth, and other forms of body maltreatment; he also might be put through humiliating experiences in the presence of his age peers and his elders.

If the boy passed these preliminary tests, he received intensive instruction concerning tribal institutions and customs, and his responsibilities and privileges as a male adult of his particular society. Allegiance to, and membership in, a family unit changed to group membership and allegiance. The young man assumed the right to fight and to hunt with other male adults, and the privilege to marry, raise a family, and become the head of his family unit. The newly initiated male adult also was permitted to garb himself appropriately for adult status, to change his body appearance in accordance with tribal custom, and to carry hunting implements or war weapons.

Failure to pass any of the preliminary tests of endurance returned the boy to his family as still a child; he suffered the humiliation of being excluded from participation in the activities of the boys in his peer group who had earned adult status. Since he had been adjudged a "weakling," his parents shared in his disgrace. Consequently, most parents refrained from pampering their son during childhood years lest he fail to pass the rigid tests associated with the pubic ceremonies. Although young boys were not expected to engage in adult activities, they were encouraged by their parents to develop strong, healthy bodies and to achieve self-control and physical endurance in preparation for the ordeal of initiation into manhood.

## The Girl's Preparation for Adulthood

In primitive society, initiation rites associated with the assumption of adult status were much less rigorous for the sexually maturing girl than for the boy. She was prepared by her mother and tested by the women of the group in the kinds of activities that represented the duties and responsibilities of a wife and mother. She also was encouraged to develop womanly "wiles" as a means of attracting the attention of eligible young tribesmen. Like the boy, she was expected to discard childish interests with the coming of puberty, and immediately to display mature attitudes, emotional control, and adult behavior patterns.

In many of the simple cultures a woman was regarded as "unclean" during her menstrual period. This attitude applied especially to a girl's first menses. At this time she usually was isolated from the other members of the group. It was the custom in some tribes to remove the girl from her family and to place her, for several weeks or a month, in a hut which was completely closed except for a small opening through which water and food were passed to her. At the end of this period of relative or entire solitude, the girl's parents arranged dances, feasts, and special ceremonies to indicate that their daughter had reached adult status and was eligible for marriage.

With the beginning of the pubertal period girls were restricted in their behavior. Rigid taboos were placed upon their association with members of the opposite sex. Boys were allowed some freedom in sexual activities, but the chastity of the girl was rigidly protected by parents and group leaders. Among most of the early peoples, as well as in later cultural groups, premarital and extramarital sex-stimulated behavior was condoned for males but strongly disapproved for females, sometimes to the point of expulsion from the societal group.

## Life Values in Simple Cultures

The primitive child's freedom is restricted to a certain extent by his lack of opportunities within the family environment to engage in activities that go beyond accepted convention. Moreover, adult responsibilities also follow relatively simple routines. The boy and the man become well acquainted with their physical environment. From it the adult male must wrest food and other life necessities for himself and his family. Primitive warfare represents face-to-face combat. Recreational outlets are limited to participating in, or watching, physical feats of skill, games, dancing, and similar activities. Girls are inducted early into an appreciation of the female role of childbearing and rearing, housekeeping and home management, and submissiveness. Their duties may entail much physical activity, but the work is relatively simple and follows a traditional pattern of performance.

Since primitive culture usually represents a handing down from generation to generation of customs and mores that are modified only gradually, the transition from childhood to adulthood may seem to be a simple matter for which little preparation is needed and which can be achieved with little of the stressful experience and conflict arousal that are relatively common among modern adolescents. In a conventional society the individual can exercise only a minimum of freedom of choice in the conduct of his daily affairs. His activities are controlled by the accepted mores and taboos of his people. He may experience security in these restrictions.

Since he knows no other way of ordering his affairs, he is willing to pattern his life activities according to the standards set for him by his elders.

The wants and needs of the average primitive young person are simple and usually satisfied easily. Hunting, engaging in warfare, and performing feats of physical skill and prowess afford him opportunities for utilizing youthful energy and for satisfying the urge for adventure. In spite of taboos concerning sex-stimulated behavior, there is found among most simple peoples a frank and accepting attitude toward the role of sex in the life of the individual or the group. Facts concerning the sexual organs and sexual functions are not shrouded in the mystery that is characteristic of more "civilized" cultures.

## Adjustment Problems of Youth

Although in some simple cultures adolescence and young adulthood may seem to be relatively tranquil periods of transition, it cannot be concluded that all primitive young people are free from "growing-up" difficulties. The young male is free to choose a mate and start a home, but he must be able to present satisfactory evidence of his ability to provide a suitable home for the girl of his choice. The girl is ready for mating, but she and her family may experience difficulties in their attempts to mate her with an acceptable young man. Among some primitive groups class distinctions and taboo limitations, especially those that reflect cultural attitudes toward heterosexual relations, are the bases of youthful turbulence and conflict that are as serious as those experienced by modern young people in their attempts to adjust to existing societal standards.

At this point, we may note briefly the emotional effects upon young people from present-day simpler societies when their traditional beliefs and customs come into juxtaposition with youthful attitudes and behavior patterns that are habitual in so-termed "higher forms of civilization." Improved and increasingly far-reaching means of world travel and communication, in conjunction with war-induced contacts of young people who possess different cultural backgrounds, are posing problems of assimilation and cultural leveling. Increased spread to every part of the world of certain elements of modern Western culture now has stimulated new approaches toward self-realization and culture evaluation among more traditionally reared young people. Much of existing youthful unrest and confusion can be explained as the predictable outgrowth of conflict between democratic ideals and rigid traditional convention.

We sometimes attempt to explain difficulties experienced by our adolescents as rooted in their misunderstanding and misuse of the democratic culture in which they have been reared. How much greater must be the stresses, the frustrations, and the conflicts experienced by those young people who have been reared in a culture that is very different from our own. These youths become aware of the differences without fully understanding what they are and how they can be applied to their own life patterns. Consequently, youthful struggles for freedom from traditional conventions, for greater and different educational opportunities, and for self-realization and self-direction are resulting in conflicts between young people and their tradition-indoctrinated elders. Increasing intercommunication over a period of years may be needed before the leveling process is completed to the point that difference in cultural background will constitute a negligible factor in adolescent development and adjustment.

## The Adolescent and Greek and Roman Cultures

In relatively modified form some primitive attitudes toward transition from childhood to adulthood continued to persist. The trend in early historical cultures, however, was toward extending the period of adolescence beyond that of primitive peoples. Attention gradually came to be given to criteria other than sexual maturity by which to measure the attaining of adult status.

The Greeks and Romans recognized the significance in their respective cultures of producing young men and women who were adequately prepared to assume their appropriate adult functions. Differing cultural emphases tended to bring about differences in adolescent training programs. We shall now describe briefly adolescent experiences in Sparta, Athens, and Rome.

### Growing up in Sparta

Like primitive youths, Spartan boys were expected to become physically strong and virile soldiers who would fight successful wars for their country. During their growing years they were subjected to rigorous training that would fit them to endure hardships, to develop a spirit of bravery and of complete loyalty to their nation, and to accept suffering of any kind. Emphasis was placed upon the girls' physical strength and good health in order that they might later bear strong, healthy sons. Although Spartan women were not expected to participate in war combat, they were rigidly disciplined during girlhood so that they would be worthy mates of their soldier-husbands. No child of a good Spartan family was coddled or pampered, even during early childhood days. In fact, newborn babies who appeared to lack promise of becoming stalwart men of war, or worthy mothers of soldiers, supposedly were allowed to die as the result of exposure to the death-inducing elements of nature. Physically fit boys and girls were reared by their mothers until they were 7 and 8 years old, respectively. From 7 to 20, boys lived in public barracks where they received professional training to become soldiers. Until the age of 30 they received practical army experience at frontier posts. They then were admitted to full citizenship and compelled to marry, although they continued to live in the barracks and participated in the military training of boys. Although girls and women stayed in the home, where they learned from their mothers about home management, they received gymnastic training as well, in order to help them become strong and robust mothers of healthy, virile sons. The academic education of adolescents was limited to the rote memorization of a few selections from Homer and the laws of Lycurgus, except for what the boys could learn from listening to the conversation of older, experienced men.

## Growing up in Athens

Athens probably represents the first cultural group in which the child and the adolescent were recognized to be individuals and in which parents were given some freedom of decision concerning the education of their sons. As in Sparta, unpromising infants were "exposed." Accepted children of both sexes were reared together in the home by mothers and nurses. Self-control and good discipline were stressed, but the youngsters engaged in much free play. At the age of 7, girls and boys were separated from one another.

The girls were trained by the older women in household arts. They might be taught to read and write; they became proficient in weaving, sewing, spinning, and embroidering, as well as in music. Until about age 16, boys devoted much of their time to the study of literature, declamation, and music, in addition to some physical training. During this period parents were responsible for the boys' education, which was obtained at home or in schools paid for by the parents. If a boy's parents were financially unable to keep him at school until the age of 16, he might be compelled to leave school at age 13 or 14 and engage in some form of work.

To achieve full citizenship a boy was expected to continue his education to the age of 20. We find here the beginnings of a recognition of the need of an extended period of adolescent training aimed at preparation for the assumption of adult responsibilities, especially for participation in government activities. From the ages of 16 to 18 these boys continued to attend schools in which the emphasis was placed largely upon athletic development. The next two years were devoted to military training. Throughout his childhood and adolescence the boy was trained to be moral and upright in terms of accepted cultural standards, to revere the gods, and to be a gentleman. Except in rare instances girls had no share in this educational program. It must be noted also that probably no more than a small fraction of the male youth benefited from this extended adolescent period of education. It is significant, however, that the Athenian cultural pattern considered adolescence as a period of development as a person.

## Adolescence in a Changing Roman Culture

In general, early Roman ideals concerning the development of youth were almost completely practical. Emphasis was placed upon four civic virtues: courage, duty, justice, and virtuous behavior. The mother trained her daughter to become a good wife, mother, and housekeeper; the father prepared his son to perform the practical duties of a man and citizen. There was much learning through doing. Attention also was given to the development of good health and physical strength. Adolescence was regarded as a period of continued preparation for adult responsibility. The tremendous influence, after 300 B.C., of Greek culture upon Rome led to the inauguration of schooling through the university level for a small fraction of the population of Rome.

It is not our purpose to consider here the great contributions of Rome to successive world cultures. We can refer briefly, however, to the fact that the Hellenization of Rome, built as it was upon the practical attitudes of the Roman people, provided favored Roman youths excellent opportunities for preparing themselves to become leaders in many fields of endeavor. Their constructive achievements still constitute the bases of many modern practices. Eventually, however, those elements that were inherent in "the grandeur that was Rome" finally led to its downfall. An increasing involvement with intellectual pursuits and self-satisfying cultural interests was closely associated with Roman decline of emphasis upon religion and morality. No stress was placed upon the development and maintenance of physical vigor and virility.

Rome's changing attitude toward life values was reflected in the self-indulgent and morally lax attitudes exhibited by the Roman leaders and imitated by those youths whose responsibility it later would become to continue and advance the prestige of Roman culture. Consequently, Roman civilization was supplanted, temporarily at least, by the more primitive culture of the physically strong and virile Germanic tribes. During the later years of Roman supremacy, however, the influence of the ideals of Hebraic and Christian culture patterns began to exercise a potent effect upon the general citizenry.

# Adolescence during the Middle Ages and Early Modern Times

By the Middle Ages the concept of adolescence as a period of preparation for adult living had moved far in kind and in length from the pubic phase of development that was characteristic of primitive culture. As the organizational patterns of cultural groups increased in complexity, the adolescent period took on greater significance.

## The Medieval Adolescent

During the Middle Ages schooling for all children and young people was the exception rather than accepted custom. In the days of "chivalry" boys of the upper class served as pages to women until about the age of 14, when they became squires and were inducted into the arts of knighthood by the men whom they now served. Adult status was achieved when, or if, a young man gave evidence of having developed those behavior characteristics that were considered to be knightly. Courage, chastity, and loyalty to God, country, and his "fair lady" supposedly were knightly qualities. The adolescent girl was prepared to be an attractive, tender, and submissive mate to her spouse. Considerable attention was devoted to the acquiring by "upper-class" youth of grace, charm, wit, and sprightly manner.

## The Adolescent and the Beginnings of Modern Cultures

Through early modern times children of lower social classes enjoyed little, if any, adolescent preparation for adult responsibility, except what they received as members of hard-working family units. Elizabeth Browning's poem "The Cry of the Children" presents a tragic picture of the lives of small children who worked in the mines of England. The novels of Charles Dickens and his contemporaries paint vivid word pictures of the sad experiences suffered by young people of the time, even where some schooling was made available for the masses. As was the situation in earlier cultures, economically and socially favored youth enjoyed superior educational advantages.

The Reformation and the Industrial Revolution, which were the outgrowths of general dissatisfaction with existing European cultural patterns, exercised a tremendous effect upon the place of the child and the adolescent in the societal group. As a result of the Reformation, responsibility for achieving spiritual salvation was transferred from the religious leaders to the individual himself. Through the Industrial Revolution, the provision of life necessities was taken out of the home, thus weakening to that extent the closeness of cooperative effort within the family unit. Both of these societal upheavals were accompanied by significant changes in adult attitude toward most children and adolescents.

By the beginning of the eighteenth century some schooling had been made available for children of all social classes, including some schools for adolescents. For the most part, however, whatever educational opportunities existed were subsidized and controlled by the Church and were established to serve religious purposes. The developmental needs of children and adolescents were not considered, however. Some two hundred years ago fundamental schooling in the vernacular started to become a state function; educational opportunities for adolescents and young adults increased. Yet not until men like Rousseau, Basedow, Pestalozzi, and their followers propounded revolutionary theories concerning the education of children was recognition given to concepts that stress the unfolding capacities of the child, the natural urges, interests, curiosities, and activities of young people, and the possibility of potential differences in ability to achieve successfully.

Early modern times witnessed disagreements among religious and political leaders, educators, and psychologists that dealt with the growth and developmental needs of adolescents as well as children. There was difference of opinion concerning the purpose to be served by, and the extent of, education that should be made available for all young people. Also considered were the ways in which appropriate learning opportunities should be subsidized and organized. The research and experimental contributions of psychologists, biologists, and sociologists of early modern times have resulted in the gradual development, especially among the Western cultures, of a new attitude toward the maturing child and adolescent, a greater appreciation of individual differences among young people, a more intelligent understanding of the problems of adjustment that may be experienced by a young person in his struggle to achieve adult status, and a trend toward granting him increasing freedom of action and decision making during his maturing years.

## Changes in Adolescent Status

Summarized briefly, the gradual changes in cultural patterns from early authoritarianism to present-day widespread democratic ideology have been accompanied by changing adult attitudes toward the growing-up years, as shown in Table 4.

As we consider the changes that have gradually taken place in adolescent status and in adult attitude toward the significance in the life of the individual of his growing-up years, we must be cognizant of the fact

*Table 4.* Changes in Adolescent Status

| FROM | TO |
|---|---|
| A short pubertal period between childhood and adulthood (primitive cultures) | An ever-increasingly longer period (four to seven or eight years) of preparation for the assumption of adult responsibility |
| The experiencing of rigid rites and ceremonials as tests of readiness for adult status (primitive cultures) | Relatively little emphasis upon such procedures, except for religious observances (confirmation) during early adolescence and some social recognition ("coming-out" parties) for girls at the end of the adolescent period |
| Early marriages and the raising of large families for the benefit of the societal group | No restriction upon age at marriage or size of family |
| Mating controlled by parental authority | Individual freedom of mate selection |
| Specialized training of upper-class boys for war or political leadership (Greek culture) | Many-sided education as preparation to engage in one or another occupational or citizenship activity |
| Little, if any, education for girls beyond some training in homemaking (Athenian and Roman culture) | Increasing trend toward equalization of educational opportunities for the two sexes |
| Great emphasis upon superiority in physical strength and endurance | Concern about the mental as well as the physical health of young people, and decreasing emphasis upon mere physical strength and endurance |
| Educational advantages available to a relatively small number of young people | Educational advantages available to all |
| Schooling, for the most part, the responsibility of parents, religious institutions, or national organizations, usually on a fee basis, especially for adolescents and young adults | Nontuition, citizen-supported education available for all from the preschool level through adolescence and, in some communities, through the graduate-college or university level |
| No recognition of individual differences among children except in physical structure and constitution | A recognition and acceptance of the fact that young people are different as well as alike, physically, mentally, and emotionally |
| Almost complete disregard and non-understanding of young people's developing interests, aptitudes, and needs | Increasing interest in, and study of, the developmental pattern of the needs, wants, interests, and aptitudes of maturing children and adolescents |
| Emphasis upon the submission of young people to the authority and will of parents and other elders | Encouragement of individual freedom of behavior from early childhood through adolescence within the framework of the general welfare of a democratic society |

that deviations from traditional practices can be found even among some of the earlier cultural groups. Moreover, certain traditional attitudes toward adolescence have persisted to the present. Perhaps it is possible to find in the conflict that still exists between former authoritarian attitudes of adults toward young people and modern, democratic ideals one of the most serious causes of the problems experienced by today's teen-agers.

## Adolescent Development in a Complex Society

Simple communal living no longer is possible in any part of modern Western civilization. Cultural patterns have become increasingly complex. Hence, the differences that are found among different societal groups represent degrees of complexity of ideology and differences in political, economic, and social status. The impact upon developing young people of the many stress-arousing conditions and situations inherent in Western civilization is tremendous. Many complex cultural elements are so intertwined with factors inherent in the developmental process that it is difficult, if not impossible, to separate the two areas of influence on adolescents. Scruton describes the relationship in these words:

Each of us lives in a universe composed of natural and social elements, but while the two aspects are in fact quite different, in our experience they are merged inseparably. For us, certainly for those whose experience is mainly urban, the world is largely a cultural thing, and in this culture-world, this artificial, man-created universe, each of us is nurtured, grows, and absorbs, unconsciously for the most part, the expectations, habits, beliefs, and attitudes which are appropriate to our several places in society. This extraordinary process of inculcation is so successfully accomplished that by adolescence the "natural" child has ceased to exist, if such an individual is even imaginable. This is the chief argument to this point— that man and culture are one; that men, who create the elements of culture are, at the same time, utterly dependent upon these elements, and other humans organized in terms of them, to survive. We say, further, that the unique and shared experiences which come to each person act upon the genetic potential of each individual to produce a personality, and that this personality, which bears so indelibly the mark of a particular social group, *is*, for all practical purposes, the individual.[1]

## Modern Youth

As has been indicated earlier in this chapter, the culture in which, as a child and an adolescent, an individual grows and develops comprises

[1] David L. Scruton, "Culture and Adolescence," in Merle T. Strom (ed.), *Needs of Adolescent Youth*, The Interstate Printers and Publishers, Inc., Danville, Ill., 1963, pp. 101–102.

the physical and material elements of the environment in which he is reared and all the factors of influence that are inherent in the traditions, mores, beliefs, attitudes, and behavior patterns that represent the cultural pattern of the young person's social or community group. In their abilities and tendencies to respond to and to mold their personalities according to the stimulating forces of their physical and social environment, modern American adolescents do not differ from the youth of earlier cultures. The simpler in form and the more consistent the culture, the more rapid and easier the transition from childhood to adult understanding of personal and group rights and responsibilities probably is. The complex interrelations of all the facets of so-called "modern American culture" include many heterogeneous classifications and groupings of personal and social attitudes and activities. The achievement by the adolescent of satisfactory preparation for adult living is dependent, therefore, upon the breadth and depth of his experiences during preadult years.

In his discussion of the relationship between adolescence and adulthood, Havighurst[2] suggests that self-support is a sign of a young person's assumption of adulthood. He divides young people into three groups according to the age at which they become self-supporting: (1) those who become self-supporting only after the completion of four or more years of education after high school, (2) those who complete a secondary school education and then engage in satisfying work experiences, (3) those who leave school at the age of 14 to 16 and seek gainful employment. The length of the preadult period differs, of course, among these three groups. Different also are the experiences that help to prepare these young people for adult responsibilities.

Concerning the first group Havighurst says:

Postponement of adulthood puts these young people in a favored economic position. Most of them come from middle-class families that have taught them to postpone immediate pleasures for greater future satisfaction. They see this pattern in their own parents and identify with it. They have learned the art of sublimation of their impulses. The Kinsey studies show that these young people seek direct sex outlets later and less frequently than young people with less education and with working-class expectations. Until recently they postponed marriage until they were ready to take up an adult work role.

But a considerable number of these young people are now marrying in their early twenties. This means that for this group marriage is a part of adolescence and not the beginning of adulthood. This is probably a useful adaptation to adjust the disparity between biological and cultural realities.[3]

[2] Robert J. Havighurst, "Adolescence and the Postponement of Adulthood," *School Review*, pp. 52–62, Spring, 1960.

[3] *Ibid.*, pp. 54–55.

The second group is described as follows:

The second and largest group at present consists mainly of those who complete secondary school and then go to work. This group also includes a few who quit school a year or so before high-school graduation to take a job and a few others who start college but drop out by the end of the first year.

This group makes a gradual entry into adult roles between the ages of seventeen and twenty. They re-gard high-school graduation as a necessary step toward the kind of job they want. Their high-school dating leads them rather smoothly toward marriage; more than half of the girls in this group are married by the age of twenty, and more than half of the boys are married by the age of twenty-three. For this group marriage marks the end of adolescence.[4]

Various personal and social problems arise among members of the third group. Havighurst comments about these young people as follows:

These boys and girls generally drop out of school at the age of fifteen or sixteen after a history of failure, frustration, and frequently of bad behavior. Maladjusted to school, many of them are also maladjusted to work and family life, and make little or no progress toward responsible adulthood during the next few years. . . .

At about the seventh or eighth grade the members of this group begin to have trouble in school. They have been slow, dull students. They have known failure. Coming from the wrong side of the tracks they have known discrimination in social life. They realize that school will be no easy pathway to adulthood for them, as it is for most of their schoolmates.

When they reach the legal school-leaving age, they drop out of school. By this time many of them have a police record for minor delinquency. Others have become apathetic and intimidated, and have lost confidence in themselves.

At this point, at the age of fifteen or sixteen, they are no longer chil-dren, but they cannot find their way into adulthood through high school. About two-thirds of them are fortunate enough to break into an adult role by successful work or successful marriage. . . . They go to work on the farm or in an unskilled occupation, and they make good at it. By the age of eighteen or nineteen they are well established in a work role which has low social status but is nevertheless an adequate adult role. The girls are likely to be married by this age. . . .

The 8 or 10 per cent who drop out of school and then do not find a way to adulthood through work are indeed the failures of our society. Juvenile delinquency is heavily concentrated in this group. In nearly every case families are inadequate and have not provided their children with a base of character on which to build.

When the boys in this failing group get work, they generally prove to be untrustworthy, or aggressive and hostile, and cannot hold a job for any length of time. Nor are they successful if they enter military

4 *Ibid.*, p. 57.

service. If they are not rejected on the ground of mental or personal incompetence, they are likely to be let out of the service after a few unsatisfactory months. . . . This tragic group of 8 or 10 per cent of our youth, who are not able to grow up through the school, through work, or through marriage, suffer not so much from postponement of adulthood as from a set of roadblocks that may prevent them from ever achieving adulthood. They will never achieve self-definition or identity. They have had their share and more than their share of conflict with teachers, parents, and policemen. Whether they are apathetic and fearful, or hostile and delinquent, they have been defeated.[5]

Cultural influences are bringing about changes in most of today's world. Increasing media of communication and transportation are tending to level traditional differences among peoples. The East is rapidly adopting some Western customs. Especially are these attitudes evident in the younger members of countries in which century-old traditions are considered to be sacred by some of their elders. For example, a recent visitor to Africa described conditions there in this way:

All of the large cities are noisy and crowded, with autos dashing about. A good percentage of the natives wear colorful costumes. They carry baskets of produce on their heads or strapped on their backs (the women with the inevitable baby). The city men appear in every degree of modern attire—to the type photographed for men's shirts and collars. Even more spectacular are the young girls! You cannot conceive of their extreme styles of heels, skirts, blouses, pocketbooks, and especially "hair-dos."

The writer also commented on the appearance of various cities. Some of the coastal cities are interesting because of the Arab and Indian architecture and narrow streets. One city has beautiful, modern buildings and another is just a rough-and-tumble place, with big and little buildings jammed together. In most of the cities there are Western-style hotels. Yet these may be situated among traditional surroundings. It is understandable that developing young people experience difficulties in adjusting to such differences between old and new cultural influences.

The American cultural pattern has become a different but equally serious problem of adjustment for the young. The United States often is referred to as a "melting pot." Many different peoples, representing diverse cultural backgrounds, have continued to make this country their home. Ideological differences among them exercise an influence upon what we like to refer to as "the American way of life." These various peoples attempt to adjust their traditional beliefs, attitudes, and forms of behavior

[5] *Ibid.,* pp. 58–60.

to our democratic ideal. Their interpretation of, and ability to conform to, democratic standards concerning individual rights and responsibilities increase the complexity and heterogeneity of American culture to an extent that is not experienced by other national groups whose citizenry represents more homogeneous grouping.

Many children of foreign-born parents have been and still are the victims of conflict between old-world traditions and modern American ideals. Conflict situations caused by the recent influx into the United States of young Puerto Ricans is a case in point. Within the freedoms guaranteed us by the Bill of Rights can be found some of the roots of adolescent difficulties, since these individual rights are not understood by all our adult and adolescent citizens and are sometimes misinterpreted in terms of the common good.

An adolescent's development in, and adjustment to, his or her particular school, occupational, community, religious, political, and economic conditions and situations are discussed in later chapters. At this point we shall consider some of the fundamental changes in modern culture that are affecting the lives of young people.

## The Effects of Mobility

Mobility can be interpreted in either of two ways: as geographic change or as movement from one social class, or "caste," to another. Either aspect of mobility represents a trend away from traditional stability of home environment and social class status toward populational fluidity.

*Trend from Rural to Urban Life.* Until about three centuries ago, most countries contained many rural communities. Family ties were strong; large families were necessary so that the children might help care for the farms and provide life necessities. Early marriage was the custom. In fact, some small communities were composed almost entirely of close or more distant family relatives. Young people grew up in a relatively peaceful environment in which work, recreation, religious experiences, and schooling were centered in the home and the community.

The rise of industrialism led to a rapid urbanization of Western peoples. Beginning in the nineteenth century the trek of young persons from the farm to increasingly crowded urban industrial centers is continuing. For example, by referring to Figure 1 it can be seen that in 1900 about 60 per cent of the population of the United States lived in rural areas. Today more than 63 per cent are urbanites or suburbanites, with expected continuing increase. These population changes constitute the bases of many adjustment problems for both rural and urban youth. Many of those who migrate from the farm to urban centers are older adolescents and young adults. From a relatively sheltered existence, including much physical work and simple social and recreational activities, adjustment must be made to crowded living conditions, bustle and confusion, impersonal and businesslike relationships with fellow workers and even with neighbors, extended educational and vocational opportunities, and many different kinds of recreational activities and commercialized entertainment.

Both rural and urban communities differ among themselves and within themselves in terms of the respective subcultures that comprise them. Children and adolescents mingle with others of their own age groups who have been reared in homes that represent attitudes and behavior patterns that may differ greatly from their own. They are then confronted with the problem of determining what cultural values are most worthwhile. Children of migrant workers are especially sensitive to differences among the various communities in which they must live for shorter or longer periods of time, as their parents go from place to place

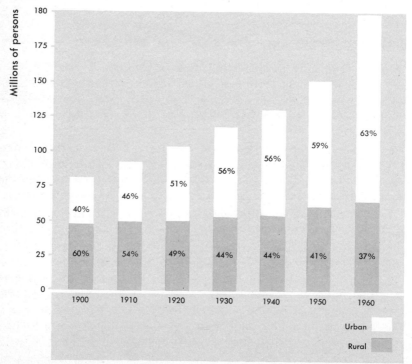

*Figure 1.* Population trends in the United States, 1900–1960, showing trend toward urbanization. Under the current urban definition the 1960 urban population would be 69.9 per cent, and the rural 30.1 per cent. (Based on United States census data.)

for seasonal work. Adequate provision for the education and social needs of these young people has become a serious problem.

*Social Class Mobility.* Various caste systems were characteristic of earlier forms of culture and still are relatively strong in some parts of the world. The democratic ideal of equality of opportunity for all people according to their ability to achieve vocational and/or social recognition has tended to break down artificial class barriers. There are extant in our modern civilization, however, certain class differentiations that are peculiar to differences in educational level, religious affiliation, occupational activity, or economic status. There also is much social mobility. Some of our most respected, admired, and revered leaders in every area of social betterment have risen from lowly beginnings to great heights of achievement.

The concept of social mobility is an essential concomitant of the democratic ideal, yet it constitutes one more factor of possible adolescent conflict. Personal and parental ambitions in relation to personal capacity to achieve may initiate the arousal of youthful feelings of frustration that are less characteristic of caste-controlled societies.

## Effects of Technological Progress

To survey even briefly all the changes in mode of living that accompany technological progress would go far beyond the limits of this discussion. Certain material and mechanical advancements are affecting the development and life adjustment of young people. We shall refer here to some of the general factors of influence upon young people in this age of technology.

During earlier days of Western civilization, many life necessities were produced in the home; others were made by hand in the shops of community artisans. The adolescent shared in production, either as his parent's helper or as an apprentice to the village producer. In any case, the young person participated in the work activity and followed the making of an article from the first operation to completion. Care and accuracy of workmanship were stressed. Mass production constitutes a different situation for the young person who must select the kind of work in which he wishes to engage, prepare himself adequately for it, and then seek and hold a job, sometimes in face of much competition. Vocational opportunities are constantly changing with technical advances. Increase in mechanical power is accompanied by decrease in need of man power. It is often difficult for the young adolescent to decide upon his life work. An occupational field that is open when he starts to train for it may be closed by the time the prospective worker is prepared to enter it.

Modern technological advances are accompanied by considerable emphasis on scientific and mechanical "know-how." The creation of Sputnik, for example, led to a great demand for workers with some educational background in the physical sciences. Continued experimentation with atomic energy and exploration in space constitute the bases of a growing need for able young people, girls as well as boys, to major in science, mathematics, and related fields. Other areas of endeavor, such as the humanities and the arts, cannot be neglected, however. We are living in an era during which specialization rather than general over-all knowledge and skill is required. This intensifies adolescent problems of vocational selection.

Another effect upon youth of improved mechanical devices can be found in the release of young people from former home responsibilities. The many timesaving and laborsaving household gadgets that are available to most housewives make it unnecessary for mothers to assign household chores to their children. Young people are motivated to devote to leisure-time activities the hours that once were given to household tasks. Recreational opportunities available to young people as well as to their elders also reflect the spirit of mechanical progress. Radio, television, motion pictures, automobiles, airplanes, and other inventions offer so many diverse and ever-changing ways of filling one's time and stimulating one's interests that they have become a threat to family unity, adolescent stability, societal standards of wholesome behavior, and religious values. Significant technological changes can exercise a disturbing influence upon youth during the growing-up period.

## Effects of War Conditions

Youthful confusion and instability brought about by the factors of mobility and technological change that are inherent in our present culture have been intensified by disturbed world conditions. Although there is actual combat in some areas, at the time of this writing the world at large supposedly is waging a cold war, which, unless great care is exercised by politically strong nations, can develop into world-shattering combat. Hence most countries are maintaining peacetime military units. The United States, for example, has many such units stationed at strategic points, both at home and abroad.

Serious problems of adjustment are experienced by older adolescents and young adults who become members of the armed services. They take with them to their new life conditions those patterns of behavior that reflect accustomed school or work interests and adjustments. They are relatively immature; they may not yet thoroughly understand adult-pointed responsibilities; too many of them lack an appreciation of the significance of accepted moral codes and of the power of self-discipline.

Efforts are being made to do a better job of preparing men and women for entrance into the armed services. For example, at a conference of the American Social Health Association, Charles I. Carpenter, then Chief of Chaplains of the United States Air Force, spoke forcibly concerning problems that are associated with the attitudes and behavior of young military personnel here and in foreign countries. He stressed the need of basic preinduction preparation that would begin early in the life of the young person. Parents and educational and religious leaders, as well as the young people themselves, must share in bringing about an emotionally stable and mature attitude in the young inductees toward their responsibilities as representatives of the American democratic state, especially in their relationships with people of a culture different from their own.

## The Changing Status of Women

In the foregoing discussion we have pointed up some of the major elements of modern American culture that have a tremendous impact upon a developing young person. Another significant factor is the rapidly changing status of girls and women. Traditionally minded older men and women regard with dismay and even horror the increasing trend throughout the world toward equality between the sexes in educational, vocational, and political opportunities for self-realization. Some younger men resent the inroads of women into supposedly male fields of activity. Many girls and young women do not yet feel secure in their new-found freedom.

Relaxed control of boy-girl relationships, combined with technologically provided increase of leisure time, has resulted in confusion concerning proper standards of behavior of one sex toward the other. As adolescent boys and girls struggle to achieve adult status in the group, keen competition may arise between the sexes. At the same time, members of each sex are motivated by maturing sex urges toward the building of new and different relationships between men and women. These new interests are especially disturbing to young people during their earlier adolescent years, but may continue through the teen-age years unless boys and girls have achieved a wholesome understanding of, and a feeling of security in, their own sex roles.

## Responsibility of Society for Adolescent Adjustment

Since an individual's development during childhood usually takes place within the family unit and in a relatively small neighborhood group, he is likely to assimilate the mores and habitual attitudes and behavior patterns that are common to the subcultural community of which he is a member. When, however, as an adolescent, he comes to grips with the elements of wider, more heterogeneous cultures, he begins to experience feelings of insecurity, confusion, or conflict. During this period he is expected to gain an understanding of the many facets of the democratic way of life, and to prepare himself adequately for active participation in national and world affairs.

In modern Western culture adolescence probably represents the most critical period of an individual's life. An adolescent's position is anomalous. The average life span has risen from about 22 years in 1500 to more than 70 years at the present, with an expected continued rise. The age at which adult responsibilities are to be assumed is delayed, in some instances to as late as an age of 25 or older. Yet some 18-year-olds or younger teen-agers are gainfully employed. They also may be married and have children. While an adolescent may be treated by his elders as if he were a child, he is expected nevertheless to display mature judgment in the management of his affairs.

The difficulties inherent in adolescent development and adjustment are increased by the fact that cultural mores still are in a state of flux. There is no clear-cut and generally accepted adult interpretation of the connotation and significance of adolescence. Young people's behavior is affected by the various adult cultural influences surrounding them. At the same time, since adolescence represents a developmental period during which its members no longer are children and have not yet achieved adult status, it is understandable that there emerges a kind of adolescent society. Behavior motivations of teen-agers often grow out of their experiences in educational institutions. James S. Coleman has this to say about the emergence of an adolescent subculture:

This setting-apart of our children in schools—which take on ever more functions, ever more "extra-curricular activities"—for an ever longer period of training has a singular impact on the child of high-school age. He is "cut off" from the rest of society, forced inward toward his own age group, made to carry out his whole social life with others his own age. With his fellows, he comes to constitute a small society, one that has most of its important interactions *within* itself, and maintains only a few threads of connection with the outside adult society. In our modern world of mass communication and rapid diffusion of ideas and knowledge, it is hard to realize that separate subcultures can exist right under the very noses of adults—subcultures with languages all their own, with special symbols, and, most importantly, with value systems that may differ from adults. Any parent who has tried to talk to his adolescent son or daughter recently knows this, as does anyone who has recently visited a high school for the first time since his own adolescence. To put it simply, these young people speak a different language. What is more relevant to the present point, the language they speak is becoming more and more different.[6]

In their relationships with the fundamental social institutions—religious, family, governmental, educational, and occupational—adolescents need to experience a generally consistent pattern of attitudes and behavior. Instead, they may be exposed to cultural uncertainties. They may receive autocratic treatment from one of these institutions; they may be expected by another to understand democratic ideals and to pattern their behavior accordingly. In addition, one or another of these institutions, failing to achieve a nice balance between needed authority and desirable democracy in their relations with immature adolescents, may adopt a generally permissive or laissez-faire attitude toward youth training.

Many adolescents resent absolute adult authoritarianism; they are likely to fumble in their efforts to achieve their democratic rights and to fulfill their responsibilities in a democratic society. Too great permissiveness accorded them by their elders, who themselves display a laissez-faire attitude toward cultural standards, may have dangerous consequences. In the resulting adolescent confusion, insecurity, and conflict experiences are rooted the basic causes of youthful delinquency, mental and emotional disturbance, and the continuance of immature inadequacy to meet and to adjust successfully to the personal and social obligations that accompany the reaching of adult status.

Many modern young people succeed in bridging the gap between childhood and adulthood with a minimum number of disturbing experiences. They give evidence of a zestful attitude toward the many challenges that are inherent in the growing-up process. Good inherited potentials and wise adult guidance during childhood and adolescent years make it possible for them to develop stable emotional status and to adjust adequately to the many differing stimuli situations that can have devastating effects upon less fortunate adolescents. In general, however, young people tend to conform to the cultural influences to which they are exposed. Scruton has this to say:

Our adolescent reacts, as we all have reason to know, in a strikingly predictable way in various circumstances. For example, adolescent behavior with respect to clothing, music, food, group attitudes, and parental authority, to name but a few areas, is sufficiently standardized in this culture that we have a pretty good idea what to expect in specific circumstances. These preferences, habits, outlooks, and attitudes are reflections of personalities, and their repeated appearance

[6] James S. Coleman et al., *The Adolescent Society: The Social Life of the Teenager and Its Impact on Education*, The Free Press of Glencoe, New York, 1961, p. 3.

in young people in our society can only be the result of being exposed to a common body of understandings and expectations, which is to say, culture. Culture, then, creates the world in which the adolescent lives. It creates hopes, and needs, and it creates the means of achievement, and it creates the mode of expressing frustration when they are not met. It creates obstacles, and the means of overcoming them, or escaping from them. It creates problems and crises and the means of solving and resolving them. Culture, in company with biology, creates the adolescent.[7]

In this chapter the biological and cultural factors that influence the developmental progress of maturing boys and girls have been presented. Psychologists and educators are not so much concerned about adolescents *in toto* as they are with specific patterns of development. Hence we shall consider next some of the techniques currently utilized to study teen-age needs, urges, interests, attitudes, and displayed behavior patterns, as well as the interpretation and possible application of the results of study techniques utilized with adolescents.

## Questions and Problems for Discussion

1. Outline ways in which (*a*) biological inheritance and (*b*) cultural heritage influence adolescent development. As you consider them suggest the impact of each on adolescent development.
2. Indicate the extent to which life values found in earlier primitive societies during adolescence continue in such countries as Mexico, the United States, Japan, Canada, France, Russia, and Italy. What are the influences in each country that promote good adolescent adjustment?
3. Discuss the advantages and disadvantages of the short period of adolescence found in primitive societies and the extended period found in most countries today.
4. List problems caused by the concentration of adolescent population in large urban areas. Compare the problems of adolescents reared in a rural setting with those of adolescents reared in an urban setting.
5. In what ways, if any, has the growing concept of "one world" affected the adolescent's attitude toward his problems and his peers?
6. *Special Exercises:*
   *a.* Study and report the extent to which present-day adolescents participate in practices similar to those of adolescents of primitive societies.
   *b.* Study the behavior of adolescents living in at least three different countries, on different continents. Note similarities and differences

---

[7] Scruton, *op. cit.*, p. 98.

that you find, including types of adjustment problems met. Indicate possible causes for any differences that you find.

c. From your resource material, try to discover the important stresses and strains that were faced by growing youth during the early part of this century. Also report the stresses and strains that you experienced during your growing years. Interview two or more adolescents to discover what bothers them today. Report your findings.

## Selected References

Benedict, Ruth: Patterns of Culture, Houghton Mifflin Company, Boston, 1934.

Coleman, James S., et al.: The Adolescent Society: The Social Life of the Teenager and Its Impact on Education, The Free Press of Glencoe, New York, 1961.

Grinder, R. E.: Studies in Adolescence, The Macmillan Company, New York, 1963.

Havighurst, Robert J., and Hilda Taba: Adolescent Character and Personality, John Wiley & Sons, Inc., New York, 1949.

Havighurst, Robert J., et al.: Growing up in River City, John Wiley & Sons, Inc., New York, 1962.

Hechinger, G., and F. M. Hechinger: Teen-age Tyranny, William Morrow and Company, Inc., New York, 1963.

Hollingshead, A. B.: Elmtown's Youth, John Wiley & Sons, Inc., New York, 1949.

Kelley, E. C.: In Defense of Youth, Prentice-Hall, Inc., Englewood Cliffs, N.J., 1962.

Knapp, R. B.: Social Integration in Urban Communities, Bureau of Publications, Teachers College, Columbia University, New York, 1960.

Kuhlen, R. G.: The Psychology of Adolescent Development, Harper and Row, Publishers, Incorporated, New York, 1952.

Mead, Margaret: Coming of Age in Samoa, William Morrow and Company, Inc., New York, 1928.

Mead, Margaret: Male and Female: A Study of the Sexes in a Changing World, William Morrow and Company, Inc., New York, 1949.

Patterson, F., et al.: The Adolescent Citizen, The Free Press of Glencoe, New York, 1960.

Smith, E. A.: American Youth Culture, The Free Press of Glencoe, New York, 1962.

Stier, L. D.: "Adolescents and Other Western Cultures," Journal of Secondary Education, vol. 36, pp. 398–405, November, 1961.

# Chapter Three

## Approaches
## to the Study
## of Adolescence

A large body of information concerning child and adolescent growth and development is available for utilization by parents, teachers, and other adults interested in the welfare of children. For the most part, data obtained concerning child development have scientific validity and practical value. To the present, however, we do not have equally valid study results dealing with adolescent growth and development. One reason for this differnce can be found in the relative simplicity of the developmental pattern during childhood as compared with complex adolescent adjustment. Furthermore, the significance in the life of an individual of his childhood experiences was recognized earlier by psychologists and educators than was the need to gain a realistic understanding of the changes that take place during the adolescent period of development. A growing awareness of the problems experienced by young people during their growing-up years has stimulated among psychologists a vital interest in the factors of adolescent adjustment. Consequently, some helpful beginnings have been made in the study of adolescent personality.

## Basic Considerations in Adolescent Study

In 1904, G. Stanley Hall published the findings of his study of adolescents in the two-volume *Adolescence*. The book served as an impetus to other psychologists to concentrate their efforts upon analyses of youthful attitudes and behavior. As a result of his monumental study, Hall concluded that adolescence represents a period of "storm and stress" in the life of an individual. This interpretation came as a shock to those persons who either had regarded adolescence as no more than a continuation of childhood development or had given little, if any, serious thought to adolescent preparation for adult status. Some of the studies that followed Hall's work, therefore, were attempts to refute his findings by showing that growth and development are continuous processes that run along smoothly from early beginnings to the attainment of adult maturity.[1]

---

[1] It was claimed that Hall's conclusions had been based upon data obtained through the utilization of the questionnaire technique and that such a method may or may not yield valid and reliable results.

More recent work in this field indicates greater objectivity of approach, with more variation of findings. Among psychologists, some controversy still exists, however, concerning the amount and kind of stressful experience that is general among teen-agers.

## Adult Need to Understand Adolescents

Twentieth-century psychologists have emphasized the importance of recognizing differences as well as likenesses among human beings. Probably at no age period are individual differences so marked as they are during adolescence. As was noted in Chapter 2, the impact of differing cultural influences upon differing biologically inherited potentialities is extremely strong during these years. Hence variations in rate of growth and maturation, combined with differences in attitude and behavior development and adjustment, require that adult treatment of, and attitudes toward, young people reflect an appreciation of (1) common personality characteristics of adolescents at different age levels, i.e., early adolescence versus late adolescence, (2) individual differences among adolescents of the same age period, and (3) the progressive changes that occur in the developmental pattern of a single adolescent.

Parents become concerned when their younger adolescent children exhibit behavior different from that which had been displayed by their older sons and daughters during early adolescent years. Some fathers and mothers are unable to reconcile themselves to the fact that their adolescent children seem to lack certain qualities that were characteristic of parental adolescent personality. Many of the problems of home and family adjustment discussed in Chapter 14 could be avoided if parents and other relatives possessed a greater understanding of adolescent nature.

Most school people who have taught in both elementary and secondary schools admit that in many ways it is easier to work with elementary school children than it is to motivate learning among secondary school pupils. Although energy-filled youngsters may need firm guidance, they usually are malleable and respond readily and cheerfully to overt expressions of adult friendliness toward them and interest in them. It is much more difficult for the secondary school teacher to achieve rapport with all his pupils, especially if the members of his class include young people at different stages of maturation. Each pupil is an individual who may need to be treated differently from every other pupil. Unless the teacher is aware of the ways in which young people differ and knows something of the background history of each of his students, pupil cooperation may be difficult to achieve.

That there is a need for much extensive and intensive study of adolescents and their problems is evidenced by many examples of unintelligent handling of youth problems by parents, school people, courts, and civic leaders. Adults must understand adolescents and recognize and fulfill their responsibilities toward them. For example, a teacher who forbids an adolescent stutterer to participate in class discussion because, according to the teacher, the student's struggles to express his thoughts "make me nervous," is failing to recognize the young person's need for teacher understanding and help.

Our discussion to this point may seem to place major emphasis upon adult obligations to youth. It is equally necessary for young people to understand themselves, their problems, and their own share of responsibility for the kinds of changes that are taking place during this critical period. Unfortunately, one of the results of adolescent study has been the development among some adults of a sentimental compulsion to condone or minimize adolescent participation in asocial or delinquent behavior. To understand the causes of such behavior does not mean to excuse it. We can probably serve youth best by studying them, preventing or ameliorating unhealthful physical and social conditions, and then providing stress-and-strain-free opportunities for them, through their own efforts, gradually to achieve independence from adult control, self-determination, and self-realization.

## Areas of Adolescent Study

Psychologists agree generally that an individual's personality represents a complex interrelated total organism that functions constantly in response to inner and outer stimulating forces according to developed reaction habits and the strength of natural drives, urges, and acquired interests and ambitions. We can learn much about adolescent personality from an intensive study of the various characteristics of one adolescent.

There is value also in studying each of the various aspects of the whole personality, provided that attention is given to the possible effect upon a particular personality trait of the interaction that may be taking place between it and other personality traits. We sometimes refer to the various phases or aspects of the total personality pattern as *personality traits* or *characteristics*. For operational purposes a trait can be defined as a single, persistent mode of response to a stimulus situation that tends to evoke it. A trait does not function in isolation, however. Hence it is not enough to discover that one adolescent appears to be more industrious, cheerful, cooperative, alert, aggressive, timid, or courteous than another. Since a behavior trait is a learned reaction habit and is an expression of an acquired attitude, the source of its acquisition also must be understood, as well as its interrelation with other segments of the individual's whole personality pattern.

During adolescence the personality-patterning process that is taking place within a maturing young person is affected by the physical and physiological changes which he is experiencing, by the expansion of his intellectual powers and his increasing skills and broadening knowledge, by his developing urge to attain adult status and to achieve satisfactory group relations, and by his growing concern about life values. Adolescent personality development is a two-way process. Environmental conditions and situations set the stage for the kinds of experiences which help or hinder the boy or girl in his development and adjustment. In addition, the attitudes, behavior habits, degree of emotional control and self-understanding, and kinds of personal-social relationships that are carried over from childhood to and through the adolescent period determine in great part the extent to which teen-age experiences result in the development of well-adjusted or maladjusted life patterns.

To be worthwhile any approach to the study of adolescent personality must take into consideration (1) the changes that are taking place during adolescence in physical structure and physiological functioning, and in personal and social urges and interests, (2) environmental stimulations and opportunities for development, and (3) childhood background of development and training. Moreover, valid and reliable findings that result from studies of adolescents should then be utilized by those adults whose responsibility it is to help youth develop personality qualities that will enable them to be competent, forward-looking, and well adjusted in the various phases of life activities. Among the areas of study and application, therefore, can be included factors that are inherent in the achievement of independence from parental control; heterosexual adjustment, wise choice and marital and parental success; satisfactory vocational selection, preparation, and participation; intelligent and cooperative citizenship; and prevention, or reconditioning, of maladjusted or delinquent adolescent behavior.

## Reasons for Study Inadequacies

Various obstacles are encountered by psychologists, educators, and other evaluators when they attempt to study all the various phases of adolescent life and adjustment. Some of these difficulties are common to all study projects that involve analyses of complex human behavior. It is almost impossible to isolate one phase or segment of the total, integrated personality pattern. Furthermore, the subtle interrelationships that may exist between human reactions and environmental stimuli constitute elusive elements that interfere with one's efforts to discover valid cause-effect relationships as these affect human behavior. The fact that the human being has potential for behaving in many ways in a given situation makes it difficult to predict how any one individual will behave in a particular situation. There are influences both within and outside him that predispose toward one or another type of behavior. For example, his inherited abilities and capacities, his physical condition at the time, and his basic learning are potent factors of influence on his behavior at any given moment.

Other general factors of inadequacy in currently utilized evaluating procedures include lack of clear understanding of the purpose of the study, lack of accuracy in the administration of evaluating techniques, and lack of correctness and completeness in interpreting the obtained data. In addition, it would seem to be a matter of general understanding that a study has value only when the findings are checked for validity and reliability and then applied constructively. Unfortunately, there still are too many instances of study projects that are carefully completed, and the results perhaps published in a professional journal, with little or no practical utilization of their implications.

Attempts to study adolescents present certain specific problems. The adolescents themselves may resent what to them appears to be a form of prying into their affairs. They are sensitive to possible adult criticism of their attitudes, beliefs, or behavior. For example, an adolescent will agree with his teacher that he is weak in mathematics or that he is not achieving as well as he would like in some other school subject, but he rarely will tolerate a suggestion from an elder that his grooming, dress, manners, expressed attitudes, and convictions need to be changed or improved according to adult standards. The young person may seem to agree with the suggestion; he is more likely than not to continue the criticized practice, however. Adolescent secretiveness and lack of cooperation with adults whom they do not know well and in whom they do not have confidence often have the result of making it impossible for an investigator to obtain accurate or truthful responses from young people who are the subjects of an evaluative study.

Although the reasons for adult lack of cooperation vary, parents, teachers, and other leaders of youth are not always helpful in their attitudes toward study approaches. Some parents fear that questions presented to them concerning their adolescent children may carry implications of parental failure in child rearing. Moreover, it is difficult for a father or mother to be completely objective in the evaluation of his child's strengths and weaknesses, especially to a stranger.

Even though a parent admits that his adolescent child has erred in one way or another, there is evidenced an attitude of placing the blame for the situation on conditions outside the home, or of criticizing other adults for not understanding the young person, or for failing to give him a "fair deal." An example of this parental attitude recently came to the authors' attention. A teen-age boy of a good family was brought into court twice because of delinquent behavior. In both instances the parents criticized the presiding judge for his harshness and lack of understanding of their son's problems. They also have been consistent in their expressed attitude of placing the blame for the boy's delinquent behavior upon factors and conditions outside his own and the family's control.

Some school administrators and teachers are reluctant to devote school time to participation in study projects that involve their pupils. Except for matters that deal with school progress, any information possessed by school people concerning students and their families is supposed to be held in confidence unless an individual pupil and his family are willing to release it to other persons or agencies. This school-home relationship functions as a barrier to the obtaining of much valuable information that otherwise might be available through the administration of questionnaires to teachers and pupils, the setting up of series of fact-finding interviews, or the utilization of other mediums of investigation. The time-consuming demands of an extensive and intensive investigation, even though receiving parental and school administrator approval, interferes with the teaching-learning activities that are needed to "cover" the materials of overcrowded school curriculums. Hence teachers often believe that they dare not "waste" time on an investigation that may not have specific and immediate educational value.

Growing concern about adolescent maladjustment and delinquency among professionally minded men and women, as well as among the general citizenry, is tending to modify former resistance to participation in adolescent study projects. An increasing recognition of the value as an educational aid of the results of studies that already have been conducted is stimulating interest in continued research. Some of the study difficulties referred to in this part of the discussion still exist, however. With the improvement and expansion of techniques of study and evaluation, some of these obstacles may be removed. As we consider the various techniques and approaches to adolescent study, we shall attempt to indicate ways through which greater reliability of methodology and validity of findings may come to be achieved.

## Commonly Used Study Approaches

There are various possible approaches to the study and evaluation of human characteristics. More or less consciously, everyone is constantly attempting to discover why another person acts or thinks in one or another way. For the most part, the layman's evaluation of his respective associates is conducted informally and reflects his own attitudes, standards of values, and biases or prejudices. To be valid, a study of the development and adjustment of a young person of any age must represent an objective approach and follow scientific procedures to as great an extent as is possible. Conclusions subjectively arrived at can be avoided or minimized only if the person or group engaging in the study or evaluating process makes careful preparation for the project, observes or measures accurately and objectively, classifies obtained data completely, summarizes the results of the study correctly and impartially, and verifies the final conclusions through continued research and application.

## Limiting Factors of Study Approaches

Regardless of the study technique employed and the carefulness of its utilization, general applicability of the resulting conclusions may be questionable. For example, many of the existing studies of adolescent development and behavior have centered around research concerning young people who have been reared in middle-class urban communities. In Chapter 2 we emphasized the effect of subcultural influence upon the developmental pattern of youth, as well as the effect of differences in biologically inherited potentialities. Hence, as we consider the various commonly utilized techniques of adolescent study and evaluation, we need to be alert to at least two significant facts: (1) generalizations resulting from research applicable only to members of the group studied, e.g., behavior or attitudes that may seem to be general for younger adolescents or for teen-agers who are born and reared in a large metropolitan community such as New York City may not be representative of older adolescents or youth in the small agricultural village of Dundee, Ohio; (2) within the group studied there are likely to be some adolescents who, for one or another reason, deviate from the generally accepted norm of development or adjustment, e.g., an adolescent's personal and group behavior may be affected by too great difference between himself and the majority of the group in physical structure and constitution, mental potential, emotional balance, or socioeconomic status. With these cautions concerning the acceptance of study results, we now shall consider some of the generally used approaches to the study of adolescent nature.

## The Horizontal Study Approach

Many of the data now available concerning adolescents have been obtained through the utilization of horizontal or cross-sectional study approaches. By means of this technique, often referred to as a "normative" study, specific characteristics of a large group of subjects, supposedly of the same status, are investigated to discover what the general trend or average for that particular group appears to be. When a norm has been reliably ascertained, any individual who falls into the group studied can be compared with his group's average to determine the extent of his deviation from it, i.e., with the degree to which he is atypical.

The utilization of cross-sectional studies has provided us with considerable information concerning general growth and development trends. Height and weight charts represent the results of studies that have been conducted at various age levels. The same is true of mental growth and of other phases of child and adolescent development. Comparisons of these developmental "average ages" have led to the acceptance of certain expected norms as standards for the evaluation of individual growth and progress. The many carefully conducted cross-sectional studies that have been made and continue to be made have value in that they represent a convenient basis for evaluating the status of a young person at any given stage of his development.

The study inadequacies referred to in the preceding section apply to the utilization of the horizontal approach. If we critically examine all the factors involved in this method, we recognize the danger of accepting without question any norm, no matter how reliable it may seem to be. The results of a cross-sectional study usually are supposed to represent a sampling of the whole population at a given stage of growth or development. Since it is difficult to obtain an adequate sampling, the obtained norm may not be representative of all possible cases. Hence apparent deviation from that norm may not be a reliable measure of individual evaluation. It is only as many different studies are conducted in the same area of investigation, and yield comparable results, that valid conclusions can be drawn.

Another cause of error in cross-sectional studies of growth and development lies in the fact that rate of progress differs with individuals. One cannot assume, for example, that all persons who have the same chronological age, say, 8, 10, 12, or 14 years, have reached the same maturational stage. Yet most of them may be fully mature by age 20. The factor of growth and development rate is particularly significant during the adolescent years. Another weakness lies in the fact that an 8-year-old group may yield a greater range of differences than is found in older age groups, with consequent unreliable "averages."

This situation may be illustrated by supposing that in a school or school system a simultaneous group study is undertaken to discover the average increase in mental ability that can be expected to take place in pupils from the fourth to the eighth grade. Undoubtedly the study project will show that children grow mentally during these years. The average difference, however, between age and grade levels cannot be explained entirely in terms of the growth and development factors alone. Unless the school or school system is organized in terms of social promotions, i.e., according to chronological age, with no regard for success in learning progress, the pupils of the higher grades constitute a more selective group from the standpoint of mental alertness. Since the mentally slower members of the fourth-grade group have not been able to keep pace with their brighter classmates, the norms of intelligence in the upper-grade groups represent not only increasing maturation but also greater homogeneity in mental ability.

## The Longitudinal or Vertical Study Approach

Parents, teachers, and other adults who are responsible for the welfare of young people usually are interested in general "psychological" principles only to the extent that they apply to specific boys and girls. Parents are concerned about the developmental progress of their child. The teacher at any school level needs to understand each of his pupils in terms of the young person's particular developmental history, his present status, and probable future progress. The child, and especially the adolescent, should gain some awareness of personal strengths and weaknesses. These data can be obtained only by means of a continuous study of the individual from the prenatal period through the maturing and developing years. Such longitudinal or vertical studies are time-consuming and costly projects. They necessitate the continued application of research techniques which may be difficult to manage. Moreover, reliable conclusions concerning the individual's pattern of developmental progress cannot be made until he has reached maturity. Longitudinal studies are extremely valuable, however. We are now beginning to get the results of such studies that were begun in the 1920s and 1930s. Some of these research projects will be described later in this chapter.

## Specific Techniques of Evaluation

Various techniques and instruments of evaluation are utilized in the study of adolescent development and adjustment. Among those commonly used are (1) observational techniques, (2) interviewing, (3) questionnaires, (4) standardized testing instruments, (5) evaluation through self-expression, (6) experimentation, and (7) the case study or case history. Each of these study approaches is described briefly below.

### Observational Techniques

Observation of displayed behavior is a common method of discovering what a person is like. Roughly, this method can be classified as (1) informal, unplanned observation of behavior that takes place daily among associates, and that may be interpreted in terms of personal bias or may place emphasis upon certain aspects of behavior and disregard others, (2) planned observation that is conducted by a trained person, is controlled in terms of specific purposes of study, and is relatively free from personal prejudice, or (3) observation that is conducted through a one-way vision screen or through motion pictures of displayed behavior that had been taken without the subject's or subjects' awareness of being observed.

Planned, controlled observation often is used by the teacher in the classroom. This form of study technique will be discussed later. The utilization of the one-way screen or the motion-picture technique is an excellent method of studying what can be termed "natural reactions." Arnold Gesell's detailed studies of the behavior patterns of young children exemplify the value of this mode of observation. Many institutions of teacher education are employing one-way vision screen and sound amplifying techniques as means of helping teacher trainees become acquainted at firsthand with children's behavior patterns under varying conditions.

Although well-organized observational techniques are excellent approaches to the developmental study of children, their utilization in the study of adolescents tends to be less successful. Teen-agers usually are quick to realize that they are the subjects of observational study. They are sensitive; they may be suspicious of stimuli situations that seem to focus upon themselves and their behavior. They react unfavorably to observational note taking in their presence. Hence in a situation of this kind they are likely either to become unresponsive or to display artificial rather than habitual behavior patterns. Moreover, some young people have learned about one-way vision screens; they resent attempts to interview them in rooms which they believe to be thus equipped. A 16-year-old boy expressed his attitude to one of the authors in these words: "What do they think I am—a performing monkey in a cage? Well, I'll give them their money's worth."

If an adolescent is the subject of planned observation, the situation should be made to appear informal, and no notes should be taken until the observational period is ended and the subject has withdrawn from the situation. Similarly, an adolescent should not be observed through a one-way vision screen, or have motion pictures taken of his activities, unless the person in charge of the project is certain that the subject is unaware of the presence of the mechanical aid, or is willing to cooperate in the project, with full knowledge of the fact that he is being observed and of the purpose of the observation.

## Interviewing

An interview is a helpful method of gaining greater understanding of an individual's attitudes, interests, beliefs, and thought patterns. The success of the interview technique is in direct ratio to the interviewing skill and receptive attitude of the interviewer. Summarized briefly, the characteristics of effective interviewing include (1) careful preparation for the interview situation by a trained interviewer; (2) the maintenance of an informal and relaxed atmosphere during the interview, as a result of the interviewer's display of a sympathetic, understanding, and sincere attitude toward the interviewee and the purpose of the interview; and (3) the provision of ample opportunity for the interviewee to express himself freely, frankly, and without undue interruption or pressure by the interviewer.

Adolescents tend to respond to the interview situation in much the same way as they react to the utilization of the observational technique. As was said earlier, they tend to be secretive about their affairs and are suspicious of what may seem to them to be adult prying. Consequently, they resent note taking during the interview unless they are permitted to see what is written. If they have confidence in the integrity and understanding of the interviewer and are convinced that he is sincerely interested in them and their welfare, they usually are extremely cooperative. They then report honestly concerning their attitudes, feelings, and interests; they discuss their problems freely in an individual interview with an adult who can convince them that he or she is concerned primarily with their welfare rather than with the accumulation of data about them.

## Utilization of Questionnaires

The questionnaire technique is one of the oldest and most commonly used in the study of adolescents. Much of Hall's data concerning adolescence was obtained in this way. A questionnaire that deals with the submitting of factual data in uncomplicated form is useful as a means of gathering objective information. These data can be helpful to an interviewer in his preparation for individual interviews with the adolescents who submitted answers to the items included in the questionnaire. Interview time then can be devoted to more personal matters.

Questionnaires that are intended to discover adolescent emotional, attitudinal, or other personal attributes should be used sparingly. Unless the questions are presented in simple, clear form and can be answered objectively and briefly, the resulting data may be inadequate. Furthermore, adolescents may be unwilling to respond truthfully unless the purpose of the questionnaire is explained to them and their cooperation secured. Too often, conclusions based upon the results of the administration of questionnaires concerning personal reactions are invalid and unreliable.

## Standardized Testing Instruments

Standardized intelligence and achievement tests, and interest inventories that are administered to young people at different age and development levels, yield considerable data concerning maturational and experiential progress. Self-evaluating and personality rating scales also provide some significant material helpful in adolescent study. The value of these instruments depends in part upon the care with which they have been constructed and in part upon the accuracy of young people's responses. Rating scales that are devised for the evaluation by others of an individual's attitudes, behavior, or other personality characteristics have validity to the extent that the raters are sufficiently acquainted with the subject of the rating to give adequate opinions concerning him, and are able to divorce their judgments from personal bias or prejudice.

Other more or less standardized aids to adolescent study include (1) projective techniques such as the Ink Blot Test and the Thematic Apperception Test, by means of which the adolescent is provided an opportunity to give free expression to his attitudes and feelings; (2) artificially structured situations, in which the individual's behavior is observed; and (3) role playing, in which the subject is asked to present certain specified forms of behavior. Only trained psychologists should administer these tests.

## Evaluation through Self-expression

Adolescents usually like to talk and write about themselves. They exchange confidences with their peers concerning their interests, their likes and dislikes, and their developing philosophy of life. They hesitate to share their thoughts, aspirations, and emotional reactions with an adult, however, unless they feel certain that he or she is trustworthy. If they discover that a confidence is betrayed by an adult, they become resentful, their ego becomes deflated, and they may become suspicious of other adults.

During the growing-up period, many girls and some boys keep diaries. Boys' diaries usually are written in the form of logs that present, in chronological order, an objective account of interesting activities or events. Among girls, however, daily or weekly reports of happenings, interests, and attitudes tend to be emotionally charged. To this extent a girl's diary does not represent a factual account of adolescent experience.

Moreover, girls, and less often boys, who engage in this activity go to great lengths to maintain the secrecy of what they write. Consequently, it may be almost impossible for adults to gain access to their diaries. The authors have been fortunate in having diaries written by adolescents turned over to them. They also have found that it is not easy to achieve this. For example, they were promised a diary that was written during her adolescent years by a woman who now is in her early twenties. However, on second thought, she decided against releasing it, saying, "It is too personal."

Another approach to the study of adolescents is an attempt through a written list of clearly and simply worded questions to discover their attitudes toward their peers and their adolescent experiences. The authors have collected from adolescents of various ages written answers to questions such as the following: What characteristics do you like (dislike) in members of the opposite sex? What can you do to become popular with members of your own sex or of the opposite sex? What are some of the things that you would like to do that appear to be disapproved by your parents or other adults?

Although many of the thousands of responses that have been obtained seem to be honest reports of youthful reactions, there still is the possibility that the answers to questions like these represent what the responders consider to be acceptable answers rather than true expressions of their feelings or beliefs. Existing emotional involvement is likely to result in distorted reports of actual facts. Questions such as those above have value insofar as they indicate that most adolescents know what they should admire in their peers rather than what actually stimulates their interest in a particular peer associate. Responses to questions of this kind tend to be much more objective if they are answered in retrospect by young adults who have come to understand some of their own adolescent vagaries. Adult evaluation of youthful attitudes and behavior may suffer from memory lapses, however, or experiential changes in personal or social values. For example, the authors are acquainted with an able and talented woman who, at the age of 15, adored a college man whose only asset was his brilliance as a student. If this girl had been asked at that time to name the characteristics that she most admired in a member of the opposite sex, she would have described this young man, stressing his academic achievements. As an adult, however, she is able to recognize this man's many weaknesses. In retrospect, therefore, she underplays her actual 15-year-old evaluation.

Some informal study approaches to adolescent development and adjustment involve objective adult appraisal of various forms of written expression that are submitted by young people in connection with their schoolwork. Alert, experienced secondary school teachers are valuable sources of information concerning their students, especially when the teachers are able to establish good rapport with the adolescents themselves and with parents.

## The Experimental Approach

Basically, the experimental method of study is a form of directed observation of an isolated factor under carefully controlled conditions. Although controlled experiments dealing with animal behavior have yielded relatively successful results, experimental investigations of human characteristics are difficult to organize and conduct satisfactorily in any area of behavior except those concerned with simple reaction patterns.

For the results of an experiment to yield conclusive results in the field of adolescent study, for example, many complex factors must be controlled, e.g., sex, age, and maturation level of the subjects of both the study and the control groups, as well as their past developmental experiences and their present physical, mental, and emotional status. Attempts have been made, for instance, through the application of the experimental technique, to discover the truth of the common belief among some school people and employers that high school and college girls are less successful than their brothers in the study of the physical sciences. In this area of ability to achieve, as well as in others, experimentally derived results would seem to indicate that differences between the sexes may have their origin in factors other than that of sex alone. Consequently, little has been done to date in the utilization of the experimental method in the study of adolescent development or adjustment.

## The Case Study Approach

The case history or case study represents an accumulation by a trained person of data concerning an individual. A complete case history contains correct and adequate information about the subject's physical and physiological, mental and emotional development from birth to the time of the study, home conditions, educational, vocational, and social experiences, and any other factors of influence that are pertinent to the study. These data are obtained through the utilization of all or many of the study approaches that have been described in the preceding pages. Then they are organized by the investigator and accompanied by interpretations and recommendations.

The case history approach is employed by the staffs of psychological clinics in their study and treatment of young people referred to them because of an existing problem situation. This approach also is utilized as a genetic study of developmental changes in the attitudes, interests, and behavior patterns of adolescent boys and girls.

## Study Approaches Utilized by the Secondary School Teacher

It is almost axiomatic to say that a teacher's degree of success in motivating his students toward effective learning activity depends largely upon his recognition of learner needs, abilities, interests, ambitions, and attitudes toward the school, the teacher, and the value of educational offerings. Probably on no other school level is the teacher's understanding of his pupils so much needed as it is in the secondary school. In spite of crowded school conditions, the interested high school teacher has many opportunities to study his pupils and thereby obtain considerable information about them and insight into their adjustment problems. Data concerning adolescent attitudes and behavior that are contributed by classroom teachers are extremely helpful as aids in investigations concerning adolescent development. These data can be obtained in various ways by the teacher as he works with and studies his adolescent pupils.

### Observational Study and Reporting

Compared with the controlled observational techniques that were described earlier, a teacher's observation of student behavior is relatively informal and may be affected by the teacher's prejudice or lack of insight. Yet there is value in the day-by-day teacher observation of the fact that a certain student displays a particular behavior pattern in his relationships with his classmates and his teacher. The validity of teacher observation is increased when several teachers agree in their interpretation of a young person's personality characteristics, either during the same school year or during much or all of his stay in the school.

In an increasing number of secondary schools it is becoming customary to encourage teachers to submit written reports concerning their pupils to the school dean or other appropriate administrative officer. These observational reports, or *anecdotal records,* usually consist of brief descriptions of classroom incidents involving the display by one or another specific student of significantly atypical behavior that either is superior to the so-called "norm" or would seem to need readjustment. From an accumulation of such teacher reports concerning a large number of adolescents, an understanding of adolescent behavior trends can be achieved that is extremely valuable to the student of adolescent psychology, as well as to the guidance personnel of the school.

## Autobiographical Materials

The secondary school teacher of English is in an excellent position to gain insight into adolescent interests and attitudes as these are displayed by his students in their written compositions or themes. Young people often divulge more about themselves in their writings than they realize. Many teachers of English have their pupils write autobiographies, or discuss in written form their interests or ambitions, their unusual experiences, or the problematic situations which they have encountered. Interesting bits of information concerning adolescents can be gathered through the utilization of this study approach.

However, too much credence cannot be given to what adolescents write about themselves. Some young people are honest and frank in their accounts about themselves, their background history, and their experiences; they feel secure in their relationships with their peer and adult associates, and are achieving successfully in their various areas of activity. There also are many teen-agers who are uncertain of their group status. They are sensitive to the economic, social, and personal ability differences that they believe exist between themselves and their peers. Hence in their written accounts of themselves they tend to misrepresent or to exaggerate personal experiences or conditions. If a young person's report about himself can be checked against other valid data, any inconsistencies between them yield valuable information about adolescent attitudes. Regardless of the accuracy of his autobiographical material, however, an adolescent is given an opportunity through participation in self-descriptive writing projects to evaluate himself and his experiences more objectively than he might otherwise do.

## The Sociometric Technique

The construction by the teacher of a sociogram to discover peer relationships among the members of his class is more common on the elementary school level than it is in secondary schools. The utilization of this technique involves the teacher's asking each of his pupils to submit to him the names of two or three classmates who are his best friends or with whom he would like to work on a project, or the name of the pupil next to whom he would like to sit in class. The purpose of the pupil selection is to discover which members of the class are most popular with their peers and which pupils are rejected by all or most of their classmates.

This technique helps the teacher discover the isolates in the class so that he can then attempt to assist these young people to develop personal characteristics that will gain for them acceptance in their peer groups. The application by secondary school teachers of this study approach affords opportunities for investigating some of the bases of adolescent peer acceptance or rejection. By comparing the behavior patterns of popular teen-agers with those of the isolates, some insight can be gained concerning adolescent relationship values. Care must be exercised by the investigator, however, that sensitive young people do not become emotionally disturbed by discovering that their classmates have rejected them. Hence teachers need to be cautious in their utilization of the sociometric technique.

## Types of Studies and Investigations of Adolescence

The past thirty-five years have witnessed a rapidly developing trend among psychologists, sociologists, and educators to engage in systematically organized investigations of adolescent development and adjustment. Many studies that have been completed or that are still in progress represent short-time attempts to refine our understanding of areas of adolescent nature that are limited to one age; other investigations are comprehensive, include many phases of adolescent development and/or adjustment, and are long-time projects. The results of the simpler studies usually are based upon findings that are procured through the utilization of one or a few of the study approaches described in the preceding pages. In the more ambitious and elaborate investigations, all or most available and acceptable informal and formal techniques are employed.

## Normative versus Individual Studies

The type of study approach to be used depends upon the particular purpose of an investigation. Parents, teachers, social workers, or any other adults who are working with adolescents of the same age group, for example, recognizing the fact that individual differences exist among the members of the group, need to know what is considered to be relatively normal in one or another phase of development at a particular age level. They must discover to what extent specific members of the group deviate from a "norm" that has been established as a result of supposedly accurate measurement or evaluation of many individuals on the group level. By means of such investigations of large groups, generally referred to as *normative studies,* we are enabled to compare a young person's various physical characteristics, degree of mental alertness, or display of other personal attributes with the accepted average of his peer group.

Normative studies of respective developmental stages have provided a wealth of information concerning the *probable* general rates and kinds of changes that can be expected to take place during the adolescent period. On the basis of obtained findings it is possible to determine the existing status of individual young people and to predict their progress in one or another area of development. The correctness of evaluation of any one adolescent in comparison with the norm of his peer group, however, is dependent upon two factors: the reliability of the established "norm," and the effect upon him of various environmental influences that are peculiar to his particular experiences but not common among the great majority of the group with which he is being compared. Hence it is necessary for comparisons to be made in terms of conclusions that are based upon data resulting from wide, representative cross-sectional investigations. These studies must have been conducted with scientific care and their findings interpreted objectively in terms of clear and definite criteria of evaluation. Moreover, to obtain an adequate understanding of a particular adolescent's developmental pattern of progress and changing patterns of adjustment, not only should he be evaluated in terms of group norms but also he should be the subject of an intensive long-time progressive study aimed at discovering the interrelationships that exist between his potentialities of development and the molding effects of environmental influences upon his various trait potentials.

The *individual study* approach yields significant data concerning the adolescent who is studied, and may give insight into the nature of other similar young people. In order to arrive at valid conclusions concerning general trends of adolescence, however, there would be needed many individual studies that paralleled one another both horizontally and vertically and that represented adequate sampling. An increasing number of such studies are under way, but the establishing of completely valid and reliable generalizations from obtained data probably still is in the distant future.

## Variation in Purpose of Studies

Adolescent studies vary in the purpose they are to serve. Many investigations are focused upon obtaining greater understanding of adolescent growth progress. Others represent attempts to discover something about young people's interests, attitudes, ambitions, beliefs, opinions, and habitual behavior patterns at progressive stages of their development and in terms of their background experiences. As a result of an apparent increase among adolescents of delinquent behavior and of mental and emotional disturbance, considerable attention is being given to the study of adjustment problems experienced by adolescents, the possible or probable causes of these problem situations, and ways in which maladjustive conditions can be removed or ameliorated.

## Studies of Adolescent Attitudes and Interests

A few of the many investigations in these areas are presented briefly here in order to acquaint the reader with some of the study approaches utilized and the significance of the findings.

In an extensive study, Remmers and his associates attempted to discover something about adolescent interests and attitudes. The investigation was based on the Purdue Opinion Poll (constructed by Remmers and Davenport), involved some 15,000 young people, and extended over several years.

One area of the study dealt with a comparison of the attitudes of high school students in rural areas and small towns of Indiana and Illinois with those of their fathers, mothers, and teachers. From the obtained data it was concluded that, in general, greater similarity of attitude was evidenced between parents and children than between teachers and children or teachers and parents; the attitude patterns of younger adolescents were more similar to those of their parents than were the attitudes of older adolescents; the degree of likeness of attitude between youth and adults varied somewhat with the specific nature of the attitude.[2]

From among the various aspects of the investigation a brief reference is made here to two other sets of findings: (1) young people's concern about their bodies and (2) their attitudes toward their school experiences. Adolescents indicated in their responses to questions in the first area that they were especially concerned about their weight, body build and posture, acne, and awkwardness. Attitudes toward school experiences included fear of failure and concern about study habits, concentration, difficulties in expressing themselves, teacher-student relations, homework, school progress, and the like.[3]

In a later investigation, Remmers and Radler studied the attitudes of 3,000 high school students in various parts of the United States. Half or more of the young people studied listed the following as their most serious problems: improving figure and posture, wanting people to like

[2] H. H. Remmers and N. Weltman, "Attitude Interrelationships of Youth, Their Parents, and Their Teachers," *Journal of Social Psychology*, vol. 26, pp. 61–68, 1947.

[3] H. H. Remmers and C. G. Hackett, *Let's Listen to Youth*, Science Research Associates, Chicago, 1953.

them, experiencing stage fright before a group, wanting to gain new friends, and desiring to change their weight.[4]

A significant study was a comparison by Harris of the interests in 1935 of the high school students in New York City and in Tulsa, Oklahoma, with those in 1957 of young people (grades seven through twelve) in Minnesota. Various interest changes were apparent. Sex adjustment ranked higher in 1957 than in 1935, as did getting along with people and home relationships. A sharp drop was shown in interest in manners and courtesy. Interest in health and recreation was relatively high in both 1935 and in 1957. Civic interest ranked fourteenth (of fifteen items) in both studies. Some significant differences were found between the interests of boys and girls.[5]

A recent study of adolescent attitudes deals with young people's religious experiences. A group of 144 ninth-grade students (67 boys and 77 girls) in a junior high school of Natick, Massachusetts were asked to write two paragraphs in answer to these questions:

1. When do you feel closest to God?

2. Have you ever had a particular experience when you felt especially close to God? [6]

An alternate question to the foregoing was: "Why does God permit war, murder, and disease?"

The students tested included 36 young people of high ability and 108 of average school achievement. The religious affiliation of most of the group was Protestant, although 27 were Roman Catholic and 25 Jewish.

Some of the findings of the study were:

1. There were six types of recurrent and five types of acute religious experiences.

2. There were differences among boys and girls and between honor and average groups.

3. Frequency of reported religious experiences differed among Roman Catholic, Protestant, and Jewish young adolescents.

Various studies have been made concerning adolescent interest in television. According to Witty and Kinsella,[7] favorite television programs

[4] H. H. Remmers and D. H. Radler, "Teenage Attitudes," Scientific American, vol. 198, pp. 25–29, June, 1958.

[5] Dale B. Harris, "Life Problems in Interests of Adolescents in 1935 and 1957," The School Review, pp. 335–343, Autumn, 1959.

[6] D. Elkind and S. Elkind, "The Varieties of Religious Experiences in Young Adolescents," Journal for the Scientific Study of Religion, vol. II, pp. 102–112, 1962.

[7] Paul Witty and Paul Kinsella, "Children and TV—A Ninth Report," Elementary English, vol. 35, pp. 450–456, November, 1958.

change from year to year. These investigations also report that the average number of hours spent weekly with television by adolescents in the Chicago area varied as follows: 1951—19 hours, 1952—23, 1953—24, 1955—24, 1957—22, and 1958—20.

## Some Investigations Concerning Adolescent Development and Adjustment

The materials concerning adolescence that constitute the bases of discussion in the remainder of this book represent the findings of normative and individual studies of various types. We have described briefly a few of the relatively short-time investigations that have yielded some significant data concerning adolescent attitudes and interests. We now shall turn our attention to several studies of adolescent problems during the growing-up years.

One of the earlier challenging investigations is reported in Howard Bell's *Youth Tell Their Story*.[8] This study, begun in 1935 under the sponsorship of the American Council on Education, represents an attempt to discover the problems experienced by 13,528 Maryland adolescents who ranged in age between 16 and 24, and most of whom were out-of-school youth. The study approach utilized consisted of interviews conducted by a staff of thirty-five field interviewers during a period of seven months. The data obtained from these interviews gave indication of the attitudes of these young people toward home, school, work, recreation, and religious affiliation. Some of the more serious problems reported appeared to be associated with educational offerings, recreational facilities, and employment opportunities.

Another of the early studies in the California Adolescent Growth Study, a seven-year investigation that was begun in 1932 with 215 young people. Under the direction of Harold Jones, they were measured every six months by means of various study approaches, including physical and physiological testing, psychological tests and inventories, teacher ratings, and other similar mediums.[9]

At this point attention can be directed to the approaches utilized by Jones, with the assistance of staff members of the Institute of Child Welfare of the University of California, in the study of an individual adolescent.[10] From among 80 boys of a grade group who participated in the

[8] H. M. Bell, *Youth Tell Their Story*, American Council on Education, Washington, 1938.

[9] Harold E. Jones, "California Adolescent Growth Study," *Journal of Educational Research*, vol. 31, pp. 561–567, 1938.

[10] Harold E. Jones, *Development in Adolescence*, Appleton-Century-Crofts, Inc., New York, 1943.

seven-year study, one boy, called John Sanders, was selected as the subject of an individual report. Included in the report were phases of this adolescent's experience and adjustment over a seven-year period, in relation to his home, school, and social relationships; his physical development, motor and mental abilities, interests and attitudes, self-evaluation, and his struggle for maturity. From the data obtained through this individual longitudinal study Jones concludes:

The study of single cases is likely to yield conjectures and hypotheses rather than general conclusions. At least one conclusion, however, can be lifted out of the developmental history presented here. It is, perhaps, a little like the conclusion to be drawn from a Horatio Alger story. John Sanders was a boy with an extraordinary accumulation of personal handicaps: physical, social, emotional, economic. He was unsupported by any special sense of security in his family; unaided by any special gift of intelligence or by any special insights on his part or on the part of his teachers.

He reached a low point in adjustment, but he did not remain there. The greater personal stability and the more adequate social relationships he achieved in the last year of high school were carried forward during college. His college years also brought a successful record in courses and in an enterprising variety of outside activities. So marked an upturn in John's personal fortunes is evidence not only of the toughness of the human organism but also of the slow, complex ways in which nature and culture may come into adaptation.[11]

Other comprehensive studies of adolescence have yielded data that have improved our insight into adolescent nature and adjustment problems. The Committee on Human Development of the University of Chicago conducts intensive and extensive studies that are related to the development of children and adults. One phase of their program deals with the study of character development. In this connection a "broad-gauge" investigation was undertaken in a Middle Western community, "Prairie City," having a population of less than 10,000. Although the study included young people who became 10 and 16 years old during the calendar year 1942, the report by Havighurst and Taba[12] deals with data concerning 68 boys and 76 girls of the 16-year-old group. Both statistical and individual approaches were used. The study was based upon the postulate that character is learned through reward and punishment, as well as through unconscious imitation, and that "character develops through reflective thinking." The various substudies yielded interesting data concerning the interrelationships that may exist between adolescent

[11] Ibid., p. 161.
[12] R. J. Havighurst and H. Taba, Adolescent Character and Personality, John Wiley & Sons, Inc., New York, 1949.

character development and various factors of influence that lie within and outside the individual. These data will be considered in greater detail in a later chapter.

Another University of Chicago project deals with the impact upon adolescents of social class status. The subjects were 175 boys and girls of high school age who lived in the Prairie City area, and the locale is called "Elmtown." The study presents a realistic and relatively depressing picture of the effect upon youthful attitudes and behavior of belonging to the "lower social classes." [13]

A recent report of the work of the Committee on Human Development of the University of Chicago deals with the growing-up experiences of young people in "River City." [14] In this study the factors in the developmental pattern of boys and girls that are related to their achievement of competence as young adults are considered. The study contains an objective report of social class and social adjustment problems in the lives of young people from childhood through adolescence to young adulthood.

In an attempt to discover young people's reactions to the growing-up process, Ruth Strang[15] conducted a study in which some 1,500 junior and senior high school students were invited to write compositions on "How It Feels to Be Growing Up." The young people involved in the study came from various environments: urban, suburban, semirural, rural; public, private, and parochial schools; lower-, middle-, and upper-socioeconomic levels, although the majority represented urban and rural areas, and middle- and lower-socioeconomic groups.

The dominant feelings about growing up, in which is represented "a combination of the desire to be independent and a willingness to assume responsibility," are presented in Table 5.

A study of the data in Table 5 reveals that four of the first five categories about which more than 20 per cent of the adolescents were concerned are in the area of their relationships with other people: boygirl, social, marriage and family, and feeling of independence. Concern about vocation and the future, although somewhat personal, may have an association with desire for effective family life and social recognition. It is interesting to note that among boys concern about military service is not so prominent as some adults have been led to believe. Also, concern about money is near the bottom of the list of included items. Strang found

[13] A. B. Hollingshead, *Elmtown's Youth*, John Wiley & Sons, Inc., New York, 1949.

[14] R. J. Havighurst et al., *Growing up in River City*, John Wiley & Sons, Inc., New York, 1962.

[15] Ruth Strang, *The Adolescent Views Himself*, McGraw-Hill Book Company, New York, 1957, pp. 132–176.

*Table 5.* Attitudes of Adolescents toward Their Responsibilities (In per cents)

| RANK | CATEGORY | PER CENT |
|---|---|---|
| 1 | Concern with boy-girl relationships...................... | 33.4 |
| 2 | Feeling of increasing independence and self-direction...... | 27.6 |
| 3 | Concern about vocation or the future................... | 26.4 |
| 4 | Concern with social relationships...................... | 25.6 |
| 5 | Concern with marriage and raising a family............. | 23.1 |
| 6 | Awareness of increased responsibility................... | 19.9 |
| 7 | Feelings about religion or morality..................... | 17.6 |
| 8 | Concern about school success or grades................. | 17.5 |
| 9 | Problems of sibling relationships...................... | 14.9 |
| 10 | Dissatisfaction with school experiences................. | 12.9 |
| 11 | Interest in sports.................................... | 12.3 |
| 12 | Concern with larger social problems (national, international) | 10.5 |
| 13 | Concern with clothes or appearance.................... | 10.3 |
| 14 | Feel "good," it is "fun," it is "nice" time of life......... | 9.4 |
| 15 | Feeling of frustration that independence is not recognized.. | 8.4 |
| 16 | Viewpoint that adults do not "understand" adolescents.... | 6.1 |
| 17 | Problems about money................................ | 6.1 |
| 18 | Suggestion of reluctance to lose dependence............. | 4.4 |
| 19 | Awareness of increasing acceptance in the adult world..... | 4.1 |
| 20 | Concern with military service......................... | 3.6 |

SOURCE: Ruth Strang, *The Adolescent Views Himself,* McGraw-Hill Book Company, New York, 1957, p. 138. Reprinted by permission.

a variation in tone of adolescent responses in the respective compositions and suggests that they range from "delight to despair."

Whether one agrees with the conclusions evolved from data obtained by well-trained and experienced investigators, the fact remains that many scientific and semiscientific studies have been and are continuing to be undertaken for the purpose of increasing our understanding of adolescence as a life period and of refining our insight concerning the problem situations experienced by developing adolescents in their struggle toward the achievement of adult maturity. Important as is the process of reaching sound conclusions based upon reliable study, an academic interest in study results is not enough. Approaches to the study of adolescents are valueless unless their results are utilized by parents, school people, and other social agents as foundations of better adolescent adjustment. Home rearing, school curriculums and teaching, vocational and recreational opportunities, social and political ideals and practices, and general adult example—all these constitute the background experiences of developing young people and determine the individual adjustments that they are likely to achieve in terms of their particular rights and responsibilities during their teen years and later. Hence, throughout the remainder of this book emphasis is placed upon the practical application of significant study results as these findings apply in our discussions of evolving principles that are fundamental to wholesome adolescent development and adjustment.

## Questions and Problems for Discussion

1. Illustrate by use of examples that you could participate in a cross-sectional approach to the study of adolescent development and yet not be able to conduct a longitudinal study during the current term.
2. Examine at least two longitudinal studies in the area of adolescent development. Note differences between them, and indicate what you like in one that you do not like in the other.
3. Present both the value and the limitations of the use of observation in the study of adolescent behavior.
4. Decide on a study that you, with three other students, would like to undertake concerning some phase of adolescent behavior. Identify the problem and suggest a research design that might be used to complete the study.
5. *Special Exercises:*
   a. Go with one or two other students to observe a child or an adolescent in a common setting for a period of thirty minutes. (This is easily arranged in colleges in which children are in action behind a one-way screen.) Write down everything you observe about the individual during the thirty minutes without consultation with the other observer(s). Read the report in class, and ask the class to note differences between your report and the other(s).
   b. Go with one or two other students to observe several children or adolescents in a common setting for a period of thirty minutes. Write down everything you observe in the setting. Read the report in class, and ask the class to note differences between your report and the other(s).
   c. If you can arrange to observe an adolescent over a three-week period, keep an anecdotal record of his behavior during that time.
   d. Ask an adolescent to write a short autobiography on the topic "My Experiences during the Past Summer." Study it to try to learn more about the individual.

## Selected References

Ames, Louise B., et al.: *Adolescent Rorschach Responses,* McGraw-Hill Book Company, New York, 1959.

Ausubel, D. P.: *Theory and Problems of Adolescent Development,* Grune & Stratton, Inc., New York, 1954.

Bayer, Leona M., and Nancy Bayley: *Growth Diagnosis: Selected Methods for Interpreting and Predicting Physical Development from One Year to Maturity*, The University of Chicago Press, Chicago, 1959.

Harrower, Molly: *Personality Change and Development: As Measured by the Projective Technique*, Grune & Stratton, Inc., New York, 1958.

Havighurst, R. J., and others: *Growing up in River City*, John Wiley & Sons, Inc., New York, 1962.

Hollingshead, A. B.: *Elmtown's Youth*, John Wiley & Sons, Inc., New York, 1949.

Holtzman, W. H., et al.: *Inkblot Prediction and Personality: Holtzman Inkblot Technique*, University of Texas Press, Austin, Tex., 1961.

Jennings, Helen H.: *Sociometry in Group Relations*, rev. ed., American Council on Education, Washington, 1959.

Jones, Harold E.: *Development in Adolescence*, Appleton-Century-Crofts, Inc., New York, 1943.

Kaplan, Bert: *Studying Personality Cross-Culturally*, Harper & Row, Publishers, Incorporated, New York, 1961.

Klopfer, Bruno, and Helen H. Davidson: *The Rorschach Technique: An Introductory Manual*, Harcourt, Brace & World, Inc., New York, 1962.

Kuhlen, R. G., and G. G. Thompson: *Psychological Studies of Human Development*, 2d ed., Appleton-Century-Crofts, Inc., New York, 1963.

Maier, N. R.: *The Appraisal Interview: Objectives, Methods and Skills*, John Wiley & Sons, Inc., New York, 1958.

Mussen, Paul H. (ed.): *Handbook of Research Methods in Child Development*, John Wiley & Sons, Inc., New York, 1960.

Stone, A. A., and G. C. Onque: *Longitudinal Studies of Child Development*, Harvard University Press, Cambridge, Mass., 1959.

# Part 2

## ADOLESCENT DEVELOPMENT

# Chapter Four

## Physical and Physiological Growth

The early stage of adolescent development is referred to commonly as the pubertal period. The term *puberty* is derived from the Latin word *pubertas*, "the age of adulthood." For a young person to have reached this period of growth signifies that physically he or she is able to participate in the reproduction of the human species.

## The Significance of Puberty

Manhood or womanhood, as we interpret the term, is not achieved suddenly or completely with the onset of puberty. The physical and physiological changes that are associated with adolescent development represent a continuing process that begins early in the life of the individual. Certain forewarnings of sexual development may be evidenced to a greater or lesser extent during the later years of childhood. These years are commonly referred to as the prepubertal or preadolescent period of growth and maturation.

### General Characteristics of Puberty

A child can be said to be asexual. Ordinarily, he accepts without question the physical growth changes that are taking place and mingles freely with members of the opposite sex. As observable signs of sexual maturing begin to show themselves, however, the young person becomes aware of definite body changes, may experience "feelings" that are new to him and consequently not understood, and is likely to develop a changed attitude toward the opposite sex. These personal and social aspects of sexual adjustment are discussed in Chapter 9. In this chapter, sexual growth and maturation are considered in relationship to the physical and physiological changes that are characteristic of adolescent growth and maturation.

It is difficult to determine ahead of time precisely when puberty will begin for an individual. For boys, the overt evidence may be the first nocturnal emission; for girls, the pubertal period may begin with the *menarche* or first menstruation. According to findings obtained from the

71

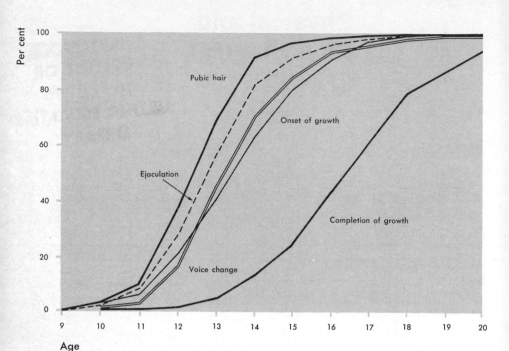

*Figure 2.* Physical development in adolescent boys. (Courtesy of A. C. Kinsey et al., *Sexual Behavior in the Human Male,* W. B. Saunders Company, Philadelphia, 1948, p. 185.)

retrospective reports of some individuals and by actual examination of sexually maturing young people, the age at which pubic hair (a pubertal characteristic) appears varies with individuals. Seven per cent of boys have pubic hair by the age of 11, 68 per cent by the age of 13; up to 1 per cent of boys do not have pubic hair until the age of 17.

Other physical and physiological changes that begin at puberty and continue through adolescence include changes in physical growth and general body contours, breast development in girls, and voice change in boys. Many individual differences can be found in the rate and sequence of growth and maturation among these various characteristics of adolescent development. Patterns of sexual development in adolescent boys are presented in Figure 2.

## Effects of Pubertal Changes on Behavior

Adults who are associated in any way with developing young people need to understand the significance in the life of a young adolescent of the physical and physiological changes that are inherent in pubertal and later growth and maturation. Unless parents, and teachers especially, have some insight concerning the effects of physical changes upon adolescent behavior, they may find themselves almost, if not entirely, bewildered by what often are termed "adolescent vagaries."

Structural and functional changes constitute the factors of adolescent mental, emotional, and social development. The rate and upper limits of physical growth and physiological maturation are closely related to a developing adolescent's self-appraisal in relation to his peers. Either retarded or accelerated physiological maturation may induce emotional reactions that interfere with the achievement of the adolescent's desired social status. Moreover, a recognition of the impact upon adolescent behavior of the interrelationships that exist among the various aspects of adolescent development can help adults to be objective in their critical evaluation of young people's attitudes and conduct.

A pubescent tends to display more or less suddenly acquired but definite attitudes and modes of behavior that are different from childhood reaction patterns. Furthermore, an adolescent's behavior is likely to change from year to year. The growing awareness of body changes is accompanied by changing behavior in relations with adults, members of his or her own sex, and especially members of the other sex. Observation of the activities and expressed attitudes of an individual at the ages of 6, 12, 15, and 18 years yields data that give indication of the changes that take place during this twelve-year period of development. The processes of physical growth and sexual maturation are the determining factors of differences in behavior development.

## Anatomical Growth

In terms of adolescent development, significant areas of body structure are height, weight, body build, and dentition.

## Growth in Height

Comparative growth studies of males and females yield considerable data concerning significant differences between boys and girls in their respective growth patterns. At birth the boy is slightly longer (taller) than the girl. When he is 10 years old, the boy loses his height advantage for several years. During the middle teens he regains his advantage, which he continues to maintain. The construction of the presented curves is obtained from longitudinal studies of many developing young people. Hence the represented height trends are not characteristic of individuals. Rather, significant individual differences are observable at all ages.

Height differences are less observable or measurable at birth and in infancy and childhood than they are during adolescence or at maturity. Many longitudinal studies have been made of height and weight growth trends of boys and girls through the age of 18 years. Shuttleworth,[1] for example, has found that girls who menarche earliest also attain their greatest height earliest; girls who reach their menarche later attain their greatest height later, yet often become taller than girls who began to menstruate at an earlier date. There is a rapid deceleration of growth in stature after the menarche. The inner adjustments of the body are preparing for possible motherhood, and the growth-stimulating action of the glands is diminishing rapidly.

Some data from a growth study made by Nancy Bayley[2] are presented here. In Figure 3 three girls who have different rates of maturing are presented, and in Figure 4 the actual heights of those three girls at various ages of their development are illustrated. It can be observed that the girl who attained the menarche last was the girl who reached the greatest height.

Studies of growth progress among boys, as among girls, give evidence

[1] F. K. Shuttleworth, "Physical and Mental Growth of Boys and Girls Aged Six through Nineteen in Relation to Age at Maximum Growth," *Monographs of the Society for Research in Child Development,* vol. 4, no. 3, pp. 248–249, 1939.

[2] Nancy Bayley, "Individual Patterns of Development," *Child Development,* vol. 27, p. 52, March, 1956.

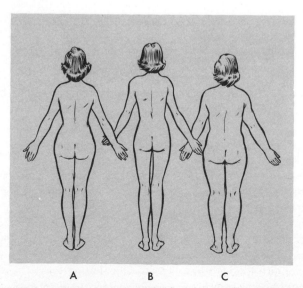

A          B          C

*Figure* 3. Three 18-year-old girls who matured differently. A was accelerated; B was retarded; C's growth was irregular.

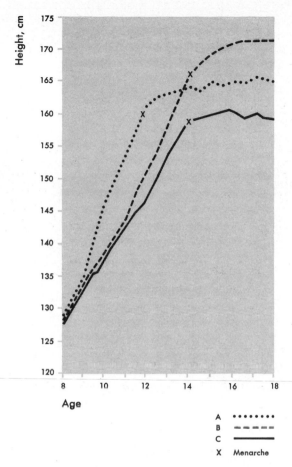

A ••••••••
B ━ ━ ━ ━
C ━━━━━━
X Menarche

*Figure 4.* Curves of height and skeletal age of girls
A, B, and C. Age at menarche for each is indicated
by an *x*.

of an apparent average trend upward from early adolescence to adult
height status. Height growth of any young person may deviate from this
average trend, however. A range of height difference is common among
all boys and all girls. During the developing years growth increments
vary with age. For example, for some girls the growth rate at, or just
prior to, puberty is greater than at any other time; for boys greater growth
increment occurs during the middle, or slightly after the middle, of the
pubertal period.

There are significant differences in height growth among boys of the
same age. This is illustrated in the variation in height of the five boys in
Figure 5, in which each boy is 16 years of age. For purposes of identification, we shall call the boys (left to right) A, B, C, D, and E. The extent

*Figure 5.* Height differences among five 16-year-old-boys.

to which the height leveled off by the age of 24 is illustrated in Figure 6 for three of the boys, A, B, and D. Since not all the boys in Figure 5 were available for the picture in Figure 6, we present in Table 6 the present height, at age 24, of each of the boys in Figure 5.

*Table 6.* Actual Heights of the Five Boys in Figure 5 at Age 24

| BOY | HEIGHT FEET | INCHES |
|-----|------|--------|
| A | 5 | 10½ |
| B | 5 | 11½ |
| C | 6 |  |
| D | 6 | 3 |
| E | 6 | 4 |

## Growth in Weight

Another aspect of growth is weight. Growth in height alone does not give an accurate picture of the story of growth during adolescence. It is important to know that Benjamin is 5 feet tall, but the fact that his relative shortness is accompanied by a weight of 160 pounds is still more descriptive of his growth pattern. Even more significant is the knowledge that he is 15 years old, that his weight one year earlier was 110 pounds, and that his height at that time was about what it is now. The relative height and weight increments are helpful in the understanding of the adolescent.

Reed and Stuart conducted a longitudinal study in which they measured the height and weight of 134 individuals (67 boys and 67 girls) from birth to age 18. We present the normative data by sex for each age.

From a comparison of results of studies we can conclude that average weight differences between the sexes follow trends that are somewhat similar to those for height. Before puberty, girls usually are lighter than

*Figure 6.* Height, at age 24, of the second, third, and fourth boys (reading from the left) in Figure 5.

*Table 7.* Means of Height and Weight According to Age and Sex (67 boys and 67 girls)

| AGE* | HEIGHT, cm† | | WEIGHT, kg | |
|---|---|---|---|---|
|  | BOYS | GIRLS | BOYS | GIRLS |
| 1 | 75.4 | 73.9 | 10.2 | 9.6 |
| 2 | 87.8 | 86.2 | 12.6 | 12.1 |
| 3 | 96.4 | 95.4 | 14.5 | 14.3 |
| 4 | 103.7 | 103.3 | 16.4 | 16.4 |
| 5 | 110.3 | 110.2 | 18.3 | 18.6 |
| 6 | 116.7 | 116.6 | 20.3 | 20.8 |
| 7 | 121.5 | 121.3 | 22.8 | 23.2 |
| 8 | 127.4 | 127.1 | 25.4 | 26.0 |
| 9 | 133.0 | 132.7 | 28.3 | 28.9 |
| 10 | 138.1 | 138.4 | 31.6 | 32.5 |
| 11 | 143.2 | 144.7 | 35.3 | 36.6 |
| 12 | 148.9 | 151.2 | 39.4 | 42.0 |
| 13 | 155.7 | 156.8 | 44.8 | 47.2 |
| 14 | 162.7 | 160.3 | 50.8 | 51.3 |
| 15 | 168.9 | 162.0 | 56.1 | 53.7 |
| 16 | 172.8 | 162.7 | 60.5 | 54.6 |
| 17 | 175.1 | 163.1 | 63.4 | 54.9 |
| 18 | 176.3 | 163.5 | 65.8 | 55.6 |

* Each of the 134 children is represented in the data for every age.
† Supine length to age 6, standing height from 6 to 18 years.
SOURCE: R. B. Reed and H. C. Stuart, "Patterns of Growth in Height and Weight from Birth to Eighteen Years of Age," in *Supplement to Pediatrics*, Charles C Thomas, Publisher, Springfield, Ill., November, 1959, p. 905. By permission of publisher and American Academy of Pediatrics.

boys; during earlier puberty, girls tend to become heavier than boys. It is shown in Table 7 that the average weight of boys at age 11 is 35.3 kilograms and the average weight of girls is 36.6 kilograms. At age 15 the relative weights of the sexes are reversed. Also, as a group, once boys become heavier or taller than girls they maintain this advantage throughout the remainder of their lives. Individual curves of growth in weight of five boys and five girls from the Nancy Bayley study are shown in Figures 7 and 8.

## Changes in Skeletal Structure and Body Proportions

We know that the skeletal structure of a neonate is composed mostly of cartilage. During childhood a process of ossification takes place as the result of the depositing in the cartilage of calcium, phosphate, and other minerals. The pubescent's skeletal structure consists of about 350 bones.

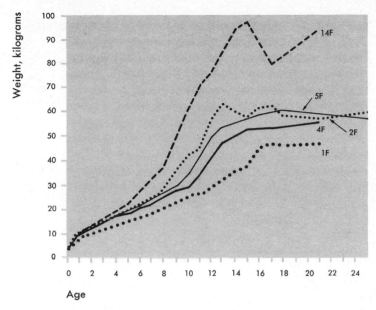

*Figure 7.* Individual curves of growth in weight by age for five girls in the Berkeley Growth Study. (From Nancy Bayley, "Individual Patterns of Development," *Child Development,* vol. 27, pp. 64–65, March, 1956.)

By adulthood the number is reduced to about 206 bones. The process of ossification, or hardening, also continues during the adolescent years to maturity. Although the growth process of the bony structure appears to be relatively regular for most young people, there can be found some individual differences.

As a result of research studies it has been concluded that degree of ossification may be dependent upon nutritional factors. In addition, since the process of ossification is still continuing during the adolescent years, young people are accident-prone as their youthful energy impels them to participate in activities for which their skeletal growth status is not yet ready. Hence boys especially become the victims of broken collarbones, strained or broken ankles, and hip and arm injuries.

Significant changes in body proportions or contours are characteristic of adolescent physical growth. There is relatively little difference in body contour between the male and female child. Inherent in the body changes that occur during puberty are the beginnings of marked contour differences between boys and girls. The adolescent boy's form usually is characterized by straight leg lines, slender hips, and broad shoulders. A girl's leg lines usually become curved and her hips wider, although her shoulders may remain narrow.

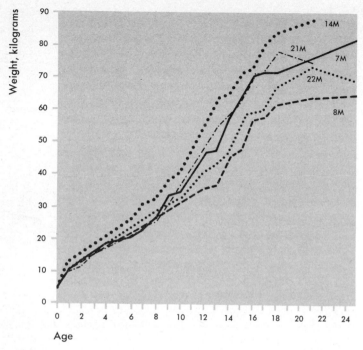

*Figure 8.* Individual curves of growth in weight by age for five boys in the Berkeley Growth Study. (From Nancy Bayley, "Individual Patterns of Development," *Child Development,* vol. 27, pp. 64–65, March, 1956.)

Of course, the individual boy's or girl's deviation from what can be considered average rate and amount of growth progress in body proportions is similar to individual differences in height and weight. Some of these differences can be attributed to the age at which puberty begins.

As one compares variations in size among 15-year-old adolescents, he is able to recognize some of the physical growth factors that play important roles in adolescent peer and adult relationships. Many instances could be cited of young people experiencing adjustment difficulties that stem from physical growth. For example, a short, slender, narrow-shouldered college student recalls vividly the many embarrassments he suffered, especially during his early high school years, when his classmates nicknamed him "Baby" and excluded him from rough-and-tumble play. This young man still is trying to compensate for his body structural inadequacies through meticulousness of grooming, attempted monopolization of class discussion, and "witty" comments that annoy his peer associates.

Another annoying situation is that of a small, undeveloped-appearing 17-year-old girl who is denied certain socializing privileges that are granted to her tall, physically well-developed 15-year-old sister who, according to the parents, is "big enough to take care of herself." Attention also can be directed to the boy who at 16 years of age was about 6 feet 4 inches tall and well developed. His sister, 1½ years older than he, was tall for a girl but some 5 inches shorter than he. When he was about 14 years old, however, his sister, in line with expected growth progress, exceeded her brother in height by at least 6 inches, as well as in proportionate weight and general physical status. Consequently, the boy resented not only his physical inferiority to his sister but also the attitudes that he imagined his family and peer associates had toward his apparently retarded growth. He became emotionally disturbed by the thought that he would "take after his mother," who is relatively short and slender in comparison with his father, who is 6 feet 6 inches tall and weighs over 300 pounds.

## Classification of Body Build

Attempts have been made to classify adolescent and adult body build in relation to behavior and attitude concomitants of physical structure and proportions. Interest in the significance to an individual of his body build is not new. As early as 400 B.C., Hippocrates attempted to classify "personality" types according to so-called "body humors." During the first quarter of the present century Kretschmer concluded that an individual's personal characteristics can be classified according to his body build as

Athletic—muscular and responsive to desirable adjustments

Asthenic—tall and thin, critical of others but sensitive to criticism of themselves

Pyknic—short and stout, easygoing and popular with people

Dysplastic—abnormal build with characteristics growing out of the abnormality

An extensive study between body build and type of personality among men has been undertaken by Sheldon and his coworkers.[3] Basing their findings upon results obtained by the utilization of anthropometric measurements with more than 4,000 college men, conclusions were reached that males cannot be classified according to discrete types of body build. Rather, they represent a kind of combination, with one type of build predominating over the others. Hence in their studies they have employed various digit evaluations to indicate the degree to which characteristics of each of three body types are present in an individual.

[3] W. H. Sheldon, S. S. Stevens, and W. B. Tucker, *The Varieties of Human Physique*, Harper & Row, Publishers, Incorporated, New York, 1940.

Certain personal attributes are supposedly associated with these body types. The categories according to which, with some variations, male build can be classified are termed somatotypes. They include

Endomorphic—body soft and round, abdominal region prominent

Mesomorphic—muscular and bony, hard and heavy physique, and thick skin

Ectomorphic—thin body with relative prominence of skin and neural structure

In an analysis of human physiques, no one individual completely represents one physical type. However, as an easy way of identifying the extent to which an individual displays each of the somatotypes, a scale from 7 to 1 is used. If an individual's rating is 7–4–1, it indicates that he has prominent endomorphic features, some mesomorphic features, with a minimum of ectomorphic features. Likewise, a rating of 2–7–1 would represent a predominantly mesomorphic physique; and a rating of 1–2–6 would represent a predominantly ectomorphic physique.

Attempts at body typing have gained some popularity, especially insofar as emphasis has been placed upon the association of body build and personal attributes or kinds of temperament. Scientifically, however, the various conclusions that have emerged from studies in this area are questionable. The extent to which one or another tendency in body build seems to be associated with the overt expression of a specific kind of temperament probably represents a paralleling rather than a cause-and-effect relationship. Factors other than physique alone can be said to influence personality development among adolescents (see Chapter 7). In conclusion, however, it can be repeated that in deviant height, weight, and body proportions may be rooted many of the social problems of maturing young people. Extreme tallness or shortness may lead to difficulties of adjustment. Abnormal overweight induces ridicule or more or less good-natured name calling among the peers of the fat boy or girl. Adolescent misery can be caused by such peculiarities of body contour resulting from irregularity of growth rate as, for example, large hands or feet, or long torso and short legs.

## The Significance of Dental Growth

The number of permanent teeth erupted usually represents a reliable measure of maturity level. The dental scale presented in Figure 9 is based upon the examination of about 12,000 children of north European stock at different age levels. It is evident from the scale that girls are more advanced than boys at each age level. As is found in other areas of physical growth, there can be detected a definite spurt in dental development during the preadolescent state. The closeness of the erupted teeth,

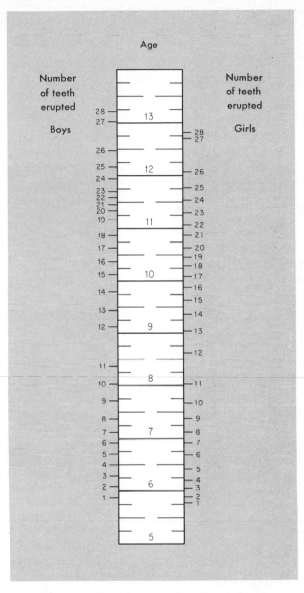

*Figure* 9. Dental age scale. (Courtesy of
Psyche Cattell, *Dentition as a Measure of
Maturity,* Harvard University Press, Cam-
bridge, Mass., 1938.)

by number, indicates that the frequency is greater at one time than at another.

The shape, arrangement, and "health" of a young person's teeth probably are innate. The enamel may be hard or soft. It has been determined, however, that proper nutrition and periodic dental care are significant factors of teeth preservation. The "first" teeth benefit from care, but it is imperative that a young person learn to use rather than misuse his "second" or permanent teeth. During the growth period, as well as throughout life, healthy teeth are achieved and maintained only insofar as they are cared for properly.

## Physiological Maturation

Adolescent changes in anatomical characteristics are observable. Their progress can be evaluated by the periodic utilization of objective measuring instruments. The maturational progress of physiological characteristics, however, represents functional change that usually is reflected in the behavior reactions of the maturing young person. Generally included among physiological aspects of physical constitution are the nervous, circulatory, respiratory, and digestive systems, the muscles, and the endocrine glands.

### Physiological Changes during Adolescence

As we have seen, the effect upon individual adolescent adjustment of particular patterns of anatomical or structural growth can be far-reaching. Of much greater significance in the life of the maturing young person, however, are the emotional behavior and attitudinal concomitants of the physiological changes that are taking place within him. It is possible that the variability of behavior characteristics of many teen-agers can be explained by the fact that they have difficulty in understanding and adjusting to all the forms of physiological functioning which they are experiencing.

The functional potentialities of the major organs of the body are dependent upon rate and limit of growth, as these are accelerated or retarded during growth. Interest in physiological functioning is evidenced by the increase in the number of studies that deal with the growth progress of the internal organs of the body, in comparison with earlier investigations concerning the growth patterns of height, weight, body contour, and other anatomical aspects of individuals.

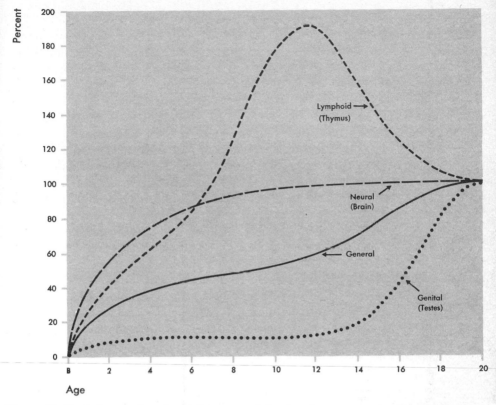

*Figure 10.* Typical examples of growth curves of the four basic types of tissue growths. (From R. E. Scammon's "The Measurement of the Body in Childhood," in J. A. Harris et al., *The Measurement of Man,* The University of Minnesota Press, Minneapolis. Copyright 1930 by the University of Minnesota.)

Studies of the various organs of the body reveal interesting data concerning growth progress of individual organs, as well as growth inter-relationships among the various organs. In one study, for example, consideration was given to the rates of growth of four basic types of tissue: lymphoid, neural, genital, and general all-over external body dimensions.

The findings of this and other studies seem to indicate that the growth of some internal organs is similar in many respects to height and weight growth patterns. It appears also that immediately preceding and during puberty there is considerable increase in the rate of growth of certain internal organs. It can be seen in Figure 10 that neural tissue has its most rapid growth before the age of 6, lymphoid between the ages of 6 and 12, and genital between the ages of 13 and 20.

## Growth of the Heart and Circulatory System

By the time an individual is 12 years old his heart can be expected to weigh about seven times as much as it did at birth. Although there may be a lag in growth during preadolescence and early adolescence, the heart appears to double in size between the ages of 12 and 17. Although arterial growth is positive, it progresses at a much slower rate than does heart size.

The growth ratio between the heart and the arteries results in an increase of systolic blood pressure from young babyhood to the later adolescent years. Moreover, during early childhood the sexes differ little in blood pressure; from about puberty onward, however, boys tend to have higher blood pressure than girls. Pulse rate is highest at birth, decreasing with age. The decrease is steady between the ages of 12 and 18. During adolescence the pulse rate of girls is from 2 to 6 beats per minute faster than that of the boys.

In an effort to study physiological instability during adolescence Eichorn and McKee examined the longitudinal data from the *Adolescent Growth Study* by Harold E. Jones. They compared basal metabolic rate (BMR), oral temperature, pulse rate, and systolic and diastolic blood pressure as functions of age among boys and among girls. Some of the results of their study are illustrated in Figures 11 and 12. In interpreting the results Eichorn and McKee say:

Except for temperature, the curves for the two sexes are rather similar for any given physiological function, but the age trends are not the same for all functions. For BMR, intra-individual variability declines irregularly, while for pulse rate and the blood pressures there is an increase. For temperature, the boys' variability decreases erratically and the girls' curve is so unsystematic that chance appears to be the most reasonable explanation. In general, the curves fall into two groups. Those for pulse and the blood pressures tend to parallel each other as do the curves for BMR and oral temperature. The latter parallel is somewhat more marked for boys than for girls. This is not surprising since we have already observed that, for these subjects at least, body temperature and BMR are correlated in boys and uncorrelated in girls. Although more of the curves in the two figures show a rise than show a fall, the data do not support the notion that there is a *generalized* physiological instability during adolescence. Rather they suggest that some functions become more stable and others less. Nor do the data support the view that such a hypothetical instability is *temporary,* for in no case does the curve first rise and then fall.[4]

[4] Dorothy H. Eichorn and John P. McKee, "Physiological Instability during Adolescence," *Child Development*, vol. 29, no. 2, pp. 255–268, June, 1958.

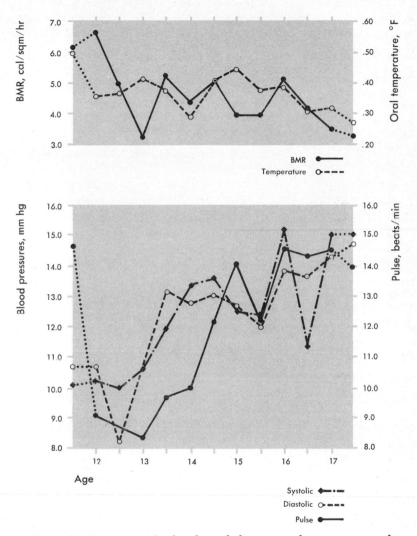

*Figure 11.* Mean range for basal metabolic rate, oral temperature, pulse rate, and systolic and diastolic blood pressure as a function of age (boys). (From Dorothy H. Eichorn and John P. McKee, "Physiological Instability during Adolescence," *Child Development,* vol. 29, no. 2, p. 259, June, 1958.)

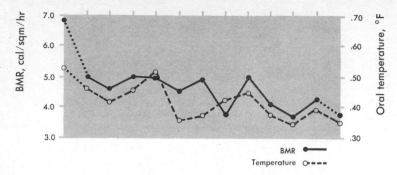

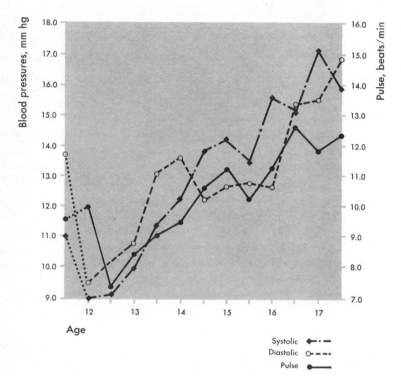

*Figure 12.* Mean range for basal metabolic rate, oral temperature, pulse rate, and systolic and diastolic blood pressure as a function of age (girls). (From Dorothy H. Eichorn and John P. McKee, "Physiological Instability during Adolescence," *Child Development*, vol. 29, no. 2, p. 261, June, 1958.)

## Growth Trends in Muscular Strength and Coordination

Muscular strength increases during adolescence. There are differences between the sexes, however, in the degree of muscular power achieved during these years. Although the muscles of an adolescent girl become longer and heavier than they were during childhood, she actually has less muscular strength than do boys. Superior male strength during the growing years also can be attributed partly to the fact that boys usually are more active than girls and engage in more strenuous exercise. Moreover, male superiority in physical sports is based upon the advantage of greater leverage resulting from the possession of wider shoulders, longer arms, and larger hands.

Most teen-age boys take great pride in exhibiting their increasing muscular strength. Traditionally, the prestige value in this area is great for the boy; for the girl the displaying of exceptional muscular power may act as a deterrent toward the achieving of desired popularity, especially among boys of the same age. Consequently, a boy often attempts by strenuous exercise to develop his muscles; a girl tends to refrain from muscle-developing activity. Modern girls are beginning to participate successfully in various forms of athletics, however, although sports rules usually are modified for them in terms of their endurance and performance potentialities. Numerous measurements have been taken to discover differences between boys and girls in relative strength of grip, speed of running, height of jumping, distance of throwing a ball, and width of broad jump.

It is relatively easy to discover a person's strength of grip, for example, by measuring the number of pounds of pressure he can exert. The difference between male and .female strength of grip as reported by Jones is given in Figure 13. It can be observed that the average grip of boys is greater than that of girls at all ages. The difference remains fairly constant from ages 11 to 14; although from that time the strength of grip of girls continues to rise, the rate is slower than that of boys. Significant differences are shown between the sexes in both "pull" and "thrust" (push-ups). In these tests girls are superior by several pounds to boys between the ages of 11 and 13. However, there are significant differences between the girls and the boys after that time. After age 13 the ability of girls to thrust appears actually to drop, while it rises rapidly for boys between the ages of 13 and 16.

In the California Adolescent Growth Study, Jones compared right-hand strength for two groups of girls, early maturers whose average age at menarche was 11.7 and later maturers whose menarche did not occur until an average age of 14.5. There is a rapid rise in strength of grip for the early-menarche group prior to the age of about 12; this is followed by a very slow rate of increase. During their earlier years the girls who mature latest show relatively regular but retarded growth in strength of grip.

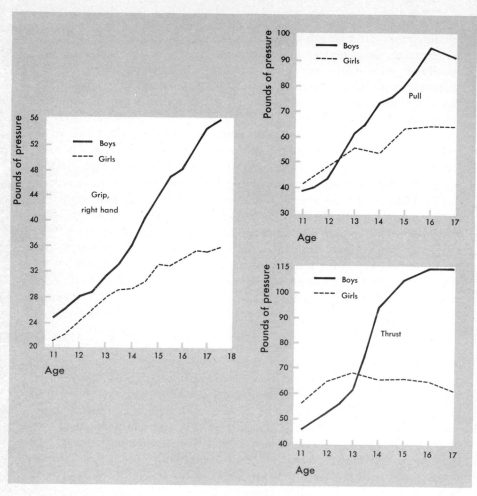

*Figure 13.* Growth in strength. (From H. E. Jones, "Motor Performance and Growth," *University of California Publications in Child Development,* vol. 1, pp. 35, 36, 1949. Used by permission of the University of California Press, publishers.)

## Functions of the Endocrine Glands

Located in various parts of the body are ductless glands known as endocrine glands. Although small in size, they exercise an extremely important influence on the growth and proper functioning of other body organs. The endocrine glands contain chemical laboratories for the production of substances called *hormones,* which are discharged into the blood stream. Each of these glands (see Figure 14) produces its special hormone that is distributed, through the circulation of the blood, to the part of the body where it performs its special function. Some hormones influence the rate of body growth, some affect basal metabolism, others affect mental development and emotional behavior, and still others play important roles in the development of both primary and secondary sex characteristics. As we discuss the functioning of these glands we shall make extensive use of ideas formulated by Thomas H. Eames, who has presented some excellent ideas on the influence of endocrine glands on learning.

The Pituitary Gland. The pituitary gland secretes growth hormones, which control general bodily growth, and gonadotropic hormones (sex hormones), which are necessary for the functioning of the sex glands. It consists of the anterior lobe, the pars intermedia, and the posterior lobe. Each part secretes one or more hormones. The anterior lobe of the gland secretes both the growth hormone and the gonadotropic hormone. During the prepubertal years there is a marked increase in the number of hormones secreted by the anterior lobe, which remains active throughout the reproductive period of life. Eames's comments on the pituitary gland follow:

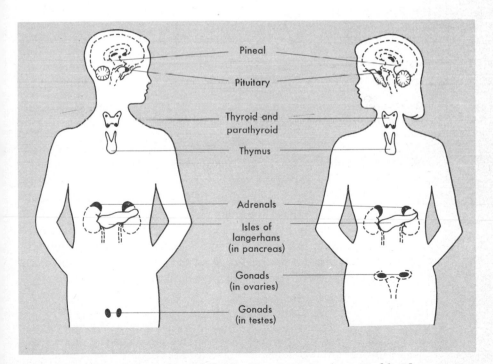

Figure 14. Position of the endocrine glands. (By permission from Health Observation of School Children, by G. M. Wheatley and G. T. Hallock. Copyright 1951, McGraw-Hill Book Company, New York, p. 93.)

This gland regulates the entire endocrine system. A variety of hormones are produced and evidences of excess or deficiency depend on which hormone is affected. The gland is a small, round, grayish-red organ, attached to the brain by a stalk and lying in a depression in the sphenoid bone near the hypothalamus. In other words it is in the head, closely attached to the brain. It has three lobes. When the anterior lobe is affected any of several general reactions are likely to occur. Deficiency of the growth hormone makes the child symmetrically dwarfed. He is a tiny but well-formed person. When the gonadotrophic hormone is deficient the child remains small and immature and he retains his appearance of immaturity into adulthood. Such children are often overweight and exhibit personality changes. Digestive difficulties are not infrequent and they interfere further with the child's ability to work at top efficiency. Anterior pituitary deficiency is often accompanied by *mental retardation* and inability to compete with pupils of normal intelligence. . . .

Sometimes the hormones of both the anterior and posterior lobes of the gland are affected and there is a deficiency of the hormones they produce. This results in what is known as Frohlich's Syndrome. It occurs more commonly in boys, who take on a feminine shape with female distribution of fat and hair, and may exhibit either no mental change or some degree of retardation. They tend to be *inactive and sleepy, are not aggressive, make a poor showing in their studies*, seem to be *unable to attack the work* and exhibit some emotional disturbance which is, at least partly, the result of their changed appearance and the unkind jibes of their classmates. Visual defects, including blind areas and other changes in the visual fields, occur. This may *interfere with the ability to use texts* and to perform other tasks requiring good vision. There may also be *impairment in the eye span* with consequent *increase in the number of fixations required per line of material read*. Some may be *unable to use texts* at all, especially in advanced cases.[5]

*The Thyroid Gland.* The thyroid gland secretes a complex hormone known as thyroxin. This secretion, partly influenced by the anterior lobe of the pituitary gland, aids in the control of metabolism and the normal development and functioning of the body. Thyroid enlargement resulting from cell increase (puberty hyperphasia) in young adolescents is a common cause of emotional instability. When a serious deficiency in thyroid secretion exists from birth or infancy, it gives rise to a condition known as *cretinism*—stunted physical development or deformity. According to Eames:

The thyroid gland regulates body metabolism and its degree of activity is often expressed in terms of the

basal metabolic rate. When this approximates the norm the individual lives at a pace similar to that of the

[5] Thomas H. Eames, "Some Neural and Glandular Bases of Learning," *Journal of Education*, vol. 142, no. 4, pp. 25–26, April, 1960.

majority but when the rate is higher or lower than the average he can be thought of as *living* at a corresponding rate. Intelligence is greatly influenced by the degree of activity of this gland. When activity falls off, metabolism slows down, the metabolism of the brain cells is reduced, and intellectual capacity diminishes. When the gland is overactive the pupil appears highly stimulated and may achieve more than he did formerly. The highly stimulated child is nervous, active, and often more emotionally tense than before, while the one whose metabolism is diminishing experiences a dulling of emotional response, loses interest, makes less effort in school, and is generally inattentive.

Thyroid gland deficiencies are probably the commonest endocrine disorders that influence school achievement. Their effect varies from mild to severe and usually yields promptly to adequate medical treatment with corresponding improvement in school accomplishment. The thyroid gland is located in the neck in front of the trachea (windpipe). It consists of two lobes connected by an isthmus. Its hormone regulates metabolism.

Both educational and medical authorities recognize the relationship of thyroid disease to intelligence and the ability to do good work in school. Hardly any course in psychology, either general or educational, passes without reference to and sometimes discussion of cretinism and myxedema, which are manifestations of rather marked thyroid deficiency. One of the chief differences between these conditions is that cretinism exists from birth, while myxedema comes on later. The cretin tends to be dwarfed, placid, and mentally deficient. He is usually good-natured, has a hoarse, rough voice, his tongue is oversize and although he may learn to speak, his speech is likely to be somewhat defective. The cretin lacks energy and is not strong. He is likely to feel cold more than others of his age. . . .

Cretinism and myxedema are not the only types of thyroid deficiency. A mild type occurs among young pupils and older students. It is often overlooked because parents, teachers, and sometimes doctors, are fooled by the apparent *disinclination to work, the lack of interest, the dislike for school, poor achievement in studies, and poor attention.* Teachers sometimes say such children are "woolgathering." When you have a "woolgatherer" in your class it is time to wonder how he got that way. Ask yourself if his achievement is below what would be expected in relation to mental age, whether his achievement and grades are poorer than they were six months or a year ago, whether he perspires less than others in the same activities, and whether he has slowed up a little on the playground. Look at him. Are his skin and hair dry? Is he putting on weight? If the answer to most of these questions is "yes" it is time to request that he receive a physical examination.[6]

*The Parathyroid Glands.* The parathyroid glands, four in number, are located near the thyroid gland. They regulate the calcium metabolism of the body. An insufficient supply of parathyroid secretion gives evidence

------

[6] *Ibid.*, pp. 27–28.

of an increase in physical response to motion, habit spasm, emotional upset and outbursts, and sudden uncontrollable impulses. According to Eames, "They predispose to spasms of accommodation, sore eyes, and rapid *fatigue in book and desk work*."

*The Adrenal Glands.* There are two adrenal glands, one above each kidney. Each gland is composed of two parts: the adrenal *cortex* (the outer layer) and the *medulla* (the inner core). The hormones secreted by each of these parts have widely different functions. The medulla secretes *adrenaline,* a hormone which seems to energize the body when demands for sudden action occur. The cortex produces a hormone known as *cortin,* which is vital to life and appears to be related to sexual development. An insufficiency of the cortin hormone sometimes occurs during or following an acute infection. Extreme deficiency of cortin may produce a condition known as *Addison's disease,* which is characterized by weakness in various areas. There is likely to be progressive weakness, excessive fatigue, lowered resistance to disease, low blood pressure, weak heart action, and diminished sex interest. Normal health may be restored by the injection of adequate amounts of cortin. Overactivity of the cortex, on the other hand, may result in premature puberty. Concerning adrenal glands and the pancreas, Eames says:

The adrenal (suprarenal) glands exert some influence on learning. It is not fully understood but they are of importance to education in their effect on the pupil's *drive and his fatigability.* There are two glands; one situated on the upper pole of each kidney. They are divided into a central or medullary part and an outer or cortical part. The central part forms the hormone, adrenalin (epinephrine). When the individual is under stress this hormone reenforces sympathetic nervous action and is said to be a sustaining agent for it. If the hormone is deficient in quantity or quality, the ability to withstand stress is impaired. The cortical part of the gland forms the hormone, cortin, which affects growth and development. When this hormone is deficient all the muscles—visceral, skeletal, and cardiac—tire quickly. It seems probable that moderate, perhaps subclinical, degrees of deficiency may explain the problem of some of those pupils who are constantly tired or who tire rapidly.

Sometimes there is overgrowth of the outer part of the gland and this may result in bodily changes in both boys and girls. Emotional and psychological difficulties may result. At first, growth may become rapid but it does not continue so, since there is premature union of the epiphyses (ends) of the bones with the shafts. Pupils so affected tend to take on the characteristics of the opposite sex. The *psychological effect* on the adolescent pupil is often a considerable handicap. Comparatively recent developments in the medical treatment of this condition make it possible to overcome it to a very considerable extent.

*The Pancreas.* The pancreas is both an exocrine and an endocrine gland. It secretes a group of digestive solutions as well as forming the hormone, insulin. This gland is situated in the abdomen. Its exocrine function is of less importance in learning than its endocrine activity. The former has to do with ordinary processes of digestion and, when deficient, may interfere with pupil performance to the extent that any digestive upset would be expected to do. No studies so far have shown any striking relationship between the two. On the other hand the hormone, insulin, is a major factor in carbohydrate metabolism. When deficient, the child develops the disease known as diabetes (diabetes mellitus).

Until the discovery of insulin and its application to the treatment of diabetes, a child with this disease ran a downhill course and came to an early end. When a child receives adequate medical treatment for diabetes (which usually means that he is getting a carefully adjusted dosage of insulin), there is no reason why he should not do as well and live as long as others. However, there are a good many pupils who may not be able to follow the regular program. This is not the usual condition, however.[7]

*The Thymus and Pineal Glands.* The thymus and pineal glands are believed to have some influence upon sexual development. The thymus is located in the neck, below the thyroid gland. It consists of two lateral lobes and secretes a hormone that appears so to influence the gonads as to hold in check the development of the reproductive organs in the young child. The pineal gland is a small cone-shaped structure about the size of a pea, lying at the base of the brain, behind and above the pituitary gland. The exact function of the gland is not known. It is believed that its secretions also affect sexual development by inhibiting it until the age of puberty is reached. This gland gradually degenerates so that by adulthood it seems to serve no definite function.

*The Gonads.* The gonads are sex glands. The testes secrete hormones in the male that are different from those secreted by the ovaries in the female. The testes produce sperm cells. The ovaries of the female produce ova or egg cells. These functions are connected directly with reproduction and utilize ducts. Hence they do not represent strictly an endocrine function. The hormone produced by the *interstitial* cells in the testicles of the male account for the development of secondary sex characteristics, however. The hormones secreted by the *corpus luteum* of female ovaries also are connected with secondary sex characteristics. *Theelin,* one of the sex hormones, is active until the menopause. It stimulates the breasts and reproductive organs as well as secondary sex characteristics.

The gonads remain in an underdeveloped state until puberty, although there may be some hormonal benefits through a slight functioning. On the average, the ovaries are not fully developed until about age 20; likewise, at age 14 the testes are only about 10 per cent of adult size,

[7] *Ibid.*, pp. 29–30.

but at age 20 they are relatively mature. It is likely that no sperm cells are secreted by these glands before puberty. Nevertheless, certain hormones, the *androgens* and the *estrogens,* begin to be secreted early and show rapid increase at puberty.

Both boys and girls excrete small amounts of estrogenic and androgenic hormones into the urine. The amount of excretion is not significantly different for either sex until the beginning of puberty. At this time the male continues to excrete estrogens at about the same rate as he had been doing earlier, but the female excretes them at a tremendously increased rate owing to a cyclic excretion which appears some years before the menarche. There is change also in the secretion of androgens, although the rate difference is not so great as for the estrogens. Approximately 50 androgens are found in the sex hormone of both the male and the female at the age of 3. The number of androgens secreted through the years rises until the age of 14 when, for the female they reach a total of about 180 and for the male about 250. Approximately 20 estrogens are excreted by both the female and the male at the age of 3. The number of estrogens excreted rises slowly until the age of 10 for both the female and the male (slightly higher for females than for males). Between the ages of 10 and 12 the excretion rises rapidly for females to more than 240 by the age of 12, when the number recedes slightly. It rises again to more than 380 by the age of 14. The excretion of estrogens by the male, however, never rises above 30 by the age of 14.[8]

## Menstruation as an Endocrine Function

In his discussion of the effects of an endocrine function on achievement, Eames reports that menstruation may at times tend to interfere with best achievement. He says:

An endocrine function that interferes with achievement in some cases is menstruation. It is a completely normal function resulting from cyclic activity in the pituitary which causes the gonadotrophic hormone to increase and accumulate for successive periods of about 28 days, during which time the lining of the uterus (endometrium) is prepared and held ready for pregnancy. If one has not occurred by the end of the interval the gonadotrophic hormone starts to diminish. With its influence withdrawn the endometrium disintegrates and its fragments mixed with blood from many tiny ruptured blood vessels is cast off. When the process goes on normally the girl has little difficulty with it. Others have painful menses, due to various malfunctions or defects of the parts involved (dysmenorrhea). Girls who expe-

[8] See I. T. Nathanson, L. E. Towne, and J. C. Aub, "Normal Excretion of Sex Hormones in Childhood," *Endocrinology,* vol. 28, 1941.

rience this may lose as much as a week each month through absence. Those who come to school with considerable discomfort short of prostration are distracted and cannot profit fully from the instruction. Such girls should seek competent medical advice since many of the disturbing causes can be corrected.[9]

## The Male Sex Organs

The male sex organs are both external and internal to the body. They consist of the testes, the penis, the *vas deferens*, and the prostate gland (see Figure 15). The testes are located in a small sac called the *scrotum*. The function of the testes is to secrete the sperm cells which are needed to fertilize the egg cells produced by the female. Although the sperm cells are produced in the testes, they pass up through the tube and the *vas deferens*, to the seminal vesicles, and on to the prostate gland. They are mixed with certain fluids in the *vas deferens* and the prostate gland, and they are propelled by muscular contraction through the penis in the form of semen, in which millions of sperm or reproductive cells float.

The penis is composed of a spongy tissue that can become permeated with blood, hardened, and extended. With proper erection, the penis can be used to introduce the semen containing sperm cells into the vagina of the female sex organ, thus inducing fertilization.

[9] Eames, *op. cit.*, p. 31.

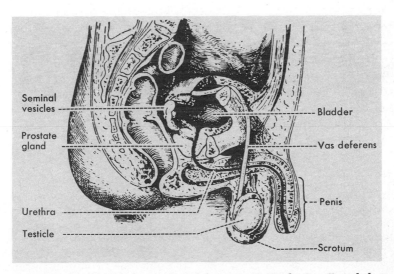

*Figure 15.* Male sex parts. (Adapted from G. McHugh, *Sex Knowledge Inventory, Form Y,* Family Life Publications, Inc., Durham, N.C., 1950, p. 2. Courtesy of G. McHugh.)

*Ejaculation.* The first ejaculation, or the fact that maturational status is adequate for it to occur, marks the onset of the pubertal period. The appearance of the first ejaculation may be hastened by mechanical or other means. The extensive findings of Kinsey and his coworkers concerning the ages and sources of first ejaculations are given in Table 8.

*Table 8.* Sources of First Ejaculation in Relation to Age at Onset of Adolescence

| SOURCE OF FIRST EJACULATION | PER CENT DEPENDING ON EACH SOURCE WHEN AGE AT ONSET OF ADOLESCENCE IS | | | | |
|---|---|---|---|---|---|
| | 8–11 | 12 | 13 | 14 | 15+ AND LATER |
| Masturbation......... | 71.6 | 64.8 | 58.9 | 55.0 | 52.1 |
| Nocturnal emissions... | 21.6 | 28.2 | 35.6 | 38.9 | 37.1 |
| Petting............. | 0.0 | 0.3 | 0.6 | 0.3 | 2.2 |
| Intercourse.......... | 0.6 | 1.4 | 0.9 | 0.9 | 3.2 |
| Homosexual......... | 2.6 | 3.2 | 1.2 | 2.0 | 2.2 |
| Animal............. | 0.3 | 0.3 | 0.2 | 0.3 | 0.0 |
| Spontaneous......... | 3.3 | 1.8 | 2.6 | 2.6 | 3.2 |
| Total............. | 100.0 | 100.0 | 100.0 | 100.0 | 100.0 |
| Cases.............. | 306 | 722 | 984 | 650 | 186 |

SOURCE: A. C. Kinsey et al., *Sexual Behavior in the Human Male,* W. B. Saunders Company, Philadelphia, 1948, p. 300.

Kinsey fixes the date of puberty in boys at the date of the onset of the first ejaculation, without regard to the cause of the ejaculation. He especially makes the point that if the pubic hair and the first ejaculation make their appearance during the same year, there can be no doubt about the year of the beginning of puberty. Since the larger percentage of the boys studied by Kinsey stimulated ejaculation by mechanical or other means, he believes that the date of puberty might better be determined by the physical development, which in some cases is some years in advance of first ejaculation.

There seems to be a definite relationship between the onset of puberty as determined by the first ejaculation and social or educational level. Kinsey concludes:

In the male the age of first ejaculation varies by nearly a year between different educational (social) levels: the mean is 14.58 for boys who never go beyond eighth grade in school, 13.97 for boys who go into high school but not beyond, and 13.71 for boys who will go to college. The differences are probably the outcome of nutritional inequalities at different social levels, and they are in line with similar differences in mean ages of females at menarche, where nutrition is usu-

ally considered a prime factor effecting variation.[10]

## The Female Sex Organs

The female sex organs can be considered to be internal, since they are contained within the body cavity. They consist of the ovaries (two in number), the Fallopian tubes, the uterus, the vagina, the labia (major and minor), the hymen, and the clitoris (see Figure 16).

The ovaries secrete the ova or egg cells; the Fallopian tubes carry the ova to the uterus or permit the sperm to move up for fertilization; the uterus houses the fertilized ovum and provides a place for its nourishment throughout the period of prenatal development; the vagina is the organ into which the penis deposits the male sperm cells during sexual intercourse as the result of an orgasm (the ejaculation of the semen into the vagina).

The growth of the ovaries is slow during childhood. At puberty they grow rapidly, and they reach their full growth at age 20. Sometimes the ovaries grow more rapidly than corresponding parts of the abdomen and

[10] A. C. Kinsey et al., *Sexual Behavior in the Human Male,* W. B. Saunders Company, Philadelphia, 1948, p. 187.

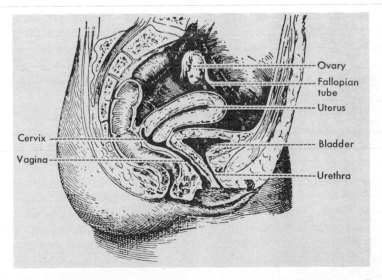

*Figure 16.* Female sex parts. (Adapted from G. McHugh, *Sex Knowledge Inventory, Form Y,* Family Life Publications, Inc., Durham, N.C., 1950, p. 2. Courtesy of G. McHugh.)

thus create a pouchy appearance, which usually disappears within a relatively short time. The walls of the ovaries are lined with follicles that contain the immature egg cells. These ova begin to ripen at the start of puberty and continue to mature at the rate of one every month. Usually the ovum originates in one ovary one month and in the other ovary the next month. The ovum is discharged by the bursting of the follicle at the time of ripening of the egg cell. It then makes its way through the Fallopian tube to the uterus, where the egg, if it has been fertilized by a sperm cell, is nourished and protected during the period of prenatal development. Fertilization of the egg is known as conception. The fertilized ovum then continues to live and grow in the uterus for approximately nine months, and is expelled through the vagina as a new individual. If the matured egg is not fertilized when it reaches the uterus, it deteriorates and passes from the body.

*Menstruation.* In preparation for the start of the new life the body of the female provides extra blood to nourish the fertilized ovum. At first the menstrual flow usually is at the rate of once every lunar month, unless fertilization takes place. Within a relatively short time, however, the regular cycle of approximately every twenty-eight days will be established and will continue until, in the late forties or early fifties, the menopause or change of life is reached.

There is an increase in blood pressure during the three or four days preceding menstruation; there also is a drop in body temperature about one day before the onset of the menstrual flow. These facts often cause a girl to feel different from her usual self. She may become fatigued or depressed. The girl recovers from these physical discomforts shortly, however, and she feels physically fit until the approach of the next menstrual period. Pains accompanying menstruation are not uncommon during the early years.

The first menstrual flow can be terrifying to a young girl who has had no warning of its appearance. Hence every girl needs to be prepared in advance to understand that it is a natural function and cannot be avoided. Sensitive girls especially should be spared the shock that may accompany the discovery that something suddenly seems to be wrong with them. It may be better for an adult to describe menstruation in relatively scientific terms than to wait until uninformed girls discuss it among themselves in undesirable surroundings and thus acquire inadequate and emotion-stirring ideas. Moreover, mothers can be good examples to their daughter by exhibiting emotionally controlled behavior during their own menstrual periods.

The menses soon become regular and the physical discomfort becomes less and less. The present attitude of women toward the menstrual function has reduced the number of individuals who suffer so much pain that the aid of a physician is necessary. In those instances in which a physical examination is indicated it should be had without delay. All girls should be encouraged to meet most of their responsibilities during these periods, however, especially since the following of daily routine is made possible through the utilization of modern sanitary aids.

## Effects of Physical Status upon Adolescent Adjustment

All human beings respond adversely to those conditions which interfere with vital urges. If fulfillment is endangered, there is a possibility that herein may germinate what may become a basic frustration. Both size and strength are influential in assessing a boy's place among his fellows. A study of twenty boys among seventy-eight 17-year-old boys revealed that the ten strongest boys achieved better personal adjustment and gained greater social prestige than were attained by the ten weakest boys. The stronger boys were more at ease with others and freer from emotional tensions. The weaker boys showed many symptoms of maladjustment, suffered from poor health, and manifested inferiority, tensions, anxieties, and worries.

Adolescent boys and girls are greatly disturbed by deviant physical features. Among the features that disturb adolescent boys are smaller-than-average stature, extreme stoutness, facial blemishes of any kind, small and rounded shoulders, small genitals, and poor physique in general. Girls are disturbed by such physical features as extreme tallness or shortness, excessive stoutness or thinness, underdeveloped breasts, acne, and any features in which a girl believes she is much different from other girls of her age.

Physical features exert a powerful influence on adolescent attitudes and behavior. Girls desire those physical and physiological attributes that will make them attractive to boys and accepted by girls. Boys desire to be strong and well built. They want to be regarded as masculine. Girls take pride in their femininity. Adolescents continually want their peer associates and their elders to admire their physical appearance. Members of both sexes desire their faces to be free from acne or other blemishes.

### Questions and Problems for Discussion

1. Based on your study and observation of adolescents, list as many physical changes as you can that occur on entrance into puberty.
2. Recall the physical changes that occurred in your life and the preparation you received in the understanding of them. In what way, if any, did these changes create problems for you?
3. Interpret to the class the meaning that Figure 7 is expected to convey.
4. Study the "dental age scale" and report growth differences you find between boys and girls.

5. Suggest ways in which the problems of short adolescent boys differ from those of tall adolescent boys. Do the same for short and tall adolescent girls. What can be done to help them meet these facts of life?

6. *Special Exercises:*

   *a.* Talk individually with each of four adolescent boys, 13 or 14 years old and of wide differences in height or weight, about any problems that have disturbed him. Report your findings in class.

   *b.* Talk individually with each of four adolescent girls, 13 or 14 years old and of wide differences in height or weight, about any problems that have disturbed her. Report your findings in class.

   *c.* Describe differences in secondary sex characteristics that you observed among the four adolescent boys or girls in *a* and *b* above.

   *d.* Prepare a paper discussing the various ways in which the endocrine glands affect adolescent behavior and development.

## Selected References

Baller, W. R., and D. C. Charles: *The Psychology of Human Growth and Development,* Holt, Rinehart and Winston, Inc., New York, 1961.

Cole, Luella: *Psychology of Adolescence,* 5th ed., Holt, Rinehart and Winston, Inc., New York, 1959.

Crow, Lester D., and Alice Crow: *Human Development and Learning,* rev. ed., American Book Company, New York, 1964.

Horrocks, J. E.: *The Psychology of Adolescence,* 2d ed., Houghton Mifflin Company, Boston, 1962.

Hurlock, Elizabeth B.: *Adolescent Development,* 3d ed., McGraw-Hill Book Company, New York, 1956.

Jersild, A. J.: *The Psychology of Adolescence,* 2d ed., The Macmillan Company, New York, 1963.

Jones, H. E.: *Motor Performance and Growth,* Appleton-Century-Crofts, Inc., New York, 1949.

Kuhlen, R. G.: *The Psychology of Adolescent Development,* 2d ed., Harper & Row, Publishers, Incorporated, New York, 1963.

Levine, L. S.: *Personal Growth and Development: The Psychology of Effective Behavior,* Holt, Rinehart and Winston, Inc., New York, 1962.

McGuigan, F. J.: *Biological Basis of Behavior: A Program,* Prentice-Hall, Inc., Englewood Cliffs, N.J., 1963.

Mussen, P.: *Developmental Psychology,* Prentice-Hall, Inc., Englewood Cliffs, N.J., 1963.

National Society for the Study of Education, Forty-third Yearbook, part I, *Adolescence,* The University of Chicago Press, Chicago, 1944.

Stolz, H. R., and L. M. Stolz: *Somatic Development of Adolescent Boys,* The Macmillan Company, New York, 1951.

Symonds, P. M., and A. R. Jensen: *From Adolescent to Adult,* Columbia University Press, New York, 1961.

Tanner, J. M.: *Growth at Adolescence,* Charles C Thomas, Publisher, Springfield, Ill., 1962.

# Chapter Five

## Maturing
## Mental
## Abilities

During the present century, much attention has been focused upon the developmental patterns of mental functioning. Intensive and extensive study has been devoted to attempted solutions of problems arising out of the observed fact that children and adolescents differ in their degree of successful reaction to situations that involve the utilization of complex mental processes. Some of the major questions to which answers have been sought deal with the refinement of skill competence, the mastery of book knowledge, and the gaining of accurate understanding of meanings and relationships. Numerous investigations have been conducted, various theories have been evolved concerning mental growth and development, and differing interpretations of "intelligence" have been formulated.

The varying results of research in this field have stimulated considerable controversy among psychologists. Consequently, continued research and study are needed to resolve existing disagreements among investigators. Tentative conclusions, based upon available data, seem to present evidence of certain growth and development trends in mental abilities from childhood through adolescence, however. In the following discussion we shall consider some of the basic aspects of mental development, the interpretation and significance of intelligence, the evaluation of intellectual progress, and characteristic adolescent changes in mental potentialities.

## The Functioning of Intelligence

The terms *degree of mental ability* and *intelligence status* often are used interchangeably. Viewed developmentally, a young person's degree of mental ability at any age represents his existing stage of mental growth as it has been accelerated or retarded in terms of environmental experiences. When we speak of a person's intelligence, however, we are referring more specifically to the way in which he functions in a situation that requires the utilization of mental activity. In fact, there is a growing trend toward substituting the term *intelligent behavior* for the word *intelligence*, in order to stress the functional implication of its meaning.

## The Concept of Intelligence

Considerable controversy continues to exist concerning the formulation of a definition of intelligence that would be acceptable to all the various schools of psychological thought. Earlier definitions emphasized the innate aspects of intelligence. According to this concept, an individual was supposed to possess at birth whatever "intelligence" he might display throughout his life; his possible degree of mental achievement was thought to be limited in terms of natural intellectual endowment. More recent investigators emphasize the influence of environmental experiences upon intellectual development, especially during the adolescent stage of mental growth.

Many attempts have been made to define intelligence. These vary in their emphases. For example, intelligence has been interpreted variously as the ability to learn or to profit from experience, or as the ability to adjust to novel situations. Some psychologists conceive intelligence to be the operating of the higher mental functions, i.e., memory, conceptual and abstract thinking, reasoning, and problem solving.

Until the relatively recent past, it was customary to refer to "general intelligence" as opposed to specific aptitudes. As early as 1920, however, Thorndike suggested that intelligence can be considered to have three aspects—abstract, mechanical, and social—and that an individual may give evidence of differences of ability among the three. Other investigators have attempted to break down general intelligence into component parts or mental traits. As a result of their researches, Kelley, Thurstone, and Burt concluded that the following individual mental traits may exist: perception, number, visualization of space, verbal relations, deduction, and problem solving. According to Stoddard:

*Intelligence is the ability to undertake activities that are characterized by (1) difficulty, (2) complexity, (3) abstractness, (4) economy, (5) adaptiveness to a goal, (6) social value, and (7) the emergence of originals, and to maintain such activities under conditions that demand a concentration of energy and a resistance to emotional forces. . . .*

1. *Difficulty* is a function of the percentage passing. Throughout any series of mental measure-

ments, it must increase with chronological age, so long as we postulate mental growth.

2. *Complexity* refers to the breadth or area: not only how difficult the task, but how many kinds of tasks may be successfully undertaken. Attributes (1) and (2) are related in the sense that high accomplishment is pyramidal in structure.

3. *Abstractness* is a means of connecting mental ability to symbolic relationships. It eliminates,

as such, physical and motor acts.

4. *Economy* is another name for speed—the accomplishment of the most mental task in the least time. It calls for early good choices, for faster insights.

5. *Adaptiveness to a goal.*—It is not enough to perform speedily difficult and complex tasks. There must be a goal, a purpose as against aimlessness, and plasticity as against rigidity.

6. *Social value* as an attribute is useful in keeping intelligent ac-

tions within the normal range of human behavior. Thus insanity is not, from this standpoint, something that the human mind may endure without loss of intelligence.

7. *The emergence of originals* is included because of its special place at the upper end of any valid distribution of intelligence. It is characteristic of genius. While related to high ratings in the six preceding qualities, it is not an inevitable outcome of such ratings.[1]

## Theories Concerning the Nature of Intelligence

The trend toward analyzing the composite of intelligence into individual mental traits is an outgrowth of the promulgation of various theories concerning the nature of intelligence. In 1923 Spearman formulated the theory that intelligence consists of a general factor ($g$) and various special abilities ($s$). Basing their research upon Spearman's statistical analysis of intelligence, Kelley, and later Thurstone, arrived at the conclusion that a *multiple-factor* theory represents a better explanation of the nature of intelligence than did Spearman's two-factor theory. Thurstone listed thirteen components of intelligence, seven of which, considered to be the primary mental abilities, are among the foregoing definitions of intelligence.

Morgan names and describes his seven factors as follows:

1. *Verbal comprehension* (V)—ability to define and understand words

2. *Word fluency* (W)—ability to think rapidly of words, as in extemporaneous speech or solving crossword puzzles

3. *Number* (N)—ability to do arithmetic problems

4. *Space* (S)—ability to draw a design from memory or to visualize relationships

5. *Memory* (M)—ability to memorize and recall

6. *Perceptual* (P)—ability to grasp visual details and to see differences and similarities among objects

7. *Reasoning* (R)—ability to find rules, principles, or concepts for understanding or solving problems[2]

[1] George D. Stoddard, "On the Meaning of Intelligence," *Psychological Review*, vol. 48, pp. 255–256, 1941.

[2] From Clifford T. Morgan, *Introduction to Psychology*, 2d ed., McGraw-Hill Book Company, New York, 1961, pp. 445–446. Reprinted by permission.

Guilford has presented a *structure of intellect* that includes three basic factors: (1) "the kind of process or operation performed, (2) "the kind of material or content involved," and (3) "the kinds of products." [3] We present the cubical model that Guilford developed to represent the structure of intellect. We also present his interpretation of the respective factors.

Although each factor is sufficiently distinct to be detected by factor analysis, in very recent years it has become apparent that the factors themselves can be classified because they resemble one another in certain ways. One basis of classification is according to the basic kind of process or operation performed. This kind of classification gives us five major groups of intellectual abilities: factors of cognition, memory, convergent thinking, divergent thinking, and evaluation.

Cognition means discovery or rediscovery or recognition. Memory

[3] J. P. Guilford, "Three Faces of Intellect," *The American Psychologist*, pp. 470–471, August, 1959.

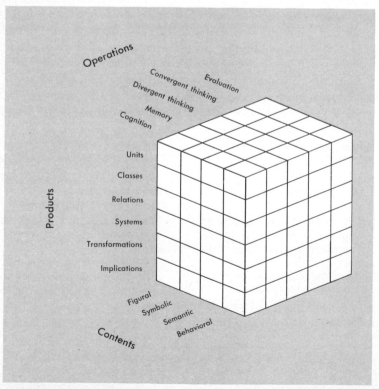

*Figure 17.* A cubical model representing the structure of intellect.

means retention of what is cognized. Two kinds of productive-thinking operations generate new information from known information and remembered information. In divergent-thinking operations we think in different directions, sometimes searching, sometimes seeking variety. In convergent thinking the information leads to one right answer or to a recognized best or conventional answer. In evaluation we reach decisions as to goodness, correctness, suitability, or adequacy of what we know, what we remember, and what we produce in productive thinking.

A second way of classifying the intellectual factors is according to the kind of material or content involved. The factors known thus far involve three kinds of material or content: the content may be figural, symbolic, or semantic. Figural content is concrete material such as is perceived through the senses. It does not represent anything except itself. Visual material has properties such as size, form, color, location, or texture. Things we hear or feel provide other examples of figural material. Symbolic content is composed of letters, digits, and other conventional signs, usually organized in general systems, such as the alphabet or the number system. Semantic content is in the form of verbal meanings or ideas, for which no examples are necessary.

When a certain operation is applied to a certain kind of content, as many as six general kinds of products may be involved. There is enough evidence available to suggest that, regardless of the combinations of operations and content, the same six kinds of products may be found associated. The six kinds of products are: units, classes, relations, systems, transformations, and implications. So far as we have determined from factor analysis, these are the only fundamental kinds of products that we can know. As such, they may serve as basic classes into which one might fit all kinds of information psychologically.[4]

The various theories concerning the functioning of mental abilities do not represent a complete dichotomy. Continued study of individual performance on so-called "tests of intelligence" would seem to indicate that differences in success of response are quantitative rather than qualitative (Thorndike), since test results indicate that the more successful do not give evidence of new kinds of intellectual behavior. Rather, they are superior in their reactions to the same sorts of stimulating material as those to which the "less able" respond unsatisfactorily. Further, an analysis of the clusters of factors that constitute the materials of any situation involving the display of intelligent behavior yields data that would seem to justify the implications of the multiple theory of intelligence suggested by the followers of Spearman. We shall now consider briefly the significance, in the mental development of an individual, of the differentiations (traits) in intelligent behavior that characterize progress in mental maturation, and the organizational patterns of those traits.

[4] *Ibid.*, p. 470.

## Trait Differentiation and Organization

Fundamental to a consideration of changes in intelligent behavior as accompaniments of mental development is the acceptance of the theory that evidenced intellectual power at any age level not only is dependent upon innate capacity but also reflects the influence upon mental activity of environmental factors. To substantiate this theory many investigations have been undertaken that represent studies comparing the performance of younger children with that of older children and adolescents.

The results of these studies seem to indicate that young children give evidence of a great degree of generalized intelligence. With increased mental maturation and enriched environmental experience, individual performance is characterized by differentiation of response and specialization of abilities. It has been discovered, for example, that space perception changes from tactual-visual during early childhood to visual localization by the age of about 13. In general, specific mental traits seem to have become fairly well stabilized by the beginning of adolescence.

The fact that within limits native mental potentialities progressively are affected by experienced environmental influences poses important questions concerning the kinds of learning situations to which the mentally maturing young person should be exposed. It may be recalled that two of the primary mental abilities listed by Thurstone are the verbal and number functions. During childhood, verbal facility is basic to overt display of intelligent behavior, especially in our culture. The truth of this statement was brought to the attention of the authors during a two-day visit to their home of three little boys, aged 5, 4, and 3. The children were born and have been reared in Asia Minor and spoke only Arabic. Verbal intercommunication was almost impossible, although the eldest boy was able to understand a few English words. Because of the language barrier, it was difficult for them to relate to us or for us to understand them. Consequently, we were unable to evaluate their respective degrees of mental alertness, except what we could assume as a result of our observation of their reactions to toys and other objects around them.

Mental traits are characteristics of an individual's behavior to the extent that he gives evidence of possessing specific intellectual abilities that are relatively stable, that have predictive value, and that may differ to a greater or lesser degree from the characteristics of other individuals. The "primary mental abilities" proposed by Thurstone—verbal comprehension, word fluency, number, space, associative memory, perceptual speed, and induction or general reasoning—can be considered to be group factors that represent "aggregates of more elementary units." The elementary units may be said to have *functional unity* or serve as *operational unities*.

The factors of intelligence, as these constitute the variables of individual performance (on an intelligence test, for example), provide descriptive categories of responses rather than serving as the causes of the responses. By means of the sampling approach,[5] or the application of statistical techniques of factor analysis,[6] it is possible not only to study the organization of intelligence but also to investigate special areas of vocational and academic abilities. One of the major problems of the adolescent, for example, is rooted in his uncertainty concerning his plans after high school. He needs help to determine in what areas of continued study or of occupational activity he can be expected to perform successfully. To reach an objective and realistic decision it is necessary for him to know the ability demands of various areas of study or work, as well as his probable or possible chances of meeting the intellectual requirements of any one or more of them. Factorial techniques may be applied in the construction of tests of specific abilities, or of special aptitudes such as speed of reaction, number facility, mental flexibility, insightful reasoning or problem solving, clerical perception, or artistic appreciation. Through the administration to interested young people of appropriate test batteries, some predictive evidence might be obtained concerning their special strengths and weaknesses in the areas tested.

## The Evaluation of Mental Abilities

In their day-by-day activities individuals differ in the ability to perform successfully, especially in situations that require responses that go beyond the fulfillment of routine or habituated tasks. A trained observer often is able to evaluate roughly, over a period of time, the degree of intelligent behavior that a young or older person displays as he engages in one or another form of activity. A secondary school teacher once remarked that after he had worked with a class of students for a school term, he had a fairly accurate impression of the intelligence level of each of his students. He may have been correct in his belief. He probably could have done a better job of guiding the learning activities of the mentally different members of the class, however, if early in the term he had consulted the official records of performance of these young people on standardized intelligence tests. The value of observing individuals in action cannot be questioned. This is a time-consuming technique; the

[5] G. H. Thomson, *The Factorial Analysis of Human Ability*, 3d ed., Houghton Mifflin Company, Boston, 1948.

[6] J. P. Guilford, *Psychometric Methods*, 2d ed., McGraw-Hill Book Company, 1954. Also, D. L. Wolfe, *Factor Analysis to 1940*, Psychometric Monograph no. 3, 1941.

utilization of more formal instruments may not yield completely accurate data, but their results represent certain general intellectual trends or special abilities that then can be checked for validity against performance in actual situations.

## Instruments of Intelligence Testing

During the past fifty years or more many so-called "intelligence tests" have been constructed. These testing instruments can be classified according to various categories: (1) individual or group; (2) paper-and-pencil, verbal and nonverbal, or performance. Intelligence tests also differ in range of difficulty. Some tests are designed to measure the mental alertness of young children. These tests are nonverbal, paper-and-pencil tests, or performance tests, and usually are administered to one child at a time. Other tests are constructed for use with older children and/or adolescents; they may be given individually or in groups. For the most part they are verbal or pencil-and-paper tests, although they may include nonverbal material or performance tasks. Still other tests are designed to evaluate the functioning of the higher mental processes of older adolescents and adults. Certain batteries of tests are so constructed that they can be utilized with various age levels and the results interpreted in terms of increasingly higher norms.

A survey of even the most reliable and valid group tests of intelligence would go beyond the space and function limits of this chapter.[7] Attention is directed at this point, therefore, to a brief description of several individual tests that can be used with adolescents. One of the best-known individual tests is the Stanford Revision of the Binet-Simon Intelligence Scale (1960 Terman-Merrill revision). Although the 1960 revision of this scale can be used on all age levels, beginning at age 2 and extending to the level of superior adult, it is considered to be especially adequate for use with older children. Most of the test items for the higher age levels are presented in verbal form and test the individual's ability to recognize relationships, to make adequate judgments concerning situations and conditions, and to engage in problem solving.

Another individual intelligence test that is gaining in popularity among clinicians for evaluating the degree of mental acuity of older adolescents and adults is the Wechsler-Bellevue Intelligence Scale (WBIS).[8] Insofar as possible, this scale avoids the inclusion of tasks that involve the kinds of school experiences that, according to Wechsler, are

---

[7] For a detailed discussion of various types of intelligence tests and their functions see the Selected References at the end of the chapter.

[8] D. Wechsler, *The Measurement of Adult Intelligence*, 3d ed., The Williams & Wilkins Company, Baltimore, 1944.

characteristic of many intelligence tests. The Wechsler-Bellevue Scale includes verbal and performance subtests. As used at present, it consists of eleven subtests. These are (1) six verbal subtests: general information, general comprehension, arithmetic reasoning, digits forward and backward, similarities, and vocabulary; and (2) five performance subtests: picture completion, picture arrangement, object assembly, block design, and digit symbol. A comparison of this test with others in the field will show that the tasks follow traditional clinical syndromes. Abbreviated forms of the test sometimes are utilized to evaluate specific areas of abilities.

In addition to the Wechsler-Bellevue Scale, Wechsler and his associates have constructed the Wechsler Intelligence Scale for Children (WISC),[9] based upon the Wechsler-Bellevue Scale and intended for use with children between the ages of 5 and 15. The WISC gives evidence of greater care in standardization than does the WBIS. A recently revised form of the WBIS, called the Wechsler Adult Intelligence Scale (WAIS), is a well-standardized and valid individual intelligence test. The Wechsler scales as well as the Terman revision of the Binet-Simon Intelligence Scale can be administered and interpreted adequately only by trained psychologists and clinicians.

As commonly utilized by school people, intelligence tests represent techniques to discover how successfully a young person can be expected to learn. Since most tests administered to school pupils above the early grades are of the paper-and-pencil variety, at least some verbal facility is needed to respond to the test items. In addition, the ability to deal with even simple mathematical concepts presupposes an understanding of numerical relationships. Hence it may seem difficult to discover the extent to which performance on such tests is the result of innate capacity rather than of acquired knowledge. The test items contain learned materials but the manipulation of those materials presented in novel form requires the ability to recognize principles or relationships. If the individuals who take the test have a common background of learning, any difference among them in manipulating test material usually is regarded as the innate or unlearned factor.

## Interpretation of Intelligence Test Results

Raw scores, representing the number of correct responses on a specific test, have little value as a measure of comparison with results of other

[9] D. Wechsler, *Intelligence Scale for Children,* The Psychological Corporation, New York, 1949. Also, H. Seashore, A. Wesman, and J. Doppelt, "The Standardization of the Wechsler Intelligence Scale for Children," *Journal of Consulting Psychologists,* vol. 14, pp. 99–110, 1950.

tests on the same performance level or different age or grade levels. Hence raw scores need to be interpreted according to statistically computed norms for the test, or in terms of conversion into one or another accepted type of derived score. Among the more commonly used bases of interpretation of individual performance on an intelligence test are mental age, intelligence quotient, and percentile rank.

The concept of mental age is an outgrowth of a form of test organization, primarily the Binet-Simon type, in which the respective test items represent units of increasing difficulty. In terms of established age norms, an individual's performance on the test can be interpreted as an indication of the fact that he possesses a certain mental age regardless of his chronological age. For example, a young person whose chronological age is 13 may appear to have a mental age of 10, 13, or 16. In other words, he is below, at, or above what can be considered "normal" for his chronological age group. This is a commonly used method of interpreting actual performance on a test.

In order to obtain more definite information concerning an individual's relative dullness or brightness, Terman devised a technique to discover the relationship that can be expected to exist between an individual's chronological age and his demonstrated level of mental maturity. This type of derived score is called the *intelligence quotient* (IQ). The IQ is obtained by dividing the mental age (resulting from performance on an intelligence test) by the chronological age and multiplying the quotient by 100 to eliminate the decimal point. This is a statistical device that is relatively meaningless unless the IQs are classified into categories that represent continuous but differing levels of ability to perform. The spread of intelligence quotients as indicated in Table 9 ranges from a low near 0, to a high that is believed to exceed 200.

*Table 9.* Classification and Distribution of Intelligence Quotients

| IDENTIFICATION OF GROUPINGS | IQ RANGE |
| --- | --- |
| Near genius | 140 and above |
| Very superior | 130–139 |
| Superior | 120–129 |
| Above average | 110–119 |
| Normal or average | 90–109 |
| Below average | 80–89 |
| Borderline | 70–79 |
| Feebleminded | 0–69 |
| Moron | 50–69 |
| Imbecile | 25–49 |
| Idiot | 0–24 |

The distribution of mental abilities among the general population can be illustrated graphically as shown in Figure 18. For purposes of comparison with the intelligence quotients, the approximate lines of demarcation between the various IQ groupings are superimposed on the figure by means of broken lines. This *percentile ranking* approach is receiving increased attention from psychologists and educators in working with earned raw scores of individuals who are competing in a particular situation. The scores earned by all the members of the group are arranged in percentile rank order. The significance of an individual's performance is indicated by his place in the group, i.e., if subject L has a percentile rank of 92, this means that only 8 per cent of his group represents an intelligence status that is higher than his, and 92 per cent are less able mentally than he is (according to the results of the specific measuring instrument applied); the raw score of subject R, on the contrary, earns for him a percentile rank of 28, indicating that 72 per cent of the group are brighter than he is. The application of this interpretative device has validity only to the extent that the members of the group tested are similar in educational and experiential background.

## Constancy of Mental Development

The extent of constancy that is maintained between increase of age and mental maturation has been a matter of much controversy. Especially do questions arise among school people concerning the constancy of the IQ. Since mental age status commonly is determined by performance on a test of intelligence, the validity and reliability of the testing instrument becomes an important factor. Moreover, one must take into account certain other elements of influence. Rate of growth may not parallel increase in chronological age; environmental experiences not only affect mental growth during all the maturing years, but may exercise a more potent influence upon mental development at certain ages than at others; training stimulates more extended and greater development among the mentally superior than among the mentally retarded.

We know that inherited potential sets limits to the extent of mental growth but that kind and amount of environmental stimulation affect rate of development. The child who remains in a relatively constant environment probably will maintain a ratio between his chronological and mental age that may vary no more than about 5 points when expressed as IQ. With changes in environmental conditions, these point differences may become greater. The IQs of children tend to be more constant than the IQs of adolescents, probably as a result of the latter's wider variation in experience and possibly because of differences in the tests used for the two age periods. A young person, however, who continues to experience

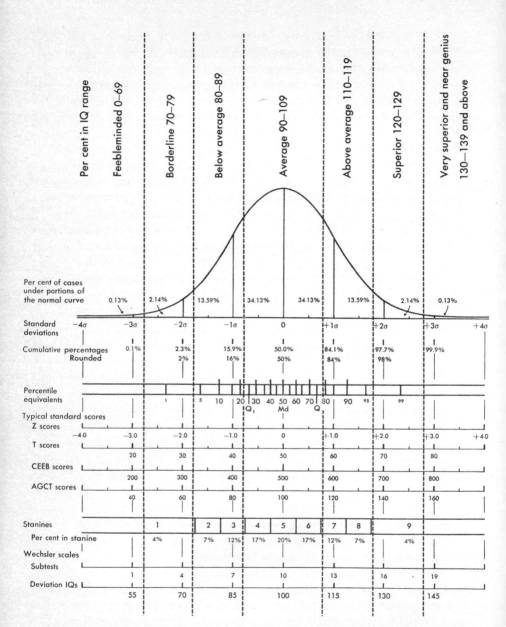

*Figure 18.* Distribution-of mental abilities, with intelligence quotients superimposed. (From *Test Service Bulletin,* no. 48, p. 2, January, 1955. Courtesy of The Psychological Corporation.)

relatively constant educational advantages tends to give evidence of comparative constancy of mental development. His IQ can be expected to have predictive value for several years at least.

The degree of mental alertness displayed during the early years of childhood has little, if any, predictive value for adolescence. Not only is it difficult to construct and administer appropriate tests of mental ability for use with the very young child, but his experiential background is still too meager for him to display whatever mental potentialities he possesses.

In her study of growth of intelligence (Berkeley Growth Study of Children from Birth to 21), Nancy Bayley[10] reported a variety of findings. Bayley organized these according to 16 $D$ scores. The 16 $D$ scores mean that the scores of each individual at all ages are expressed in terms of the 16-year standard deviations from the mean score at 16 years. In Figure

[10] Nancy Bayley, "On Growth of Intelligence," *American Psychologist*, vol. 10, pp. 805–818, December, 1955.

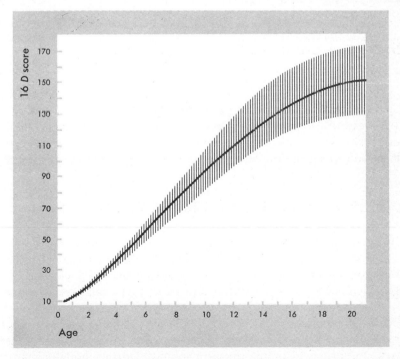

*Figure 19.* Curves of means and SDs of intelligence by 16 $D$ units, birth to 21 years, Berkeley Growth Study. (Adapted from Nancy Bayley, "Individual Patterns of Development," *Child Development*, vol. 27, no. 1, p. 67, 1956.

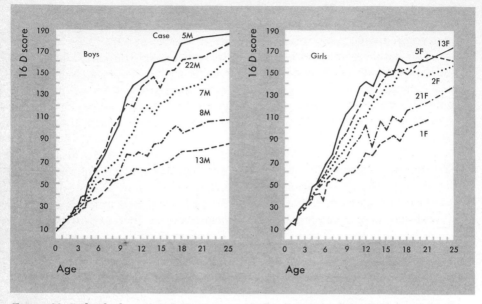

*Figure 20.* Individual curves of 16 D scores showing growth of intelligence of five boys and five girls from 1 month to 25 years. (Adapted from Nancy Bayley, "Individual Patterns of Development," *Child Development,* vol. 27, no. 1, p. 67, 1956.)

19 are presented all scores for all ages expressed as deviations from the 16-year level, e.g., based on the means and SDs of the 16 D scores.

In her study of individual patterns of development Nancy Bayley prepared two patterns that show growth of intelligence in 16 D scores for five boys and five girls from 1 month to 25 years of age (see Figure 20).

## Mental Development during Adolescence

A significant characteristic of the adolescent years is the fact that the interests and activities of young people in the secondary school tend to become more specialized than they were during the childhood years. In general, elementary school children are exposed to relatively the same educational stimulation, i.e., they are expected to learn what can be termed the fundamentals. Emphasis is placed upon the mastery of primary language skills and numerical concepts, and upon the development of power to engage in simple problem solving. During the later maturational stage, however, the beginnings of preparation for adulthood are evidenced. Secondary school students select different curriculums or courses in terms of their own ambitions and interests, or as the result of parental pressures. Their out-of-school interests and activities also are likely to differ from those that were experienced during earlier childhood years. Hence the mental growth patterns of young people are influenced by differing environmental situations and conditions, resulting in variation of mental development that is reflected in their performance on tests of intelligence. For example, an individual utilizes speaking, listening, reading, and writing in the development of mental capacities. The extent to which the progress of mental development varies is illustrated in Figure 21.

## Characteristics of Adolescent Mental Development

Although general adaptability in mentally stimulating situations (the g factor) may continue to show itself in adolescent behavior, special mental abilities (the s factors) become much more evident than they were during the less challenging childhood years. Yet it must be kept in mind that the mental reactions of the adolescent do not suddenly change completely. The potentiality to develop certain special abilities has always been present. During the teen years increasing mental growth and appropriate environmental conditions encourage the development of these abilities. Perhaps this point can be clarified by reference to the development of a particular form of physical prowess, such as weight lifting. Because of his lack of strength, a small child cannot lift a heavy weight. As one child develops physically his strength increases, but he may not become sufficiently interested or able, or receive sufficient training in this form of physical activity, to become a champion weight lifter. Another child who gives no or little evidence of superior ability in this area pos-

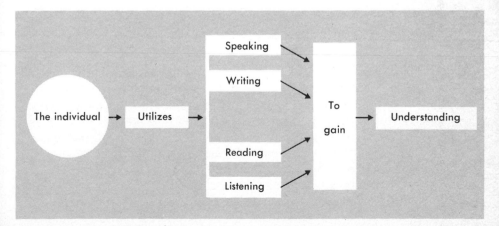

*Figure 21.* Mental development depends on the stimulation given to individual capacities.

sesses undeveloped potential that later, through training, enables him to excel as a weight lifter.

There are certain popular misconceptions concerning changes in mental capacities from childhood to adolescence. Contrary to the opinions expressed by some, there appears to be no valid evidence that the onset of pubescence is accompanied by a sudden spurt in mental development. It is possible that the earlier physical development of girls, as compared with that of boys, gives the former some advantage in test-determined general status of mental development over boys of the same chronological age. The developmental pattern of specific mental functions represents a continuum of growth and development from early years onward, however. For the most part, age differences in overt display of one or another aspect of intelligence can be explained in terms of general growth trends and environmental enrichment.

## The Ability to Concentrate

Adolescents as well as children exhibit differences in their ability to concentrate. From the adult point of view most children are distracted easily from one situation to another, especially if the second stimulus is more closely related to personal interest than the first. Fundamentally, the child's attention span is short. Parents and teachers recognize this fact. A child asks a question that appears to represent great personal interest; before an adult has formulated the answer the questioner's attention may have focused upon something else. He is scarcely aware of the fact that he asked a question and was receiving an answer.

Attention span gradually increases with age, i.e., an individual develops greater power to return to the original attention-demanding situation from which he was momentarily distracted. Therefore it can be expected that the adolescent is gaining the ability to concentrate upon a task at hand. Yet personal interest in the activity remains a significant factor of his willingness or ability to concentrate successfully. Adults sometimes deplore the lack of concentration shown by the teen-ager. In many instances the difficulty is, however, not so much his inability to concentrate as his tendency to concentrate on matters other than those to which adults, in terms of their wishes or desires, expect him to devote his entire attention. Sometimes a secondary school teacher seems unable to understand that an adolescent boy or girl may have so many interests and "worries" that he or she cannot concentrate upon school study so well as the teacher expects or demands.

Environmental conditions may interfere with concentration. Differences among high school students in the preparation of home assignments may result from differing study conditions in the home. One student may be fortunate enough to have his own room in which he can work without outside interference. Another boy or girl is expected to concentrate upon school tasks in a room shared by other members of the family who engage in interesting conversation or turn on the radio or television; a parent may interrupt the young person's study to have him "run errands" or participate in other family chores. So accustomed do some adolescents become to distractions that they claim that they can concentrate upon their studies better while they are listening to the radio than if the room is quiet. The telephone also may be a strongly disturbing preventer of young people's gaining the power to concentrate successfully on mental work. Fundamentally, however, successful concentration is linked with adolescent interests.

## The Ability to Memorize

Memory is considered to be a special mental trait. People differ in what they remember, and how well or how long they retain in memory those situations or conditions that they have experienced or the persons or things with whom or with which they have been associated. We know that the intensity, vividness, or duration of a stimulus, as well as the kinds of personal feelings that are attached to it, determines the strength of one's memory of it. Pleasant experiences are supposed to be remembered longer than annoying ones. Yet the vividness or the affective influence of an unpleasant experience may seem to impress itself indelibly on one's memory. For example, an embarrassing situation caused mainly by an adolescent's social immaturity or awkwardness may so greatly affect his self-regard that he becomes emotionally involved at the time of its occurrence. More serious is the fact that he remembers it for a long time, unless he later redeems himself by displaying greater social ease or until, as a mature adult, he can recognize the relative unimportance of the incident.

Memory can be classified as *rote* (verbatim reproduction of memorized material) or *logical* (recall of meaningful ideas presented in one's own words). Early psychological studies concerning memory placed almost complete emphasis upon the functioning of rote, or verbatim, reproduction. Hence it was concluded that children's memories are better than those of adolescents and adults. According to the findings of later investigators, however, the probabilities are that children are willing to memorize by rote certain materials such as poems or prose passages, but that adolescents or adults find verbatim memorization monotonous or time-consuming. Moreover, a child may not understand the meaning of the material that he has memorized. Since the older person is more interested in ideas than in the words themselves, he is more willing and able than the child to master content logically.

It has been found that if an adolescent or adult is motivated to memorize certain material by rote, such as a part in a play or another selection which he desires to reproduce exactly, he usually is better equipped to do so than is the child. The task is relatively easy for the older person since he understands the meaning of what he is memorizing, experiences a personal interest in the material to be memorized, and expects to obtain commendation for his performance. Unless personal interest or desire acts as a motivating force, however, an adolescent usually dislikes intensely to be required to memorize by rote any material such as scientific or mathematical formulas, grammatical rules, the spelling of words out of context, or other similar study tasks.

Although an adolescent needs to memorize some material by rote, much of his learning consists of associating new ideas with those that he already knows. The more correct associations that are made, the greater will be the comprehension and "fixing" of the new ideas. A student's success in mastering ideas depends on factors such as his degree of interest in the material to be memorized, his recognition of its value to him, and his ability to organize it according to major concepts and related details. Moreover, whether the memorizing is rote or logical, rarely is one exposure to the material sufficient for the learner to remember it. Many repetitions (overlearning) of facts or ideas in differing contexts are needed to prevent rapid forgetting.

For a time psychologists repudiated the value of any drill or rote learning, placing emphasis upon the understanding of concepts as one of the main functions of learning. Since understanding is not always tantamount to knowing and remembering, *overlearning* through functional repetition of significant facts or concepts is coming to be utilized in secondary schools and colleges to a greater extent than it had been during the recent past.

## The Functioning of Imagination

During early childhood the imaginary and the realistic worlds are so closely related to each other that a youngster sometimes finds it difficult to distinguish between imagined and real experience. The imaginative lying of the young child is rooted in this interrelationship of his two worlds. During the elementary school years, however, the child becomes so intrigued by his many real experiences that he is likely to give little or no attention to imaginary situations, conditions, or people. There are exceptions to this generally displayed attitude, however, especially among lonely "only" children.

It is difficult to measure by way of standardized measuring instruments the progress of a maturing individual's powers of imagination. Growing young people differ in their display of creative imagination. These differences may be rooted in inherited potentiality or they may result from environmentally stimulated experiences. Moreover, the functioning of the imagination may constitute one of the basic factors of a special aptitude that, with training, expresses itself in superior performance. For example, relatively few persons, in comparison with the general population, exhibit great superiority in areas of performance such as music, representative art, writing of prose or poetry, or other specific fields of ability.

These brief comments concerning the development of special aptitudes have been introduced at this point because of the close relationship that exists between aptitudinal potential and the functioning of the imagination. The exceptional musician, artist, or writer possesses the ability to interpret realistic materials in such a way that he stimulates the imagination of others. To accomplish this goal the artist in any area of expression must be able to recognize and subtly combine the ideal and the real. In other words, he must possess an active but controlled imagination.

As was noted in the foregoing, developmental changes in the functioning of imagination cannot be evaluated successfully by means of standardized tests. During the course of class activities, however, teachers can discover some significant differences between the child and the adolescent in the use of imagination. For example, an imaginative story written by a child usually deals with action that is unusual or different from that which he actually experiences. Except in rare cases, a child's production takes the form of objective presentation of imaginary people, situations, or conditions; his drawings are based upon observed material; his music performance is related to his present simple experiences. Usually a child is willing to practice scales and to play simple musical compositions that often are performed with musical accuracy, but with relatively little expression of emotionalized imagination.

Adolescents, on the contrary, tend to give their imagination free rein. With little or no adult stimulation, they are moved to express their imaginative dreams in poems or idealistic stories which often reflect their developing philosophy of life or personal ambitions. Adolescent symbolic drawings or musical renditions reflect the expression of personal mood at the moment or the play of the imagination. Technical accuracy of performance may be disregarded. Adolescents are more concerned with the imagined feelings and thoughts of the people in their stories than are children. High school and young college students also tend either to introduce much immature humor into their writings or to stress human misery and deprivation to the point of extreme tragedy that is unrelieved by any lighter touch of humor.

Most young people can be encouraged to develop realistically controlled imagination. A varied background of experience is an excellent stimulator of adolescent imagination. The interested and imaginatively inclined teacher is able to recognize the kinds and levels of functioning imagination exhibited by the various members of his classes. He is alert to the signs of superior potentiality displayed by some of his students. He accepts as his responsibility the improvement of their abilities; he encourages them to continue their training toward the development of superior performance in the area of a specific aptitude. This teacher attitude represents a phase of adolescent guidance that to the present has been relatively neglected. At the same time, it must be remembered that regardless of the strength of an aptitude, the achievement of superior performance depends upon the young person's general mental ability and the appropriateness and intensity of the training program.

Sometimes complete absorption on the part of an adolescent in specific, time-consuming study in one area of study activity denies him opportunities to develop satisfactorily those other phases of his personality that will enable him to establish desirable interpersonal relationships. It also happens that an adolescent boy or girl may give evidence of one or another specific aptitude which he is willing to develop, but other maturing interests demand his time and attention. Hence this young person may dissipate his energies rather than concentrate upon improvement of the special ability. Consequently, his imagination functions to his detriment insofar as he attempts to reconcile his various interests and behavior reactions. To illustrate this point, reference can be made to the case of Joan.

During her high school and college days Joan constantly was commended by her teachers for her imaginative ability and especially for her "flair" for writing. She was encouraged to continue training in this field and thus channel her imagination into the production of thought-challenging fictional writings. Although Joan has continued to experience the urge to engage in this activity, she has come to be involved in so many other imagination-stimulating projects and responsibilities involving human relationships that her time and energy are expended almost entirely in outgoing, group-centered activities. Whatever writing she finds time for is associated with her work. Many talented adolescents find themselves in the position of selecting one of various areas of activity upon which to concentrate their imagination, or of drifting into a field or fields other than the one in which their exceptional powers of imagination could be utilized most effectively.

## The Development of Success in Reasoning and Problem Solving

There is a close relationship between imagination and judgment or reasoning. Moreover, the mental processes involved in thinking, reasoning, and problem solving do not vary qualitatively from childhood through adolescence. The child thinks; he can reason about the simple situations and conditions with which he has experience; with training he is able to solve problems that lie within his limits of comprehension. The continuance of mental growth and the expansion of experience inherent in intellectual development are basic factors of adolescents' increasing power to engage in the manipulation of concepts, ideas, and relationships.

The degree of skill attained by an adolescent at any age depends upon the rate and upper limit of his mental development. From results obtained through the administration of testing techniques, it has been found that adolescents differ from one another in their ability to think objectively, judge correctly, or obtain adequate insights concerning people or objects in their environment or about situations or conditions by which they are affected. Yet, for the most part, teen-agers give indication of better intellectual discrimination than is characteristic of children. Possible reasons for this may be found in the increased vocabulary of the older group, as seen in Figure 22.

Harrell studied the relative lengths of written and oral compositions of boys and girls at various ages. The results of his study are presented in Table 10.

Table 10. Approximate Mean Lengths of Compositions at Different Ages for Boys and Girls

|  | WORDS IN WRITTEN COMPOSITION | | WORDS IN ORAL COMPOSITION | |
| --- | --- | --- | --- | --- |
| AGE | BOYS | GIRLS | BOYS | GIRLS |
| $9\frac{1}{2}$ | 200 | 210 | 250 | 255 |
| $11\frac{1}{2}$ | 205 | 250 | 330 | 320 |
| $13\frac{1}{2}$ | 245 | 280 | 290 | 275 |
| $15\frac{1}{2}$ | 285 | 310 | 360 | 335 |

SOURCE: Based on a figure in Lester E. Harrell, "A Comparison of the Development of Oral and Written Language in School-age Children," *Monographs of the Society for Research in Child Development*, vol. 22, no. 66, p. 29, 1957.

In her study of consistency and variability in the growth of intelligence throughout the growing years of 33 cases, Nancy Bayley organized

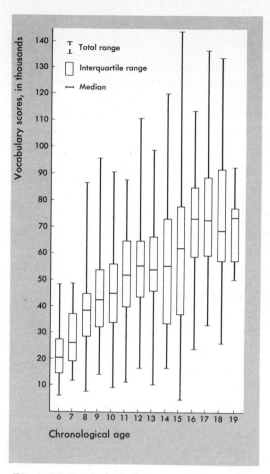

*Figure 22.* Total vocabulary scores of chronological age groups. (From Mary K. Smith, "Measurement of the Size of General English Vocabulary through the Elementary Grades and High School," *Genetic Psychology Monograph*, vol. 24, p. 319, 1941.)

the data into age curves for several learning functions, as shown in Figure 23. In her summary statement she says:

We have evidence that intelligence, as measured by repeated tests on the Wechsler-Bellevue scale, increases (about equally for both sexes) from 16 to 18 to 21 years of age. The gains occur at all levels of intelligence and education found in this sample. There are indications that some persons appear to have reached their own top capac- ities by 16 to 18 years, while others may still be growing at 21.[11]

Training plays an important role in the development of adolescent reasoning and problem solving. Too often immature young people are encouraged to make judgments concerning one or another situation or condition with which they have not yet had sufficient experience to gain adequate insight into its subtle elements. They sometimes are expected to attempt solutions of social, economic, political, or other major problems that may defy a mature adult's power to solve. Lacking adequate experiential background for objective reasoning, adolescents are likely to

[11] Nancy Bayley, "Data on the Growth of Intelligence between 16 and 21 Years as Measured by the Wechsler-Bellevue Scale," *Journal of Genetic Psychology*, vol. 90, p. 14, 1957.

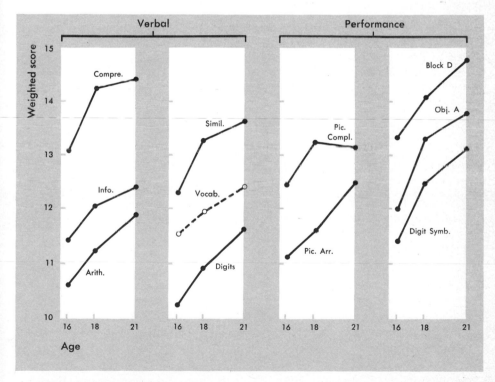

*Figure 23.* Wechsler-Bellevue categories, mean weighted scores by age for the total Berkeley Growth Study sample. (From Nancy Bayley, "Data on the Growth of Intelligence between 16 and 21 Years as Measured by the Wechsler-Bellevue Scale," *Journal of Genetic Psychology*, vol. 90, p. 14, 1957.)

depend upon imagination, or to repeat, parrot-fashion, statements which they find in newspapers or magazines, hear on radio or television, or garner from the conversation of adults who themselves may be poorly informed or prejudiced in their thinking.

From a democratic point of view it certainly is desirable for young people to become aware of the many problems that need to be solved in the interest of general human welfare; realistically, however, adults as well as young people need to recognize the fact that reasoning or judgment, to be valid, must represent the mental maturity and experiential background that are lacking even among so-called "adults." Consequently, there is a growing trend among psychologists, sociologists, and educators to motivate maturing adolescents to give major attention to problems that are within their developing comprehension limits, and to encourage them to reason objectively about their own youthful problems of adjustment. Teen-agers can be helped, step by step, to achieve control of their imagination through improved appreciation of the realities of life; they can be inducted gradually into situations that possess problem potential. To the extent that these educative processes succeed, it is found that young people gain increased power to become sensitive to subtle elements of their environment, to achieve improved insight, and to engage in objective, unprejudiced, and constructive reasoning and problem solving.

## Relation of Mental Function to Other Aspects of Adolescent Development

The importance to the adolescent of the kind and amount of development that are taking place in his various mental functions is great. The degree of mental acuity that he possesses and is trained to utilize adequately during his teen years represents a significant factor of his adjustment to his responsibilities as an adult. Yet one cannot disregard the interrelationships that exist among the various personality aspects of the developing individual. We have referred briefly to the relation between physical and mental growth. Attention also needs to be directed toward the role of the mental functions in the emotional development and social adjustment of the adolescent.

Too many parents of the past disregarded the effect upon their maturing children of adolescent emotional changes. A growing boy's or girl's participation in social activities was considered to be a matter of almost complete parental decision. High school teachers and administrators were accustomed to consider intellectual achievement to be the primary concern of their pupils. More recent educational philosophy has stressed adolescent emotional development and social adjustment almost to the exclusion of intellectual advancement. Many psychologists and educators are recognizing the dangers inherent in either of these extreme approaches to adolescent education. Hence the present trend is toward greater educational emphasis upon a young person's achievement of adjusted and adjustable patterns of behavior and attitudes that involve adequate functioning of his physical, mental, and emotional potentialities in the management of his personal affairs and in his relationships with individuals of all ages.

## Questions and Problems for Discussion

1. Mental development during adolescence is deeply rooted in the experiences of the individual. Explain additional factors that contribute to an adolescent's mental development.
2. Explain the relationship between habits and mental development. Indicate the extent to which a habit once formed can be broken.
3. Discuss the relationship between mental attitudes and school success.
4. Present the underlying psychological factors that indicate the undesirability of keeping an adolescent at an intellectual task that does not challenge him.
5. Present ways in which study habits are associated with the development of mental abilities. What study habits are among the good ones that you possess?
6. *Special Exercises:*
   a. Ask permission to administer a group form of an intelligence test to one of the adolescents you have been observing and studying. In what way can this information be helpful to a teacher?
   b. Study the IQ scores of ten adolescents and compare these results with the extent of achievement in one or more school subjects. Report your findings.
   c. Prepare a weekly study schedule and follow it. Discuss the impact on mental development of knowing and using good study procedures.

## Selected References

Anastasi, A.: *Differential Psychology,* 3d ed., The Macmillan Company, New York, 1958.

Bayley, Nancy: "On Growth of Intelligence," *American Psychologist,* vol. 10, pp. 805–818, December 1955.

Clark, W. W.: "Boys and Girls— Are There Significant Ability and Achievement Differences," *Phi Delta Kappan,* pp. 73–76, November, 1959.

Corsini, R. J., and K. K. Fassett: "Intelligence and Aging," *Journal of Genetic Psychology,* vol. 83, pp. 249–264, 1953.

Cronbach, L. J.: *Essentials of Psychological Testing,* 2d ed., Harper & Row, Publishers, Incorporated, New York, 1960.

Ells, K., et al.: *Intelligence and Cultural Differences,* The University of Chicago Press, Chicago, 1951.

Ghiselli, E.: *Theory of Psychologi-*

*cal Measurements,* McGraw-Hill Book Company, New York, 1964.

Guilford, J. P.: "Three Faces of Intellect," *American Psychologist,* pp. 469–479, August, 1959.

Hunt, E. B.: *Concept Learning: An Information Processing Problem,* John Wiley & Sons, Inc., New York, 1962.

Hunt, J. M.: *Intelligence and Experience,* The Ronald Press Company, New York, 1961.

Inhelder, B., and J. Piaget: *The Growth of Logical Thinking from Childhood to Adolescence,* Basic Books, Inc., Publishers, New York, 1958.

Morgan, Clifford T.: *Introduction to Psychology,* 2d ed., McGraw-Hill Book Company, New York, 1961.

Sherman, M.: *Intelligence and Its Deviation,* The Ronald Press Company, New York, 1945.

Stoddard, George D.: *The Meaning of Intelligence,* The Macmillan Company, New York, 1937.

Terman, L. M., and Maud A. Merrill: *Stanford-Binet Intelligence Scale: Manual for the Third Revision Form L-M,* Houghton Mifflin Company, Boston, 1960.

Viaud, G.: *Intelligence: Its Evaluation and Forms,* Harper & Row, Publishers, Incorporated, New York, 1960.

Wechsler, D.: *The Range of Human Capacities,* The Williams & Wilkins Company, Baltimore, 1952.

# Chapter Six

## Changing Emotional Patterns

The development of the emotions begins at birth and continues through adolescence. The very young child's emotional experiences constitute general all-over patterns of response. Gradually the various emotional reactions become localized and definitive. By the time an individual has attained emotional maturity (sometimes well into the period of adulthood) characteristic patterns of emotional behavior have become habituated.

An adolescent is sensitive to the many emotion-arousing stimuli in his environment. His affective experiences become vital to him in a way that they had not been earlier. He responds to social stimuli differently; he is building a personality out of the environmental influences that produce one feeling tone today and another tomorrow. Although emotion plays a leading role in the development of the individual through his entire life, during adolescence he is emotionally aroused by stimuli that may not have affected him as a child. The emotional changes are caused largely by the physiological development that is taking place or has taken place within him.

A girl who is preparing for her first date spends all day arranging and rearranging her hairdo, painting and repainting her fingernails, and trying to decide which dress to wear. Yet she has not completed her preparations when her date arrives that evening. This girl's behavior exemplifies the emotional strife experienced during adolescent years. Another girl may react to her first date by worrying all day about whether she will know what to talk about. Her anxiety changes to delight when she discovers during the evening that conversation flows freely. The first date may be an emotion-arousing experience for the boy as well as for the girl. The adolescent boy also fusses about his grooming, he is anxious about his "manners," he ventures a quick parting kiss which causes him to feel as though he were walking on air even though the kiss is no more than a peck on the cheek.

### The Bases of Emotional Experiences

An emotional experience is a stirred-up state of the individual. Although there may be increasing storm and stress during adolescence, emotions are experienced both before and after this age period. Hence they are not peculiar to the adolescent stage of development. Emotional reactions during adolescence differ, however, in certain respects from earlier emotional expression.

## The Nature of Feeling

A feeling state is an affective experience that accompanies an individual's daily experiences. The attitude of the individual at the moment has a profound influence upon the way he may react. An anticipatory attitude toward, and an attitude of acceptance of, the environmental conditions aid the individual at the time to experience *pleasantness* or *unpleasantness*. Of necessity, feelings are subjective and introspective. Only the individual can experience the feeling state; if the situation is accompanied by a feeling of pleasantness, there is a desire to repeat it; if unpleasantness is experienced, there is a tendency to exhibit avoidance behavior. There is a strong adolescent drive to continue activities that bring enjoyment and thus prolong pleasant experiences, and to reject, avoid, or terminate unpleasant situations or conditions.

An adolescent feels differently about participation in certain activities at various age levels. Some activities in which he may have been intensely interested and which were pleasant to him at age 13 or 14 become extremely unpleasant to him at 18 or 19. For example, a 19-year-old girl writes:

One attitude I had when I was 13 that changed my growing up was a concept I had about friends. At 12 I found them essential in my life. We girls formed a club and I was very friendly with all the members, although at that time I was more concerned about myself than about others. At 14 I was still friendly with the same group, but decided that their feelings were important and should be considered if I wanted to keep their friendship. At 15 I found myself too mature to be friendly with them. I had a "boy friend" and decided to spend most of my time with him. I was very happy as I saw this boy most of the time; I spent little time with the girls. By the age of 17 I had cut off my friendship completely with the girls and was interested only in the boy. After I had entered college I decided that it is as important to have girl friends as well as a companion of the opposite sex. I became friendly with a few girls; these friendships have continued until the present. Now, at 19, I see how much I missed by not having closer friendships with girls, at least during part of my adolescent years.

The stimuli that produce pleasantness or unpleasantness change with the circumstances surrounding them. Changes in age, interests, and attitudes contribute to these changes in feeling. At one time the attitude and behavior of one individual may arouse pleasant feelings in another person.

If, however, the second person loses interest in the other, the former pleasant feelings are not experienced. The girl who is the present object of an adolescent boy's affection stimulates him to experience feelings of pleasantness at the sight of her, at the sound of her voice, or at the touch of her hand. No matter how deep these feelings toward her may be, they are lost if another girl becomes the center of his interest.

Thompson and Witryol conducted a study that deals with adult recall of unpleasant experiences that occurred in each of three periods of childhood.[1] These periods were the first 5 years of life, ages 6 to 12, and ages 12 to 18. Fifty young women, college students between the ages of 18 and 24, participated in each of the recall studies. The subjects of the experimental project were asked to respond in terms of recall to each item of a list of twenty-two categories of unpleasant experiences for each of the three designated age levels. Recently the experiment was further extended by the authors of this book, using the same twenty-two categories and gathering data from college students of both sexes, 100 women and 100 men.

In both studies the items group themselves into three generally meaningful "clusters": (1) "unpleasant or painful sensory and emotional experiences"; (2) "unpleasant experiences during process of learning to live in a social world"; (3) "unpleasant experiences generating feelings of inadequacy and insecurity." The findings of these two studies would seem to indicate that the subjects' unpleasant memories of experiences that occurred during early childhood fall into the first group of items, especially "painful injuries" and "illness"; during the ages 6 to 12, the unpleasant experiences were clustered around "forced to do unpleasant things" and "verbally disciplined"; in the 12- to 18-year-old group, unpleasant experiences appear to be closely related to adolescent attitudes of personal inadequacy and insecurity, as is indicated by their unpleasant experiences with "death of relatives and friends," "school failure," and being "refused desired objects."

The percentage difference in responses between the studies is slight. The students in the Crow and Crow study reported many more unpleasant experiences in these items: (1) ages 1 to 5, "illness," "verbally disciplined," and "visit to doctors"; (2) ages 6 to 12, "illness," and "feelings of inferiority"; (3) ages 12 to 18, "quarrels with parents," and "feelings of guilt." The students in the Thompson and Witryol study reported significantly more unpleasant experiences in (1) ages 6 to 12, "forced to do unpleasant things"; and (2) ages 12 to 18, "school failure," "refused desired objects," and "loss of friends."

[1] G. G. Thompson and S. A. Witryol, "Adult Recall of Unpleasant Experiences during Three Periods of Childhood," *Journal of Genetic Psychology,* vol. 72, pp. 111–123, 1948.

## The Nature of Emotion

Emotions resemble feelings to the extent that the entire body participates in the reactions that accompany the experience. Both feelings and emotions are concerned with the affective experiences that involve general reactions of the individual during the time he is affected by stimuli that arouse or excite. An individual is not born with set patterns of emotional behavior. Emotional responses are the outgrowth of interactions between inherited constitution and environmental factors of influence. An emotionalized state may be accompanied by a dynamic drive to action, but the emotion cannot be regarded as the cause of the drive. Individuals and groups differ in their emotional reactions. The following suggestions offered by Smith are enlightening:

It is difficult to generalize about expressiveness in a society as large and complex as the United States. We probably are not as inhibited as the Balinese, as expressive as the Haitians, as hostile as the Sioux, as fearful as the Hopis, nor as affectionate as the Arapesh. However, we are less aware of these cross-cultured differences than of the differences within our own society, for the Maine lobsterman, the Vermonter, the Georgian, and the Texan all have their somewhat unique styles of emotional expression. We note the greater inhibition of the New Englander and the freer expression of the Southerner, and we see that women in our society more fully express their emotions than do men.[2]

Some adults erroneously attempt to explain a young person's expressed urge "to go places and do things" as symptomatic of the strong emotions that are considered to be characteristic of adolescent development. As we know, however, the physiological and psychological changes that are taking place during the growing-up years give rise to the arousal of new wants. The extent to which these adolescent "needs" are satisfied or thwarted determines the kind and intensity of consequent emotional reactions.

## The Arousal of Emotions

An emotion results from the fusion of complex sensory and perceptual experiences with patterns of attitudes and behavior already established. The perception of an appropriate stimulus starts the emotion, which is fully experienced as soon as the feeling tones and other affective elements have been aroused through the functionings of the autonomic nervous system. The feelings and impulses thus aroused are basic to an

[2] Henry Clay Smith, *Personality Adjustment*, McGraw-Hill Book Company, New York, 1961, p. 138.

emotional experience. Moreover, stimulus situations that are associated with interest or desire can become emotion-arousing. For example, if an individual has developed an interest in another individual, an object, or a situation, it is possible that emotional reaction will result from stimuli that emanate from the presence of the individual, object, or situation, or from thoughts about the stimulator of the emotional state.

There is a close relationship between the stimulus that arouses the emotion and the emotion itself. A particular stimulus arouses one emotion at a time; it cannot arouse two opposite emotions simultaneously. Moreover, the stimulus situation may arouse an emotion at one time and not at another, even though the conditions appear to be similar at both times. Contrariwise, similar stimuli may arouse different and even opposing emotions at different times. Difference in perception of the stimulus will change the inner reaction of the individual to it. Stroking may arouse the emotion of anger at one time; at another it may elicit the emotion of affection.

The rate of change from one emotional state to another can be rapid. A person may be aroused by anger or jealousy at one moment; if he is exposed to an appropriate stimulus, he immediately may experience a more pleasant emotional state. The intensity and duration of emotional responses depend upon the physical and mental condition of the individual as well as upon the persistency and strength of the stimulus. An emotional state is likely to continue if the stimulus that aroused the emotion is present and the individual is aware of it. If the stimulus is removed, however, or the individual's attention is distracted from it, the emotion either disappears or is reduced considerably in strength.

## Physiological Bases of Emotion

Many physical and physiological changes accompany an emotional experience. These changes are made possible through the functioning of the endocrine glands, which are controlled by the autonomic nervous system. This nervous system has three main divisions; they are concerned with glandular action and the action of many vital organs. The *cranial* and *sacral* divisions work together and in direct opposition to the *sympathetic* branch. The cranial and sacral therefore are sometimes called the parasympathetic branch. Nerves from all branches run to the vital organs of the body, such as the heart, blood vessels, lungs, stomach, liver, intestines, spleen, salivary glands, sweat glands, kidneys, bladder, colon, and genitals.

The sympathetic branch inhibits digestion, constricts blood vessels, dilates the pupils of the eyes, causes the hair to stand erect, releases blood sugar from the liver, stimulates the secretion of sweat glands, releases adrenaline from the suprarenal glands, increases the blood pressure and pulse, and checks the flow of saliva. The action of the cranial and sacral divisions is opposite to that of the sympathetic. There is a constant struggle for normal balance between these sets of nerves. During an emotional state the sympathetic branch is in ascendance; as the emotion subsides, the parasympathetic branch assumes control until normal balance is restored.

The sympathetic nervous system is not under voluntary control; a person cannot direct his heart to beat faster, his glands to secrete more or less fluid, or his eyes to dilate. Nor can he experience an emotion unless there is an actual stimulus to arouse it. He also is unable to stop the emotion if external and internal conditions are set for its continuance. Overt expression of one's feelings can be partially concealed, but the emotion itself cannot be controlled. The keen observer can recognize certain overt signs of emotionalism, such as a bulge of the eyes, a flush on the face, a flow of tears, a choke in the voice, an attempted retreat from the situation, or a display of aggressive behavior. The conditions that arouse emotional states are as varied as the range of human experience. An emotion may be aroused when an adolescent's desires are fulfilled, when his efforts are thwarted, or when he is confronted with personal danger. Usually any force that affects his view of himself or interferes with his self-concept is likely to give rise to an emotion.

An emotion, therefore, represents affective feeling tones, is characterized by inner adjustment, conditioned by the functioning of the autonomic nervous system, expressed overtly through behavior responses peculiar to the particular emotional state experienced, and aroused by the interaction between an external stimulus situation and the inner mental status. The stirred-up state of the individual, as represented by a combination of these factors, represents an emotional experience. Thus an emotion is a dynamic internal reaction that protects and satisfies the individual or causes him discomfort or annoyance. These various aspects of an emotional experience can be condensed into a summary definition of emotion as *an affective experience that results from the fusion of complex sensory and perceptual stimulation with established patterns of behavior, accompanied by inner adjustment of stirred-up states and expressed in one or another form of overt behavior.*

## Significance of Adolescent Emotional Experiences

Anyone who lives with or associates closely with teen-agers cannot help being aware of the fact that adolescent emotional experiences constitute an extremely important accompaniment of the growing-up process. Even apparently well-adjusted adolescents have their trials and tribula-

tions, as well as highly satisfying and thrilling experiences. Their emotionalized attitudes tend to fluctuate between optimistic, enthusiastic
cooperation and withdrawing, pessimistic depression. To a parent or a
teacher an adolescent's behavior may seem to be unpredictable.

For no area of development during the "in-between" years is adult
understanding of the changes that are taking place more needed than in
regard to emotional development and adjustment. Previous chapters have
referred briefly to the impact of emotion-arousing situations upon the
sensitive young person, especially as these are related to adolescent study
approaches. Although various methods of studying adolescents already
have been described, we now shall indicate how some of these techniques
may be applied specifically to the study of adolescent emotions, thereby
gaining greater insight into the affective phases of adolescent experiences.

## Approaches to the Study of Adolescent Emotions

The method of direct observation might be employed with relatively
good success in the study of the emotional reactions of young children.
Considerable difficulty may be encountered in attempts to evaluate the
emotionally stimulated behavior of preadolescents and adolescents. Certain aspects of a child's emotional state may be noted and recorded by
competent observers. Included among these might be such as: (1) the
situational stimuli that give rise to the child's behavior during an emotional experience; (2) the duration of the emotion; (3) the attempts to
control the emotion on the part of the child, his parents, or his playmates;
(4) the child's behavior during the entire emotional experience. Since
the child usually is under continuous and close supervision throughout
the day, he probably will not become aware or suspicious of any special
observation of his behavior.

To discover the emotional behavior of adolescents presents a much
more complicated situation. Direct observation no longer is a reliable
study approach. As has been said earlier, the teen-ager is alert to, and
sensitive about, close study of his behavior and is likely to resent the fact
that he is being studied, especially when he is emotionally excited or
disturbed. Since the adolescent considers adult observation of his actions
to be an intrusion into his privacy, a recognition by him of the fact that
his behavior is being observed and evaluated may arouse a display of
angry resentment that replaces whatever other observed form of emotionalized behavior he had been expressing.

The investigator who attempts to study the emotional behavior of
adolescents wisely utilizes other techniques, even though the latter may
be less reliable than direct controlled observation. Data obtained from
adolescent diaries and judicious use of questionnaires have been helpful.
Similarly, the utilization of one-way vision screens for direct observation

of adolescents' behavior in interview situations is proving fruitful to large numbers of college students and other observers who thus can study and record behavior and compare interpretations of reactions.

It is possible for a trained observer to conduct studies of adolescent emotional behavior by mingling with adolescent groups, thereby making records of the behavior reactions of numerous adolescents in the situation. To study adolescent emotions is so difficult a task that the results are not too reliable. Perhaps the "mingling" technique may yield data that are only relatively valuable. Yet it can give a little insight into the emotional life of adolescents in situations in which they are completely off guard.

A long-term predictive study of children's personal and emotional adjustment was conducted by John E. Anderson.[3] The subjects of the study included more than 2,400 children and young people, ages 9 to 17 years, living in Nobles County, Minnesota. A follow-up project attempted to discover changes in the behavior patterns of the subjects of the study. It was found that changes with age tended to take place in various areas such as cognition, skill, and knowledge, but that the emotional and personality areas were little affected by the age factor.

## Characteristics of Adolescent Emotions

The child may express joy by squealing and dancing with delight, but the adolescent expresses his feelings and emotions in more subdued fashion. The latter is expected to be less demonstrative as he gives expression to his emotional appreciation. His gaining in knowledge and wisdom and his utilization of the apperceptive mass or the total background of experience condition adolescent attitudes. Even a single experience in a sequence of events may alter the total behavior reaction thereafter. An adolescent's recognition of another teen-ager as his rival for peer status, for a date with the same girl, or for a place of honor in scholastic achievement may arouse anger, fear, hate, or jealousy when the competing rival is present. Or, if great joy has been experienced in a particular situation, any subsequent situation that is similar may arouse a pleasurable emotion. Interest, desire, and degree of thwarting are the chief components that largely determine the intensity, duration, and direction of emotional expression.

Both the child and the adolescent seek social approval. The intensity of interest is less in the child than in the adolescent. The child gradually learns that emotional outbursts bring forth disapproval; hence he changes

[3] In Raymond G. Kuhlen and George G. Thompson (eds.), *Psychological Studies of Human Development*, 2d ed., Appleton-Century-Crofts, Inc., New York, 1963, pp. 559–574.

his behavior to conform to the wishes of those elders whose approval he craves. During puberty a young person experiences a strong urge for the approval of his peers. His attitudes are influenced by inner changes and by external social stimuli. He sometimes seems to lose control of his behavior in his eagerness to express himself. He is stirred from within to become overtly aggressive or submissive; he is stimulated from without to become affectionate or jealous, tolerant or intolerant, approving or disapproving.

The stimuli that give rise to the emotions during early adolescence actually are less important than they seem to him at the time. Heightened emotional experiences during early puberty may become a source of embarrassment to an adolescent. He may experience great emotional turmoil and become thoroughly ashamed of himself. He engages in constant battles with his elders and his peers, especially with siblings near his own age. He resents parental control of his behavior. For example, he is aroused emotionally by problems suggested by the following statements:

My parents seem to reject me. They act as though I had interfered with their life.

I have a stepfather who hates me to the point of perpetual malice.

Every time I say something my father passes a sarcastic remark. I am now afraid to say anything.

If my mother approves of my doing something, my father is sure to disapprove.

My father has become very nervous and jumpy; he is always starting arguments.

I am the youngest child and treated as though my opinions are insignificant.

I would like to have privacy in my home, but my letters are opened and my bureau drawers are looked through.

I cannot make my mother realize that I want just as much freedom as my brother has.

My mother finds faults in me that I believe I do not have.

My sister is 13 and I am 18. She is very jealous of privileges given to me that are denied her.

My younger brothers and sisters insist on staying around when I have a guest.

When I displease my parents, I am required to remain in my room for hours at a time.

When I am introduced to someone I do not like, I show my feelings at once.

Because of my good nature I am "walked on."

These are but a few of the emotion-arousing situations that adolescents face as they move slowly through the teen years. Many more could be cited. According to William G. Hollister,

Psychiatrists and psychologists who have studied the emotional problems of normal teen-age youth point out that adolescence is a period marked by the appearance of new kinds of adult feelings that the boy or girl really doesn't understand. Sometimes these strong surges of emotion are so mystifying that they even create uncertainty or anxiety. If the teen-ager has been strongly attached to his parents, the flood of new feelings may change his attitude toward them. Without be-ing able to put it into words, he senses that his very growing up is endangered by the temptation to fall back into the emotional closeness of childhood. Thus that closeness becomes something he feels he must avoid.[4]

## Types of Emotional Reactions

The young adolescent displays a wide range of emotions almost daily. At one moment he may exhibit a state of great joy; but as a result of a shift in conditions, interference with his plans, or other thwarting circumstances, he may be moved to great anger. An increasing consciousness of the self and of physical awkwardness combines to disturb him. He is called upon to become more active in social situations; he often is embarrassed by his inability to manage his arms and legs, and by other signs of the sudden growth to which he has not yet fully adjusted. He develops a feeling of inadequacy and self-distrust.

Young people should and do engage in socializing experiences. Adults, however, may disapprove if, for example, a girl giggles when she is experiencing joy, happiness, elation, or affection, or sheds tears as an expression of unpleasant emotions such as fear, anger, jealousy, or worry. Yet there may be some value for girls in these behavior reactions since they provide tension release that is denied boys who build up inner tensions that find no overt outlet. It has been suggested that there may be some relationship of female tension release and male tension inhibition to the longer life span of women as compared with that of men.

An adolescent boy's emotional response to a pleasurable experience often is by a show of sheepish, embarrassed behavior; an unpleasant emotional experience may call forth strong imprecations, either audible or under his breath. During an emotional state a boy's facial muscles may twitch, he may shift his body weight from one foot to another, he may twist a tie or an ear, or squirm. He may have difficulty in speaking distinctly, or he may display a general clumsiness of movement. Unpleasant emotions often are accompanied by negative attitudes such as glumness and refusal to participate in conversation. Although an emotionally stimulated girl may exhibit some of the characteristic responses of a boy, she is likely to be more outgoing in her behavior.

The temper tantrum of the young child usually is expressed in overt

[4] William G. Hollister, "Emotional Ills of Adolescents," *The PTA Magazine*, p. 10, January, 1962. Reprinted by permission.

behavior that is relatively fleeting and easily observed by anyone in the child's presence. During the adolescent years exhibitions of temper tantrum behavior sometimes are classified as moods. If overt expression of an experienced emotion continues to be repressed, the mood condition becomes intensified. The adolescent appears to be gloomy; his moodiness is exhibited in his lack of interest in people, inability to make decisions, carelessness, and laziness. He tends to be preoccupied by his own thoughts and feelings; he becomes gruff, surly, and rude to all who are near him or who seemingly thwart his wishes.

## Causes of Emotional Disturbances during Adolescence

Not only may adolescents give expression from time to time to one or another variety of emotionalized reaction, but they also differ in their emotional experiences and observable emotionalized behavior. These emotional differences depend largely upon their training and other environmental experiences in the home and the school, as these interact with certain innate potentialities. Attitudes and patterns of behavior that are formed during childhood years are very important.

Among the factors that influence the emotional reactions of adolescents can be included health status, intelligence level, sex, day of week, time of day, order of birth, degree of school success, amount of social acceptance, and kinds of vocational interests. In addition, the emotion-arousing stimuli of the radio, television, motion picture, sex-pointed literature, and jazz music represent the kinds of exciting experience situations that bombard adolescents almost daily. It is not surprising, therefore, that less stable young people are impelled to engage in highly emotionalized and socially disapproved forms of behavior.

There is a significant relationship between health condition and emotional reaction. On any age level poor health tends to be a cause of heightened emotionality. Emotional disturbance often occurs more readily when a person is suffering from one or another form of ill-health than when he is free from physical ailment. A physically frail or sickly adolescent is physiologically set for the arousal of unpleasant emotional reactions. Stimuli that ordinarily might be ignored almost completely by the healthy young person become extremely annoying to the less robust boy or girl. Moreover, when a usually well-controlled child or adolescent develops an uncooperative attitude or is quick-tempered or sulky, the cause of the emotionalized state may be associated with temporary illness.

Similarly, the experiencing even by the supposedly well-adjusted adolescent of situations or conditions that are not satisfying to his ego or that, temporarily at least, appear to interfere with his personal interests, ambitions, or drive toward the achievement of adult status, may constitute the emotion-arousing bases of more or less disturbed behavior and of feelings of thwarting or unhappiness.

The influence upon adolescent emotional reactions of some of the "problem" situations in which young people find themselves is discussed more fully in another section of this book. We next shall direct our attention to specific areas of emotions experienced during adolescence.

## Specific Emotional Experiences during Adolescence

We know that definite changes take place in emotional development as the child passes through preadolescence and adolescence into adulthood. The young child's emotional manifestations cannot easily be classified as fear, anger, disgust, hate, affection, joy, pleasure, delight, envy, distrust, and jealousy. Adolescent affective experiences, however, can be classified more readily as falling into one or another emotional area. Emotions show themselves as the individual lives in various situations and comes into contact with other persons. Hence an adolescent's emotional behavior can be appraised with relative accuracy insofar as he develops a set of values, desires, and ideals; to the extent that his interest in, and attitudes toward, the acceptance of responsibilities assume a more definite mode; and to the degree that he responds to the points of view and ideals of others. Although the research work related to stimulus-response patterns of adolescent emotions has been limited in scope, the following discussion represents an attempt to analyze the behavior of adolescents as they experience different emotions in their growing-up process.

### Fear

Early observation and experimentation in the field of emotional behavior led to the generalization that there may be only three unlearned emotions: *fear, rage,* and *love.* Concerning "natural" fear, for example, John B. Watson, as a result of extensive research with infants, concluded that fear is aroused naturally by very few forms of stimulation. A child does not fear the dark, fire, snakes, strangers, and similar emotion arousers without conditioning (exposure to learning situations). According to Watson, factors of insecurity, such as loud noises, loss of support, or falling a short distance, may elicit the fear response without previous conditioning.

At all age levels a common behavior response during fear is flight. Physical responses include perspiring, paling, panting, trembling, and becoming rigid. These physiological conditions appear to represent symptomatic preparation for fleeing from the fear-arousing situation, since either actual or symbolic flight from fearsome conditions appears to be a natural and satisfying mode of achieving emotional equilibrium.

## Nature of Adolescent Fears

The usual fear reactions of adolescents are similar to those of children. In fact, fears that are begun in childhood tend to continue into adolescence. Once a child responds with fear to a specific situation, he is likely during his later years to experience fear reactions in situations which are similar to those of his childhood. For young people especially, an element of the *unknown* in a situation has fear-arousing potential. For example, sudden noises or sights tend to be fear producers; inability to foresee the possible end results of activities in which one is interested is a strong stimulator of fear arousal. As an adolescent comes to discover, however, that particular sounds or sights are harmless and that certain situations

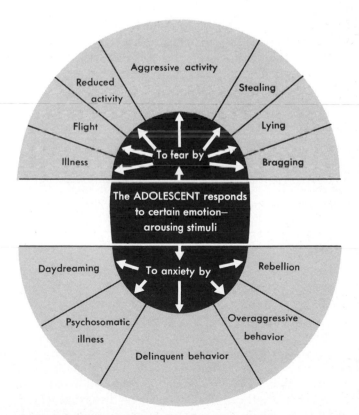

*Figure 24.* Typical adolescent responses to stimuli that arouse fear or anxiety.

are not dangerous, his fear responses to them gradually are modified and finally may cease.

Unless they have achieved considerable understanding of themselves and of their personal and social relationships, older adolescents may have such emotional experiences as fear of illness, of social or vocational failure, of the loss of relatives or friends, of the possibility of an unhappy marriage, or of poverty. In fact, one or more of these fears can continue to plague an individual through much or all of his adult life.

Fear is characterized by inner excitement with tendencies toward withdrawing from or avoiding situations. The subtleness of the reaction is increased with age. An adolescent may learn that by anticipating a possible fear-arousing stimulus he can run away from it in advance, thus avoiding emotional disturbance. This flight behavior sometimes is not noticed by his associates; yet it is basic to many personality difficulties. If a child is afraid to engage in a competitive activity, his attitude is understood and accepted by those about him; for an adolescent to retreat from an activity in which others expect him to participate may earn for him the disapproval of both adults and his peers. Flight is not the only behavior reaction displayed by the adolescent who is experiencing a specific fear or is in a state of anxiety concerning possible difficulties that he may encounter. He may tend to advance rather than retreat; he may engage in socially disapproved behavior; he may experience actual or imagined illness (see Figure 24).

## Control of Fear

The practice of self-control is important to the adolescent in all emotional areas. Even if complete elimination of fear might be considered desirable, it would be impossible to accomplish. The recognition of certain stimuli as fear producers changes with age, but at no maturity level is there indication of absence of any fear. Intelligently controlled fear has value. Fear can be a safeguard against harm to the extent that it encourages an attitude of cautiousness. Fear of consequences can help an adolescent restrain impulsive behavior until he becomes increasingly adept in coping with the many novel interpersonal relationships which he experiences during the growing-up years.

Fear of the loss of prestige, or fear of failure in the opinion of others, may lead to increased and improved activity, more careful preparation for study or work tasks, and the exercise of greater caution in the management of one's affairs than would result from indifference to the significance to himself of others' evaluation of his behavior. The desire for approval from those whom one respects is based upon a fear of possible adverse criticism if one does not perform at the level expected.

Disregard of cautious fear can cause mental or physical ill-health or loss of life. One characteristic of emotional maturity is the recognition of the value of intelligent fear or caution as a restraining influence, when one is tempted to engage in activities which possess elements of potential danger to oneself or to others. For example, upper-class college students in a metropolitan area are participating, as a phase of their teacher-training experiences, in volunteer community agency activity. To get to some of the agencies the students need to travel through sections of the city that might arouse in these young people some fear for their safety. The college has taken the responsibility of avoiding possible harm to them by providing proper supervision for them during their travel. Thus disturbing fear is eliminated; yet wholesome fear under control is being given attention.

The beneficial effects of sensible fear are evidenced by its sociological value. To become an acceptable and respected member of a societal group one must sacrifice many personally satisfying modes of behavior. This is more easily accomplished when the adolescent fears loss of prestige or loss of the friendship of members of either sex whom he admires very much. If mental attitudes provide the directing stimuli, fear can act as a guide to the attainment of many social virtues.

## Worry

Some of the most devastating fears are products of the imagination. Fear in the form of *worry* emanates from imaginary rather than real causes. Emotional reactions resulting from imagined terrifying situations are likely to produce more serious results than those that originate in actual fear-producing situations. The motivating factors of worry are always near at hand. All the individual needs to do is to call upon his imagination for the stimulus that will arouse a state of worriment.

To worry is a common emotional reaction; it usually is of longer duration than fear. Worry may be based upon past events that have not been personally satisfying; it may represent anticipatory emotionalism concerning future activity in which the individual desires strongly to achieve success. Worry may appear at any age period; it is likely to be characteristic of the adolescent years. Young people are especially worried about their relationships with their associates of both sexes. The authors conducted a study of teen-age problems that included a consideration of adolescent worries.[5] In this study, college students (120 women and 100 men) were invited to list their worries in various areas of life

[5] Lester D. Crow, "Teen-Age Traits, Interests and Worries," *The Educational Forum*, pp. 427–428, May, 1956. By permission of Kappa Delta Pi, owners of the copyright.

*Table 11.* Adolescent Worries Relative to Friends as Recalled by College Juniors

| MALE WORRIES | FEMALE WORRIES |
|---|---|
| Arguments with friends | Are friends true friends |
| Friends may not like me | Not to let friends down |
| To be worthy of good friends | To be popular |
| How to make friends | How to be leader in a group |
| Friends continue good opinion of me | How to overcome inferiority feeling |

during their teen years, 14 through 19. The responses of the men and the women were organized separately. Consideration was given to two life areas, e.g., "friends" and "boy and girl relationships." The results are presented in Tables 11 and 12.

*Table 12.* Adolescent Worries Relative to Boy-Girl Relationships as Recalled by College Juniors

| MALE WORRIES | FEMALE WORRIES |
|---|---|
| Not being popular | Being accepted |
| Desire for more dates | Sexual conflicts |
| Inferiority | Loss of boy friend |
| Displease parents with date | Sexual relations to maintain |
| Too few girl friends | Feeling of inferiority |
| Persistency of female | Boy I like doesn't like me |
| Girl I like doesn't like me | Boy who could hold my interest |
| | Little mixups |

The authors also investigated the worries of 658 fifteen- and sixteen-year-old high school students (352 girls and 306 boys) by giving them an opportunity to list their worries during the teen years according to the following ten areas: school life, homelife, boy-girl relationships, recreation, friends, vocational choice, religion, health, clothes, and money. The results of the study are presented in Table 13.

These investigators found sex differences worthy of note. The two sexes tend to worry about similar matters, but women seem to worry more than men about their possible inability to attain the degree of success in their work to which they aspire. Men seem to worry more than women about such things as not working hard enough, growing old, and living in shabby homes. Other studies suggest that college freshmen worry about personal, academic, and social problems.

Worry is transitory and disappears with the removal of the causal factors. Often there is a feeling of inadequacy that is associated with an attitude of inferiority. If there is a belief that adjustment in the situation may be difficult or impossible, the worry is increased and prolonged. If an adolescent's worry is to be controlled, the person must take positive action in order that adequate adjustments may be made. He should take

*Table 13.* Adolescent Worries in Various Life Areas

| LIFE AREA | MALE WORRIES | FEMALE WORRIES |
|---|---|---|
| School life | Homework<br>Getting along with teachers<br>Tests<br>Marks<br>Failure<br>Reciting in class<br>Grade for parents' sake<br>College entrance<br>Being accepted | Homework<br>Getting along with teachers<br>Tests<br>Marks<br>Failure<br>Reciting in class<br>Parents' attitude toward grade<br>Being accepted<br>College entrance |
| Homelife | Arguments with sister or brother<br><br>Arguments with parents<br>Arguments between parents<br>Strict parents<br>Conflicts with parents<br>Arguments about dating<br>Treated unjustly | Younger brothers get what they want<br>Parental domination<br>Parents object to going steady<br>Conflicts with parents<br>Fear of mother<br>Conflicts on values<br>Arguments in home |
| Boy-girl relation-ships | How to get a date<br>Girls I like don't like me<br>Girls cost too much<br>How to be invited to parties<br>Mother objects to my going steady<br>How to have a girl go steady<br>Inability to dance<br>Does girl love me?<br>Girls of another religion<br>How to forget girl who jilted me | How to meet new friends<br>Boys I like don't like me<br>How to be popular<br>Boys are too demanding<br>I would like to go steady<br>Loss of boy friend<br>Behavior of boy friend<br>Sexual relations to maintain<br>Girls who try to steal boy friend<br>How to get over love for boy<br>How to refuse a date tactfully |
| Friends | Are they true friends?<br>Friends may not like me<br>To be worthy of good friends<br>How to make friends<br>To be popular | Are they true friends?<br>Not to let friends down<br>To be popular<br>How to be a leader in a group<br>Feelings of inferiority |
| Vocational choice | State of indecision<br>How to get a job | State of indecision<br>How to get into show business |
| Religion | Should I marry out of my religion?<br>Indecision<br>Not attending religious services | Should I marry out of my religion?<br>Doubt about religious values<br>Fear parents will discover that I wish to change my religion |
| Health | How to grow more<br>How to lose weight<br>Pimples<br>Disease | Thinness and smallness<br>Fear of losing good health<br>Disease<br>Illness tendencies |

action, become informed, face the situation, and evaluate the cause of the worry. If it seems necessary, he should seek the cooperation of experienced adults to help him eliminate the cause of the worry and finally the worry itself.

### Anger

An angry person usually displays aggressive behavior and tends to cast off, remove, or eliminate disturbing or thwarting stimuli.

## Nature of Adolescent Anger

The angry adolescent tends to avoid a direct attack upon the individual who arouses his anger; he may throw the first thing that comes into his hands, or turn to some form of strenuous exercise. Sometimes he mutters under his breath about the things that he will do when he gets a chance. He is mentally prepared to do many things that will show those at whom his anger is directed that he will not tolerate their attitude or behavior (see Figure 25).

The temper tantrum of a small child usually takes the form of striking, crying, biting, kicking, tearing, or even holding the breath. If tantrum

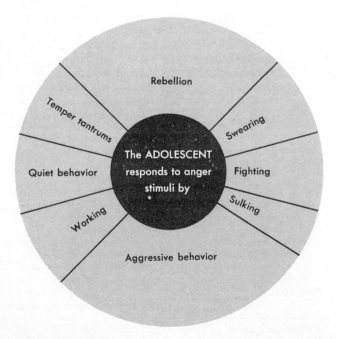

*Figure 25.* Typical responses of adolescents to anger-producing stimuli.

behavior is permitted to continue, it may become quite troublesome during adolescence. The overt expression of the adolescent's irrational emotional state is more subtle than that of the child. The tantrum state may be displayed through the extensive use of profanity in the presence of others, the "silent treatment," the use of extreme sarcasm directed with bitterness at the object of the tantrum, and sometimes deep self-pity and antisocial moods.

An adolescent may display tantrum behavior when his social plans are interrupted or interfered with, when his routines are changed, when he believes that he is not understood by adults (especially parents and teachers), when siblings preempt his property, when things in general are not going right, when elders "boss" him unduly, or when he believes that he is being imposed upon or denied his lawful rights. The general causes of adolescent anger are rooted in social relationships. The angry state usually reflects a form of thwarting experience such as interference with self-assertion or habitual activity.

In his continuing attempts to achieve adult status the adolescent is constantly subjected to many petty annoyances, the cumulative effect of which can be the arousal of strong resentments or bitter hostility. A young person may regard a situation or another person's attitude toward him as inimical to his best interests even though it is not so. His pride is easily hurt. Failure to achieve satisfactorily in school or apparent lack of acceptance by peers tends to become a stimulator of anger. The teenager is prone to respond unfavorably to anyone or anything in his environment that seems to him to be a threat to his self-esteem. The adolescent also may direct his anger at himself insofar as he recognizes limitations within himself in realizing those ideals and aspirations that represent the effect upon him of adult expectations.

In light of the foregoing discussion, it can be understood that in the adolescent's struggle to achieve self-reliance and independence of action he experiences various types of thwarting or frustrating situations and conditions. He may be insecure, fearful, and uncertain concerning what he should do and how he should do it. Consequently, he is stimulated to respond to unsatisfying experiences in one of two ways: flight or fight. Whether a young person in a stressful situation retreats (a fear response) or becomes aggressive (an anger response) depends in large measure upon the kind of behavior that had become habitual and relatively satisfying during his childhood years.

## Control of Anger

The close relationship that exists between affective stimuli and emotion arousal can be recognized easily as applying to anger. Remove the stimulus that causes a particular angry state and the emotion tends to disappear. An angry adolescent can be changed into a happy, self-respecting individual through the application of appropriate stimulation by those with whom he works and socializes. To ignore or show disapproval of the angry behavior will not improve the situation. New and appropriate stimuli should be provided to help the young person regain his self-respect. He needs his ego bolstered and protected.

If the adolescent's disturbed state is to be alleviated, the adult needs to understand the background of the anger-arousing situation and the habit patterns of the young person involved. It is usually easier to cope with the anger of an adolescent if the motives or reasons underlying the behavior are known. Moreover, a period of waiting for the cooling-off process to function may be helpful if there is a justifiable reason for the anger state. Then provocations of the anger can be minimized or removed. Parents and teachers find the use of praise or commendation to be effective in assisting an adolescent to overcome his real or fancied hurt. Further arguments with the thwarted young person, or attempts to reason with him by directing attention to the cause of the anger, will increase rather than decrease it. A pleasant remark, preferably unrelated to the emotionalized state, may divert the wrath and reduce the tension.

## Affection

Pleasant experiences build up emotional reactions that are classified as *affection, love,* or the *tender emotions.* As members of the family or family friends pick up, hold, and play with the baby, they are giving him affectionate attention. Receiving affectionate care and interest from others in his day-by-day living becomes one of the most important factors in the emotional development of the young child, and continues to be important throughout life.

## Changes in Affectionate Behavior

During childhood pleasant emotions are associated not only with solicitous adults but also with pets and familiar objects, especially toys. As the individual grows into adolescence, the tender emotions are associated almost entirely with human beings, although some attachment to pets may continue.

The child usually showers his affection on anyone who extends it to him; the adolescent becomes discriminating in his selection of individuals to whom he gives his affection. Within the limits of available associates the adolescent becomes attached to a select few. Girls pair off in two-somes; boys, after passing through the gang or large-group stage, tend to reduce the number of close friends to one or two, toward whom an attitude of strong attachment is displayed. The adolescent boy or girl is "choosy" about the age peers or older people with whom he is willing to associate and toward whom he evinces affectionate regard.

An adolescent, as does a child, needs to feel secure in the affection of another, to know that he is liked and wanted. He also needs to experience concern about the interests and welfare of others. This adolescent need can be satisfied by encouraging a young person during childhood to perform kindly acts. As a result, by the time he reaches adolescence, a co-operative attitude will be characteristic of his habitual behavior pattern. Affection is the dominant emotion that a child or an adolescent boy or girl experiences in a well-adjusted home. Even as a member of an affectionate family group, however, there are times when jealousy and varying degrees of resentment are exhibited if the adolescent believes that he is not receiving his rightful share of affectionate attention from his parents or others in the home.

The adolescent usually does not express his affections through uncontrolled demonstrations but rather by desiring to be with the loved one, by attending to the latter's every wish, by attempting to do whatever he can to make the other person happy, and by responding to everything the loved one says and does. An adolescent is stirred deeply by his love for another; the affections of a child may be somewhat lukewarm and fleeting. Since the adolescent experiences a need for the companionship of the present object of his strong affection, he feels insecure in the absence of the loved one; he devises numerous methods to "keep in touch" with him or her. He may visit, telephone, or send letters or telegrams in order that he may continue the close affectionate relationship.

## Affection between the Sexes

Adolescents want their friends of the opposite sex to show affection toward them, but they usually desire to follow accepted social customs in matters dealing with relations between the sexes. For example, a conventional kiss must not be given in the presence of others lest it cause embarrassment. When girls or boys ask questions concerning desirable dating behavior, they actually are attempting to discover appropriate methods of showing affection. The questions in this area asked by members of both sexes include the following:

How can a boy or girl overcome blushing?

If I do not like someone I cannot help showing my feelings. How can I remedy this?

What should one do if he has the feeling that others are laughing at him?

How does one get out of a goodnight kiss?

How can you refuse a man a date? Do you think necking is wrong? Should a girl invite a boy to take her out? Should a girl show a boy that she likes him? How can I overcome my bashfulness in the presence of girls? After you have broken off with a girl, how would you go about getting her back?

Can a boy of 19 be true to two girls? Should I tell my friend the things I dislike in her? How can I become a part of an in-group? How can you compete with others and still remain their friends? Is it necessary to break certain friendships as you acquire new friends?

Problems that cause emotional experiences center around the fact that the adolescent wants to be held in high regard by members of the opposite sex. The boy or girl does not always know how to behave in order to hold the affection of another and at the same time retain self-respect. What love means to adolescents can best be described in their own terms. The replies of five teen-agers are revealing.

Love is a mutual affection that grows until you can't see any other person. Love is undeniable. I just don't live unless I see this person. Love is a gradual thing. You must see this person night and day. Your thoughts become part of his life and thoughts. Love is putting your heart and life in someone else's hand. Love is a gradual process that fuses two hearts, making them one.

## Jealousy

Jealousy reflects a combination of anger, fear, and possible loss of affection. Jealousy results from emotion-arousing stimuli inherent in a social situation. If there is loss, or fear of loss, of the affection wanted from another, of a coveted honor, or of the attainment of any strongly desired goal, jealousy is aroused. For example, a high school senior may fail to be elected class president by his classmates, an honor which he had coveted and had worked hard to attain. He may become extremely jealous of the winner of the position and find it difficult to cooperate in class affairs. If a boy is forced to stand by while another dates the girl in whom he has become interested, both his pride and self-esteem may be wounded. Jealous reactions inevitably result when a young person is denied a privilege that is granted to another. This is true whether it occurs in the home, the school, or any other societal group.

Jealousy shows itself in boy-girl relationships, especially as adolescents move from larger group activities to twosome dating. The emotional attitudes of the adolescent change from an interest in group activities to an interest in a particular person of the opposite sex who now has become the "best girl" or the "boy friend." In a study made by the authors concerning traits disliked in members of the opposite sex, it was found that among behavior qualities, boys dislike girls who have a tendency to flirt, talk about other dates, mingle with a fast crowd, sulk and pout, be catty, or show immature behavior; girls dislike boys who are boastful, display poor manners, are unfriendly, act conceited, act foolish at parties, are fresh, use bad language, talk too much, ridicule others, or are moody.

A girl becomes jealous when her "date" at a party appears to have forgotten her and devotes his attention to another girl. Likewise, a boy becomes extremely annoyed if his "girl" acts toward another boy at the party as though she enjoyed his company more than that of her "date." Behavior during these experiences varies with the degree of maturity of the young person involved. The girl may regress to infantile behavior, such as whining or crying, or she may decide to avoid future embarrassment by refusing to have dates with the boy; the boy may become sarcastic, make derogatory remarks about the individual whom he considers to be the intruder, or ridicule the latter when he is not present to defend himself. The emotionally immature boy may resort to bodily attack, as does the young child when his jealousy is aroused.

## Curiosity

Learning through experience is stimulated by curiosity. The desire to explore the new and the different is very strong from early childhood through adolescence. The form that it takes varies with the satisfactions that are experienced through the growing years. His attempts to discover how things work or what makes them "tick" often get the child into a great deal of trouble. He may be able to take objects apart but he frequently damages them because of his inexperience and lack of knowledge, especially in his attempts to put them together again. Although he sometimes is punished for such activities, he persists in his attempts to satisfy his curiosity in one way or another.

During adolescence a young person's exploratory procedures are somewhat restrained since he now has learned that a good child does not destroy or damage objects but rather learns to take good care of them. Curiosity continues to function in other ways, however. The pubertal changes that are occurring within him, for example, arouse a strong interest in his own physical development as related to that of members of the opposite sex.

Adolescents continue to be interested in the new and the different in their enlarging environment. They have abundant opportunities to satisfy this urge. Yet, to their consternation, many of their exploratory activities are planned minutely for them by adults. As a result of too great adult direction of their exploratory interests, some adolescents come into conflict with their elders, leave home, join the Armed Forces, become delinquent, or engage in socially disapproved sex behavior. Less-aggressive and better-controlled young people plan parties or other social activities to satisfy their spirit of adventure and curiosity.

Chief among the newly aroused interests during this age period are those associated with sex. Many boys and girls are becoming informed at an early age regarding their physiological and psychological sexual development. There still remains, however, enough that is new for them in phases of growing up to stimulate their curiosity toward more complete knowledge concerning boy-girl relationships and adjustment (see Chapter 9 for a detailed discussion of this problem).

## Effect of Emotional Experiences on Adolescent Behavior

Emotions are essential to the complete development of adolescent behavior patterns. When an adolescent is trained to do what is socially acceptable, he should be ready to assume independent control of his behavior. His self-directed decisions tend to be conditioned by his emotions, however. Since an adolescent's emotions exercise a potent influence upon his attitudes and behavior, unbridled emotional reactions may interfere seriously with a young person's power to use the freedom of decision making and of behavior that he craves and should be granted. Hence the achievement by the adolescent of habitual control of his emotions is essential to his enjoyment, adjustment, and success.

### Emotions as Behavior Molders

Fear, anger, affection, and curiosity can be thought of as motivating forces. They can drive an individual toward constructive action; they may inhibit or slow down worthwhile activity or encourage participation in destructive forms of behavior. Therefore it becomes extremely important that an individual learn to control his actions during an emotional experience. For example, for a teacher to control his overt behavior during an emotional experience associated with pupil misbehavior means that the adult weighs carefully what he should do in the situation rather than saying the first thing that comes to mind. A teacher's or a parent's display of emotional control is of value not only to the adult but also to the young people who are stimulated by adult example.

The adolescent who, during a state of anger, restrains himself from bursting forth in an emotional tirade is giving evidence that he has achieved a high degree of emotional maturity. Rather than keeping the emotional state penned up, however, he should attempt to release the emotional tension in an activity outlet that is socially and individually acceptable. Strong emotions of anger or fear may produce undesirable paralyzing behavior. If emotions are basic to the motivation of behavior, they should be controlled in such a way as to serve the adolescent rather than to become his master.

An adolescent whose pattern of life is satisfactory, whose urges and desires meet with fulfillment, and whose interests and needs are met with satisfaction tends to enjoy life and to be emotionally mature. Contrariwise, if his urges, desires, interests, or needs are frustrated, his emotional experiences may lead to the development of instability or patterns of maladjustment. Many adolescent responses are representative of behavior of objective reasoning and judgment; yet there are times when emotional urges and drives almost completely influence youthful thinking and behavior. For best adjustment, enjoyment, and productivity, the emotions should influence behavior but not control it.

## Effects of Emotions upon Physical Status

Excessive fears, including phobias, intense anger, prolonged and too deep affection, and similar emotional experiences, may have detrimental effects upon health. The normal process of digestion may be inhibited by changes occurring in the glandular secretions during states of fear, anger, anxiety, or worry. The mouth may become dry, and the rate of heartbeat, the blood pressure, and the action of the entire digestive system may change during emotional excitement. It does not follow, however, that all emotions affect digestion adversely. On the contrary, pleasant and relaxing emotional states act as aids to digestion; annoying or tension-producing emotional states interfere with the secretion of the correct amount of digestive juices, however. The cause of most stomach ulcers is not entirely organic; an ulcer condition often results from a prolonged emotional state of fear or worry. In such instances the cure usually depends in part upon the removal of the worry or fear that produced the glandular imbalance. Fortunately, relatively few adolescents suffer from stomach ulcers; their fears, worries, or affections usually are not sufficiently prolonged to cause digestive impairment, although stomach upsets based upon emotional disturbance are found frequently among adolescents. For instance, it is not unusual for an adolescent girl or boy to be unable to eat properly if he is emotionally stirred by a new love.

Emotional disturbances have been found to be the cause of many speech difficulties with which adolescents are afflicted. When a speech difficulty appears without evidence of physical deformity in the speech organs, the cause usually can be explained in terms of pent-up emotions. It is believed that emotional strain may cause a person to stutter or stammer. When he is relaxed, his speech is relatively fluent; but with the introduction of emotion-arousing stimuli, he quickly exhibits deviate speech behavior.

## Emotional Bases of Adolescent Attitudes

A young person's appraisal of people and objects tends to reflect his emotional maturity. For the immature teen-ager, self-respect must be maintained at all cost. If he suffers humiliation because he has been mistreated in school by his teachers, or in the home by his parents, he may retreat into reticence or even flee from the situation altogether. Attitudes of timidity or aggressiveness often result from emotional tension or frustration experienced by adolescents in social settings. Consequently, inherent in an adolescent's evaluation of people, situations, or conditions are the emotional reactions that are associated with personal interrelationships.

The emotionalized attitudes of many adolescents are wholesome, outgoing, and subject to intellectual control. We quote from *Preinduction Health and Human Relations*. Since this manual deals with the development and adjustment of adolescents and young adults, it may be noted that the term *person* as used in the following cited materials connotes, for the most part, *young* person.

### THE EMOTIONALLY HEALTHY PERSON

The emotionally healthy person has certain attitudes and characteristics that are discernible in the way he regards himself, other people and day-to-day situations.

He has a good opinion of himself. He neither denies nor overestimates his capacities and character. He sees room for self-improvement. This challenges rather than depresses him. His sense of humor makes him view himself objectively and permits him to be amused at his own foibles when others expose them. He sees the absurdity that often exists in human situations, yet does not despise others for the weakness or foolishness that creates such situations.

Such a person enjoys the company of other people and respects them whether he happens to like them or not. He refuses to permit prejudice to come between him and his fellowmen and refuses to sit in judgment on them. He may, and sometimes must, disapprove of what they do, but he feels no unhealthy compulsion to tell them so unless it is his clear duty to do so. He does not actively dislike people for their faults, knowing that one can "hate the sin and love the sinner."

Although the emotionally healthy

person enjoys work, play and co-operative activities with others, he is not lonely when by himself. Because he is self-sufficient, he can use privacy and solitude for his hobbies and for reflection, planning and sorting things out in his own mind.

Others' opinions of him are important to him, but they do not throw him into panic and alarm if they are not uniformly approving. He weighs criticism as objectively as possible, tries to determine its validity and uses it in his efforts to improve himself. He does not dwell on criticisms nor resent the person who made them.

A person with good emotional health has a philosophy of life that helps him do his best at all times. Into this philosophy of life—not necessarily fully developed in a young person but nevertheless a guiding factor in his behavior—go his spiritual values and his attitudes towards himself, other people and society generally. His philosophy guides him in viewing the world around him, in evaluating current history, in planning his own future and in making the best possible contribution to his community and country.[6]

Many adolescent problems are rooted in emotional experiences and stress conditions. In this chapter we have considered some of the basic and more general aspects of emotional development and adjustment during the growing-up years. Specific problems related to adolescent emotional status are discussed later in Chapters 14–17.

## Questions and Problems for Discussion

1. Observe the behavior of adolescents in a group situation to discover the extent to which it is sex-directed behavior. Then discuss the need for an understanding of the effect of emotions on adolescent behavior.
2. Give examples to illustrate how peer approval or teacher approval can be a motivating force in the life of an adolescent.
3. Present emotional experiences that interfere with adolescent acceptance and/or success. Suggest what might be done to alleviate stress situations so that the individual could feel at ease in a group, and/or succeed at his study or other activity.
4. What are some incentives that have aroused your curiosity and/or stirred you to successful achievement? To what extent can these be used by teachers to motivate adolescents?
5. Most of our emotions can serve useful purposes, although some of them often hinder or interfere with our success in one or another area of interest. Report three useful purposes to which you have put such emo-

[6] E. E. Sweeney and R. E. Dickerson (eds.), *Preinduction Health and Human Relations*, American Social Hygiene Association, New York, 1953, pp. 46–47. Reprinted by permission of the American Social Health Association, copyright 1953.

tions as anger, fear, and affection; report situations in which each of them has interfered with your success.

6. *Special Exercises:*
   a. Report differences in fear, anger, and love responses of four adolescents whom you have known or with whom you are presently working.
   b. Present a situation during which anger, hate, or fear became contagious in a crowd. Explain why emotions tend to spread quickly and widely in a group.
   c. From your own experience, illustrate that emotions have a powerful influence on health.
   d. Indicate the extent to which your emotional experiences have influenced your vocational choice; your avocational activities.

## Selected References

Arnold, M. G.: *Emotion and Personality,* Columbia University Press, New York, 1960.

Bennett, E.: *The Search for Emotional Security,* The Ronald Press Company, New York, 1959.

Blaine, G. B., Jr., C. C. McArthur, et al.: *Emotional Problems of the Student,* Appleton-Century-Crofts, Inc., New York, 1961.

Diamond, S.: *Personality and Temperament,* Harper & Row, Publishers, Incorporated, New York, 1957.

Gallagher, J. R., and H. I. Harris: *Emotional Problems of Adolescents,* Oxford University Press, New York, 1958.

Havighurst, R. J., et al.: *Growing Up in River City,* John Wiley & Sons, Inc., New York, 1962.

May, R.: *The Meaning of Anxiety,* The Ronald Press Company, New York, 1950.

Mechanic, D.: *Students under Stress: A Study in the Social Psychology of Adaptation,* The Free Press of Glencoe, New York, 1962.

O'Brien, P. V.: *Emotions and Morals,* Grune & Stratton, Inc., New York, 1950.

Pearson, G. H. J.: *Adolescence and the Conflict of Generations,* W. W. Norton & Company, Inc., New York, 1958.

Reymert, M. L.: *Feelings and Emotions,* McGraw-Hill Book Company, New York, 1950.

Sherif, M.: *Intergroup Relations and Leadership: Approaches and Research in Industrial, Ethnic, Cultural, and Political Areas,* John Wiley & Sons, Inc., New York, 1962.

Wilkinson, B.: *Understanding Fear in Ourselves and Others,* Harper & Row, Publishers, Incorporated, New York, 1951.

# Chapter Seven

## Personal and Social Aspects of Personality Development

The term *personality* connotes, variously, physical attractiveness, charm, good nature, ease of manner, "outgoingness," or any other form of behavior or attitude that induces a favorable impression. One person can be heard commenting upon the fact that another has "personality," implying thereby that the one reacts pleasantly to the other. An adolescent is particularly prone to regard personality as a desirable characteristic to possess and as something to be sought in his associates, especially those of the opposite sex. The psychologist and the better-informed layman recognize the inaccuracy of such use of the term. Everyone possesses personality characteristics. Although one's so-called "personality" may be "good" or "bad," in that it either attracts or repels, the term itself defies accurate definition.

The personal attributes that earn social acceptance or rejection cannot be isolated easily. The aspects of an individual's personality that arouse either admiration or dislike often are subtle elements that can be detected with difficulty, if at all. By the utilization of a scientific rather than a popular approach to the interpretation of personality, it has been concluded that both hereditary factors and social experiences have significance in determining the kind of person an individual becomes. Personality is the resultant of those integrating forces that involve innate potentialities and habitual attitudes and behavior tendencies. Consequently, not only are an individual's manifested personality traits important, but the type of integration that is taking place continuously is even more significant.

## The Dynamic Nature of Personality

The primary purpose of this discussion is to consider the development of adolescent personality. Development trends during adolescence have their roots in earlier growth and developmental patterns and are relatively predictive of the kind of adult the maturing young person is likely to become. At this point, therefore, we shall consider the inherent

157

and environmental bases of the dynamic changes that characterize an individual's personality from birth onward.

Certain potential tendencies begin to show themselves early in the life of a child; their overt manifestations, however, are conditioned by the various stimulus situations to which an individual progressively responds. One's personality, as expressed in his behavior at any developmental stage or in any situation, is dynamic; it provides the inner motivation through which is sought the satisfaction of personal and social needs, wants, interests, and ambitions. Hence, in its functioning, personality reflects the changes that are peculiar to a particular individual's physical, intellectual, and emotional pattern of development.

## Significance of Personality Traits

The concept of personality as an integrated functional pattern of the whole person has value to the extent that it represents a kind of gestalt or general framework for the many facets of personality that are interrelated in their respective functioning. An attempt to evaluate an individual's personality requires the utilization of specific descriptive terms to discriminate between the significant constituents of his personality as compared to the personal characteristics of one or another individual. For example, a person is categorized as predominantly quick or slow in speed reactions, introverted or extroverted, honest or dishonest, cheerful or moody, industrious or lazy, excitable or phlegmatic. In fact, thousands of terms ordinarily are used to designate specific personality characteristics.

A particular aspect or "dimension" of personality that tends to manifest its functioning to a high degree of consistency in an individual's behavior is termed a *personality trait*. A personality trait typifies a characteristic reaction that represents a developed constitutional potentiality, e.g., tallness, speed of reaction, gait, or degree of excitability. In terms of social interrelationships, however, the significance to an individual of his predominant personality trait or traits is determined for the most part by the reactions of other persons to his display of trait-controlled behavior. When the manifestation of a particular trait or cluster of traits, such as personal integrity, is evaluated as "good" or "bad" or self-aggrandizing or selfless, it can probably be regarded more significantly as an aspect of personality.

In any case, the dynamic nature of personality traits is evidenced by their possibility of changing with changing conditions and situations. This fact holds especially for those traits that have social or ethical implications. Most adolescents, for example, are sensitive to the overt reactions of others toward themselves—their physical appearance, their emotionalized attitudes, and their habitual behavior patterns, as these reflect developing personality adjustments. Moreover, young people seek the attention, if not always the approval, of their associates. Hence most teenagers react to others in terms of the latters' reactions to them; as a result certain behavior-controlling traits are strengthened, others consciously are weakened or changed insofar as habit patterns can be modified.

An individual's reputation among his associates may be related closely to the effect upon them of one or another aspect of what to them is regarded as his personality. The concept of personality, however, represents more than the mere combination of traits or personal characteristics or attributes. Rather the term *personality* signifies the dynamic interrelationship of all an individual's physical, mental, and emotional potentialities as these interact with environmental forces. During the maturing years especially, the functioning of the many phases of personality organization becomes habituated. Insofar as an individual tends to respond to environmental stimuli in terms of habitual modes of behavior, his personality traits represent general personality trends.

## Functional Aspect of Personality

A personality trait operates as a dynamic behavior motivator; it has permanent aspects in that it may exert a controlling influence upon an individual during much or all of his life; it varies in degree or extent of dimensional significance. Personality trait differences are quantitative rather than qualitative. A comparative study of personal characteristics usually involves the utilization of a scale that begins at the near-zero point and extends to the opposite extreme of near or total possession of the trait.

For example, degree of intellectual ability as measured by performance on an intelligence test may range from a low of 25 IQ, or lower, to a high of about 200 IQ. Similarly, the results of the administration of a test of "sociability" might range from a low of extremely inadequate social interrelationships to a high of exceptionally successful social adaptability and adjustment. Woodworth and Marquis[1] presented twelve basic or primary trait dimensions with their quantitative extremes. For example, *primary trait:* "dominant, ascendant, self-assertive"; *opposite:* "submissive, self-effacing."

Acceptance of the quantitative nature of specific personality traits is closely related to one's appreciation of possible trait organization and relative trait strength. Although traits describe rather than explain behavior, it is possible to differentiate conceptually between those traits that are relatively deep-rooted or fundamental aspects of personality and

[1] R. S. Woodworth and D. G. Marquis, *Psychology*, 5th ed., Holt, Rinehart and Winston, Inc., New York, 1947, p. 92.

other traits that represent environmentally stimulated manifestations of the more fundamental personal attributes.

Certain qualities or traits tend to dominate an individual's behavior. Hence probable behavior in certain situations can be predicted with relative reliability since the various components function as a generalized whole. It cannot be predicted with certainty, however, that the trait will be displayed in every situation. An adolescent, for example, may be extremely cooperative with his teachers, but argumentative and ungracious in his attitudes and behavior toward the members of his family. The particular personality traits displayed in any given situation emanate from the deep-seated reaction pattern of the individual as it is motivated by the social stimuli that are inherent in the specific situation.

The general and specific nature of trait functioning can be illustrated by the many incidents experienced almost daily by most individuals. For example, a near relative or a close friend of a habitually honest and outspoken individual is suffering from what may be a fatal illness. The individual is asked by the sick person to tell him honestly what his chances of recovery may be. How honest an answer should be given? Should the patient's morale by bolstered by a tactful response, or should he be apprised of the seriousness of his illness? The kind of answer given depends upon various determining factors in the situation, e.g., the understanding by the person questioned of how the questioner is likely to react to the truth about his illness, and the former's willingness or ability to adapt his habitual truthtelling attitude to meet the exigencies of the situation. Again, as a result of the pressure of too much work, or because of illness or extreme thwarting, a generally cheerful and sociable person may become irritable, moody, and/or asocial.

## The Adolescent Personality

The term *adolescent personality* probably is a misnomer in that it seems to connote that all teen-agers display similar personality traits, or that any one adolescent's personality pattern remains relatively consistent during his growing-up years. Nothing could be further from the truth. To the adult who regards himself as the victim of inconsistent adolescent vagaries, sensitivities, rebellions, and intolerances, the more correct term would be *adolescent personalities*, with emphasis upon the chameleonlike changes in behavior and attitude that may seem to occur almost momentarily.

Although an adolescent's reactions often are unpredictable, this apparent inconsistency is evidence of the dynamic behavior motivators that are rooted in the physical, mental, and emotional phases of the growing-up process. Interpreted in terms of the meaning and purpose of adolescence, we can describe adolescent personality as a syndrome that represents the symptomatic aggregate not of a physical disease but rather of a mental and emotional struggle for the achievement of adult maturity.

## Adolescent Personality Development

Personality development during adolescence can be expected to continue in the form that it has been following during the childhood years, but it will be conditioned by more and more of the social influences that help the individual attain status in his peer group. Although individual differences appear at birth, they are not always recognized as such. The process of personality development begins with what the individual possesses in the way of heritage and continues to develop, even though the process is much more irregular and complex than is the development of specific skills and habits.

Self-awareness, self-realization, and self-assertion develop gradually. From a relatively vague recognition of an urge to fulfill certain physical needs, the child gradually comes to achieve understanding of the objects and persons in his environment that are associated with his developing feelings of comfort and discomfort. He enlarges his needs to include satisfying relationships with many environmental factors and to discover that he is a recipient of adult attention. Thus he develops an awareness of self, and becomes self-assertive within the confines of his relatively narrow social environment.

Throughout adolescence the developing individual becomes increasingly cognizant of the impact upon himself and his expanding needs and urges of the customs and mores of his culture, its rules and regulations, and the accepted patterns of behavior that are peculiar to the group of which he is a member. He is confronted with the necessity of evaluating his behavior in terms of the social standards and ideals of his group. His personality is undergoing vital changes during this period. The success of his activities depends upon his ability to adjust himself and his urges and interests to group demands in such a way that he can become an active, accepted member of the group.

Fundamentally, the personality traits displayed during childhood do not change suddenly with the onset of puberty. The alert, cheerful, and cooperative 10-year-old can be expected to give evidence of similar behavior characteristics when he is 15 years old. The adolescent who as a child had learned to get what he wanted by "throwing a temper tantrum" probably will continue to employ tantrum behavior when his strong desires are thwarted. An individual's general pattern of personality organization is relatively consistent throughout the growing years. Yet personality differences appear to become more marked with the changing awareness of self that accompanies pubescent physical changes, combined with a growing recognition of the significance of cultural values.

Adolescent personality structure is affected by family structure. This has been found by Peck who studied thirty-four adolescents who represented a cross section of all children born in Prairie City in 1933. These adolescents were interviewed and tested yearly from age 10 to age 18. Peck discovered that in the full range of personality adjustment and moral responsibility, there appeared to be "a significant pattern of relationship between family experience and personality." [2]

## Some General Characteristics of Adolescent Personality

Although certain needs, wants, urges, and interests are common to the majority of adolescents, it should be emphasized that the overt expression of these behavior motivators differ from one young person to another. These differences are the resultants of societal or cultural influences upon developing personality patterns. Adolescents tend to be exceedingly active in their attempts to satisfy their wants and needs according to the standards of their group. This is amply revealed in the personality traits listed for *The Personality Sphere* by Guilford. They are:

1. Liking for friends and acquaintances
2. Social leadership
3. Social poise
4. Liking for the limelight
5. Freedom from shyness or bashfulness
6. Gregariousness
7. Liking for social affairs
8. Being conspicuous
9. Maintaining one's rights
10. Self-defense
11. Social initiative
12. Lack of fear of social events [3]

As indicated earlier, the expression of deeply rooted personality traits varies with environmental atmosphere. From childhood onward an individual's personality is shaped by culture-dominated influences. Probably at no other period in his life is he so susceptible to societal pressures as during the teen years. The adolescent has strong desires to compete, to succeed, to demonstrate his physical and mental strength, to have freedom of choice, to reform and improve, and to experience pleasure of various forms, including that of a sensual nature.

Anyone who is closely associated with adolescents can recognize the

[2] Robert F. Peck, "Family Patterns Correlated with Adolescent Personality Structure," *Journal of Abnormal and Social Psychology,* vol. 42, pp. 347–350, 1958.

[3] J. P. Guilford, *Personality,* McGraw-Hill Book Company, New York, 1959, p. 80. Reprinted by permission.

extent to which all or most of these compulsions function to influence personality traits. The expression of a culturally directed want varies with individual personality patterning and differing value emphases. We shall comment briefly concerning the effect upon adolescent personality development of each of the listed compulsions.

*The Competition-Success Pattern.* Most adolescents display a spirit of competitiveness but the area of competition is not the same for all. Some high school and college teachers display an attitude of believing that their students' major want should be competition for success in scholastic attainment. Although some young people meet their teachers' expectations in this regard, many adolescents are more concerned about striving for superior status in their peer group, especially with members of the opposite sex.

*The Desire for Bigness, Strength, Growth, and Greatness.* Competition is implicit, for example, in an adolescent boy's desire to excel in school sports. Thereby he can demonstrate his superior strength and power. The physically small, undeveloped lad who is denied the opportunity to compete in athletic activities with bigger, stronger boys, directs his efforts toward the achievement of greatness in other areas. He may consciously imitate the dress, manners, and other supposed personality characteristics of a small but admired friend or acquaintance, or of a small man who has achieved current or historic fame.

*Individual Freedom and Personal Expression.* One of the strongest of an adolescent's behavior drives is the urge for freedom of decision, action, and self expression. The manner in which he displays this felt need depends partly upon his previous experiences and present adult example. An adolescent who as a child had developed attitudes of cooperation and of submission to adult authority may be so conditioned by his own temperament and his earlier training and experiences that he finds it difficult to give overt expression of his need for independence. Outwardly he may appear to be the same submissive, cooperative individual that he had been during his earlier years; inwardly, however, he gives vent to feelings of deep resentment and frustration, thereby undermining his mental health and discouraging the development of a constructive, outgoing personality.

The effect upon an independence-seeking adolescent of contacts with differing cultural standards is well illustrated by the experiences of the teen-age children of foreign-born parents. During their childhood these young people usually develop personality patterns of the family's close-knit subcultural neighborhood group. As secondary school students, however, they are exposed to the more permissive, self-determining influences of democratic standards of behavior.

The struggles that the young person experiences as he attempts either to achieve a compromise between differing cultural mores or to disavow the old for the new may induce the development of aggressive and defiant attitudes, especially toward his parents and their ideals. Further, he may fight for a place in his chosen cultural group without a realistic understanding of the group's standards. Hence he may engage in what he considers to be acceptable behavior, but discover that he is earning the strong disapproval of his new associates rather than the acceptance which he had sought. Consequently, he becomes an insecure, confused young person who may be driven to satisfy through asocial acts his natural urge for freedom and self-expression.

Equally serious is the situation of a teen-age boy or girl who in the family circle has been and continues to be granted extreme freedom of behavior. If he has been encouraged by his parents and other relatives to develop a self-regarding personality to the extent that he is concerned almost entirely with the satisfaction of his own wants and urges, he is likely to suffer many deflating experiences when he attempts to dominate or defy the wishes of associates of his own age.

*The Notion of Progress, Reform, Improvement, and Change.* At one and the same time an adolescent may be a self-centered realist and a selfless idealist. A growing boy or girl may become very much concerned about human welfare. His sympathies go to geographically near or more distant groups that he believes to be oppressed, suffering economic lack, deviating from acceptable behavior standards, or giving evidence of any forms of underprivileged status. The idealistic boy or girl is motivated to change "this sorry scheme of things."

The direction of his emotionally stimulated urge to serve humanity depends upon the strength of environmental influences. Hence an adolescent variously wants to become a social worker, a physician, a missionary, a great statesman, a chaplain in a penitentiary, a philanthropist, a labor leader, or teacher who understands adolescents. Yet an adolescent who is filled with ardor to save or help the world may disregard almost completely the many opportunities for service that he could find in his immediate environment.

For example, the adolescent grumbles when he is asked to perform a family chore; he teases siblings or neighborhood children and torments cats or dogs; he selects the most comfortable chair in a room; he pushes his way into a crowded streetcar or dives for a seat in which he sprawls himself so that other passengers fall over his feet, to his vocalized annoyance; he plays tricks on his teacher and then resents deserved reproof. These are a few of the many evidences of adolescent thoughtlessness that unfortunately are condoned by some adults who, at the same time, may express amusement or ridicule of adolescent idealism. There are young people, however, who combine their idealistic dreams of service with realistic appreciation of the many ways in which they can and do help the members of their home, school, and community groups. These adolescents gradually are developing personality traits that impel them as adults to become our humanitarians or our social and civic leaders.

*The Desire for Pleasure and Sensual Enjoyment.* An individual of any age needs "time out for play" and opportunities to satisfy his desire to gain emotional satisfaction from the contemplation of natural and man-created beauty or to derive pleasure from participation in relaxing activities. The adolescent is sensitive to the elements in his environment that stir him emotionally. He wants to satisfy his craving for that which he believes will release him temporarily from the pressures of work or study responsibilities, or will free him from environmental restraints or personal adolescent worries.

The environmental influences by which the adolescent's interests and activities are motivated, and his own developing tastes and appreciations, condition him to derive pleasure from one or another form of emotionally satisfying activity. He may spend many hours in an art gallery; he may carry around with him, and at convenient times lose himself in, the writings of his favorite poet; he enjoys singing, dancing, and listening to music that stirs him emotionally. Usually an adolescent's preferred form of leisure-time activity reflects his general temperament. However, his degree of physical energy, his intellectual level, his emotion-stimulating needs, and the kinds of pleasurable activities in which he engages are representative of the interests of his cultural group.

One cannot fail to recognize the potent, sometimes subtle, influence upon adolescent personality of the interaction that is constantly taking place between individual desires and cultural factors. During the growing-up years the relative significance of inner motivation and of outer stimulation varies from person to person. It is impossible to predict with certainty that one type of cultural influence pattern provides the most favorable environment for personality development. Moreover, youthful potentialities and drive may differ so greatly among individuals who are reared in the same cultural environment that evolving personalities vary considerably. The factors that affect adolescent personality are illustrated in Figure 26.

## Effect of Adolescent Goal-seeking

Changing adolescent interests and attitudes (see Chapter 8) can be regarded as both the causes and results of personality changes that occur during the teen-age years. Basically, these personality changes are effected as innate needs, wants, and urges find expression in developing interests and attitudes. The kind and strength of an adolescent's interest are dependent upon the nature of the goal toward which he is striving. The

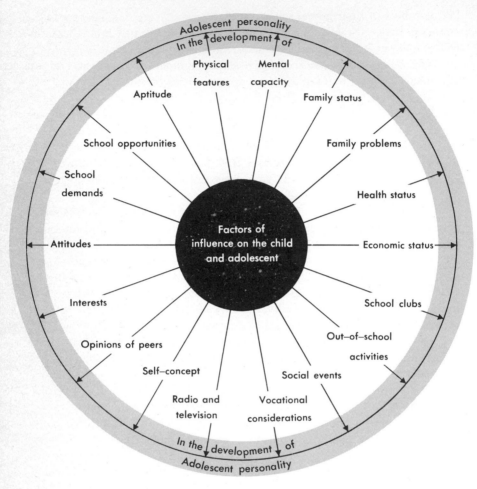

*Figure 26.* Factors that affect adolescent personality.

degree of successful goal achievement that the young person experiences exercises a powerful influence upon his attitudes and consequently upon the evolving pattern of his personality.

Vocational ambition is a specific adolescent goal that enters personality structure early in life. Most children tend to think and talk about what they are going to do when they grow up. Childhood vocational ambitions usually are fleeting, temporary interests, however, and are motivated by changing personal wants or by admired adult example.

The child's vocational ambitions usually are unrealistic in that they reflect a desire to possess something in which he is interested at the moment, or to be like someone who seems to him to be very important.

At various times a boy may decide to become a candy store owner, a fireman, a policeman, a rich businessman, a veterinarian, or a famous public figure. He may want to follow his father's vocational activities. A 7-year-old youngster, for example, insisted that he was going to drive a bus when he was a man; his father deals in the buying and selling of buses. When the child was asked if he were going to sell his father's buses, he was vehement in his assertion that he would keep all of them because he wanted to have more buses than anyone else in the world.

Little girls dream about their future. A young "mother" of many dolls is going to have a lot of babies; especially is this the ambition of an only child or one who has only one brother or sister. Variously, girls also may want to be teachers, nurses, motion-picture stars, singers, airplane hostesses; girls tend to be interested in vocations that represent service or glamor.

A childhood vocational interest may become so much a part of a youngster's developing personality that it persists and reaches adult fulfillment. Usually children's attitudes toward adult vocational choice are ephemeral and change with experience. Adolescent interests in this area of goal-striving are likely to be more meaningful; they reflect to a greater degree the direction being taken by certain aspects of the developing personality. Yet changing ambitions are characteristic of the adolescent years as well as of childhood. For example, the authors asked 175 college students (mostly first-semester juniors) to list in order their remembered vocational interests from the age of about 15 to 19. Since the responders were preparing to become teachers, it can be assumed that all or many

*Table 14.* Aspirations and Goals about which Adolescents Dream during the Ages of 15 to 19

| FEMALE ASPIRATIONS | MALE ASPIRATIONS |
|---|---|
| Teacher | Teacher |
| Marriage | Writer |
| Writer | Musician |
| Fashion designer | Lawyer |
| Nurse | Chemist |
| Social worker | Dentist |
| Actress | Athlete |
| Doctor | Policeman |
| Lawyer | Doctor |
| Musician | Social worker |
| Artist | Ballplayer (major league) |
| Interpreter | Engineer |
| Secretary | Airplane pilot |
| Ballet dancer | Detective |
| Psychologist | Radio announcer |
| Athlete | Artist |

of them had made their final vocational choice. That teaching had not been a persistent ambition during their growing-up years, however, is evidenced by the results of their introspective reports as presented in Table 14.

These young men and women probably were motivated by various factors to decide upon teaching as a vocation. The extent to which they will achieve success in this field is closely related to their respective personality traits as these function in teaching-learning situations, in college classrooms during their training period, and later in their own school activities.

## Social Development during Adolescence

As has been said repeatedly, no individual of any age acquires in a vacuum whatever he comes to possess in the way of specific interests, attitudes, and behavior patterns. To consider in detail at this point the adolescent's interactions with his social milieu might seem to be repetitious. Yet there are certain aspects of adolescent social development that can be regarded as fundamental influences upon a young person's maturing personal characteristics.

### Developing Social Awareness

The neonate is not a social being; he is a physical organism. He responds to his environment only to the extent that it can satisfy his primary needs: food, shelter, sleep, elimination, and some all-body activity. Yet by the end of the neonatal period the very young child displays simple beginnings of social awareness. The other human beings in his environment, of course, are associated with the satisfaction of his physical needs. He is completely but unconsciously self-centered. As is proper, he takes from others but gives nothing except himself in the form of a helpless infant dependent for survival upon the loving care provided by parents or other adults.

The young child's natural growth and maturation are accompanied by increasing recognition of the relationships between the "me" and the "you" that cannot be ignored. Social development has begun, and it continues through the preadult years. Throughout his life an individual's personality is affected constructively or adversely by the impact upon his personal potentials of the people by whom he is surrounded.

Too often the isolate, the hermit, or the socially nonconforming radical has become what he is because of the detrimental effects upon his developing personality of social pressures. Contrariwise, favorable and constructive social relationships can motivate an individual to develop outgoing, cooperative, useful, and personally and socially satisfying qualities. Hence, except for the first weeks of his life, an individual's personality reflects his interrelations with human beings. Probably at no age period, however, is a person more sensitive to the success or lack of success of his intersocial relationships than he is during the teen years.

## Adolescent Need for Social Acceptance

Whatever may be the wants, interests, and ambitions experienced by the adolescent that constitute the bases of his developing personality, one characteristic appears to be outstanding. He wants to be liked by his peers. The goal toward which he strives especially is acceptance of himself by the members of the group that he strongly admires and in which he believes that he best can achieve self-realization. The young person is helped in this goal-seeking struggle by gaining some understanding of the degree of interdependence that exists between his own personality characteristics and those of his chosen associates. He observes their behavior and tries to emulate it. Regardless of whether their attitudes and conduct are approved by parents or other adults, he attempts to model his behavior according to what he considers to represent the standards of the peer group.

In terms of the "fashion of the times," adolescents usually want to improve their personal assets. They tend to devote an increasing amount of time and attention to such matters as personal grooming, style of dress, and manners, often to the dismay of their elders. They read books on etiquette and seek advice from sympathetic adults concerning proper social behavior, especially in relation to dating procedures. They believe that their drive for popularity can be satisfied by emphasizing these aspects of personality.

They not only are interested in their own appearance and outward behavior but also in the conduct of their family and in the appearance of their home. A high school girl, for example, was embarrassed when she was asked about her father's vocational activity. Young people want to be proud of what their parents have done or are doing. Moreover, they soon learn which personal or family characteristics are approved by their peers and which are not. Young people attempt to "reform" their families as well as themselves in terms of what they consider to represent their peers' social demands.

As has been suggested repeatedly in previous discussions, an adolescent is constantly striving for status. He wants to be recognized as a person rather than as an undistinguished member of a herd; yet he does not wish to be too different from others of his group in those aspects of his behavior and attitude that are characteristic of his group in comparison with other adolescent or societal units. Hence he may seem to rebel against what he terms conventionality but, at the same time, he is likely to conform to group standards.

The means utilized by an adolescent to effect a compromise between the two desired goals—individuality and social conformity—exercise a potent influence upon his changing traits. The kind of person he eventually becomes reflects his adolescent goal-seeking experiences in the home, in the school, on his first job, and among his community associates. Although a young person appears to be most concerned about his relationships with his peers, he also wants to direct adult attention to himself.

Much of what seems to be defiance of all adult authority or intolerance of adult-approved standards (especially those of parents, teachers, or employers) is an expression of an adolescent's struggle to achieve status among his elders. The still-immature young person may not yet have become sensitive to differences among adult attitudes toward himself. Some teen-agers, however, seem able to recognize rather quickly whether adults respect them as individuals or regard them merely as representatives of a group inferior in age.

A young adolescent, for example, resents adult reference to himself as a "child." During the early high school years a boy's ego is bolstered when he is called "Mr." by his teachers, and a girl's when she is called "Miss." As they approach adult status, however, their increasing self-security tends to reduce their urge to have their growing-up status recognized, particularly by adults with whom they have achieved a satisfying relationship. To illustrate, a college instructor had been careful not to use the first names of the members of a class of juniors, although this was a common practice among some of the instructors. Toward the end of the semester the students expressed their regret that the formal mode of address had been followed. They claimed that the fine rapport established in the class and the instructor's sincere attitude of friendly understanding of their differing personalities should have been accompanied by the use of their first names, which represented them in a more personal fashion than did their family names. They further asked their instructor to use the given names of the members of the next class as soon as instructor and student *accepted one another as individuals* rather than as instructor and students.

In another adult and older adolescent situation, however, the adolescent, who was a student-teacher in a high school class, resented the classroom teacher's referring to her by her first name in the presence of the young students, since the members of the class followed the teacher's example. In the college classroom situation referred to, the students felt that they had achieved adult status, with resulting personality expansion;

in the high school situation, contrariwise, the teacher-trainee evaluated the older adult's attitude as representative of a feeling of superiority that was aimed at deflating late-adolescent personality status.

The foregoing illustrations of adolescent reactions to their human interrelationships—peer and adult—have significance in that they exemplify the many relatively subtle elements that combine to affect personal and social changes during the in-between years. Although some of the fundamental personality traits formed during childhood tend to persist, the stresses and strains that are likely to accompany adolescent goal-satisfying struggles are stimulating factors of personality change. There is some investigatory evidence of the nature of trait changes.

For example, a study of changes in adolescent personal-social development was conducted by Kuhlen and Lee.[4] The mode of procedure was to have sixth-, ninth-, and twelfth-grade pupils evaluate, according to a given list, the personality characteristics displayed by their respective classmates. The findings of the study indicate significant changes in behavior, attitudes, and interest from grades 6 through 12. A comparison of the relative percentages not only presents evidence of differences between the sexes in some characteristics for all ages but also shows sex and age trends in trait manifestations.

It would be interesting to compare the results of this study with a follow-up comparison of the responses of the sixth-grade subjects when they reached the twelfth-grade level. This would necessitate keeping the entire sixth-grade group together for six years, a situation that is difficult to achieve with our mobile school population.

## Adolescent Groupings and Social Class Status

During early adolescence the "gang" organizations of later childhood, each composed of children of the same sex, become social groups or "crowds" comprising both sexes. Membership in a peer group satisfies an adolescent's urge to belong, helps him learn to get along with others of his kind and to develop an attitude of loyalty toward them, enables him to adapt himself to his new relationships with the members of the opposite sex, and may offer him an opportunity to exercise potential leadership ability within the group. The many advantages that accrue to adolescents through their formation of close-knit social groups are offset to the extent that several such school or neighborhood groups become snobbish, exclusive "cliques" that vie with one another in socially unacceptable ways to gain social prestige.

[4] R. G. Kuhlen and B. J. Lee, "Personality Characteristics, and Social Acceptability in Adolescence," *Journal of Educational Psychology*, vol. 34, pp. 321–340, 1943.

In Chapter 2 we referred to the fact that in the United States there is considerable social mobility. Yet in some communities there still exist definite social class barriers that exercise a potent effect upon adolescent social attitudes and activities. A notable example of "class" differentiation is reported by Hollingshead.[5] For the purpose of this study the families of 16-year-old adolescents living in a small Middle Western community were classified according to economic status into five groupings, almost mutually exclusive. The adolescents of families in Group I represented the "elite"; most of those of Group V (85 per cent) were regarded as "grubbies," or socially nonacceptable by young people in the higher "classes"; no one in Group I or Group II was regarded as a "grubbie," although about 1 per cent of Group III and 20 per cent of Group IV were so categorized by their peers. There were good children in each social group.

The possible relationship among social stratification and individual mental ability, school achievement and continuous vocational plans, and social participation is shown in Figure 27. A careful study of the presented data will alert the reader to the inequalities that are experienced by young people living in a community of the type represented by Elmtown.

In some respects the study dealt with an extreme situation. Yet even in larger, less stratified communities, circumstances over which an adolescent has no control can cause him to be rejected or tolerated by associates whose approval he seeks and in whose social activities he strongly desires to participate.

Some adolescents, as well as adults, are not particularly interested in social activities of large groups. Although they desire social acceptance, they are content to engage in study, work, or recreational programs either alone or with a few close associates. These individuals are not isolates. If they are expected to take part in larger-group social activities, they are willing and able to do so gracefully and effectively, even though they might prefer to devote their time to activities that would seem to them to be more worthwhile. Hence the authors believe that parents and teachers should not attempt to force a young person against his will to become "one of the crowd."

Other teen-agers who are not members of any peer social group simulate a behavior attitude of self-sufficiency which is not an expression of real desire or interest. They are eager to be members of one or another group but feel that they are neither acceptable nor accepted by other young people. They believe that they are physically unattractive; their clothes seem to them to be unsuitable; they think that they lack poise, charm, or the ability to engage in social "chitchat"; they are sensitive

[5] A. B. Hollingshead, *Elmtown's Youth,* John Wiley & Sons, Inc., New York, 1949.

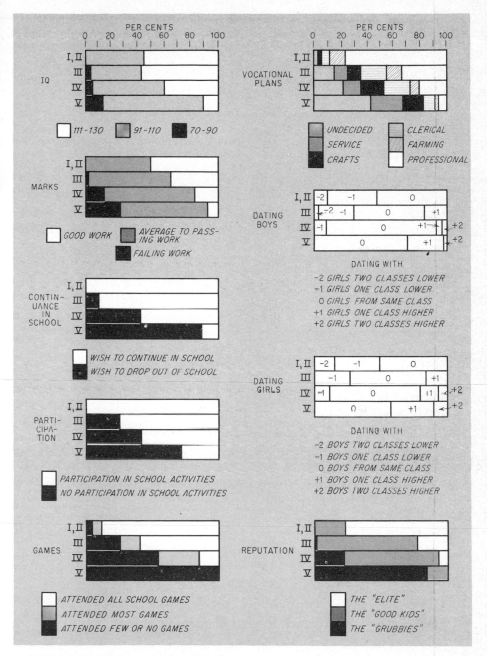

*Figure* 27. Influence of social class upon attitudes and activities. (Reprinted from L. Cole and I. Hall, *Psychology of Adolescence*, 6th ed., Holt, Rinehart and Winston, Inc., New York, 1964, p. 359.)

about any adverse criticism, real or fancied, that is aimed at them by adults or other adolescents. These adolescents are isolates.

A young person who seemingly is rejected by his peers should receive help from his elders. Teachers especially need to be alert to the social inadequacies of these students and attempt to improve their social relationships with other schoolmates. Through the construction of a sociogram based upon young people's responses concerning their "preferred" classmates, a teacher can discover the apparent isolates in his class. This technique needs careful administration; otherwise, sensitive teen-agers can become extremely distressed if they discover that they are not among the "popular" members of the class. Ingenious school people can plan various types of socializing activities and encourage the participation in them of withdrawing, socially insecure young people.

Some of the most serious adolescent problems have their roots in feelings of social insecurity. Young people ask many questions concerning their intersocial relationships. Some of these questions are included in a later discussion that deals with the social adjustments of adolescents (see Chapter 17). It must be remembered, however, that social acceptance is related closely to personal adjustment. Hence an adolescent's developing personality can be regarded as both the cause and the result of the social interactions he experiences during the maturing years.

## Personality Patterning

It is not unusual for an adolescent to invent what he considers to be a personality-describing nickname for a peer associate or an adult, especially a teacher. The "private" name supposedly represents an outstanding personality characteristic of the individual to whom it is applied. In terms of the adolescent's experiences with the one so named, it may be complimentary or disparaging. In any case, the applying of a nickname by a young person constitutes an emotionalized impression of the type of person the other seems to be. This youthful play of the imagination finds its counterpart in serious psychological attempts to classify various personality manifestations according to type.

### Attempts to "Type" Adolescent Personality

We have stressed consistently the integrative relationship that exists among the various dynamic aspects of human development. Certain personality trends appear to motivate the display of what can be considered an adolescent's characteristic behavior patterns. If we accept the "nuclear cluster" organizational concept of similar or related traits, it is possible to assume that one fundamental trait cluster can function so effectively that it overshadows the significance of other traits. Consequently, the dominant cluster or group of traits may appear to motivate behavior reactions to the point that it becomes descriptive of the total personality.

Various attempts have been made to "type" personality according to one or another group of traits or characteristics. In Chapter 4 reference was made to Kretschmer's and Sheldon's comparisons between body build and personality. Endocrinologists have associated the display of certain personality characteristics with the ductless glands, i.e., degree of balance or imbalance.[6] Some of the supposed effects upon personality of glandular imbalance are:

*Hyperthyroid*—overambitious and domineering

*Hypothyroid*—lazy and intellectually dull

*Pituitary type*—good humored, patient, considerate, docile, diffident, tolerant of physical and mental pain

*Adrenal cortex* (cortin)—the prematurely developed; in females leading to adiposity and beards

*Parathyroid* (calcium metabolism)—the explosive type; showing aggressive conduct

*Gonads, hyperactive*—the more aggressive personality

*Gonads, hypoactive*—the less aggressive personality, interested in art, literature, and music

Psychologists are loath to accept completely the conclusions of earlier endocrinologists, however. Although an overactive thyroid may cause a person to be domineering and overambitious, for example, not all domineering or overambitious people are suffering from thyroid imbalance. A personality characteristic thus explained in terms of the functioning status of a ductless gland actually may be more closely associated with environmental influences or other causative factors.

Attempts have been made to classify individuals into "types" in terms of their accustomed modes of reactions to people, things, and conditions. An interesting theory propounded by Jung[7] is based upon differences among people in the ability to "relate" oneself to others. According to Jung, two significant personality classifications are *extroversion* and *introversion*. The extrovert is outgoing, interested in people, and socially adaptable; the introvert tends to be interested in his own feelings and reactions, and to be retiring and shy in his social relationships.

Various lists have been promulgated to indicate the specific characteristics that are associated with extroversion and introversion. One finds,

---

[6] W. B. Cannon, *Bodily Changes in Pain, Hunger, Fear, and Rage*, Appleton-Century-Crofts, Inc., New York, 1929; L. Berman, *The Glands Regulating Personality*, The Macmillan Company, New York, 1921; A. T. Cameron, *Recent Advances in Endocrinology*, J. & A. Churchill, Ltd., London, 1933.

[7] C. G. Jung, *Psychological Types* (H. G. Baynes, trans.), Harcourt, Brace & World, Inc., New York, 1923.

however, that an individual may exhibit so-termed "extrovert behavior" in one situation but, under different circumstances, give evidence of introversion. Hence most people are described as *ambiverts*, possessing both introverted and extroverted characteristics. Since adolescents are so sensitive to attitudes displayed by others toward themselves, they are likely to respond to the social atmosphere either by outgoing or withdrawing behavior. Moreover, to cover their feelings of insecurity or fear, some young people consciously attempt to appear friendly and unembarrassed in social situations.

Since an adolescent's behavior characteristics are affected by many factors within and outside himself, it rarely is possible to classify his personality according to a particular type. An adolescent's reputation stems from the kinds of personality traits to which he gives expression in the presence of his associates. Differences in personal values among the members of his various groups, as well as individual attitudes toward, or interests in, the young person concerned, may influence their evaluation of his personal characteristics to the extent that his reputation may vary from group to group or person to person.

A common illustration of this variation is found in differences in attitude among teachers toward the same high school student. A boy who excels in mathematics but who is poor in English probably will be cooperative and outgoing in his mathematics class but retiring and apparently lazy in his English class. Consequently, his reputation among the teachers and classmates of the two classes will be very different. Similarly, a young person's dress and grooming, habitual mannerisms, behavior toward the opposite sex, opinions, artistic appreciations, and other aspects of personality expression are evaluated by his peers and elders according to their own personal standards and ideals as well as according to their insight concerning his behavior motivations.

One or another nuclear cluster of personality traits may seem to be more characteristic of some adolescents than of others. To the extent that a particular young person gives evidence of the persistent display of cluster-related traits, he can be considered to belong to that particular type group. To illustrate, upon the completion of nineteen adolescent case studies, Havighurst and Taba considered that, on the basis of similarities, the members of the group studied could be classified as self-directive, adaptive, submissive, defiant, and unadjusted. Although these groupings of their 16-year-old subjects were reached empirically, conclusions were not formulated until the data were analyzed and reanalyzed, similarities among certain subjects carefully observed and grouped together, and common characteristics of each subgroup described. Personality profiles constructed by Havighurst and Taba are presented in Table 15.

Sigmund Freud [8] is well known for his work in personality. His theory of personality embraces three basic concepts as follows: (1) the personality core becomes fixed as patterns during the early years of life, (2) drives are direct or indirect forms of the sexual urge, and (3) personality has three levels: the *id*, the *ego*, and the *superego*.

In an attempt to separate certain personality components, Kurt Lewin developed a "field" theory in which he postulated that both individual perception and behavior take place. He believed that external stimuli affect the individual through his perceptions rather than directly. Thus he conceived the wholeness of the representation, but held that the component parts can be analyzed.

The utilization of type analysis such as described in the foregoing has value when one is dealing with a particular group of young people whom one can study intensively in specific situations, thereby gaining insight into the background history, motivational patterns, and interrelationships of the individuals concerned. One needs to be wary, however, in applying the profiles in any attempts to type young people in terms of observed behavior in one or a few situations only.

## The Evaluation of Adolescent Personality

It is difficult to achieve a completely adequate evaluation of an adolescent's developing personality. The continuously changing subtle interactions among the many phases of the total personality pattern may so affect a young person's attitudes and behavior that his reactions appear to differ almost from one week to another. Any attempted evaluation of a young person, therefore, can be expected to yield reliable data concerning him only insofar as it represents what he is like at the time of the evaluation. Prediction is uncertain except for deep-rooted, persistent personality trends that may be characteristic of the individual throughout most of his life.

## Varieties of Evaluation

In Chapter 3 the various approaches to the study of adolescence and some of the difficulties encountered in attempts to evaluate accurately the components that comprise the integrated whole personality were considered. We also described briefly some of the generally utilized techniques of evaluation such as observation, interviewing, standardized

[8] Sigmund Freud, *An Outline of Psychology*, W. W. Norton & Company, Inc., New York, 1949.

*Table 15.* Personality Profiles of Adolescents

| AREA | INSTRUMENTS OR METHODS | PERSONALITY TYPE | | | | |
|---|---|---|---|---|---|---|
| | | SELF-DIRECTIVE | ADAPTIVE | SUBMISSIVE | DEFIANT | UNADJUSTED |
| Social personality | Observation Sociometric tests Interest inventory Essays | Ambitious Conscientious Orderly Persistent Introspective | Outgoing Confident Positive, favorable reactions to environment | Timid Does not initiate action Stubborn Avoids conflict | Openly hostile Self-defensive Blames society for failure | Discontented Complaining Not openly hostile |
| Character reputation | Reputation instruments | High Higher on H and R than on F | High Higher on F than on H and R | Average to high Higher on H and R than on F | Very low Higher on MC than on other traits | Low to average |
| Moral beliefs and principles | Student beliefs Life problems Essays | Variable High uncertainty | High Little uncertainty Adopts current standards | High Some uncertainty | Low | Low to average |
| Family environment | FR-CR Test Interviews and reports on family Interest inventory Mooney Problem Check List | Strict family training Some conflict with family | Permissive family training No conflict with family | Severe family training No conflict with family | Family training inconsistent, provides no basis for constructive character formation Conflict with family Early neglect | Variable family training Conflict with family |

| | Measures | Leader | Very popular | Follower | Unpopular | Unpopular |
|---|---|---|---|---|---|---|
| Social adjustment with age mates | Sociometric tests<br>Interviews<br>Observation | Active in school affairs<br>Awkward in social skills | Active in school affairs<br>Social skills well developed<br>Popular with opposite sex | Nonentity<br>Awkward in social skills | Hostile to school activities<br>Quarrelsome | Hostile or indifferent to school activities |
| Intellectual ability | Intelligence tests | Average to high | Average to high | Low to average<br>Seldom high | Low to high | Low to high |
| School achievement | Academic grades | High, or higher than IQ would imply | Fair to high | Fair<br>Seldom high | Low, or lower than IQ would imply | Low, or lower than IQ would imply |
| Personal adjustment | Interviews<br>Personality inventory<br>Interest inventory<br>Thematic Apperception Test<br>Rorschach<br>Mooney Problem Check List | Self-doubt<br>Self-critical<br>Some anxiety, but well controlled<br>Concern about moral problems<br>Average aggressiveness<br>Moves away from people<br>Lack of warmth in human relations<br>Gains security through achievement | High on all adjustment measures<br>Self-assured<br>No signs of anxiety<br>Unaggressive<br>Moves toward people | Self-doubt<br>Self-critical<br>Submissive to authority<br>Unaggressive | Hostile to authority<br>Aggressive impulses<br>Inadequately socialized<br>Moves against people | Aggressive impulses<br>Feelings of insecurity |

SOURCE: Reprinted with permission from R. J. Havighurst and H. Taba, *Adolescent Character and Personality*, John Wiley & Sons, Inc., New York, 1949, pp. 118–119.

testing materials, individual self-expression, experimentation, and the case study.

To avoid repetition, the discussion at this point will be confined to a consideration of various standardized and informal instruments of personality measurement. The purpose to be served by the administration of an evaluating instrument may be either (1) to discover the degree of possession of one or more traits or dimensional aspects of personality, or (2) to gain insight concerning the functioning in a given situation of the total integrated personality pattern.

## Areas of Dimensional Evaluation

The commonly measured personality aspects or dimensions are physical condition, general intelligence and specific aptitude, quality of study achievement, personal interests and attitudes, and emotional status. Although all these areas of measurement represent dimensional aspects of personality development, the term *personality evaluation* generally is limited in usage to refer specifically to interests, attitudes, and emotional status. Since an adolescent's physical and mental status and his achievement level may exercise a potent effect upon his total personality, we shall give attention to these areas before we discuss the evaluation of the so-called "personality attributes."

## Measurement of Physical, Intellectual, and Achievement Status

Since physical constitution and health status exercise a powerful effect upon the total pattern of personality integration, an adolescent's physical condition is of primary importance. An apparent deviation from habitually expressed interests, or an emotionally or socially disturbing experience, may stem from a real or imagined physical defect. Hence a thorough yearly physical examination should become an established practice from childhood onward. Periodic health checkups are needed especially during pubescence and early adolescence, since the physical and physiological changes characteristic of these growth periods may seriously affect the health status of a young person. Tests of physical fitness should be administered by a physician. Parents, teachers, and other adults, however, should be able to interpret height and weight charts and the results of physical performance tests.

Degree of mental acuity and of the possession of a special aptitude are basic factors of the direction of an adolescent's personality development. Various approaches to the measurement of intellectual capacity are presented in Chapter 5. No more will be said here than to emphasize the fact that if test results are to be reliable and meaningful, the test must be administered carefully according to specific testing directions and the obtained results interpreted intelligently according to standardized norms of performance.

The utilization of relatively reliable and valid aptitude tests has value as a means of helping an adolescent discover any special ability that he may possess. In terms of his displayed potential he can then be guided toward participation in appropriate educational and vocational areas of activity. The trial-error-success approach to educational and vocational exploration is costly and often inadequate.

Vocational tests are intended to serve one of two purposes. A vocational aptitude or prognostic test is an evaluating device administered to discover potential ability in an area of performance for participation in which there has been no training. A vocational achievement or success-attainment test, on the other hand, is utilized to determine the degree to which a potential aptitude has been developed through training. Vocational tests usually include items that measure both mentally stimulated or informational materials and manipulatory performance.

The results of these tests are not infallible. The fact that an adolescent appears to possess a test-determined aptitude cannot ensure his attainment of success in the particular vocational activity. Personality factors other than the possession of a specific aptitude are influential in determining an adolescent's eventual vocational selection and successful accomplishment in his chosen field. Nevertheless, vocational tests have some value as aids to adolescent occupational adjustment. Recently constructed measuring instruments in this area include the Differential Aptitude Tests (DAT), developed by the Psychological Corporation, and various classification instruments devised for use in the armed services, such as the Army General Classification Test (AGCT) and the Armed Forces Qualification Test (AFQT).

Achievement tests and scales have been constructed to serve one or more of the following functions: (1) discovering the level of achievement attained by an adolescent or a group of adolescents; (2) discovering the degree of readiness of the adolescent to enter into another area of learning (Test for High School Entrants); and (3) diagnosing the specific learning difficulties of an adolescent in a particular field of learning.

The present trend is away from specific achievement tests in isolated areas of learning toward survey or general achievement batteries and comprehensive examinations. Many of these batteries, or comprehensive examinations, are geared toward evaluating achievement progress on the secondary school level. Included among these are the Cooperative General Achievement Tests (CGAT), the Iowa Tests of Educational Development (ITED), the Scholastic Aptitude Test (SAT), and the Tests of

General Educational Development, prepared by the United States Armed Forces Institute (USAFI-GED). The growing interest in comprehensive examinations reflects an educational trend toward effecting greater integration in the teaching-learning process.

## Measurement of Personality Traits

Personality tests or inventories include more or less standardized measuring instruments that are designed to evaluate an individual's personal qualities, interests, attitudes, and behavior patterns apart from physical constitution, general intelligence, specific aptitude, and achievement or performance. The reason for administering personality tests is to attempt to measure such qualities as cooperativeness, perseverance, honesty, sincerity, social adaptability, attitudes toward customs or beliefs, initiative, responsibility, introversion or extroversion, ascendancy or submissiveness, and emotional stability or neurotic tendencies.

*Rating Scales and Inventories.* These tests are devised (1) to enable an individual to rate himself concerning his interests, attitudes, emotional states, temperament, and other aspects of his personality, or (2) to help teachers, employers, psychologists, or other interested persons to evaluate an adolescent's status in one or more personality characteristics. Most rating scales and inventories are paper-and-pencil questionnaires. There are many such instruments available today, representing varying degrees of validity and reliability.

Many of the earlier questionnaires were so devised that the items were answered by "yes" or "no." Some inventories allow for three categories in the answer: "yes," "no," or "?". Examples of such tests are the Bell inventory and the Bernreuter Personality Inventory. By the administration of six different keys to the same answers, the Bernreuter inventory attempts to measure six different aspects of personality: neuroticism, self-sufficiency, introversion, dominance, confidence, sociability. Some recently constructed personality tests employ ingenious evaluating approaches. Their results are not yet reliable, however, since they are still in the experimental stage of construction.

For many years the Brooklyn College department of education has been using a personality report form for evaluating the personality traits of its students. The form has undergone numerous refinements. The most recent adaptation consists of five major categories.

*Interest Inventories.* These consist of systematically arranged series of questions designed to discover the kind and intensity of an individual's major likes and dislikes among specifically listed activities and attitudes. These inventories are of value in the study of an adolescent's personality qualities, even though their results are not indicative of persistent or stable interests. Probably two of the most useful instruments are the Strong Vocational Interest Blank for Men, Revised, and the Strong Vocational Interest Blank for Women, Revised. Other significant interest inventories are:

Allport Study of Values, Revised
Guilford-Schneidman-Zimmerman Interest Survey
Kuder Preference Record—Personal
Kuder Preference Record—Vocational
SRA Employee Inventory
Thurstone Interest Schedule

## Evaluation of Personality Integration

As we know, the total personality is more than the sum of its traits. Hence the summation of all the data gained from the measurement of personality components or traits does not equal the composite whole; nor does it represent an adequate evaluation of an adolescent's total personality. The interactions of those traits which make for personality integration cannot be discovered through the administration of the paper-and-pencil type of trait measurement. Consequently, certain forms of evaluation called *projective techniques* have been developed to permit the individual to display in an integrated fashion his habitual attitudes, aspirations, ideas, aggressions, fears, or worries.

During the administration of a projective technique the individual is presented with relatively unstructured situations, to which he reacts freely with a variety of possible responses. It is believed that, as he describes or explains the situation, he is giving overt expression to inner attitudes and ideas that are representative of his personality pattern. Among the various types of projective techniques are the verbal techniques; drawing and painting; play and dramatic techniques; the Rorschach ink-blot technique; and pictorial techniques.

*Verbal Techniques.* Verbal techniques include such procedures as the "free association" test, the sentence completion test, and the picture association test. The "free association" test consists of a list of words, to each of which the subject is asked to respond with the first word that comes to his mind. The time of reaction to each word is recorded, since both the response itself and the length of time between the stimulus and the response are considered significant indicators of amount of emotional tension. This test can be used to discover something about an individual's thoughts, ideas, and specific emotional states.

Another form of the verbal technique is the *sentence completion test*, in which the subject is given, in either written or oral form, the beginnings of sentences and asked to complete them. Some examples are:

I like. . . . I enjoy. . . . My father. . . . I prefer. . . . The words or phrases used by the subject to complete the sentences may have value as clues to his attitudes, opinions, or emotional status. The individual also might reveal significant aspects of his relations with his peer associates, his breadth of understanding, or his social beliefs.

An interesting approach to the study of emotionalized attitudes is exemplified in the Rosenzweig Picture-Frustration Study. The test consists of a series of comic-strip-type pictures. Each picture depicts a realistic, frustrating situation, to which the subject responds by writing in an empty "balloon" included in the picture. The subject is instructed to write down "the first reply which comes to mind," and to "avoid being humorous" (see Figure 28).

It is assumed that consciously or unconsciously the subject will identify himself with the frustrated individual in each of the pictures. Consequently, the written response will reflect the testee's habitual expressions of aggressive behavior in response to differing frustration-arousing stimuli.

Psychologists are experimenting with the so-called "lie detector," an adaptation of the verbal technique. By means of a mechanical device consisting of instruments that measure intensity of visceral emotional reactions, the investigator determines the effect upon the subject's emotional

*Figure 28.* Picture association study for assessing reactions to frustration. (Copyright, 1948, by Saul Rosenzweig, reproduced by permission.)

state of specific question-answer combinations. It is hoped that the action of the lie detector can be sufficiently refined to yield accurate indication of the degree of truth or falsity of the subject's responses to emotion-arousing questions.

*Self-expression through Drawing and Painting.* Children and adolescents increasingly are being encouraged to give expression to their interests, creative abilities, and inner tensions through mediums such as finger painting, drawing, and water-color or oil painting. Resulting procedures can be diagnostically evaluated to discover a young person's conceptual appreciation of persons or things in his environment, his imaginative power, or his emotional attitudes. To the extent that an adolescent projects his personality into his "creative" production, insight can be achieved concerning apparent emotional disturbance. The interpretation of obtained data is extremely subjective, however, and should not be undertaken by anyone except those who have been trained in the use of this type of evaluative technique.

*Play and Dramatic Techniques.* The techniques of play therapy and sociodrama were explained earlier. Here comment will be directed to the value of these techniques as mediums of personality interpretation. Attitudes displayed by a subject either in a free-play situation or in self-expressing role playing may offer clues concerning the emotional difficulties suffered by the individual, thereby serving as a basis for possible rehabilitation. These techniques can be used effectively with adolescents. As a young person enacts one or another role on a stage, or as he participates in artificially constructed situations, he is likely to project his inner feelings and attitudes into the role or roles he is playing. The interpretation of the displayed behavior is subjective, however, and may or may not be valid.

*The Rorschach Technique.* The Rorschach projective technique, known as the Ink Blot Test, is an excellent device to discover personality traits of adolescents or adults. The test consists of ten cards containing ink blots of various shapes similar to the sample given in Figure 29. Five of the ink blots are in shades of black and gray; the other five contain two or more colors. The subject is asked to look at each card and then to report to the examiner what he *sees* in the whole blot, or in any one or more segments of it. The subject is given a second showing of the card and asked to point out as exactly as he can the area or areas which represent the various objects or situations that he saw in the first showing. Although interpretation of the results is based upon established norms, these are not yet sufficiently reliable for scientifically accurate conclusions concerning a subject's personality pattern.

*The Thematic Apperception Test.* A projective technique much used by clinicians to evaluate personality by means of picture presentation is the Thematic Apperception Test (TAT). The test material consists of twenty cards, nineteen of which represent situations involving one or more persons who are pictured against a relatively vague background. The twentieth card is blank. The test administrator gives the subject a card and asks him to tell a story about it. While the subject tells the story, the administrator writes down what is being said. This procedure continues until a story has been told for each of the nineteen cards. Then the subject is handed the blank card and asked to imagine a picture that appears on it and to tell a story about it. The picture that appears on one of the cards is presented in Figure 30.

The utilization of the TAT, as well as of other projective techniques that currently are administered to evaluate the functioning of an individual's total personality, gives evidence of their future promise as evaluating techniques. Since they still are in an experimental stage, however, caution needs to be exercised in their administration and interpretation. The techniques themselves are continuing to be improved and clinicians are gaining greater insight into the significance of testee responses. Eventually their utilization may come to have considerable value in helping adults guide adolescent personality development and adjustment. No one except a trained person should administer or interpret one of these projective techniques.

Whether it ever will be possible to categorize the personality components of every individual adolescent is a moot question. Probably the best that we, as adults, can accomplish is to reflect in our own personal-

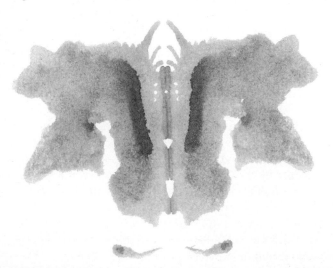

*Figure 29.* Ink-blot sample similar to those used in the Rorschach test.

Figure 30. Example from the Thematic Apperception Test. (Reprinted by permission of the publisher from Henry A. Murray, *Thematic Apperception Test,* Cambridge, Mass., Harvard University Press. Copyright 1943 by the President and Fellows of Harvard College.)

ities those qualities and attributes that we want adolescents to develop; then we can be alert to ways in which youthful attitudes and behavior seem to deviate from an acceptable norm, and attempt to help the adolescent make whatever personality changes seem desirable.

## Questions and Problems for Discussion

1. Present the important psychological bases of personality. Show how any one of them is interrelated with the others.
2. Discuss the extent to which an individual's personality is in the mind of another person. To what extent do you have personality? To what extent is it given to you by another?
3. What qualities do you look for when seeking a friend of the same sex? Of the opposite sex?
4. Discuss the impact of change of environment on personality development. How important to the adolescent is a change of environment?
5. Discuss the use of play and dramatic techniques in the evaluation of personality.
6. Differentiate between the Ink Blot Test and the Thematic Apperception Test in personality evaluation. Indicate reasons why a teacher should not attempt to utilize these procedures in personality evaluation.
7. *Special Exercises:*
   *a.* Analyze the differences and similarities in the personalities of adolescents you have observed. What accounts for these differences?
   *b.* Observe the behavior of an adolescent as he meets a new group of adolescents for the first time. Describe as much of his behavior as you can recall.
   *c.* Observe the behavior of an adolescent when he deliberately attempts to impress a peer of the same sex; of the opposite sex. Report your findings.

## Selected References

Allport, G.: *Pattern and Growth in Personality,* Holt, Rinehart and Winston, Inc., New York, 1961.

Bennett, E.: *Personality Assessment and Diagnosis,* The Ronald Press Company, New York, 1961.

Blum, G. S.: *Psychoanalytic Theories of Personality,* McGraw-Hill Book Company, New York, 1953.

Dalton, R. H.: *Personality and Social Interaction,* D. C. Heath and Company, Boston, 1961.

Diamond, S.: *Personality and Temperament,* Harper & Row, Publishers, Incorporated, New York, 1957.

Fisher, S., and S. E. Cleveland: *Body Image and Personality,* D.

Van Nostrand Company, Inc., Princeton, N.J., 1958.

Guilford, J. P.: *Personality,* McGraw-Hill Book Company, New York, 1959.

Hall, C. S., and G. Lindzey: *Theories of Personality,* John Wiley & Sons, Inc., New York, 1957.

Jennings, Helen H.: *Leadership and Isolation: A Study of Personality in Inter-personal Relations,* 2d ed., David McKay Company, Inc., New York, 1950.

Lazarus, R. S.: *Personality and Adjustment,* Prentice-Hall, Inc., Englewood Cliffs, N.J., 1963.

Leuba, C.: *Personality: Interpersonal Relations and Self-Under-*

*standing*, Charles E. Merrill Books, Inc., Columbus, Ohio, 1962.

Lundin, R. W.: *Personality: An Experimental Approach*, The Macmillan Company, New York, 1961.

Maslow, A. H.: *Motivation and Personality*, Harper & Row, Publishers, Incorporated, New York, 1954.

Patty, W. L., and L. S. Johnson: *Personality and Adjustment*, McGraw-Hill Book Company, New York, 1953.

Sarnoff, I.: *Personality: Dynamics and Development*, John Wiley & Sons, Inc., New York, 1962.

Schneiders, A. A.: *Personality and Adjustment in Adolescence*, The Bruce Publishing Company, Milwaukee, 1960.

Smith, H. C.: *Personality Adjustment*, McGraw-Hill Book Company, New York, 1961.

Stagner, R.: *Psychology of Personality*, 3d ed., McGraw-Hill Book Company, New York, 1961.

# Part 3

## ADOLESCENT BEHAVIOR MOTIVATIONS

# Chapter Eight

## Importance
## of Interests
## and Attitudes

The terms *interest* and *attitude* often are used together to express an individual's pattern of reactions toward himself, his physical environment, his associates, and the situations in which he may find himself. Interests and attitudes have much in common. Except as certain potentials can be considered to be inherited characteristics, a person's interests and attitudes develop from early childhood onward as a result of experience.

Interests and attitudes are personal. Although one or another group may seem to possess similar interests and to give evidence of likeness in attitude toward this or that factor of environmental experiences, each member of the group can be regarded as evincing his own particular interest in, or attitude toward, a person, thing, or condition. His interest or attitude may be influenced, of course, to some degree by his association with other members of the group.

An *interest* can be interpreted roughly as a motivating force that stimulates an individual to participate in one activity rather than in another. As a result of influences outside himself, he may engage in certain behavior in which he personally is not interested. A situation of this kind may reflect a habitual attitude on the part of the individual to be willing to satisfy the interests of others rather than his own. Left to himself, he might act very differently.

The term *attitude* refers to a person's feeling toward other people, conditions, or situations. Attitudes are specific and born of experience. They are personal and tend to reflect themselves in the individual's relations with his fellows. Certain attitudes become so habituated that they influence much of an individual's behavior.

A motivating interest that has resulted in successful achievement in a particular situation may become the basis of a pleasant attitude toward the elements that constitute the situation. Lack of success in attempts to realize a felt interest may lead to the development of unpleasant attitudes, biases, or prejudices toward the people or things comprising the situation that resulted in failure to achieve. Moreover, a strong attitude may give rise to an equally strong motivating interest. One difference between interest and attitude, however, must be kept in mind. Given an opportunity to express an interest, an individual usually is conscious of his interest in expressing it; contrariwise, an individual's attitude may be consciously recognized by himself, or he may be unaware of the real attitude that influences his behavior. With this brief interpretation of what differentiates interests and attitudes, we shall proceed to discuss those interests and attitudes that seem to be characteristic of adolescents.

## The Development of Interests through Childhood

From his early years an individual's interests are affected by his physical condition, his mental and emotional status, and the social environment in which he is being reared. Hence adolescent interests do not appear full-born with the beginning of puberty. Rather, they are built upon interests that are peculiar to the childhood years.

A person's interests constantly undergo changes. Toward the later years of adolescence and the beginning of adulthood some interests become relatively fixed. The adult then, if asked what his special interests are, can list those which have become habitual aspects of his personality.

### Interests during Early Childhood

Of necessity, the young child's interests center around the home and family associates and activities. He evinces an interest in discovering the purpose or meaning of his surroundings in relation to himself. His activating interests seem to follow patterns set by his family or playmates.

Both little boys and little girls are interested in playing with the simple toys provided for them. Yet even at this early age there are differences among children's interests. Some children prefer playing with toys in which other children may be disinterested. The same holds for games. Most children enjoy playing with marbles, looking at picture books, and engaging in play activities that reflect home or neighborhood life. Some children, however, show little or no interest in these activities.

Physical, mental, and emotional differences among children not only influence the amount of interest they exhibit in one or another activity but also affect the way in which they express the interest. Moreover, unless differing interests between the sexes are encouraged by adults, little boys and girls appear to have relatively similar interests.

### Interests during Later Childhood

During the elementary school years a child's interests broaden and take on a more definite pattern. His former almost complete concern with self and the fulfillment of personal wants changes somewhat to include interest in other people, including his teachers and schoolmates. He wants to learn about places, people, and conditions outside his immediate environment. He gradually develops a greater interest in organized play activities with others of his age group. His earlier sporadic interest in hoarding favorite toys takes on a more definite form of collecting one or another type of article such as stamps, political campaign buttons, dolls, pictures, bits of string, or any other type of collectable article that may strike his fancy. The child of this age level also becomes interested in participating in creative activity. Magician sets, airplanes, or other construction mediums may challenge his ability to produce something that will attract the attention of his peers or elders.

The elementary school child usually becomes interested in listening to the radio, watching television, or reading stories and comics appropriate to his mental level. Certain differences between the interests of boys and girls begin to show themselves in the choice of these areas of interest. Both boys and girls like action, but boys seem to enjoy the portrayal of more strenuous activity than do girls.

This is the age of interest in "gang" activities among boys and of "best pal" interest among girls. Some insight can be gained concerning children's interests by listening to their conversations. Topics may center around their daily activities, radio, television and motion-picture programs, books and comics, and their likes and dislikes. Many older children are interested in discussing with their pals their feelings and opinions—the beginnings of a developing philosophy of life.

During this period each of the two sexes is interested in activities that exclude the other. At present there seems to be a growing trend among older boys and girls to participate together in dancing, group dates, and other activities that generally are associated with the interests of adolescents. The degree of maturity displayed in children's interests reflects in good part the level of their social development.

## Characteristics of Adolescent Interests

The interests of the adolescent change with age as do those of the child. Like the child, the adolescent is interested primarily in himself and his own welfare. At the same time there is an expansion of his former intense interest in his family and immediate environment, and thus he is more able to include the welfare and activities of many other persons and groups.

## Development of Interests

Interests developed during childhood, such as play, creativity, radio, television, motion pictures, reading, socializing, gaining knowledge, and planning for the future, are characteristic of the adolescent but vary in form and intensity. Adolescent interests as well as those of children are influenced by factors such as physical and mental ability, emotional attitudes, and environmental or social status. Interests serve as tension reducers during this period of change from the status of childhood to that of adulthood. They also help prepare the teen-ager for his gradual assumption of adult responsibilities. In fact, adolescent interests tend to reflect changing adult concerns. For example, in recent years some young people have exhibited an increasing interest in world affairs and in life values.

Adolescence may be a difficult period of adjustment for some young people, although an evaluation by earlier psychologists of adolescence as a period of "continual stress or strain" no longer is generally accepted. There are certain interests that are common to most adolescents. Some young people evince interests that deviate to a greater or lesser degree from so-called "normal" interests. Such deviation need not be undesirable, however. In any case, if any adolescent interest is thwarted, problems of adjustment may occur. To the extent that a situation of this kind arises in the life of an emotionally insecure adolescent, stress, strain, or conflict may result. In the main, however, adolescent interests are healthful and forward-looking.

In the following pages some common adolescent interests will be discussed briefly. As these are described, the reader will come to recognize the fact that during this age period the interests of the two sexes may show greater differences than are evidenced during childhood.

Dale Harris[1] compared sex differences in the interests of 1,641 students who, in 1935, attended junior and senior high schools in Tulsa and New York City with those exhibited in 1957 by 1,165 junior and senior high school students in a Minnesota community.

The results of the study are presented in Table 16. Although geographic location and cultural changes probably affected the findings, the following results are significant: high interest of boys in recreation, health, and money; lack of interest by both sexes in safety and study; greater interest of girls than boys in personal attractiveness; increasing interest by 1957 for both sexes in love and marriage, home and family relationships, and getting along with other people; decreasing interest in manners.

Physical, mental, and social status become greater determiners of

[1] Dale B. Harris "Sex Differences in the Life Problems and Interests of Adolescents, 1935 and 1957," *Child Development,* vol. 30, pp. 453–457, 1959.

Table 16. Ranks Accorded Issues Considered as Interests by High School Boys and Girls in 1935 and in 1957

| | BOYS | | | | GIRLS | | | |
| | 1935 | | 1957 | | 1935 | | 1957 | |
| ISSUE | MEAN RANK | RANK | MEAN RANK | RANK | MEAN RANK | RANK | MEAN RANK | RANK |
|---|---|---|---|---|---|---|---|---|
| Health........ | 5.6 | (2) | 6.4* | (2) | 6.6 | (4) | 7.0 | (6) |
| Love, marriage. | 9.3 | (13) | 7.7* | (8) | 9.4 | (12) | 6.5* | (4.5) |
| Safety......... | 7.8 | (7) | 8.7* | (11) | 9.2 | (10) | 10.2* | (14) |
| Money........ | 7.1 | (3) | 6.5* | (3) | 8.1 | (8) | 8.2 | (10) |
| Mental hygiene | 9.6 | (14) | 9.5 | (13) | 9.8 | (13.5) | 8.0* | (9) |
| Study habits... | 8.7 | (11) | 9.4* | (12) | 9.3 | (11) | 9.9* | (12.5) |
| Recreation..... | 4.9 | (1) | 5.6* | (1) | 5.6 | (2) | 7.8* | (8) |
| Personal, moral qualities..... | 7.7 | (5.5) | 7.3* | (6) | 7.6 | (7) | 7.1 | (7) |
| Home, family relationships. | 8.4 | (10) | 7.2* | (5) | 8.3 | (9) | 6.4* | (2.5) |
| Manners...... | 7.5 | (4) | 8.6* | (10) | 6.3 | (3) | 8.5* | (11) |
| Personal attractiveness..... | 8.1 | (8) | 8.0 | (9) | 5.4 | (1) | 6.0* | (1) |
| Daily schedule. | 10.5 | (15) | 10.9 | (15) | 10.4 | (15) | 11.4* | (15) |
| Civic interest.. | 9.0 | (12) | 9.6* | (14) | 9.8 | (13.5) | 9.9 | (12.5) |
| Getting along with other people...... | 8.2 | (9) | 7.1* | (4) | 7.0 | (5) | 6.4* | (2.5) |
| Philosophy of life....... | 7.7 | (5.5) | 7.4 | (7) | 7.3 | (6) | 6.5* | (4.5) |

* Change from 1935 significant at the 1 per cent level.
SOURCE: Dale B. Harris, "Sex Differences in the Life Problems and Interests of Adolescents, 1935 and 1957," *Child Development*, vol. 30, p. 454, 1959.

the extent to which interests can be realized. The interests of the younger adolescent represent a gradual change from those of childhood; the interests of the older adolescent often are similar to those of the young adult. In this fact can be found one reason for the difficulty of determining at what point in an individual's life he has changed from adolescence to adult status.

## Specific Adolescent Interests

Some psychologists classify adolescent interests in terms of three categories: personal, social, and vocational. For discussion purposes there are merits in this classification. It is difficult, however, to place a particular interest in one category only. The expressing of an interest has personal and social implications; to a lesser degree it may influence a young person's vocational choice.

This discussion of adolescent interests follows no set pattern of presentation. Adolescent interests will be treated in such a way as to indicate their value—personal, social, or vocational—to the adolescent.

## Physical Attributes, Grooming, Voice, and Dress

The onset of adolescence usually is accompanied by a changed attitude toward personal appearance and an increased interest in one's own and others' physical characteristics. Boys and girls alike develop a new awareness of their body size and proportions, body odors, hair and skin, and voice quality. Boys and girls differ, however, in their reactions to their physical appearance.

*Differences in Growth Status and Physical Condition.* Young people, especially during early adolescent years, are much concerned about the observable indications of the developmental changes that are taking place within them. They are sensitive to the possible reactions of their associates. Lack of size or a too sudden growth spurt may instigate considerable disturbance, as may certain physical conditions that tend to be characteristic of this age period. The young adolescent boy whose physical and general appearance still is that of a child often suffers great mortification as he compares his appearance with that of boys who have begun to mature physically. Moreover, his short stature and relative lack of strength may deny him participation in the games played by huskier boys.

The young adolescent boy who "shoots up" quickly may experience the problem of being rejected by boys his own age but smaller, as well as by older boys whose equal he is in height and weight. Because of the general unevenness of physical growth, the boy who develops early may seem to be all hands and feet. Since he has not yet learned how to manage his body, he may be awkward in his movements and stumble and drop things. He becomes the prey of good-natured or less kindly bantering by his peers.

Like the boy, the young adolescent girl develops great interest in her physical appearance. The small girl usually is not bothered by her short stature. The girl who has suddenly become taller and perhaps heavier than other adolescents of the same age, especially if she is taller than boys, is very much aware of her abnormal size as she attempts to participate in their social activities. For example, she finds dancing with a shorter boy to be a humiliating experience. Unevenness of physical growth may cause her considerable anguish. She is especially conscious of the size of her hands, feet, nose, and abdomen, which during early adolescence may be large in comparison to other body parts.

The presence of acne or skin blemishes frequently is a source of much concern among young adolescents. Regardless of the cause of acne —improper diet, hormone imbalance, or uneven development of the oil glands—the sufferer regards it as a condition that will cause him or her to be rejected by associates. In the same category can be included body odors that result from unusual activity of the sweat glands during this period. These indicators of physical imbalance have a significant effect on young people's behavior.

*Grooming.* Good grooming becomes increasingly important to the adolescent boy. Whereas to him, as a child, bathing and "washing behind the ears" were nuisances, the boy now exhibits an increasing interest in cleanliness. Hairdo also is important. He experiments with various styles of haircuts and is likely to become a devotee of hair oils and pomades.

Girls like to spend many hours in the bathroom. They are consistent users of sweet-scented bath salts and talcum powder. A girl tends to shampoo her hair often and to experiment with one hairdo after another. Straight hair seems to be a major affliction. Hence a girl may spend considerable time and money in attempts to adapt her hair style to what she considers to be the latest mode for her age group. Her facial appearance and the state of her complexion may become an absorbing interest. Unless she is guided intelligently, her use of cosmetics may represent quantity rather than quality of application.

Both boys and girls develop an interest in the appearance of their fingernails. Boys usually are satisfied if their nails are well trimmed and clean. Girls, on the other hand, may express their interest in their appearance by wearing abnormally long nails and by experimenting with various shades of nail polish.

*Voice.* Voice tone and quality become exceedingly important to adolescents. The free shouting and laughter of childhood days give way to greater control of the vocal organs. The boy is interested in developing a deep, manly voice. The period of voice change is a difficult time for him. Although voice change is not so noticeable in the adolescent girl, she consciously attempts to adopt an adult voice tone and quality. Except in off moments, she strives to achieve feminine modulation of tone and dignified smiling instead of loud speech and uncontrolled laughter. So interested may the girl become in her voice pattern that she adopts an affected form of speech that is based upon what she considers to be the voice and speech pattern of her currently favored actress.

*Dress.* Adolescents usually are extremely clothes-conscious. Young adolescents like bright colors and unusual combinations. Later they develop an interest in more subdued colors and more conventional dress.

Girls generally are interested in the wearing of costume jewelry. At first, these ornaments tend to be bright in color, worn on every occasion, and large in quantity. As the girl nears adulthood there is greater selectivity in the kind and amount of jewelry worn.

In all matters concerning appearance and clothes, adolescents are extremely interested in the appropriateness of their appearance as judged by the standards of their peer groups. It was believed formerly that the members of each sex were most interested in the effect of their appearance upon the other sex. At present it would seem that young people's interest in this respect includes the achievement of self-satisfaction in appearance and the approval of the members of their group, regardless of sex. They also wish to please their elders, but adult approval usually is of least importance to them.

## Conversation

Both boys and girls are interested in expressing their opinions about many things. Common topics of conversation include individual or group interests such as sports, school activities, dates, books read, radio, television, motion-picture and musical programs attended, personal achievements, future plans, and evaluations of persons, situations, or conditions known to the speakers.

Adolescents seem to enjoy engaging in debates or arguments with other members of their group. They like to "talk one another down." Often it would seem as though the less adolescents know about a topic, the more heated are their arguments. In later adolescence, however, discussions appear to be more serious, with a greater emphasis upon factual knowledge. They also are showing an increasing interest in world affairs.

It is generally agreed that both sexes tend to talk about schoolwork and common experiences. Boys seem to be interested in matters dealing with sports, fraternities, dates, mechanics, and government and politics. Adolescent boys enjoy telling stories, and sometimes questionable jokes, and engaging in more or less good-natured banter.

Girls' conversations include the discussion of topics such as dates, clothes, books, motion pictures, other girls, school activities, parties, family affairs, and personal interests. Modern girls, however, are evincing an increasing interest in subjects that at one time were associated with the conversational interests of adolescent boys.

Upper-term high school and college boys and an increasing number of girls participate in group discussions that can be referred to as "bull sessions." These are excellent mediums for the expression of personal interests in, and attitudes toward, all sorts of things, people, and conditions. It is here that the adolescent can begin to develop an idealistic or a realistic philosophy concerning life values.

## Writing

The writing of adolescents is more or less motivated by school requirements. If adolescents are given a chance to write freely, inner thoughts, interests, and attitudes are transferred to paper. Boys as well as girls may try their hands at versification. Topics usually selected by boys include sports, mechanics, and personal opinions about political and governmental affairs, although other topics may challenge their interest. Girls are interested in writing about themselves and their experiences, and their friends and families.

During early adolescence both boys and girls show interest in the writing of autobiographies, which may or may not be completely truthful accounts of their experiences. The ages between 14 and 16 are the diary-keeping years. If a boy keeps a diary, it usually is written in the form of a log, reporting incidents and experiences in chronological order. A girl's diary is much more personal. Although she too may list incidents and experiences, her diary is likely to include expressions of her attitudes toward her dates or associates and her hopes and ambitions.

## Study

An adolescent's urge for independence, his growing awareness of himself as a person, and the increase in the number and intensity of his interests exert a powerful effect upon his attitude toward study and work. The high school and college student's study interests comprise an area of consideration that well could fill the pages of an entire book. Hence no more than a few significant points can be mentioned here.

As a result of his intellectual status, his previous study experiences, and the study attitudes of school friends, an adolescent begins his study in one or another area of subject matter with preconceived ideas concerning his chances of successful achievement. Consequently, his interest in attempts at mastering the subject is dependent in part upon the attitude that he has developed toward it. Moreover, a student may have a definite interest in one area of study in which he performs diligently. The study of other subjects may seem to him to represent no more than a waste of time.

A young friend of the authors is a college sophomore whose career interest is journalism. He spends much time and effort and has earned creditable success in his writing classes and in his work as the editor of the college newspaper. He is bored by required subjects such as history, foreign languages, science, and mathematics. Recently he complained to the dean of the college that he is very much dissatisfied because he is not getting from his college work what he believes he wants and needs. The dean then suggested that this 19-year-old boy try to get a job in a newspaper office and continue his college studies at night. This suggestion met with the boy's interest and he now is attempting to organize a plan of activities that will include work in his field of interest and continued study toward the attainment of a college degree—another interest goal.

One of the most difficult phases of teaching is the motivation of apathetic students toward the development of interest through successful study achievement. There is a present trend toward adapting learning methods and materials to learner interests. One difficulty, however, is the question of the extent to which teaching should follow the path of immediate and probably changing learner interests, or be aimed at fulfilling more fundamental and permanent interests of individuals in terms of their ability to become successful learners.

## Work

Adolescents like to work if the work is of their own choosing and represents a felt interest. A boy or girl may resent the doing of household chores. Hence parents often respond to an adolescent's interest in money to acquire things which he wants by paying their child for performing household tasks that should be his responsibility as a family member. At the same time, many young people are very much interested in part-time jobs which will provide for them the luxuries that the family budget cannot include. Their interest in the purpose of the work is so keen that they do a good job.

It is only as the adolescent reaches the stage of adult responsibility for his own welfare and that of others that he is willing to work at a job in which he has no particular interest. Even then the adolescent is more likely to achieve success in his work if his interest in the activity is great.

## Social Activities

The normal adolescent is interested in parties, dates, dances, or any other form of social activity in which he can engage with his peers.

*Parties.* Interest in parties is not characteristic solely of the adolescent period. From early childhood onward, birthdays, special holidays, or other special events are celebrated by parties. Even during the early years most children's parties include members of both sexes, although during these years girls usually are more interested than boys in party activities. The girls enjoy the games as well as the food; boys may tolerate playing games with little girls, but are enthusiastic about plenty of good eats.

During the junior high school years, parties become popular with boys as well as with girls. The development of interest in members of the opposite sex brings about an interest in these gatherings as a means of adjusting to this new relationship. Since girls mature more quickly than boys, the former tend to prefer to have parties with older boys rather than with those of their own age groups. This discrimination on an age basis is likely to decrease with later adolescence.

Young people do not like formal parties. They like to gather together to have fun—play games, talk, and eat "goodies" which they themselves have selected and helped prepare. The party situation also aids the boys and girls to discover members of the other sex who have interests similar to their own and whom they find attractive.

*Dating.* Members of the opposite sex who meet at parties as well as in connection with school activities soon begin "dating." At first young people go out in groups or on double dates. As two young people become increasingly interested in each other, they may engage in "twosome" recreational or social activities.

The date is one of the primary interests of young people. It may afford an adolescent his or her greatest thrill. Failure to date may be regarded as a tragedy. Parental attitudes, lack of self-confidence, or supposedly unattractive appearance may deny an adolescent the satisfaction of one of his greatest interests. A situation of this kind is experienced more often by girls than by boys and requires intelligent help from adult associates.

*Other Social Activities.* Many high schools and colleges are meeting their responsibility to provide opportunities for boys and girls to participate in social activities. In some high schools there are classes in social as well as group dancing, in which boys and girls together receive instruction. School parties also are planned for the boys and girls. By participation in such school activities the timid, insecure adolescent can develop social poise and self-confidence.

One difficulty encountered by the school, however, is the fact that adolescent girls tend to be interested in "older men" as their dancing partners or for dates of any kind. Some adolescent boys, on the other hand, seem to be afraid of girls of their own age and are more at ease in a social situation with slightly older girls or with women. As adolescents become more mature, age differences appear to be less important. Interest then comes to center in the appearance, attitudes, and conversational ability of the member of the opposite sex with whom the older adolescent or young adult shares social activities. In an attempt to discover differing social interests at ages 13–14 and 16–17, a study was conducted by the authors in which college students were invited to indicate their social interests at these respective ages.

The social interests of adolescents were discovered by asking college juniors to indicate preferred social activities, as they remembered them, for the stated age periods. The twelve most frequently named interests for each age were listed. The items, as they appear in Tables 17 and 18,

*Table 17.* Social Interests at Ages 13–14 as Ranked by 160 College Juniors

| RANK | | |
| --- | --- | --- |
| MEN | WOMEN | SOCIAL INTEREST |
| 7 | 5 | Attending parties (school and neighborhood) |
| 8 | 4 | Attending social gatherings |
| 3 | 1 | Finding a place in peer group |
| 5 | 3 | Being neat in appearance |
| 2 | 9 | Participating in sports activities |
| 9 | 6 | Wearing attractive clothes |
| 10 | 7 | Participating in dancing |
| 6 | 10 | Collecting items of interest |
| 1 | 2 | Having a best friend of the same sex |
| 4 | 8 | Attending motion pictures |
| 11 | 11 | Smoking cigarettes |
| 12 | 12 | Writing poetry |

*Table 18.* Social Interests at Ages 16–17 as Ranked by 160 College Juniors

| RANK | | |
| --- | --- | --- |
| MEN | WOMEN | SOCIAL INTEREST |
| 1 | 1 | Developing social skills |
| 4 | 3 | Attending parties |
| 8 | 5 | Becoming a member of a social club |
| 7 | 9 | Attending dances |
| 3 | 2 | Being concerned about dress and appearance |
| 2 | 8 | Participating in sports |
| 9 | 6 | Having twosome dates |
| 5 | 4 | Impressing members of the opposite sex |
| 11 | 10 | Attending picnics |
| 10 | 12 | Attending motion pictures |
| 12 | 11 | Choosing a mate |
| 6 | 7 | Becoming independent of parents |

were then given to other college students for the purpose of ranking in "the order of your greatest interest when you were at each age listed."

Involved in the study were 160 college students (100 women, 60 men). The rank order of the items is given separately for men and women.

There appears to be some difference between the sexes in the extent of social interest as ranked by these students. For example, the item "participating in sports activities" is ranked higher by the men for both age groups. The rank order of two items is reversed between the sexes, thus indicating a difference of interest in these items, e.g., "participating in dancing," and "collecting items of interest." Apparently girls aged 13–14 have greater interest in dancing than do boys; boys have a greater interest in collecting than do girls.

The differences in rank of items seem to become less as both move into older age groups. The items in which the spread of difference is more than one rank difference are "participating in sports activities," referred to earlier, "becoming a member of a social club," and "having twosome dates." Girls appear to have stronger interest in these social activities during ages 16–17 than do boys.

## Recreational Interests

The kinds of recreational interests developed by adolescents and the leisure-time activities in which they are likely to engage are determined to a great extent by available opportunities. The adolescent whose family enjoys a better-than-average socioeconomic status can develop interests and fulfill them to an extent that is almost, if not entirely, impossible for the adolescent whose parents are among the underprivileged.

Recreational and social interests and activities are closely allied. In both areas of interests adolescents differ in what they wish to do with their leisure time from what gave them pleasure during childhood. Also, recreational interests take on new forms from early adolescence to early adulthood.

Recreational activity or play can be thought of as activity in which an individual engages solely for the pleasure he experiences therefrom. This is true of most child play. For the adolescent, recreation may possess elements of cultural or educational value. In both instances, however, the reason for participation is the interest of the growing person in a form of leisure-time activity. One difference between boys and girls in recreational interests is that the former are more concerned with stress and the latter with fancy.

*Games and Sports.* Adolescents are keenly interested in organized games. Both boys and girls engage in team activity. The bright and the dull find here a common interest. Participation in athletics is one of the most desired forms of activity to most teen-age boys and to some girls.

The average high school or college provides for student participation in organized games such as basketball, football, and baseball.

Team play possesses interest factors not only for the participant but also for those who watch the game and root enthusiastically for their team. Too, in team play young people learn the value of group cooperation. In the past, strenuous play was limited almost entirely to boys; at present, however, girls also are engaging in basketball and baseball games, but the rules for girls' teams are aimed to prevent some of the "roughness" that may be characteristic of the play of boys.

There is much discussion concerning the value of interschool competition, especially on the high school level. Studies may be neglected by the team members unless the school maintains a relatively high standard of scholarship as a requirement for playing. School interest in winning a game may run so high that an undue amount of time and energy is expended on practice. Often only a few members of the student body participate actively. As a result, some high schools place emphasis on the formation of many school teams that compete among themselves. This practice encourages many adolescents to satisfy their interest in play activity and to achieve muscular development.

During the early and middle years of adolescence there is great interest in participation in games and sports. Older adolescents, except for the relatively few who have become school or community heroes because of their superior achievement in athletics, shift their interest from sports to other social and recreational activities such as dating, dancing, or watching big-league games.

*Radio, Television, and Motion Pictures.* Adolescents are no less interested in radio, television, and motion-picture programs than they were as children, but they become much more discriminating. Girls tend to continue their interest in romantic plays, but they want the programs to be realistic and well presented. Boys of junior high school age prefer mystery stories to the Wild West shows that thrilled them as children. Older adolescents of both sexes seem to be most interested in programs that present comedy, popular song and dance, and historic, romantic, and general drama. They also show some interest in programs dealing with political events and international affairs. The average number of hours per week they spend in watching television is about fourteen.

In homes where there are television sets, children are avid watchers of programs dealing with their interests. Attendance at motion-picture theaters has decreased somewhat for all age groups since the advent of television. Adolescents, however, still seem to prefer the motion pictures. This is largely because of an interest connected with going there with a member of the other sex, thus engaging in a social activity away from the home. One adolescent girl expressed her attitude in these words: "Television is fine. Some of the programs are very interesting, but everyone has to keep quiet. I like to talk."

*Reading.* Interest in reading for enjoyment is strong for both sexes during adolescence. Unless other activities interfere, young people spend many hours reading their favorite newspapers, magazines, and books. The type of reading material preferred differs in terms of degree of intelligence, sex, and family status.

Interest in comics begun during childhood appears to persist during adolescence. Both boys and girls enjoy reading newspapers. To the extent that they are motivated in school to keep up with daily world happenings, both boys and girls evince interest in newspaper reports of national and world politics and of social conditions. Of greater interest to boys, however, are the sports pages, and to girls the woman's page and reviews of motion pictures. Crime news and advertisements have some appeal for both.

Magazines are popular, but the type read depends upon the intellectual status, age, and sex of the adolescent. The duller adolescent, especially if his financial allowance is limited, likes the cheaper, more popular magazine; the more intelligent boys and girls generally read those magazines that can be found in the home, with a few additions of their own choice. In general, adolescent boys prefer magazines that deal with science and mechanics, adventure, and the lives of heroic men. Although girls may show some interest in periodicals read by boys, they continue throughout adolescence to prefer magazines containing romantic stories and adult fiction, and, in some cases, home-interest magazines.

Probably because of their greater availability, adolescents tend to read more magazines than books. The public libraries, however, offer splendid reading opportunities for young people. Hence many adolescents are constant patrons of their local library. In book choice, boys and girls usually follow their magazine-reading interests. Girls give evidence of greater interest in the reading of poetry than do boys. During this age period girls also show interest in long stories, while boys prefer shorter articles or stories. There are some boys, however, who are intensely interested in long adventure stories or biographies.

The development of reading skills is an important area of high school learning. Young people need to be encouraged to want to read and to profit from reading materials that can serve them later. Unfortunately, too many adolescents lack interest in the writings of authors included among the school's required reading. The study of literature on the high school and college level is aimed at the development of good reading interests among young people. If the school's purpose fails, one reason for the failure probably can be found in inadequate teacher motivation and non-stimulating teaching methods.

## Vocational Selection

The child's interest in glamorous vocational activities may persist with modifications well into adolescence. The boy gradually shifts from interest in adventuresome fields of activity to a desire to become a brilliant and successful professional worker. As the girl loses her interest in becoming a motion-picture star, she is likely to turn her attention to humanitarian vocations. Young people tend to be extremely altruistic. They are eager to be of service. A boy whose pet dog becomes ill or dies decides to become a veterinarian. A girl who helps a sick member of her family believes that she should become a nurse.

The vocational interests of most adolescent boys are unrealistic. By the time they reach middle adolescence they are motivated in their career selection by the prestige of a vocational field rather than by its service opportunities. Some boys dream about gaining great fortunes, either through business activities or by discovering hidden treasures. They give little attention to their own abilities or to the requirements of their chosen field. During their later adolescent years boys become more interested in selecting an occupational field that will give them financial security, accompanied by prestige if possible, but not necessarily. At present, there is a trend even among younger adolescent boys to be more realistic about their vocational choice. A study to discover the vocational preferences of high- and low-achieving junior high school students was made by Stanley Krippner.[2] His investigation included 350 seventh- and eighth-grade students in an upper-middle-class community near Chicago. His findings are reported in Table 19.

In the past, the problems associated with the selection of a vocation were not so serious for adolescent girls as for boys. For most girls the primary interest was eventual marriage to a man who could support her and their children. Many modern girls plan and expect to work after marriage. One reason for this decision may be a strong interest in continuing a professional career. Many young women from poor to average families have little choice, however. Living costs are such that it is necessary for the wife as well as the husband to work. Girls who can afford to do so go to college and prepare themselves for one or another professional career. Those on a lower socioeconomic level must prepare themselves for entering the world of work, either upon graduation from high school or by the time they reach the age of 17. Choices are limited for these girls. Their chief interest usually is related to the already-crowded secretarial field. They then may have to become industrial workers.

Vocational interests of adolescents may be influenced by the occupa-

[2] Stanley Krippner, "The Vocational Preferences of High-achieving and Low-achieving Junior High School Students," *Gifted Child Quarterly*, pp. 88–90, Autumn, 1961.

*Table 19.* Occupational Preferences of High-achieving and Low-achieving Junior High School Boys and Girls (In per cents)

| OCCUPATIONAL PREFERENCE | HIGH-ACHIEVING BOYS | LOW-ACHIEVING BOYS | HIGH-ACHIEVING GIRLS | LOW-ACHIEVING GIRLS |
|---|---|---|---|---|
| Armed forces......... | 3.0 | 2.0 | 0.0 | 0.0 |
| Arts................ | 3 | 2 | 0 | 0 |
| Aviation............ | 0 | 9 | 10 | 12 |
| Business, clerical, sales. | 4 | 9 | 13 | 27 |
| Education........... | 0 | 0 | 43 | 15 |
| Engineering......... | 16 | 9 | 0 | 0 |
| Farming and forestry.. | 3 | 5 | 0 | 0 |
| Housewife........... | 0 | 0 | 3 | 4 |
| Law................ | 10 | 5 | 0 | 0 |
| Medicine and nursing.. | 23 | 16 | 10 | 15 |
| Professional sports.... | 6 | 5 | 0 | 0 |
| Science............. | 10 | 0 | 3 | 0 |
| Skilled trades........ | 0 | 15 | 0 | 0 |
| Other occupations..... | 3 | 2 | 3 | 0 |
| Undecided.......... | 10 | 21 | 2 | 15 |
| Total............. | 100 | 100 | 100 | 100 |

SOURCE: Stanley Krippner, "The Vocational Preferences of High-achieving and Low-achieving Junior High School Students," *Gifted Child Quarterly*, p. 89, Autumn, 1961.

tional activities of members of the family or older friends who have achieved success in their field. They also may be affected by the attitudes of members of their peer group. Parental interests may differ from those of their children. This poses a problem of adjustment. Available opportunities also may constitute a factor to be considered by the adolescent as he or she attempts to discover a vocational interest and perhaps to achieve it.

# The Development of Adolescent Attitudes

An individual is known by his expressed attitudes. These are individual and personal, and relate to the way a person thinks or behaves in situations. The feeling tones that accompany each experience constitute the quality components out of which attitudes are constructed. As an individual is stimulated by an idea, an activity, an object, or another person, he makes certain responses in the form of approval or disapproval, i.e., he is kind or unkind, friendly or unfriendly, critical or uncritical, tolerant or intolerant. The previous experiences of an individual determine in large part the acceptance or rejection that is aroused within him by the forces and influences in the total situation.

## The Nature of Attitude

Every human experience is accompanied by feeling tones and affective responses. Sensations possess feeling aspects of pleasantness or unpleasantness, satisfyingness or annoyance. The summation of these experiences constitutes a feeling tone or affective experience. These human qualities or attitudes influence an individual's thoughts, interests, and behavior.

Attitudes constitute values that relate to self and are quite subjective. An individual is concerned about the things that are of special interest to him or that affect him directly. One person will experience concern about a different set of problems, a different possession, a different situation, a different person, or a different condition than will another. Each individual evaluates and appraises situations or issues in terms of his degree of interest in, and attitude toward, them.

Behavior, then, is determined by attitudes and affective qualities. Attitudes become dynamic forces in human behavior. They give mental set to experience. In a conflict situation, the more intense the desire, the stronger is the accompanying attitude. An individual's attitudes do not necessarily remain constant toward a person or situation. As a result of his experiences, a young person develops desirable or undesirable attitudes toward himself, his parents, relatives, adult associates, members of his peer group, authority, religion, politics, world conditions, and any other persons, situations, or conditions that affect his interests or activities. Fortunately, undesirable attitudes can change as the young person gains greater understanding of their fundamental bases.

## The Power of Attitudes

Attitudes can exert a potent influence upon an adolescent. His attitudes are developing moment by moment. Some of them are formed without direction; others are the result of careful planning by a person— or persons—who desires to encourage the development of certain wholesome attitudes in others. One function of teaching is to stimulate young people toward the acquisition of attitudes that are individually and socially desirable. Much of personal development and citizenship training is a matter of attitude formation.

Adolescents are great imitators of attitudes; these are caught as they are taught. Adolescents learn many of their attitudes from their parents, their teachers, and their other associates. Consequently, teen-agers tend to develop similar attitudes without always realizing that they are doing so. If the adolescent can learn to be of service to others, he gains in personality characteristics that are essential to winning appreciation from others.

## The Influence of Unconscious Attitudes

Adolescents do many things without an awareness of the forces that prompt their behavior. Much of their inner conflict is attributable to these unconscious attitudes. The force of these attitudes is not fully appreciated by adolescents because they are not aware of the effect of their behavior upon others; they do not recognize the fact that their motives may appear different to others than they had intended them to be. An adolescent may not be aware of the attitudes of selfishness, insincerity, domination, or self-interest that he exhibits, even though they are known to others. Grandmothers and in-laws usually are sincere in their belief that the advice given by them is unbiased and aimed at the total good of everyone concerned. They usually are unaware that their advice is resented and looked upon as coming from an intruder.

Unsocial attitudes should remain dormant in the unconscious. Hates, prejudices, and resentments are best left in an inactive state. It seems wise for an adolescent so to order his behavior that his attitudes are wholesome and aimed at socially desirable goals. The skilled and proficient worker builds into his habit patterns many attitudes that become a part of his everyday living. It is in retrospect that an adolescent appreciates the satisfactions that were his during his former experiences.

## Attitudes as Directive Forces

An adolescent's thinking is influenced as he considers his interests in relationship to the environment. His behavior, in turn, is affected by the dynamic nature of sensory and perceptual experiences as they give rise to dominating ideas. The changes occurring among the ideas and thought processes, as these are experienced from time to time, are based upon the fact that one idea is in focus at one moment, a different one at another. The dominance of one idea over another is a selective process that is motivated by an individual's attitudes or feeling tones at the moment.

The directing influence of an attitude or an interest is apparent in an adolescent's responses to any given situation. An individual who is mentally ready to obtain information on a particular topic is likely to comprehend what is being said much more quickly than is the person whose mental set is different. For example, you have prepared a tasty drink containing fruit juices. As it is being praised by the guests, the question is asked, "Did you use lemon concentrate?" You may answer "Yes," since you

believed that the question referred to the fact that you had used un-
adulterated fresh lemon and lime juice; but the individual who asked the
question has in mind the frozen or canned juice called a "concentrate."

## Opinions and Attitudes

Expressed words often convey opinions rather than reflect deep-
seated attitudes. A spoken or written expression may or may not reveal the
actual beliefs or feelings of an individual. Attitudes revealed through
behavior are more reliable in evaluating reactions or thinking in situations
or issues. Deep-seated attitudes are less likely to be affected by verbal
expression than by actual circumstances that may exist at the moment.

In many situations an adolescent's expressed attitudes and his actual
behavior are not in agreement. It is more important for him to live his
"Excuse me" or "I am sorry" than it is that he merely verbalize those
words. It is better to be tolerant than merely to discuss the importance of
tolerance. Proper attitudes toward other people can be inculcated into an
adolescent's behavior so that greater understanding of people different
from himself can be achieved.

Adolescents usually express definite attitudes toward issues. When
action is required, however, they may respond by behavior that is quite
different from that expressed verbally toward the issue. If the behavior of
one adolescent is approved by most members of a group, another adolescent who otherwise may disapprove the behavior also may express his
approval of it. Yet when he is with another set of friends, he may criticize
the faults of the individual whom he was ready and willing to praise
earlier. This illustrates the influence of others on the expressed attitudes or
opinions held by adolescents at any one time.

Since an adolescent is not always aware of all his attitudes, it may be
difficult for him to distinguish clearly between an attitude and an opinion.
Expressed opinions often are at variance with deep-seated attitudes,
partly because individuals rationalize their beliefs. Hence an adolescent
may appear to be tolerant toward others when their activities do not
adversely affect his life. Attitudes reveal themselves in situations in which
an individual's interests are at stake.

## Characteristic Adolescent Attitudes

Although children, adolescents, and adults are physically and psychologically more alike than different, there are many variations or differences among individuals and within the individual himself. All adolescents seem to want to assert a rightfully developing attitude of independence and release from earlier accepted adult control. They are

neither children nor adults. The more they recognize their anomalous position, the more likely they are to indulge in one or more of the vagaries that are characteristic of the adolescent period of development. The teen-ager may seem to defy adult authority in spite of, or perhaps because of, a realization of his insecurity.

Elias Tuma and Norman Livson[3] conducted a study of the relationships between family socioeconomic status and adolescent attitudes toward authority. They summarize their findings as follows:

Attitudes to authority, ranging from conformity to rebelliousness, were evaluated in three interpersonal situations (at Home, in School, and with Peers) for the same sample of adolescent boys and girls at ages 14, 15, and 16 years. These inferential ratings, based on interviews with the subjects and their parents and on data provided by teachers and classmates, were analyzed for sex differences (a slight tendency toward greater acceptance of authority in girls), for generality among the three ratings at a given age (moderately positive intercorrelations), and for stability of a given attitude over the three age levels (considerable fluctuation). Most striking is the consistently negative relationship between degree of conformity experienced by the male adolescent (in all situations and all ages) and the socioeconomic status of his family (measured separately by a composite index, by the Berkeley Social Rating Scale, and by mothers' and fathers' educational levels). No consistent trend is apparent for girls. Mothers' education is the single, most powerful predictor of boys' attitudes to authority, yielding signicant negative correlations in eight of nine instances. There is a suggestion, for both sexes, of variation in degree of conformity relatable to an interaction between socioeconomic factors and the physical maturity level of the adolescent. The results are evaluated in the context of reported social class differences in parental values and practices and their corresponding socialization goals.[4]

A boy may become unduly aggressive; he may act as though his parents' chief function is to serve him and to cater to his wants; he may tend to wear sloppy or overconspicuous clothes; he may assume a superior attitude toward younger children as well as toward adults; at the same time, in various ways he may attempt to impress his peer groups, both boys and girls. An adolescent boy may become moody and unduly sensitive to the attitudes displayed toward him by others in his group, or he may develop a boisterous, self-assured attitude that serves as a coverup of his inner feelings of insecurity.

For a teen-age boy to "lose face" among his peers is a major tragedy. Adults are not always aware of the things that may be tragic incidents.

[3] Elias Tuma and Norman Livson, "Family Socioeconomic Status and Adolescent Attitudes to Authority," Child Development, vol. 31, pp. 387–399, June, 1960.
[4] Ibid., pp. 398–399.

For example, a baby girl was born into a family of an 18-year-old boy. The lad loved his baby sister and was very proud of her. In fact, her cute ways became the subject of many talks between him and his pals. His mother made the mistake, however, of expecting this boy to take the baby for a daily airing in her carriage. Much as he liked her, this was going too far for the sensitive adolescent. What would his pals think of his being a nursemaid? This boy was too well trained to disobey his mother's request, but, as he laughingly said later, he could have throttled the child. The fact that his friends admired the baby he was wheeling along the streets did not lessen his embarrassment. Perhaps indirectly this incident caused him later to major in pediatrics and place emphasis in his professional career upon child care and parental attitudes toward children.

The behavior of growing girls is as unpredictable as that of their brothers, if not more so. They also struggle for self-realization, usually in more subtle ways than boys. Since a girl tends to mature earlier than a boy, she is likely to become sensitive sooner to changing relations between the sexes. Her tentative attempts to attract boys' attention may take various forms such as coyness, affected mannerisms and speech, daydreaming, apparent indifference to boys or rudeness in their presence, extremes of dress, make-up, and hairdo, or even encouragement of, and participation in, more or less serious petting activities.

There are indications that present-day young adolescents are developing relatively more mature attitudes toward certain aspects of their life experiences than those that were evident in the past. For example, a study was conducted to compare the attitudes of ninth-grade students in Oakland, California, during the years 1935, 1950, and 1959.[5]

As a result of the findings, it was concluded that during the 1950s ninth-grade boys and girls gave indication of greater maturity of heterosexual interests, more serious purpose, and more tolerant attitude toward social issues than was found in the 1935 sampling. The later groups also evidenced less interest in "childish" activities. Jones suggests that these changes in attitudes may be associated with earlier maturing, parental influences, altered school curriculums, and changes in world affairs.

## Attitude Problems of Adolescents

Adolescents experience various problems associated with attitudes. According to a recent survey of 3,000 high school students in the United

[5] Mary Cover Jones, "A Comparison of the Attitudes and Interests of Ninth Grade Students over Two Decades," *Journal of Educational Psychology,* vol. 51, pp. 175–186, June, 1960.

States, it was found that 50 per cent or more of those contacted were concerned with the improvement of their figures or posture, wanting people to like them more, experiencing stage fright before a group, wanting to make new friends, and wanting to gain or lose weight. The entire list of concerns centered around personal and social activities.[6]

The adolescent's attitudes are rooted in his personal constitution. His physical constitution becomes to him an important element in his relationships with others. His behavior is affected by such factors as his physical size, uniformity of physical features, health, and degree of emotional stability and energy. These are significant to him because of the way in which they may influence the attitudes of others toward him. Socially undesirable attitudes may be traced to an overemphasis upon any one or more of the aforementioned conditions.

The behavior of elders that interferes with an adolescent's freedom may stimulate antagonisms within him. The teen-ager believes that adults are intolerant of adolescent wishes, interests, and behavior. The adolescent considers himself to be open-minded; yet he has many deep biases based upon his desires and felt needs. He often is motivated by an attitude of self-sufficiency or a belief in his rightness. Adults too have their own biases toward their work, family experiences, and other factors that affect their life. The kind of attitudes displayed by adults in the presence of adolescents may cause the latter to develop either desirable attitudes or attitudes of bitterness or of personal futility. Both boys and girls can give evidence of aggressive behavior when their interests are thwarted. There are sex differences, however, although boys generally are considered to be more aggressive than girls.[7]

Overaggressive teen-agers often are permitted to develop habits that interfere with their present and later interpersonal relationships. Some adolescents become demanding for the fulfillment of their desires. They are likely to increase these selfish demands as they grow and develop unless someone assists them in redirecting self-aggrandizing motives. This clearly becomes the duty of parents and teachers. Parents often are torn between what they think is their duty and what they believe may be expected of them. Teachers are becoming more responsive to social pressure in their dealings with adolescents.

In general, an adolescent's attitudes are outgoing. He often is driven by an urge to reform the world. Although his attitude toward a child or an older person may be one of impatience, the teen-ager has a kindly

---

[6] H. H. Remmers and D. H. Radler, "Teenage Attitudes," *Scientific American*, vol. 198, pp. 25–29, June, 1958.

[7] See Leonard M. Lansky et al., "Sex Differences in Aggression and Its Correlates in Middle-class Adolescents," *Child Development*, vol. 32, pp. 45–48, March, 1961.

feeling toward children as a group and pity or sympathy for those who are many years his senior. His attitudes toward his own group, however, are conditioned by his immediate relationship with them. He may be resentful of those who possess superior advantages or who seem to receive more attention than he does. Also, he may exhibit an attitude of superiority toward other young people who appear to be less able or less successful than he is.

## Overt Expressions of Attitudes toward the Opposite Sex

It is an observable phenomenon that as boys and girls approach the adolescent period, they begin to develop as individuals and to display attitudes toward members of the opposite sex that gradually come to differ markedly from their earlier childhood interpersonal relationships. These changing social attitudes result partly from newly awakened interests and urges that are rooted in physical and physiological growth changes. Adolescent social attitudes are influenced also by social pressures that affect themselves as well as their peer and older associates.

The preadolescent boy suddenly seems to lose interest in girls of his own age. With his boy pals, he tends to engage in games and other activities from which girls are excluded. It would seem, however, that preadolescent boys are participating in social activities that include girls.

Adolescents develop attitudes toward themselves and their peer associates that give evidence of subtle differences that are not completely understood by them and that change with increase in age. Girls may become shy in the presence of their former boy pals. They may "moon" over the pictures of popular motion-picture actors or television stars. Little cliques of preadolescent girls may display silly, giggling attitudes in the presence of boys, or may seem to evince an attitude of superiority to boys of their own age.

Both boy and girl behavior represents a kind of "battle of the sexes" that is rooted in a developing but not fully recognized awareness of one another that results from the glandular changes that are taking place within them. As children approach puberty, they come to realize that their attitude toward members of the other sex is different from what it was during childhood. Their newer social approaches are uncertain unless their parents have prepared them for changing social status and situations. The fact that boys and girls do not mature at the same time, the girls becoming mature first, may cause attitude difficulties to arise that have educational implications. In the junior high school, for example, there may be girls who are developing adolescent attitudes and boys who are still children. Maturing girls and immature boys tend to think differently. They have differing interests. Their approach to study activities may not be the same. Teachers, as well as parents, have the responsibility of meeting the developmental needs of both sexes.

In their evaluation of, or their attitudes toward, the members of the opposite sex, girls are supposed to stress the possession of good looks, brawn rather than brains, and a "smooth line." Boys are expected by adults to fall for a "cute trick," extremes of dress and make-up, a minimum of intelligence, and a tendency to be "free and easy." Perhaps adults are mistaken. The following data give insight into the personal characteristics of boys and girls that are admired or disliked by members of the opposite sex.

In order to discover more clearly the attitudes of teen-agers, a study was made concerning what young people consider to be desirable and undesirable qualities in associates of the opposite sex. About 4,900 young people (2,500 girls, 2,360 boys), representing a cross section of junior and senior high school students in New York City and environs, were asked to write answers to the following questions:[8]

1. What are the personality characteristics that you admire in girls (boys)?
2. What traits do you dislike in girls (boys)?

3. What do you do to increase your popularity with the girls (boys) whom you know?

Resulting data were organized according to the ages of the adolescents responding: the younger group, ages 12 through 14; the older adolescents, ages 16 through 18. Most of the younger teen-agers emphasized physical characteristics and overt behavior. The more mature teen-agers stressed attitudes and behavior associated with inner motivations and character traits. There were certain qualities, however, that were considered desirable by most teen-agers. The characteristics of girls admired by boys and of boys admired by girls are presented in Table 20. The items are listed in the order of frequency of expressed interest by the teen-agers responding. Personality traits of boys disliked by girls and traits of girls disliked by boys are presented in Table 21. The attempts made by each sex to impress members of the other sex are presented in Table 22.

Younger girls dislike boys who want to kiss and "paw" them. Many of the younger boys like girls who have good figures and with whom they can have fun, but dislike girls who are fresh and try to act older than they are. A few of the younger boys say that they do not like anything about girls or that girls are usually nuisances. Girls like boys who are

---

[8] The teachers who submitted these questions to their students were enrolled in the graduate guidance and counseling program at Brooklyn College.

*Table 20.* Personality Traits Admired by Members of the Opposite Sex (Arranged according to frequency)

| PERSONALITY TRAITS OF GIRLS ADMIRED BY BOYS | PERSONALITY TRAITS OF BOYS ADMIRED BY GIRLS |
| --- | --- |
| Good personality | Good personality |
| Good-looking—beautiful face, dress, and figure | Good-looking—not necessarily handsome |
| Look nice in a bathing suit | Good character |
| Neatness and cleanliness | Neatness |
| Helpful to others | Clean and appropriate dress |
| Consideration for others | Intelligent |
| Appropriate dress | Good conversationalist |
| Dependable | Consideration for a girl's wishes |
| Good talker | Respect for girls—not fresh |
| Good listener | Willingness to take a girl on dates |
| Friendliness | Boy to be older than girl |
| Ability to dance | Good manners |
| Good manners | Good-natured |
| Acts her age | Smart in school |
| Courtesy | Clean-shaved and hair cut |
| Politeness | Clean-minded |
| No show-off | Kind, generous, tall |
| Interest in hobbies of boys | Acts his age |
| Modest but not shy | Has a sense of humor |
| Act grown-up, not like a baby | Not too shy |
| Clean-minded | Honest and fair |
| Able to take a joke | Respect for rights of girl |
| | Punctuality |
| | Not to try to be a big shot |
| | Able to get along with others |
| | Has self-control |
| | The way he kisses |
| | Good listener |

older than themselves. They like boys who are willing to meet a girl's parents and who like sports and hard work. They dislike hot-tempered, rude boys, and those who take a girl to a party and then pay no attention to her.

Boys in their later teens seem to admire girls who are even-tempered, lively, less intelligent than the boy (but not stupid), a good listener, modest, and sincere. Many of the older boys object to a girl's excessive use of make-up and wearing of slacks or sweaters that exaggerate her figure. Some of the boys prefer a girl to wear her hair long rather than too short.

Many of the older adolescents (both boys and girls) stress as desirable the possession of qualities such as "good character," consideration for older people, mature behavior, self-respect, and ambition. Some girls

*Table 21.* Personality Traits Disliked by Members of the Opposite Sex (Arranged according to frequency)

| TRAITS OF GIRLS DISLIKED BY BOYS | TRAITS OF BOYS DISLIKED BY GIRLS |
|---|---|
| Sloppiness of appearance | Sloppiness of appearance |
| Overweight or underweight | Boastfulness |
| Tendency to flirt or "two-time" | Act like big shots |
| Talk too much | Display poor manners |
| Extremes of dress | Stinginess |
| Little regard for money | Being conceited |
| Too much interest in self | Poorly groomed |
| Lack of punctuality | Laziness |
| Snobbishness | Foolish behavior at parties |
| Talk about other dates | Exhibit fresh behavior |
| Too much make-up | Shyness |
| Sulking and pouting | Smoking excessively |
| Being conceited | Using bad language |
| Bites nails | Discourtesy to elders |
| Smokes and drinks | Talks too much |
| Giggling or talebearing | Wants to be center of attention |
| Inability to dance | Moodiness |
| Immature behavior | Sponging off other boys |
| Mingling with a fast crowd | Asking for date at last minute |

say that they do not want boys to spend money on them unless the boys have earned the money. Although they do not say specifically that they like only young people who have the same religious affiliation as themselves, they do seem to approve of a young person's having some religious convictions.

The results of this study reveal the sound thinking, high ideals, and wholesome attitudes of many adolescents. Whether or not their expressed likes or dislikes actually are the motivating forces that influence their own

*Table 22.* Attempts Made by Boys and Girls to Increase Their Popularity with Members of the Opposite Sex (Arranged according to frequency)

| ATTEMPTS MADE BY BOYS TO IMPRESS GIRLS | ATTEMPTS MADE BY GIRLS TO IMPRESS BOYS |
|---|---|
| Develop good taste in dress | Become careful about appearance |
| Participate in school activities | Try to be friendly |
| Avoid annoying habits in school | Develop sincerity |
| Be considerate of the other person | Be popular with girls also |
| Develop similar interests | Try not to be catty |
| Become lively | Not go to expensive places on a date |
| Be as friendly as possible | Be a good conversationalist |
| Eliminate all annoying habits | Go in for school activities |
| Always be dependable | Avoid ridicule of others |
| Be polite to everyone | Have respect for elders |

choice of girl or boy associates, they at least give evidence of knowing what should be admired.

## Adolescent Interests and Behavior in Relation to Parents

Whether a growing boy or an adolescent girl causes parents greater concern is a moot question. Since the girl usually is expected to be more amenable to parental direction than the boy, the teen-age girl may find her problem of growing up different from that of the boy, but not easier. Her forms of adolescent rebellion are likely to be centered in the family. Home customs and conditions sometimes receive the teen-age girl's disapproval. She may be "ashamed" of her parents' mannerisms, speech patterns, and dress modes. Furniture arrangement or old-fashioned furnishings may "make it impossible" for her to take her friends into the home. The presence of younger children in the home, especially when they engage in teasing their older sister, can be a cause of youthful frustration unless parents are able to cope with the situation.

A teen-age girl seems to tend more than a boy toward the development of intense but short-lived fads and fancies. Joan, the 15-year-old daughter of socially and economically middle-class parents, was fortunate enough to have her own room. She decided that her room was entirely too conventional. Her mother wisely agreed to permit Joan to redecorate the room if the girl herself did the work and kept the cost low. Joan gleefully accepted the challenge. She spent months planning, painting, and rearranging. The results? The room was a startling study in severe black and white: black walls and floor, white furniture, inexpensive white draperies and bedspread. No hint of any other color was permitted. Never before had Joan been so careful about keeping her clothing in closets and dresser drawers. Nothing must interfere with her color scheme. For another month the room was the object of great admiration among her girl companions, some of whom received permission to follow her example.

During this period Joan's mother commented upon the fact that Joan's interest in the ultramodern would wane. The mother was right. Before a year had passed, the girl began to be annoyed by her earlier "childish" ideas, and the room was again redecorated. This time it oozed dainty, lacy femininity.

Many examples might be cited similar to the foregoing. Manners, dress, hairdo, and objects of adoration keep changing as the adolescent attempts in one way after another to assert himself as a person with all the rights and privileges that are owed him by adults. Parents need to understand their teen-age children and, at the same time with kindly firmness, guide adolescent vagaries. No rigid rules can be constructed whereby all parents can be expected to influence all adolescent attitudes and behavior. The mental and emotional characteristics of both parents and adolescents enter the situation.

## Cultural Differences in Attitudes

Attitude qualities are not found in isolation. An individual's attitudes have emanated from his biological drives, his mental sets, his state of readiness, his verbal responses, his muscular adjustment, or his generalized behavior. These are interrelated in various ways and serve to color opinion. The attitudes possessed by a particular person reflect in large part the kinds of environment that have had an impact upon the individual.

### Attitudes toward the Behavior of Others

Social behavior is understood by considering the attitudes aroused in a group or crowd which conform to the characteristic behavior of the particular group. Thus, in order to understand adolescent attitudes it is necessary to know something concerning the differences in views and values which characterize the different subcultures in which adolescents mature.

Each adolescent has a readiness to respond to the presence of people, regardless of who they are. Each has a set attitude to conform to the behavior expected of him by others. Certain attitudes prevail in many social situations concerning problems such as courtesy of the road or respect for the rights of others. This readiness promotes certain behavior actions and inhibits others. In fact, attitudes toward cooperation, courtesy, or dignity determine the nature of an adolescent's behavior.

Attitudes are contagious and, as they appear in the behavior of others, are likely also to be displayed by adolescents. Suggestion stimulates attitudes that have social values. Social attitudes should be started early so that by the time an individual becomes a teen-ager, he already has developed wholesome attitudes toward others, regardless of race, color, or creed.

The growing person discovers the values of life through associating with others. A baseball game is enjoyed partly because an individual's friends enjoy it; picnics are selected activities partly because others have had fun at them; a play, a toy, an automobile, or anything that can be mentioned is enjoyed to some extent because others have had satisfying emotional experiences in connection with it. The adolescent who matures among people who display wholesome personal attitudes enjoys a richness of living that is worthy of imitation.

Even though a high school student has had no personal experiences with a teacher, he is likely to regard him favorably if other students report that he is "tops." It is not until the student himself becomes a member of the teacher's class, however, that an individual attitude is formed. Although the adolescent is mentally set to like the teacher, he must discover for himself that the adult knows his subject matter, understands that adolescents are not children, has high but fair standards of learner accomplishment, and evaluates learner achievement justly and intelligently. Through experiences of this kind good adolescent attitudes toward teachers are developed.

## Racial and National Attitudes

The development of suitable attitudes toward racial, national, and religious groups is one of the great needs of today. The one-world ideal hinges upon the ability of civilization to eliminate bias, prejudice, and intolerance. In the article "Attitude Development for International Understanding," one of the authors suggested:

Educational objectives are expanding in their meaning to include considerations that now extend well beyond the national boundaries of any one nation. Hence, attention must be given to developing adolescent orientation toward national attitudes as well as toward international responsibilities. Gone are the days when any nation could live unto itself alone. World conditions today require that the education of teachers include not only an understanding of individual learners but also an appreciation of the attitudes and customs of people everywhere. A nation has individuality as much as does a child. The interests, habits, and customs peculiar to itself constitute the rightful heritage of a particular polity. An individual should be encouraged to develop his potential abilities to the fullest. Likewise should a nation be given a chance to promote its own customs, cultures, and mores for the purpose of becoming a successful unit in the family of nations. The pattern of human relationships that is being developed in any one nation must become a living part of the ideational background of all young people of that country. To this end both national and international indoctrination should go hand in hand toward the achievement of the larger ideal of international understanding, respect, and peace.

All should be alerted to an understanding of international needs and to an appreciation of the interrelationships that exist among and between nations. As we attempt to inculcate democratic attitudes and ideals, however, we must not make the mistake of believing that we should pattern our procedures upon the models set by other countries, and especially we must *not* attempt to impose our form of democratic living upon any other nation. Each nation should be permitted its own individuality, and be given freedom in the educational processes that may be utilized to maintain it. Interference from another nation should not be tolerated by any nation if the purpose of such interference is aimed at changing drastically those traditions which characterize it as a nation. Let teachers be educated, therefore, so that through their attitudes and behavior they will help their students develop a respect for the rights of nations just as we ask respect for the rights of individuals within a nation. International understanding must rest upon mutual appreciation of the rights and responsibilities that are practiced by teachers and students in all lands.

Important traits are exhibited by teachers who have shown that they have a fundamental understanding of human values in the area of national and international relationships. *The internationally-minded teacher shows through his attitude and behavior that:*

1. He can work with individuals as individuals and assist them in the development of an understanding of the larger society in which they live.

2. He is mindful of his status in his family, in his city, in his state, and in his nation, but at the same time he can be world-minded.

3. He has an appreciation of individuals without regard to race, color, or religion.

4. He is concerned with the culture and the problems of all national groups, wherever they may be.

5. He believes that desirable influences should be shared by all people.

6. He wishes to achieve these goals without involving himself or his learners in any undesirable foreign entanglements.

7. He has patience, courage, and a deep faith in people and their motives.

8. His purpose is to help individuals develop the capacity to live together in harmony in a world united.

9. He is aware that desirable human relationships must be developed from within; they cannot be purchased in any form that is ready for use.[9]

In "No Matter Where They Live," one of the authors further elaborates:

International understanding and world-mindedness are becoming increasingly necessary aspects of our daily living. We are in need of a faith in people that will include individuals from all lands, the development of sincere interest in people as persons without reference to nationality. The value of such an attitude was demonstrated by the writer's experiences with Japanese educators during a year's assignment as visiting expert in Japanese teacher education. . . .

The young are great imitators of adult behavior. Consequently, the former tend to acquire the attitudes of the elders with whom they asso-

[9] Lester D. Crow, "Attitude Development for International Understanding," *American School Board Journal*, pp. 25–26, December, 1953.

ciate. It has been gratifying, as shown in their letters to me, to learn that the Japanese educators with whom I worked have not lost the fine attitudes they were developing while I was in Japan. Perhaps most important is the fact that they are trying consciously to inculcate similar attitudes among their college students. Since these students are the future teachers in Japan, the influence can be endless. I believe that my Japanese friends have come to realize that teacher example, even on the college level, plays a dominant role in individual development. Consequently, attitudes displayed will influence greatly the attainment of the goal of friendship among the people of the world. Through precept and example teachers can exhibit desirable attitudes toward other nations and nationals. A teacher's eventual effectiveness and worth perhaps depend mostly upon the extent of his influence upon his learners.

I sincerely hope that my Japanese co-workers have become convinced that:

1. Teachers should develop an appreciation of the problems basic to international friendship.

2. Men and women responsible for the education of youth should make conscious efforts to attain the goal of better understanding among the people of respective nations.

3. International friendships rest upon mutual appreciation of *rights* and *responsibilities* as practiced by the teachers, students and other responsible leaders of all nations.

4. Respect for one another, combined with a sincere attempt to bridge superficial differences, can do much to spread that ideal of international cooperation expressing itself in personal friendliness and mutual give and take. When one pushes aside superficialities and prejudices, people are people, no matter where they live.[10]

## The Role of Attitudes in Behavior Motivation

Attitudes are basic behavior motivators. In this chapter the authors have attempted to present an overview of the kinds of attitudes exhibited by adolescents and the ways in which attitudinal tendencies influence the various phases of teen-age personal and social adjustments. To clarify the discussion, descriptions, explanations, and illustrations have included home, school, vocational, and social experiences.

In the remaining chapters of Part III, as well as in all of Part IV, the reader will find that an adolescent's attitude constitutes the foundation upon which is built the kind of personality he eventually achieves. From this point onward attention will be directed toward the functioning of attitudes as behavior motivators and as adjustment or maladjustment inducers.

[10] Lester D. Crow, "No Matter Where They Live," *Phi Delta Kappan,* vol. 35, no. 8, pp. 333–335, May, 1954.

## Questions and Problems for Discussion

1. Illustrate, by use of examples, how interest differs from attitude. Indicate also the extent to which attitudes are acquired as a matter of living in a particular environmental setting.
2. Cite an instance in your experience in which one of your strong interests led to the arousal of an equally strong attitude toward certain people or situations.
3. Compare your radio, television, motion-picture, and reading interests as a child, as a young adolescent, and at present. Discuss likenesses and differences.
4. Recall five of your interests as a child (exclude those mentioned in question 3) and the ways in which you expressed them. List these activities. Then, next to each, indicate (a) the activity through which you attempted to satisfy the same interests when you were 15 years old, and (b) how these interests are expressed at present.
5. What likenesses do you find to exist between your present interests and those of a close friend of the opposite sex? What differences?
6. Enumerate the factors that influenced you in making a decision in a vocational area. If you have not yet decided on a vocation, to what extent is interest motivating you toward one or another choice?
7. Compare your present attitude toward adult authority with that when you were in your early teen years. Suggest reasons for any changes.
8. Explain why it is easier today to develop friendly attitudes toward people of various countries than it was fifty years ago.
9. To what extent should women participate in the work world? Be shielded from hard work? Be placed on an equal footing with men in the world of work?
10. *Special Exercises:*
    a. Confer with three adolescent boys and three adolescent girls to discover their interests in areas such as (1) members of the opposite sex, (2) teachers, (3) subjects in school, (4) athletics, (5) life work. What differences do you find among them?
    b. Study the interests of two members of your own age group, and the interests of two adults beyond the age of 30 years. Report any differences you find.

## Selected References

Allport, G.: *The Nature of Prejudice*, Addison-Wesley Publishing Company, Inc., Cambridge, Mass., 1954.

Boyer, W. H.: "A Survey of the Attitudes, Opinions & Objectives of High School Students in the Milwaukee Area," *Journal of Educational Sociology*, pp. 344–348, March, 1959.

Cohen, A. K.: *Delinquent Boys: The Culture of the Gang*, The

Free Press of Glencoe, New York, 1955.

Crow, Lester D., and Alice Crow: *Mental Hygiene for Teachers: A Book of Readings*, The Macmillan Company, New York, 1963.

Crow, Lester D.: "Teen-age Traits, Interests and Worries," *Educational Forum*, pp. 423–428, May, 1956.

Crow, Lester D.: "Attitude Development for International Understanding," *American School Board Journal*, pp. 25–26, December, 1953.

Havighurst, R. J., et al.: *Growing up in River City*, John Wiley & Sons, Inc., New York, 1962.

Harris, Dale B.: "Life Problems and Interests of Adolescents in 1935 and 1957," *School Review*, pp. 335–343, Autumn, 1959.

Merry, F. K., and R. V. Merry: *The First Two Decades of Life*, 2d ed., Harper & Row, Publishers, Incorporated, New York, 1958.

Norvell, G. W.: *Reading Interests of Young People*, D. C. Heath and Company, Boston, 1950.

Norvell, G. W.: *What Boys and Girls Like to Read*, Silver Bur-

dett Company, Morristown, N.J., 1958.

Remmers, H. H.: *Introduction to Opinion and Attitude Measurement*, Harper & Row, Publishers, Incorporated, New York, 1954.

Roe, Anne: "Early Determinants of Vocational Choice," *Journal of Counseling Psychology*, vol. 4, pp. 212–217, 1957.

Steiner, B. A.: *The People Look at Television: A Study of Audience Attitudes*, Alfred A. Knopf, Inc., New York, 1963.

Strong, E. K.: "Satisfaction and Interests," *American Psychologist*, vol. 13, pp. 449–456, August, 1958.

Super, D. E.: *The Vocational Maturity of Ninth-grade Boys*, Bureau of Publications, Teachers College, Columbia University, New York, 1960.

Tannenbaum, A. J.: *Adolescent Attitudes toward Academic Brilliance*, Bureau of Publications, Teachers College, Columbia University, New York, 1962.

Wilson, W. C.: "Development of Ethnic Attitudes in Adolescence," *Child Development*, vol. 34, pp. 247–256, March, 1963.

# Chapter Nine

## Sex Behavior
## of Adolescents

Adolescent sexual adjustment constitutes a personal and social problem that begins early in adolescence and continues as a potent force during this period. Often there is conflict between adult standards and evolved adolescent codes of behavior pertaining to dating, petting, mate selection, courtship, and premarital or extramarital sexual intercourse. The achievement by young people of culturally acceptable attitudes toward their developing sex urges is a major problem not only for the adolescents themselves but for parents, school personnel, religious leaders, and workers in social and welfare agencies. The current increase of delinquency among young teen-agers, including sex experimentation and rape, is alerting thoughtful adults and adolescents to the needs of boys and girls during their growing-up years to be helped toward an understanding of the role of sex in an individual's life and the development of wholesome patterns of sex-stimulated behavior.

Chapter 4 dealt with the physical and physiological aspects of sexual growth and maturational processes during adolescence. We shall now consider, in terms of recent research findings, the development of adolescent sex-stimulated attitudes and behavior in relation to societal sex restrictions and taboos.

## Significant Aspects of Heterosexual Relationships

The sex drive eventually becomes a powerful behavior-motivating force in the life of most people. It usually develops gradually, from little or no manifestation of its presence during childhood to full maturation by the age of 18. Adolescents differ from one another in the rate and intensity of sexual development, however, and in the effect upon them of the emotional concomitants of the sex urge.

### Importance of Attitudes and Knowledge

Many adults are coming to believe that there is an urgent need to provide adequate sex education for children and adolescents. There is no general agreement, however, concerning the best method of educational approach. Some parents are unable to meet the problems of sex guidance with the same objectivity and frankness that they employ in other areas of child training. Basic to this parental attitude may be such factors as (1) uncertainty concerning the when, what, and how of appropriate education at the various developmental levels, (2) conflict between personal standards and socially condoned practices, and (3) parent-experienced sexual maladjustments.

It would seem that whatever is done in the area of sex education should start early in the home and continue throughout the adolescent years. Since the success of the training during adolescence rests upon what is done during the early years, it becomes important that wholesome attitudes toward sex be developed during childhood. Sometimes adults unconsciously embarrass children and young adolescents by seeming to shroud in mystery, or by subjecting to ribald jest, those aspects of sex that in themselves are suitable topics of discussion in the presence of young people.

No phase of human development represents an isolated process. Hence it can be understood readily that developing attitudes and behavior associated with sexual maturation tend to be influenced greatly by the direction taken by other aspects of development. It has been found that there is a significant relationship between constructive and emotionally nondisturbing sexual development during adolescence and wholesome childhood attitudes and behavior patterns. These include healthful habits of body care, energy-filled work and play activities, cheerful assumption of appropriate home and school responsibilities, friendly and cooperative relations with peer associates, and complete confidence in parents' interest in a child's problems and ability to help solve them.

As a result of unfavorable childhood experiences, many boys and girls bring with them into their prepubescent years a meager or negative background of preparation with which to meet adjustment problems associated with adolescent sexual development. The child who has been reared by rigid parents usually is fearful, shy, submissive, and perhaps bound by unrealistic convention.

Even though a child has been helped to develop socially cooperative attitudes and behavior habits, he may have received from his elders little or no information concerning physical structure and sexual functions, or still worse, he may have gathered from other young people a confusing mass of misinformation. Most children are curious about their origin, the relationship between their parents, and other matters that deal with sex. Hence when the overt signs of the onset of puberty appear before the young person is properly prepared for these new experiences, the resulting shock or fear may interfere seriously with his power to adjust objectively and without emotional turmoil to his changing physiological and psychological status.

Every pubescent or young adolescent experiences changing emotional reactions as accompaniments of the physical and glandular processes of growth and maturation. In common parlance, he is being inducted into the "mysteries of sex." Probably at no other time in his life does an individual need more help in achieving a sensible and objective attitude in relationship to himself than he does at this stage of his development.

Many adolescents attempt to solve their own problems in this area of experience. A few adolescents, however, seek advice and help from adults. Unless the young adolescent has built up a close, understanding relationship with his parents, he is likely to take his questions concerning his new sex status to persons outside the home. Sympathetic religious leaders, teachers, and counselors often are chosen as the confidants of confused adolescents with problems in this area. Hence constructive personal guidance of this kind should be made available to young people by churches and secondary schools.

## Changing Heterosexual Relationships

A normal or natural trend appears to operate from babyhood through adolescence in respect to a growing and maturing individual's attitudes toward members of the opposite sex. Heterosexual development begins in an infant's almost complete absorption with himself, moves through levels of changing sex-differentiating attitudes, and culminates in the young adult's displayed readiness for marriage. During this period there are periodic displays on the part of boys and girls of seeking, accepting, and rejecting behavior toward the other sex. These activities are significant only to the extent that they are general trends toward heterosexually stimulated behavior that inevitably occurs between members of the opposite sex.

Most girls mature sexually earlier than boys. Consequently, young adolescent girls may annoy or amuse boys of the same age by what the latter often refer to as "silly-girl giggling and nonsense." A girl who has older and younger brothers, however, may be extremely objective in her relations with boys, even during the supposed giggly, self-conscious pubescent stage of development. Similarly, a boy who has older and younger brothers and sisters may give little or no evidence of antagonism or aversion to, or overconcern about, girls at any developmental stage. An only child who continuously has been "protected" by overanxious parents from association with members of the opposite sex not only may fail to exhibit varying heterosexually stimulated behavior during the developmental years but, even with the approach of adulthood, may be shy and withdrawing in the presence of members of the opposite sex and, consciously or unconsciously, attempt to repress natural sex urges.

The general pattern of the development of heterosexual interest is relatively consistent for the majority of young people. Yet childhood experiences, environmental conditions, and cultural influences play major roles in determining the way in which, and the extent to which, an adolescent's overt behavior gives evidence of the functioning of his developing sex-stimulated urges and drives. For example, before adolescents "find" themselves in relation to peer members of the other sex, they may project their developing emotionalized feelings in the direction of an adult member of the same sex, often an admired and sympathetic teacher. The girl's "love" for an older woman is designated a "crush"; a boy's extreme admiration for a man becomes a case of hero worship.

Homosexual relations with the older person rarely are desired or sought. The adolescent is likely to imitate the dress, mannerisms, and general behavior of the idealized adult. A girl may become so involved in her emotional regard for her crush that she follows her around the school, writes letters to her, telephones her at home and in various other ways makes a nuisance of herself, becomes extremely shy in the woman's presence, or is sensitive to any real or fancied slight or lack of attention on the part of the adult.

Adolescent crushes and hero worship appear to serve as natural outlets for newly experienced emotional needs. Situational factors may encourage the display of crush behavior, e.g., a girls' school staffed by women teachers only. Moreover, in some girls' schools every student must have for herself a crush about whose admirable and lovable qualities she boasts to her schoolmates. Adolescent idealization and daydreaming thus are satisfied in an emotion-releasing situation.

If a few women are added to the instructional staff of a boys' school, the hero worship usually directed by the boys toward admired men teachers is diverted to the women, especially if the latter are relatively young, attractive, and friendly. The attitude of the boys toward their women teachers may resemble somewhat that of a crush. Similarly, a small minority of men instructors in a girls' school may serve as a stimulator of early heterosexual feelings.

In a coeducational secondary school, staffed by a faculty that includes a relatively even representation of both sexes, crushes and extreme hero worship rarely constitute serious problems of adolescent development. Moreover, when boys and girls are provided many opportunities to participate together in energy-releasing and pleasurable school-sponsored work and recreational projects, these activities serve as excellent mediums for the development of wholesome heterosexual relationships.

It is not unusual for a boy or girl to direct his or her first heterosexually pointed interests toward an older member of the opposite sex. Since a girl matures sexually earlier than a boy of the same chronological age, she seeks the attention of older men. The object of her affection may be a glamorous motion-picture or television star; she collects pictures of him, and may spend many hours in gazing at them while she day-dreams about thrilling situations in which she is the heroine and he is the hero. It is a well-known fact that much of the fan mail received by successful young male entertainers is written by starry-eyed young adolescents.

A girl may develop a strong emotional attachment for an older man such as a close friend of the family. More frequently, however, she tends to lavish her "love" upon a male high school teacher. She may manifest her feelings in various ways: preparing her home assignments meticulously, lingering after class to ask questions or otherwise to focus his attention upon herself, gazing at him dreamily during class periods, becoming shy in his presence, or otherwise paralleling behavior that characterizes crushes on women teachers. One difference is that adoration of an unmarried male teacher may take the form of regarding him as a possible mate when the girl is old enough to marry; if the man is married, the girl may experience deep jealousy of the wife who, in the young adolescent's opinion, is not worthy of her great honor. The situation becomes almost unbearable if the girl meets the woman and is forced to watch the latter's possessive attitude toward her husband.

The young adolescent boy, consciously or unconsciously recognizing the greater maturity of girl schoolmates of his own age, is usually awkward and unsure in their presence and resents their seemingly cruel and superior attitude toward him. He seeks the attention of older women, often an admired young teacher who bolsters his self-esteem by her apparently sympathetic and understanding attitude toward him. He may think of himself as a knight in shining armor, whose life is dedicated to protecting his fair lady from any danger that may beset her. The boy may be shy in her presence or consciously avoid focusing her attention upon himself lest his schoolmates get wrong ideas about her or him. Yet he will fight with any other boy who speaks disparagingly about her or who annoys her in any way.

## Effect of Others on Heterosexual Relationships

Adolescents must be helped to establish the sex role. Each adolescent must be able to internalize his or her sex role. Each must come to feel that he or she is developing the behavior associated with the masculine or the feminine role. This may be influenced by early experiences that may have distorted sexual identity. Anyone's ability to internalize the proper feelings depends on established relationships between the inner feeling and the enactment. For example, if a girl is required to act in a feminine manner when she believes being a girl is debasing she has difficulty in harmonizing her inner feelings, and conflicts often arise. If she is to achieve an adequate sex role she needs to gain emotional strength from her own resources as well as from other persons. She needs to become effectively involved with the activities of other members of her own sex in order to avoid a feeling of "emptiness." She needs to strive for an acceptance of herself by others and by herself.

In an urban culture a boy generally has greater difficulty in constructing his sex role than does the girl. The boy usually wants to meet situations in which he can demonstrate his strength, his courage, and his developing masculinity. In urban life there are limited activities for the growing boy to demonstrate these qualities. He needs to have situations provided in which he can make social contributions, show work responsibilities, and in general prove his worth. Parents, educational leaders, and other citizens share in the responsibility to provide these.

A young and relatively inexperienced teacher of either sex who becomes the object of adoration of adolescents of the same or the opposite sex often finds it difficult to handle the situation in such a way that these early sex-stimulated emotional attachments can be changed to objective, friendly, teacher-pupil relationships. Unless the teacher's approach is tactful and motivated by a sincere interest in the young person involved, there is danger that the latter may experience serious emotional conflict. Strong feelings of resentment toward the adult who apparently has rejected him, combined with loss of self-respect and of needed security in the affection of another, may cause the still-immature boy or girl to seek the satisfaction of his growing sex urge through forms of activity that may be harmful to himself and others.

For most young adolescents the focusing of emotionalized reactions upon an adult is a passing phase of their sexual development during which they are getting ready for normal heterosexual relationships. Hence teachers need not become too concerned about youthful crushes, especially if the school provides opportunities for the boys and girls to engage together in work and recreational activities. Serious problems then arise only in the cases of young people who, for one or another reason, appear to be unable to adjust to sex relationships with persons of the same age and the opposite sex. An adolescent who cannot achieve satisfying heterosexual associations with his peers may continue, even on the college level, to identify himself or herself with a sympathetic instructor. If the adult is unmarried and the age difference is not too great, mutual sex attraction may lead to a temporary romantic attachment or eventual marriage.

If a male married instructor becomes emotionally involved with a girl student who lacks boy admirers among her peers, the man may engage in extramarital sex relations with the girl, divorce his wife to marry her, or extricate himself from the situation with little or no consideration for the serious effects of his rejection of her upon the girl's already mal-adjusted emotional status. Situations of this kind are not limited to college campuses; young girls in the business world often experience similar in-volvements with married male employers or supervisors.

Sooner or later an adolescent's sexual drive impels him to seek the attention of members of the opposite sex who are more nearly his own age. The age at which the so-called "boy-crazy" or "girl-crazy" period is reached varies with individual rate of physical development and differ-ences in stimulus situations. By the time most young people are about 16, their earlier emotionalized interest in older adults is transferred to peer associates of the other sex. For some adolescents the crush or hero-worship stage is of short duration or practically nonexistent. A few young people pass quickly from this period to that of boy-girl attraction. In many instances the transition from one stage to the other represents a gradual process, with some conflict between loyalties.

Some adolescents begin early to become boy-crazy or girl-crazy. In spite of adult disapproval, a young adolescent girl may be so eager to attract male attention to herself that she flaunts her physical charm before every boy she meets. She crudely applies pancake make-up, mascara, vivid lipstick, and fingernail polish. She stands and walks in such a manner as to emphasize her budding breasts or even resorts to the wearing of "fal-sies" to accentuate them. A boy-crazy girl may assume a sophisticated manner and try to impress an older adolescent boy with her worldliness and her willingness to accede to any sex-stimulated behavior that she is able to arouse. Young servicemen are considered by her to be easy prey. Sometimes an immature girl whose sex drive has been overstimu-lated by too much reading and viewing of sex-filled materials with-draws in fright and confusion when a boy, believing that she wants what she seems to desire, starts to engage in heavy petting with her or sug-gests that they have sexual intercourse.

A young boy who early develops strong sexual drives is likely to annoy younger girls, corner them when no one is looking, and then lift up their skirts, attempt to touch their bodies or in other ways try to satisfy his sex urge through contact with little girls. These situations represent manifestations of strong sex urges that are experienced before the young person has learned to control them in a socially acceptable fashion. Re-gardless of habits of emotional control learned during childhood, how-ever, most boys and girls pass through a stage of "puppy love." They seem to be in love with love itself and attach their maturing sexual interest to any member of the opposite sex who is in the immediate environment.

For many young people the beginning of sex-stimulated behavior constitutes no more than a stolen, awkwardly administered kiss, holding hands, or walking with arms around each other. One can observe such behavior in school corridors or on the street, especially during spring. Young romance usually does not focus upon one member of the opposite sex. It represents a kind of trial-and-error process until the "right" one is found. Unhappiness or conflict is experienced either by the boy, or more usually the girl, who has become seriously involved in a love affair and then discovers that the other's apparent attachment represents no more than a fleeting phase in the search for the true love.

## Significant Characteristics of Heterosexual Behavior

Much of the sex experimentation in which some adolescents indulge can be explained in terms of the functional aspects of personal and environmental factors of influence. An adolescent's individual sexual behavior and attitude toward sex may be rooted in (1) the strength of his sex drive, (2) the role of sex in his culture, and (3) the adequacy of his factual knowledge concerning body structure and the functioning of body organs that are operative in the satisfaction of the sex drive.

Since the sex drive probably reaches its height during late adolescence or early adulthood, a developing adolescent needs to gain an adequate and accurate understanding of the psychology and physiology of sex. He should be helped to know and appreciate the biological aspects of sex, the hygiene of sex in his culture, as well as societal attitudes toward sex-stimulated behavior. Cultural differences in attitudes toward sexual maturation were considered in Chapter 2. A description of primary and secondary sex characteristics was included in Chapter 4. At this point attention is directed toward physical and physiological reactions in sex experience. Later we shall discuss the psychology of sex.

### The Physiology of the Sex Function

The sex drive is fundamental to the continuance of the human race. Normal sex activity does not represent one-person performance only, but requires the cooperative efforts of two individuals, one of each sex. Moreover, sex-stimulated behavior involves the whole body; it is not localized in the region of the sex organs. In some of its more general aspects the sexual behavior of the male and the female are relatively similar. Certain specific aspects of the sexual process reflect anatomical and organic differences between the sexes.

Nature has provided for the male's experiencing an orgasm during sexual intercourse. Semen is thereby deposited in the vagina of the female and a male sperm cell is enabled to fertilize the ovum of the female.

Normally the latter also experiences an orgasm or a rhythmic contraction of the walls of the vagina and sometimes of the uterus. The female orgasm varies from complete contraction in both vagina and uterus to no orgasm (*frigidity*). Failure of an orgasm to occur in the female, however, does not interfere with the possibility of conception. An erection (a swelling of the tissues in the sex organ) in the male is essential for sexual intercourse; if erection cannot be achieved by a male, he is considered to be *impotent*. Most women also experience some degree of turgescence.

## Amatory Activity

*Amatory* and *erotic* are terms used to describe love feelings toward, and sexual interest in, a person of the opposite sex. Amatory feelings may manifest themselves solely in attempts to be with and enjoy the company of a member of the opposite sex. Usually, however, the emotional state is accompanied by a strong desire for physical contact with the other person. If conditions are favorable to the arousal of intense excitation, the drive may become so strong that the amatory behavior culminates in sexual intercourse.

The sight of a loved one or the sound of her voice may cause a male to experience erotic thoughts or feelings. In some men characteristic female odors may produce amatory effects; hair coloring and texture or quality of skin may attract others. The female also may "love" a male for his height, strength, hair, voice quality, or any other outstanding physical characteristic. A response to sensory stimuli is not amatory, however, unless it produces sexual love or desire in the person stimulated thereby. Erotic feelings that at first are aroused by physical characteristics may be strengthened or weakened by behavior traits that are discovered later. Sometimes physical attraction may serve as a motivator of marriage but soon lose its holding power, especially if the admired mate displays self-centered, uncooperative, or other undesirable attitudes during the intimate relationships of married life.

## Deviant Sex Behavior

Considerable data already have been gathered about human sexual behavior in the areas of masturbation, homosexuality, nocturnal sex dreams, petting, coitus, and animal contacts. These data have been gathered in a variety of ways including the interview and questionnaire. For example, Kinsey and his coworkers interviewed a limited sample of individuals. In the final analysis, the validity of data on sexual behavior depends on the veracity and the ability of the informants. There seems to be sufficient evidence to conclude that some uniformity of sexual activity occurs within large population groups.

When consideration is given to the general pattern of adolescent sexual development, emphasis usually is placed upon the changes that are likely to occur in a young person's heterosexual activities. Circumstances may interfere with the supposedly normal development of the sex drive in relation to members of the oposite sex. Consequently, other means may be employed by the sexually maturing individual to satisfy his sex-stimulated urges or desires.

As a result of strict childhood rearing or because of self-evaluated personal unattractiveness, an adolescent may tend to avoid association with members of the opposite sex. The fact that an adolescent or young adult is a student in a segregated school or is attached to a one-sex institution also may deny the boy or girl needed companionship with members of the other sex. Then sex tensions are likely to find release in forms of behavior that deviate from heterosexual relationships. The two most common aberrations are masturbation and homosexuality. Each of these sex-stimulated behavior patterns is discussed below.

## Masturbation

Masturbation includes those activities of self-induced sex pleasure in which the genital organs or other parts of the body are stimulated. It represents sexual excitement of the self through the use of the hand or other artificial means. Masturbation is a common practice during adolescence and may be continued throughout adulthood. Investigations have revealed that at some time in life nearly all males and more than half the females of the human species practice self-stimulation.

Masturbation begun in childhood may become an obsessive habit. It is more likely to start at puberty, however, when erotic responses are developing rapidly and an orgasm can be experienced. The frequency of masturbation may decrease in a few years; in some cases it may continue for a long period of time. The effects of this form of sex perversion are not yet fully known.

The frequency of masturbation for the male before the age of 21 runs as high as 99 per cent of the males. Kinsey found that by 20 years of age, about 92 per cent of the males had masturbated. He estimated that fewer than 16 per cent of the males masturbate before the age of 10 years. The time of starting this practice varies with the time of reaching puberty. Boys who reach puberty earlier usually start to masturbate earlier than boys whose puberty is delayed. As males approach maturity, masturbation preoccupies them less and less; yet for some it remains the primary sexual outlet before marriage. Active masturbation is highest during the early teen years among males of low socioeconomic level, and during later adolescence among those of higher social status. However, those males destined to go to college from the low social level masturbate with greater frequency throughout adolescent years than do those who complete their schooling early.

The number of females who masturbate during the teen years is considerably smaller than that of males. This holds for the number of females who masturbate prior to puberty as well as for those who masturbate at a later period of life. It is estimated that from 30 to 60 per cent of the females masturbate sometime during their teen years. However, women who expect to go to college are more likely to masturbate during their late teens than are those females who complete their formal education at an earlier age. According to William R. Reevy:

In the late teens, especially, girls from the lower social levels and educational backgrounds turn to coitus and away from masturbation as a type of sexual response. Those who will go to college, compared to those who accept other educational levels and are from lower social backgrounds, consider masturbation more desirable than coitus. Consequently, for them, masturbation becomes a major source of sexual stimulation. Particularly is this trend true up to the age of 15 (Kinsey, 1953), when as much as 90 per cent of the total release to orgasm is through masturbation (it is approximately 50 per cent for the grade-school level at this age). This trend for the college-destined girl continues through to maturity for the single girl, and at almost any age or year she achieves more of her outlet in orgasm from masturbation than those girls of lower social level and educational promise. By late adolescence girls of all social levels become more accepting of coitus. However, its incidence is still relatively low among girls of all social levels, even in late adolescence.

As is the case with boys, petting and coitus are the two major activities that tend to displace masturbation, when both accumulative and active incidence are considered. At practically all ages, not only are the incidence and frequency of masturbation for females during adolescence much less than for males, but it is a much more sporadic activity. Among girls greater individual differences in frequency exist and the range of variation is much greater. Some girls report a frequency of masturbation as little as once or twice a year, while others may masturbate as many as ten to twenty times a week. The modal frequency is probably less than once a month.

For all adolescents adherence to a strict religion (devoutness) has a restraining effect upon masturbation, affecting total incidence, active incidence, and frequency. Its restraining effect, in general, appears to be greater upon girls than boys.

The techniques of masturbation, of course, vary somewhat as to sex. But the techniques employed by adolescents are, in the main, no different from those employed by adults. Genital manipulation by hand is the most frequent technique employed by both sexes. Vaginal insertions are sometimes employed by girls. Thigh pressure is a little less frequently used by girls than vaginal insertions. Boys, however, seem to be almost unaware of this technique as a means of inducing orgasm, although it is effective in the male sex also. A few girls rub their vaginal areas against objects such as pillows, bedclothes, covers, edges of chairs, and the like. Similar techniques are infrequently used by boys, who rub their genital organ against bedclothes, pillows, and the inside of mouths of bottles and other holes.[1]

## Premarital Sexual Activity

Sex codes vary throughout the world. In early American society sex purity as a highly desired goal of achievement was taken for granted. Recently, however, there are evidences of considerable deviation from this code of behavior. Although the ideal of chastity still remains as part of our culture, many teen-agers seem either to be indifferent to it or to disregard it almost completely. Definite changes in adolescent sex behavior are extant. For a variety of reasons, sex-stimulated behavior is becoming more active among adolescents and young adults of both sexes.

Since the Kinsey study, attitudes toward premarital coitus, especially among females, have changed. Now the attitudes of married women toward premarital intimacy are of interest. In a recent study of 171 married women it was found that 73 had had premarital coitus with their spouses. The social class status of these 171 women was as follows: lower class, 13.5 per cent; middle class, 45 per cent; and upper class, 41.5 per cent. The incidence of these sexual intimacies was reported by Eugene J. Kanin. He found that:

The upper-middle class women reported the smallest incidence of premarital coitus, 31.0 per cent; the middle class female came next with 41.6 per cent, and the highest incidence was reported by the lower class female, 82.5 per cent. The social status of the male was not in itself significantly associated with any type of premarital sex behavior.[2]

In a study of mother and daughter attitudes to premarital sexual behavior Bell and Buerkle[3] found that there were significant differences

[1] William R. Reevy, "Adolescent Sexuality," from *The Encyclopedia of Sexual Behavior,* by A. Abarbanel and A. Ellis, copyright © 1961 by Hawthorne Books, Inc., 70 Fifth Avenue, New York 11, N.Y.

[2] Eugene J. Kanin, "Premarital Sex Adjustments, Social Class and Associated Behaviors," *Marriage and Family Living,* pp. 258–259, August, 1960.

[3] Robert R. Bell and Jack V. Buerkle, "Mother and Daughter Attitudes to Premarital Sexual Behavior," *Marriage and Family Living,* pp. 390–392, November, 1961.

in such matters as remaining a virgin until marriage. Nearly 90 per cent of the mothers believed it to be "very wrong" to have coitus prior to marriage, as compared with 55 per cent of the daughters (see Table 23).

*Table 23.* Relative Opinions of Mothers and Daughters about Premarital Coitus (In per cents)

| | RELATIVE OPINIONS | | | | | |
| | VERY WRONG | | GENERALLY WRONG | | RIGHT IN MANY SITUATIONS | |
| QUESTIONS | MOTHERS | DAUGH-TERS | MOTHERS | DAUGH-TERS | MOTHERS | DAUGH-TERS |
|---|---|---|---|---|---|---|
| Do you think sexual intercourse before marriage is . . . ? | 88 | 55 | 12 | 34 | 0 | 13 |
| Do you think sexual intercourse during engagement is . . . ? | 83 | 35 | 15 | 48 | 2 | 17 |

In their conclusions Bell and Buerkle say:

*Conclusions.* The responses of the mothers and daughters lead to the following probabilities:

1. The attitudes of daughters toward the importance of premarital virginity may be like those of their mothers until they have spent some time in college and have reached their adult years.

2. Around age 20 there emerges sharp differences between mothers and daughters in regard to premarital sexual attitudes. Behavioral studies indicate that it is at this point that sexual activity is greatly intensified. Perhaps because it is at this age that college girls are entering engagement. A suggested pattern is that the college girl of 20 or 21 years of age, in her junior or senior year and engaged, has a strong "liberal" pattern toward premarital sexual behavior and attitudes.

3. The responses of the college educated mothers raise some interesting questions. The "liberality" of the college girl as to premarital sexual behavior and attitudes may be a temporary phenomenon. It is possible that later in her life the daughter may be as "conservative" as her mother, when her attitudinal rationales are not related to herself, but to her own daughter. It is therefore possible that the "sexual emancipation" of the college girl exists only for a short period of time, centering around her own engagement.

4. The findings in this study indicate that premarital sexual behavior provides one of the greatest potential areas of mother-daughter conflict. Because this is such an emotionally laden area of human behavior the differences in orientation take on great

| | |
|---|---|
| intensity. This may be even more upsetting to those mothers | who remember their own "liberality" as coeds.[4] |

The sexual behavior of today's adolescents seems to function on a group-code basis. Young people appear to be enjoying an increasing amount of freedom in their social activities. This freedom from adult supervision of teen-age behavior is setting the stage for adolescents to establish their own standards of what should or should not be done in given social situations. Traditional mores still prescribe that chastity is the ideal; yet more and more it is becoming the responsibility of youth to interpret and apply this ideal. To have the privilege to make their own decisions concerning sexual behavior in terms of the accepted mores of the majority of their elders constitutes a challenging opportunity for adolescent decision making. Submission to rigid adult behavior control may arouse inner resentment or outwardly displayed rebellion. Personal freedom in behavior control is likely to be accompanied by the arousal of many problems and conflict situations, however.

## Homosexuality

Homosexuality is sexual behavior in which the cooperation of another person of the same sex is needed. The findings of Kinsey and his associates would seem to indicate that homosexual activity is more common than was believed. As a result of his investigations, Kinsey found that, contrary to popular opinion, homosexual experiences are no more frequent among females than among males.

Kinsey also concluded that there seems to be some relationship between participation in homosexual activities and the age at which individuals develop sexual maturity. He says:

Homosexual activities occur in a much higher percentage of the males who became adolescent at an early age; and in a definitely smaller percentage of those who became adolescent at later ages. For instance, at the college level, during early adolescence about 28 per cent of the early-adolescent boys are involved, and only 14 per cent of the boys who were late in becoming adolescent. This difference is narrowed in successive age periods, but the boys who became adolescent first are more often involved even ten and fifteen years later. It is to be recalled that these early-adolescent boys are the same ones who have the highest incidences and frequencies in masturbation and in heterosexual contacts. It is the group which possesses on the whole the greatest sex drive, both in early adolescence and throughout most of the subsequent periods of their lives.[5]

[4] *Ibid.*, p. 392.
[5] A. C. Kinsey et al., *Sexual Behavior in the Human Male*, W. B. Saunders Company, Philadelphia, 1948, p. 630.

In his discussion of the dynamics of homosexuality Robert J. Campbell, M.D., says:

Accidental homosexuality (faute de mieux—for lack of anything better), that kind of homosexuality seen in prisons and on ships when women are not available, indicates that most males are probably capable of a homosexual object choice. But the true homosexual must exclude women as his object choice for some other reason. Factors predisposing to homosexuality include fixation at pregenital (and especially anal) levels, fear of castration, intense oedipal attachment to the mother, narcissism and narcissistic object choice, and readiness to substitute identification for object relationships as is seen in identification with sibling rivals with secondary overcompensatory love for them. The sight of the female genitalia provokes castration anxiety by providing concrete evidence that castration is a reality and, through association with old oral anxieties, by perception of the genitalia as a castrating instrument. Such castration anxiety favors retirement from rivalry with the father by a denial and renunciation of all women.[6]

Homosexuality is a social problem to the extent that other individuals are involved. Since an adolescent often is approached by a homosexual adult, a young person sometimes becomes a victim of this practice because of the chance factor of meeting with an experienced homosexual. If parents and other adults interested in adolescent welfare discover that a young person is being inducted into homosexual practices, they should attempt to remove him from the stimulus situation in order to prevent any repetition of such experiences and to help him forget them. Unless this is done, one or a few forced participations in homosexuality may earn for him social rejection because of his seeming willingness to engage in abnormal sexual behavior. The innocent victim of societal disapproval then may be stimulated by his felt need for human interrelationships and group approval to seek the company of homosexuals and find a place for himself among them by engaging with them in homosexual practices. However, an occasional homosexual act might better be minimized, especially if it occurs in early or middle adolescence.

## Emotional Concomitants of Boy-Girl Relationships

For a boy and girl to engage in social activities as an unchaperoned twosome now begins as early as the seventh grade and sometimes continues throughout the secondary school years. A girl recently reported that

[6] Robert J. Campbell, "Masturbation and Homosexuality," in William C. Bier, S.J. (ed.), *The Adolescent: His Search for Understanding*, Fordham University Press, New York, 1963.

she went "steady" from the age of 12 to 15, after which she broke off her close association with the boy, and started to go out with different boys. Such boy-girl relationships, either pairing or shopping-around approaches, tend to stimulate highly emotionalized behavior. The extent of resulting stresses and strains will be conditioned by the standards of conduct set for the adolescent by his family, the school, and other socializing agencies in his environment, and by the personal and social values that are respected by his peer group.

Parents are becoming increasingly concerned about the possible effects upon their children of the modern custom of "pair dating" at an early age. A growing practice in adolescent social gatherings is for a boy to dance only with his date. The two cannot avoid the emotional effect of close body contact during dancing, combined with the stimulation of romantic dance music. Developed feelings of intimacy may lead to participation in sex-stimulated activities off the dance floor. The pair relationship then may become a struggle to determine what code of behavior shall be the controlling factor of their conduct. Every new date involves elements of speculation on the part of each concerning the code of behavior to which the other will adhere. In small communities the individual standards of each adolescent become generally known; hence speculation is less common than in larger urban areas in which young people are more likely to go on "blind dates" or pair off with mere acquaintances.

The fact that preadolescents are involved in boy-girl relationships is clearly shown in a recent study of needs and interests of more than 1,000 boys, ages 11, 12, and 13, who are members of Boys' Club of America.[7] In this countrywide sample 32 per cent of the members said that they "go steady" with a girl; 61 per cent either take girls to parties or attend parties at which girls are present; 40 per cent accompany girls to the movies; and 44 per cent either take girls to dances or attend dances as "stags."

In a study of the dating problems of 288 teen-age boys and 286 teen-age girls, Landis and his coworkers[8] discovered some of the important issues or problems that arise between parents and high school students. Among his findings were: (1) more girls than boys asked parents' permission for the first date; (2) about half the parents required that both boys and girls be home by 10 P.M. but permitted them to stay up until midnight; (3) only a few parents imposed no time limits; (4) the number of dates permitted per week was limited usually to two, with

[7] *Needs and Interests Study of 11–12–13-Year-Old Boys' Club Members,* Boys' Club of America, New York, 1963, p. 60.

[8] Paul H. Landis, "Research on Teen-Age Dating," *Marriage and Family Living,* pp. 266–267, August, 1960.

boys given more freedom than girls in this matter; (5) parents reserved the right to veto the date of the girl but seldom of the boy; (6) most parents permitted either single or double dates; (7) parents showed concern about the serving of liquor and the places the young people attended; (8) girls discussed their dates more freely with parents than did boys; (9) the young people expressed their preference for dating as compared with being with members of their own sex or with members of their family.

## Mate Selection and Courtship Behavior

With few exceptions, adolescents look forward to marriage and the raising of a family. As was pointed out in Chapter 2, early and parent-arranged marriage was an accepted custom among primitive people. In our present society responsibility for mate selection, courtship behavior, and time of marriage is assumed by the young people themselves, with little or no interference from parents or other adults. Various elements inherent in modern living exercise a potent effect upon youthful attitudes and behavior toward mate selection and marriage. Adolescent attitudes toward premarital sex relations, boys' participation in military service, girls' career interests, or extended educational requirements for entrance into certain occupational fields can become the basic causes of much youthful confusion or conflict.

### Attitudes toward Sex Relations

The ideal of chastity continues to constitute the cultural standard according to which our unmarried young people are expected to regulate their sexual behavior. Although deviation from this standard on the part of a member of either sex is regarded by society as a form of youthful delinquency, the behavior of a male sex delinquent often is condoned, but that of a female delinquent usually receives severe social disapproval. Many adults still believe that the sex drive is much stronger in the male than in the female. In spite of the great freedom in their social activities that young people now are permitted, it is taken for granted by many adults that a "good" girl has sufficient emotional stability to exercise control over a boy's need to release sex tensions stimulated by his nearness to the girl in an unchaperoned situation.

Contrary to popular misconceptions concerning the sex urge, the findings of scientific investigations seem to indicate that the sex drive is as strong in the human female as in the male. The fact that premarital sexual intercourse may result in the girl's becoming pregnant is responsible for her apparent resistance to participation in the climactic sex act. So long as society continues to reject the illegitimate child, a girl must inhibit her natural sex desires or experience fear or anxiety in her sexual relationships. Hence the adolescent girl, more than the boy, is impelled to maintain the moral code by being selective in her dating. Thereby she can avoid situations which may be embarrassing if she resists a boy's importunities and her own desires, or may lead to tragic consequences if she submits.

Adolescent girls and young women are beginning to resent the so-called "double standard" of morals that permits the male to indulge at will in uncontrolled sexual behavior but bans promiscuity on the part of the female. Although their demands for a single standard would seem to imply that both sexes should develop a greater adherence to the ideal of chastity, available data present evidence to the effect that some girls are lowering their moral standards to the level of the male code.

Young people's attitudes toward heterosexual relations are potent factors in mate selection. Many young men and women still tend to choose a mate in terms of values, such as similarity of interests, apparent compatibility, and respect for and admiration of personal qualities, as well as sexual attraction. The present increase in hasty mate selection and marriage can be explained, in part at least, as resulting from the impact upon immature adolescents and thoughtless young adults of the many sex-stimulating situations and conditions that characterize modern living. Some of the significant factors of influence are:

1. Increased freedom of opportunities for the two sexes to participate in social activities of their own choosing without adult chaperonage.

2. Increased participation by adolescents and young adults in cocktail parties and similar social activities.

3. Night automobile drives by twosomes, and stops on deserted roads.

4. Tacitly accepted, though openly disapproved, participation by "respectable" girls in premarital heterosexual experimentation.

5. Knowledge that the broken hymen does not necessarily represent loss of virginity.

6. Glamorous and detailed newspaper, radio, and television reports of the love life of national celebrities; unrealistic love stories in some of the popular magazines; sex-pointed novels and motion pictures; sexually arousing music, representative art and dancing, and similar exciting mediums of entertainment.

7. Decrease of religious influence in the home.

8. Apparently easy procural of a divorce and the high divorce rate. (The reply of a newly engaged college student to a question concerning

her attitude toward her fiancé: "Think it will work out all right; if not, there are always divorce courts.")

9. Knowledge about, and availability of, contraceptives.

10. Apparent ease of setting up a home by means of installment-plan buying.

11. Examples of lack of sexual control among older adults.

12. Existing confused state of world conditions and possible outbreak of war.

## Toll of Teen-age Marriages

Of the more than 1.7 million marriages that took place in the United States in 1962, almost 500,000 involved individuals in their teen years. About 40 per cent of the females who married and 13 per cent of the males were teen-agers. These figures in and of themselves need not be alarming, yet when it is known that the divorce rate of these brides under 20 years of age is three times the national average there is need to give thought to the desirability of early marriage for many individuals. When two out of five teen-age marriages end in divorce it becomes a matter of public concern. Contributing to this condition are many and varied factors, among them immaturity, lack of full independence of behavior, lack of economic stability, and after a brief period, strong desire not to be tied down. Fortunately some of these teen-age marriages are happy and some are hopeful. Tragedy strikes in those cases in which there is anger, despair, or divorce.

## Factors (Other than Sex)
## of Mate Selection and Marriage

Although the modern youth is permitted an amount of freedom in mate selection that formerly was almost unknown, he still is limited in his choice of mate and subsequent marriage by factors outside himself and by his own interests and attitudes. The state sets the minimum age at which young people can marry without parental consent, may demand that certain health conditions be met, and establishes a waiting period between the issuance of a marriage license and the date of the marriage. Some parents attempt to control the mate selection and marriage of their children, but parents have no legal rights in this respect except in the case of a young person who is under marriageable age as set by state law.

*Extended Education.* Another possible limitation upon mate selection and marriage for some young people is the trend toward extended educational preparation for entrance into some professions, especially medicine, law, engineering, and teaching on higher school levels. It is during this training period that the sex urge is likely to be at its peak. To be denied lawful, marital sexual intercourse places a tremendous emotional strain upon a sexually mature young man. Repression of the urge may interfere seriously with study achievement; illicit sex relations may induce feelings of guilt or result in venereal infection. Recognizing the difficulties inherent in such situations, society is encouraging early marriage among this group of young people. Educational institutions welcome married students because of the likelihood that release of sex tensions will encourage serious study.

The married college student may experience financial difficulties, however, unless he is subsidized by his parents, the college, or a Federal, social, or professional agency. In some cases the young wife engages in gainful employment while her husband is attending an institution of higher learning. This situation may give rise to emotional difficulties. The young husband may feel humiliated by the fact that his wife is supporting him, even though it is a temporary situation. The need for delayed childbearing may give rise to emotional conflict and nonsatisfying sexual relations.

*Girls' Career Interests.* Formerly, the educational opportunities that were available to girls were aimed at preparation for wifehood and motherhood. Today adolescent girls are becoming increasingly interested in preparing themselves for participation in one or another form of occupational activity. Many girls regard their vocational training merely as preparation for a job which they expect to hold only temporarily until they marry, and to which they may return later if a financial emergency arises.

An adolescent girl may become so interested in a particular occupational field, however, that she decides to prepare for it as a career. While she is completing her education, or after she has earned success in the field, she "falls in love" and wants to marry her chosen mate. There then arises a conflict situation, especially if the young man is opposed to her continuing to work and wants to have a family. Although a compromise may be reached in that he agree to her working until a child is expected, her career interest may interfere with the development of desirable marital and family adjustment. The girl who renounces marriage for her career also is likely to experience emotional and sexual conflict. She may become so engrossed in her work that she denies herself needed social and recreational emotional outlets, or else she may attempt to release sexual tensions through more or less temporary "love affairs" with unmarried or married business or professional associates.

*Courtship Behavior.* In spite of a belief to the contrary, young people are marrying at a younger age today than at any time, on the average, since 1890, when the median age for men at the time of marriage was 26.3 years. By 1950 it had dropped to 22.8; it is estimated that it has now fallen to approximately 22. The median age of marriage for girls in 1890 was 22.0; in 1950 it was 20.

Early marriage has a definite effect upon the courtship period. The term *courtship* can be regarded either as including all the sex-stimulated behavior that is characteristic of the young person who is passing through the process of selecting a mate, or as the period that elapses between a couple's decision and the wedding date. Interpreted either way, the length of the courtship is lessened when young people marry in their early twenties.

Successful adjustment to the marital state usually is achieved with relative ease by a man and woman who knew each other for a sufficiently long period before marriage, so that each could discover and be ready to accept the other's weaknesses and peculiar habits and mannerisms. In "quick" mate selection and hasty marriage good marital adjustments may come slowly or not at all. Hence unless the young husband and wife were adolescent schoolmates or neighbors, they may experience problems of marital adjustment as they attempt to become acquainted with each other. Youth is adaptable, however. If each of the young pair brings to the marriage habitual control of the emotions and attitudes of cooperation, satisfactory interpersonal relationships will soon be achieved.

Marital adjustment also is related closely to courtship experiences. Older adults sometimes wax sentimental over young lovers. Holding hands, embracing, kissing, and in other ways giving evidence of complete engrossment with each other represent accepted forms of courtship behavior. Interested adults, as well as the young people themselves, do not always appreciate the extent to which these physical contacts may induce sexual overstimulation in one or both of the pair to the point of causing them to attempt to release sexual tensions through copulation. Participation in such behavior may lead to the arousal of guilt feelings, repulsion, or fear of pregnancy or sexual inadequacy.

During a long period of courtship the two individuals are likely to experience conflict between the ideal of chastity and their strong urge toward sexual gratification. A short courtship period affords a young couple greater opportunity to exercise emotional control and sexual restraint. Activities associated with preparation for an early marriage and planning for their future together can help keep the young couple relatively free from extreme sexual involvement.

The fact that modern young people are permitted considerable freedom in the selection of a mate has caused many boys and girls to give serious attention to the constituent factors of success in the marriage relationship. They attend lectures and read books in preparation for marriage, and often seek counsel from older married adults.

From the findings of studies in this area of human relationships young people discover that emphasis usually is placed upon items such as childhood experiences, present attachment to parents, parents' attitudes toward each other and toward their children; personal qualities, including degree of emotional control, cooperativeness, interest in children, and adaptability; religious affiliation; socioeconomic and educational status; national or cultural background; age at time of marriage; and an understanding of the sexual aspects of marriage.

Some young men and women are alert to the significance of these factors as they may apply to themselves. They recognize the fact that no one of the items is all-important, but they are willing to discuss these matters frankly and freely during the courtship period and come to some agreement concerning compromises that may need to be made by each if they are to achieve a successful marriage relationship.

There are other young people who plunge into marriage with little or no concern about the adjustments that may be necessary after the glamour and thrill of the honeymoon have passed. The boy and girl honestly may believe that the sexual attraction which brought them together and colored their courtship behavior will continue its hold upon them throughout their married life.

Although too great emphasis upon physical attraction as the primary basis of mate selection and marriage is to be deplored, its importance as a factor of adjustment cannot be disregarded. Even though the mates have many interests in common, a marriage in which there is lack of sexual compatibility between husband and wife is likely to fail. Unless religious ideals or moral scruples prevent it, one or both will be strongly impelled to gain sexual satisfaction through extramarital sex relations. Some psychologists and other writers in the field, therefore, tend to place considerable stress upon a couple's being certain that they are well mated sexually. Consequently, some young people are motivated thereby to engage in sexual experimentation during the courtship period lest they discover too late that the woman is frigid or the man impotent.

The results of premarital experimental intecourse rarely are successful. In spite of the use of contraceptives or other preventive measures, the woman may experience fear of pregnancy. Because of situationally unfavorable circumstances, copulation may bring no satisfactory release of sexual tensions. Moreover, even though immediate gratifications are achieved, the experiences may become so habituated that, with marriage, the couple will be denied the normal thrill that accompanies discovering one another at the beginning of a supposedly permanent life relationship.

In addition, it is possible that the primitive male urge to force a resisting female to submit to his sexual desires is not completely lacking in civilized man. Hence continuous premarital sexual activities with his fiancée may lessen her sexual attractiveness to the extent that the man loses interest in the contemplated marriage. He may have doubts concerning her suitability as a mate; he may come to believe that she is potentially promiscuous; or he may find himself attracted by another girl who stirs him to want to possess her rather than his fiancée.

A woman is sensitive to a man's reactions to her. Hence the engaged girl may recognize the fact that "her man's interest in her is waning." Although her sexual experiences with him may have strengthened her love for him, she is torn between her desire to hold him and her feeling that he has become apathetic toward her. Still more conflict-arousing is the situation of a girl who in good faith submits to premarital sexual intercourse as a preparation for marriage and who then discovers that the man has no marital intentions. On this point Bowman makes the following observations:

*A couple who start with the idea that their sexual relationship will bind them closer to each other may find that their experience serves as a means of separating them.* If one or both regret the episode or become ashamed, they may lose respect for each other and build up a barrier between themselves, even though they are engaged.

*The relationship is often one-sided because the boy seeks only his own satisfaction, with no thought for the girl or her feelings.* She may be left emotionally stirred up but frustrated, or she may be left with the attitude that sex is masculine only. For her it is all give and for him all take. This depersonalizes a relationship that should be highly personalized. The girl, instead of being wanted for all her personal qualities, is wanted only because she is female. Such a relationship, too, affords one of the privileges of marriage without entailing its responsibilities. Under such circumstances the boy may grow to think of marriage as a trap, a price for privilege. *There is often little opportunity* for adequate preparation on the part of the girl. As we shall see in a later chapter, this is a *sine qua non* of a satisfying relationship.

*The relationship may mean more to the girl than it does to the boy.* She may yield to him because she loves him, while he is interested only in physical satisfaction and has no wish to fall in love or to marry her. If such be the case, he may drop her when his appetite has become satiated or when he discovers that she is in love with him. If the relationship does mean more to the girl than to the boy, even though the experience does not cause the boy to lose interest in her, she may be deeply disappointed because it does not increase his interest. She assumes that it will make him care for her more, and he does not change.

*Sometimes a woman focuses her life around the man with whom she first has intercourse.* The fact that with him she passes a milepost in her life causes her to develop a strong attachment for him. This attachment may be accentuated if she feels that, being no longer virgin, she would not be worthy of another man. If the man for whom she develops the attachment happens to be a loving husband, this attachment contributes toward happy marriage. If, however, he is a man she would not want as her husband or a man with whom she could not be happy in marriage, her attachment may distort her whole future.

*A girl who yields to gain popularity, or to do a man a favor, destroys the mutuality of the relationship and reemphasizes in her own think-ing the traditionally accepted but spurious belief that sexual desire is a masculine prerogative.* Eventually, if we are to found our attitude toward sex on facts instead of fables, we must get over the notion that women are neuter, that intercourse is something that men demand and to which women reluctantly submit. The girl who submits voluntarily but reluctantly, in order to become popular or to get dates, commercializes the relationship and is in a class with any woman who yields to masculine impulses for economic return.[9]

Some sociologists report with pride that commercialized prostitution is decreasing. This decrease probably can be explained by the increasing number of immature young girls who are sexually ignorant but who are so stirred emotionally by environmental sex elements that they easily are persuaded to have coitus with male associates. Existing overconcern with sexual gratification seems to be a cause of the prevalence in our society of disturbing conditions such as adolescent delinquency, divorce, venereal disease, and mental illness. Any one of these conditions constitutes a tremendous challenge to parents, educators, and civic leaders. Problems associated with juvenile delinquency are discussed in Chapter 12; some basic aspects of mental illness are included in Chapter 11; a brief consideration of venereal disease is presented below.

## Venereal Disease as an Individual and Social Problem

Although much headway has been made in developing controls of venereal disease, it continues to be a dangerous accompaniment of promiscuity.

### Active Venereal Diseases

Diseases that usually are introduced into the body through the genital organs by means of sexual contact are referred to as venereal diseases. They are extremely contagious and harmful. Since two persons are involved in spreading them, they are often called the *social diseases*.

[9] Henry A. Bowman, *Marriage for Moderns*, 4th ed., McGraw-Hill Book Company, New York, 1960, pp. 169–170. Reprinted by permission.

The two most prevalent venereal diseases are *syphilis* and *gonorrhea*. After infection the syphilis germs (*Treponema pallidium*) multiply rapidly and soon make their way into the blood stream and thereby distribute themselves throughout the body. During the first stage a pimple may be observed at the point of infection but may disappear within a short time. The damage to the individual continues, however. During the second stage, the devastating effect of the disease upon the body is manifested in the form of severe impairment of many vital organs. The disease is contagious during its first two stages.

Gonorrhea is more widespread than syphilis and is caused by a paired germ (gonococcus). This disease, localized in the region of the genital organs, does not spread its influence to other parts of the body. Severe damage, however, may be done to the organs of the reproductive system, sometimes causing blindness in newborn children of infected mothers, and sterility, especially in the female.

As a result of present-day scientific knowledge, recovery from either syphilis or gonorrhea can be achieved easily if the disease is discovered early and treatment started immediately. In spite of this fact, the actual reduction of the incidence of the disease is small, caused partly by the fact that there is an increase in sexual promiscuity. It is fortunate that under most circumstances a person is unlikely to acquire syphilis from ordinary contacts, since the germ does not live long outside the body. Self-protection, as well as protection of others from a venereal disease, is facilitated if an individual who suspects that he has been exposed to possible infection goes at once to a competent physician for diagnosis and treatment.

The following salient facts about syphilis and gonorrhea should be known by all young people as well as adults:

SYPHILIS

Caused by a spiral germ called the spirochete *treponema pallidium*.

Primary sore, secondary symptoms, latent period and late manifestations. (No detailed symptomatology.)

Treatment and cure by standard and new measures; dangers of quackery and self-medication.

Transmission by sexual and nonsexual methods.

Prostitutes and other sexually promiscuous persons as sources of infection.

Symptoms often not readily detected; possibility of infection by seemingly healthy person.

Physician should be consulted if individual thinks there is any likelihood of infection.

Effectiveness of continence; limited effectiveness of mechanical and chemical prophylaxis and personal hygiene as preventive means.

GONORRHEA

Caused by a spherical germ called gonococcus.

Genital and non-genital manifestations of the disease.

*Table 24.* Infectious Venereal Disease by Diagnosis and Age

| CALENDAR YEARS | 0–9 YEARS | | 10–14 YEARS | | 15–19 YEARS | | 20–24 YEARS | | 0–19 YEARS | | 0–24 YEARS | |
|---|---|---|---|---|---|---|---|---|---|---|---|---|
| | P & S | G | P & S | G | P & S | G | P & S | G | P & S | G | P & S | G |
| 1956 | 11 | 1,222 | 75 | 2,425 | 1,093 | 44,264 | 1,778 | 74,755 | 1,179 | 47,911 | 2,957 | 122,666 |
| 1957 | 33 | 1,628 | 80 | 2,363 | 1,192 | 43,705 | 1,857 | 70,777 | 1,305 | 47,696 | 3,162 | 118,473 |
| 1958 | 23 | 1,164 | 90 | 2,706 | 1,228 | 48,723 | 2,005 | 76,964 | 1,341 | 52,593 | 3,346 | 129,557 |
| 1959 | 39 | 1,325 | 90 | 2,601 | 1,620 | 50,088 | 2,699 | 80,801 | 1,749 | 54,014 | 4,448 | 134,815 |
| 1960 | 20 | 1,619 | 139 | 3,261 | 2,577 | 53,649 | 4,691 | 87,823 | 2,736 | 58,529 | 7,427 | 146,352 |
| 1961 | 35 | 1,615 | 210 | 2,567 | 3,215 | 52,131 | 5,575 | 90,686 | 3,460 | 56,313 | 9,035 | 146,999 |

P & S—primary and secondary syphilis.
G—gonorrhea.

SOURCE: Association of State and Territorial Health Officers, American Venereal Disease Association, and American Social Health Association, *Today's VD Control Problem*, American Social Health Association, New York, 1963, p. 63.

Modern use of the antibiotics (penicillin, aureomycin) to effect cure; dangers of quackery and self-medication.
Sexual and (rare) non-sexual transmission.
Prostitutes and other sexually promiscuous persons as sources of infection.
Effectiveness of continence; limited effectiveness of mechanical and chemical prophylaxis and personal hygiene as preventive means.[10]

## Attitudes toward Social Diseases

The incidence of venereal disease has been high throughout the ages. In the past the disease was so prevalent in some cultures that it was accepted as an inevitable concomitant of sexual intercourse; in other societies an infected person became a social outcast, unworthy of medical care. In our culture vigorous campaigns are being waged to prevent the spread of venereal disease and to cure those who are infected.

Venereal disease is important both to the individual and to the society in which it flourishes. The new sex freedom practiced today, together with the ease of mobility from one place to another, makes it difficult to isolate either syphilis or gonorrhea in communities in which infections occur. Authorities are trying to locate the various contacts of the syphilitic and treat each of them with known remedies. Unfortunately, in spite of known drugs that help cure both syphilis and gonorrhea, both are increasing. The data in Table 24 indicate that the incidence of syphilis and of gonorrhea is increasing in spite of efforts to hold it in check.

A study of the incidence of early syphilis for various countries has changed considerably during the decade 1950–1960. Figure 31 shows a downward trend for the population over 15 years of age from 1950 until about 1957, when the trend was reversed and has continued upward ever since. In light of known cures for syphilis this is an alarming fact. The spread of these germs is important to everyone since they are destroyers. For example, syphilis may cause blindness, paralysis, insanity, or death.

### Questions and Problems for Discussion

1. Explain why both boys and girls during their adolescence should understand the structure and function of human sex organs.
2. Discuss ways in which behavior associated with sex of boys can be

[10] E. E. Sweeney and R. E. Dickerson (eds.), *Preinduction Health and Human Relations,* American Social Health Association, New York, 1953, pp. 137–138. Reprinted with the permission of the American Social Health Association, New York, from *Preinduction Health and Human Relations,* copyright 1953, by the American Social Health Association.

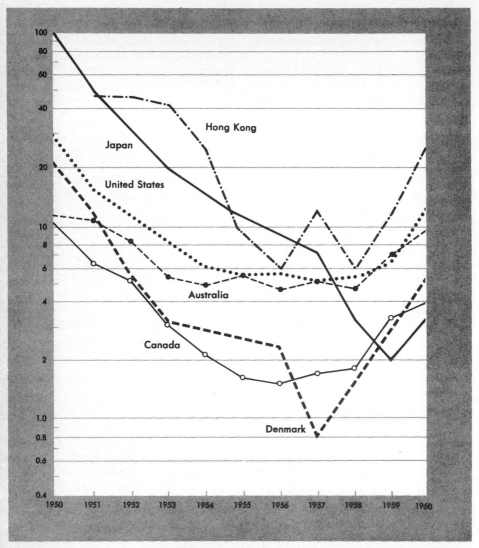

*Figure 31.* Early syphilis, 1950–1960, in selected countries in the Americas, Western Pacific, and Europe (rates per 100,000 adult population over 15 years of age). (From Association of State and Territorial Health Officers, American Venereal Disease Association, and American Social Health Association, *Today's VD Control Problem,* American Social Health Association, New York, 1963, p. 63.)

explained to girls; ways in which behavior associated with sex of girls can be explained to boys. What benefits can accrue to each if this is well done?

3. Consider such sex practices as masturbation, homosexuality, and pre-

marital sexual intercourse. Evaluate their effect (a) on the individual who practices them and (b) on the society in which they occur.

4. Explain why syphilis and gonorrhea are sometimes called "social diseases." What can be done to guard against their spread?

5. What instruction in matters of sex should individuals be given to prepare them for the fulfillment of the marriage function?

6. *Special Exercises:*

   a. Inform yourself on earlier procedures in mate selection. Then compare them with present-day practices. Do this for individuals in at least three countries. Discuss the advantages and disadvantages of each.

   b. If you have had training in sex education and are a male student, talk to two prepubescent boys about the physical changes taking place within them; if a female student, explain to two prepubescent girls the significance of menstruation.

   c. Visit a marriage clinic to discover what is being done to help young people understand and meet problems during marriage. Report your findings.

## Selected References

Baruch, D. W.: *New Ways in Sex Education,* McGraw-Hill Book Company, New York, 1959.

Bowman, Henry A.: *Marriage for Moderns,* 4th ed., McGraw-Hill Book Company, New York, 1960.

Brown, F., and R. T. Kempton: *Sex Questions and Answers,* McGraw-Hill Book Company, New York, 1950.

Caprio, F. S.: *The Power of Sex,* The Citadel Press, New York, 1962.

Christensen, H. T.: *Marriage Analysis—Foundations for Successful Family Life,* 2d ed., The Ronald Press Company, New York, 1958.

Crow, Lester D., and Alice Crow: *Sex Education for the Growing Family,* The Christopher Publishing Company, Boston, 1959.

Davis, M.: *Sex and the Adolescent,* The Dial Press, Inc., New York, 1958.

Duvall, E. M.: *Love and the Facts of Life,* Association Press, New York, 1963.

Havighurst, R. J., and Hilda Taba: *Adolescent Character and Personality,* John Wiley & Sons, Inc., New York, 1949.

Kinsey, A. C., et al.: *Sexual Behavior in the Human Male,* W. B. Saunders Company, Philadelphia, 1948.

Kinsey, A. C., et al.: *Sexual Behavior in the Human Female,* W. B. Saunders Company, Philadelphia, 1953.

Kelly, G. A.: *The Catholic Youth's Guide to Life and Love,* Random House, Inc., New York, 1960.

Landis, Paul H.: *Your Marriage and Family Living,* 2d ed., McGraw-Hill Book Company, New York, 1954.

O'Brien, J. A.: *Sex-character Education,* The Macmillan Company, New York, 1952.

Olsen, H.: *Sexual Adjustment in Marriage,* Grove Press, Inc., New York, 1962.

# Chapter Ten

## Physical, Mental, and Emotional Deviation

The words *normal* and *average,* as applied to human development or behavior, are commonly used to describe individuals who seem to display developmental patterns of personal characteristics that are similar to those of the majority of their peer group. In any attempt to determine normalcy, the size and constitution of the group studied is a significant point of reference, however. For example, in terms of height a Japanese man is normally much shorter than an average Norwegian. Yet there are some Japanese who are taller than some Norwegians. Hence an established height norm for the entire population of the world might have little meaning if it were applied to the population of a particular racial or geographical group. The most accurate conclusion, therefore, might be that there are average height trends in specific groups that have some validity for other groups, e.g., the results of height studies seem to indicate that the average man is taller than the average woman.

## Deviation from the Norm

A comprehensive and scientifically conducted statistical study of any phase of development or behavior in a particular group will yield an adequate norm for this characteristic that can be applied in a comparative evaluation of the individual members of the group. It then may be discovered that no individual is representative of the exact numerical norm. Some individuals cluster so closely around the statistical average, however, that for practical purposes they can be considered to be normal for their group.

## Normal Adolescent Trends

Chapters 4 to 6 dealt with some of the major characteristics of physical, physiological, mental, and emotional development during adolescence. In those chapters we were dealing primarily with what can be considered to be relatively normal development progress as the individual changes gradually from childhood status to adult maturity.

In the previous discussions we gave attention to some of the biological and environmental factors that operate as directive influences upon adolescent development. We emphasized the fact that each individual differs from every other individual to the extent that there are differences in inherited potential and variation in the effect upon the growing and maturing adolescent of his environmental experiences.

Insofar as in any area of development and consequent behavior patterning an adolescent's deviation from a statistically determined norm is relatively slight, he can be helped to achieve satisfactory personal and social adjustment to the ordinary life experiences of teen-agers. As a result of unusual inborn potential, atypical development, or uncommon environmental experience, an adolescent may deviate so greatly from the average in one or another area of development that he encounters difficulties of adjustment that are not experienced by his more normal peer associates. Hence he can be regarded as an atypical or exceptional adolescent.

## Significance of Exceptionality

An adolescent is classified as exceptional or atypical if in any characteristic he differs markedly from that which is considered to be normal for his group, and if the deviation is sufficient to warrant that special attention be accorded him by the members of his family and school personnel, as well as by society in general. The greater the degree of exceptionality, the more important it is that it receive intelligent and constructive consideration.

## Meaning of and Areas of Exceptionality

Interpreted broadly, *exceptional* or *atypical* refers to a condition of an individual that, even to the casual observer, may seem to set him apart from other more normal members of his group. From the point of view of those persons who are responsible for an atypical individual's developmental or learning experiences, the concept of exceptionality is exposed succinctly in the words of Lloyd M. Dunn:

By definition, then, *the exceptional pupil is one who deviates from the average in mental, physical, social, or emotional characteristics to such an extent that he is unable to profit adequately from the regular high-school curriculum alone, and requires special educational services in order to have educational opportunity equal to that provided the usual pupil.*[1]

[1] L. M. Dunn, in *The Education of Handicapped and Gifted Pupils in the Secondary School,* reprinted by permission from the Bulletin of the National Association of Secondary-school Principals, p. 4, January, 1955.

If the atypical adolescent is to be helped to meet his developmental and adjustment needs, the specific kinds of service rendered in his behalf must differ in terms of his particular form of exceptionality. Consequently, the various types of exceptional individuals usually are classified as:

PHYSICAL CONDITION

1. Blind and partially sighted
2. Deaf and hard of hearing
3. Defective in speech
4. Crippled
5. Otherwise physically handicapped
6. Health handicapped, i.e., epileptic, tubercular, cardiac, and delicate

MENTAL STATUS

7. Mentally superior, i.e., genius, near genius, and specially talented
8. Mentally retarded, i.e., dull normal, moron, imbecile, idiot

EMOTIONAL AND SOCIAL ADJUSTMENT

9. Emotionally disturbed
10. Socially maladjusted

It can be noted that the physical and emotional types of exceptionality represent below-average conditions, but that mental deviation may tend toward either superior or retarded status.

## Extent of Exceptionality

No complete census is available for school-age exceptional children and adolescents. Various estimates have been made, however, that place the percentage of school-age atypicals at about 10 per cent of the total school population. Included in a recent survey of education in the United States are data concerning the types of exceptional children and adolescents who are enrolled in urban schools, including elementary and secondary schools. From these data can be estimated, for each of the types of exceptionality, its percentage of incidence in the total school population, approximately 31 million elementary school pupils and 10 million secondary school pupils.

The number of atypical pupils classified according to type of exceptionality and to school level with percentage of incidence of each type for the total school population is presented in Table 25.

Although the percentage of exceptionality as presented in Table 25 totals 14.73 per cent of the total school population, some of the atypical

*Table 25.* Percentage of Exceptional School-age Population

| TYPE OF EXCEPTIONALITY | PERCENTAGE OF SCHOOL-AGE POPULATION | ESTIMATED NUMBER, 1963–1964 | |
| --- | --- | --- | --- |
| | | ELEMENTARY | SECONDARY |
| Blind...................... | .03 | 9,300 | 3,000 |
| Partially seeing............. | .20 | 62,000 | 20,000 |
| Deaf and hard of hearing.... | 1.50 | 465,000 | 150,000 |
| Speech handicapped......... | 4.00 | 1,240,000 | 400,000 |
| Crippled.................... | 1.50 | 465,000 | 150,000 |
| Special health cases......... | 1.50 | 465,000 | 150,000 |
| Mentally retarded........... | 2.00 | 620,000 | 200,000 |
| Gifted..................... | 2.00 | 620,000 | 200,000 |
| Socially maladjusted........ | 2.00 | 620,000 | 200,000 |
| Total.................... | 14.73 | 4,566,000 | 1,500,000 |

pupils may represent more than one type of exceptionality. For example, a blind child may be crippled, or a speech-handicapped pupil may be mentally retarded and socially maladjusted. Hence we probably are safe in estimating the percentage of handicapped individuals to be about 10 per cent.

There probably are relatively more exceptional pupils in the elementary schools than in secondary schools. This can be explained partly by the fact that the subpar condition may become severe enough for the older child to be hospitalized or otherwise institutionalized. Certain unfavorable health conditions may not be evidenced until the adolescent years, however. In addition, many mentally retarded children do not reach the senior high school, but the gifted may not seem to require special educational opportunities until their secondary school years. Consequently, the relative percentage of atypical pupils on the respective school levels is not so important as the difference in educational opportunities that may be needed.

## Adjustment Needs of Exceptional Adolescents

Atypical adolescents can be expected to experience the inner drives, urges, and interests that are characteristic of other teen-agers. The fact that a young person is a deviate does not lessen or eliminate his fundamental physical and psychological needs. Since the satisfaction of his felt needs may be limited by his atypical condition, he often encounters frustration-arousing situations. The way in which, and the extent to which, feelings of thwarting or frustration are experienced are closely related to the adolescent's particular type of exceptionality and its effect upon the behavior of others toward him, as well as the attitude he develops toward himself, his atypical status, and his associates.

During his maturing years the atypical individual's home and school relationships are particularly important. It is his democratic right, for example, to be the recipient of all of the educational advantages enjoyed by his peers insofar as he is able to profit from participation in learning activities. He must be understood and accepted by school people.

In the following pages we shall discuss adolescent adjustment problems that are linked with each type of exceptionality. We also shall attempt to suggest for each some of the adjustive approaches that can be utilized by adults and peer associates in their relationships with young people who give evidence of one or another type of deviation from the accepted norm.

## Physical Exceptionality

The adolescent who suffers a sensory or motor defect or is a victim of chronic ill-health needs to receive from others a sympathetic understanding of his difficulty. At the same time, he wants to develop an attitude of self-dependence and self-realization insofar as it is possible for him to do so. He usually resents oversolicitous attempts on the part of others to do things he can do for himself. Contrariwise, he becomes emotionally disturbed if persons in his immediate environment seem to avoid him or tend to show by their behavior that they consider him inferior to, or very different from, themselves.

These general characteristics are common to most young people. Each type of exceptionality is accompanied by specific problems of adjustment, however.

### The Blind and Partially Sighted

The blind adolescent suffers from complete lack of vision; the vision of a partially sighted young person falls between 20/70 and 20/200 vision in the better eye after all attempts at possible correction have been made. Although the percentage of the entire school population with impaired vision is relatively small (less than 0.25 per cent), the young people thus afflicted represent a group of seriously handicapped individuals who experience social maladjustment. The visually handicapped adolescent's ability to relate to his physical and social environment is dependent upon time and intensity factors, i.e., blindness or impaired vision at birth, or total blindness or defective vision acquired during childhood.

The individual who never has been able to see things and persons needs training to develop his other sensory equipment to the point that he is enabled to create at least some visual images. This is a difficult task since neither the blind person himself nor his parents or teachers can be certain that he is acquiring adequate mental pictures. The adolescent who was once sighted possesses a background of visual imagery upon which he can be helped to build mental images of present phenomena in terms of memory. In some ways the young person who attempts to compare remembered sights with existing changed visual stimulations experiences greater frustration than does the individual who has had to learn from birth to adjust himself to an unseen world.

The problems of the partially sighted adolescent are different from those of the totally blind. The individual who is born with weak eyesight constantly is faced with the necessity of interpreting what he sees in terms of what others say they see. The difficulty is intensified if neither he nor others recognize the fact that his vision is impaired. If he fails to report accurately about what he is supposed to see, he may be accused of being uninterested, inattentive, or stupid. Persons with visual acuity of 20/200 or less are termed "clinically blind" and in some states are eligible for sight classes, sight-saving materials, and other services.

The adolescent whose vision has become defective as a result of an accident, illness, or too great eyestrain that is caused by excessive reading or other close eye work is likely to recognize his difficulty. If he is sensible, he consciously reduces eye work to a minimum. It is not always easy for an individual to change his habits, however. An adolescent or young adult may persist in completing his education through the college level or beyond. Then he discovers that he thereby has ruined his eyes to the extent that he is prevented from engaging in the occupational activity for which he had prepared. His ambition may have been so great that he was impelled to ignore the fact that he was overtaxing his eyesight.

For example, even as a child the eyesight of a young man known to the authors was below par. Although he was aware of his visual impairment, he tried to convince himself that he would outgrow the difficulty. His vocational ambition was to prepare himself for the legal profession. By the time he had reached his senior year at college he was willing to admit that, in spite of delayed ophthalmological treatment, his eyesight was becoming worse rather than better. Consequently, he was compelled to change his vocational plans. He needed to limit his vocational choice to a form of activity in which there would be a minimum of reading. Since he possessed an outgoing socially attractive personality, he entered the sales field, in which he achieved considerable success. He does not find this type of work suited to his interests and abilities, however. Now, at the age of 36 he is restless and dissatisfied; he keeps searching for an occupational opportunity in which he can find an outlet for his vocational ambitions in spite of his visual impairment.

Physicians, parents, and school people have become increasingly alert to the child's need of eye care. Physicians treat the eyes of newborn infants to prevent possible venereal infection. The pediatrician watches carefully the visual development of the infant and young child. Parents are learning to recognize early symptoms of abnormal vision. In most school systems periodic eye examinations for all pupils are mandatory; appropriately lensed glasses are recommended for those children who appear to need them. Usually parents are expected to provide the glasses. In cases of parental economic inability to do so, many schools assume the financial responsibility, either entirely or in part. Although the school is obliged to make certain that a pupil's visual defect is corrected insofar as possible, strong resistance to the carrying out of school recommendation may be displayed either by the young person concerned or his parents. Ignorance or indifference may cause the adults to refuse or delay the procuring of glasses for the adolescent. It is not uncommon for a parent to assert variously that the "eye doctor" will damage the child's eyes by putting "drops" into them; that all the members of the family have good enough eyesight (grandfather died at the age of 80 without ever having worn glasses, even though his increasing old age had resulted in almost complete blindness); or that there is no need to bother about glasses now, since most children have some trouble with their eyes which they outgrow as they become older.

For a child or an adolescent to dislike wearing glasses is understandable. They interfere with a child's participation in active play. He may break or lose them, thus incurring the anger of his parents, or earn teachers' disapproval by forgetting to take them to school. An adolescent girl is likely to believe that wearing glasses detracts from personal attractiveness or is a symbol of overstudiousness. The trend toward the manufacture of differently shaped and colored eyeglass frames, some of which are decorated with rhinestones or in other ways made to look distinctive, is tending somewhat to break down the adolescent girl's resistance to wearing them. For the adolescent boy who is sports-minded, however, the wearing of eyeglasses continues to constitute an intolerable situation to which he may react by consciously refusing to wear them. Among older adolescents and young adults who need eyeglasses there is a trend toward wearing contact lenses.

As a result of the prejudice on the part of young people against sight conservation or improvement, many relatively mild and easily corrected visual defects are allowed to develop into cases of chronic visual impairment. Fortunately, the preservation of adequate eyesight is receiving increased attention from the citizenry at large. Scientific experimentation has resulted in the production of light bulbs that reduce eyestrain. Publishers are giving greater consideration to the size of type, spacing of letters, and kind of paper used in books, especially textbooks. The wearing of glasses during the early years as a means of strengthening a child's vision is coming to be accepted by a greater number of parents and children than formerly was the case. The adjustments of those young people whose visual defects cannot be improved by artificial aids or by treatment continue to be serious problems, however. Among these problems can be included: satisfying their sex curiosity, dating, mobility (e.g., inability to drive a car), and concern for the future.[2]

One of the most significant problems of the blind and partially sighted is the development of good social attitudes. These handicapped young people need to find a place for themselves among their sighted peer associates. This objective probably can be achieved best through sharing as many school experiences as the handicap will permit. Hence on the secondary school and college levels many receive their education in regular classes. Since there is no relation between blindness or sight impairment and mental status, rapid learners can be helped to master academic subjects and some skills, especially if sight-saving materials are available.

Blind students can be trained to read Braille and to use a typewriter. Some commonly used textbooks have been translated into Braille form, thus helping the blind person to master some subject matter without the aid of a "reader." The ability to read Braille and to gain skill in typewriting, combined with careful listening to, and participation in, class discussions, has an excellent psychological effect upon a blind adolescent. Thereby he is helped to develop an attitude of self-dependence. This prevents the arousal in him of feelings of self-pity or inadequacy that result from dependence upon others, who by their zealous attempts to help the handicapped may give evidence not only that they feel sorry for their blind classmate but that they are conscious of their superiority to him.

The attitude displayed by sighted adolescents toward a blind classmate has a potent effect upon the latter. An interesting situation recently came to the attention of the authors. Jane had been a member of an elementary school class for the blind, in which she had gained a commendable amount of self-dependence and self-assurance. She then went to a high school in which there were sighted young people who had had no previous experience with the blind. Consequently, Jane's classmates, assuming that she was completely dependent upon others, felt so sorry for her that they overwhelmed her with attention. They led her from

[2] See Bertha Lowenfield, "The Blind Adolescent in a Seeing World," *Exceptional Children*, pp. 310–314, March, 1959.

classroom to classroom, made certain that she was seated comfortably in each room, and reported to her in detail what was happening. In turn, they read the assignments to her, explaining each point of a lesson as though she could not think for herself.

This was a new experience for Jane. The solicitude of these adolescents resulted in the girl's losing her earlier self-assurance; she became increasingly dependent upon them. She appeared to be gaining emotional satisfaction from the fact that she was the object of peer-group attention. She demanded similar treatment from her family and out-of-school associates. A member of the school staff, recognizing the harm that had been done to the handicapped girl by her overenthusiastic schoolmates, tried with little success to help the blind girl and her school associates develop a more realistic attitude toward the handicap. It was difficult for Jane to regain her former self-dependence before she was faced with the problem of adjusting to adult experiences that required her to be willing and able to fend for herself.

The past thirty years have witnessed various studies dealing with the adjustment problems of the blind and partially sighted. A recent interesting investigation of the visually disabled is that of Emory L. Cowen and three associates.[3] The purpose of this three-year study was to determine some of the factors basic to the adjustment of visually disabled adolescents as compared with the sighted. Special attention was given to parental attitudes toward and understanding of their blind or partially sighted children. The subjects were 167 young persons in the seventh through the twelfth grades, and between the ages of 13 and 18. Some were attending public schools in New York State, others were students in residential schools in New York, Pennsylvania, and Ohio. Various measurement instruments were utilized, and certain criteria were established for the inclusion of students in the study. A general conclusion of the study is:

Comparability and overlap between visually disabled and sighted adolescents with respect to adjustment, as opposed to sharp differences and significant discrepancies, is the rule which emerges from our work. For all groups, publicly expressed maternal attitudes are ill-suited to the prediction of adjustment in the child. On the other hand, consistent and sensitive correlates of adjustment are found in the cluster of indices of maternal understanding. Progress has been made toward the development of a complex set of predictors of good adjustment to visual disability. Empirically, variables have been identified which show promise of being particularly useful in future work in this area.[4]

[3] Emory L. Cowen et al., *Adjustment to Visual Disability in Adolescence*, American Foundation for the Blind, New York, 1961.
[4] *Ibid.*, p. 176.

During their growing-up years the blind and partially sighted need to be encouraged to participate in appropriate social and recreational activities with their sighted associates of the same age. Some adolescents and adults who suffer from this handicap have been helped to acquire social skills that ensure acceptance of them by most groups. An independent, active, and accepted blind or partially sighted adolescent is likely to be cheerful, busy, and well adjusted in spite of his handicapped state.

## The Deaf and Hard of Hearing

A popular misconception concerning the interrelation of the senses is that the loss of one sense results in naturally increased acuity of the other senses. Although this belief is not founded upon actual fact, it is true that a deaf person can be trained to compensate for his hearing handicap by utilizing sight, touch, smell, and taste more effectively than does the individual who hears normally. Through the superior development of his other senses the deaf person is enabled to establish relatively adequate intercommunication with his associates and to gain knowledge of the physical environment. Since impaired hearing is less obvious than impaired vision, the individual may succeed in concealing the fact for a long time. Hearing impairment may result from any one of various defective conditions of an individual's hearing mechanism. Hence hearing may be restored through surgical operation or improved by means of a hearing aid. The totally deaf child whose hearing cannot be restored or improved needs to be helped early to adjust to a physical and social environment which he can see but the many different sounds of which lie outside his field of experience.

A child who is deaf from birth cannot speak intelligibly. Although his vocal organs are ready to function adequately, the sounds which are produced by him as a young baby cannot follow the course of progressively developing speech patterns that are acquired by the normal child through imitation of the oral speech of others. Since the deaf child cannot hear language sounds he is unable to imitate them. Formerly, therefore, the deaf were considered to be "dumb," and there was developed an elaborate system of sign language based upon the utilization of various meaningful positions of fingers, hands, and arms, accompanied by facial expressions and head movements.

By means of this "deaf-and-dumb" language, intercommunication was made possible among deaf people, as well as between the handicapped and hearing persons who mastered the appropriate manipulatory symbols. The recognition by scientists of the fact that oral speech is accompanied by throat vibrations which differ in terms of intelligible oral sounds has been a boon to deaf children. Although the process is slow and requires much patience on the part of the deaf child as well as his teacher, the former can learn to speak intelligibly by sensitizing the tips of his fingers to the throat vibrations, his teacher's as well as his own, that are associated with particular word sounds. Through this technique controlled vocalization is developed.

The deaf child also can be trained to read the lips of a speaker who is facing him. Remarkable progress has been made in the education of the deaf. Recently one of the authors engaged in a long and interesting conversation with a professional associate without knowing that the man is totally deaf. Moreover, one could attend a play produced by the pupils of a school for the deaf and find no differences from a dramatic production enacted by hearing persons, unless he were sufficiently observant to notice that the deaf actors "listened" to one another by watching the lips of the speaker.

Because of the need of the deaf person to be face to face with the speaker in order to understand what is being said, he finds it difficult to participate in large group discussions. Further, a deaf person is likely to be suspicious of a conversation which he cannot hear. Even though he is a lip reader, a group of persons may be so situated that he cannot "hear" what they are saying. If one or more of the group happen to look in his direction, he is likely to conclude that they are criticizing or ridiculing him, or commenting upon his handicapped condition. As a result, he may experience a strong feeling of resentment or frustration.

In many ways the deaf are exposed to more conflict-arousing stimulations than the blind. The latter remain unaware of the presence of certain subtle environmental stimuli that can be seen by the deaf but only partially evaluated correctly, if at all. The general attitude of nurses and social-service workers concerning temperamental differences between the blind and the deaf is that the former tend to be cheerful and cooperative but that the latter are likely to be irritable, suspicious, and demanding. We must recognize the fact, however, that there are individual differences among adolescents in each group.

The problems of the hard-of-hearing young person are different from, but often equally as serious as, those of a totally deaf child or adolescent. Both deafness and inadequate hearing may result from illness or an accident. Speech patterns developed before the onset of total deafness may continue to be of service to the afflicted individual but, at the same time, the more or less sudden loss of hearing may induce marked emotional disturbance that interferes considerably with his educational progress. Except for rapid learners, few totally deaf young people continue their schooling through the secondary level. Those who are deaf in one ear only, or are below par in both ears, usually continue their education within the limits of their mental ability and learning interests.

Even though a deaf or hard-of-hearing child attends a special elementary school in which he receives training appropriate to his type of defect, it is psychologically desirable that he continue his education in a regular secondary school. Certain adaptations of customary learning procedures may be needed, however, to meet his special needs.

Parents and teachers often misjudge the behavior of the partially deaf young person. If a child or adolescent fails to respond to an adult's question or request, he is likely to be accused of inattention, disinterest, daydreaming, stubbornness, or "psychological" deafness (failure to hear what he does not want to hear). A hard-of-hearing adolescent may be extremely sensitive about his impairment and try to conceal the fact that he cannot hear what is said. Sometimes a child, as well as an adolescent, is so reluctant to let his peers find out about his difficulty that in the classroom he will give the impression that he does not know the answer to a question asked him by his teacher rather than admit that he cannot hear the question.

If parents and teachers discover early that a child's hearing is impaired, appropriate treatment often can be administered successfully. If the defect is permitted to continue into the adolescent years, however, little can be done to remedy it. The only recourse then is the wearing of a good hearing aid. An increasing number of adults are coming to recognize the value to themselves of using an artificial device. Some adults and most adolescents are unwilling thus to attract attention to their defect, even though intercommunication would be improved thereby. Hence manufacturers of hearing aids are experimenting with the production of mechanical devices that will be less noticeable and easier to manage than those now available.

## Adolescents with Speech Defects

For practical purposes, speech defects usually are classified according to two major categories: *organic* and *functional*. At present there is some disagreement between psychologists and speech pathologists concerning the possibility that all speech disorders have an organic base. Certain speech difficulties result from structural or organic abnormalities, e.g., deafness, cleft palate, harelip, teeth formation and arrangement, malformation of the vocal organs, cerebral palsy, illnesses, or brain injury.

The incidence of specific organically caused defects is relatively low. Many adolescents and young adults give evidence of more or less serious forms of unacceptable speech, however. These include so-called "baby talk" (especially among girls, sometimes used to gain attention from male associates); slovenly speech or careless pronunciation of consonant and vowel sounds; inadequate voice control, such as excessive loudness or softness, thinness, harshness, or monotonous pitch; foreign accent; lallation; stammering and stuttering. Some defective speech patterns result from imitation during childhood of adult models that represented inadequate speech standards. The adolescent finds it difficult to alter or eliminate unattractive speech or voice habits that earlier had been developed and accepted in the home and neighborhood, and more or less disregarded outside the immediate home community.

If as a high school student the adolescent realizes that his speech is subnormal for the group, he may become embarrassed and emotionally insecure. He then may meet the disturbing situation by aggressive intensification of the unacceptable speech or voice usage, by withdrawing, by reluctance to speak unless he is compelled to do so, or by abortive attempts to model his speech or voice patterns according to what he considers to be highly acceptable standards, thereby acquiring artificial speech or voice usage.

A severe shock or a strong emotional conflict may cause a child, more often an adolescent, to develop a stammer or a stutter. A bright young person may find that his thoughts flow so quickly that they run ahead of his oral expression of them. He cannot find the right words to express his ideas. The more emotionally excited he becomes, the more difficult it is for him to utter the word that he wants or to start saying it without hesitation. Continued experiences of this kind set up emotional blocks that interfere with normal speech patterns. If this conflict-arousing situation occurs in a classroom, teacher pressure or impatience and classroom ridicule intensify the adolescent's speech difficulty.

Educators are beginning to recognize the importance to a young person of developing acceptable speech and voice patterns and of the effect upon speech adequacy of shock-producing and conflict-arousing experiences. Psychologists, speech pathologists, and speech therapists are emphasizing the need of early speech and voice patterning. Hence in an increasing number of school systems speech and voice training are being stressed to an extent that was unknown in the past.

In New York City, for example, specially trained teachers of speech improvement are being assigned to elementary schools in order to help children who have speech difficulties. With the cooperation of the parents of these children, "speech improvement" teachers diagnose specific defects and trace their causes. If the speech defect appears to have an organic base, recommendations are made for physical care. The seemingly functional disorder is treated therapeutically by the special teacher, with the aid of parents and regular class teachers. In many high schools teachers of speech utilize various techniques to improve adolescent speech and voice usage. Teacher-training institutions and teacher-licensing agencies require that a young man or woman who aspires to be a teacher possess the kind of speech patterns and voice usage that will be models worthy of imitation by pupils.

In one high school an experiment was conducted with fifteen adolescent girls who gave evidence of speech disorders that appeared to be associated with emotional maladjustment. These girls spent one period daily in a student activity lounge with the dean and teachers of health education, music, and speech. The relationships among the girls and the members of the faculty were extremely informal. The girls were encouraged to talk freely among themselves, to dance, and to sing popular songs. The dean was alert to references on the part of any of the girls to the existence of home, school, or personal problem. She then did what she could to ameliorate unwholesome conditions or to improve undesirable attitudes.

During the remainder of the school day the girls attended their regular classes. Their teachers encouraged them to participate in class activities, but avoided asking them direct questions associated with home study. All the girls reported a gradually relaxed and more secure attitude toward their schoolwork. They consciously made an effort to participate in class discussions and acquired increasing fluency of speech. Hesitancy, stammering, and stuttering became less evident, except when they became emotionally disturbed, which sometimes happened without any observable cause. This program of speech rehabilitation continued for two years. It was discontinued when the girls enthusiastically prepared for and, with little or no emotional tension and in relaxed speech, enacted a play before a large audience of fellow students. Although a project of this kind is costly and requires teacher patience, the rewards in the form of adolescent rehabilitation are well worth the expenditure of money, time, and effort.

## The Crippled and Otherwise Physically Handicapped Adolescent

Like the blind and the deaf, orthopedically handicapped adolescents possess the urges, interests, and desires that are characteristic of most physically normal young people. To the extent that the physical handicap is easily observed and bars them from the forms of physical activity in which their more fortunate teen-age associates engage, these handicapped adolescents experience severe feelings of thwarting, discouragement, and resentment toward their crippled condition, which may deny them the kinds of social participation that are so much desired. Consequently, one of the greatest needs of these young people is to learn to adjust themselves to their interrelationships in the home, school, and community in such a way that they will gain the admiration and respect of their associates in spite of the handicap.

To achieve emotional, social, and vocational adjustment is not easy for the individual who is tied to a wheelchair, cannot walk without crutches, or is the victim of any form of physical malformation or crippling condition. The adolescent who has been handicapped since birth may have been helped early to accept his handicap and to develop skill of performance in activities in which he can participate. Understanding parents and teachers can do much to encourage in the child an attitude of self-dependence insofar as his handicap will permit, and to reduce to a minimum the experiencing of self-pity and the demanding of extreme attention from other persons. Many orthopedically handicapped children are remarkable for their patience and cheerfulness, and their ability to gain satisfaction from their limited activities and to win the friendship of their peer associates.

An adolescent who more or less suddenly becomes severely crippled is deprived thereby of participation in his accustomed physical and social activities. The emotional shock that may accompany his recognition of the effect of the handicap upon his life pattern poses problems of adjustment that are difficult to solve, not only for the young person himself but also for the adults who are responsible for his care. An especially serious problem is the kind or extent of continued schooling which can be made available for him.

The handicap may be so severe that the sufferer cannot attend a regular school. In such cases some school systems provide special teachers who go to the homes of the young people and guide their learning to the point that a high school diploma can be earned. "Homebound" students are denied those social experiences that represent some of the greatest values to be gained from attendance at a regular high school.

Adolescents who are mobile to the extent that they can travel in wheelchairs or with crutches usually are encouraged to attend a regular high school where they are taught in special classes, in regular classes that meet on the first floor (if the school has no elevator), or in any class if the school building has elevator service.

Since most orthopedic handicaps are obvious, a sensitive crippled adolescent often is embarrassed by having other persons stare at him. They sometimes make comments about his condition, which he overhears, or indicate by their facial expression as they look at him that they pity him or are repelled by his appearance or by his uncontrollable body movements. In spite of the fact that they are fond of him, it sometimes is difficult for members of the handicapped adolescent's family, his teachers, and his close associates to treat him objectively or to disregard his infirmity. The adolescent who experiences such situations is likely to become extremely emotionalized; he is impelled to withdraw from social situations; he may develop an attitude of apathy even toward those activities in which he could participate successfully and thereby earn recognition and commendation. It is possible, however, for a handicapped young person to force himself aggressively into situations he is not physically able to handle, thus adding to his difficulties.

The achievement of self-direction and self-realization is not always easy for the normal adolescent; for the adolescent who is the victim of a severe orthopedic handicap it often is impossible. He may need psychiatric or other specialized treatment and guidance that can help him acquire socially and vocationally useful skills, accept his physical limitations, and cultivate attractive, cooperative, and outgoing personality characteristics.

Some crippled conditions are localized, especially those that are caused by an accident. Absence of a limb, or a crippled or malformed hand, foot, arm, or leg, may limit an adolescent's physical activities but does not impair his general physical constitution or mental status. It is possible for him to learn to adjust so well to his infirmity that he is enabled to achieve a high degree of competence in his school studies or occupational activities, and to develop outstandingly fine personality traits. Consequently, his contributions are such that they divert attention from his physical handicap, and he becomes an esteemed and sought-after member of his group.

Other serious orthopedic conditions tend progressively to exert detrimental effects upon the individual's physical constitution and physiological functions. For example, in progressive muscular dystrophy, beginning at about age 5, the voluntary muscular tissues gradually degenerate and waste away, at first causing the child to fall easily. He begins then to drag his feet and finally becomes a wheelchair patient. Cerebral palsy, characterized by motor-function impairment originating in injury to, or abnormal development of, specific brain areas, may result in mental retardation, defective hearing, vision, and speech, or impaired activity of the arms and legs.

Improved surgery, physical and occupational therapy, and appropriate medication are contributing much toward improving the condition of individuals who suffer from one or another form of physical handicap. The emotional strain that is likely to accompany an adolescent's submission to ameliorative or cure-inducing experiences often is so great that the patient requires psychological or psychiatric care as well as surgical or therapeutic treatment.

Moreover, the attitude of parents toward their crippled child is extremely important. The parent who is oversolicitous or continuously gives expression to his feelings of guilty responsibility for his child's unfortunate condition creates a home atmosphere that is conducive to the arousal in the adolescent of self-pity, overdependence upon others, or deep resentment. Parentally displayed attitudes of acceptance, understanding, and helpfulness (when needed) usually motivate the handicapped adolescent to develop constructive, self-orienting attitudes and behavior. Similarly, since the teacher of handicapped adolescents exercises a potent influence upon his students' attitudes and behavior, those qualities that are desirable in dealing with normal adolescents need to be intensified in teachers of the handicapped.

## The Health-handicapped Adolescent

As a result of the strain upon their physical constitutions of the organic changes that are taking place within them, adolescents are susceptible to cardiac and tubercular difficulties and epileptic seizures. The health condition of the so-called "delicate" child may improve as he matures. If an adolescent's health is not watched carefully, however, his developing urges and interests may cause him to become a victim of a serious health defect or may intensify his delicate health status. Most high schools require their students to undergo a yearly health examination. In some school communities all teachers and pupils are given periodic chest X rays. It is especially important that predisposition to ill-health be recognized by parents, school people, and young people themselves.

We know that adolescents tend to resent adult attempts to curb youthful interests and activities. It is especially difficult for a health-handicapped boy or girl to submit to the imposition of special restrictions upon his activities, particularly participation in sports and dancing. He may dislike early retiring hours and rest periods during the day. Adolescents who are interested in their school studies are irked by the necessity to carry "limited" subject programs or by prolonged school absences caused by illness.

As we know, habits acquired during childhood tend to persist throughout most of an individual's life, unless changes in undesirable modes of behavior can be effected during the teen years. The delicate or frail child is likely to be pampered and relieved of all responsibility in the home. His oversolicitous parents mistakenly believe that his every wish or whim should be satisfied. His elementary school teachers also may allow their sympathetic attitudes toward his delicate condition to cause them to grant him privileges that the more robust children do not enjoy. Consequently, by the time the child reaches adolescence he is thoroughly spoiled.

In his school and social relationships the spoiled, sickly adolescent expects his teachers and peer associates to accord him the special considerations which he earlier had come to demand as his rights. To the extent that his expanding needs and interests do not receive immediate fulfillment through the efforts of his new associates, he experiences many frustrating situations. The impact upon him of these thwartings tends to intensify his already warped personal characteristics.

Although the delicate adolescent needs care and proper consideration of his health limitations, he should not be pampered. Rather, he should be encouraged to perform tasks within the limits of his health and intellectual status. Parents and school people working cooperatively can help a young person whose vitality is low or who is the victim of ill-health to develop those outgoing, socially acceptable attitudes that will prevent his becoming a self-centered and health-involved adult.

## Mentally Atypical Adolescents

An individual is considered to be mentally atypical if his performance of mental tasks deviates to so great an extent in either direction from an established norm of intelligent behavior that it is difficult or impossible for him to adapt his thinking patterns to those of the majority of his group. The deviation may represent extreme mental retardation or so great subnormality that no amount or kind of training can induce behavior that is normally intelligent. Or the mental deviate may display behavior that is so superior to that of the normally intelligent individual that intellectual feats far beyond the ability of the mentally average are possible of achievement.

### Interpretation of Mentally Atypical

Both mental retardation and intellectual superiority represent exceptional mental status, although the term *exceptional* often is applied mistakenly only to the superior or gifted. As is true of a physical or health type of exceptionality, a mentally atypical adolescent displays evidence of characteristically deviant attitudes and forms of behavior in terms of his particular type and degree of exceptionality. Formerly many parents and school people assumed that children differed little, if at all, in their ability to learn. Superior performance was explained in terms of superior adult motivation or the innate "goodness" of the child. Inadequate achievement was supposed to result from the learner's unwillingness to learn, laziness, or "badness."

With the acceptance of the psychological concept of individual differences, school people and parents (sometimes reluctantly) came to recognize the fact that some young people are rapid learners and others are below normal or slow learners. It further was recognized that educational offerings and procedures must be fitted to the degree of learning potential possessed by respective children and adolescents. Various techniques, therefore, have been utilized to discover rapid and slow learners.

One study was conducted to discover the "types of identification procedures used to determine mental exceptionality among secondary school pupils." [5] Of the 1,200 secondary schools to which questionnaires were sent, returns were received from 814.

The questionnaire contained twenty items, each representing a possible identification procedure. The rank of the respective items as identifiers of rapid and slow learners is presented in Table 25. The ranking for most of the items is quite similar for both the rapid and the slow learners. It can be seen by inspection of the listed data that the highest-ranking techniques are teachers' marks, group intelligence tests, teachers' estimates of school achievement, standardized achievement tests, and information on physical health.

It is not enough to discover mental differences among adolescents. Not only do the behavior characteristics of the mentally retarded adolescent differ from those of the intellectually gifted, but also their respective mental and emotional needs differ. Hence school people share with parents the responsibility of helping mentally exceptional adolescents achieve satisfying adjustments to their particular mental potentialities and in their interpersonal relationships.

Informal and formal education that is either broad in scope or intensive in form represents the medium through which can be fulfilled the adjustment needs of exceptional young people. Although we shall consider the fundamental adjustive factors that function in the developmental process for both the retarded and the superior adolescent, emphasis will be placed upon the value to both mentally atypical groups of their educational experiences.

The gifted and mentally retarded do not profit similarly from their schooling, no matter how excellent the learning opportunities may be. Nevertheless, no matter what the adolescent's capacity for learning is, there should be made available to him the best that can be provided to meet his special needs. The principle of individual differences in mental ability will continue to operate as a limiting factor of the amount of learning and the adjustments that can be achieved by a particular learner. The equality of educational opportunity needs to be broadened in its interpretation to include the kind of understanding and acceptance of intellectual variation, on the part of the adult public, that will permit

[5] A. Jewett and J. D. Hull (coordinators), *Teaching Rapid and Slow Learners in High Schools,* U.S. Department of Health, Education, and Welfare Bulletin, 1954, no. 5.

*Table 26.* Techniques Used in Discovering Rapid- and Slow-learning Pupils

| | RANK ORDER | |
| --- | --- | --- |
| ITEM | RAPID LEARNERS | SLOW LEARNERS |
| Teachers' marks............................... | 1 | 1 |
| Group intelligence tests........................... | 2 | 2 |
| Teachers' estimates of school achievement............ | 3 | 3 |
| Standardized achievement tests.................... | 4 | 5 |
| Information on physical health.................... | 5 | 4 |
| Guidance counselor's appraisal of pupils' interests, aptitudes, and abilities........................... | 6 | 6 |
| Information on vocational plans................... | 7 | 7 |
| Information on reading interests and habits.......... | 8 | 8 |
| Information on home environment................. | 9 | 9 |
| Anecdotal reports and records..................... | 10 | 10 |
| Information on personality adjustment.............. | 11 | 11 |
| Teachers' estimates of aptitudes................... | 12 | 12 |
| Information on physical maturity................... | 13 | 13 |
| Homeroom adviser's appraisal of pupils' interests, aptitudes, and abilities........................... | 14 | 15 |
| Information on social maturity.................... | 15 | 14 |
| Information on hobbies........................... | 16 | 16 |
| Teachers' estimates of intelligence................. | 17 | 18 |
| Standardized aptitude tests in specific fields.......... | 18 | 19 |
| Individual intelligence tests...................... | 19 | 17 |
| Parental appraisal of pupils' interests, aptitudes, and abilities....................................... | 20 | 20 |

SOURCE: Adapted from A. Jewett and J. D. Hull (coordinators), *Teaching Rapid and Slow Learners in High Schools,* U.S. Department of Health, Education, and Welfare Bulletin, 1954, no. 5, pp. 16–17.

school authorities to provide school equipment and facilities, teaching techniques, curriculums, and programs that will enable each adolescent to develop to the maximum whatever learning potential he possesses.

## The Mentally Superior or Specially Gifted Adolescent

Society usually selects as its leaders those individuals who give evidence of keen insight, objective and impartial judgment, and comprehensive and intensive understanding, as these qualities are related to successful leadership in any given area of endeavor. Present-day advances in science and technology and the increasing need for interworld cooperation require the services of able and well-trained men and women in various fields of activity. It is imperative, therefore, that potential leaders be discovered early. These young people then should be motivated by their parents and school personnel to expand and refine their special endowments.

## Educational Needs of the Gifted

The intellectually gifted adolescent can be expected to attain a high degree of skill performance and subject matter mastery. The best educational outcomes usually result if the gifted individual, after experiencing a broad, enriched background of fundamental education, is stimulated to focus his study activity upon intensive learning in the field of his special abilities.

Too many exceptionally bright young people are permitted to dissipate their energies by attempting to become partially trained in various areas as these in turn attract their changing interests. Others develop a kind of intellectual snobbery that excludes any individuals whom they consider to be mentally inferior to themselves. Hence, as important as, if not more important than, the bright adolescent's intellectual challenge is his recognition of the comparative values of education and his willingness to be helped to achieve emotional stability and adequate adjustment in his interpersonal relationships with mentally less able associates as well as with his intellectual peers.

## Physical Characteristics of the Gifted

Contrary to popular belief before the twentieth century, the physical constitution and health status of the intellectually superior child or adolescent are superior to the physical condition of the mentally normal young person. In general, mentally superior adolescents are superior in height, weight, strength, physique, health, emotional stability, sociability, and length of life span.

## Intellectual Characteristics of the Gifted

It is usually considered that intellectually superior young people are those whose intelligence quotient (resulting from the administration of a valid and reliable standardized test of intelligence) is 120 or higher. With some exceptions, the mentally gifted can learn quickly and achieve a high degree of success in schoolwork. In a statement concerning general policies on education of intellectually gifted students in the Los Angeles city schools, Everett Chaffee suggests that gifted pupils may possess some or all of the following characteristics:

1. Are alert, intellectually curious, and keenly observant.
2. Have a wide variety of interests and versatility.
3. Are perceptive.
4. Are creative and inventive.
5. Understand concepts, recognize relationships, make generalizations, and reason clearly.

6. Learn easily and rapidly with a minimum of drill.
7. Are highly verbal.
8. Are persistent and have power of concentration and retention.
9. Have the ability to work independently and responsively.[6]

Home conditions and parental status, as well as heredity, seem to play an important role in the development of mentally superior young people. For example, a study of the family backgrounds of 456 gifted pupils in the public schools of Cleveland, Ohio,[7] yielded, among others, the following findings: For the most part, the homes represented upper-middle-class status; more than 80 per cent of the gifted subjects were reared by their own parents; 40 per cent of the parents were in professional and managerial positions; 22.4 per cent in the clerical and sales, and 21.5 per cent in skilled labor, with only 3.7 per cent in unskilled labor. From the results of studies, it can be concluded that many gifted children are reared in homes that represent professional or near-professional attitudes and interests. Hence not only do these children probably inherit superior parental potential but they also are exposed to environmental advantages in the form of books, magazines, and other educational facilities, as well as enriching experiences such as association with alert and challenging family friends, and opportunities for extensive travel.

The fact that, on the average, mentally superior children and adolescents tend also to be physically and emotionally superior does not guarantee that every gifted individual is representative of the group norm physically or emotionally. Whether a particular young person achieves good health status and emotional stability during his childhood and adolescent years depends in great part upon his parents' reactions to his mental superiority as well as upon his relationships with teachers and peer associates. Parents may expect too much of their gifted child or lack understanding of his emotional or social needs. Teachers sometimes emphasize unduly a young person's mental superiority with the result that he is resented by his fellow classmates. Hence the bright child or adolescent can experience difficulty in achieving a satisfactory adjustment to

[6] Everett Chaffee, *Education of Intellectually Gifted Pupils in Los Angeles City Schools,* in Lester D. Crow and Alice Crow (eds.), *Educating the Academically Able: A Book of Readings,* David McKay Company, Inc., New York, 1963, pp. 18–19.

[7] Walter B. Barbe, "A Study of the Family Background of the Gifted," *Journal of Educational Psychology,* pp. 302–309, May, 1956.

his various relationships with people and conditions. The following situational experiences illustrate this point.

A bright little boy or girl is likely to "pick up" one or another form of "cute" behavior, e.g., reciting bits of verse, singing popular songs, or executing simple ballet steps. If the parents' pride in their child's accomplishments is greater than their understanding of child nature, they may insist that he repeatedly display his special talent for the benefit of visiting friends and relatives. Parental encouragement of childish "showing off" can affect a youngster's self-regarding attitude in either of two ways. An aggressive child becomes too sophisticated for his age or overdemanding of attention; a shy or modest youngster is sensitive to the behavior of the adults who are expected by his parents to be amazed by his superiority. He is reluctant to be the center of attention; he refuses to give a "demand" performance. The aggressive child bores his victims; the shy child embarrasses his parents and may be regarded by them as stubborn or uncooperative. Parental overemphasis upon a child's brightness tends to excite unfavorable emotional reactions.

Parents may become so concerned about the intellectual development of their gifted child that they deny him the fulfillment of other normal interests. For example, some years ago a boy received considerable newspaper publicity because of the fact that not only was he the youngest winner of the degree of doctor of philosophy from a well-known university but also he had written one of the best doctoral dissertations ever presented. As a child this boy attended a private school. His mother had him driven to and from school daily and brought him his lunch, the eating of which she supervised in a room containing just the two of them. Moreover, the mother insisted that the boy should not be permitted to mingle with other children, refusing to allow him to participate in play activities lest he catch a germ. Consequently, he became stout and physically lethargic. To the chagrin of his devoted parents, he rebelled against the mode of life to which he was being subjected. After he received his doctorate during middle adolescence, he refused the professional offers that he received, withdrew from the family circle, and struck out for himself as an employee of a business firm. The reason given by him for his action was that he wanted to be a normal man, released from the emotional tensions that had accompanied his being a "brain" rather than a whole person.

In her own way, a high school sophomore, now a college freshman, settled the problems of adjustment that she recognized to be accompaniments of exceptional mental superiority. She found that during her elementary and junior high school periods her intellectual superiority was interfering with normal relationships with her peers. Her classmates, as well as her teachers, had come to regard her as a special person who was not expected to be interested in the everyday social interests and play activities of the other children. Consequently, she decided that she would become no more than an average student. She studied just enough in high school to earn an over-all 83 per cent, the lowest rating that would gain entrance for her into the college of her choice. At the same time she became a well-accepted leader in high school student activities. This high school graduate could not control her responses to the items in the college entrance examination, however, with the result that she earned the highest score ever obtained by an applicant to this college. When her college counselor asked her to explain the discrepancy between her high school average and the results of the entrance examination, she expressed her great desire to be like other girls. Asked how she is progressing in her freshman college studies, she answered, "I have just written an essay for English; I made it a B paper."

In most secondary schools too many young people can be found who are termed "bright underachievers." These students fail to achieve academic success commensurate with their apparently high mental potential. This situation can be explained in various ways. During his earlier school experiences, the young person may have earned satisfactory marks with little or no effort on his part. Hence he had never learned how to study; his superior intelligence had not been recognized by his teachers and he had not been motivated to excel in his school work. Another cause of his underachievement in high school can be the result of the effect on him of the physical and emotional changes that take place during adolescence. He becomes so involved in satisfying his newly felt personal and social needs that meeting the school's standards of academic achievement appears to him to be of minor importance. Yet he may exhibit considerable interest in other areas of knowledge.

School people are becoming increasingly concerned about the bright underachiever and are attempting to discover what stimulates intellectual curiosity and in various ways to motivate him toward engaging in the kind of school study activities that will ensure for him a high degree of mental accomplishment without denying him the satisfaction of his other strong interests and urges.

These few examples illustrate the experiences of some gifted young people. Adults can err either in failing to recognize, or in placing too great emphasis on, intellectual superiority, thereby stifling the usual personal, emotional, and social needs of maturing children and adolescents. It is possible for a gifted boy or girl to achieve a good life adjustment in spite of his superior mental ability provided that outgoing attitudes are fostered from early childhood onward. For example, a college upper junior, a student in a class taught by one of the authors, has maintained a consistent grade of A to this point in her college studies. Yet she is married, participates with enthusiasm in college and community agency activities, and is extremely well liked as well as respected by her instructors and fellow students. Sensible parents and understanding teachers have helped this young woman to achieve wholesome, all-around development.

## Psychological Procedures

In an attempt to meet the educational and social needs of the gifted adolescent, various plans have been tried. A program of rapid advancement (acceleration) has been advocated and found helpful within limits. The separation of the exceptionally bright from less able students in special classes (segregation) has been tried with some appreciable degree of success. An educationally valuable approach is to keep the gifted in regular classes where superior intellectual needs are met through supplementary assignments and additional materials (enrichment), but participation in recreational and social activities with peers is not denied. There are advantages and disadvantages in each plan.

Through acceleration intellectual accomplishments can be furthered, but at the expense of social and emotional development. This is an especially hazardous procedure to be employed with socially sensitive adolescents. The organization of special classes enables gifted students to achieve high scholastic averages; the consequent lack of opportunity for these young people to mingle with the rank-and-file school population, however, is likely to encourage among these special students the development of superior, conceited, or snobbish attitudes. Although enrichment within the regular class situation may appear to be the desirable solution, it taxes the ingenuity of the teacher and places an extra study burden upon the learner, which he may resent. The special attention accorded him by the teacher may earn the enmity of the other members of the class. Moreover, the teacher may encounter difficulty in evaluating objectively the mentally superior student's achievement in terms of the study results of the mentally inferior class members.

Regardless of the administrative approach utilized by a school or school system for the education of intellectually superior young people, teachers who earn success in motivating rapid learners toward the development of effective study habits place emphasis upon learner participation in extensive supplementary work that has practical application. Some gifted young people give evidence of a high degree of scholastic interest; others can recognize no value to themselves of many subjects which they are compelled to take, and consequently do no more studying than is needed to "get by" in comparison with their less able classmates.

To overcome mental inertia on the part of the bright student, many teachers attempt to discover his specific interest and provide for his particular needs. High school and college instructors increasingly are introducing many different types of activities appropriate for meeting individual differences in the needs and interests of gifted students, whether the particular teaching-learning area is mathematics, science, language usage, social studies, home economics, or another subject that has application or appreciation value. The success of any plan approach requires the cooperation of parents, community agencies, and the young person himself, as well as teacher effort. Moreover, whatever teaching-learning procedures are employed, mentally superior young people should be helped to achieve the following objectives, listed by Charles E. Bish, the director of the Academically Talented Student Project:

1. Become intellectually curious, searching for meanings and seeking to find new relationships rather than old facts.
2. Improve the ability to do independent study and carry on research with attention to basic work habits, study skills, and methodology.
3. Learn to apply a wide range of knowledge and principles to the solution of many life problems.
4. Gain skill in self-evaluation.
5. Develop skills in critical thinking, gain a passion for truth, become open-minded with a sense of suspended judgment.
6. Realize the responsibilities as

well as the power of knowledge.
7. Develop leadership ability including personal poise, respect for the worth of others, and skill in group dynamics and person-to-person relationships.
8. Extend any tendency toward creativeness of various types.
9. Sense the implications of change.
10. Perfect skills in communication.
11. Develop the breadth of vision to see the possibilities of the future, the realities of the present, and the heritage of the past; to see in all this the continuing stream of man's ideas and questions and concerns.[8]

## Mentally Retarded Adolescents

The mentally subnormal group includes all individuals who represent the deviation from normal mental status to that of the moron, imbecile, or idiot. Much research has been and is being undertaken concerning the possible causes of mental retardation, but it is not our purpose here to review the literature in this field.[9] Since idiots and many imbeciles need

[8] Charles E. Bish, *Administration Procedures and School Practices for the Academically Talented Student in the Secondary School,* National Education Association, Washington, 1960, pp. 17–18.
[9] See *Proceedings of Two Conferences on Research Opportunities in Mental Retardation in Pennsylvania,* The Woods Schools and Residential Treatment Center, Langhorne, Pa., 1962.

to be institutionalized during their childhood years, they rarely, if ever, gain entrance into a secondary school. Hence the discussion here deals with those adolescents whose degree of mental ability, according to a valid and reliable intelligence test, falls approximately between IQs of 50 and 75, and who commonly are termed *mentally retarded* or *mentally handicapped.*

Although mentally retarded adolescents constitute no more than about 2 per cent of the adolescent school population of the United States, their developmental needs become as important parental, school, and general community responsibilities as do the needs, urges, and interests of mentally average and superior young people. In fact, the displayed inability of many mentally handicapped teen-agers to adjust adequately to ordinary life situations tends to earn for them the more or less sympathetic attention of adults and peer associates.

## Characteristics of the Mentally Retarded Adolescent

On the average there is little, if any, physical difference between the mentally retarded and the mentally average adolescent. For both, growth in height and in total muscular weight, the age at which pubescence is reached, and the development of motor ability and eye-hand coordination follow approximately the same patterns of individual variation. A mentally retarded individual, however, has incomplete or impaired mental development. In comparison with the mentally more able, he learns less and learns it more slowly. He tends to be ineffective in situations that demand the exercise of reasoning and judgment, and finds it difficult to adjust satisfactorily to new conditions or experiences. In general, he can be expected to perform at a lower level than do mentally average young people.

The mentally handicapped adolescent displays a degree of intellectual development that approximates the mental status of an average 10- or 11-year-old child. As is true of the child, the retarded adolescent's memory may be good; he may improve in the ability to give voluntary attention to, and to concentrate upon, a concrete situation. This young person, however, usually fails to acquire an average adolescent's ability to deal with abstractions. Power is lacking to make adequate comparisons, to arrive at accurate, objective generalizations, or to be successful in creative activity. The vocabulary is meager, and verbal expression may be relatively colorless and stilted. Written composition is concerned with the concrete and present rather than with the imaginative, remote, or fanciful. Also, the fact that the slow learner may be retarded two or more grades in reading ability gives rise to difficulty in mastering the content of textbooks that usually are geared to the reading power of his brighter classmates. Moreover, since many mentally retarded young people represent low socioeconomic family background, they lack the kinds and amounts of home advantages that are experienced by members of the higher socioeconomic groups.

Significant differences between mentally retarded adolescents and their more intelligent peers are evidenced in their attitudes toward recreational and social activities, home relationships, and peer associations. Mentally slow teen-agers like action. Both boys and girls enjoy outdoor games and sports, various forms of dancing, exciting (often syncopated) rhythmic exercises, and some table games. Girls usually are interested in home activities, reading simple love stories, viewing television or motion-picture programs; boys like to read about and make useful objects and are interested in factual history, sports, and adventure; adolescents of both sexes prefer remunerative, activity-stimulating jobs to study or school attendance.

When the mentally retarded young person recognizes his limitations, he becomes extremely sensitive to the attitudes displayed toward him by adults and associates of his own age. He resents intensely any attempts on the part of his elders to "smooth the way" for him by directing his behavior and trying to protect him from situations in which he might be at a disadvantage. He also tends to be emotionally disturbed if his peers either treat him with too much consideration or reject him because of his retardation.

The school-attending retarded boy often can gain status among his schoolmates through the display of physical prowess in sports activities. A retarded adolescent girl who is "pretty," good-natured, and apparently submissive may attract the attention of more able boys; but her lack of pep soon bores them and they reject her for more alert girl associates. Some dull adolescent girls, however, begin early to become interested in members of the opposite sex and continue to experience the urge to have a boy friend. They are compelled to fulfill their desire by seeking the company of boys of the same age or dull older boys.

Although the mentally retarded adolescent is at a disadvantage in most of the situations in which he finds himself, his mental status cannot always be evaluated by introspection. Hence as he attempts to adjust to his relationships with his associates, he is enabled to develop whatever success-effecting social qualities he can achieve. There are evidences of overlapping in social competence between mentally slow and brighter young people, even though the average adjustment of the slow group may be considerably inferior to that of more intelligent groups. Since evaluating instruments designed to measure degree of social maturity are still in an experimental stage, many of the subtle elements that combine to produce social competence continue to elude test constructors and test-performance interpreters.

## Adult Attitudes and the Mentally Handicapped

Parental attitude toward the handicap of the mentally retarded adolescent exercises a potent influence upon his emotional status. Although some mothers continually prod their children from birth onward, many parents appear able and willing to accept the fact that during his early years a child does not achieve successfully in school work, or display exceptional alertness in his home or other interpersonal relationships. The parents are likely to explain his retardation in terms of slow development. When the boy or girl approaches or has passed the pubertal period, the mother no longer can blame the developmental process for the retarded behavior. The reason must be sought elsewhere.

The mother suddenly remembers that early in the child's life the father or another member of the family dropped the child, thus damaging his head. Or the father or mother recalls that the child resembles an older member of the spouse's family who always has been "queer." More often, however, parents are likely to blame school people for their adolescent child's apparently retarded behavior, especially for his poor school achievement. The teacher cannot teach; low test scores reflect teacher prejudice against or dislike of the young person. To the extent that parents are ambitious for their child, they demand that he take difficult college preparatory courses in spite of repeated failures. Attempts on the part of school personnel to fit curricular offerings and teaching approaches to the educational needs of retarded pupils may incite considerable resentment among parents. This attitude is caused by the belief that they and their child will suffer disgrace in the community.

Regardless of the way in which parents express their disappointment in, and distress over, their child's mental retardation, the adolescent himself becomes the victim of their displayed attitudes. The young person is embarrassed not only by his own inadequacy but also by his parents' inability or unwillingness to accept his mental retardation and to cooperate with the school in helping him develop whatever potential he possesses. Hence the emotionalized home situations to which he is constantly exposed are likely to encourage the development of either excessive aggressiveness or extreme withdrawal behavior.

In school the retarded adolescent may have frustrating experiences. His feelings of personal and social insecurity are not always recognized by his teachers. They may consider him to be indifferent to learning, uncooperative, or socially immature. He may seem to lack individual responsibility and to have delinquent tendencies. Unless the school in cooperation with parents can provide adequate opportunities for the mentally retarded to find a respected, even though humble, place for himself in his community, he is likely to become emotionally disturbed as well as being mentally retarded.

## Educating the Mentally Slow Adolescent

In states where the school attendance law permits young people to leave school at age 16, many slow adolescents drop out of school when they reach that age. Since a 16-year-old dropout rarely is prepared for any except a menial job, educators are attempting to keep these adolescents in school by providing educational offerings for them that will be interesting and profitable.

Although both the mentally superior and the mentally retarded are receiving considerable attention from educational leaders, the learning problems of the latter group were recognized earlier than those of the bright. Hence various approaches have been made toward fitting curriculums and teaching procedures to the learning level of the slow adolescent. For example, comparative studies have been undertaken to discover the difference in value of certain teaching-learning situations to rapid and slow learners. In a study conducted by the U.S. Office of Education it was found that among thirty instructional provisions and procedures utilized in the teaching of English in the secondary schools, rapid and slow learners differ in the extent to which any particular teaching approach has value. The data indicate that for slow learners the teaching of English must be geared to their present needs and interests. Similar emphases hold for the other nine subject areas included in the study.

Attention is being directed toward fitting slow learners for vocational activities that are suited to their ability level and interests and in which they will achieve satisfying adjustment. They need much intelligent vocational guidance. Provision also is made for helping them to improve their personal habits and their relationships with adults and other young people, as well as to achieve a better self-concept. Emphasis is placed on participation in out-of-class school activities. The sociodrama can serve as a good medium for encouraging slow learners to change certain undesirable social attitudes.[10]

The secondary school population of the mentally retarded can be expected to increase as teaching materials and procedures become suited to their level of learning. One significant approach is to provide special

[10] Ethelwyne Arnholter, "Social Drama for Retarded Adolescents," *Exceptional Children,* pp. 132–134, January, 1955.

classes with specially trained teachers. These classes usually are small in size, making it possible for the teacher to meet the learning needs of each adolescent enrolled. There are two types of special classes: (1) the integrated special class, which allows the pupils to attend the special class for part of the day and then to mingle with other, more able pupils for general instruction, and (2) the segregated special classes, which keep the slow pupils together during the entire day for all their schoolwork. The latter plan represents a type of isolation that may be socially undesirable for them as well as for the others who will come into contact with them in out-of-school situations. Moreover, a stigma is attached to this type of organization that is difficult for the segregated pupils and their parents to accept.

Some school systems (especially those in urban areas) have established vocational or trade schools presumably for the benefit of mentally less able adolescents. It has been found, however, that the achieving of competence in many of the skills to be developed in these schools requires a higher degree of mental alertness than is possessed by some of the mentally handicapped. Hence vocational and trade schools are becoming selective in their admission policy. Although some retarded learners can be helped to master simple skills, we must not lose sight of the fact that others will be able to perform adequately only in a job that represents no more than unskilled labor.

Many secondary schools are organizing cooperative programs. During his junior or senior year the learner's schedule of classes is so arranged that he can alternate for one- or two-week periods between work at a job and attendance at school. This enables the student to continue his schooling and at the same time begin to bridge the gap between the school and the community. The employer and the school authorities share the responsibility of the activities of the two adolescents who alternate their programs. Thus the school and the employer together can help the paired individuals achieve success in the schoolwork learning. These experiences have value for any high school pupil, but they are especially worthwhile for the mentally retarded adolescent who needs to experience success in practical work in order to bolster his ego and his dignity.

In their attempts to meet the educational needs of mentally slow adolescents, high school administrators and curriculum constructors have made some significant errors and have experienced interesting repercussions. For example, at one time dull students who could not succeed in so-called "academic" subjects, especially mathematics and modern foreign languages, were scheduled for commercial subjects such as typewriting, stenography, and bookkeeping. This procedure placed a stigma upon the latter area of study, which teachers in the field resented strongly and which caused brighter students to hesitate to elect them. More serious, however, is the fact that the retarded student finds stenography and bookkeeping as difficult to master as foreign language and mathematics. Hence business training for the slow student has been limited in scope to typing from copy, filing, "receptioning," and other routine office chores. Contrariwise, some schools provide for the retarded a nontechnical and practical course in applied chemistry which has become so popular with more able students that it now is accepted for college entrance.

The kind of curriculum provided and the teaching procedures utilized vary with degree of retardation. In any case, subject-matter materials should be geared to the practical needs of the retarded individual. Teaching approaches must be adjusted to the young person's present level of understanding and his immediate interests, with a hope on the part of his teachers that, within his mental limitations, he gradually may improve his understanding and refine his interests. One of the authors once was told by a supervisor that exceptionally bright young people manage to learn in spite of poor teaching. Regardless of the truth of this statement concerning the bright, there can be no doubt about the fact that the teacher, as well as the parent, of the retarded needs patience, emotional control, ingenuity, keenness of insight, and a sympathetic (but not sentimental) attitude toward the mentally handicapped, as well as the power to motivate successful learning to the limit of individual capacity to achieve.

## The Emotionally Disturbed or Socially Maladjusted Adolescent

Throughout this chapter the reader's attention has been directed to the possible emotionally disturbing and socially maladjustive concomitants of any form of adolescent exceptionality. The atypical adolescent is likely to experience situational problems and difficult interpersonal relations that exercise a potent influence upon his emotional status and social adjustment. For an adolescent to differ markedly either in physical constitution or in mental ability from the average of his group tends to set him apart from his peer associates. If the others can learn to accept his possession of the isolating factor, satisfactory personal and social adjustment can be achieved.

There are, however, some apparently physically and mentally "normal" adolescents who, without any easily discovered reason for their condition, show so great evidence of serious emotional disturbance or social maladjustment that they are considered to be atypical or exceptional. Special attention needs to be given to these individuals to prevent their condition from becoming more serious. Parents and teachers can be of help in alleviating tensions.

## Characteristics of the Emotional or Social Deviate

Normal adolescents tend on occasions to be aggressive, rebellious, or withdrawn. Hence it sometimes is difficult to differentiate between more or less typical adolescent behavior and that which is exceptional to the degree that the young person concerned requires special attention. We know that an attitude of resentment, insecurity, or rebellion against authority either in the home or in the school may express itself in any one of various forms of behavior. For example, Greta Mayer and Mary Hoover list certain behavior reactions of developing adolescents that can be justifiable causes for adult concern. The behavioral symptoms that probably need special attention are presented separately for younger and older adolescents.

The 11- to 14-year-old group:

Justifiable causes for concern include:

1. Inability to make any friends at all, or intense, exclusive preoccupation with dating.
2. Excessive eating to the point of becoming significantly overweight—or extremely poor appetite resulting in undesirable weight loss.
3. Severe nail biting.
4. Refusal to take any responsibility both at home and at school; *excessive* rebellion against au-

thority—*some* rebellion is good.
5. Persistent failure in school after having initially done well.
6. Preoccupation with and too frequent, indiscriminate use of obscene language.
7. Persistent general lack of interest in life, constant joylessness.
8. Excessive childishness or fear of growing up as shown by a child's continuing unwillingness to look or act his age and by his playing *only* with younger children.[11]

The 14- through 17-year-old group:

Signs of possible trouble include:

1. Constant open rebellion against *all* authority, or inability to see the need for *any* limits on his behavior.
2. Excessive withdrawal, lack of interest in friends but no interest in solitary pursuits either, seeming to be constantly lost in his own thoughts.
3. Intense preoccupation with dat-

ing—to the exclusion of everything else.
4. More than an isolated episode of overt homosexuality.
5. Use of narcotics; *excessive* smoking and drinking.
6. Inability to stand up for himself, crying a great deal, always seeking out the company of younger children.
7. In spite of normal intelligence,

---

[11] Greta Mayer and Mary Hoover, *When Children Need Special Help with Emotional Problems,* The Child Study Association of America, New York, 1961, pp. 13–14.

absolutely no interest in any pursuits more demanding than television or the movies.

8. Frequently expressed fears of not being able to amount to anything, of not being able to live up to his own or his parents' expectations.

9. Preoccupation with schoolwork to the exclusion of any close friendships or any leisure-time activity.

10. Constant need for parental approval and help in making even minor decisions.[12]

An adolescent needs to be studied carefully and perhaps receive therapeutic treatment if his behavior is characterized by extreme and prolonged tendencies toward shyness, withdrawal, or overaggressiveness. Equally serious are habitual lying and stealing, bizarre actions, vandalism, or the display of other forms of behavior that are symptomatic of emotional instability or asocial attitudes. The causes of the atypical behavior may be deep-seated. Unfavorable environmental conditions may serve to intensify an already-developed personality defect.

## Adjustive Procedures

The incidence of extreme emotional instability during adolescence is discussed in Chapter 11. At this point we shall consider briefly some of the educational procedures commonly utilized with adolescents whose emotional difficulties are so severe that it is inadvisable to keep them in regular classes for instructional purposes. An emotionally disturbed or socially maladjusted young person usually requires much of the teacher's time and attention. To permit him to remain in a class of better-adjusted students would be unfair to both the teacher and the class.

Some school communities have established special schools for the training of emotionally atypical young people, as, for example, the "600" schools in New York City. The purpose of these schools is to provide educational opportunities for adolescents who are not mentally retarded but whose behavior problems are so severe that a teacher of a regular class cannot cope with them.

To the present, relatively few special secondary schools and classes have been provided for emotionally and socially atypical adolescents. Therefore many of these young people must remain in regular classes. The situation is helped somewhat, however, by an increasing trend on the secondary school level toward adding specially trained guidance workers and counselors to the regular school staff. Disturbed young people can thereby receive individual help. The trained social worker is finding a place for himself in most communities, where he can serve as a

[12] *Ibid.*, pp. 14–15.

liaison officer between the home and the school. In dealing with difficult cases the assistance of the court may be needed. Little can be accomplished in the way of adolescent rehabilitation by the members of the school guidance staff, however, unless they receive commendable cooperation from parents, organized community agencies, and the school's administrative and teaching personnel.

## Questions and Problems for Discussion

1. Suggest reasons why exceptional individuals have special adjustment problems. Show what can be done to help them.
2. Compare the adolescent handicapped by deafness with the adolescent who is blind. What differences do you find between their adjustment problems?
3. What relationship, if any, is there between speech defects and emotional disturbance? List a speech defect for which you can suggest therapy.
4. Outline the kinds of adjustment problems experienced by mentally retarded adolescents; by academically talented adolescents. What differences are found between them?
5. Enumerate some of the needs of gifted adolescents that are not being met today.
6. Suggest ways in which teaching approaches to the motivation of mentally retarded learners and of gifted learners might differ.
7. *Special Exercises:*
   a. Prepare two lists of characteristics: one to identify mentally retarded learners and another to identify mentally gifted learners. Report the differences you find between them.
   b. Recall an adolescent of superior ability and describe the traits that led you to believe he was mentally superior.
   c. Talk with two adolescents who are mentally retarded and try to discover their worries. Do the same for two adolescents who are intellectually gifted. What differences do you find?

## Selected References

Abraham, W.: *Common Sense about Gifted Children,* Harper & Row, Publishers, Incorporated, New York, 1958.

Baker, H. J.: *Introduction to Exceptional Children,* 3d ed., The Macmillan Company, New York, 1959.

Ball, J. C.: *Social Deviancy and Adolescent Personality: An Analytic Study with the MMPI,* University of Kentucky Press, Lexington, Ky., 1962.

Barbara, D. A. (ed.): *The Psychotherapy of Stuttering,* Charles C Thomas, Publisher, Springfield, Ill., 1961.

Cowen, Emory L., et al.: *Adjust-*

*ment to Visual Disability in Adolescence,* American Foundation for the Blind, New York, 1961.

Crow, Lester D., and Alice Crow: *Educating the Academically Able: A Book of Readings,* David McKay Company, Inc., New York, 1963.

Cutts, N. E., and N. Moseley: *Teaching the Bright and Gifted,* Prentice-Hall, Inc., Englewood Cliffs, N.J., 1957.

Daniels, A. S.: *Adapted Physical Education: Principles and Practices of Physical Education for Exceptional Children,* Harper & Row, Publishers, Incorporated, New York, 1954.

Davis, H.: *Hearing and Deafness,* rev. ed., Holt, Rinehart and Winston, Inc., New York, 1960.

D'Evelyn, K.: *Meeting Children's Emotional Needs: A Guide for Teachers,* Prentice-Hall, Inc., Englewood Cliffs, N.J., 1957.

Eisenson, J.: *The Psychology of Speech,* Appleton-Century-Crofts, Inc., New York, 1938.

Fiedler, M. F.: *Deaf Children in a Hearing World,* The Ronald Press Company, New York, 1952.

Freehill, M. F.: *Gifted Children: Their Psychology and Education,* The Macmillan Company, New York, 1961.

French, J. L.: *Educating the Gifted: A Book of Readings,* 2d ed., Holt, Rinehart and Winston, Inc., New York, 1964.

Garrison, K. C., and D. G. Force, Jr.: *The Psychology of Exceptional Children,* 3d ed., The Ronald Press Company, New York, 1959.

Gowan, J. C.: *An Annotated Bibliography on the Academically Talented,* National Education Association, Washington, 1961.

Haring, N. G., and E. L. Phillips: *Educating Emotionally Disturbed Children,* McGraw-Hill Book Company, New York, 1962.

Heck, A. O.: *The Education of Exceptional Children,* 2d ed., McGraw-Hill Book Company, New York, 1953.

Hildreth, G., et al.: *Educating Gifted Children,* Harper & Row, Publishers, Incorporated, New York, 1952.

Ingram, C. P.: *Educating the Slow-learning Child,* 2d ed., The Ronald Press Company, New York, 1953.

Kirk, S. A.: *Educating Exceptional Children,* Houghton Mifflin Company, Boston, 1962.

Lichter, S. O., et al.: *The Dropouts: A Treatment Study of Intellectually Capable Students Who Drop Out of High School,* The Free Press of Glencoe, New York, 1962.

Magnifico, L. X.: *Education for the Exceptional Child,* David McKay Company, Inc., New York, 1958.

Mathews, D. K., et al.: *The Science of Physical Education for Handicapped Children,* Harper & Row, Publishers, Incorporated, New York, 1962.

Sarason, S. B.: *Psychological Problems in Mental Deficiency,* 3d ed., Harper & Row, Publishers, Incorporated, New York, 1959.

Torrance, E. P.: *Guiding Creative Talent,* Prentice-Hall, Inc., Englewood Cliffs, N.J., 1962.

Witty, P. (ed.): *The Gifted Child,* D. C. Heath and Company, Boston, 1951.

# Chapter Eleven

## Conflicts and Behavior Disorders

The adolescent undergoes a continuous process of adjusting. His personal and social behavior does not develop in a vacuum. Those interests, attitudes, and modes of behavior that are peculiarly his result from the relationships that exist between his personal desires, needs, or inherent potentialities and the existing environmental conditions by which he is stimulated. Frustration and conflict situations may confront the adolescent almost continuously in his growing-up process. In his attempts to meet his personal and social needs the adolescent makes a variety of adjustments. He may satisfy his own needs and those of society; he may experience inadequate adjustments; he may fail so completely to adjust that emotional or mental breakdown results.

## Effects of Adolescent Frustration

It is a matter of common observation that some adolescents are able to make needed adjustments without undue stress. Yet even for them the process of adjusting involves a certain amount of stress and strain. An adolescent who adjusts well can be regarded as a young person who experiences relatively little tension in his daily activities. Contrariwise, an adolescent who habitually adjusts poorly tends to experience tension to a marked degree.

## Bases of Frustration

It is difficult for an adolescent to engage in any form of activity without meeting social or personal barriers of one or another kind. A barrier becomes a psychological obstacle when the individual recognizes it as a threat to his self-realization. Existing goals outside the adolescent's interest range do not become psychological barriers to him. Among the forces that may cause mental and emotional disturbance are the behavior and interests of others, school or group rules and regulations, social codes, unfulfilled desires, goals beyond achievement, and similar thwarting situations. Hence frustration can be considered to be *the result of an unsatisfied need or a thwarted desire.*

An adolescent's needs, wants, and interests become more extensive and intensive as he develops an increasing awareness of the objects and people that constitute his environment. The satisfaction of his various needs becomes more and more complex as these needs are influenced by his developing tastes and the customs of his group. The adolescent becomes extremely sensitive to the accepted mores of his culture. He wants attention, he seeks the approval of his associates, he strives for security, and he needs the ego satisfaction that accompanies successful achievement in one or another of his areas of activity. Failing in one or more of these, he develops a feeling of frustration, thus causing conflict to arise within himself or between himself and the constraining factors of his external environment.

## Sources of Frustration

Innumerable forces appear to block an impulse. What often appears to the onlooker to be no more than a petty source of annoyance may be productive of strong feelings of frustration in the individual concerned. Emotional stresses often are produced by happenings which, ten years later, cannot be recalled. During adolescence such experiences as the following become exciting factors of influence: the doorbell rings when a teen-ager wants to complete a typewritten report; a boy friend appears before his girl expects him; a 15-year-old boy has a date but is not permitted to drive the family car; a teen-ager is sent to bed in the middle of an exciting television program he is watching; a coach in a basketball game plays a boy who failed to meet practice conditions; the parents of a 14-year-old girl decide that she is too young to have twosome dates, with the result that the boy "hates" her parents; a teen-ager cannot convince his parents that they are "old-fashioned" because they disapprove of a boy and a girl dancing only with each other at a party.

Frustrating situations similar to those listed are common adolescent experiences; their frustrating influence, however, usually is temporary. At the time of their occurrence adolescents become emotionally upset. Later such experiences are recalled as amusing incidents by the same young people who earlier had regarded them as major tragedies. Yet adolescents sometimes seem to believe that everyone is conspiring against them to thwart their immediate plans or interests.

The nature and extent of frustration are associated closely with adolescent motives or goals. For example, a study[1] was conducted by high

[1] M. Brown and V. Martin, "The University High School Study of Adolescents: Characteristics of High School Students," *University High School Journal*, vol. 12, pp. 177–219, 1941.

school counselors of the interests and behavior-motivating goals of their students. Through the utilization of evaluating techniques such as the obtaining of introspective reports from the adolescents themselves, observation of their overt behavior, and reference to student cumulative record folders, the investigators found that for 105 high school students there was evidence of the possession of 287 identifiable goals that could be classified according to definite categories such as vocational, school, social life, economic independence, and marriage and family life. Adolescents face insurmountable obstacles such as the arousal of strong feelings of frustration with respect to lack of competing drive, conflict with parents, and lack of social prestige situations. The sources of some frustrations are rooted in the attitudes, motives, and interests of the adolescent himself; other obstacles to self-realization are products of environmental conditions.

Unfortunately, not all thwartings and annoyances can be overcome without undesirable aftermaths. If the frustration situations lie outside the adolescent's control, he may experience extreme emotional stress and strain. To be unprepared for an available coveted job; to be recommended for a position and then to fail the preliminary test; to be denied by parents the privilege of wearing dungarees to high school when other young people wear them; to contract a contagious disease at a time of contemplated marriage; to be called to serve in the Armed Forces against the desire to serve; to be apprehended by the police in an act of vandalism; or to "lose face" by failure to meet an important commitment—all these represent environmentally stimulated frustration situations that may produce emotional reactions varying with the degree of emotional stability possessed by the person or persons concerned.

Many more frustration situations would be experienced if laws that restrict asocial behavior were enforced more fully. Many of these laws and codes of behavior are established for the general welfare; yet these laws sometimes interfere with the desires or interests of the adolescent. Sex laws or sex codes are broken by some teen-agers; traffic regulations are disobeyed by adolescent drivers. Acquisition by adolescents of a willingness to obey traffic laws that are made for the benefit and safety of everyone would go far toward reducing the more than 36,000 traffic deaths that occur annually.

The arousal of a feeling of frustration is a common experience of an adolescent who believes that he cannot meet peer competition in any area of activity. For example, the economic status of his family may be a strong source of frustration both to the adolescent himself and to his parents who are eager to meet his monetary needs and interests. The democratic ideal, based upon the concept of equality of opportunity within individual limitations to attain desired goals, has helped to reduce former rigid class distinctions. Nevertheless, an adolescent feels frustrated if he cannot afford to have or to do things for which many of his friends seem to have sufficient money.

## Frustration Tolerance

The extent to which an adolescent is able to endure frustration without becoming emotionally disorganized can be considered to be his *degree of frustration tolerance*. An individual's frustration tolerance depends upon various factors, including his age, health, and past experience, as well as the nature of the situation or the personal motive that can become the cause of the frustration. The kind and size of the obstacle that is encountered and the extent to which it is mastered are indications of an adolescent's degree of frustration tolerance.

A particular situation or set of circumstances may constitute a possible source of annoyance to each of a group of young people. Their respective reactions are evidences of differences in frustration tolerance. For example, students of relatively equal ability are assigned the same set of problems to solve. A few of the students may look at the problems and decide that they are too difficult, thus exhibiting low frustration tolerance; others display high frustration tolerance by persevering in the task until they complete the assignment.

A procrastinator has good intentions but also has low frustration tolerance; he seldom starts an activity until the last minute or after it is too late to complete it. High frustration tolerance is shown by those adolescents who carry out their good intentions according to a schedule; they become the individuals upon whom others can depend for the completion of tasks in spite of factors of annoyance, disappointment, or thwarting.

Behavior that reflects low frustration tolerance may have serious consequences. To illustrate this point take the case of John and Harry, two equally able young men who were college classmates. John was selected to be the student supervisor of the dormitory in which both boys lived. Although Harry was not annoyed by the fact that he had not been chosen for the post, he could not resist teasing John about the great responsibilities connected with the job and all the things that John should or should not do. Harry's attitude was not malicious, but the other boy became very much disturbed by what he considered to be unjust criticism of his behavior. Finally, in an emotional frenzy John procured a gun and shot Harry. This exhibition of completely uncontrolled behavior is an indication of John's extremely low degree of frustration tolerance.

# Adolescent Conflicts

Conflict arises when an adolescent wants to satisfy two opposing interests or desires at the same time. He may want to obey his parents by remaining at home to complete his study; at the same time he has a strong desire to be with his crowd. He wants to indulge in petting behavior; yet he wishes to be considered a model boy. Too often an adolescent wants to play both sides of the fence by being all things to all peer associates and adults. Sooner or later these attitudes are certain to arouse emotional turmoil. Once a young person makes up his mind, i.e., arrives at a constructive decision, he resolves his conflict. The adolescent encounters this kind of conflict situation many times during his development. If he decides to become a major athlete, he is likely not to become a medical student; if he strongly desires to be a social leader in his school, he is likely not to be on the high school or college honor roll; if he wants to be known as the class clown, he probably will not be selected as the school's representative in academic competition.

## Bases of Conflict

An unsatisfied need may be the cause of mental or emotional conflict. The struggle among opposing desires sets up tensions that often are increased by the repression of an unsatisfied drive. If these tensions are not lessened, many problems of personal and social adjustment may arise in the life of the adolescent. Mental or emotional conflict occurs when an adolescent's various ideas and feelings tend to find their respective outlets in his psychic experiences.

Mental conflicts sometimes take the form of a combat with reality. When the demands of nature are too severe for the adolescent, he may develop neurotic tendencies and attempt to retreat into a world of fantasy. It is easy for him to satisfy his desires in this dreamworld. Some adolescents find it difficult to subject themselves to the hardships that they encounter in routine activities; others are unwilling to submit to any form of authority. In both cases the emotions are highly sensitized. These adolescents dislike everything that interferes with their desire to assert their individuality or that adds to the difficulty of dominating their peers, elders, or surroundings.

An adolescent endows each new experience with emotional values. His daily activities are colored by feeling tones attached to earlier experiences. His past experiences and his attitudes toward them are mental and social factors that may arouse feelings of insufficiency. The adolescent often finds that he is scolded for his mistakes or ridiculed for his short-comings more than he is praised for his accomplishments. If he is clumsy or inept in performance, he is thereby constantly denied participation in desired activity. This kind of conditioning imposes handicaps that are difficult for the already inhibited adolescent to overcome.

The intricate pattern of human nature and the complex character of human relationship preclude the possibility of any adolescent's achieving a completely placid, nonthwarted state of self-satisfaction. An unresolved conflict may persist in varying forms and situations. Unless the afflicted person can achieve a reasonable resolution of his conflict, he may attempt to escape from the situation in one of various ways. Unresolved conflicts affect the individual's entire behavior pattern; they may predispose toward disintegration of personality.

## Adjusting to Frustration and Conflict

It has been pointed out that frustration arises whenever goal-seeking activity is obstructed. Interference by things or people, or by individual or environmental deficiencies, may be the cause of mild or extreme forms of frustration. There is no standard remedy that can be applied to assist an adolescent who is experiencing a frustration or a conflict. Parents, teachers, and community leaders can help an adolescent achieve self-building experiences, yet a preventive program is fraught with innumerable problems on the social level.

Whatever its source may be, the adolescent who is experiencing a conflict can approach the problem situation in one of three ways: he can launch a direct attack, he can attempt to compromise, or he can retreat from any attempt at the solution of the problem. According to the first approach, he attempts to do something about his difficulty. In the second, he seeks ways and means of alleviating the stresses and strains with as little personal disturbance as possible. If he follows the third, he becomes a victim of the conflict situation, and may become mentally ill as a result of the nonresolution of it.

Various factors need to be considered before direct action or compromise is applied to a conflict situation. Direct action may be too impulsive; it may omit some factors that are basic to the situation. Immediate solutions are successful only when they are based upon an intelligent understanding of all the factors that have contributed to the conflict. Too often an adolescent uses direct action to solve a conflict situation and later regrets his decision.

Compromise usually is the approach of a person who can meet his conflict situation with some intelligent understanding of its basic factors, and who is willing to make concessions rather than to demand complete satisfaction of his wants. An adolescent who is willing to compromise to free himself from a conflict situation discovers that any action he takes to relieve tension is better for him than passive acceptance of emotion-disturbing conditions. We shall now consider briefly some of the devices and approaches that are frequently employed to resolve conflict and frustration.

## Adolescent Struggles toward Adjustment

The struggle for adjustment is a continuous process. Personality adjustments or maladjustments during adolescence do not develop suddenly and without cause. In adolescent attempts to meet the problems of growing up there is constant utilization of various techniques of adjustment. When adolescents' motives are blocked, they tend to react in one or another of several different ways. There is a tendency to control, remove, or destroy the obstacle, or to effect a satisfactory compromise in the resolution of a conflict. Consequently, the adolescent utilizes one or more forms of behavior adjustment that sometimes are referred to as substitute responses in the situation. The implications of the most important patterns of adjustment are described here.

### Compensatory Behavior

Compensation can be interpreted as a general concept that includes many specific forms of adjustment to failure or inadequacy, or as a specific attempt to reduce tensions that result from a recognized defect. In compensatory behavior the individual tends to emphasize the functioning of another trait so that the attention of his associates will be directed away from his real or imagined defect.

A physically strong teen-age boy who cannot excel in his studies may aim to become a successful athlete. A small adolescent boy may try to compensate for his short stature by excessive talking or by highly opinionated behavior. A teen-age girl may wear startling clothes to compensate for her lack of physical beauty. An invalid may become exacting or violent in his demands to gain the attention he craves. In each instance an attempt is being made to earn social approval by calling attention to what the person believes to be his strong characteristics. In most forms of compensatory behavior there is a suggestion of maladjustment which may be either mild or extreme.

## Attention-getting Behavior

Occasionally an adolescent who is on the defensive seems bent upon attracting attention to himself. Young adolescents sometimes make faces, gesticulate foolishly, walk in stiff-legged fashion, or manage in some other way to "show off." Older adolescents employ more subtle tactics to attract attention to themselves. They want to receive recognition, since to be recognized is more satisfying than to be ignored. It is only when ordinary behavior fails them that individuals attempt to bring attention to themselves by means of spectacular or unconventional behavior. This urge is especially strong during adolescence.

A few of the attention-getting activities of adolescents include boasting of family status or personal prowess; displaying bad manners; engaging in hobbies; affecting peculiar dress or speech patterns; or teasing and tormenting. These activities often are resorted to when ordinary behavior does not gain for teen-agers the amount and kind of recognition which they crave.

Many of these simple attempts represent innocuous adjustment techniques. For example, a boy in a freshman high school class with others who are mentally superior to himself is able to pass in his work, but is usually near the bottom of his class in achievement. Hence to gain recognition from his classmates he collects unusual specimens of whatever the current interest of the group may be. Any peer approval that he receives acts as an impetus toward further efforts on his part to collect shells, stones, marbles, pictures, political campaign buttons, or whatever else may be handy or desirable.

It is possible for adults to overencourage attention-getting behavior. If the habit of thrift is being developed, a young person may become so much interested in the size of his account in the school bank that he develops undesirable traits such as miserliness or dishonesty. In order to avoid possible ill effects of undue competition, wise teachers refrain from placing too great emphasis upon competition among their pupils.

Sometimes the adolescent's desire for attention is so strong that he engages in abnormal and asocial behavior as a means of gaining the approval of his peers. For example, in order to gain prestige, a teen-ager who feels inferior to his peers may perform many tasks demanded of him by a group of which he strongly wants to become a member. Often delinquent behavior can be traced to the attempt of adolescents to satisfy their urge for attention.

## The Utilization of Identification

It is normal for an adolescent to identify himself with a person whom he considers to be his superior and to experience satisfaction from the achievement of his associates. An adolescent wants to be identified with successful individuals. The person for identification may be his father, his favorite teacher, a famous athlete, a successful businessman, or a statesman. These forms of identification are beneficial to the extent that they help the young person develop fine personality characteristics. Personal loyalty is engendered by identification with worthwhile individuals and groups.

A baseball fan identifies himself with his favorite team; he then rejoices in the success of any team member or of the team and considers it to be a personal victory. An adolescent tends to identify himself with specific groups: gangs, select clubs, fraternities, or social and civic organizations. He takes pride in the good reputation of his organization. The higher the qualification for entrance, the greater is his tendency to boast of his group's achievements. This is especially true if he is the weak member of the group. He takes pride in the group's accomplishments. Likewise, the mediocre member of an outstanding family may find it comforting to boast about the accomplishments of his relatives.

Identification is undesirable if the adolescent so loses his individuality in that of his ideal that he is no longer conscious of himself as a person. The identification should not become so close that he takes on in thought and action the personality of his hero. There is some cause to fear that as boys identify themselves with the heroes of undesirable motion pictures or thrilling bad men on television, they may imitate in their own behavior the acts of their heroes.

## Projection of Blame

A tendency to blame another person or object for one's own shortcomings is not uncommon. Most adolescents dislike to admit their errors of judgment or their inability to perform with success. It is much more satisfying to *project* responsibility than to assume it. A social worker, for example, working with a group of teen-agers might attribute her lack of skill to inadequate facilities, poor supervision, or other less personal elements in the situation.

Many examples of the use of projection can be cited. His wife is to blame if the driver makes the wrong turn; the teacher is responsible for the poor grades of the student; a girl's tallness is the cause of her unpopularity and her lack of dates; interference of parents is the basis for a boy's being ignored at parties; the unbecoming dress is the reason for a girl's being a wallflower. Most of these statements represent excuses for the real reason of personal inadequacy.

If an attitude of inferiority dominates the individual, he may experience failure in various situations such as those associated with school, social, or civic life. If projection becomes habitual to the extent that the adolescent blames all his failures on others, deep-seated attitudes of resentment may develop and emotional disturbance may eventuate.

## The Utilization of Introjection

An adolescent gradually acquires ideas, emotional attitudes, and ideals from his associates. As he lives in his home and as he attends school and various social gatherings, the ideals exhibited by the individuals in the different situations are gradually and unconsciously acquired by him. The adolescent experiences his own feeling tones, his own emotional reactions, his own frustrations, but his beliefs result from the beliefs and ideals of parents, brothers and sisters, and others in his environment. It is through *introjection* that behavior is acquired when stimulated by the forces and influences just outlined. The adolescent, however, develops his own ideals and values through the interaction between himself and his home and educational influences. Since imitation of behavior is practiced and introjection tends to function indirectly, there is great need for parents and other adults, especially teachers, to exhibit the kind of behavior that is worthy of being used as a model.

## Self-deception through Rationalization

Rationalization is a form of self-deception employed by an adolescent when he has done something that he knows is undesirable or foolish. He attempts to explain his behavior in such a way that he will avoid criticism from others and bolster his own ego. He finds that if there is no valid reason for the self-satisfying behavior in which he has indulged, he must produce what to him is a sensible justification of it. Janet, 16 years old, is permitted to drive her father's automobile; hence 16-year-old Tom decides to drive his father's car although he has not asked permission to do so. Tom justifies his attitude on the basis of privileges granted to others.

It is very difficult for an adolescent to admit to himself or to others the real reasons for his acts or the actual motives for his behavior. Correct behavior is expected of adolescents. Hence it is almost unbearable for them to admit that their behavior is actuated by unworthy motives. If this type of self-deception is practiced too often, it is likely that no one will believe the young person when he is completely truthful.

Many rationalizations serve as self-bolstering forces in peer relations. Yet the persistent use of rationalization as a means of self-justification may lead to the development of a false appreciation of one's own personal attributes. The effects are not serious if the rationalizations are accompanied by an attitude of determination to try to avoid behavior that needs to be explained or excused.

## Daydreaming

Daydreaming is not always an indication of retreat from frustrating situations. There is a constructive aspect of daydreaming that is productive of art, music, and discoveries in science. There is a form of daydreaming, however, in which the adolescent attempts to gain satisfaction from imaginary successful achievement that might earn the approval of others which he could not earn through personal achievement. This is a popular form of self-satisfying adjustment for many adolescents.

Daydreaming permits the imagination to play with ideas that are immediate satisfactions of desired goals or purposes. When the adolescent recognizes the ephemeral character of his dreams or uses these daydreams as preparation for actual accomplishment, this form of mental activity is beneficial. Inadequate adjustment results when the world of fantasy is divorced completely from reality so that the individual is forced to rely upon daydreaming as a self-satisfying device.

The healthy adolescent is in no way harmed by his youthful dreams or fantasies if he is given sufficient opportunity for successful achievement within his abilities. The adolescent is known for his ability to drape himself over an armchair and indulge in idle dreaming. His thoughts wander from one half-formed dream to another; he is only mildly conscious of his surroundings. Yet shortly thereafter he is busily engaged in a realistic, constructive activity.

## Mental and Emotional Disorders

Sometimes his frustrations and conflicts are so severe that the adolescent is unable to find a way to resolve them in a socially acceptable fashion. The result is that his attitudes and behavior become increasingly unacceptable to his peers and other associates. The first failure to make a satisfactory adjustment to an emotion-disturbing situation is likely to become the basis of continued failure, resulting in serious maladjustment.

### Causes of Mental and Emotional Disturbances

Inability to master a disturbing situation may result either in flight from the annoying condition or in an unwarranted and abnormal attack upon the person or object involved. Flight is characterized by fleeing from the situation, self-criticism, envy, alcoholism, drug addiction, some form of neurosis, a psychotic state, or even suicide. Attack takes the form of overt aggression, grouchiness, delinquency, crime, or physical combat. Although laymen may not recognize the milder forms of these disturbances, the trained person, the psychiatrist, and many psychologists usually are sensitive to them. Many mental disorders originate in thought and feeling and need to be treated through constructive mental and emotional stimulation. The advance of psychiatric knowledge has done much to assist the afflicted and to dispel the once-held belief that irrational or antisocial behavior stems from heredity. Lay people are coming to understand that an emotionally disturbed state may be the resultant of social or other life experiences that serve as exciting factors.

The basic causes of maladjustment may be classified as *predisposing* and *exciting*. Most predisposing factors that cause mental and emotional disorders result from environmental influences. They emanate from conflict between the individual's psychobiological drives and the restrictions of his environment. Thus certain social, occupational, and sexual interests are significant barriers that may call for a detour if their form of expression is to be considered acceptable in our culture.

An adolescent whose life pattern is free from unusual stresses or strains can adjust satisfactorily to his daily activities, even though his frustration tolerance is relatively low. Conflict situations, however, may arise in the young person's life that act as exciting causes of more or less serious mental and emotional disorders. Some mental disturbances may be temporary in nature; others may persist until the victim can be helped only through hospitalization or the application of appropriate therapy.

## Psychosomatic Illness

The term *psychosomatic* implies an interrelationship of mind, body, and disease. A disturbed emotional state is believed to be accompanied by various physiological changes, e.g., change in rate of heart beat, gastronomical dysfunctioning, and increased muscular strength during extreme anger or rage. Normal functioning usually is restored with the reduction of emotional tension. The victim of a persistent fear or rage situation may be unaware of the strength of the emotional state. Yet he suffers physical discomfort or pain, which is interpreted by him to be symptomatic of a disease condition.

Some physical disorders that formerly were considered to have an organic origin now are regarded as psychosomatic, in that they involve emotional factors. The more common types of psychosomatic disorders include the common cold, ulcers, asthma, hay fever, colitis, eczema, arthritis, disorders of the circulatory system, obesity, and sterility. The habit acquired in childhood of emphasizing physical pain rather than emotional stress can influence an adolescent's reactions in similar situations. Moreover, it generally seems more acceptable to complain of physical illness than to reveal the fact that one is suffering from mental or emotional disturbance.

## Psychoneurosis

A neurosis or a psychoneurosis is a mild form of mental or emotional disturbance. It is a nervous disorder that usually is characterized by the apparent absence of any organic difficulty. There are many adolescents who are unable to make direct and straightforward adjustments. These individuals tend to meet certain exacting demands of life by developing one or another form of neurosis. Although the neurotic person may not be physically ill, he is far from well. Emotionally he is very unhealthy. The ailments of the neurotic person presume an interaction between physical and psychological aspects of his total personality. Emotional stress is accompanied by a type of bodily activity that tends to interfere with normal processes.

A psychoneurotic disorder usually is caused by a conflict between an individual's strong desires or ambitions and the restrictive force of the conduct standards of his culture. The thwarted urges of adolescents often represent highly personalized attitudes that were developed during childhood. These habitual attitudes tend to serve as predisposing conditions of emotional disorders. Contrariwise, actual symptoms of mental disorder are exhibited when the adolescent meets a shock-inducing situation, or when he can no longer repress his conflict condition successfully. In terms of their behavior manifestations, psychoneurotic disorders usually are classified as neurasthenia, psychasthenia, anxiety states, and hysteria.

A *neurasthenic* is self-preoccupied and depressed, and seems to be suffering from feelings of physical and mental fatigue. He frequently complains that he is suffering from one or another form of physical ailment such as indigestion, constipation, heart pains, eyestrain, or shortness of breath. Certain areas of his body seem to be more sensitive to pain than others; in fact, some areas become hypersensitive to pain, others are insensitive.

*Psychasthenia* is characterized by mental and emotional symptomatic conditions such as extreme fears or phobias, compulsions, or obsessions. One or more of these inner states seem to possess the individual completely. He is concerned about his health status and displays strong feelings of inadequacy. He may experience an extreme phobia such as *acrophobia,* fear of high places; *claustrophobia,* fear of closed places; *agoraphobia,* fear of open places; *achlophobia,* fear of crowds; or *zoophobia,* fear of animals. The adolescent may have a fixed idea or an obsession from which he is unable to free himself; yet he recognizes it to be irrational. He may have a tendency to perform meaningless motor acts that also are recognized as irrational. The psychasthenic is possessed by a compulsion to act, but seems to be unable to control his behavior.

An *anxiety state* is revealed in the adolescent's behavior when he experiences vague fears and feelings of apprehension. He feels that something terrible is going to happen but is unable to explain what it is. During an anxiety state the adolescent cannot concentrate, he easily becomes depressed and excited, and he may be irritable and quick-tempered. Feelings of inferiority or inadequacy often form the basis of his fears. He finds it difficult to assert himself or to appreciate what success he may be achieving.

*Hysteria* is characterized by apparent symptoms of serious physical or mental disorder that may be somewhat similar to the symptoms of psychosomatic illness. Often it is difficult for the trained person to discover whether the physical symptoms are imagined or have an actual organic base. Hysteria usually is caused by the adolescent's unconscious attempt to escape from an unresolvable conflict situation, inadequate adjustment to a real or fancied sexual shock, or unsuccessful attempts to compensate for other personality limitations.

## The Psychoses

The adolescent who suffers from a serious type of mental and emotional disorder is considered to be mentally ill. His *psychosis* (form of mental illness) usually represents complete or almost complete withdrawal from reality. The frequency of occurrence of six different psychoses among first admissions to mental hospitals is presented in Table 27.

*Table 27.* First Admissions to State and County Mental Hospitals in the United States by Selected Psychoses, 1950–1960

| PSYCHOSIS, NEW NOMENCLATURE | YEAR | | | | |
|---|---|---|---|---|---|
| | 1950 | 1951 | 1952 | 1953 | 1960 |
| Meningoencephalitic syphilis......... | 3,205 | 2,501 | 2,009 | 1,608 | 526 |
| Acute brain syndromes, alcohol intoxication................... | 5,771 | 5,618 | 5,726 | 6,085 | 8,662 |
| Cerebral arteriosclerosis............. | 17,766 | 18,311 | 17,602 | 16,155 | 18,012 |
| Senile brain disease................. | 14,691 | 15,226 | 15,205 | 6,167 | 9,155 |
| Manic depressive and psychotic depressive........................ | 10,115 | 8,906 | 8,044 | 3,688 | 4,195 |
| Dementia praecox.................. | 31,548 | 32,172 | 32,507 | 25,881 | 28,556 |

SOURCE: National Institute of Mental Health, Bethesda, Md.

## Causes of Mental and Emotional Disorders

Common predisposing and exciting causes of temporary or persistent mental and emotional disorders are:

1. Fixed parental prejudices, denials, or shocks experienced during childhood.

2. Inability to satisfy a fundamental want (often the sex urge) in terms of socially accepted behavior.

3. Abnormal fatigue, worry, anxiety, or boredom.

4. Physiological epochs such as puberty or the menopause.

5. Pressures arising out of disturbed economic, political, and social conditions.

6. Climatic conditions, as those indirectly produce a state of exhaustion and toxemia.

7. Disease, especially syphilis.

8. Trauma or injuries, especially to the head or spine.

9. Toxic infections brought about by alcohol or narcotics, or by poison that originates in the body, especially in the gastrointestinal tract.

10. Severe emotional shock such as fright, sudden death of a beloved, or the sight of the wounded or dying, as in severe accident or on a field of battle.

## Symptoms of Mental or Emotional Disorders

A significant symptom of mental illness differs in *degree* rather than in *kind* from abnormal behavior that is common to most normal people at one time or another. As has been suggested earlier, any one of us is more or less likely to experience temporarily, in our physical condition, attitude, or behavior, certain characteristics that may deviate from customary status. The situation becomes dangerous only when an abnormal state persists and becomes more or less fixed. Mentally disturbed persons may display many characteristics that seem to deviate from the norm and consequently be symptomatic of a psychosis. It often is difficult. however, to determine whether these symptoms are imagined, feigned, or real.

Persisting or fixed symptoms of mental and emotional disorders can be classified roughly as (1) physical, (2) mental, (3) emotional, and (4) behavioral. Symptoms for the respective classifications are presented below:

1. *Physical Symptoms*
   a. Change in pulse, temperature, and respiration.
   b. Nausea, vomiting, headache, and dizziness.
   c. Loss of, or abnormal, appetite.

  *d.* Extreme change in weight.
  *e.* Excessive fatigue, pain (actual or imagined), coughing, or pupillary activity.
  *f.* Motor incoordination, speech disturbances, or writing peculiarities.
2. *Mental Symptoms*
  *a.* Distractability, flight of ideas, delay or retardation of mental association, and blocking of the thought processes.
  *b.* Loss of understanding or of ability to produce language (*aphasia*).
  *c.* Loss of the power to perceive existing relationships in the world about him (*agnosia*).
  *d.* Complete loss of memory (*amnesia*).
  *e.* Phobias or strong irrational fears that are attached to generally harmless situations, such as abnormal fear of the dark, closed rooms, high places, dirt, insects, or possible illness.
  *f.* Compulsions to engage in certain forms of behavior, some of which may have serious consequences, such as an urge to take property belonging to another regardless of its value to himself (*kleptomania*) or a compelling desire to start fires (*pyromania*).
  *g.* Fixed ideas or obsessions that may concern themselves with the attitudes of other people toward the patient or his own attitudes toward himself or others. For example, an obsession might take the form of a fixed belief that certain foods are poisonous or that the end of the world is imminent.
  *h.* Disturbances of perception such as *illusions* and *hallucinations*. An *illusion* is a faulty perception of an object. An abnormal mind set may lead to a distortion of what is seen, heard, or touched. A stranger may be mistaken for a close relative, a tree may become a menacing enemy brandishing a lethal weapon, the voice of an associate may be recognized as that of a person no longer alive.
  *i.* *Hallucinations,* on the other hand, have no basis in immediate and actual sensory stimulation. They are imaginary perceptions and represent disorders of the imagination. The patient hears voices or bells, or sees objects or persons that are nonexistent except in his imagination. He seems to experience muscular sensations that are not present or taste sensations without food.
  *j.* *Delusions* or significant disorders of judgment are false beliefs that cannot be corrected by an appeal to reason, that have no basis in fact.
3. *Emotional Symptoms*
  *a.* A state of emotional indifference or apathy, accompanied by

expressions of worry, sighs, crying, and an almost complete refusal to eat or speak. The patient sits and broods; he is morbid
and depressed, gloomy and downhearted.

b. The display of an unnatural state of happiness that shows itself
in singing, dancing, excited talking, and much laughter. The
patient has no cares or worries; he views the world through
rose-colored glasses and seems to be unaware of anything in a
situation that is not completely satisfactory or is in any way
undesirable.

4. Behavior Symptoms

a. Increased psychomotor activity wherein the individual is impelled toward constant motion, crying, laughing, shouting, or
whispering.

b. Decreased psychomotor activity showing itself in the slowdown
of motion, hesitation, or indecision (abulia); rigidity; and halt-
ing speech or refusal to talk.

c. Behavior that is impulsive or unduly responsive to external suggestion, as shown by the persistent repetition of the words or
movements of another, or by an attitude of refusal to respond,
or of doing exactly the reverse of what might be expected.

d. Constant repetition of the same act (stereotypy).

e. A display of unaccustomed vulgarity or profanity of language,
and peculiar mannerisms such as shuffling walk, queer movements of the hands or shoulders, and facial grimaces.

The symptoms of mental illness cannot be sharply defined and classified. They are interrelated and appear to a greater or lesser degree in
varying combinations. Many of these symptoms are exhibited in a mild
or temporary form by individuals who are usually normal. For that
reason, in their early stages they are not always recognized as signs of
mental disorders. It is only when these symptoms, individually or in combination, become extreme or tend to persist that they arouse among the
members of the family or among the associates of the patient an awareness of a developing mental illness.

The most startling and attention-demanding symptom of severe
mental disorder is the overt expression of a false belief or a delusion. The
expression of an unreasonable or false belief may be based upon lack of,
or inadequate, knowledge. The false belief of an otherwise normal person
can be corrected through improvement of knowledge. The family and
associates of a mentally disturbed person cannot fail to recognize the fact
that something is wrong, however, if he persists in giving expression to
unrealistic attitudes of grandeur, persecution, or melancholy, in the form
of factual statements, although normally he would recognize their falsity.

The patient who is suffering from delusions of grandeur imagines that he is a person of great power or influence. He may believe himself to be Napoleon, a noted inventor, a possessor of great wealth, a savant, or even God. His behavior is imitative of his imagined attitude and the actions of the one with whom he identifies himself, and he demands from others the attention that is appropriate to his exalted position.

*Delusions of persecution* are mental states that represent an attitude which is completely opposite from that evidenced by the sufferer of delusions of grandeur. The patient who suffers from intense feeling of persecution imagines that he is the object of hatred, jealousy, and malicious influences aimed at interference with, or destruction of, his welfare.

A person who is suffering from an extreme case of *melancholia* tends to imagine that he has committed an unforgivable crime or that he is suffering from an incurable disease. He may spend most of his time in self-abnegating acts and in attempts to right wrongs that he never has committed. There is no joy in life or hope of recovery for the seriously afflicted sufferer from melancholia.

## Dementia Praecox (Schizophrenia)

Special attention is given to this particular psychosis because of its frequency and its importance as a behavior disorder during the adolescent years. Schizophrenia is the most common form of mental disorder. Its victims are found principally among adolescents and young adults, although the psychosis occurs occasionally after age 40. There are four different types of this psychosis: simple type, hebephrenic type, catatonic type, and paranoid type.

*Simple dementia* or the *simple type* is characterized by idleness, daydreaming, lack of interest in others, and shiftlessness. The early symptoms are difficult to recognize and evaluate. An attitude of indifference is exhibited toward the victim's family, his friends, or his schoolwork.

The *hebephrenic type* is characterized by a more abrupt onset than is the case of simple schizophrenia. There is a tendency in the individual to become silly, to smile or laugh without provocation, or to indulge in fleeting hallucinations or changeable or fantastic delusions.

The *catatonic type* is characterized by negativistic reactions accompanied by stupor or excitement. Headaches, insomnia, confusion, and listlessness may precede the chronic onset. Muscular tension is associated with the catatonic stupor, as evidenced by the rigidity of body position. The patient may become mute and refuse to talk; or he may become excited and inflict injury upon others or destroy objects within his reach.

The *paranoid type* is characterized by delusions of grandeur and by ideas of persecution, which may be accompanied by vivid hallucinations to the discomfort of the victim.

# Therapeutic Treatment
# of Mental and Emotional Disorders

Even for the well-trained psychiatrist, the diagnosis and treatment of mental and emotional disorders are extremely difficult. Early discovery of symptoms is a great aid to the psychiatrist in his treatment. Successful rehabilitation after a case has a prolonged history depends in large measure upon many personal and situational factors. Improved methods of treatment having mental hygiene implications are proving beneficial. Included among the approved methods are psychosomatic medicine, psychotherapy, psychoanalysis, group therapy, and occupational and recreational therapy.

## Psychosomatic Medicine

Psychosomatic medicine places the emphasis upon the relationship that exists between emotional reaction and the nature and extent of a physical disease. Almost one-half of all symptoms of physical disorders are rooted in emotional disturbances. Hence treatment of the organism as a whole becomes the concern of the physician or psychiatrist. It is now recognized that in rehabilitation the mental cannot be separated from the somatic. Much exploration is needed in the area of attitude development toward a physical illness if cure or amelioration of the condition is to be effected. Although emotion plays an important role in physical illness, it is difficult to explain to an individual, especially to an adolescent, that his illness may have an emotional origin.

The application of psychological approaches to the patient simply means that the physician and nurse recognize the relationship that may exist between emotional reactions and the possibility of recovery from a physical illness. The patient must be willing to cooperate with the physician, however. In fact, according to Vaughan:

The value of the psychosomatic approach is in its emphasis upon the treatment of the *whole* person, involving a study of his *physical* condition *and* an exploration of his *mental* outlook. The traditional medical concentration upon the organic will be corrected by the psychosomaticists who call attention to the importance of including the psychological angle too. The doctor who is wise will consider the personality of the sick person in addition to taking his temperature, thus obeying the famous dictum of Sir William Osler: "It is more important to know what kind of patient has a disease than to know what kind of disease a patient has." [2]

[2] W. F. Vaughan, *Personal and Social Adjustment,* The Odyssey Press, Inc., New York, 1952, p. 210.

# Psychotherapy

Psychotherapy is aimed at the improvement of the sufferer's attitudes, emotional reactions, and overt behavior. Suggestion and reeducation are among the chief techniques utilized in the treatment of a disturbed individual. Suggestion and reassurance can relieve physical or emotional tensions. Repeated encouragement is given to reassure the patient who seeks help to cure some form of ailment. The psychiatrist employs morale-building procedures. Yet the effectiveness of therapeutic techniques that are based primarily upon reassurance and encouragement is usually limited. Most physicians, psychologists, social workers, and school teachers, however, apply psychotherapy in one way or another. Psychotherapy is broad in its application and, according to Maslow, takes place in six main ways:

(1) by expression (act completion, release, catharsis) as exemplified in Levy's release therapy; (2) by basic need gratification (giving support, reassurance, protection, love, respect); (3) by removing threat (protection, good social, political, and economic conditions); (4) by improved insight, knowledge, and understanding; (5) by suggestion or authority, and (6) by positive self-actualization, individuation, or growth. It is probable that all systems of psychotherapy use all these basic medicines in varying proportions. For the more general purposes of personality theory, this also constitutes a list of the ways in which personality changes in culturally and psychiatrically approved directions.[3]

In the application of psychotherapy consideration needs to be given to the fact that during his developmental years the adolescent has a unique set of dynamics that are different from those either of childhood or adulthood. Those that are specific for this period need to be identified and appropriate therapy devised to resolve any special problems associated with them. Alfred R. Joyce, M.D., in writing about psychotherapy with adolescents suggests ways in which the psychoanalyst selects his patients for treatment and the attitudes that need to be displayed by the therapist.

How does the psychoanalyst select his patients for treatment, especially among adolescents? Diagnosis is important, but it is felt that an evaluation of the ego is even more important. We evaluate the following components: (1) the individual's ability to form relationships; (2) his ability to form relationships with the opposite sex; (3) his motility towards a realistic goal; (4) his sense of reality; (5) his conception of himself; (6) his intellectual functioning.

[3] A. H. Maslow, *Motivation and Personality*, Harper & Row, Publishers, Incorporated, New York, 1954, p. 306.

The adolescent who does well in a majority of these areas seldom requires psychoanalysis. If he is disturbed in several of these areas, then intensive therapy is indicated. Should these disturbances be left untreated, the adolescent can crystallize into a character-disorder individual whom no amount of therapy will help later on. In the initial sessions, the therapist listens with a third ear to what the adolescent is saying, without making any comments or judgments. The adolescent has to recognize that the therapist is there to help him and he eventually has to become aware of his own difficulties.

For his part, the therapist has to be an extremely flexible person, able to swing with the alternation of moods in the adolescent. The negativism that is so prominent in the adolescent is usually a defense against underlying infantile aggressive and sexual feelings. A couch is hardly ever used with the adolescent because it could encourage excessive fantasy and regression. The therapist becomes a real person who understands, protects and serves as a healthy model for identification. Eventually, the adolescent's ego grows under this atmosphere of understanding and unconditional love. At this point the ego has become sufficiently healthy for the youngster to leave the analyst and face the anxieties of the real world.[4]

It is possible through psychoanalysis to elicit from a disturbed person a body of significant information concerning his past mental and emotional life. The patient discloses incidents in his past life that may have continued to exert a potent influence upon his behavior. The psychoanalyst hopes to discover the experiences that may have led to the pathological state, then to offer suggestions for treatment. There is an attempt to attack the underlying emotional conflict rather than symptomatic behavior. Merely to remove the particular symptom by suggestion may not be very helpful unless something is done to resolve the underlying conflict.

Freud believed that the symptoms of neurotic patients were in reality the expressions of mental conflicts. He suggested that a dream was a "wish fulfillment," a conscious expression of unconscious wishes or fantasies. Freud utilized free association to elicit the actual meanings which the censor of the unconscious prevented from coming into waking life, except as these meanings were disguised or masked in symbolic form.

Psychoanalysis has become useful both as depth psychology in the study of personality and as a therapeutic method. It has contributed to the dynamic approach in the study of personality and to the elaboration of a systematic theory of personality and behavior. Psychiatrists are making practical use of this method in some of their work with emotionally disturbed adolescents.

[4] Alfred R. Joyce, "The Professional Psychotherapist," in William C. Bier (ed.), *The Adolescent: His Search for Understanding*, Fordham University Press, New York, 1963, pp. 182–183.

## Group Therapy

The application of group therapy was started by Moreno when, in 1911, he encouraged children to participate in a form of psychodrama. Children were encouraged to give expression to their fantasies by dramatizing them in group situations. The psychotic and the neurotic usually have difficulty in meeting their life problems on a mature adult level. Hence they need help to achieve independence by gradual steps until they are brought to maturity in easy stages. Preparation for group therapy under the supervision of trained personnel includes the interviewing of all participants, a study of all data relative to each, and a classification of each participant according to his dominant psychopathological pattern. Proper dramatic action can then be planned for evaluation and therapy.

## Occupational and Recreational Therapy

The purpose of occupational therapy is to divert the attention of the victim of the disorder from himself and give him an opportunity for self-expression. Physical and mental coordinations are improved through its use. This type of therapy acts as a morale builder. The completed product is not the important goal; the process, the actual work itself, is the therapeutic agent. Choice of occupation, however, should be within the cultural background, intelligence, aptitude, and general ability of the individual.

Occupational and recreational activities have therapeutic value for those afflicted by emotional disturbances. These therapeutic techniques tend to divert the attention of the mentally ill person from his fears, worries, or other disturbances which may be the bases of his present disorder. Tensions are reduced through the use of occupational activities and physical recreation. The individual can be diverted from his troubles through participation in recreational programs that utilize music, books, magazines, radio, motion pictures, dances, television, and social activities. The particular psychosis is to be considered before the therapeutic activity is planned. For example, the singing of "Annie Laurie" may calm one patient but stimulate another to violent activity.

The utilization of recreational therapy also provides opportunity for afflicted individuals to associate with one another in situations devoid of tensions. Recreational therapy combines in a wholesome way some of the benefits of group therapy with play attitudes, thereby enabling the individual concerned to forget self as much as possible. Forms of recreational activity that have been used successfully in therapeutic treatment may be carried over into the later activities of the individual when he has regained the ability to manage his own affairs adequately.

## Questions and Problems for Discussion

1. Show that conflict may be valuable in adolescent adjustment. Also, illustrate ways in which conflict may interfere with good adjustment.
2. Describe the behavior of a greatly frustrated adolescent. Indicate ways, if any, in which frustration may (a) assist adolescent adjustment and (b) result in adolescent maladjustment.
3. Illustrate how both conflict and frustration may operate in social situations.
4. Examine your own behavior to identify any compulsion. Give reasons for believing this behavior to be a compulsion and report ways in which this compulsion directs your behavior.
5. Present factors that predispose toward the development of mental disorders.
6. Describe the behavior of an adolescent who shows a tendency toward regression.
7. Illustrate, by specific examples, ways in which parents, teachers, and employers can promote the mental health of young people.
8. Explain how adjustment can be effected through psychotherapy, group therapy, psychoanalysis, free association, and psychodrama.
9. *Special Exercises:*
   a. List an item you would like to purchase but which, because of limited funds, you cannot. Explain your behavior and your feelings.
   b. Give at least one example from your experience of each of the following adjustment mechanisms: (1) compensation, (2) identification, (3) rationalization, (4) projection, and (5) daydreaming.
   c. Visit a hospital for the mentally ill. Describe the behavior of an adolescent who shows symptoms of negativism, stupor, depression, or delirium.

## Selected References

Bandura, A., and R. Walters: *Adolescent Aggression,* The Ronald Press Company, New York, 1959.

Berkowitz, L.: *Aggression: A Social Psychological Analysis,* McGraw-Hill Book Company, New York, 1962.

Bernard, H. W.: *Toward Better Personal Adjustment,* 2d ed., McGraw-Hill Book Company, New York, 1957.

Boulding, K. E.: *Conflict and Defense: A General Theory,* Harper & Row, Publishers, Incorporated, New York, 1962.

Carroll, H. A.: *Mental Hygiene,* 4th ed., Prentice-Hall, Inc., Englewood Cliffs, N.J., 1964.

Crow, Lester D., and Alice Crow: *Mental Hygiene for Teachers: A Book of Readings,* The Macmillan Company, New York, 1963.

Farber, S. M., H. Roger, and L. Wilson: *Conflict and Creativity: Control of the Mind, Part II,* McGraw-Hill Book Company, New York, 1963.

Jones, M. R., et al. (eds.): *Nebraska Symposium on Motivation,* University of Nebraska Press, Lincoln, Nebr., 1962.

Jourard, S. M.: *Personal Adjustment*, 2d ed., The Macmillan Company, New York, 1963.

Lindgren, H. C.: *Psychology of Personal and Social Adjustment*, 2d ed., American Book Company, New York, 1961.

Rosenbaum, M., and M. Berger (eds.): *Group Psychotherapy and Group Function*, Basic Books, Inc., Publishers, New York, 1963.

Sarnoff, I.: *Personality: Dynamics and Development*, John Wiley & Sons, Inc., New York, 1962.

Scheflen, A. E.: *A Psychotherapy of Schizophrenia: Direct Analysis*, Charles C Thomas, Publisher, Springfield, Ill., 1961.

Schneiders, A. A.: *Personality and Adjustment in Adolescence*, The Bruce Publishing Company, Milwaukee, 1960.

Shaffer, L., and E. J. Shoben, Jr.: *Psychology of Adjustment*, 2d ed., Houghton Mifflin Company, Boston, 1956.

Slaton, T. F.: *Dynamics of Adolescent Adjustment*, The Macmillan Company, New York, 1963.

Smith, H. C.: *Personality Adjustment*, McGraw-Hill Book Company, New York, 1961.

Thorpe, L. P.: *The Psychology of Mental Health*, 2d ed., The Ronald Press Company, New York, 1960.

Woodworth, R. S.: *Dynamics of Behavior*, Holt, Rinehart and Winston, Inc., New York, 1958.

Yates, A. J.: *Frustration and Conflict*, John Wiley & Sons, Inc., New York, 1962.

# Chapter Twelve

## Behavior Delinquencies

When the first edition of this book was published, the major purpose of the authors was to direct the attention of parents, teachers, and other youth leaders to teen-age interests and activities, and problems of adjustment, with special emphasis upon youthful delinquency, which at that time was widespread. National and community leaders were hoping, however, that if sufficient time, thought, and energy were devoted by concerned adults to ways and means of countering the rise of adolescent asocial behavior, the problem might be solved at least partially, if not entirely. Unfortunately the situation now appears to be more serious than it was then. Although many young people are well-adjusted citizens, the incidence of delinquent behavior has been rising steadily.

### Personal and Social Significance of Delinquency

Juvenile delinquency is both a personal and a social problem. For the teen-age group, it draws more attention than any other social problem. It is one that knows no national boundaries; no large urban area is free from its devastating effects. It is an unfortunate aspect of the dynamic process of social change and of the exposure of individuals to differing cultural groups. During and immediately after war it is more easily accepted; however, its present increase in most parts of the world is a matter of great concern to the citizens in those areas. The increase in all forms of delinquent behavior, such as rape, theft, burglary, and vandalism, testifies to the need for building behavior patterns that will function more effectively in our complex social structure. The goal of the individual in a democratic society is to develop such self-discipline that he can be an asset rather than a liability.

### Meaning of Delinquency

A maladjusted person usually is his own worst enemy. The disturbed adolescent may be afraid, resentful, or uncooperative. He does not necessarily become aggressively antisocial, however. He hurts himself rather than others. If a young person definitely interferes with the rights of others, appropriates their property, causes damage, or violates the sex

316

code, he is interfering with the life of another person and is *delinquent*. According to the Ohio Code, "A delinquent child is defined as one who violates a law, is wayward, habitually disobedient or truant, or who behaves in a way that endangers the health or morals of himself or others, or who attempts to enter the marriage relation without the consent of parents or guardian."

Delinquent behavior, as reported by school people in leading cities throughout the world, includes, in the order of frequency, truancy, petty larceny, sex offenses (for girls), general incorrigibility, breaking and entering, running away from home, vagrancy, disorderly conduct, drinking, destructive acts, and injury to persons.

Legally, a delinquent is a teen-age person who has been brought to court, not as a criminal who is mature enough to recognize the seriousness of his offense, but as a maturing person who needs to be taught the responsibilities of adjusted citizenship. However, some adolescents are guilty of delinquent acts, but either are not detected or are protected from court action by their parents or others. In a broad social interpretation of the term these young people are delinquents, even though they have not been apprehended for their antisocial behavior.

Whether delinquency is considered in its legal connotation or according to a more comprehensive and lay point of view, it is one of the most serious problems with which present day society is confronted. Possible solutions must be aimed not only at so guiding adolescent behavior as to avoid court action, but also at encouraging needed improvement in the fundamental attitudes and behavior of the young people concerned. Desirable behavior cannot be *legislated*, but can be *trained*, into the life pattern of a boy or girl.

Many well-known men and women, including the leaders of those organizations which concern themselves with the welfare and education of young people, are giving serious thought to the problems of juvenile delinquency, and are seeking workable solutions. In almost every community, committees have been organized for the dual purpose of preventing delinquency and rehabilitating the delinquent. The ingenuity of the community leaders will express itself not in one general solution but in many specific recommendations for the meeting of the particular needs of the respective communities.

Young people themselves must be included in the working-out of whatever programs are developed. Although they may hesitate to accept plans that are superimposed by adults, they can be depended upon to aid in the execution of plans that they themselves may be encouraged to carry out under intelligent adult supervision. Here, as in other adolescent relationships with adults, youth welcomes adult leadership but resents dictation.

## Characteristics of Delinquents and Their Behavior

Although many delinquents have low IQs, there also are many socially acceptable adolescents of the same intellectual level. Low intellectual level alone cannot be considered a contributing factor of delinquency. Physical abnormalities may act indirectly to cause delinquent behavior. In studies of delinquency a tendency (to the extent of about 8 per cent) is found toward physical defects, greater than among nondelinquents in dental care, poor dental hygiene, and defective tonsils. Chronic deficiencies lead to restlessness and a lack of concentration. However, poor physical conditions without complicating emotional factors cannot be considered independent characteristics of delinquents.

A delinquent differs from a normal adolescent mainly in his emotional reactions. He is emotionally unstable and is not satisfied with society; he resents discipline and refuses to submit to normal social restrictions. He is egocentric and immature in his appreciation of right and wrong. His emotional ties with his family usually are not well knit; he rejects their advice and guidance, and becomes disobedient. If he has been rejected by his parents, he may develop undesirable behavior in his attempts at becoming adjusted to his lack of parental love.

In general, the problem of delinquency is the same today as it was earlier, but the form of the behavior seems to have become more violent. Juvenile delinquency now seems to involve the type of adolescent behavior that no longer can be classified as adolescent pranks. Today the behavior is more dangerous, including robbing, raping, and killing.

## Nature and Extent of the Problem

Fortunately, about 95 per cent of all adolescents are law-abiding and fine upstanding citizens. Nevertheless, these satisfying data cannot eliminate the fact that there is a sordid side to the behavior of a number (although small in percentage) of adolescents. The low rate of delinquency cannot alleviate the suffering of the person who has been assaulted, raped, or otherwise injured by an adolescent hoodlum. The percentage of adolescents who get into trouble with the police may be low, yet the number of adolescents between the ages of 10 and 18 who are apprehended annually exceeds 1 million; of these, about one-half are actually brought into the juvenile courts.

According to J. Edgar Hoover, the three most prevalent juvenile offenses in 1963 were burglary, larceny, and auto theft. Hoover also reports that the three most vicious crimes of youth are rape, assault, and criminal homicide. He reports the following percentages for crimes committed by youth under 18 during 1963: assault, 14; criminal homicide, 19;

rape, 18; robbery, 26; burglary, 50; larceny, 53; and auto theft, 63. (See *Crime in the United States*, July 20, 1964.)

# Causes of Juvenile Delinquency

Opinion on the causes of criminal behavior has changed with time. Early in the nineteenth century it was thought that the physical constitution of the body of a criminal was different from that of a normal person. Later, genetic studies led to the theory that most criminals are feeble-minded. Malfunctioning of the endocrine system and mental conflict also were proposed as causes of delinquency. All these ideas have been proved false or nonconclusive. The present-day theory stresses emotional insecurity, social inadequacy, and cultural conflict as the main causes of delinquent behavior.

## Contributing Factors

Many adolescents become delinquent because they express social talents through antisocial behavior. These adolescents usually do not get along with parents or school officials even when they participate freely and naturally in other activities. Many of them are more successful with their peer associates than are more academically minded adolescents. Thus these individuals, lacking academic competence, have social competence and, if properly guided, might be helped to avoid delinquent behavior.

The problem of juvenile delinquency is so complex that there is no one cause and no simple cure. The cause seems to be rooted in the home, the school, the community, the church, and the courts. Among the factors that contribute toward delinquency can be included (1) the relaxation of home control and parental supervision; (2) the moving of workers from small-town or rural areas to cities; (3) economic conditions in family life that may cause neglect of children; (4) poor health or physical defects which may result in feelings of inferiority, discouragement, or bewilderment; (5) inadequate recreational facilities; (6) inadequate school buildings and equipment; (7) inadequate teaching; (8) public indifference; (9) unsettled world conditions; and (10) ineffectual attempts to prevent delinquency.

## Effect of Change in Parental Supervision

Parents have carried the brunt of the blame for the spread of juvenile delinquency. Their present trend of abdication of authority in areas of primary responsibility tends to create a problem of appalling proportions. It places a heavy burden on school people and law-enforcement officers. According to J. Edgar Hoover:

We in the FBI are in a unique position to observe the criminal and to survey the background which led to his implication in a life of crime. It is on the basis of this experience and this observation that I draw my conclusions regarding the growing problem of youth in crime and the tragic implications inherent for the future.

What is at the root of the juvenile crime problem? I believe that this problem is the result of an abdication of authority in many areas, foremost of which is the home. Recently a distinguished jurist expressed his opinion in a forthright article on this subject. He held that relinquishment by the father of his rightful place as head of the household is a basic cause of delinquency in this country. I agree wholeheartedly with this position. In addition, we Americans have allowed the word "discipline" to fall into bad repute both in the home and in the school. For too long we have listened to the apostles of anarchy label any mention of that good, sturdy word with the brand of brutality.

To me, discipline is the reasonable concept set forth in Webster's— "training which corrects, molds, strengthens or perfects." It does not mean punishment for the sake of punishment, but rather a "rule or system of rules affecting conduct or action."

Human beings need rules to live by—children as well as adults. The small child, incapable of making proper decisions, needs—and wants —a boundary line of rules which are clear-cut and definite. A world without moral and legal disciplines becomes a jungle of anarchy, whether it is an adult or a juvenile world. A child should have all reasonable freedom within specific bounds, but he should be taught from babyhood that when he steps beyond the bounds swift but fair punishment—discipline, if you will —is certain to follow.[1]

Parents should accept their rightful share of the responsibility for the spread of juvenile delinquency, but they cannot be held accountable for the social change that surrounds them and is beyond their control. In a discussion of the problem of delinquency under the title "Who's to Blame?" one of the authors made the following observations:

It is imperative that we attain a fuller understanding of the effects of a well-planned and constructive education upon growing children. Each child needs careful and patient guidance of his behavior from birth onward. This can be left neither to chance nor to the whims of the person giving the guidance. Children, at any time, will behave as they have been allowed to behave. This means that adults carry the responsibility of providing the kind of training that will serve chil-

---

[1] J. Edgar Hoover, "We Must Choose between Discipline and Barbarism," *American Legion Magazine*, September, 1958.

dren's needs as well as the needs of others with whom young people associate.

What then is the answer to the question: "Who is to be blamed for the delinquent behavior of an increasing number of adolescents?" Should the guilt rest entirely or even largely on the shoulders of the social individual? If it does not, can the cause of such behavior be located so that the problem can be dealt with more effectively at its source?

Why is there so much juvenile delinquency at the present time? Can it be that such adolescent behavior is rooted in the cumulative effect of the educational practices that have been associated with child behavior? Does delinquent behavior result from a possible overemphasis upon the rights, the stimulated initiative, and the unguided freedom of the individual?

During the past several years the blame for the rapid increase in juvenile delinquency has been attributed largely to parental mistakes in child development.

The problem is much larger than one which can be solved by parents alone. Someone should come forward with an answer to why some parents suddenly became careless in matters dealing with the supervision of child behavior. Is it possible that these parents are trying feebly to implement an educational philosophy with which they are not very well acquainted and which appears to grant almost unlimited freedom of action to their children?

It has been urged for many years that parents and teachers should avoid any practice that might frustrate children. They have been encouraged to stimulate the child's initiative and to permit him to do what he wants to do with as little adult interference as possible. Perhaps we have erred in this respect. A child needs supervision of his behavior to the extent that some of his desires or immediate wants should be left unsatisfied at the moment. This is essential to good social development. Personal and social adjustment include the giving of one's self as well as the getting or receiving of attention or favors from others. These self-denying experiences need to accompany any attempts that are aimed at the guidance of child behavior.

Overaggressive children often are permitted to behave in ways that develop habits which interfere with their present and later interpersonal relationships. Some children early become demanding for the fulfillment of their desires. They are certain to increase these selfish demands as they grow and develop unless someone assists them in redirecting self-aggrandizing drives. This clearly becomes a duty of parents and teachers. Parents, however, are torn between what they believe is their duty and what they believe educators expect of them in the matter of child rearing.

Is it possible then that some children inadvertently have been trained by parents to develop tendencies toward delinquent behavior? Have teachers, too, permitted children to engage in self-centered behavior lest deep-seated conflicts be established or lasting feelings of frustration developed? In other words, have these adults been led to believe that, in the redirection of misbehavior, corrective measures should be used sparingly? [2]

[2] Lester D. Crow, "Who's to Blame?" *Ohio Parent-Teacher*, vol. 33, no. 2, pp. 20–21, October, 1954.

## Areas of Community Responsibility

The ten delinquency inducers listed earlier in the chapter reflect community failure to meet its responsibility for the welfare of young citizens. In our discussion concerning adolescent physical, mental, emotional, and social development, we included a consideration of the various constructive or detrimental factors of influence by which a maturing young person is affected during his adolescent years.

According to the law, parents are primarily responsible for their children's welfare. Yet in order for them to fulfill their parental obligations adequately, they need the cooperation of other community agencies such as the school, the church, the courts, and other youth-serving agencies. Through its leaders each of these community organizations and institutions is giving voice to an increasing awareness of its particular area of responsibility.

Although world conditions continue to be unsettled, there is evidence that public indifference is giving way to a definite growing concern about youthful delinquency. Moreover, the fact that many attempts to prevent delinquency have been ineffective has motivated youth leaders toward (1) more intensive and extensive study of the basic causes of child and adolescent asocial behavior, (2) better preventive approaches, and (3) improved remedial techniques. We are not now facing a new problem. Youthful misconduct or immorality appears to be a concomitant of local, national, or world crises.

## Teen-agers in Trouble with the Law

Before presenting the opinions of youth leaders, we shall comment briefly on the usual procedures followed in dealing with young people who get into trouble with the law. As we know, more than 1 million young people a year are apprehended by the police. The most serious cases of delinquent behavior, about 800,000 offenders, are brought to the juvenile courts either by the police or by parents. Various dispositions of these cases are made.

On the basis of the seriousness of the offense or of the number of "repeat" delinquencies, the young person may be returned to the care of his home and of community service agencies, placed on probation, or sent to a detention home for a shorter or longer period. Apparently incorrigible delinquents are sent to training schools, usually state institutions where, it is hoped, there may be some chance of rehabilitation before they are returned to their homes. In the following statements by leaders of various youth-serving organizations are indicated some of the weaknesses inherent in current treatment approaches to youthful delinquency, as well as suggestions for improvement.

# The Problem of Delinquency as Viewed by Leading Citizens

The first edition of this book contained the expressed opinions of several leaders of youth concerning possible causes, preventive measures, and therapeutic suggestions in relation to juvenile delinquency. Here we present the current thinking of leaders in education, religion, social agencies, police departments, and the Federal Bureau of Investigation.

## Suggestions on Juvenile Delinquency by an Educational Leader

When William Jansen was the New York City superintendent of schools, he emphasized the seriousness and breadth of the problem of juvenile delinquency, the many possible causal factors, and the shared guidance and care responsibilities of all adults. At present, during his retirement, he believes in much that he wrote earlier. He has, however, given us certain modifications that we have incorporated into his statement. The following represents his current thinking:

As to the problem of juvenile delinquency, I should like to emphasize the need for a complete attack on this problem from every angle. The situation is serious; society may be facing a crisis. There is a ray of hope in the fact that society is, but all too slowly, becoming aware of the seriousness and complexity of the problem. We shall make progress when individuals cease to put the blame on any one factor, and cease proposing a single cure.

We cannot expect much progress when we provide one type of assistance to a delinquent or potential delinquent, while at the same time he is being subjected to a number of evil influences which more than nullify the help that he is being given. All young people need affection, appreciation, a feeling of success in some endeavor, and more good education. If their psychological needs are not met by good people, then they will find the answer in the gang. Below are some suggestions:

1. An educational program should be developed that points up the responsibility of parents for the behavior of their children. If we answer in the affirmative to the question, "Am I my brother's keeper?" how much more emphatic must be our answer to the question, "Am I my children's keeper?"

2. We must arouse among all adults a greater sense of responsibility for the welfare of children. It would be especially

helpful if we could have greatly increased adult participation in the voluntary agencies that work with children. Every delinquent needs individual help.

3. We must have more recreational facilities associated with our schools, churches, and parks. Such facilities are particularly useful in the evenings, on weekends, and during vacation periods. These are the times when youngsters get into trouble, not during the school day.

4. Guidance services, both in and out of school, must be increased and improved.

5. A larger teaching staff is essential if we're to provide smaller classes for special groups.

6. Social services must be better coordinated.

7. Religious institutions must work more closely with other social institutions.

8. Child care agencies must be extended.

9. Psychiatric and mental health facilities must be increased to care for those who are emotionally unstable or mentally ill.

10. Residential treatment centers, with educational and psychiatric facilities must be provided.

11. Improved and expanded probationary services must be developed.

12. Mass media: the radio, television, newspapers, magazines, publishers of comic books, and movie producers must be induced to cooperate in a socially wholesome program.

13. A central source for materials, reports of research and programs should be set up.

Juvenile delinquency, like adult crime, is a civic disease. The war against it can never cease. There never can be a complete victory, but we must constantly strive to improve our situation.

## Suggestions on Juvenile Delinquency by a Religious Leader

As could be expected, religious leaders are deeply concerned over modern trends toward materialism and a lessening appreciation of spiritual values. We present the current ideas of the Right Reverend Monsignor Charles E. Bermingham, executive director of Catholic Charities for the diocese of Rockville Centre, Long Island.

Moral training and discipline are words being revived in the education of youth. It is at this level that religion and the Church make their greatest contribution. The normal child wants cogent reasons for a pattern of living. He finds this in an awareness of a Supreme Planner of life who is God. He is taught that God is a loving and just Father. God is not a vacillating "softie."

Ultimately, He will ask for a reckoning and has promised both rewards and punishments. Aside from those youths who are pathologically disturbed, religious morality laid down by a living God is a source of stability to modern youth. The emphasizing of this factor in daily life is the important role of the Church toward the prevention of delinquency.

# Released Time and Juvenile Delinquency

Linden M. Lindsay, executive secretary of the Greater New York Coordinating Committee on Released Time of Jews, Protestants and Roman Catholics, Inc., provided the authors with the following statement concerning the effect of released time on juvenile delinquency:

Released Time for Religious Education is a deterrent to Juvenile Delinquency. It is not a panacea, but one of the numerous approaches toward the solution of this growing problem.

The Released Time movement has been in existence since the early twenties. It has functioned successively in forty-nine of the fifty states. It was introduced to New York City in February, 1941. During these twenty-two years, over two million children have attended classes in Religious Instruction in hundreds of churches and synagogues.

Mayor Robert F. Wagner stated in a proclamation dated September, 1963 "Released Time is a constitutionally approved plan whereby home, school and church or synagogue closely cooperate in providing additional opportunity for moral and spiritual training." He further urged "All parents and guardians to make available to their children this convenient way of fortifying them in their faith and developing in them, a love of God and neighbor."

Released Time is a spiritual supplement to education. Its major emphasis is upon moral and spiritual values. It is a character and personality building program. Few, if any, of the children enrolled in Released Time for Religious Education become delinquent.

# Suggestions on Juvenile Delinquency by Law-enforcement Agencies

Law-enforcement personnel are called upon constantly to deal with the problem of youthful offenders. We present the thinking of a representative leader in the law-enforcement area. It is a statement that presents the viewpoint of the Police Department on its responsibilities in the area of youth crime. These are excerpts from an address made by Police Commissioner Michael J. Murphy at the annual conference of the Police Department and the New York City Youth Board. Commissioner Murphy said:

The problem of juvenile delinquency and youth crime is not new to mankind. Because of this, too many people have adopted a complacent attitude towards this social problem. However, this department has not been and will not be complacent about it. We know that no organized society can long prevail if it allows the unlawful activities of individuals or groups of individuals formed into youth gangs to go uncontrolled. It is for this very reason that laws are enacted. To enforce these laws, the Police Department was created as the agent of the community to protect life and property, prevent crime and maintain the public peace. The manner in which the police implement these duties is very much intertwined with the prevailing needs of society.

This department's policy has been publicly stated many times and I will repeat it, because this policy applies equally to delinquents and youthful criminals as well as adults. We have been accused of being either, "too soft or too tough." The truth of the matter is that we ascribe to neither approach. There is only one policy for this department to follow: The police will take correct legal action as prescribed by law against all law breakers; and this action must, and shall be, taken with due respect for the rights of all people no matter what their age, economic condition or any other accidental characteristic.

In our democratic society, the police function is geared, as it should be, to the maintenance and preservation of civil liberties. This is our mandate and we are determined to fulfill it.

Our police approach to juveniles gone astray is consonant with the philosophy of the newly-created Family Court Act which stresses prevention rather than punishment. It is important to note that this new law recognizes that the community bears a significant responsibility for the unlawful activities of its youth population. The police have been stressing, for many years, the importance of community involvement in the prevention of juvenile delinquency and youth crime. As far back as 1943, this department sponsored community councils to obtain active cooperation of the civic-minded citizens within each patrol precinct. This grass-roots approach has been further intensified under the direction of a Deputy Commissioner in Charge of the Youth Program. The police must be regarded as part of the total community effort enlisted in the prevention of delinquency, youth crime and particularly violence by members of teenage gangs. It is high time that the public realize that this problem is their problem too!

## Suggestions on Juvenile Delinquency by Social Agency Leaders

In writing on ways of dealing with the problem of juvenile delinquency, Esther Emerson Sweeney, former director of Community Services of the American Social Health Association, says:

We believe that, although we would pursue a program of education for personal and family living if there were no problem of juvenile delinquency—because of its countless positive values for the individual and society—such a program is bound, in terms of its very nature, to play an important preventive role. Consequently, we believe that education for personal and family living is a contribution to the prevention of juvenile delinquency, providing for young people, as it does, insights into patterns of human behavior, understandings of social responsibilities, motivation toward sound interpersonal relations, and opportunities to give serious consideration to the reasonableness of the moral code.

As an Association, we have been vigorous in working for social change in many areas which have a bearing on juvenile delinquency. We have urged communities all across the country to develop consultant and treatment services for families experiencing internal conflict, and to develop social services in their courts which would help families considering separation or divorce.

Similarly, we have urged communities to repress prostitution and allied conditions which, if permitted to exist, offer an unwholesome community environment for youth, suggest to young people that laws can be violated with impunity if there is enough police protection (while at the same time youngsters are expected to be law-abiding citizens in the very towns where others are not), and, of course, expose young people to the emotional and physical hazards of promiscuous sexual relations.

Apparent in Esther Sweeney's statement is a conviction that delinquency or moral turpitude grows out of family and community apathy to the detrimental effects upon a young person of exposure to the "emotional and physical hazards of promiscuous sexual relations," as well as adult condoning of adolescent (also adult) violations of the law.

As members of the board of directors of the education section of the American Social Health Association, the authors are well aware of, and thoroughly in accord with, the association's program for personal and family living. Although projects of this kind necessarily move slowly, considerable headway has been made toward the realization of the association's purposes and objectives as listed by Esther Sweeney, both in the area of preventive education and in the field of therapeutic rehabilitation of adults as well as adolescents. The degree of success achieved by the ASHA to this point can be explained partly in terms of the untiring efforts of its active members, and partly as a result of the close working relations it has established with other interested groups, e.g., parents, school people, local community agencies, Federal and state bureaus, and military personnel.

# Constructive Approaches to the Problem of Juvenile Delinquency

There is much current evidence of community cooperation to stem the rising tide of juvenile delinquency by getting at the roots of the problem. Parents, church groups, businessmen, industrialists, educational leaders, community councils, and others are doing much to give youth some mobility within the limits of desirable social acceptability. The increasing number of parks and afterschool playgrounds, community centers, teen-age clubs, and camps; the continuing provision for better housing conditions, including school buildings; the improving control of crime comic books, radio and television programs; the more tactful supervision of adolescent social activities; and the greater availability of counseling services for teen-agers and their parents—all these represent areas of community-sponsored attempts to solve this vexing problem.

Some assistance may be gained from observing England's apparent degree of success in reducing the number of delinquents. The British are emphasizing respect for the law and are prepared to deal harshly with repeated violations. They believe that a healthy fear of the law is useful in the solution of the problem of juvenile delinquency. This does not mean that an offender is never given a second chance; it suggests that he is less likely to get a third chance. They believe that misguided leniency is one of the factors that cause juvenile misdemeanor to become juvenile crime.

In the United States there still are differences of opinion relative to the value of harsh treatment. More and more, however, there seems to be a general tendency to tighten up. The courts are moving away somewhat from so-called "soft handling" or "coddling" of young offenders. Yet there are certain limitations to the administration by the courts of punishment as a cure. Juvenile-court judges are influenced in their disposition of cases by the lack of adequate penal institutions, the shortage of trained personnel, and their fear of public disapproval, especially of parents and relatives, if in their sentences they exhibit objective consideration for public welfare rather than subjective "understanding" of youthful impulses.

Delinquency is a state of an individual. The boy or the girl who is a potential or actual juvenile delinquent must be treated individually. However, those elements of society which are responsible for this young person's maladjustment (or that of all other delinquents) must combine to form a social program reflecting the behavior and attitudes of all members of society and requiring the concerted action of all citizens in their home, school, business, community, and government relationships, if desirable environmental changes are to be effected.

The development of delinquency is similar to the development of any other form of behavior. When a young person becomes delinquent, there may be inherent in him certain potentialities of emotional maladjustment or socially disapproved behavior. Since individuals possess within themselves differing degrees of strength or weakness to combat unhygienic environmental influences, any treatment of the individual delinquents should include a consideration of these factors.

A young person possessing a physically and emotionally strong constitution may be expected to make an excellent personal adjustment in a wholesome environment if given sound guidance. Likewise, in a similar environment, with similar guidance, a weaker individual usually succeeds in attaining emotional stability and socially acceptable behavior.

The strong person may be able to, and often does, fight his way through many unfavorable environmental situations and thereby achieve a degree of desirable adjustment that may seem to be strengthened by the very intensity of his struggle. It is the potentially unstable young person who, if he is unfortunate enough to find himself in a vicious environment and denied wise guidance, is likely to achieve not adjusted but maladjusted behavior, and to become not a respected leader but a delinquent.

## Delinquency and the Home

Although the home situation does not constitute the only causative factor of youthful delinquency, the potency of the effect upon young people of parental attitudes and behavior cannot be denied. The truth of the above statement is affirmed by men and women who have engaged in extensive and intensive study of the causes of delinquency.

As a result of their study of 1,000 delinquents, the Gluecks[3] concluded that the home conditions of many delinquents tend to be characterized by such factors as clashes of adult and adolescent customs, lack of desirable educational equipment, low socioeconomic home conditions, unwholesome parental attitudes, mental deviation of one kind or another, inadequate supervision because of broken home, and poor behavior models. Any one or more of these factors tend to serve as bad examples for members of the teen-age group.

J. Edgar Hoover, in discussing the role of the Sunday School in relation to the total problem of juvenile delinquency, says:

We are responsible for the climate in which we live. Our sins of commission and of omission are reflected daily in the life about us. We need no sheaf of statistics to make us aware of the growing scourge of juvenile delinquency or the developing blight of crime. One glance at a daily paper is enlightening on that score. And, we may ask ourselves, Are we directly at fault?

What do the eyes of today's child mirror on the bookshelves at the corner drugstore, the magazine racks, on the cinema screen, and on television? Does he, perhaps, see violence and immodesty emphasized? Decency and honesty ridiculed? May he not, from what he sees and hears, assume that graft and corruption are normal incidents of daily living?

[3] S. Glueck and Eleanor T. Glueck, *One Thousand Juvenile Delinquents, Their Treatment by Court and Clinic,* Harvard University Press, Cambridge, Mass., 1939, pp. 80–82.

And what of the home in which today's youngster lives? Is it a place in which faith, love, discipline, sympathy and understanding form an island of security in an uncertain world?

Today, against the background of delinquency, crime, and threat of world conflict, what should be the role of the Sunday school?

There is immense and vital power in the Word of God. But knowledge is needed to release that power. It is the role of the Sunday school to disseminate knowledge of the basic truths upon which our civilization rests. . . .

We must assess the moral climate of today with a most critical eye and ascertain the degree to which it is responsible for the present scourges of crime, delinquency, and subversion. If we are to change that climate—if the rampant materialism that is at the base of so many of today's evils is to be forced into retreat—we must look to every spiritual weapon at our command. Certainly the Sunday school is such a weapon.[4]

In his study of maternal employment and adolescent roles, Prodipto Roy arrived at the following conclusions concerning the effect of maternal employment on academic performance and on the increase in delinquency:

3. The employment of the mother does not generally lower the academic performance or aspirations of the children. The results suggest a residential differential: the employment of town mothers lowered the academic performance and aspiration of their children, and the employment of rural mothers raised the academic performance and aspiration of their children.

4. The general fear that delinquency would increase due to the employment of the mother was not borne out. The results indicated that rural children seemed to manifest less delinquency when their mothers were fully employed than when their mothers were not employed. The other scales devised to measure affection, fairness of discipline, democracy and cooperation did not give consistent predictions in any one direction: that is, the employment of the mother did not seem to affect the amount of affection, fairness of discipline, democracy and cooperation as perceived by sons and daughters in the family. The results suggest that rural families in general benefited from the employment of the mother, in that the girls, and, in part, the boys, showed less delinquency, more affection, more fairness of discipline, more democracy and more cooperation in their families.[5]

In addition to the factors already named, reference should be made to delinquent-provoking conditions that may exist in apparently well-

[4] J. Edgar Hoover, "The Role of the Sunday School," *Sunday School Times*, Feb. 23, 1957. Revised, August, 1962.

[5] Prodipto Roy, "Maternal Employment and Adolescent Roles: Rural-Urban Differentials," *Marriage and Family Living*, p. 349, November, 1961.

adjusted homes. Among these are questionable business practices of an apparently successful father, parental sentimentality, and encouragement by parents of childish cruelty toward animals. Insufficient adolescent participation in home responsibilities, with an accompanying surplus of free time, which the young person may employ in undesirable social activities, is conducive to the formation of gangs of boys who hang around street corners with no constructive activities for the utilization of their boundless energy.

What can be done in the home? So subtle are the influences to which a child is exposed in his family relationships that it may seem that no one adequate answer can be given. However, there are at least three ways in which improvement can be encouraged: (1) the right to parenthood should be in direct ratio to an individual's physical, mental, and emotional fitness to be a parent; (2) an extended and detailed program of parent education by men and women qualified to offer it should be made available to all present and future parents; and (3) provision should be made by community agencies for remunerative and personally satisfying work opportunities for all citizens and the consequent elimination of slum areas. Although delinquency is a responsibility of society as a whole, it cannot be denied that the roots of delinquency lie in unadjusted home conditions. Hence it is in the home that the work of delinquency prevention must begin.

## Delinquency and the School

Most delinquents show a history of dislike of school, and they are apt to be truants. When they are questioned concerning their unsatisfactory school records, their answers seem to place emphasis upon factors such as inability to master the subjects of study, with consequent discouragement and retreat from embarrassing classroom experiences; harsh and unsympathetic treatment by teachers; regimentation of pupils in oversize classes; lack of opportunities for play and recreation; and illegal detention from school on the part of parents.

Educational leaders are aware of these teen-age criticisms of school procedures and attitudes and are gradually eliminating or modifying those school factors which in the past have militated against the educational progress of all children within their limits of achievement. When the citizenry as a whole recognize the importance of investing public funds in well-equipped and well-staffed schools, rather than in prisons and reformatories, forward-looking educational programs will be accelerated.

The delinquent boy or girl has been found not only to have home problems but also to be a misfit at school. Hence modern educational procedures and practices are being adapted to the learner in school so that these aids will be of value to each individual throughout his educational advancement. Teachers are friendly, sympathetic persons who attempt to understand adolescents and their problems. Consideration is given to a program of activities that is adapted to learner needs and to individual differences. It is a live, vital program that is varied in terms of abilities and interests of learners.

New teachers are trained to think of the pupil rather than merely of the subject matter. They are encouraged to know each pupil, his assets, and his liabilities, and to administer guidance in terms of his discovered potential. In addition, special psychological services are offered both within the school and as adjuncts to the school, available to the school personnel when needed. According to Kvaraceus and his coworkers, teachers can be educated to work effectively with disturbed children. Kvaraceus suggests:

The teacher who works effectively with disturbed youngsters:

1. Has a strong liking for children, including the disturbed and disturbing; attracts children and is attracted by them
2. Does not feel a compelling urge to be loved by every child
3. Can distinguish between the child and his behavior; rejects misbehavior without rejecting the child as a person
4. Realizes there are at least three phases to an action: what one does, how one does it, and why
5. Has some knowledge of the variations in child-rearing practices among different cultural groups and has some understanding of the relation between child-rearing practices and personality formation
6. Has some over-all knowledge of modes of living of the local community, with its implications for child and school program
7. Can define and maintain his role as *teacher*
8. Has adequate awareness of his own problems and takes care not to work these out through the child
9. Is able to distinguish between delinquent behavior that reflects cultural influence and that which reflects emotional disturbance
10. Accepts the child as he is and encourages his healthy aspirations
11. Recognizes that all behavior is functional for the child
12. Has sufficient strength to absorb some direct hostility and defiance, recognizing that hostility and defiance can be an essential part of growth
13. Has some perception of his own academic, cultural, and personality limitations
14. Can establish limits which are neither overrestrictive nor overprotective[6]

---

[6] William C. Kvaraceus et al., *Delinquent Behavior: Culture and the Individual,* Juvenile Delinquency Project, National Education Association, Washington, 1959, pp. 110–111.

## The Delinquent and the Community

Community indifference to, or actual responsibility for, delinquency cannot be treated lightly. As long as community leaders are unaware of the deplorable condition of some of their community neighborhoods or do nothing officially about it, they are a little like the old lady who is reported as having objected strenuously to suggestions that the slums of London be eliminated. Her disapproval of any such plan was based on the fact that people like herself would thereby lose their opportunity to gain eternal salvation by obeying the Biblical admonition that good people should visit the "fatherless and widows" and help those in distress. How could she do this, if there were no longer any available slums in which she could carry on her good work?

Worse than community apathy is the actual contribution to delinquency through the permitting of commercially run questionable dance halls, gambling devices, beer gardens, and grills, obscene or low-standard magazines on newsstands; and advertisements encouraging the "sophisticated" use of cigarettes, alcohol, and the like. There is an almost general lack throughout the country of adequate recreational facilities. Those which are adequate, from the point of view of uplifting rather than degrading influences, are often hampered in their programs by insufficient funds. Hence they are unable to compete with the better-equipped and more glamorous commercial forms of entertainment, which may not be wholesome.

Many communities have begun or are in the process of inaugurating a program of city planning. Sanitary conditions, comfort, beauty, and decent standards of living are the goals toward which such programs are aimed. Opportunities for youthful participation in community service and recreational projects also are being made available. In crowded city neighborhoods it is difficult to provide sufficient wholesome recreational facilities, however. Hence the young people are likely to form themselves into street-corner gangs that soon become the centers of organized participation in unlawful activities.

In recent years several cities have been making use of local men who talk the language of the youngsters. They visit the trouble spots to help the boys before they get into the clutches of the law. Two such projects are reported in *Newsweek* as follows:

New York City's Youth Board sends "street-club workers"—men between 20 and 30—into a neighborhood to win a gang's confidence, eventually channeling the energy of the boys into more normal social pursuits and sports. The results so far have been encouraging. Teen-age gang wars have abated recently as a result of street-club workers' efforts, and in case after case the gangs have ceased being sources of trouble, after Youth Board efforts to change a gang into more of a club. One street club worker summed it up this way: "If we can go into a neighborhood and break the pattern by which older gang boys lead their younger brothers into antisocial activity, then we've got something. Maybe not much, because the problem is bigger than we are. But maybe, too, a society that's willing to spend a couple of billion dollars on a new highway will decide some day to spend that kind of money to rehabilitate its kids."

The Chicago Area Project attacks the problem on the broader canvas of the entire neighborhood. Picking some of the most troublesome areas in the city, this project has enlisted aid from the people who live there —even ex-convicts, in some instances—to help the people change the pattern of their lives. That is a job no outside social worker can do, the Project authors reason. A run-down of what Steve Bubacz, one "alley-wise" leader, does in the course of his work gives an idea of how the Project works. "Mothers complained that their sons who were shoeshine boys were staying out too late; Steve investigated and induced the local saloonkeepers to refuse the kids admittance," John Bartlow Martin reported in *Harper's*. "A couple of junk dealers were buying hot, or stolen, merchandise from neighborhood children and encouraging them to steal; although unable to obtain convictions the Committee put on so much pressure that today the dealers telephone Steve before buying any doubtful junk. The Committee has closed several blind pigs and taverns which have sold liquor to minors. When 14-year-olds turned up drunk consistently the Committee discovered the identity of their bootlegger and tipped off the FBI, which sent him to Leavenworth. . . ." [7]

There is a trend toward combining reasonable penalization with attempted rehabilitation of the offender. In line with this philosophy, ideal treatment can be pictured as setting up special courts for the handling of delinquents. Therapeutic, rather than penal, juvenile court sessions are held informally in small rooms, rather than in large fear-inspiring courtrooms. These meetings are conducted by specially selected judges, whose attitude and training reflect sympathetic understanding of adolescent problems and who, unsentimentally, may be able to guide the young delinquent toward a more desirable form of living.

Physicians, psychologists, psychiatrists, social caseworkers, and probation officers cooperate with these courts in the work of rehabilitating the young offender. Cooperation with the home and other social agencies is encouraged. Here again community budgetary planning is a factor. Some such juvenile courts are functioning at present, but many more are needed to meet the needs of our young delinquents. Of course, as conditions that encourage delinquency are gradually eliminated, we hope that there will be a decreasing need for juvenile courts and juvenile aid societies.

[7] "Juvenile Delinquency: How Can We Meet the Challenge?" *Platform*, published by *Newsweek*, pp. 19–20, November, 1954.

Apart from the whole problem of suitable job placement, which will be considered in connection with the vocational adjustment of young people (see Chapter 16), employers too have a part in the rehabilitation of delinquents. One of the causes of reverting to former delinquent behavior after treatment is the fact that it is often difficult for a young offender to obtain a job, even though he wants to make a new start. Employers often are afraid that there may be a recurrence of the earlier difficulty. Their fear may be grounded in fact. However, unless such boys or girls are given an opportunity to make a normal adjustment under normal conditions, there can be little hope of improved attitude or behavior.

Other community agencies that are potential delinquency promoters are newspapers and broadcasting and motion-picture organizations. Many columns of our daily newspapers cannot be devoted to detailed accounts of criminal acts and sex offenses, or our motion-picture films and radio and television programs present the "blood-and-thunder" variety of entertainment, without exciting unduly the emotions of energetic and imaginative young people. Fortunately, there is a growing attitude of desirable censorship of such programs.

*Figure 32.* The combining of forces as a bulwark against juvenile delinquency. (From *Helping Delinquent Children,* Children's Bureau Publication 341, 1953, p. 37.)

A good beginning has been made in our fight to combat delinquency. However, it is perhaps not too old-fashioned to believe that results will not be commensurate with the efforts expended unless there is a return to religion on the part of American people.

The school and other community agencies that are dealing actively with juvenile delinquency are illustrated graphically by the Children's Bureau in Figure 32. Although all serve as a bulwark against juvenile delinquency, the home, the school, and the church appear to be of greatest importance.

## Recommendations for Prevention and Treatment

Throughout the chapter various suggestions have been made to meet or alleviate the problem of juvenile delinquency. High on any list of recommendations are (1) helping the adolescent to develop a deep sensitivity to the needs and rights of others, and (2) the formation of behavior patterns of self-discipline. In order to achieve these goals, each individual needs to develop certain feelings and attitudes toward himself and others. He needs to understand his rights and his responsibilities. He needs to acquire curiosity for knowledge, a willingness to share, and a recognition of his worth as a person. In a recent study concerning the rights and responsibilities of teen-agers the beliefs in Table 28 were found to prevail in regard to family, school, and social relationships.

Additional recommendations for the prevention and treatment of juvenile delinquency can be summarized as follows:

1. An extension of parent education

2. A renewed emphasis upon parental responsibility for the behavior of children

3. Greater vigilance by the police for the discovery of delinquent behavior

4. Wider utilization and extension of juvenile courts

5. Closer cooperation among home, school, church, courts, and other social agencies

6. Elimination of slum areas as rapidly as is possible

7. An extension of health services

8. An increase in recreational opportunities for all young people

9. A greater use of school facilities for community projects

10. A reduction of class size in schools

11. An increase in school personnel and guidance service

12. An increase in trained personnel for social work

13. An extension and enforcement of regulations governing the employment of minors

*Table 28.* Teen-agers' Rights and Responsibilities (Based on opinion of college students)

| RIGHTS | RESPONSIBILITIES |
|---|---|

### In Family Relationships

| RIGHTS | RESPONSIBILITIES |
|---|---|
| 1. To have status as a respected member of the family | 1. To accept parental guidance and discipline, especially concerning dating, friendships and recreational activities |
| 2. To be loved and cared for | |
| 3. To participate in over-all family discussions dealing with everyday life | |
| | 2. To display respect, gratitude and consideration for parents |
| 4. To express one's opinions freely and be listened to with interest | 3. To understand the economic limits to which the parents can afford to meet one's demands for "extras" |
| 5. To voice a point of view concerning one's future career, education, goals, etc. | |
| | 4. If financial assistance is needed, to help by taking an afterschool job |
| 6. To have freedom within reason to select one's friends, invite them to the home, and engage in social activities outside the home | 5. To perform household chores: keeping one's room clean, washing dishes, marketing, etc. |
| 7. To receive correct information concerning matters dealing with the sex life | 6. To care for one's own belongings and for grooming and clothing needs |
| 8. To have equality of treatment with other siblings | 7. To respect the personal belongings of others in the family |
| 9. To be permitted to arrange and decorate one's room as one pleases | 8. To be loyal to one's family |
| | 9. To visit relatives with parents |
| 10. To be accorded the right to have personal property respected and to have privacy of mail, telephone conversations, etc. | 10. To protect one's own health and the health of the family |
| | 11. To take care of younger siblings, as needed |
| 11. To receive an appropriate allowance, if not working | 12. To keep parents informed of one's activities |
| 12. To be given increasing independence and responsibility with increasing maturity | 13. To cooperate with all members of the family |

### In School Relationships

| RIGHTS | RESPONSIBILITIES |
|---|---|
| 1. To be provided with proper facilities to gain an education | 1. To cooperate with teachers and schoolmates |
| 2. Not to be compared unfavorably with classmates | 2. To attend school regularly |
| 3. To have curricular offerings and teaching methods suited to one's ability level | 3. To obey school rules and regulations |
| | 4. To appreciate and utilize the right to a free, public education |
| 4. To receive teacher recognition of successful study achievement | 5. To take an active part in school affairs |
| 5. To have reasonable freedom in choice of subjects to be studied | 6. To respect school property |
| 6. To receive help in vocational selection and planning | 7. To uphold school standards: honesty in examinations, attention in class, etc. |
| 7. To have freedom in the expression of one's opinion in class | 8. To accept deserved disapproval of one's work or conduct |

*Table 28.* (Continued)

| RIGHTS | RESPONSIBILITIES |
|---|---|

**In School Relationships**

8. To have the opportunity to join clubs or to participate in extra-curricular activities in terms of one's interests
9. To ask pertinent questions in class
10. To receive expert counseling when it is needed

9. To respect the rights of other students
10. To meet school obligations by completion of homework, proper grooming and dress, etc.

**In Social Relationships**

1. To join groups of one's own choice
2. To have status in a group
3. Not to be discriminated against because of creed or race or nationality
4. To choose one's hobbies and other activities, such as sports, dancing, etc.
5. To be accepted for one's self rather than for another's worth
6. To lead or to follow, depending on one's ability and interest, and the situation
7. To develop a normal interest in the members of the opposite sex
8. To exact loyalty and justice from group members
9. To have such prestige as one merits
10. To be permitted sufficient time each week for constructive and relaxing activities

1. To conform with desirable group standards but maintain proper individuality
2. To be a good sport
3. To share in group activities
4. To trust parental guidance of one's social activities
5. To abide by all safety and sanitary codes of the community
6. To manifest no superiority or prejudiced attitude
7. To avoid influences and situations which might lead to trouble, such as gang war, vandalism, loitering late at night
8. To respect the opposite sex (for boys especially)
9. To be careful of one's language
10. To be loyal to friends

SOURCE: Alice Crow, "Three R's for Teen-agers: Rights, Responsibilities, Relationships," *High School Journal*, pp. 370–371, May, 1958.

14. The establishment in every community of a youth commission consisting of parents, adolescents, and leaders of all community, social, and civic organizations

15. The provision of opportunities for young people to establish reasonable codes of morals for the direction of their conduct

16. Improved control of radio, television, and motion-picture programs

17. Decrease of emphasis in newspapers and newscasts upon incidents of violence and immoral behavior

18. The banning of "cheap" magazines that feature lurid unrealistic stories, including undesirable comics

19. Lessening adult concern with material possessions and materialistic advantages

20. A general return to religion and an increased appreciation of moral values

Many procedures can be used in the treatment of delinquent behavior. Group therapy, for example, holds promise as a form of psychotherapy that can be used for the treatment of disturbed offenders. It needs to be understood, however, that not much is known about the actual positive results of this process. Treatment of the drug addict, for example, requires much more than dealing with him in a community setting. Experimental treatment of some drug addicts in a group situation is being attempted, and other addicts who have been convicted of possession of narcotics are being placed on probation for careful supervision. The results of these efforts are not yet very promising. There is hope, however, that as experiments of this kind are continued, ways will be found to restore the victims to good social living.

In his summary statements of the diagnosis and treatment of delinquent behavior, Paul W. Tappan suggests the following:

4. Treatment of the criminal must be based to a considerable extent on considerations other than the causes of his crimes, partly because the dynamics of criminality are still largely obscure and partly because our methods are not yet sufficiently refined to enable us to treat the apparent causes.

5. Considerations of social protection, individual freedom, and economy seriously limit appropriate correctional treatment methods. Excessive risk to public interests cannot be taken. On the other hand, the individual's deprivations should bear some just relation to the risk he creates. The duration and intensity of treatment are limited by the public purse and by our concern for the values of freedom.

6. It is quite probable that the treatment methods most effective with the ordinary offender today are not based specifically upon etiological information. We must rely more largely on deterrent sanctions, the use of influence and persuasion, the indoctrination in ideals, and the modification of the environment. We are least effective in treating the minority of offenders with deep emotional difficulties who have been closely studied and diagnosed by psychiatrists and other clinicians.

7. Much research remains to be done, particularly in relation to rapid and group treatment methods, in order that we may discover less expensive and more effective ways of preventing crime and of reconditioning the offender.[8]

## Questions and Problems for Discussion

1. Describe a case of juvenile delinquency that seems to be rooted in the home; another rooted in the school; a third rooted in the neighborhood.

[8] Paul W. Tappan, Crime, Justice and Correction, McGraw-Hill Book Company, New York, 1960, p. 538.

2. Arrange an interview with a known teen-age delinquent. Discover all you can about the deep-seated causes of his behavior, his attitudes toward his delinquent behavior, and persons or influences upon whom he places the blame for his asocial behavior.

3. List ten or twelve influences, in order of importance, that you believe are closely associated with the causes of juvenile delinquency. Explain why you placed certain ones at the top and others at the bottom of your list.

4. Explain what parents can do to reduce the spread of juvenile delinquency.

5. Recommend changes in the school program that might help to mitigate delinquent behavior.

6. What may be the basic explanation of the great rise in delinquent behavior in the light of greater emphasis upon human relationships in teaching?

7. *Special Exercises:*

   *a.* Interview one of the following: a religious leader, a judge of a juvenile court, a social worker, a member of the Youth Board, or anyone officially working with delinquent youth. As you prepare for the interview, construct several questions to which you would like to get answers. Write a report of the interview.

   *b.* Interview two 16-year-old adolescents to discover the types of temptations with which they must cope.

   *c.* Prepare a list of suggestions that you believe might help prevent juvenile delinquency.

## Selected References

Belman, H. S., and B. Shertzer: *My Career Guidebook: for Students at the Junior High School Level,* The Bruce Publishing Company, Milwaukee, 1963.

Block, H. A., and F. T. Flynn: *Delinquency: The Juvenile Offender in America Today,* Random House, Inc., New York, 1956.

Block, H. A., and A. Niederhoffer: *Gang,* Philosophical Library, Inc., New York, 1958.

Clinard, M. B.: *Sociology of Deviant Behavior,* rev. ed., Holt, Rinehart and Winston, Inc., New York, 1963.

Cloward, R. A., and L. E. Ohlin: *Delinquency and Opportunity,* The Free Press of Glencoe, New York, 1960.

Cohen, A. K.: *Delinquent Boys: The Culture of the Gang,* The Free Press of Glencoe, New York, 1955.

Despert, J. L.: *Children of Divorce,* Doubleday & Company, Inc., Garden City, N.Y., 1962.

Fine, B.: *1,000,000 Delinquents,* The World Publishing Company, Cleveland, 1955.

Garbarini, M.: "Delinquency: Dropout and Related Problems," *Michigan Educational Journal,* vol. 40, pp. 349–350, January, 1963.

Glueck, S., and Eleanor T. Glueck: *Family Environment and Delinquency*, Houghton Mifflin Company, Boston, 1962.

Herbert, W. L., and F. V. Jarvis: *Dealing with Delinquents*, Emerson Books, Inc., New York, 1962.

Johnston, N., et al. (eds.): *The Sociology of Punishment and Correction*, John Wiley & Sons, Inc., New York, 1962.

Kvaraceus, William C., and I. M. McInnis: "Selected References from the Literature on Exceptional Children: Juvenile Delinquency," *Elementary School Journal*, vol. 31, pp. 353–355, March, 1963.

Kvaraceus, William C., and W. B. Miller: *Delinquent Behavior: Culture and the Individual*, National Education Association, Washington, 1959.

McDowell, J.: "Jd: Community Attitudes," *Clearing House*, vol. 36, p. 176, November, 1961.

Martin, L. M.: "Three Approaches to Delinquency Prevention," *Crime and Delinquency*, vol. 7, pp. 16–24, 1961.

Neisser, E. G.: *School Failures and Dropouts*, Public Affairs Pamphlet, no. 346, New York, 1963.

Robinson, S. M.: *Juvenile Delinquency: Its Nature and Control*, Holt, Rinehart and Winston, Inc., New York, 1960.

Schreiber, D.: "Dropout and the Delinquent: Promising Practices Gleaned from a Year of Study," *Phi Delta Kappan*, vol. 44, pp. 215–221, February, 1963.

Tait, C. D.: *Delinquents: Their Families and the Community*, Charles C Thomas, Publisher, Springfield, Ill., 1962.

Tappan, Paul W.: *Crime, Justice and Correction*, McGraw-Hill Book Company, New York, 1960.

Travers, J. F.: "Critical Problems of the School: Delinquency," *Clearing House*, vol. 36, pp. 337–342, February, 1962.

Trese, L. J.: *Delinquent Girls*, Fides, New York, 1962.

Wolfgang, M. E., et al. (eds.): *The Sociology of Crime and Delinquency*, John Wiley & Sons, Inc., New York, 1962.

Yablonsky, L.: *The Violent Gang*, The Macmillan Company, New York, 1962.

# Chapter Thirteen

## Significant Life Values

As was explained in Chapter 8, an attitude can be regarded as an affective by-product of experience. Attitudes expressed by an adolescent of any age reflect the effect of environmental influences upon his inner urges and his acquired interests. A young person's developing ideals represent the goals or life values he is attempting to build for himself. They have their origin in his gradually habituated attitudes toward self, self and others, religion, and morality. The functioning of these attitudes in his daily experiences characterizes the actualization of whatever life values the adolescent is struggling to achieve.

## The Development of Personal Ideals

Most children are conformists. Their attitudes and behavior patterns reflect imitation of adult example. Their wants and interests are relatively simple and usually can be satisfied in terms of adult care of their needs and adult guidance of their behavior. They do not have any clear concept of life values. They usually are eager to earn adult approval of their actions, and their behavior is influenced by what adults seem to consider to be right or wrong conduct for them.

With preadolescence comes greater understanding of personal responsibility for behavioral attitudes. A preadolescent's actions tend to be motivated by his developing conscience; he may experience feelings of guilt concerning actual or fancied wrongdoings. He is becoming more interested in the welfare of others. He is beginning to recognize the fact that some of his age peers have different standards of right conduct from those to which he had learned to adhere during childhood years. Adolescents gradually develop tentative or more permanent ideals that are based in good part on their earlier experiences. Yet the physical and physiological changes that occur during the teen years may cause young people to experience many and sometimes conflicting wants, interests, and attitudes that can exert considerable influence on the achieving of positive life values.

## Adolescent Attitudes and Group Standards

An adolescent often is uncertain concerning the value to himself of imitating the conduct "models" of any one or more of his associates. Through a kind of trial-error and trial-success process he attempts to effect a compromise between his own interests and attitudes and what he believes to be significant behavior ideals of his group. To the extent that he thereby achieves personal satisfaction and group approval, his developing attitudes are strengthened, become constructive ideals, and represent worthy life values.

A young person often finds himself in a situation, however, in which his expressed attitudes seem to fulfill a personal want but fail to achieve for him the social approval he desires. If there is a conflict between an adult's expressed attitudes and those of his group or groups, resulting emotion-induced problems can be resolved in one of several ways. Personal attitudes or ideals can be modified in terms of group ideals; group standards can be defied or ignored; superior leadership ability can enable the supposed nonconformist to change or modify group attitudes so that they are more nearly in accordance with his own ideals.

In dealing with his peers a young person may utilize any or all the problem approaches listed in the foregoing to achieve self-realization. Seldom if ever, however, is he a strong enough leader to influence the attitudes of his elders. Consequently, when adult and adolescent interests or ideals clash, severe struggles between them may result. The young person then is compelled to readjust his ideals in terms of adult standards or to establish a set of values that is satisfying to himself, regardless of adult acceptance of his attitudes.

## Sources of Adolescent Ideals

The life values or ideals that an adolescent gradually acquires serve as motivators of his behavior and reflect his maturation and his recognition and acceptance of those standards of conduct that he encounters during his growing-up years. He may imitate, often unconsciously, some of the attitudes of individuals whom he admires.

Many of a young person's life values have their beginnings in the home. He tends to agree with parental attitudes in areas such as social issues, political affiliation, and similar general components of the life pattern. Disagreements between the ideals of an adolescent and those of his parents or of other adults usually center around the teen-ager's personal interests, felt needs, and desired activities. The developing boy's or girl's standards of conduct also are affected by his or her religious experiences. Other factors of influence are radio and television programs, reading materials, and the expressed points of view of associates of the same age and older.

The cultural milieu in which an individual grows up exerts a potent but subtle and somewhat indirect influence on his developing ideals. Concerning the significance of cultural factors, Schneiders says:

Influences exerted by the home, school, church, and neighborhood are closely related to the cultural impact on value systems. These social units are often the wellsprings as well as the repositories of cultural values. Thus the values derived from the home are often nothing more than cultural concepts that have filtered into the minds of parents and other family members. Somewhat the same situation exists with respect to the school as a social institution, although here the relationship is complicated by the added influence of educational philosophies that are the product of tradition, experience, and experimentation.[1]

Various studies have been conducted to discover possible differences among the life values of national groups. An early study, for example, indicated that Swedish children were more concerned about intellectual and artistic qualities than were English, American, and Prussian young people.[2] A study of the attitudes of young people in ten countries led to the conclusion that adolescents in the United States are less interested in social development and more concerned about their personal affairs than are teen-agers of the other national groups.[3]

Morris attempted to compare the life values reported by college students in India, Norway, Japan, China, and the United States. His purpose was to discover the kind of life they would like to live as represented by the following: social restraint and self-control, enjoyment and progress in action, receptivity and sympathetic concern, self-indulgence, and withdrawal and self-sufficiency.[4] The results of the study as adapted by Smith are presented in Table 29.

Living conditions related to socioeconomic status may affect standards of behavior. Young people reared in low socioeconomic neighborhoods seem to emphasize aggression and self-assertion. Middle-class

[1] Alexander A. Schneiders, *Personality Development and Adjustment in Adolescence*, The Bruce Publishing Company, Milwaukee, 1960, p. 295.

[2] Elizabeth B. Hurlock and C. Jansing, "The Vocational Attitudes of Boys and Girls of High School Age," *Journal of Genetic Psychology*, vol. 44, pp. 175–191, 1934.

[3] J. M. Gillespie, in G. W. Allport, *The Nature of Prejudice*, Addison-Wesley Publishing Company, Inc., Reading, Mass., 1954.

[4] C. W. Morris, *Varieties of Human Value*, The University of Chicago Press, Chicago, 1956.

*Table 29.* The Relative Dominance of Various Philosophies in Five Nations

| RESTRAINT | ACTION | RECEPTIVITY | SELF-INDULGENCE | WITHDRAWAL |
|---|---|---|---|---|
| India | China | China | *United States* | Japan |
| Norway | India | India | Japan | India |
| Japan | *United States* | Japan | Norway | Norway |
| China | Norway | Norway | India | *United States* |
| *United States* | Japan | *United States* | China | China |

SOURCE: Adapted from C. W. Morris, *Varieties of Human Value*, The University of Chicago Press, Chicago, 1956, in Henry C. Smith, *Personality Adjustment*, McGraw-Hill Book Company, New York, 1961, p. 230. Reprinted by permission.

young adolescents appear to be more conventional and conforming. Other differences between the two groups are found. Florence Heal compared the values listed by eleventh-grade students, 34 of whom represented lower socioeconomic standards and 42 of whom were in the middle socioeconomic group. The results of the study are presented in Table 30. A

*Table 30.* Values Listed by Eleventh-grade Students

| VALUE | SOCIOECONOMIC GROUP LOWER (34) NUMBER | PER CENT | MIDDLE (42) NUMBER | PER CENT |
|---|---|---|---|---|
| Faith................. | 23 | 67.7 | 42 | 100.0 |
| Love................. | 26 | 76.5 | 42 | 100.0 |
| Honesty............. | 16 | 47.0 | 40 | 95.2 |
| Money.............. | 23 | 67.7 | 33 | 78.5 |
| Security............. | 22 | 64.7 | 36 | 85.6 |
| Education........... | 26 | 76.5 | 30 | 71.4 |
| Friendship.......... | 26 | 76.5 | 27 | 64.3 |
| Health.............. | 16 | 47.0 | 21 | 50.0 |
| Loyalty............. | 10 | 29.4 | 21 | 50.0 |
| Respect............. | 13 | 38.2 | 21 | 50.0 |
| Dependability........ | 10 | 29.4 | 21 | 50.0 |
| Peace of mind........ | 2 | 5.9 | 5 | 11.9 |
| Privacy............. | 5 | 14.7 | 5 | 11.9 |
| Leadership........... | 2 | 5.9 | 10 | 23.8 |
| Material wants........ | 10 | 29.5 | 10 | 23.8 |

SOURCE: Florence L. D. Heal, "Values in a Group of Lower Socio-economic Students," *Marriage and Family Living*, p. 371, November, 1960.

study of the table reveals considerable difference of values in some areas, e.g., faith, honesty, loyalty, dependability, etc., and a closer relationship between group values in items such as education, friendship, health, and material wants.

Also, the ethical values of young people tend to change with changing adult attitudes and practices over a period of years. In Table 31 are

Table 31. Differences in Students' Rankings of "Worst Practices" in 1919 and in 1954

| 1919 | RANK | 1954 |
|------|------|------|
| Killing or murdering | 1 | Killing or murdering |
| Sexual misbehaving | 2 | Using or selling narcotics |
| Stealing | 3 | Sexual misbehaving |
| Cheating | 4 | Stealing |
| Lying | 5 | Drinking (alcohol) |
| Drinking (alcohol) | 6 | Cheating |
| Gambling | 7 | Lying |
| Swearing, vulgar talk | 8 | Being cruel |
| Not being religious | 9 | Not being religious |
| Being selfish | 10 | Reckless driving |
| Gossiping | 11 | Swearing |
| Idleness | 12 | Being undependable |
| Snobbishness | 13 | Gossiping |
| Extravagance | 14 | Being inconsiderate |
| Smoking | 15 | Smoking |
| Dancing | 16 | Being conceited |

SOURCE: Ruth Strang, The Adolescent Views Himself: A Psychology of Adolescence, McGraw-Hill Book Company, New York, 1957, p. 115. Adapted from R. E. Horton and H. H. Remmers, Some Ethical Values of Youth, Compared Over the Years, Report No. 38, Purdue Opinion Panel, vol. 13, no. 2, April, 1954, pp. 1–3. Reprinted by permission.

presented the findings of Horton and Remmers concerning changes in what high school students consider to be "worst practices" in 1919 and in 1954. It can be noted that several practices maintain their relative ranks in both lists, e.g., "killing or murdering," "not being religious," and "smoking." Others appear on one list but not on the other, e.g., "using or selling narcotics," and "reckless driving," on the 1954 list, and "gambling" and "dancing" on the 1919 list.

## Functioning of Ideals

An adolescent's ideals are based on the fulfillment of his own fundamental needs as well as on consideration for the needs of others. He wants safety, freedom from pain, and happiness that he can share with those who are near and dear to him. A young person is a thinking, feeling, doing individual. He constantly is attempting to gain self-realization through self-actualization. He must give overt expression to his inner drives. Further, he does not live in a vacuum but in a world peopled with many different kinds of individuals. If he is to achieve a nice balance between self-serving and others-serving attitudes and activities, he must develop ideals by which his behavior can be guided toward the attainment of his goals. Moreover, he needs to acquire an objective understanding of the relationship that exists between life values which are self-serving and his chances of becoming a useful, contented, and socially accepted group member.

The democratic ideal of equality of opportunity for self-realization within the limits of ability to achieve is not completely understood by all individuals. Young people, encouraged by some of their elders, are placing great emphasis upon material satisfactions and the experiencing of self-bolstering gratifications. The swift pace of modern living can interfere with the development of serene and appreciative attitudes.

Character development is a dynamic process that involves progressive interrelationships between inner urges and environmental influences. Yet the character traits that emerge as a result of continuing interaction of inner and outer factors rarely, if ever, represent an exact ratio of 1 to 1. The attitudes, ideals, and life values that become habitual motivators of an adolescent's behavior certainly are affected by environmental forces. Fundamentally, however, the kind of person an adolescent becomes, the character traits he gradually develops, are rooted in his innate power to profit from his experiences with people and things about him.

A young person learns to recognize the extent to which he is controlled by cultural mores, and he gradually frees himself from dependence upon their influence. The gaining of personal freedom of action does not imply, however, that the young person's attitudes and ideals will come to be directed toward self-indulgence and defiance of socially acceptable standards of conduct. Rather, he achieves freedom of choice through the development of self-control. He attains a degree of realistic self-discipline that reflects the influence upon him during his early years of wise adult guidance of his uncontrolled, childish impulses.

The transition from childhood conformity to adult standards and dependence upon parental care and guidance to adult self-determination and self-dependence is not effected without uncertainty, doubt, bewilderment, thwarting, and possible conflict. The utilization of a positive approach to experiences in the building of ideals results in the establishment of a sound, forward-looking set of personal values. The individual can achieve thereby a contented, happy, calm, serene, and peaceful personality.

# The Adolescent and Religious Values

Basically, present cultural values are related directly or indirectly to religious concepts, beliefs, forms of expression, and extent of influence upon individual and group attitudes and behavior. An individual's ideals, conduct standards, and appreciation of the meaning of life are inextricably interwoven with the kind and amount of his religious experiences during his formative years. Attitudes toward religious values acquired during adolescence exercise a potent influence upon developing personality and character trends.

## Significance of Attitudes toward Religion

Among primitive peoples, as well as in more civilized societies, organized religion has played an important role in establishing moral or ethical codes of behavior. The history of great religious movements gives evidence, however, that various religious organizations or denominational institutions have tended to differ in their emphasis upon what constitutes acceptable life values. Yet all religious faiths share a basic concern over the "ultimate destiny of man." The religious concept involves an individual's relationship to his God, to himself, and to the other persons of any age that, broadly interpreted, constitute his human environment.

From the religious point of view the most important aspects of an individual's life's values are his spiritual sensitivities. The connotation of the term *religion*, even in its broadest interpretation, differs among individuals. According to Edwin E. Aubrey:

The term "religion" carries a variety of meanings. To some, it means assent to a theologically formulated system of beliefs. To others, it denotes a body of customary practices consisting of rites, mores, and private acts of devotion. To still others, it is an intimate personal experience of communion with God or of acute decision in which eternal values are at stake, or of standing under the judgment of the Ultimate. All of these are legitimate definitions, and these various aspects in religious life do not always appear in any one sequence.[5]

Considered perhaps from a more affective point of view,

Religion implies an ultimate reality to which supreme allegiance must be given. To this ultimate reality men have from time immemorial given a name—God. The religious man finds warrant for all of his con-

[5] E. E. Aubrey, "Scientia, Scientific Method, and Religion," in A. C. Wilder (ed.), *Liberal Learning and Religion,* Harper & Row, Publishers, Incorporated, New York, 1951, p. 46.

ceptions of worth, of right, of duty, and of human destiny in his relationship to this ultimate reality. There is a wide difference in the ways in which men define this concept of God, ranging from highly personal to abstract philosophical terms; from emphasis on the transcendent to emphasis on the imma-nent; from a frankly supernatural conception to one that endows the cosmos itself with spiritual purpose and power. However, religion affirms overwhelmingly a reality that transcends the flux of events and constrains men toward the true and good.[6]

The foregoing is an attempt to present a broad interpretation of religion and religious values. As the reader will discover later, the so-called "religious problems" experienced by adolescents grow out of a commonly accepted but erroneous identification of religious attitudes or belief with theology, a specific form of religious dogma, or a particular religious organization or institution. It is probable that most young people acquire their early religious attitudes and ideals as a result of association with one or another religious institution. Too much emphasis upon dogma or specific organizational taboos may have an adverse effect upon a young person's later religious appreciations.

## Religious Education in a Modern World

In the United States, as in other parts of the world, there have been established many organized religious bodies, denominations, or sects that share the responsibility of providing religious education for young people. It has been claimed that in some communities, especially in large cities, the church[7] is failing to meet adequately its educational responsibility. Hence it is losing prestige as a social agency whose primary function should be to guide the development of sound and positive attitudes, or ideals upon which can be built acceptable interpersonal and intersocial relationships. The reason for this criticism, whether or not it is valid, can be found in the fact that in our mechanical age the church continues to stress spiritual and nonmaterialistic values as opposed to compelling drives to gain material possessions.

Religious leaders are faced with the problem of meeting the challenge of a relatively popular mechanistic explanation of human nature. Moreover, to some extent psychological science has assumed a negative

[6] American Council on Education, Committee on Religion and Education (ed.), *The Relation of Religion to Public Education*, published as an appendix to N. C. Harner, *Religion's Place in General Education*, Committee of Publications of Presbyterian Church, Richmond, Va., 1949, p. 110.

[7] The term *church* as used in this discussion applies to any organized religious group, i.e., Mohammedan, Greek Orthodox, Roman Catholic, Jewish, Anglican Catholic, or Protestant.

rather than a positive approach to the study of human behavior; more attention has been devoted to human abnormalities, shortcomings, and mental and emotional deterioration than has been given to positive human potentialities, superior behavior, and mental and emotional good health. Sociology apparently also has tended to become so concerned with societal inadequacies that group strengths have been overlooked or treated lightly. It must be admitted, however, that there have been instances of similar failure on the part of organized religion to stress positive life values because of too great concern with the damnation of the "wicked."

Social scientists disagree concerning the significance of religion in the life of an individual or a group of individuals. Some express pessimism concerning the value of religious education; others, in a spirit of sincere optimism, state their belief that in the development of positive religious values among young people lies our greatest hope for the amelioration of existing social inadequacies and the improvement of present interworld attitudes. Yet, in spite of conflicting points of view among social scientists and their sincere desire to improve group morale through well-planned programs of social reform, religion and religious education still continue to exercise a considerable influence upon society's attitudes toward moral and spiritual values. The extent to which, and the way in which, programs of religious education should be organized remain controversial issues.

As the adolescent is struggling to evolve for himself satisfying standards of conduct and personal ideals, and to gain some understanding of those life values that can have meaning for him, he cannot avoid the effects upon his developing personality and character of adult attitudes toward religion. Hence we now shall consider some of the problems associated with adolescent reactions to religions as a phase of the growing-up process.

## Adolescent Religious Experiences

Perhaps in no other phase of adolescent development are individual differences more pronounced than they seem to be in the area of religious experiences. There probably are no two teen-agers who react in the same way to the transition from childhood religious concepts to mature acceptance or rejection of religious values. Differences among adolescents' developing religious attitudes and experiences can be considered to be the resultants of many variables: family attitudes toward religion, kind and amount of religious training received during childhood, religious attitudes of peer associates, adult example, influence of secular education, and extent of preoccupation with study, work and/or social activities. The most significant developmental factor, however, is the inherent nature of the adolescent himself. The kind of individual he is will determine the effect upon his religious attitudes of his changing physical, emotional, and social experiences.

Contrary to general opinion, the religious attitudes of a maturing young person, in common with his attitudes toward other aspects of experience, do not necessarily change suddenly and radically with the onset of puberty. Some adolescents appear to achieve a gradual transition from their childhood concept of a personal God who rewarded them when they were good and punished them for their naughtiness to a belief in a Supreme Being, an acceptance of the supernatural, and an appreciation of their relationship to the cosmic whole. They may achieve a deep and abiding faith, having intellectual as well as emotional components. Religious values may serve them as behavior stabilizers; from their religious appreciations may emerge their life-controlling ideals and general life values.

Even when religious growing up is relatively painless for an adolescent, doubt about certain religious tenets may be experienced occasionally, and questions concerning differences in religious practices need to be answered. The young person may think through his doubts and answer his own questions or he may seek help from his parents or from his pastor. If he belongs to a young people's church group, he may discuss his questions with the other members of the group. Usually he discovers that his doubts and questions are not peculiar to himself. Adolescents may "thrash out" their problems together or they may invite an adult in whom they have confidence to meet with them and clarify their thinking.

Not all adolescents are able to achieve an understanding and an acceptance of religious values that are broader and more comprehensive than their earlier childhood concepts. One individual may experience serious doubts concerning the value to him of religion in any form. At first these doubts are related to religious forms and ceremonies; later they center around the content of religious dogma. Eventually this adolescent may reject religion completely. He may become cynical about religious matters and scoff at his peer associates who display interest in religious belief. Another young person, who during childhood had been a regular attendant at his church school, may begin to doubt some of his earlier religious teachings. He may experience feelings of guilt; to allay these feelings he may develop a degree of religious fervor that excites him to sudden "conversion." His intellectual doubts may be thereby resolved, and religion may become for him a highly emotional, mystical experience that, for a longer or shorter period of time, satisfies all his adolescent wants or urges. Religious attitudes may be so strongly emotionalized that the boy (more often the girl) is motivated to join a religious order and thus be separated from the "wicked" world, to become a missionary who will save the souls of faraway "pagans," or to develop a great, sometimes irrational, interest in social reform.

What the attitude toward religious values may be when either the adolescent rejecter of religion or the emotionalized believer becomes a mature adult is unpredictable. Although the rejection may seem to be the result of intellectual decision making, it may be based upon emotional reactions that are as intense as those that lead to conversion. Hence to the extent that either of these adolescents is able to achieve mature emotional stability, he is likely to modify his religious attitudes. Thereby he achieves a compromise between his childhood and adolescent appreciations of religious values. He then is able to accept religion as both an intellectual and an emotional motivating force in his life.

Various studies have been undertaken to discover the kinds of changes in religious belief that can be expected to accompany adolescent maturational growth and experiential development. Probably one of the most often-cited studies in this area of investigation was conducted by Kuhlen and Arnold.[8] Statements of various beliefs were presented to 547 young people ranging in age from 12 to 18, and representing school grades 6, 9, and 12. The subjects of the study were asked to respond to each of the statements in terms of their present belief, i.e., "believe," "not believe," or "wonder about." By checking in the last column for any one or more statements, the responder would be indicating that he had thought about the religious concept contained in the statement but had not yet arrived at a satisfactory conclusion concerning it. The results of the study are presented in Table 32.

A study of the presented data will confirm the investigators' interpretation of them as representative of three general age trends: religious beliefs become increasingly abstract; tolerance in regard to religious beliefs and practice increases; areas of indecision such as the truth of every word in the Bible, the actuality of God, the hereafter, and heaven and hell represent matters of serious concern to older adolescents. These uncertainties may be the resultants of advanced study in areas such as the natural sciences and social studies, or discussions with peer or adult associates; or they may represent an attitude of suspended judgment.

A common cause of anxiety among "God-fearing" parents and other older adults is the fear that college attendance may result in an older adolescent's or young adult's loss of his belief in God and development of definite antireligious attitudes. This popular belief does not seem to be

[8] R. G. Kuhlen and M. Arnold, "Age Differences in Religious Beliefs and Problems during Adolescence," *Journal of Genetic Psychology*, vol. 65, pp. 291–300, 1944. See also Chap. 3.

*Table 32.* Changes in Specific Religious Beliefs during Adolescence as Shown by the Percentage of 174 Sixth-, 243 Ninth-, and 130 Twelfth-grade Children Who Checked Various Statements Indicating Belief, Disbelief, or Uncertainty (Wonder)

| STATEMENT | "BELIEVE" | | | "NOT BELIEVE" | | | "WONDER ABOUT" | | |
|---|---|---|---|---|---|---|---|---|---|
| | 6 | 9 | 12 | 6 | 9 | 12 | 6 | 9 | 12 |
| God is a strange power working for good, rather than a person | 46 | 49 | 57 | 31 | 33 | 21 | 20 | 14 | 15 |
| God is someone who watches you to see that you behave yourself, and who punishes you if you are not good..... | 70 | 49 | 33 | 18 | 37 | 48 | 11 | 13 | 18 |
| I know there is a God........ | 94 | 80 | 79 | 3 | 5 | 2 | 2 | 14 | 16 |
| Catholics, Jews, and Protestants are equally good........... | 67 | 79 | 86 | 9 | 9 | 7 | 24 | 11 | 7 |
| There is a heaven............ | 82 | 78 | 74 | 4 | 5 | 5 | 13 | 16 | 20 |
| Only good people go to heaven. | 72 | 45 | 33 | 15 | 27 | 32 | 13 | 27 | 34 |
| Hell is a place where you are punished for your sins on earth..................... | 70 | 49 | 35 | 16 | 21 | 30 | 13 | 27 | 34 |
| Heaven is here on earth....... | 12 | 13 | 14 | 69 | 57 | 52 | 18 | 28 | 32 |
| People who go to church are better than people who do not go to church........... | 46 | 26 | 15 | 37 | 53 | 74 | 17 | 21 | 11 |
| Young people should belong to the same church as their parents................... | 77 | 56 | 43 | 13 | 33 | 46 | 10 | 11 | 11 |
| The main reason for going to church is to worship God... | 88 | 80 | 79 | 6 | 12 | 15 | 4 | 7 | 6 |
| It is not necessary to attend church to be a Christian.... | 42 | 62 | 67 | 38 | 23 | 24 | 18 | 15 | 8 |
| Only our souls live after death.. | 72 | 63 | 61 | 9 | 11 | 6 | 18 | 25 | 31 |
| Good people say prayers regularly..................... | 78 | 57 | 47 | 9 | 29 | 26 | 13 | 13 | 27 |
| Prayers are answered......... | 76 | 69 | 65 | 3 | 5 | 8 | 21 | 25 | 27 |
| Prayers are a source of help in times of trouble............ | 74 | 80 | 83 | 11 | 8 | 7 | 15 | 10 | 9 |
| Prayers are to make up for something that you have done that is wrong.............. | 47 | 24 | 21 | 35 | 58 | 69 | 18 | 17 | 9 |
| Every word in the Bible is true. | 79 | 51 | 34 | 6 | 16 | 23 | 15 | 31 | 43 |
| It is sinful to doubt the Bible.. | 62 | 42 | 27 | 18 | 31 | 44 | 20 | 26 | 28 |

SOURCE: R. G. Kuhlen and M. Arnold, "Age Differences in Religious Beliefs and Problems during Adolescence," *Journal of Genetic Psychology*, vol. 65, p. 293, 1944.

in accord with fact. Temporarily a college student may give evidence of some skepticism, especially if the assuming of an attitude of uncertainty concerning spiritual values appears to be the fashion in his group. Most college students are intensely interested in religious values, however. Religion is one of the most popular discussion topics of college men's "bull sessions." At these meetings philosophical, religious, and social values usually receive serious and thoughtful consideration. Displayed attitudes of cynicism, skepticism, or flippancy are discouraged or not tolerated.

An adolescent or young adult may not experience too great doubt concerning the value to himself of religious belief. His earlier concepts may change but they tend to be crystallized as they become more meaningful and comprehensive. At the same time he may rebel against continuing the religious practices in which he had engaged during childhood. He may refuse to attend church school or church services and become neglectful in the observance of certain church-required obligations.

Because of his association with other young people whose respective church affiliations demand that they adhere to specific religious observances that differ from those of his own church, the adolescent considers any such obligations superficial, insignificant, and unrelated to fundamental religious truth. This adolescent's attitude is strengthened by the fact that he admires and respects the other teen-agers.

In most religious denominations the change from childhood dependence to adolescent beginnings of self-responsibility is given recognition through the application of certain rites or ceremonies, such as confirmation or *bar mizvah*. The young person may experience considerable emotional satisfaction during the period of preparation and the ceremony itself; he may accept with great seriousness his "new" church status. He may become increasingly lax about Sunday-school attendance or participation in other religious activities, however.

For some young adolescents the complete or partial withdrawal from religious practices is more or less temporary. In later adolescence or early adulthood they are likely to become active church workers. They teach in the Sunday school, attend church services regularly, and participate enthusiastically in other religious activities. But some young people drift away from the church, especially if they leave their childhood home community. They develop new interests and engage in other activities, with the result that as adults they have no church affiliation.

Some adolescents transfer their affiliation from the church of their parents' faith to another denomination. The cause of the transfer may be either a change in religious conviction or the influence of a close associate, often of the opposite sex. Many individuals, of course, maintain for one church a steady loyalty that, begun in early childhood, continues throughout life. Even though they leave the neighborhood in which the church is situated, they remain active in it, unless the traveling distance is too great. If they move to another, they immediately seek out and affiliate themselves with a church similar to the one of which they had been members, and participate in its religious activities.

In the light of the various adolescent religious experiences described in this section, it can be concluded that there is no "typical" adolescent attitude. Some of the causal factors of difference now will be discussed briefly.

## Causal Factors of Adolescent Religious Attitudes

One of the most significant factors of influence upon an adolescent's religious attitudes is the religious atmosphere of the home. A child's first experiences with religious concepts grow out of parental precept and example. Whatever he receives in the way of religious training is provided in the home or is gained from the teachings of the church with which the parents are affiliated. In past generations great emphasis was placed upon the teaching of religious dogma; the increased liberal thinking that is characteristic of our modern culture is reflected in less rigid religious tenets and teachings, except for some still-existing religious institutions.

A child reared in the home of strict adherents to certain specific denominational observances and taboos is likely to experience much mental confusion and emotional conflict when, as an adolescent, he is exposed to more liberal religious attitudes. For example, for religious reasons parents may disapprove of activities such as dancing, smoking, card playing, engaging in recreational activities on the Sabbath, or attending theatrical performances and motion-picture programs. These taboos may not affect a child to any great extent, especially if his peer neighbors are similarly restricted. When he attends high school, however, his own changing interests and the less restricted behavior of his classmates may constitute for him an intolerable situation. He becomes even more disturbed if he had been taught to fear God's wrath and eternal damnation.

The adolescent child of religious but liberal parents is likely to have less difficulty in readjusting childish religious concepts in terms of increasing maturity and broader experiences. He may display relatively little interest in religious values, however, even though he continues accustomed religious practices. Instead, he develops an attitude of extreme concern over social inequalities; he may become a radical, sometimes unrealistic, advocate of sweeping social reforms.

Contrariwise, an adolescent whose parents are irreligious and who consequently has received no religious training may suffer a feeling of insecurity; he may envy his peer associates who as children participated in religious experiences which were denied him. A young person of this kind often seeks the security he needs by affiliating himself with the religious institution of a close friend, and thereby develops strong religious attitudes. Another adolescent may accept religious ideals as his conduct standards, and learn to respect his church-attending friends, without developing any personal religious convictions.

Perhaps the most severe religious conflicts are suffered by the off-spring of mixed marriages, especially if each parent is a devout member of his particular church. In some such families, the child is expected to attend the church of each parent; in others, the stronger-willed parent is likely to guide the child's religious training, with consequent display of resentment by the other parent. If neither parent has strong religious convictions, the child experiences little, if any, church training. As a result, he either may drift along in the wake of his parents or attend a church of his own selection. In large families the situation becomes increasingly complicated.

Questionable behavior of religious leaders, Sunday-school teachers, and apparently "good" church members can stimulate adolescent attitudes of religious doubt, confusion, or disillusionment. An adolescent can become bored, or, in his own words, "disgusted," with long sermons that deal only with dogmatism or mysticism. The maturing young person, encouraged by his high school teachers to think for himself and to make practical application of the theories he is studying, wants to discover how religion can function in his own life. He is seeking answers to questions about religion that are bothering him. He does not find the desired answers in sermons that seem to him to deal only with Biblical matters or concepts which he cannot understand.

A child usually enjoys attending Sunday school. He likes to listen to or read simple Bible stories and to sing stirring hymns. He thrills to the awards he receives for good attendance. He is willing to memorize excerpts from the Bible or answers to questions in the catechism, even though he may not understand the meaning of what has been memorized. For example, a little girl who could recite the catechism without a single error had no conception of the meaning of the word "sponsor."

Unless Sunday-school procedures are adapted to meet the maturing interests of the adolescent, he soon will become disinterested. Moreover, as we know, an adolescent tends to be critical of the attitudes and behavior of all adults; hence he is not only critical of, but is disillusioned by, the bickering and jealousies of some adult church leaders and by the unethical practices of supposedly devout churchgoers.

The religious attitudes of a college student may not be too much affected by advanced study; as a result of his secondary school experiences, an adolescent who is passing through the doubting stage can become very much confused concerning the validity of some of his earlier religious beliefs. The subject matter of his study and/or the attitudes of his teachers tend to pose questions about the role of religion in the establishing of life values.

The mentally slower churchgoing adolescent is not likely to be bothered so much as is the brighter high school student by apparent inconsistencies between religious and secular education. The latter's reactions to seeming differences of emphases are dependent in great part upon the degree of strength of his religious faith. If his church affiliation represents the following of family or community convention, his awakening interest in objective and nonreligious study of natural and social phenomena may weaken his former religious beliefs. Any conflict that arises is resolved in favor of the secular approach. The young person, temporarily at least, may develop an attitude similar to that expressed by a boy known to the authors who said with youthful conviction, "Religion is bunkum, fit only for children and old folks who don't know any better."

The adolescent whose religious doubts are limited to questions concerning differences in denominational rites, ceremonies, and similar matters, but whose fundamental religious faith is strong, is likely to interpret secular learning in terms of religious belief. He is willing, perhaps eager, to learn all that he can about the world of people and things, but his faith is not shaken by his study. Yet he may be bothered by what to him appear to be nonreligious, atheistic, or agnostic attitudes displayed by teachers. His own resulting emotionalized attitude toward such an instructor may affect adversely his interest in the subject taught.

## Current Trends toward Religious Reconstruction

Many national, state, and community leaders, including church pastors, businessmen, industrialists, educators, government officials, and other men and women interested in individual and group welfare, are cooperating in a loosely organized program aimed at the revitalization of religion as a motivating force in the lives of the general citizenry. Existing world confusion and conflict, rising incidence of adult crime and youthful delinquency, increasing trends toward individualistic defiance of democratically invested authority, nonabating concern with materialistic values, and continuing display of moral laxity probably have their origin in the lack of any universally accepted code of ethical standards and in an unconcern about religious values.

Thinking people are gaining greater insight into the problems experienced by young people who are attempting to effect a compromise between the supposedly constructive ideals of the democratic way of life and the grim realities of the world in which they live. Cooperatively achievable standards for the attainment of the "good life" need to be established.

Many religious organizations are accepting the challenge of providing "core values." There are observable attempts to reduce traditional emphases upon sectarian dogma and taboos. Although fundamental religious principles are upheld, increased consideration is being given to the application of these principles to the solution of problems inherent in modern living. Sectarianism still exists and probably will continue so long as people differ in their emotional reactions to church rites and ceremonies, their attitudes toward music and pageantry, and their interpretation of the Bible and formulated creeds. Yet organizations such as the National Council of Christians and Jews and other interfaith groups exemplify a sincere effort on the part of church leaders to discover basic religious values and to encourage church adherents to live together amicably within the framework of their common beliefs.

The church is adapting its traditional organization of planned activity to meet the personal interests and social needs of maturing young people. Church-school teaching approaches are geared to meet adolescent religious doubts. Questions concerning dogma and practice are encouraged. Bible-study classes and other stimulating group discussions (led by adults or youths) are planned for older adolescents. One of the authors recalls the intellectual clarification and emotional satisfaction gained from membership in a group of 18- to about 25-year-olds, the meetings of which, under the leadership of a widely read and stimulating clergyman, were devoted to discussions on the history of religious belief.

In addition, adolescents are encouraged to engage in various church-sponsored recreational and service programs for both sexes, e.g., young people's societies, picnics, bazaars, clubs, social gatherings, voluntary services to hospitalized children, teaching of church-school classes, and similar youth-intriguing activities. Some churches also sponsor, with the aid of trained personnel, premarital and parent-child counseling services. Without neglecting their strictly religious responsibilities, many churches are becoming effective social-service agencies.

During his maturing years an adolescent can be expected to experience satisfying religious security if both his parents have been reared in the same religious faith and if all the members of the family attend the same church and participate wholeheartedly in church activities. Parents, as well as other adults, need to practice the religious observances to which they expect young people will adhere.

There is a growing movement toward providing increasing opportunities for young people to receive religious education. Many public school systems, especially in urban communities, are cooperating with church-sponsored programs of weekday religious instruction by releasing pupils from regular school attendance for an hour or more one day a week. Further, in some secondary schools and colleges religious clubs have been established and maintained as regular extraclass projects. In large communities especially, each club is sponsored by a particular religious denomination, i.e., Roman Catholic, Protestant, or Judaistic.

Public opinion differs concerning school-released time for religious education and religious clubs in public schools. Those people who favor such programs claim that thereby religious values receive increased public recognition, desirable character qualities are strengthened, and interfaith cooperation is fostered. Opposition is based upon claims that released-time instruction may be characterized by verbalism only, and that religious instruction divorced from practice and other educational experiences is inadequate. It is also claimed that a released-time program is likely to separate young people into subgroups in terms of their religious affiliations and to encourage among the various groups an attitude of religious intolerance rather than one of cooperation. Moreover, recently adherents of the principle of the separation of church and state have been responsible for legislation that denies to public schools in the United States any supposedly religious activities such as opening the school session with a prayer or the reading of excerpts from the Bible.

Other evidences of increased interest in religion-pointed education include the rising number of parochial schools that have been and are continuing to be established, particularly in urban areas, and the display of interest in religious values among institutions of higher education. Many books and articles have been written on the subject of the role of religion in higher education. Public college and university faculties are participating, either as a faculty group or in conjunction with student representatives, in planned discussions concerning religious values and the college student. The purposes of having college personnel express such interest in religious values include developing a greater recognition of religious influences, assisting older adolescents and young adults to shift from their earlier emotional religious beliefs and practices toward a more intellectual interpretation, and meeting the spiritual needs of students.

## Adolescent Moral Values

Developing ideals, changing religious understandings, and broadening moral concepts represent integrated and integrating life values. The patterning of any of these areas of character development during adolescence is not an isolated process. As we have traced the changes in attitudes toward ideals and religion that take place during the formative years, we could not avoid referring also to those elements of character formation that are rooted in the young person's developing attitudes toward *morality*. At this point, therefore, the discussion will be limited to a consideration of moral concepts and their influence upon adolescent attitudes and behavior.

## Moral Concepts

The terms *moral* and *ethical* often are misinterpreted. *Morality, morals,* and *moral behavior* carry a religious implication, while *ethics* and *ethical standards* have social or cultural significance. Another common error of interpretation is to limit the application of the term *moral* or *immoral* to unacceptable sex behavior. By dictionary definition, *morality,* derived from the Latin word *moralis,* connotes moral conduct (rectitude, chastity, virtue), or conformity or degree of conformity to conventional rules, without or apart from inspiration of guidance by religion or other spiritual influence; *ethics* refers more directly to the study and philosophy of human conduct, with emphasis on the determination of right and wrong, or the basic principle of right action.

If morality is conceived as conformity to group standards, group-accepted moral codes are pointed at achieving a *good* society. The interpretation of the term *good* may vary among social groups, however. Moreover, certain behavior may be in accord with a group's moral standards at one time but later be condemned, partly because of the long-range ill effects of the formerly approved behavior.

History offers many examples of the effects upon individuals and society as a whole of group differences in codes of morals and in changing attitudes within a group toward what is good behavior. Important in the daily life of an adolescent, for example, are differing cultural attitudes toward the acceptability of smoking, drinking, premarital sex relations, respect for authority, and other forms of conduct that may be severely condemned by his parents and their close friends, but condoned, if not entirely approved, by the cultural group of which his high school or college friends are members.

Viewed more widely, variations in moral acceptability may exercise a tremendous effect upon a society's possibility of advancement or even survival. For illustration we need only recall the effect of a lowered moral code upon Rome, the accepted "rightness" of the Spanish Inquisition and other examples of religious persecution, and socially approved child labor during the early days of industrialism. Our present problems associated with rising divorce rates, the struggle between democratic and totalitarian world powers, and differences of opinion concerning the *rightness* of utilizing atomic power in the waging of war represent some of the major differences in moral codes that constitute fundamental effecters of future cultural advancement or deterioration.

## The Adolescent's Development of a Moral Code

A child's behavior tends to be influenced by his parents' approval of what they consider to be right or good conduct for him and their disapproval of wrong conduct or naughtiness. He has little, if any, concept of morality as such. His strivings to be good grow out of his fear of punishment for wrong acts, his desire to please his parents, or perhaps a need to feel superior to other children who are not so obedient or so cooperative as he is.

A child's knowledge of right and wrong is usually associated with concrete experienced situations. He may know that he must not steal money, but to take a desired toy from another child does not mean stealing it, until he learns that this too is a disapproved form of behavior. To the extent that the child gradually gains some understanding of moral concepts, he interprets the possession of them in an all-or-none fashion, e.g., one must *always* tell the truth, a lie *always* is wicked.

Various studies have been undertaken to discover the sources of young people's moral concepts and the development of the conscience. As we have suggested earlier, children's ideas of right and wrong behavior are conditioned by experiences in the home. Hoffman's[9] review of recent research on moral behavior includes some challenging points of view. As the child reaches preadolescence his moral understandings are being influenced by the effect on him of the attitudes of associates of his own age. For example, the functions of preadolescent gangs in Australia and England were investigated by A. R. Crane.[10] Among other things he found that group life serves as a good basis for education and involves restrictions and new patterns of responding to authority figures. In the preadolescent groups the individuals feel free from imposed standards of behavior and begin to build value systems of their own. According to Crane, "The child enters the gang voluntarily and the rules, norms and codes of behavior have either been freely determined by the gang members themselves or at the very least, have been fully accepted by the members." All these experiences enable the individual to build his moral fiber.

[9] Martin L. Hoffman, "Child-rearing Practices and Moral Development: Generalizations from Empirical Research," *Child Development*, vol. 34, June, 1961.

[10] A. R. Crane, "The Development of Moral Values in Children—Preadolescent Gangs and the Moral Development of Children," *British Journal of Educational Psychology*, vol. 28, pp. 201–208, 1958.

By the time a child approaches adolescence he begins to recognize the fact that there are differences of opinion among adults as well as within his peer group concerning what is considered acceptable or unacceptable behavior. The more alert mentally the young person is, the sooner will he discover these differences and attempt to adapt his behavior in terms of particular group standards. Difficulties arise, however, when the apparent moral codes of the various groups with which he is associated differ so widely that his childhood-habituated behavior is approved by the members of one group, tolerated by others, and condemned by still others.

The adolescent becomes confused by the discrepancies in the moral codes to which he is exposed. At first he may be uncertain concerning the management of his own behavior. Consequently, he attempts to conform to the standards of whatever group he finds himself in. If the difference is between his parents' code of conduct and that of his peer associates, he tends gradually to accept the latter. Eventually he acquires his own moral code that is related closely to his developing ideals and his changing religious attitudes. The personal and social effectiveness of the moral values expressed in his behavior depends to a great extent upon the environmental factors that have operated in the building of his code.

As in other areas of adolescent development, home and school experiences are potent factors of influence. The young person's growing appreciation of moral values is affected by the attitudes of his peer associates, and by examples of adherence or indifference to moral standards as these attitudes are presented in newspapers, books, and magazines and on radio, television, and motion-picture programs, or as they are expressed in the behavior of adult members of his community.

Relatively few individuals are born, grow up, and die in an isolated community in which a traditionally rigid moral code continues to control group behavior from generation to generation. Most adolescents who are growing up in modern cultures are enabled to experience and evaluate the functioning of many different conduct standards. Opportunity is not lacking to acquire knowledge of right and wrong. For the adolescent to know what constitutes socially accepted or disapproved behavior is necessary; otherwise through ignorance he may engage in forms of conduct that are personally humiliating or socially harmful.

For an individual to *know* what is right does not always guarantee that his actual behavior will be guided by his knowledge. Many adolescents are able to answer correctly all or most of the items on a test designed to discover extent of recognition of generally accepted moral concepts. Yet in their behavior, at least some of these same young people fail to apply one or more of the conduct standards which, in the form of test items, were answered correctly. The cause of such discrepancies may be rooted in the adolescent's still-immature control of strong urges to engage in self-satisfying but socially disapproved acts, e.g., sexual indulgence; fear of failure to achieve much-desired goals, e.g., cheating in an important examination; need for peer status, e.g., stealing to obtain things possessed by schoolmates of a higher economic status than his own; youthful rebellion against adult authority or what to him represent too strict laws, e.g., driving his father's car without parental consent at 70 or 80 miles an hour on a road where the legal speed limit is 45 miles. Many more such examples could be cited.

The fact that the teen years tend to be a period of unrealistic idealism may cause an adolescent to set high standards of conduct for himself which he cannot achieve. He is then likely to become discouraged; his conscience hurts; his guilt feelings arouse emotional tensions; he may experience violent reactions of anger that are directed not only at his own inadequacy but also at other persons who are involved in any way with the failure situation. A very important but difficult responsibility of adults, therefore, is to guide the adolescent toward building for himself a high behavior-functioning code of morals, and at the same time encourage him to keep his ideals within achievable limits.

## A Mature Philosophy of Life

The end of adolescence or the beginning of adulthood does not represent an abrupt or sudden change of status. The maturing process is gradual and varies from individual to individual and among the various developmental phases of any one individual. Hence it is difficult to determine at what point in his life an individual can be considered to be completely mature.

### Meaning and Aspects of Maturity

Childhood and adolescence are regarded as stages in an individual's life during which growth and maturation of the organism and developmental experiences gradually are preparing him for the assumption of self-interested and self-directing activities on the adult level. As compared with his earlier experiences, the mature adult enjoys freedom of decision and action, is self-motivated toward establishing and fulfilling purposeful life goals, and desires contentment and a feeling of security in his life relationships.

By the time many young persons reach legal adult status, they are well on their way toward experiencing the advantages of being adults, which in their earlier years they so much coveted. Others find the reaching of adult status to be a disappointing and sometimes disillusioning experience, mainly because they are not yet ready to assume personal responsibility for their acts, or for their own or others' welfare.

Physical and intellectual maturity normally are attained by the late teens or early twenties. The age at which an individual's interests, attitudes, emotional reactions, and social adjustments can be considered to be those of a mature adult varies in terms of the degree of stability and consistency of his developed life values. Some adults in their attitudes and behavior display emotional immaturity, inadequate interpersonal adjustments, and confused appreciation of moral standards.

Since the determination of degree of maturity in those qualities of personality and character that affect human relationships does not lend itself to objective measurement, their subtle elements probably can be evaluated only by means of their impact upon personal-social interactions.

## Significance of a Philosophy of Life

Contrary to the opinion of some lay persons, the development of a philosophy of life is not an achievement that is limited to the intellectually superior, highly trained scholar. Every adolescent and adult, often unaware of what he is doing, constantly is building and rebuilding a philosophy of life. His philosophy grows out of his attitudes toward the various values that have been discussed.

Adolescents are prone to take pals of their own age into their confidence concerning their ambitions, interests, and views on the meaning of life; at the same time, they encourage the others to tell what they think about everything. Through participation in this kind of interchange of ideas, opinions, and ideals, adolescents are striving to establish an attitudinal system or set of values. With increasing maturity and broadening experiences, some of their value appreciations may change somewhat. Yet there may be retained a degree of permanency and consistency within attitude clusters. As an adolescent continues mentally to reconstruct or revise the beliefs he developed earlier, he is engaging in the task of evolving a philosophy of life that, by the time he reaches adult status, will be ready to play a significant role in determining his reactions to new adult experiences.

### Questions and Problems for Discussion

1. The period of adolescence is the time of religious decision. Evaluate.
2. What factors and influences contribute to adolescent indecision concerning religion?
3. What changes in attitudes toward religion are observable today that were less significant fifty years ago?

4. Explain present-day attitudes of adolescents toward organized religion.
5. Cite examples to illustrate individual conflict over religious values.
6. To what extent do the social taboos of a religious group affect individual adjustment to members of other peer groups?
7. Compare moral and ethical values with religious values.
8. Toward what goal should the school aim its moral teaching?
9. In what ways are attitudes associated with life values?
10. *Special Exercises:*
    *a.* Prepare a list of factors and influences that contribute to the development of religious attitudes of adolescents.
    *b.* Interview two or more adolescents to discover their attitudes and thinking toward moral values. Report your findings.

### Selected References

Baylis, C. A.: *Ethics: The Principles of Wise Choice,* Holt, Rinehart and Winston, Inc., New York, 1958.

Buckley, M. J.: *Morality and the Homosexual: A Catholic Approach to a Moral Problem,* The Newman Press, Westminster, Md., 1960.

Clark, T. B.: *What Is Honesty?,* Science Research Associates, Inc., Chicago, 1952.

Clark, W.: *The Psychology of Religion,* The Macmillan Company, New York, 1958.

De Monasce, C. G.: *The Dynamics of Morality* (B. Bommarito,

trans.), Sheed & Ward, Inc., New York, 1961.

Durkheim, Emile (ed.): *Moral Education,* The Free Press of Glencoe, New York, 1961.

Johnson, P. E.: *Psychology of Religion,* rev. ed., Abingdon Press, Nashville, Tenn., 1959.

Phoenix, P. H.: *Religious Concerns in Contemporary Education,* Bureau of Publications, Teachers College, Columbia University, New York, 1959.

Ross, M. G.: *Religious Beliefs of Youth,* Association Press, New York, 1950.

# Part 4

## ADOLESCENT
## ADJUSTMENTS

# Chapter Fourteen

## Home Adjustment of Adolescents

The home is the primary societal unit. Family relationships play an important role in an individual's life pattern from early childhood through adulthood. Especially during the adolescent period family attitudes and behavior become matters of great concern to the developing boy or girl.

## Significance of the Home

Much of an individual's personality patterning originates in the home. Not only does the child inherit certain family potentialities, but during his developing years, his attitudes, beliefs, ideals, and overt behavior reflect the influences on him of home experiences.

### The Child in the Home

The family is primarily responsible for meeting a child's basic physical and psychological needs. The degree of successful adjustment achieved by the child in his family relationships depends on various factors of influence. Of these, special attention is directed toward traditional parental attitudes toward child-rearing (rigid versus permissive), emotional reactions of family members (emotionally stable versus disturbed), and the socioeconomic status of the home (middle and upper versus lower class).

The child reared in a rigid home tends to be submissive but resentful of restrictions on his freedom; the permissively reared child is likely to be aggressive and outgoing. The child of emotionally stable parents can be expected to exhibit well-controlled behavior reactions; the child of emotionally disturbed parents or of those who display inconsistent attitudes toward him may become a confused or frustrated individual, reflecting in his own behavior the personality defects to which he has been exposed. As a result of an eight-year longitudinal study of adolescent character development, Peck[1] concluded that the personality characteris-

[1] Robert F. Peck, "Family Patterns Correlated with Adolescent Personality Structure," *Journal of Abnormal and Social Psychology*, vol. 57, pp. 347–350, 1958.

tics of the subjects of the study were "significantly related to the emotional relationships and the disciplinary patterns which they experienced in living with their parents."

The family's socioeconomic status can exert a powerful influence on a young person's developing personality. Not only is the adolescent of an economically underprivileged home denied many of the privileges and enriching experiences enjoyed by upper- and middle-class children, but his life values are affected by parental ambitions for him. For example, Kohn[2] conducted a study of the social class values of four families with children in the fifth grade of public and parochial schools in Washington, D.C. In his conclusions Kohn suggests that parents of all social classes have values that are related to their social class and that parents believe it to be important for their children to develop traits of honesty, obedience, and consideration for others. He found that working-class mothers indicated a deep appreciation for such qualities as neatness and cleanliness. They rate high those qualities that make for respectability. Middle-class parents are greatly concerned with values associated with internal standards that govern individual relationships with people including one's self. Happiness is high on the value list for boys by middle-class mothers; working-class mothers rate honesty and obedience before happiness for their sons, and place happiness first for their daughters.

The atmosphere of the home in which an adolescent is reared can advance or hinder wholesome personality adjustment. Family relationships also determine in large measure the young person's developing attitudes toward home and family life.

## Adolescent Attitudes toward Family Life

As the preadolescent's or young adolescent's world expands to include an increasing number of persons and experiences outside the home, he is motivated to evaluate his home situation in the light of other home conditions that he observes. He appreciates his father and mother as persons as well as parents. The physical and physiological changes taking place within him are accompanied by a growing feeling of independence and a strong desire for emancipation from adult control. The young person may experience more or less serious conflict in his struggle to fulfill his many new interests and needs.

Also, from about middle adolescence through young adulthood, the individual becomes increasingly concerned with his preparation for the establishment of a family unit of his own. He may experience various

[2] Melvin L. Kohn, "Social Class and Parental Values," *American Journal of Sociology*, vol. 54, pp. 337–351, 1959.

*Table 33.* Family Living Questions Asked by High School Students*

| TYPE OF QUESTION | PER CENT OF TOTAL | |
| --- | --- | --- |
| | NINTH GRADE N = 448 | ELEVENTH AND TWELFTH GRADES, N = 765 |
| 1. Problems concerning parents, intrafamily relationships; role of parents in choice and approval of dating partner, in granting permissions, inquiring into "personal" affairs............ | 11.6 | 8.8 |
| 2. Problems concerning interpersonal relationships: how to turn down dates tactfully; how to get along with others; how to regain lost love; how to get attention of opposite sex; how to overcome shyness, jealousy......................... | 36.0 | 13.5 |
| 3. Dating problems: etiquette; whom to date; what age; what to talk about; how long to stay out; where to go; what to do; age; religious differences; going steady...................... | 35.8 | 14.5 |
| 4. Problems concerning parking, necking, kissing, petting: when, how much, right or wrong, how to avoid it................................. | 4.7 | 7.5 |
| 5. Problems concerning love, infatuation, characteristic qualities of emotional maturity........ | 1.1 | 8.8 |
| 6. Lack of adequate factual information concerning physical and sexual processes and functions, such as menstruation and sexual intercourse... | 1.5 | 8.0 |
| 7. Problems concerning ethical behavior and sex problems: right or wrong of premarital intercourse; what about the person who has premarital intercourse; general conduct............. | 1.3 | 11.6 |
| 8. Problems concerning engagement: length of engagement; preparation for marriage; timing; marriage in service; personal relationship with fiancé................................. | 3.8 | 8.8 |
| 9. Marriage problems: age; religious differences; divorce; housekeeping budget; legal problems; children................................. | 3.8 | 13.0 |
| 10. Problems concerning vocations, careers; desire of some not to marry; happiness and success of single persons or of those who combine careers and marriage............................. | .4 | 5.5 |
| Total............................. | 100.0 | 100.0 |

* Douglass Brown, "Helping Teen-agers with their Family Living Problems," *Marriage and Family Living*, vol. 21, p. 390, November, 1959.

*Table 34.* Causes of Serious Difficulty in Own Marriage as Indicated by 59.5 Per Cent of Subjects*

| PROBLEM CAUSING DIFFICULTY | MEN | | WOMEN | | BOTH SEXES | |
|---|---|---|---|---|---|---|
| | N | PER CENT | N | PER CENT | N | PER CENT |
| Stubbornness.................. | 34 | 59.5 | 31 | 50.0 | 65 | 54.6 |
| Nagging or criticism by spouse.... | 21 | 36.9 | 21 | 33.8 | 42 | 35.3 |
| In-laws........................ | 8 | 14.0 | 17 | 27.4 | 25 | 21.0 |
| Selfishness..................... | 11 | 19.3 | 13 | 21.0 | 24 | 20.2 |
| Jealousy....................... | 8 | 14.0 | 9 | 14.5 | 17 | 14.3 |
| Spouse does less than (his, her) share of "family chores"........ | 4 | 7.0 | 13 | 21.0 | 17 | 14.3 |
| Health problems................ | 9 | 15.8 | 6 | 9.7 | 15 | 12.6 |
| Spouse "gets on my nerves"....... | 5 | 8.8 | 7 | 11.3 | 12 | 10.1 |
| Dishonesty..................... | 6 | 10.6 | 2 | 3.2 | 8 | 6.7 |
| Disagreement on rearing of children. | 6 | 10.6 | 2 | 3.2 | 8 | 6.7 |
| Other causes of difficulty.......... | 2 | 3.5 | 6 | 9.7 | 8 | 6.7 |
| All causes.................... | 114 | | 127 | | 241 | |
| Mean number of difficulties..... | 2 | | 2 | | 2 | |

* There were 57 men and 62 women who indicated they had serious problems.

problems of adjustment and decision making in areas such as boy-girl relations, mate selection, and the achievement of emotional and financial security. A young person's ideals for his future home often are influenced positively or negatively by his experiences in his parents' home.

Douglass Brown attempted to discover adolescents' problems of family living through the medium of 1,213 questions anonymously submitted to him by ninth-, eleventh-, and twelfth-grade high school students over a period of ten years.[3] The results of the study are presented in Table 33. Two results are worthy of comment: (1) the small percentage (about 10 per cent) of problems that deal with existing family relations and (2) the differences between the ninth-grade percentages and the upper-class percentages. Significant also is the fact that, although many of the problems deal with love, marriage, and child rearing, the subjects' exhibited attitudes toward such matters would seem to be based on the kind and amount of help they received from parents and other adults in meeting their problems.

An interesting study of the marital adjustment of college students was conducted by Florence D. Aller.[4] At least one person from each

[3] Douglass Brown, "Helping Teen-agers with their Family Living Problems," *Marriage and Family Living*, vol. 21, p. 390, November, 1959.

[4] Florence D. Aller, "Some Factors in Marital Adjustment and Academic Achievement of Married Students," *Personnel and Guidance Journal*, pp. 609–616, March, 1963.

couple studied was enrolled at the University of Idaho. The purpose of the study was to discover the extent to which 100 couples were "achieving harmony and mutual satisfaction in the marriage relationship." The median ages of husbands and wives were 23.9 and 22.2 years, respectively. The results indicated that 40.5 per cent reported no marital difficulties and that 59.5 per cent were experiencing some serious problems of marital adjustment. The causes of such lack of harmony are presented in Table 34. Although factors inherent in the situation can account for some of the problems reported, it could well be that in many instances the difficulties had their roots in the attitudes developed by these young married people during their adolescent years, that their experiences in their parental homes failed to prepare them for harmonious adjustment to homes of their own.

## Problems of Family-Adolescent Relations

As we know, an adolescent often finds that the attitudes of his enlarging social groups differ greatly from those that he has acquired in the home. Some of these differences may be relatively insignificant, but to the adolescent they may take on catastrophic proportions.

### Basic Problem Areas

The conflicts that arise between an adolescent and his parents do not limit themselves to differences of opinion on large issues. There often is constant argument concerning matters that may seem relatively unimportant to the parent although they loom large in the mind of the developing adolescent. In some instances the family group displays ideals and attitudes toward society in general, and toward the adolescent in particular, that are too different from those accepted by the majority of American people or by a particular group. The teen-age boy or girl then may be faced with serious problems of adjustment. Conflicts may arise between the adolescent and his family that are difficult to resolve if neither is willing or able to compromise.

Differences of opinion between experienced parents and their experiencing son or daughter may lead to inner conflicts on the part of the young person. The parents may neither know about nor understand these conflicts. Other resentments may have their roots in brother-and-sister relationships, relationships with other relatives, relationships between parents, financial matters, home responsibilities, and adolescent social activities. "Intolerant" parents and "intolerant" boys and girls often come to grips concerning such matters as home chores, spending money, apparent favoritism of one child over another, dates, selection of friends, vocational choice, parental rejection or overprotectiveness, and youthful impatience with parental opinion.

Moreover, there is often a lack of communication between older adults and adolescents. They do not speak the same language. For example, a college student desired to become a professional football player but was lax about engaging in preparatory physical exercises. When an older friend reminded the boy that he needed to achieve physical stamina through strenuous exercise, the latter replied "You don't understand. If a man is football material, he does not need to get into shape. They'll put him in shape when he gets on the team." Unfortunately for him, although he was drafted by one of the leading teams, he did not last the season through.

In their struggle for independence adolescents cannot tolerate family interference or domination by grandparents, uncles, aunts, or cousins. A word, a look, or a gesture often is sufficient to set off the spark of youthful antagonism. It takes all the tact and understanding that stable parents possess to handle their young firebrands. If the resentment is kept smoldering within the young person and not brought to the surface in a mild or violent eruption, the task of the parents is even more difficult.

## Adolescents' Relations with the Family

The authors have obtained from thousands of young people between the ages of 12 and 20 their questions concerning problems connected with home and family life. Certain disturbing home situations are referred to over and over again by these adolescents. Some of their most common questions are presented here.

1. Should parents treat us as if we were children?
2. Should parents open their children's mail?
3. Should a girl have the right to choose her own wardrobe?
4. Are parents always right?
5. Should my parents make all my decisions for me?
6. What can an adolescent do about a broken home?
7. What should be the relationship between a boy or a girl and a stepparent?
8. How can quarrels be avoided among brothers and sisters?
9. Should brothers and sisters borrow one another's possessions without permission?
10. Should an adolescent be compelled to take care of a younger brother or sister?
11. Should a younger brother or sister insist on staying around when a girl has a guest?

**12.** How should a girl or a boy treat grandparents or other older relatives in the home?

**13.** Should other older relatives interfere with parents' decisions concerning their sons and daughters?

**14.** Should a boy or a girl have a definite allowance?

**15.** How much should a boy or girl know about family finances?

**16.** If a teen-age boy is working, what part of his salary should he give to his parents?

**17.** Should parents allow young people to choose their own friends?

**18.** How old should a boy or girl be before he or she is allowed to date members of the opposite sex?

**19.** What is the correct time to come home from a date?

**20.** Should a younger brother be allowed to stay out later than his older sister?

Many of these problems may seem trivial to the adult and cause him to smile at the seriousness with which they are asked; to the adolescent nothing that would seem to interfere with his striving for adult status is unimportant. The situation becomes even more unmanageable if the parents or older members of the family do not realize what is going on in the thinking of the teen-ager. Adults tend to criticize young people for becoming increasingly vocal in demanding their rights. It is unfortunate that some young people tend to place too much emphasis upon their *rights* and to ignore their *responsibilities*. However, it is much more wholesome for resentments to be voiced than for them to be repressed and allowed to fester, breaking forth later in the form of a warped adult personality.

## Parental Behavior Disturbing to Adolescents

The authors also asked more than 4,000 adolescent boys and girls to state briefly those parental attitudes that seemed to them to be disturbing factors in their relationships with their parents. They reported a long list of items. Only those of major importance, however, are presented here. The items, arranged in order from the most serious to the less serious, are listed separately for boys and girls.

The items for girls indicate that parents:

**1.** Object to automobile riding with boys at night.

**2.** Scold if school marks are not so high as those of other students.

**3.** Insist that food be eaten even though disliked.

**4.** Insist that brothers and sisters be taken on trips.

**5.** Insist that exact reports be made on money spent.

**6.** Hold up sisters or brothers as models.

**7.** Won't permit use of automobile.

8. Nag concerning personal manners and habits.
9. Insist on their approval of friends.
10. Object to automobile riding with boys during daytime.
11. Pester concerning boy friends.
12. Fuss at the way lipstick is used.
13. Worry about health.
14. Object to going to dances.
15. Insist on overprotection.
16. Won't permit free choice of subjects in school.
17. Refuse to extend the privilege of selecting own clothes.
18. Won't give an adequate regular allowance.
19. Won't permit entertainment at home.
20. Insist upon criticizing what clothes are worn and how they are worn.

The items for boys indicate that parents:
1. Won't let them use the automobile.
2. Insist that they eat foods which they dislike.
3. Scold if their school marks aren't so high as their friends'.
4. Insist that exact reports be made on money spent.
5. Pester them about table manners.
6. Hold their sister or brother up as a model.
7. Won't permit a free choice of vocation.
8. Object to dirty hands and fingernails.
9. Object to rowdy behavior with other boys.
10. Won't give an adequate regular allowance.
11. Tease them about their girl friends.
12. Demand that they take their sisters or brothers with them when they go out.
13. Brag about them to other persons.

The recognition of adolescent dissatisfaction does not mean that every young person should be encouraged to follow his own impulses and urges without proper guidance. It does mean that adults should examine their own attitudes very carefully, so that they may achieve a proper balance in their thinking between the rights to which young people are entitled and the responsibilities that they should meet.

If parents themselves are emotionally disturbed, if their own marital relations are not well adjusted, if quarreling and bickering are the order of the day, then there is certain to arise within an adolescent member of the family a seething tempest, which may or may not find outlets. Such home conditions are likely to result in youthful confusion, conflict, and perhaps delinquent behavior.

Parents whose adolescent sons and daughters are achieving wholesome attitudes and habit patterns in their relationships with other people are meeting successfully the test of intelligent parenthood. Some parents, as well as their teen-age children, need specific and practical assistance in solving the more or less serious problems of home adjustment. Each emotion-arousing situation must be considered on its own merits, as well as in its relation to the entire homelife pattern, and must be treated accordingly.

Parental overprotectiveness, apparent favoritism of one child over another, inability of parents to understand some of their children's adjustment difficulties, parental example of undesirable attitude or behavior are some of the factors that give rise to adjustment difficulties among young people. No matter how carefully we may attempt to analyze human relationships into cause-and-effect sequences, we are forced to admit that certain subtle personality interrelationships cannot be analyzed out of a total situation.

Parents may get off to a bad start in their attitude toward their children, even though they themselves are basically normal in their behavior. Such parents usually respond to guidance given them by interested advisers. Hence many young people who in their early years give evidence of a nonconforming attitude can be led toward satisfactory adolescent adjustment.

## Suggestions for Improving Home Relationships

Since the home wields a powerful influence over the attitudes and behavior of young people, men and women do not dare to take lightly their responsibilities as parents. Parental influence upon a child begins long before he is born, so young men and women should prepare themselves early for future parenthood. They should develop good health habits, refraining from participation in activities that may affect their physical constitutions. Excessive smoking and drinking, the keeping of late hours, insufficient or badly balanced diet, and promiscuous sex relations are not conducive to the bearing of healthy children.

Not only should young men and women prepare themselves for desirable parenthood, but they also should use intelligence and discretion in the choice of their mates. They owe it to their unborn children that both parents shall be healthy individuals who can give to their children a sound heritage.

Much has been done in recent years for the education of parents and prospective parents in the care and training of young children. Childhood conduct is the basis upon which adolescent habits and attitudes are built. A pampered child is often an irresponsible adolescent. Stubbornness, self-will, indolence, pretense, excessive timidity, or carelessness do not suddenly change with the advent of adolescence into cooperation, industry, courtesy, poise, and carefulness. In fact, outstanding behavior patterns of childhood, whether they are good or bad, tend to become intensified as the individual develops and matures, unless environmental factors stimulate changes.

Adolescence is a training period for both the parent and the child. If the parent is able to adjust his own attitudes and behavior to the needs of his growing boy or girl, the latter will be helped immensely in the solution of those problems which are inherent in the growing-up process. In the following pages the problems of young people connected with their adjustment to home and family life are treated under six headings:

1. Rights and responsibilities of young people in the home
2. Effect upon adolescents of the marital attitudes of their parents
3. Sibling relationships
4. Effect upon adolescents of the attitudes of grandparents and other relatives
5. The teen-ager and family finances
6. Parental responsibility for the social life of young people

Under appropriate headings, suggestions are presented in as detailed and specific a form as possible for meeting some of the common problems of adolescents in the home.

## Rights and Responsibilities of Young People in the Home

It is very difficult for the average parent (especially the mother) to realize that a boy or a girl between the ages of 12 and 20 is gradually taking on the status of young manhood or young womanhood, and that parental ties must gradually be allowed to relax. The young person is no longer (if he ever was) satisfied with "You should do this because Mother says so."

## Parental Attitudes toward Child at Different Ages

In school the adolescent is expected to think things out for himself and is introduced to the relationship that exists between cause and effect. He is trained to exercise his own judgment, under guidance, in matters concerning his own welfare. He is constantly told that he is no longer a child. When a young person thus stimulated at school returns to his home, he cannot suddenly remove his attitude of growing independence as he would a coat. He is bound to resent attempts on the part of his parents to treat him as though he were still a child.

An adolescent should enjoy the same opportunity for self-direction in the home that he experiences in school life; his opinions, crude though they may seem to an adult, should receive respectful attention. If his attitudes and opinions need guidance, this should be undertaken with as much seriousness on the part of the parent as is shown by the young person. Never should his opinions be met with a smile of tolerance, a laugh of derision, or a "What do you know about such things? You are too young even to think about them."

If an adolescent attempts to do something in the home that lies within his power of execution, he should be encouraged to continue the activity, even though his first attempts are inept or bungling. This procedure may try the patience of parents. It is much easier for them to say, "Here, let me do it. You are taking all day." The task will undoubtedly be done more expeditiously and efficiently by the parent; but the young person is thereby deprived of needed practice and the recognition of himself as an active member of the family group. To encourage a young person to assume certain specific home responsibilities is desirable; but to expect an adolescent to shoulder complete care of the home is not only most unfair, but is sure to develop antagonism between parent and child, as well as possible youthful maladjustment.

At the present time there are many families in which both the father and the mother are working away from the home. Consequently, a high school daughter may be compelled to be responsible for the complete care of the home, the buying and preparation of food, and the family laundry. To expect a growing girl to assume the full responsibility for household chores and perhaps to look after younger brothers and sisters besides is asking too much.

A young person should not continue to be tied to his or her mother's apron strings. Even during childhood it is undesirable for a boy or girl to be too dependent upon his parents. During adolescence it is inexcusable. An adolescent boy or girl should never be referred to as "Sonny" or "my little girl." Parents should in no way intimate in the presence of their friends that their son or daughter thinks he has grown up but that he is still "my baby." Adolescent pride resents this parental attitude.

The weaning process should be begun early and continued until, in early adulthood, the individual is completely independent except for such guidance as is needed by everyone at any age in time of crisis. Children who were delicate or unusually attractive during their babyhood are often the worst victims of parental protection.

Parents, as they attempt to be objective in their attitude toward their children, need to be careful lest they cause them to believe that they are unwanted. One adolescent stated it thus, "My parents seem to reject me. They act as though I have interfered with their lives." It can be recognized that once this youthful attitude has been developed, it may be difficult for the parents to regain the confidence of their child.

Mothers and fathers should encourage their adolescent children to think for themselves in matters that are within the realm of adolescent decision. They should allow young people to take upon themselves a reasonable amount of responsibility for home welfare. Finally, by their words and actions, they should make it clear to their teen-age sons and daughters that they, as parents, are aware of their children's developing maturity and are proud of it, but are ready and willing to advise them whenever adult assistance is sought.

## The Problem of Opening the Adolescent's Mail

If complete sympathy and understanding exist between the adolescent and his parents, letters received by him are shared with his parents. However, a young person should have the satisfaction of opening his own mail. If the family attitude is good, the contents of the letter are then read to the parents, or the letter is given to them for reading. The fact that a young person does not want his parents to read his letters, or that a parent feels that it is necessary for him to open and read a letter before his child sees it, indicates a basic distrust and overprotection, of which the reaction toward the letter is no more than a symptom.

It is natural for a parent to be interested in his child's social life and to want to know what the latter's friends are saying to him. However, this understandable curiosity should be curbed until the recipient of the letter is present to open it. This is a right that accompanies the growing-up process. If the parent opens the letter because he is suspicious of its contents, his doing so is an acknowledgment of his own failure as a parent to train his child in desirable social relations. A parent who is too insistent in his attempts at censorship is likely to encourage the adolescent to have letters sent to another address. There is usually an obliging pal who will help out in such a situation.

## Parental Authority and the Adolescent

Everyone, no matter what his age, training, or previous experience, should realize and admit that someone else, even though this other person may be younger and less experienced, may have a better understanding of a particular situation than he has. If during childhood a young person has been led to recognize the reasonableness of his parents' decisions, there will be relatively little conflict between parents and child during the latter's adolescence. Then, when differences of opinion arise concerning desirable adolescent behavior, the young person will be likely to have confidence in parental judgment and be willing to be influenced by it.

Arguments in the home are sometimes caused by such factors as age differences, changes with the times in the general social pattern of behavior, differing cultural backgrounds, and educational inequalities between parents and children. Such family disagreements, especially if the parents are dictatorial in their attitude, encourage young people to look upon their parents as intolerant or narrow-minded. Adolescents often express the wish that their parents could be more understanding. There is a fallacy in the thinking of these boys and girls. What they do not seem to realize is the fact that they themselves are often as intolerant in their attitudes as they accuse their parents of being.

The fundamental difficulty in cases of this kind is that neither parent nor child is able or willing to understand the point of view of the other. The parent's stubbornness of attitude is duplicated in the child's. Consequently, compromise is difficult, if not impossible. Either the parent wins and the child becomes a thwarted or frustrated individual; or the parent gives up the struggle and allows his immature son or daughter a free hand, thereby depriving the young person of needed behavior guidance.

A parent is not always right, but his judgment is usually more far-reaching than that of his inexperienced child. When differences of opinion arise, the parent and the child should give serious consideration to the following questions:

1. Is the matter important enough to make an issue of it?
2. Is parental opinion based upon sound, practical reasoning and consideration of the best interests of the child?
3. Will the fulfillment of the child's wish harm him in any way, or is parental denial of it based upon a personal whim or an outgrowth of personal adolescent experiences?

Rarely, if ever, should parents criticize the behavior of young people in the presence of others, except members of the immediate family. Even then the criticism should not take the form of a comparison of one child's conduct with that of another. Sometimes public reproof is the only kind that the young person receives from his parents. Undesirable behavior in the home is overlooked because "anything goes" with the family. Discourtesy to parents or other members of the family by the adolescent boy or girl is not frowned upon, chiefly because good manners and consideration for the other person are not habitual in the family group. It is only when such parents see their son's or daughter's actions through the eyes of people outside the family group that they become excited about the undesirable behavior of their children.

If the same emphasis upon cooperative and controlled behavior holds in home relationships for all the members of the family as is expected outside the home, parents will have little occasion to be embarrassed by their adolescent child's behavior in public. Habits of courtesy, cooperation, and self-control, developed and practiced in the home, will then extend beyond the family circle, and parents will be able to feel confident that the son or daughter will be habitually considerate and charming at all times. A boy or girl who in the home is allowed to preempt the most comfortable chair, select the most desirable piece of meat, or dominate the conversation cannot suddenly change into a model of propriety in public. If, for any reason whatever, an adolescent displays undesirable behavior in the presence of people outside the family group, the wise parent ignores such behavior until he is alone with the adolescent and then voices his disapproval and discusses with his child the reasons for his attitude.

The kind and extent of guidance that should be given to adolescents when their actions merit parental disapproval is important. More important is the fact that penalties should never be administered when the parent is in an emotionalized state. There is danger that a reproof or a penalty emotionally administered may not "fit the crime." The young person is quick to recognize this. He may accept the parental disapproval or he may try to argue himself out of it, but his private opinion will be that Father or Mother "is on the rampage again." Moreover, a parent who becomes emotionalized over his son's or daughter's misdeeds may not be consistent in his attitude toward that which constitutes desirable adolescent behavior. Conduct which may stimulate strong parental disapproval at one time may be completely overlooked at another time. As a result, the adolescent is alert in recognizing a parent's good days and bad days. Hence parental guidance must be objective and consistent.

Parents often are at a loss to discover the attitude that they should exhibit toward adolescent misbehavior, in order that it may be reasonable, fit the seriousness of the offense, and be effective. Usually the kind and effectiveness of parent-child consideration of an offense during the early years of the child determine the kind to be employed with the adolescent. In some homes nothing more is needed than a quietly voiced expression of disapproval, with reasons. Long harangues, reference to the disgrace brought upon the family, or comparisons between the disapproved behavior and that of other children in the family or of the parent in his youth are seldom effective.

Perhaps one of the most desirable influences upon young people's behavior is the temporary denial of privileges when the girl or boy neglects to meet his responsibilities. There must be, however, a reasonable relationship between the seriousness of the misdemeanor and the severity of the denial. In every instance the penalty should be related to the misdeed. For example, a young person and his parents have agreed upon a specific time for his return home after a social engagement, but the adolescent arrives home late, with no valid reason for the delay. The first instance of this kind merits an expression of parental disapproval. The second offense should be penalized by the denial of permission to attend one other such social activity. The boy or girl should then be given another trial, with the reminder that he is to be home at a certain time. If the young person is again late, he should be denied the privilege of going out with this particular group but should be encouraged to have social engagements with other groups, the members of which are also expected by their parents to practice punctuality.

It is the responsibility of an adolescent to respond with improved behavior to the suggestions of his parents. It is the right of an adolescent to expect his parents to agree between themselves upon the kind of adolescent behavior that is desirable or undesirable. If a father and mother differ in their attitudes concerning desirable teen-age activities, their discussions of this matter should be held when the child is not present. They must arrive at an agreement, so that they present a solid front to the adolescent. Too often a young person bemoans the fact that if one parent says it is all right to do a certain thing, the other parent may object. This divided parental attitude causes bewilderment in the adolescent. How can standards of conduct be determined if parents themselves differ in such matters? Usually the young person plays up to the lenient parent, even though he may recognize the fact that the other parent's attitude is probably the correct one.

Either too much rigidity or too much laxity on the part of parents tends toward the weakening of adolescent confidence in parental judgment. Moreover, parents should not set behavior standards for their teenage children which they themselves do not follow. In homes where parents themselves are controlled, considerate, and cooperative, adolescent children usually follow the same pattern of behavior, except as immaturity of judgment may cause them to err. Reasonable and objective guidance will soon improve such behavior.

## Decision Making

Conflict often develops because of the tendency of parents to deny to adolescent boys and girls any freedom of choice in personal matters. The attempt on the part of the parents to dominate the lives of their children is closely allied to the fact that the parents still consider the adolescent to be a child whose judgment cannot be trusted. A few of the most common conflict-producing situations are discussed briefly.

*Selection of Clothes.* A young child cannot be trusted to select his or her own clothes. Although he may be allowed a choice between two articles of clothing, both of which would be appropriate, final selection should rest with the parents. However, as the young person progresses through his teens, he should be given more and more freedom in this matter. By example and precept he should be trained toward an appreciation of suitability, attractiveness, and good value in clothes. He should also understand the limitations of the family budget. From that point on, the young person should be given considerable freedom of selection.

During early adolescence a parent should accompany his child on shopping tours and by suggestion guide the buying. As the young person advances into the upper teen years, he should be encouraged to do most of his shopping alone, except as the parent may be invited, as a friend would be, to help in the selection. If an article of clothing is bought that does not meet the parent's standards of appropriateness or good value, he must be tactful in his appraisal of it. He should be quick to recognize the young person's reason for the choice, but he should do no more than suggest that, although the particular article has certain desirable features, he personally might have selected something different. The young person, as he wears the clothing, will probably come to agree with the parent's judgment. Although he is not likely to admit that he made a bad decision, he will probably exercise better judgment the next time.

This is an important phase of adolescent training. As an adult, the individual will need to use his own judgment in such matters, since he will not always have his parents at hand to give him advice. Hence he needs practice in the selection of clothes while he is still in the position to do so under guidance. Moreover, most adolescents receive some training in high school concerning appropriateness of dress. They want to apply this training without too much parental interference. Also, an outstanding means of asserting one's developing maturity is through personal dress and grooming. Adolescence is the ideal time to help the young person to set up for himself (not to have set up for him) accepted standards of attractive appearance.

*Smoking and Drinking.* Many parents are concerned about the possibility of their teen-age children's developing the habit of smoking or drinking hard liquor. At present these are difficult matters to handle. It is generally agreed that, for adolescents, smoking or drinking, even in moderation, is unnecessary and may be harmful. If parents smoke and if they drink an occasional cocktail or glass of wine or serve these in their home, it is natural for young people to want to be included among those who take part in such activities. Not to allow the adolescent ever to smoke a cigarette or to take a drink when he sees his elders do so is very hard on him. It might be possible to encourage him to indulge once in a while on a special occasion, but he must know why his parents believe that it is undesirable for him to do this often. If parents themselves are controlled in their smoking and drinking, young people usually are willing to conform to their parents' wishes in these matters.

Parents who themselves neither smoke nor drink must be intelligent in their attitude toward their children's possible interest in doing these things. To attempt to give the impression that such things are the invention of the devil and that no decent person indulges in them will do no more than cause the son or daughter to lose faith in parental good judgment. Young people are likely to meet fine and attractive adults who do smoke and occasionally drink liquor. Parents who are complete abstainers should admit to their children that some fine people do these things but that they themselves believe such practices to be unnecessary and perhaps injurious to the health. They should also stress the fact that they would like their children to use similar controls in their own health habits. Overindulgence in sweets, starchy foods, gum chewing, and the like can be handled similarly.

*Having One's Own Room.* Fortunate is the boy or girl who has a room of his own. More fortunate is the one who is allowed a reasonable amount of freedom in the decoration and arrangement of his room. This is an excellent medium of self-expression. A young person's ideal of attractively decorated walls or interesting color combinations may cause an adult to shudder. If a parent can live through the various phases of his adolescent child's developing appreciation of beauty, the room of the older adolescent will probably be almost austere in its simplicity. This last is especially true if other rooms in the house reflect parental good taste in furnishings and decorations.

Let the adolescent's imagination run wild if it must, but insist that the contents of the room be kept in a reasonable state of cleanliness and orderliness. Even when there are servants to do the heavy cleaning, the day-by-day care of his room should be the adolescent's own responsibility and pride. This should include making his bed and picking up and putting away his clothes. He must receive training in his parents' home that will help him keep his own home neat and attractive. The generic "he" is used advisedly here to include both boys and girls. Many mothers who give excellent training to their daughters in the care of personal belongings fail to give a similar training to their sons. Boys as well as girls should take care of their own personal belongings, learn to make their own beds, and help with the household chores.

Returning to the consideration of a young person's room, this place should serve as a haven of peace to its occupant. He should feel free occasionally to enjoy the privacy of his own domain without an anxious or curious parent's coming to find out what he is doing. Of course, if the adolescent makes a practice of withdrawing from family activities to the solitude of his own room, there is probably something wrong. Retiring from the family group may be the symptom of family maladjustment which requires the intelligent attention of parents. The teen-ager should not be scolded or teased for his attitude, but the reason for it should be tactfully sought. He may feel that his presence is not wanted, or he may be passing through a phase of mental superiority, which causes him to be bored by ordinary family conversation or activity. Whatever the cause, it is the responsibility of the parent to discover it and to draw the young person back into the family circle.

To sum up the discussion of the rights and responsibilities of young people, it should be emphasized that the habit patterns developed during adolescence and the guidance in decision making received during this period have a tremendous effect upon the young person's success as an independent adult. A dominated adolescent usually is a futile and indecisive adult. Parents who do not give teen-age children an opportunity to learn by their own mistakes are depriving them of a rightful heritage. A dominating adolescent tends to become an aggressive, self-asserting, and self-satisfied adult. It is the responsibility of parents to guide their adolescent children toward habits of cooperation and consideration for others.

## Effect upon Adolescents
## of the Marital Attitudes of Their Parents

No human being is perfect. No matter how well a man and woman may be mated, there are times when the actions of one will cause emotional disturbance in the other. It is natural and desirable to express dissatisfaction with the conduct of a spouse when it annoys or hurts. To have it out with the other person is far better than to nurse a grievance, real or fancied, and thereby develop a silent antagonism, of which the mate is conscious without knowing what the cause may be. Such matters are the personal concern of the married couple. Children should not be drawn into the situation.

## Husband-Wife Behavior

Consider the effect upon a young person who wishes to be loyal to both parents if in his presence these parents engage in emotionalized quarreling and bickering. Which parent is right? The adolescent on the sidelines is mature enough to realize that both parents may be justified in some of the things that they are saying to each other, but that many of the accusations made are foolish and even unjust. Shall he interfere? Shall he take sides?

Loyalties are strained and the young person is confused. His attitude toward the marital relation may be affected by the friction in the home. He may decide that he will never marry lest he inflict similar torture upon his own children. As he grows older, he realizes that family arguments are not necessary, and he will probably marry; but he will carry with him into his adult life the scars of emotional upsets experienced during periods of parental friction. Moreover, as the adolescent listens to unfair recriminations of one parent against another, he learns to discount similar outbursts against himself.

## Effects of a Broken Home

Although a broken home is not the only or even the major cause of adolescent delinquency, it does create an abnormal home situation which is likely to affect a young person's emotional development. Loss of a parent through death not only deprives the developing adolescent of the wise counsel and guidance of that parent but may cause development of too close a bond between the remaining parent and the child.

If the home is broken because of incompatibility between the parents, the young person is affected not only by the break itself but also by the parental friction that led to the break. If he has experienced constant parental disagreement and then is deprived of one of the parents through divorce or separation, he is exposed to further conflict without adequate emotional stability to meet it.

The parent with whom the child remains may be very bitter toward the mate who is no longer in the home. Hence he is almost certain to make disparaging remarks to the child concerning the other parent. This is hard on a maturing young person, even though his loyalty may be given to the parent with whom he lives. If he really loves the absent parent, the situation is tragic for him. To expect an adolescent to be friendly with both parents, perhaps living with each for a part of the year, or living with one and visiting the other, demands emotional adjustment to a degree that he has not yet attained.

Parents who are separated from each other (mothers especially) often encourage their children to visit the other parent and then insist upon receiving a full account of what was said and done during the visit. If the separated mate has remarried, the young person may be catechized about the new husband or wife. The adolescent does not know how to meet a situation of this kind. If the visit was a pleasant one and he reports it truthfully, he may be faced with a fit of hysterics or accusations of favoring the other parent. In order to avoid a scene, the boy or girl may give a wrong picture of the visit, leaving the desired impression that it was not enjoyed.

In this way an adolescent may learn to deceive his parent, and develop the habit of employing the same technique in matters concerning his own activities. The important fact is that the child has lost respect for his parents and is no longer willing to submit to their domination. He is like a ship without a rudder, unable to steer his way to the safety of the home port. Hence he may find his satisfactions outside the home. If he develops undesirable habits as he seeks to assert his maturing personality, he has no one to whom he can turn for wise counsel and emotional security. The whole situation is intensified if the adolescent cannot find a place in the life of either parent and is left to the care of other relatives or strangers.

It is true that one cause of adolescent maladjustment or delinquency may be found in the fact that the children of broken homes have inherited those personality characteristics of either or both parents which caused the marital friction and the final break. However, the broken home itself deprives adolescents of any supporting props that might have kept them straight. For this reason some writers claim that the family unit should be kept intact, even though parents cannot get along together. If both parents are unstable, the adolescent has little potentiality of normal adjustment. If one parent is definitely responsbile for the discord in the home and the other is emotionally stable, a young person would probably have more chance of achieving desirable adjustment if he remained with the emotionally stable parent and the other were completely removed from the situation. The sensible solution is for both parents to take their marital and parental responsibilities seriously, so that the home may represent a closely knit family unity.

## Attitude toward Stepparents

The presence in the home of a stepparent is often the basis of emotional unrest among young people. It is a family situation in which great tact and understanding must be practiced by everyone. The bringing into the intimate relations of family life of a comparatively or completely strange person, entitled by his position in the family to a certain amount of authority, is likely to cause some degree of conflict, no matter how cooperative each member of the family may be. The period in the child's life in which the stepparent comes into the family, the cause of the actual parent's absence from the home, and the attitude of the child toward the latter are factors which must be considered in a discussion of this relationship.

No matter how much independence of action a young person may consider to be his right, it is normal for him at the same time to desire security and affection in his home relationships. The presence in the home of an uncooperative or disagreeable parent, the absence of one or both parents, or the presence of a stepparent may seem to deny a child that feeling of security which he craves.

The bringing into the home of a kind, understanding stepparent may do much to bring back the atmosphere of family unity, especially if the child is young enough to form new attachments and thus gradually forget the absent parent. As half sisters and brothers appear in the family, the attitude of the older child toward them is influenced to a great extent by the parental attitude toward him in relation to the younger children. If all the children are treated alike, especially by the new parent, many half brothers and sisters are as devoted to one another as are real brothers and sisters.

It is more difficult for an adolescent to adjust to new family relationships than it is for a young child to do so. The older girl or boy has become accustomed to certain routines of family behavior, and consequently he may be unwilling or unable to include another person in the family unit. A strong bond of affection may have developed between the teenager and the remaining parent. Hence the new parent may be viewed as an interloper who is robbing the son or the daughter of the love or attention that is rightfully his. Or the adolescent may have built up an ideal image of his absent parent, which causes him to be very critical of this new person who is attempting to take the place in the home of the beloved parent. Great anguish may result from the sight of this "stranger" sitting in the favorite chair of the absent parent or using articles around the house that are closely associated with memories of him.

Maturing adolescents tend to resent too great restriction of their conduct. Even in well adjusted family units, parents find that it is not always easy to guide their teen-age children toward socially desirable behavior. It is often very difficult for a new parent to win the cooperation of an adolescent stepchild in matters concerning the latter's activities. No matter how tactfully and sympathetically the young person is approached, there is likely to be a suspicion of adult motives.

Stepparents, no matter how honest their intentions, are normal human beings, with all a normal person's emotional reactions. They are sometimes driven by their stepchildren's attitude to lose their own emotional control. This may cause family disagreement, not only between themselves and the children but also between themselves and their mates.

If there is disharmony between the adolescent and the new parent, the cause may be found in the uncooperative attitude of the young person himself, of the new member of the family, or of the remaining parent. Sometimes the real parent may be torn between his loyalty to his child and his love for his new mate. Consequently, an attempt at compromise between the two loyalties may lead to a tension that is recognized by all three and resented by the two victims of the disturbed emotional attitude. Sometimes a situation of this kind cannot be adjusted until the young person leaves the family home.

Adolescents often are uncertain how they should refer to the new mother or father. This problem may arise even though there is a very good relationship between the stepparent and the adolescent. The young person dislikes to call the new parent by the term that was used for the actual parent. One of several procedures can be followed. If the stepparent is not much older than the adolescent, the use of the first name seems to work well. If the latter had been accustomed to call his actual parent Mother or Father, the term "Ma" or "Pa," or "Mom" or "Dad" can be used.

Another factor that needs consideration is whether or not a child should assume the surname of the stepfather. This is a legal matter, but no general rules can be given for making the change. If the child is very young when the mother remarries, this may be wise. If, however, the child has reached adolescence, he may wish to continue his own identity by using his own father's surname.

### Sibling Relationships

Even though young people are the children of the same parents and are exposed to relatively similar environmental stimulations, all the children of a family do not possess similar temperaments, share similar interests, or think similar thoughts. There are bound to be differences of opinion about many things. However, if courtesy and consideration for others is the habitual attitude in a home, there will be no lasting resentments among the young people, and a temporary disagreement will very soon become a subject of amusing reminiscence.

## Causes of Disagreements

If disagreements among adolescent brothers and sisters are not too frequent and if they are not born of fundamental resentments, they are both natural and desirable. Sister-brother relationships give a young person opportunities for practice in adjusting to his peers. An only child misses this fundamental social training, in that he is denied exercise in adjusting to differing personalities and slightly different age interests in the intimate relationships of the family group

Age differences may be the basis of sister-brother discord. Younger children tend to resent domination by older children, no matter how well intentioned such apparent domination may be. The older boys and girls often think that the little ones are "getting away with murder" because the latter seem to be enjoying privileges that had been denied the teenagers when they were children. The tendency on the part of children to tease older brothers and sisters is another cause of quarrels.

Parental attitude is an important factor in the relationships that exist among the children. If parents are careful to accord to each child the rights and privileges to which he is entitled, and at the same time expect individual responsibilities to be assumed cheerfully, there is usually an excellent attitude among the children toward one another. No member of the family should be granted privileges that are denied others unless there is a valid reason for the denial and all the children understand the situation.

Parents cannot "play favorites" with their children. They must be careful that their attitude toward each child is such that antagonisms are not aroused. A delicate baby does not necessarily remain a delicate child and adolescent. As soon as he gains normal health, he should receive the same treatment as is given to the other children in the family. There should be no ugly ducking or Cinderella in the family.

Much has been said and written about girls being the father's, favorites and boys the mother's. This situation does not necessarily exist. If a child, whether boy or girl, looks like or has the personality characteristics of a beloved mate, there is a tendency on the part of the parent to feel especially drawn to that child. It is equally easy to discover and dislike traits in a child that are disliked in a mate. An amusing corollary of this fact is the quickness with which a parent may be heard to say, "He is just like his father!" or "That is her mother all over again!"

Parents of an only child are sometimes tempted to be overobjective and almost too strict in their guidance. According to a study reported in *The Adolescent in the Family,* by Burgess, an only child tends to be emotionally more closely tied to, and more dependent on, his parents than are other children, but he also tends to be better integrated into the social group and to follow social codes more fully than do other children. Middle children seem to have more social contacts than do other children, but they may feel more self-conscious. In general, however, it is probably true that family relationships are dependent upon many factors and that no one factor can be held accountable, of itself, for any family adjustment or maladjustment that may be apparent.

Unless parents themselves set an example of quarreling or give in to one child to the exclusion of others, there is little stimulation for dissension among young people. If a quarrel does arise over individual rights or responsibilities, the parent should keep out of it unless one child is definitely unfair in his accusation of, or demands from, another. The parent must always stand on the side of justice. Parents should discourage an older brother from teasing a younger brother or sister. No adolescent is always right, and very often an adolescent must be taught to recognize this fact.

## Attitude of Adolescents toward Younger Siblings

An adolescent should be an example of desirable behavior to the younger members of the family. Most adolescents recognize this responsibility and try to live up to it. However, they dislike intensely to be held up by their parents as a model. They do not want their actions to be under constant scrutiny and criticism in the light of the possible effects of their behavior upon little Johnny, Mary, or Joe. Neither do they take kindly to criticism from younger children. Parents should not allow the latter to interfere unduly with the activities of their older brothers and sisters. It is the parents' responsibility, not the children's, to decide whether or not their adolescent sons or daughters are doing desirable things.

Similarly, there are limits to the rights of older boys and girls as they appoint themselves to be guardians of the morals of their younger brothers and sisters. In general, this practice is not desirable. A few years' advantage in age does not give a boy or girl the right to dominate a younger child. This again is the parents' responsibility. It is permissible for an older child to suggest to a younger one that certain conduct is not desirable, but that is all. If an older boy or girl notices that a younger child is developing a bad habit, he should take up the matter with his parents. Where there is a mutual attitude of liking and respect among children of different ages, suggestions made by either to the other are usually accepted in the friendly spirit in which they are given.

In large families it is sometimes necessary for younger children to be placed temporarily in the care of older ones. At such times the authority of the older child should be as definite as that of the parent; but the latter must be sure that this temporary authority is used with discretion.

Parents must not expect too much from their adolescent children in the matter of taking responsibility for the care of the younger children. A teen-age boy or girl should not become a slave of the family. Adolescents should rarely be asked to take younger children with them to social engagements. Each group should have social activities suited to its own age interests. Five years' difference in age is significant when one is 15 and the other is 10, though there is no appreciable age difference when one is 40 and the other 35. Parents must remember this fact and discourage a young child from tagging along with his adolescent brother or sister.

## Special Family Problems

No boy or girl objects to giving up some of his free time to care for younger children if this does not happen too often. One member of the family (often the oldest girl) should not always be the one to sacrifice her plans in order to stay home with her little brothers or sisters. This is especially annoying to a girl if an older brother is never asked to make a similar sacrifice. Parents have failed to plan an equitable distribution of family responsibilities if adolescents resent the younger children and if they look upon each new baby as a burden on their own shoulders. Of course a mother's unexpected illness may make it necessary for an older daughter to take charge of household affairs. This situation should be no more than temporary; all the members of the family, including the father, should share in performing home chores until the mother is well again or until other arrangements can be made.

At this point a word should be said for the overworked mother. Although children should not be asked to assume an unfair share of family responsibility, every adolescent should be expected to give his or her mother some assistance in the care of the home. The mother should not be expected to do everything. Father, as well as children, should help with the household chores, marketing, looking after younger children, and the like. Even little tots should be trained to take care of their own toys and to perform simple little tasks around the home. If routine duties are well organized, the doing of them can be turned into a kind of game in which each member of the family vies with others in doing his job well and cheerfully. In such homes there are rarely neurotic mothers, disgruntled fathers, or resentful adolescents.

## Effect upon Adolescents of Grandparents and Other Relatives

Much has been written concerning the effect upon children of interfering relatives. The problem may be serious during the childhood of an individual. Some doting grandparents or aunts or uncles intentionally or unintentionally spoil the child. Others are very generous with their advice to parents concerning the proper rearing of children. On the whole, a young child is not usually too much affected by this interference except to the extent that he may learn to wheedle out of his relatives certain privileges that are denied him by his parents.

## Adolescent Attitudes

There may be definite clashes between adolescents and older relatives. It is often difficult for an adolescent to accept parental guidance of his behavior. It is almost impossible for him to tolerate any attempts at control of it on the part of other relatives. Moreover, if a grandparent lives in the home of the adolescent, there may be a constant rivalry between the teen-ager and the grandparent for the attention that each craves.

Too often a grandparent demands little attentions from an adolescent, which in themselves are unimportant but which loom large to the older person if they are not granted. An intelligent parent usually learns to accept his growing child's apparent dislike of demonstrated affection. A grandparent may not be able to accept the will for the deed, and he may become unduly miserable because of his grandchildren's apparent neglect of him. If he voices his hurt, the young people are torn between pity for the older person and annoyance at the criticism of their own behavior. At one and the same time an adolescent may feel that a grandparent is a nuisance around the house and experience a consciousness of guilt because of this feeling.

Grandparents and other adult relatives outside the immediate family circle are prone to be very much interested in the social activities, dress, and manners of their adolescent relatives. Too often they feel called upon to give well-meant advice as they criticize both the adolescent and his parents for the young person's attitudes and behavior. In this way many a family disagreement has been started, especially if the relative tends to place the blame for adolescent misbehavior upon the in-law parent, thus stimulating bad feeling between the parents, which in turn is reflected in adolescent attitudes.

## Family Attitudes toward Interfering Relatives

It is probably unpsychological to offer suggestions in the form of specific dos and don'ts, but a few seem necessary in this connection.

Relatives should not live with the immediate family of adolescents. There are instances that would seem to give evidence of the desirability of having parents live in the home of a married son or daughter. These are rare. Whenever there appears to be an excellent adjustment to an arrangement of this kind, it has usually been achieved only after struggles, or because the members of the family are unusually stable persons. All old people should be enabled to have their own homes and to pay for the care that they need in time of sickness. The feeling of independence thus stimulated will make it easier for them and their families to remain good friends. There will then be less likelihood that the family will suffer from attempts on the part of old people at a kind of domination that is really the overt expression of a basic feeling of insecurity and dependence.

In general, it is also undesirable for uncles, aunts, cousins, or married sisters and brothers to live in the close family circle for a long period of time. The presence in the home of persons who are at the same time both like and unlike members of the immediate family creates an abnormal situation. To what extent should the relative share in household chores? Whose interests or wishes should be given first consideration—those of the immediate family or those of the relatives? These and similar problems may arise and be difficult to solve tactfully.

Both grandparents and teen-age children must be helped to understand that parents, and parents alone, are responsible for the guidance of their adolescent sons' and daughters' behavior. Grandparents and other relatives should not tell young people what to do; nor, unless they are authorized to do so by the parents, should they criticize the younger members for what they have done. Adolescents must learn that they should not go to their grandparents or to other relatives for consolation if their parents deny them certain desired privileges.

## Cooperation with Family

Adolescents should be held up to a consistent standard of consideration and courtesy in their dealings with their relatives. Young people should be ready and willing to do things for members of the larger family group; but they should no more be expected to be slaves to the whims of their grandparents, uncles, and aunts than to the whims of their younger brothers and sisters. Demands upon the time of young people for care of, and attention to, other members of the family should be met by the teen-agers to the extent that such demands are not excessive or likely to interfere unduly with schoolwork or with rightfully earned recreational activities.

Young people should be expected to be on friendly terms with all members of the family and to visit them occasionally. However, parents should not demand that their adolescent sons and daughters give up their own plans in order to be present at every meeting of the older members of the family group and to be responsible for entertaining these older people, whose interests may be very different from those of teen-agers.

Some of these suggestions may seem too objective and cold-blooded as applied to the relationships of people who are bound not only by ties of blood but also by ties of family affection. This possibility of criticism is granted, but it is for the preservation of family goodwill and affection that the suggestions are offered. Fortunately, in many homes family interrelations are excellent. There are respect and affection on the part of the young people for the older relatives. The latter do not in any way interfere with the lives of adolescents except insofar as they show friendly interest in teen-age activities. In such families are found well-adjusted people living happy lives. There are too many family groups in which this fine adjustment has not yet been achieved, and where there are resulting friction, conflict, and unhappiness. It is to the members of such family groups that these suggestions are offered.

## The Teen-ager and Family Finances

One of the most important responsibilities of adult life is the management of financial affairs. The handling of money is a part of the growing-up process, and every boy or girl needs experience in using money in order to develop a better understanding of its value. An adolescent must learn that before money can be used it must be earned.

## The Adolescent's Allowance

If money flows too freely into the hands of a young person, he may develop a wrong notion of its worth. Hence every teen-age schoolboy and schoolgirl should be given an allowance and should receive definite guidance in budget making.

The size of the allowance depends upon the expenses that are to be covered by it and upon the source of income. The adolescent should gradually be given more money and greater freedom in spending it. The allowance should be set up for definite purposes. Before the amount is decided upon, one or both of the parents should work out with the son or daughter a weekly budget of expenses. If the purpose is to cover school expenses, that fact should be definitely agreed upon, and the use of the money should be restricted to that purpose.

It might be desirable to have the budget include small articles of wearing apparel such as gloves, handkerchiefs, ties, and the like. Rarely are coats, hats, suits, underclothing, and so forth, included in the weekly budget. These are seasonal items and cannot well be included in the weekly allowance of relatively untrained young people. However, as a boy or girl approaches the late teens, especially if he is attending college, it might be desirable to change the weekly budget to a monthly one, making it large enough to include most of the personal expenses. The budget should include a definite sum to be used for recreational purposes and a small amount for emergency spending, with the understanding that if the money is not needed, it will be deposited in a savings account, either through the school bank or in a personally arranged account in the local savings bank.

An adolescent should be held to a strict accounting for the expenditure of his allowance. Rarely should he be allowed to borrow on his next week's allowance; nor should he be encouraged to solicit funds from members of his family. An alert parent watches his child's spending. If it appears that the allowance is not large enough to meet reasonable expenses, it should be increased. If the young person needs money for gifts, club dues, or philanthropic purposes, the parents should expect some of this money to come out of his regular allowance. The remainder can be supplied by the parent as a gift of money to son or daughter.

The size of an allowance is less important than the training derived from its use. Many generous parents feel that an allowance is cold and objective. They prefer to provide the money whenever it is needed or to supply it in the form of gifts. Although a young person so treated may receive more money than the one who is given an allowance, he is denied thereby the satisfaction of spending his own money and of acquiring the education that is possible through this activity.

## The Adolescent and the Family Budget

Adolescent boys and girls have a right to know the economic status of the family. Too many parents seem to feel that they should grant all their son's or daughter's requests for money, even though doing so involves foolish personal sacrifice. "Keeping up with the Joneses" is a bad attitude to encourage in a young person. The state of the family exchequer should not be kept a dark secret. Young children should know that parents cannot afford to satisfy all their wants. Adolescents should be fully informed concerning the family's financial limitations. They should be included in family conferences relative to what should or should not be purchased in terms of available funds. Such matters as rent, cost of clothes, and the amount to be spent for a summer vacation should be discussed frankly and intelligently with teen-age members of the family.

A son or daughter should sometimes enjoy the privilege of deciding what should be done with any extra money that is available. Young people should have the opportunity to sacrifice some of their own interests for the benefit of other members of the family. Of course they need parental guidance in such matters. One young girl insisted upon giving up her college course when her father died, believing that it was her duty to support her mother. Since the girl was thoroughly acquainted with the state of the family finances, her mother was able to convince her that if for a few years they denied themselves certain accustomed luxuries, the girl would be able to complete her education so that they both could enjoy the larger income that would result from the extended training.

Whether there is much or little money in the family, its members are drawn closer together if they share a full knowledge of the extent to which occasional extravagances or temporary denials of wants are in order. If parents are sincere in their desire to do all that they can for their children within their financial limitations, young people usually reciprocate by modifying their own desires to meet the family income.

## The Use of Money Earned

Young people who are engaged in a full- or a part-time job often are much concerned over what proportion of their wages they should give to their parents. Some parents expect a working child to turn over to them the entire salary. The boy or girl then is given an allowance by the parents. Other parents do not require their working sons or daughters to give them any part of the money earned. Both these procedures are unwise. Half of the satisfaction of earning money is gained from the management of it. On the other hand, no young person should be allowed to expect his parents to support him entirely if he is in the position of earning money toward his own support. It is true, however, that an adolescent who earns money needs guidance and supervision in spending it.

A gainfully employed adolescent should share with his parents the cost of his living expenses. The amount of money that he should give to his parents for board or room will depend upon the size of his pay check and of the other expenses that must be covered by it. A high school or a college student often works at a part-time job in order to defray some of his school expenses. If his parents do not need his financial assistance, the amount of money that he gives to them may be very small, perhaps no more than fifty cents a week. However, even that small amount may stimulate in the adolescent a feeling of pride that he is a wage earner in the family.

If the adolescent is working full time, he and his parents should agree concerning the amount of his salary to be turned over to them. The remainder of the money should be his to budget in terms of his needs and interests. In this way he develops gradually an understanding of the value of money and a feeling of financial independence.

There are homes in which material advantages are stressed beyond the more subtle but fundamental ideals of stable home influences. Parents may sacrifice their own as well as their children's chances of experiencing normal family relations because they are too eager to supply their children with unnecessary luxuries. Unfortunately, conditions may arise that necessitate a mother working away from the home. However, in many cases of working mothers, the family unity would be increased by the mother's staying in the home, even though the family style of living might be simplified thereby. It is no disgrace to be poor. It is no special honor to be rich. Whatever the economic status of the home, young people should be aware of it and, with their parents, should adjust to what they have. If improvement is needed, they should do their share in working toward it.

## Parental Responsibility
## for the Social Life of Young People

Are parents responsible for the social life of their children? In general, the answer to this question should be in the affirmative. Parents need not be too much worried about adolescent friendships if during childhood the son or daughter has been encouraged to have desirable playmates, and if the family live in a neighborhood in which the adolescent is brought into contact with desirable young people.

## Adolescent Friendships

When a parent is tempted to criticize the companion of a teen age son or daughter, he should make sure that he has a valid reason for his attitude. Too often fathers and mothers (especially mothers) dislike to see their children form associations that tend to exclude the parents themselves. It is this fear of losing the child's complete loyalty that may cause a parent, sometimes unconsciously, to find something objectionable in the young person's new pal. The difficulty in such instances lies not in the adolescent's choice of friends but in the adult's attitude of possessiveness. If this attitude is present, a young person is quick to recognize and resent it.

A young person who has confidence in his parents' judgment is eager to have parental approval of his friendships. In those cases where the interest in the undesirable companion is so strong that parental disapproval is not heeded, one of the best procedures to be followed by the parent is that of encouraging the son or daughter to bring the friend to the home, where he may meet other members of the family and other friends of the adolescent. Usually a person who is brought into an environment in which people act differently from the way in which he himself behaves is at a disadvantage. Hence the son or daughter sooner or later tends to recognize those characteristics in the friend which are displeasing to the parents, and the friendship may end. Many parents have used this method very successfully. Although it is difficult to welcome an undesirable person into one's home, the results are usually worth the effort, since little if anything is gained by a parent's demand that a young person give up an undesirable friendship. In fact, parental objection may actually increase the bond between him and the person of whom the parent disapproves.

The situation is especially trying when an adolescent becomes too much interested in a member of the opposite sex of whom the parents do not approve. The surest way to throw a girl into a boy's arms or to stimulate a boy toward a deep interest in a girl is for parents openly to disapprove of the relationship. The fact that the boy or girl in question may be of a different faith, national group, or economic or educational level does not constitute a valid reason for parental objection to a friendship. An adolescent may not be at all interested in a particular member of the opposite sex as a possible mate unless or until adults put the idea into his head by an expression of their fears.

Young people should not have their friends selected for them by their parents. That is the right of the individual himself. Too much parental praise of a certain boy or girl may cause an adolescent to be repelled rather than attracted toward the object of all this approval. The spirit of developing independence cannot be coerced. The extent to which parents and their children can agree concerning the latters' choice of friends is a part of the whole parent-child relationship. If a parent wishes his adolescent child to select desirable companions, he must start to work toward this end during the young person's early childhood by developing in him desirable attitudes toward his playmates.

## Parents' Attitude toward Dating

No definite age can be given as the most desirable one for young people to start to "date." Judging by some of the young people one sees strolling along hand in hand on the streets of any town or the roads of any rural area, it would appear that age has nothing to do with it. To adult questioning of their behavior some young adolescents cite the case of Juliet, who at the age of 14 died for love of Romeo. The argument that those were different days has little effect upon the person in his early teens who is going through the puppy-love stage. One way of meeting the situation is that of providing for and encouraging so much participation in interesting group activities that the young person has little time for individual dating until he is mature enough to be intelligent about it.

The above suggestions are directed toward those parents who recognize the fact that sooner or later normal boys and girls have the urge to pair off, and that for emotionally controlled young people this is both wholesome and desirable. Now a word to those parents who refuse to allow their adolescent children any association with members of the opposite sex until they are old enough (in their parents' opinion) to marry. This attitude is often found among possessive parents who cannot tolerate the thought that a beloved son or daughter may develop loyalty to, or affection for, anyone except themselves.

Another type of parent who holds this attitude is the one who himself grew up in an environment of close chaperonage, especially for girls. Such parents are unwilling to allow their teen-age children to engage in any social activities except in parental company. They will not allow their adolescent children to bring friends to the home, nor will they permit them to go outside the home for social relaxation. They are then shocked if they discover that the young people are engaging in the denied social activities without parental knowledge. An ingenious young person can find many opportunities for deceiving his parents. Why force him to do so?

Another phase of the dating situation is parental attitude toward the desirable time for adolescents to return home from a date. In a small town social activities can start early and end early. In large cities, where long distances between homes and places of amusement may require several hours of traveling, time schedules must be adjusted to meet such conditions.

Policies rather than specific clock requirements can be suggested. During the school week an adolescent's social interests should be subordinated to his study needs. On his free evenings the time schedule of his social activity should be determined by the kind of activity in which he is engaging, the distance that he must travel, and the attitudes of the group with which he is associated. A young adolescent should rarely be allowed to return home later than midnight unless he is accompanied by his parents or other responsible adults. For older adolescents the time of return is less important. If a young person wishes to indulge in undesirable social practices, there are plenty of opportunities for him to do so at any time of the day. At present we are living on a twenty-four-hour schedule. Streets and transportation lines are used by people at all hours during the day and night. A parent's concern need not be directed so much toward what time the young person returns home as toward where he has been and what he has been doing. However, if the parent sets a time for the adolescent's return, the latter should be punctual.

Parental attitudes toward the social life of their adolescent sons and daughters is one phase of the whole pattern of teen-age social adjustment. Many of the questions asked by young people concerning their relationship with other young people are directly or indirectly connected with their home relationships, not only from the point of view of their parents' own social activities but also in terms of family approval or disapproval of teen-age interests.

It has not been possible in this chapter to consider all the possible problems that may arise as parents attempt to guide their teen-age children's social adjustment. More detailed consideration of these problems will be found in Chapter 17.

## Questions and Problems for Discussion

1. Give examples of what adolescents consider to be parental intolerance.
2. Give examples of what you consider to be adolescent intolerance.
3. Name five minor disagreements that are likely to occur between a parent and an adolescent. Indicate for one of them what compromise might be made.
4. Are you your father's or your mother's favorite child? Give reasons for your belief.
5. What characteristics are your parents inclined to want your friends to have? What should an adolescent do about friends of whom his parents disapprove?
6. *Special Exercises:*
   a. Prepare a list of adolescent *rights* in the home and a list of adolescent *responsibilities* in the home. What similarities and differences do you find? Ask young adolescents to prepare similar lists. Compare your lists with those of the younger adolescents.
   b. List three or four of your close relatives, excluding parents. Recall and state briefly your attitude toward each when you were a child, when you were a young adolescent, and at present. Explain any differences that you have noted.
   c. Report your experience with the use of family money (1) as a child, (2) as a young adolescent, (3) at present. To what extent have you shared in deciding how the family money should be budgeted?

## Selected References

Ackerman, N. W.: *The Psychodynamics of Family Life,* Basic Books, Inc., Publishers, New York, 1958.

Bossard, J. H. S.: *Parent and Child: Studies in Family Behavior,* University of Pennsylvania Press, Philadelphia, 1956.

Bowman, H. A.: *Marriage for Moderns,* 4th ed., McGraw-Hill Book Company, New York, 1960.

Cole, L.: *Psychology of Adolescence,* 6th ed., Holt, Rinehart and Winston, Inc., New York, 1964.

Faegre, M.: *The Adolescent in Your Family,* Government Printing Office, Washington, 1955.

Jersild, A. T.: *The Psychology of Adolescence,* 2d ed., The Macmillan Company, New York, 1963.

Lehner, G. F., and Ella Kube: *The Dynamics of Personal Adjustment,* 2d ed., Prentice-Hall, Inc., Englewood Cliffs, N.J., 1964.

Powell, M.: *The Psychology of Adolescence,* The Bobbs-Merrill Company, Inc., Indianapolis, 1963.

Schneiders, A. A.: *Personality Development and Adjustment in Adolescence,* The Bruce Publishing Company, Milwaukee, 1960.

Smith, H. C.: *Personality Adjustment,* McGraw-Hill Book Company, New York, 1961.

Symonds, P. M.: *The Psychology of Parent-Child Relationships,* Appleton-Century-Crofts, Inc., New York, 1939.

Symonds, P. M.: *Adolescent Fantasy,* Columbia University Press, New York, 1949.

# Chapter Fifteen

## School Adjustment of Adolescents

An adolescent's school experiences exert a potent influence on his developing personality pattern. The school shares with the home the responsibility of helping a young person achieve those behavior characteristics that can ensure for him the making of satisfactory adjustments to the demands on him of the various areas of his present and future life activities. The degree of success he earns as a secondary school student depends on factors such as the appropriateness of the curriculum in the light of his learning needs, the choice of major fields of study, his relationships with his teachers and fellow students, his participation in the social life of the school, the amount and kind of guidance he receives, and parental ambitions for him. Moreover, fundamental determiners of his school progress are his degree of intellectual capacity and his attitude toward continued education.

## Problems of Adolescent Adjustment

The present trend toward extending young people's education at least through high school and increasingly to college graduation is giving rise to many problems, both for school authorities and for students. To meet such problems, the time, energy, and money expended by community and national leaders toward the improvement of educational facilities are increasing. Farseeing experts are preparing for the future educational needs of which many young people already are aware.

### Educational Problems and Trends

Present educational theory and practice are far from perfect and require constant revision and improvement in order to meet the needs of the group and to satisfy the interests and abilities of the individual. No matter how well the school is organized, how excellent the curriculum, or how proficient the teaching personnel, problems will arise as individual students attempt to adjust to school life.

The ideal of the right of every citizen to avail himself to the fullest extent of those educational opportunities which fit his needs and his

404

interests has resulted inevitably in mass education. Large schools, over-size classes, quickly and sometimes inadequately trained teachers, too little understanding of child and adolescent psychology, a bewildering array of elective subjects on the high school and college levels, an orgy of experimental teaching methods—all these combine to develop a state of educational chaos, of which too many young people are the victims, resulting in dissatisfaction with schools and school people.

We are now attempting educational reorganization. We believe that we are learning from the mistakes of the past, and that we may be able to develop gradually a series of educational offerings that will meet the individual needs and interests of young people. We hope that our teaching techniques and teacher attitudes will be so improved that, through efficient teaching and sympathetic guidance, every boy and girl will be able to profit from any schooling into which he may be guided. We have gone a long way toward the realization of this educational ideal, but there is still much to be done.

At one time, a young person's school life was more or less divorced from his homelife. Parents felt that their responsibility for the schooling of their children went no further than to have them enrolled in a school. The child's teachers were expected to carry on from that point. In the same way, school authorities excluded parents from the educational program of their pupils, except as an individual boy or girl appeared to be unwilling or unable to meet study requirements or school regulations.

A definite trend toward pupil-parent-teacher cooperation is now apparent. Parent-teacher organizations function successfully in many communities. Through such organizations parents and school people together are enabled to study the needs of young people and to devise ways and means of best meeting these needs.

More important, perhaps, than the formation of such parent-teacher groups is the fact that an increasing number of parents, teachers, and young people are recognizing the value of individual conferences that include the pupil, his parents, and his teacher or school adviser. It is through such conferences, started early in a young person's high school life and continued throughout his course, that friendly relations are maintained between home and school. In this way a young person's interests, abilities, and school and future plans can become a cooperative activity. This type of intimate home-school relationship gives all those concerned a much better understanding of the importance to the growing boy or girl of a well-adjusted school life than is possible if parent, school adviser, and pupil attempt to carry out their own ideas concerning educational values independently of one another.

In the past, school administrators and curriculum makers often failed to keep pace with community progress. Consequently, many an adolescent did not get the kind of education that would best fit him for continued success in school or in his later adult activities. Tradition is an important stabilizer, and school tradition should not be treated lightly. However, traditional school practices should be continued only when such practices find their place in a changing civilization.

## Adolescent Attitudes toward School Experiences

Adolescents in school are fully aware of the problems connected with their schoolwork and they come to teachers for help. The following questions asked by adolescent boys and girls give an indication of some of the problems with which they are faced as they attempt to adjust themselves to successful school living. Like the questions raised by teen-age boys and girls relative to homelife, these have been selected as typical of the many questions asked concerning school life.

1. Should a boy or girl choose the high school that he or she will attend?

2. Should a boy be forced to go to college if he prefers to go to work?

3. Why are postgraduate courses not given in high school for students who want to take special courses but who do not want to go to college?

4. What are desirable study conditions in the home?

5. Should we be given so much homework that we have no time for rest and recreation?

6. Would it be possible to allow us to do all our work at school, since home chores and a part-time job interfere with afterschool studying?

7. Is it good to memorize the things that one does not understand?

8. Why is it difficult to get up and speak in class?

9. Should a student be compelled to go into an honor class if he believes that it is too difficult for him?

10. Should we be forced to take subjects in high school that seem to have no practical value?

11. Could the high school course be so planned that a student could change his course after two years without losing credit for some of the work he has completed?

12. Why are some students popular and others either unpopular or ignored?

13. How can one learn to work with a group?

14. Why should we join clubs in high school?

15. What should I do to get along with teachers?

16. Can a student do anything about a teacher who has a "pet" and is unfair to other students?

17. Why do teachers not have more faith in their students and listen to both sides of a story?
18. Is it very serious to have a "crush" on a teacher?
19. How friendly should teachers and students be with one another?
20. Does part-time work interfere with school success?

## Factors Affecting Attitudes toward School

When a young person enters high school, he has many adjustments to make. Learning to adapt himself to new teachers and schoolmates, deciding upon the course or subjects that he should elect, and training himself to accept personal responsibility for his success beyond what was expected of him in elementary school—all these combine to create bewilderment and perhaps serious discouragement unless there is available much sympathetic guidance and assistance in the meeting of such problems.

Further, a young person's decision concerning plans after high school must be given serious thought. Should he continue his education on the college level? Which college should he attend? What should be his field of major study? Should he enroll in a specialized school of higher learning? Would it be desirable for him to go directly to work after graduation from high school? Here again the influence of parents, advisers, and friends is potent.

After a young person has been admitted to the school of his choice, he is faced by problems that are closely connected with his achieving success, not only as a student but also as a member of the school group. Efficient methods and conditions of study, examination passing techniques, value of curricular offerings, participation in extraclassroom activities, and the desirability of engaging in part-time work while attending school may cause anxiety in the high school or college student.

Equally perplexing to these young people may be questions that concern their relationships with their teachers and fellow schoolmates. How friendly should be their attitudes toward their teachers? What may they expect from their teachers and advisers? To what degree should they engage in the social activities of the school? To what extent should they form intimate relationships with fellow students?

We must keep in mind that an adolescent brings to his school life a set of habit patterns and interests that have been developing gradually through his childhood and that have been and still are much influenced by his home relationships. Often a young person's habitual attitude toward himself and other people may make his attempted adjustment to his school life very difficult.

Fortunately, adolescent attitudes are subject to change. As an example of intelligent adult handling of a difficult situation we consider the experiences of John, a 15-year-old, attractive but stubborn and self-willed boy. He knew all the answers. His mother and aunts, according to him, meant well but did not know what it was all about. His teachers merited nothing but contempt. The only one who deserved any respect was his policeman father, except that John was not quite sure that his father was quick enough on the trigger.

At home his attitude was one of silent tolerance. In school he maintained a habitual attitude of passive resistance to any suggestion to him that he use the ability that he possessed. His answer to almost every question put to him was a shrug of his shoulders and "I don't know." He appeared to doubt the sincerity of anyone who wished to help him and was suspicious of adult intentions. The longest speech that he made to his school counselor was to the effect that all teachers were crazy. He had read it in the newspaper and "the psychologists say so." He was intelligent enough to admit that he knew that success could not be won without work, but he was not interested in success.

His family expected him to go to college, but he was negative in his response to their suggestions. Finally the family and the school counselor agreed to ignore his attitude. At home he was never requested directly to do anything nor was he drawn into family conversations or activity. At school he was treated the same way. No comment was made concerning unprepared homework. He was not called upon to recite in class and his examination papers were not returned to him.

After about five months of this treatment, John walked into his counselor's office and said, "Lay off and call the family off. I've had just about as much as I can stand and I've brains enough to know when I'm licked. Fix up my program. I am going to college and, believe me, I'm going to be on top."

He carried out his promise. He was graduated from high school with honors and then prepared himself to be a successful civil engineer. He now is married and the father of two attractive and well-reared young children. His wife sometimes wonders if any child could be as good as he expects them to be. He claims that he wants them to develop the attitude of meeting cheerfully and adequately all reasonable requests made by their parents and, later, by their teachers.

It is only through frank and objective consideration with the young person himself of his interests and abilities that satisfactory school planning can be done. It should be noted that where adolescent readjustment seems desirable, best results are usually obtained when there is close and sympathetic understanding and goodwill between parents and school advisers.

Teen-age boys and girls live a very intense life in school and take themselves and their activities much more seriously than we sometimes realize. If we, as parents and educators, were to meet our obligations conscientiously and intelligently, many fears and worries of youth could be lessened or even eliminated. Thus a more pleasant and profitable school life would be assured to adolescents.

## Suggestions for Improving School Relationships

For the majority of young people the beginning of adolescence and the entrance into the secondary level of their educational experiences coincide. The natural adolescent urges toward self-expression, independence of thought and action, and consciousness of themselves as individuals among other individuals of their own age cause young people's years at high school and college to become a proving ground in which they are prepared more or less adequately for adult living.

In all except small communities new school environment, new faces, new subjects of study, and new social and recreational activities stimulate the young teen-ager toward new forms of behavior. However, as he attempts to adjust his childhood behavior patterns to function in his new experiences, there may arise conflicts and accompanying emotional disturbances.

The activities connected with school life should be the major concern of most adolescents. The years between 12 and 20 should be devoted eagerly to the development of those skills, knowledges, and attitudes which will serve the individual well during his adult years. It is unfortunate that such factors as health, economic necessity, inability to profit from school offerings, or a personal emotional blocking may prevent an adolescent from gaining a full and rich education through these formative years.

It must be remembered by those who are responsible for the education of young people that, although school life is extremely important, teen-agers are living a homelife and a life with other groups in their community. Not only should they be guided toward effective school living, but care should be exercised that all phases of their living receive just and rightful consideration. This interrelationship of the various phases of adolescent life is sometimes forgotten by school people, with the result that students, unaided, may be unable to synthesize their differing interests. The pull of one or another interest then interferes with the development of a well-balanced personality.

The suggestions in this chapter are based upon the more common problems of young people in their school life and are discussed under the following six headings:

1. Selection of a school
2. Development of good study habits
3. Importance of the curriculum
4. School social activities
5. Teacher-student relationships
6. Other factors affecting school progress

## Selection of a School

In a small community young people usually attend the one high school that is available. In many communities the high school entrant is sent to the school that is nearest to his home. In large communities, however, there is a possibility of choice. There may be academic, commercial, vocational, technical, and industrial high schools. A few large cities include all-boy and all-girl high schools, as well as coeducational high schools. For boys and girls who live in large cities the choice of high school is an important factor in their school and vocational success.

## Adolescent Freedom of School Choice

If a high school entrant lives in a community where selection among several schools is available, the young person should be given an opportunity to participate with his parents in the final decision concerning the high school which he shall attend. Too often, parents are tempted to choose a school in terms of what *they* want their son or their daughter to become, without considering the young person's interests and abilities. If a child has made up his mind that he wishes to attend a high school where he can prepare himself for a certain vocational field, he should be allowed to do so unless it is evident that he cannot earn success there.

Either one or both parents may insist that their child enter the secondary school from which they and other members of the family had been graduated, in spite of the facts that his attending this school necessitates considerable traveling and that another good school is within short walking distance from his home.

The sentimental attachment of parents to a particular school may cause them to demand the waiving of school-district lines in order to have their child enrolled in it. The fact that the young adolescent might prefer to attend the nearby school in company with his elementary school pals is not taken into consideration. Later these parents may come to regret their peremptory decision.

When the problem of high school choice is associated only with vocational interests and abilities, for a parent to advise and yet not to dictate is a good procedure. A young person of more than average ability who has not yet discovered his definite interest should enroll in an academic or general high school, since there he probably will discover his interests. Even though he does not do this in high school, his academic or general preparation may qualify him for entrance to college, where later he will be able to determine the definite course of study in which he is most interested. There are many boys and girls, however, who, from the beginning of their high school course, should be guided into specialized schools, such as technical, aviation, needle trades, homemaking, commercial, and the like.

A word of warning should be given here. Even though a young person is definitely interested in a special field, the school to which he should be sent needs to be carefully considered. For example, a girl may be very much interested in the field of home economics. However, if she is an unusually intelligent girl, she will want to continue her study on the college level and prepare herself to be a dietitian. This girl should attend an academic high school where she can major in home economics and at the same time prepare herself for college entrance.

Rather than discouraging a child from selecting the high school that is best fitted to develop his potentialities, the parent and the child, with the help of a school adviser, should agree upon a school in terms of the young person's interests and abilities, availability of a suitable school, and later vocational opportunities in the chosen field. It is much better to select the right school and to complete a definite course in that school as a preparation for entrance into a college or into a desired field of work than it is just to go to high school. However, any high school training within the limits of his ability is of value to an adolescent and should be experienced by every young person in his teens.

## Selection of an Appropriate College

In the past when relatively few high school graduates continued their education on the college level, the college-bound student had little difficulty in gaining admission to the college of his choice, provided that he was able to meet its entrance requirements. At present, however, so many young people and their parents are recognizing the value of a college education that institutions of higher learning are not equipped to meet the increasing demands on their resources. Although the Federal government has taken steps to assist in a building program, colleges lack well-trained teaching personnel and classroom facilities. Also, in spite of what private and public colleges and universities are doing to try to meet increasing educational needs, an individual must go wherever there is room for him. Hence many young people go where they are accepted.

Because of the existing difficulties associated with gaining admission to a college, it is important that high school students prepare themselves adequately for college entrance. Moreover, they should have some understanding of what they might gain from college attendance, even though they have not yet formulated definite plans concerning the courses that they wish to pursue at college or that are available to them in the college which has accepted them. With the hope that present college opportunities will soon be expanded to meet the growing need for them, we offer certain suggestions to guide college aspirants in the charting of their college programs.

Few college students have done more than to decide on a large field of study, such as science, the arts, social science, the humanities, and so forth. Since the great majority of aspirants for college entrance are relatively uncertain about their ultimate vocational interests, such young people might do well, if they can, to enroll in a college that offers during the freshman and sophomore years an opportunity for individual discovery of potentialities and interests. These high school graduates must also consider such matters as qualifications for admission to a college of this kind, cost of the college course, and distance from home.

Some college-entrance aspirants find it most desirable to pursue a four-year course in a liberal arts college before entering their field of specialization. Still other young people unfortunately may choose their colleges for social or sports reasons.

Parents and advisers must be very tactful and understanding as they help a young person decide upon his college program. To allow a young person complete freedom in this decision is unwise. To attempt to steer him into a college course against his will may defeat the purpose of a college education. Parents must be sure that their advice is objective and that it is aimed at the best interests of their child.

To allow a young person to attend a college merely because of the social rating or the athletic reputation of the school is putting the emphasis in the wrong place. Some schools, especially colleges for girls, have long waiting lists. For that reason a socially ambitious parent may decide that his child should attend that school in spite of the fact that another type of college might be better equipped to meet the young person's interests. Again, a parent should not insist that the child attend his own alma mater unless the child definitely wishes to do so.

The cost of a college education and the distance of the college from home are two problems that should receive careful consideration. If there is a college near home that is inexpensive and that is suited to the needs of the young person, parents of limited financial means and their child can well agree upon such a school. This is especially desirable if sending the young person away from home to a relatively expensive school would cause undue sacrifice on the part of the parents and would involve the necessity of the young person's engaging in so much part-time work that he would be denied sufficient time for study and social activities.

However, if the problem of finances does not enter, there is much to be said for the values to be gained by the teen-age young person in a college away from home. The social disciplines and pleasures of living in a dormitory with other students, the personal responsibility for day-to-day decisions, and the task of making and following time schedules without parental aid are experiences that do much for an individual in the later teens. He is thus enabled to develop an independence of decision and helped to achieve a broad understanding of people in group life. Moreover, his relations with his own family are placed upon a more objective basis.

## Development of Good Study Habits

Effective learning usually comes to those who know how to study and who have desirable conditions for study. Above the elementary school level much of a young person's preparatory study for schoolwork is done in the home. Hence parents are faced with the problem of encouraging their teen-age children toward concentrated study and of providing a place in which this studying can be done with a minimum of distraction.

## Study Conditions of High School Students

An adolescent is fortunate if he has a room of his own in the home for study. A boy or girl who is really interested in his school progress experiences great satisfaction in the feeling that in his home he has a place where, undisturbed, he can calmly and effectively pursue his studies. Desirable as this is, it is not enough. The boy or girl must also be assured of the fact that his study time will not be interrupted by home interests or home chores. For this reason parents should make it their responsibility not only to provide a place for study but also to encourage a time for it.

Although a young person should be expected to take his share of home responsibilities, his home duties should be so planned that they will not interfere with the time that should be set apart for study purposes. Nor should the combination of home duties and home study exclude a little time each day for relaxation and socialization with other members of the family. Every parent, therefore, should work out with his child a definite time schedule for study and other activities.

A possible time schedule is suggested in Table 35. It is based upon a school day that extends from 8:30 A.M. to 3:30 P.M. This schedule should be known by all members of the family and by the friends of the young

*Table 35.* Suggested Time Schedule for Study

| | |
|---|---|
| 3:30–4:30 P.M. | Return to home; recreational activity such as school club, or home chores |
| 4:30–5:15 P.M. | Study—one subject |
| 5:15–6:00 P.M. | Study—another subject |
| 6:00–7:30 P.M. | Evening meal, chores, and relaxation |
| 7:30–8:15 P.M. | Study—another subject |
| 8:15–8:30 P.M. | Relaxation—socializing with family, listening to the radio, etc. |
| 8:30–9:15 P.M. | Study—another subject |
| 9:15–9:45 P.M. | Final preparation, checking, and getting books and material ready for the next day |

person concerned. The schedule may have to be revised to meet individual needs. However, after a satisfactory schedule has been prepared, it should be adhered to closely, and few, if any, exceptions should be allowed from day to day. This means that parents should cooperate in the carrying out of the study schedule.

A parent should make certain that he and the family by their actions do not become major distractions. This does not mean that the life of an entire family should be geared to the interests and activities of one person; but too often young people are forced to do their studying to the accompaniment of a blaring radio, loud conversation (sometimes quarreling) among members of the family, interruptions by younger children, and the like. Within the limitations of the home environment, study conditions should be made as conducive as possible to success for the adolescent.

## Study Conditions of College Students

Ultimate success in college is closely related to the student's study habits throughout his course. If a college student is living at home, the time schedule suggested for high school students can be used except for certain revisions in terms of the amount of time spent at the college, special library assignments, and the like.

A freshman in college away from home may find it difficult to make an adjustment to the great amount of free time at his disposal. Here the providing of adequate study conditions and the guiding of students toward successful study habits become the responsibility of the college. If the boy or girl lives in a dormitory, a study schedule may be planned for him by the college administration. He will then have a time and a place in which he may prepare his classroom assignments. However, this studying is often done in a room in which there are other students who by their actions, such as sharpening a pencil, talking to a neighbor, looking out a window, and the like, may distract the student from his work.

If a college student lives away from the campus, he may be tempted to spend so much time participating in the social activities of the school and the neighborhood that concentrated study outside the classroom may be neglected. The early adjustments of the college student away from home are many. He has to devise a completely new life pattern for himself. Other interests may tend to encroach upon the time that should be devoted to study. If the young college student has followed a definite study schedule during his high school days, he has thereby developed effective study habits that will serve him in planning his study at college.

The value of a study time schedule lies in the fact that it affords the student an opportunity for uninterrupted concentration upon study material. Yet, other factors in the immediate environment may act as distracters unless attention is directed toward their improvement. It is probably impossible to free an individual during his study time from all distracting stimulations. Such things as the pictures on the wall, the desk, the books on the desk, the lighting and heating arrangements, and the individual's own thoughts tend to attract attention away from study, but minor distractions can be disregarded if the individual is really interested in his work.

## Some Study Suggestions

Although the modern tendency in education is to offer young people more and more opportunities for learning by doing, much of the subject matter of high school and college curriculums still requires book mastery. It is true that study in its widest interpretation includes the mastery of book material, the application of such material to the solving of problems, the practice of skills, literary and artistic creation, and the like. Before a boy or girl can practice a skill or write a composition, he must have mastered certain material. Hence study fundamentally begins with an interpretation or an evaluation of what has been written or said by another. It is not easy for the young person to get the thought from a printed page unless he learns to follow a definite plan of interpretation, evaluation, and memorization.

The new student needs to understand the study assignment. Then it is not enough to read the material through once, even though this is done slowly and carefully. A better procedure includes the following steps:

1. Read through the material quickly as a kind of survey of the nature of the material, giving special attention to headings and side-headings.

2. Read the material carefully, differentiating between main ideas and supporting details. Enter significant points in a notebook, perhaps in outline form.

**3.** Raise pertinent questions and attempt to answer them.

**4.** Develop the habit of reciting sections of the material to yourself after you have read them.

**5.** Review material at regular intervals.

Following this procedure represents a kind of overlearning that helps fix ideas in the mind. After one becomes habituated to this study approach it is not so time-consuming as at first it may seem to be.

## Adult Responsibility for Adolescent Study Habits

Teachers and parents as they attempt to improve the study habits of young people should be familiar with the basic principles of effective study that are listed below.[1] The student should:

**1.** Have the right attitude toward his study.

**2.** Focus attention actively on what he is learning.

**3.** Know why a particular assignment has been made.

**4.** Study with intent to recall.

**5.** Attempt to understand what the writer is presenting.

**6.** Raise questions as he reads.

**7.** Organize the ideas in his own mind or take brief notes.

**8.** Make intelligent use of repetition or review.

**9.** Know that some material is more quickly and easily mastered than are others.

**10.** Continue practice in skill subjects.

**11.** Be alert to the points emphasized by the teacher.

It is not enough for a parent and a teacher to know that a student has devoted a definite amount of time to his study. They must also discover his methods of study and help him to make any improvements in them that may be considered desirable.

Many teachers, during the first week or two with each new group of students, help the latter to become acquainted with the most desirable techniques of learning the material of the course. Class periods are devoted to the preparation of home assignments and individual guidance is given in methods of study. Unfortunately, many parents are not well enough acquainted with desirable study techniques to be able to continue the study guidance in the home.

So much for the study of book learning. Now a few words to parents concerning ways in which they can cooperate with their sons and daughters in the perfecting of skills learned at school, the application of creative

[1] For a detailed discussion of study procedures consult Lester D. Crow and Alice Crow, *How to Study*, Collier Books, a division of Crowell-Collier Publishing Co., New York, 1963; and Clifford T. Morgan and James Deese, *How to Study*, McGraw-Hill Book Company, New York, 1957.

learning, and the carrying out of group projects. A girl who is studying home economics can be encouraged to plan some of the family's meals and to try her hand at the preparation of some of the food. A boy who is studying mechanics or carpentry can be given an opportunity to take care of minor repairs in the home or to renovate articles of furniture. The pride of young people as they demonstrate in a practical life situation what they have learned at school should more than compensate for some of the mistakes that they may make as they start to apply their learning to practical situations.

Many incidents in the lives of young people who enjoy parental co-operation in their creative efforts are illuminating as well as sometimes amusing. Jane, 15 years old, was very much interested in her high school course in clothing and costume design. She was much impressed by such principles of dressing as color harmony, relation between types of figures and pattern of material, appropriateness of accessories, and the like. She suddenly decided that her mother was so inappropriately and unfashionably dressed that her father might lose interest in his wife.

Then began Jane's attempt to change her mother into a "glamour girl." A well-developed sense of humor and an understanding of their daughter's motives on the part of both parents saved the situation. Jane's mother suggested that she and Jane consult with Jane's teacher concerning desirable changes in the mother's mode of dress, hairdo, and other details. As a result, this wise parent allowed herself to be used as a guinea pig for several class lessons on appropriate and stylish grooming for a middle-aged woman. Jane was delighted by the consequent improvement in her mother's appearance under the guidance of the teacher. She also learned in this practical and intimate fashion the difference between "glamour" and good taste in dress. Jane's mother was equally pleased and was heard to comment frequently, "My daughter has made a new woman of me!"

Sometimes a minor tragedy may result from a teen-ager's attempt to apply his practically mastered skills. Robert was studying the elements of plumbing. During his father's absence from home the kitchen sink developed a stoppage. Against his mother's advice, Robert attempted to make the needed repairs without first shutting off the water supply. When the father returned, he found his distracted wife at the telephone attempting to get a professional plumber, while water was streaming in all directions and a deflated young amateur sprawled on the floor gazing at various pieces of pipe, nuts, and the like, which did not seem to fit together. In some ways this was a costly lesson. However, young Robert specialized in expert plumbing and has several simple but excellent inventions to his credit.

Rather sad was Martha's experience with her family when she attempted to introduce them to the table manners that she had learned at school. Her efforts at improvement were resented by the members of the family, and she was told that they had done very well for all these years and did not need her newfangled notions. Her comment to her teacher as she described her lack of success was "I told them that if they want to disgrace themselves in public they can, but that I am going to mind my manners!" Who is at fault in a situation of this kind? To what extent should school training interfere with home standards? Certainly neither Martha nor her family exhibited tact; but an already bad home situation was not improved through this incident.

One more story may help to demonstrate the way in which learning by doing becomes a part of a young person's life into which the family can be drawn. One spring Arthur's class in biology was studying spring flowers and blossoms. The members of the class, after several field trips, were encouraged to hunt for unusual specimens on their own. Arthur's father, a good-natured man, who was interested in his son's schoolwork, volunteered to drive Arthur and some of his pals to places where unusual specimens might be found. Little did this father realize what he was bringing upon himself. First, he suffered extreme embarrassment because of his own ignorance concerning flora, with which these young people seemed well acquainted. Second, he became so enthusiastic about helping them that he found himself not only reading up on the subject but also consulting the teacher and leading the young people far afield in search of interesting specimens. There was a little difficulty with other members of the family concerning the use of the family car, but the companionship that was developed between this father and his adolescent son was worth the effort and the energy expended.

### Importance of the Curriculum

A curriculum should be as broad as life itself. In a democracy education should affect the physical, mental, emotional, ethical, and social development of every individual, no matter what his physical or mental capacity may be. Every citizen is entitled to training within the limits of his ability. For a democracy to function effectively, everyone must be given an opportunity to develop his specific talents so that he may make his contribution to the democratic way of life.

## Curricular Trends and Contributions

The success of a democracy depends upon the extent to which every citizen has been trained to think, to act, and to appreciate. School curriculums must be so diversified that every boy and girl will be given an opportunity to become prepared adequately for effective citizenship. Curriculums must be adapted to the individual interests and abilities of all learners. They should also include the use of all available community agencies, in order that boys and girls may become acquainted with the various phases of life activities in which they as adults may be engaged.

An individual's education should be continuous from his kindergarten days until he reaches adulthood. For that reason a developing curriculum is so constructed that there are no gaps in the young person's educational process. His elementary schooling should give him the basic tools of interrelationship with other people. This is the period of common education. As soon as the child has mastered the fundamentals of reading, writing, and simple mathematical computations, accompanied by an understanding of the simple principles of group living, he is ready for specialization in the field of his choice.

There should be no definite break between the elementary school and the secondary school. The adolescent continues to improve and extend his skill in reading and writing. He is introduced to more complex mathematical relationships. He is given a broader understanding of scientific, social, and political principles. He begins his specialization.

By the time a boy or a girl completes his high school course he should be prepared within the limits of his ability to think independently, to practice emotional control, and to recognize his responsibility as an active, contributing member of his social groups. If he is going into the world of work, he should possess skills that will assure him success in his chosen vocation. If he is planning to continue his education on the college level, he should be mentally and emotionally equipped to meet the demands of his new school environment.

The college is interested in the continued training of individuals who will be a credit to themselves and of value to society. The college curriculum, therefore, must be broad enough so that it may assist every student in the acquisition of those attitudes, ideals, and intellectual skills and procedures which will enable him to contribute to human betterment and to the establishment of a more abundant life.

## Guidance toward Appropriate Course Selection

An individual student in high school or college does not have sufficient background for the making, unaided, of wise selection of courses to be elected. Left to himself, he may select a course because he has a temporary interest in it, because he likes the teacher, or because he has learned that it is easy.

In small schools there is usually very little leeway in the selection of courses. Of necessity, such schools have a rather rigid curriculum, which must be followed by most students. As the size of a school increases, the complexity of the school's offerings usually increases also. The individual student selects one of several curriculums, or courses, and then fills in his program with free electives. These factors so complicate the problem for most individuals, regardless of their ability, that they desire help or guidance from parents, teachers, or counselors in arriving at a suitable choice of course or curriculum.

An individual may be guided in his choice by his chances for success in any study area and therefore will set his educational sails in that direction. For those students who want to make high school their last level of formal education there should be a wider range of subject choices than for those students who are preparing to continue their education on the college level. However, any individual who has pursued any organized curriculum, who has better-than-average ability, and who has done outstanding work in that area should be allowed to go to college, regardless of the fact that he may not have the specific courses that have been set as entrance requirements to a particular college.

A student should be discouraged from sidestepping a subject merely because he does not like it. If the subject fits into his program of education toward the development of a particular skill or for specialized training, he should be advised to include it in his program. If a student is extremely eager to elect certain courses, such as art, he should be encouraged to try them.

During his early secondary school years a young person may seem to exhibit exceptional interest and ability in a particular field. Whether the apparent aptitude is temporary or more permanent cannot be determined conclusively. For example, Ruth's first-year high school teachers were impressed by her unusual interest in physical education and athletics. Although she continued throughout high school to perform successfully in this field, her work was mediocre in other areas of study. The girl herself had decided that probably the best she could do would be to prepare herself for simple office work. Hence she and her parents were greatly surprised when the dean of the school suggested that she apply to a neighborhood university for admission as a physical education major. With the help of the dean, Ruth was accepted by the school. She was graduated from it with honors in her major field, although some of the more academic requirements, especially science, had been extremely difficult to master. She is now a successful recreational therapist.

Martin's experiences have been very different from Ruth's. As a child he displayed considerable ability in mechanical drawing. Encouraged by his parents, he applied for admission to a technical high school and was accepted. This meant that on each school day he spent at least three hours in travel. In addition, the school's academic standards are extremely high.

Although Martin earned some success in his art classes, his continued inadequacy in other subjects has led to difficulties in finding a college to accept him. His interest in art waned, and his inadequate preparation for college work resulted in his dropping out of school at the end of his freshman year. At present, he is an indifferently effective salesman.

If a young person who gives no evidence of a special aptitude for a given course insists upon electing it, in order to be in the class of a friend or for any other superficial reason, he should probably be advised to elect another subject more nearly related to his fundamental abilities and interests. This is more likely to keep alive within him a desire for further education, since he will probably be rewarded thereby with a greater degree of successful achievement in the subject.

Very often a student is heard to say that he just can't see any practical value in the subject he is taking. Most students feel that way about most subjects at one time or another (often when they have done poorly in an examination). If young people emphasize the immediately practical value of all the subjects that they study, teachers and parents find it very difficult to defend every subject from this point of view. Young people need to take a long-range view of their schooling. They should be helped to realize that some of the values of education are so subtly woven into the adult life pattern that their influence is often felt without being recognized.

## School Social Activities

For a young person to go to a high school or a college where he does not know any of his classmates, or many of them, may seem to him a challenge that he cannot meet and may cause him to wish to retreat from the situation. Both high schools and colleges are now engaging in numerous activities in order to orient young entrants in the new and, to them, strange environment. Elaborate trips of inspection and conferences for explaining the rules and regulations of the school are utilized. In conjunction with these efforts go planned social events, which are used as means of acquainting incoming groups with some of the upperclassmen.

No matter what plans are made in this way to help each young person to meet and become acquainted with other people on the campus or school grounds, every boy or girl must make a definite effort to acquire friends. School friendships based upon similarity of interest and experience are very much worthwhile. Joining clubs, participating in other school activities, becoming acquainted with the members of one's class, and maintaining a consistent attitude of friendliness will reap a harvest in friendships.

Many students ask how they can gain friends. Parents and teachers can give young people much indirect assistance in the building up of fine school friendships. Parents can encourage their son or daughter to bring schoolmates home or to visit the homes of other young people. Fundamentally, however, the parent's responsibility for his child's popularity in high school or college began long before the boy or girl reached these school levels.

The young person who, in his relations with his family and childhood playmates, was guided by his parents toward the development of an attitude of cooperation, friendliness, and tolerance will have no difficulty in forming satisfactory friendships. Popularity must be earned. It cannot be bought. The girl or boy who is allowed to be self-assertive, selfish, and domineering in the home cannot use these same techniques in his relations with his schoolmates if he or she wants to be accepted by them.

A mother who constantly emphasizes the fact that she and her family are superior to the neighbors is very likely to foster in her son or daughter an attitude of snobbishness and intolerance that will make it very difficult for the young person to gain popularity. Parents often fail to realize that unusual physical attractiveness, expensive clothes, and an abundance of pocket money are not an open sesame to popularity among high school and college students. Unless the possessor of the special advantage is at the same time modest, his apparent advantages of looks, clothes, and money will cause him to be viewed with suspicion by the majority of the student body. He may be able to "buy" some young people, but these will not represent the better type of student.

Young people sometimes try to convince their parents that they will be unpopular among the students if they refuse to break school rules and regulations. This is not true. In every school there is a small group of individuals who seem to feel that school rules and regulations are made to be broken. These young people take great pride in such things as cutting classes, defying their teachers, using wrong stairways and exits, and the like. In every such case there is present an actual or an incipient maladjustment which causes these young people to act as they do. To be popular with this group is not an honor. Unfortunately, the weak boy or girl who cannot find a place for himself in the school's social life is sometimes tempted to join a group of this kind.

Parents lay the groundwork for a young person's popularity in high school, and teachers can do much to help young people find a place for themselves in the school. A boy or girl may be so shy as to find it difficult to mix freely with other boys and girls. If this shyness is a symptom of a functional disorder, guidance toward normal social relationships requires much patience, with a possibility of failure to achieve the desired goal.

Teachers should help not only the shy young person but also the one who by his aggressiveness antagonizes other young people. Sometimes the apparent "cockiness" is a protective covering for inordinate shyness. Sometimes it is the result of family spoiling. It is the function of teachers to recognize the reasons for a young person's unpopularity with his peers, and tactfully help him to make whatever adjustments are necessary so that he may be accepted by other students.

A word of warning to teachers is necessary. They must never pick out one student and give particular attention to him. To gain the reputation of being "teacher's pet" is the surest way of earning the disapproval of the majority of students. This is true in college as well as in high school. Whatever a teacher does for a young person must be done tactfully and individually.

## The Value of Participation in School Club Activities

Adolescents should be not only allowed, but also encouraged, to join school clubs. Every member of the school should belong to one or more clubs and take an active part in the work of the club. The real social living of the school, whether high school or college, is usually experienced through one or another kind of extraclassroom activity. These clubs should be under the leadership of faculty advisers who know how to work with young people and who refrain from doing all the thinking and working for the members of the club.

The length of the list of clubs in most schools is being expanded yearly and is now reaching out to include every kind of activity and interest that is connected with school life. An individual who does not wish to join a club may be the very one who needs it most. He should be given special attention and helped to enter the social life of the school through these activities.

An adolescent needs to learn to live with people. If he prefers not to join a club, he thereby may be indicating a fear of people or a lack of interest in his school. The experiences that he needs most should not be closed to him. One of the problems experienced by counselors of secondary schools and colleges is rooted in some young people's "snobbish" attitude toward those of their schoolmates whom they consider to be in one or another way inferior to themselves. Educators disagree in their opinions concerning the advantages of fraternities, sororities, or other close-knit restricted student groups.

In some school systems such exclusive "clubs" are not permitted to be established in the school; yet there are few high schools in which some of the students do not organize secret societies that hold their meetings in the homes of members. In fact, high school counselors find that even among those clubs that are faculty-sponsored, the most popular ones are those that set up certain admission requirements. Likewise, membership is sought in cocurricular groups such as science, mathematics, literary, social problems, or other special-interest clubs, since membership in them would seem to represent the possession of a special interest or ability.

## Teacher-Student Relationships

It is important for a student to get along well with his teachers. Whether or not he does depends upon his attitude, which often is an outgrowth of home attitudes toward teachers. Parents should not habitually criticize teachers, but should develop in their young people an attitude of cooperation with all teachers.

If a young person is not successful in his schoolwork, it is very easy for a parent to place the blame upon the teacher's attitude toward his son or daughter, rather than upon the adolescent's own inability or unwillingness to take his share in classroom activity. An extreme instance of this critical attitude will be used as an illustration. Ruth, a high school student, had been compelled by her mother, against her own wishes, to elect algebra. The girl recognized her own mental limitations and realized that all forms of mathematics were difficult for her. Both Ruth and her teacher tried their best to achieve at least a passing mark for Ruth in the subject. However, the girl failed badly in her tests. Thereupon her mother first wrote a letter to the teacher accusing her of being unfair to Ruth and then visited the school, demanding to be shown Ruth's test papers. When these were shown to her, she insisted that the marks on them meant nothing as a teacher tends to give a girl any mark that she wishes, regardless of possible errors in the work. Ruth was transferred by her mother to another school, again in spite of the girl's wishes. Peculiarly enough, Ruth herself did not share her mother's resentment toward teachers and was cooperative in her classes.

## Teacher Attitudes toward Students

Since the classroom of the present is becoming more and more the scene of teacher-guided rather than teacher-dominated activity, there are fewer instances of old-fashioned fears and hatred of teachers. However, young people sometimes forget, as occasionally do teachers, that courtesy and cooperation are necessary in a classroom as well as in the home or any other group of persons, if they desire to be respected and admired. A domineering teacher or an indolent and uninterested student cannot expect to be popular.

A teacher is often accused of having a "pet" in class. It is easy to understand how this comes about. The student who cooperates gets a great amount of attention from the teacher. Sometimes, before either is aware of it, there has been established an understanding between the two that may become very close as the semester goes along. The teacher should not let his special interest in one of his students show itself. If desirable classroom attitudes are to be established and cooperation is to be secured from all the class members, every student should be made to feel that he is as important as every other student.

The relationship between students and teachers should always be friendly. Teachers exert a great influence upon young students and are often remembered by the latter for the influence they had upon personality development rather than for the help given in the learning situation. Sentimental emotionalism, however, is foolish and undesirable.

## Student Attitudes toward Teachers

The relationship between a teacher of either sex and a student of either sex should always be friendly but dignified. A student should never be invited to the teacher's home except for business purposes or as a member of a group. A teacher and a student should not habitually leave school together or engage in social activities together outside of school. No matter how much a teacher may admire a student and enjoy his company, the teacher-student relationship must be strictly adhered to. Any other behavior will result in the loss of the respect of other students for both the teacher and the student concerned.

High school and college students (especially girls) sometimes develop a "crush" on a teacher of the same sex or become infatuated with a teacher of the opposite sex. This is a very embarrassing situation for the teacher. His method of handling it is an indication of his strength of character. If he is weak, he may be unduly flattered by the attention he is receiving and encourage a situation that is bound to become most disagreeable and sometimes sordid. If he is strong and sincere, he will tactfully convince the emotionalized young person that he or she is wasting an affection that should be directed toward a person of his own age. If the teacher concerned is consistently objective in his attitude, yet kindly, and if he allows no privileges to this student that other students do not enjoy, he will find it relatively easy to bring about a change in the young person's attitude toward him.

These abnormal interests of students in their teachers often become serious problems among college girls, especially if there are few or no young men on or near the campus. Some college girls give an appearance of being interested in their middle-aged college professors in order to flatter the latter into giving them good grades. This is a kind of glorified "apple-polishing." Others become really attracted to their professors and may kindle a similar feeling toward them on the part of the professor concerned. Such situations are very unfortunate, especially if the man is married. Tragic consequences may result unless others connected with the persons involved show forbearance and are helpful in bringing the relationship to an end before the school authorities are forced to take drastic measures.

## Other Factors Affecting School Progress

Various other factors determine the extent to which a student earns successful achievement in his school studies. Significant factors of influence on his educational progress are (1) fear of teachers, examinations, and the like, (2) personal interest in the subjects included in the school curriculum, (3) degree of intellectual capacity to master subject matter, and (4) achievement of self-discipline.

## School-stimulated Fears

The adolescent who fears his teachers to too great an extent may trace the cause to his fear of anyone in a supervisory relationship to him. Parents who are too strict or who are unwilling to explain reasons for their corrections of youthful misdeeds, or parents or older brothers and sisters who play up the teacher as a person to be feared, are often responsible for the development of this attitude in young people. Such fear attitudes are hard to overcome, even with the sympathetic help of teachers. The individual fears not only teachers but anyone in a position of authority. This may include policemen, who have been regarded by these young people during childhood as individuals who punish children rather than protect them. Hence a young person in whom these fears have been allowed to develop comes to the new environment prepared for the worst.

Usually a student does not fear the teacher for what the teacher actually does, but rather for what he fears the teacher may do. The young person wants to feel secure in the respect and affection of the teacher. Consequently, he may be stimulated to study hard because he does not want to disappoint his teacher. He feels sorry when he cannot answer in class, not alone because he will get a poor mark but also because he fears that he thereby has lost the esteem of his teacher.

A student should be encouraged by his parents to learn to work with, think with, and get along with every teacher he may have. When right attitudes are present in both the teachers and the students, there is usually no abnormal fear. All efforts utilized to remove these fears from the classroom are rewarded by better and more effective learning on the part of every student.

Some individuals so fear the classroom situation that even though they know the answer to a question, they become tongue-tied and are unable to give it when asked to do so. These students need help in overcoming their emotional disturbance. They need to have their confidence restored. The best way to do this is to spoon-feed them at first—get a response from them and praise whatever there is in it that can be praised. Such young people should be called upon frequently to answer simple questions, so that they will develop the habit of talking in class. As they do this, the fear that they have been experiencing will gradually be replaced by a desire to answer, since they have found that they can express themselves and that, as they speak, ideas come to them. There is no place where the doing is so important as in the individual's activity in class. The teacher cannot answer for the student; other students cannot report for him; he must speak for himself if he wishes to increase his enjoyment of class participation.

Sometimes able students who do well in classroom recitations fear examinations. They become upset and are unable to do effective thinking at the time of the test. When this happens, there is usually found a history that ties the condition to the home, the pressure of the parents, the study habits of the individual, and the like. Most examinations are based upon the material covered in class, and students should approach them with eagerness to do something with the ideas previously discussed.

The young person who has prepared his lessons from day to day and has been regular in his class attendance has little cause to fear an examination unless someone is prodding him on to an attainment that is beyond the reach of his ability. An adolescent should be encouraged to do his best and no more. There should not be a goal set by his parents for him to reach, such as the top place in the class. A teen-ager often becomes increasingly nervous in school because of pressures experienced in the home. In some instances emotional disturbance results in a speech defect such as stammering.

Many young people *express* a fear of examinations that they really do not experience. This is a practice of high school seniors when they are preparing for their final examinations. They know that very few seniors fail to pass these tests. However, they talk much about the difficulties of the examinations and their fear of losing graduation because of failure in them. This is a kind of emotional preparation. They are thus impressing upon their parents the importance of this or that examination. When the news comes to the home that the examinations have been passed and that graduation is assured, there is much rejoicing, and parents who a few weeks earlier were very much worried are now inordinately proud of their successful son or daughter. The underlying reason for this display of fear of final examinations is not always realized by the young people themselves until it is called to their attention. They usually admit the truth of the accusation and discontinue their emotional outbursts.

If an individual talks too much about fearing a test, a check should be made of his study habits. He should know how to prepare his daily work and he should know how to study for an examination. It is through review that a greater understanding of the material that has already been studied is attained. The review aids not only general understanding but also specific memory.

In addition to being prepared for the examination, knowing how to approach it is helpful. This should be done with confidence, since the individual who has prepared his work is usually eager to tackle the examination. Teachers should prepare their students for major examinations by reminding them of some of the suggestions that are given here.

It is usually a good practice to read through the entire examination sheet, so that an idea will be gained of the general requirements of its contents. Questions to be answered can then be selected and time can be allotted for answering each question. It is better to write something for each question than to spend too much time on one or two questions.

Special attention should be given to the directions for the questions and to the questions themselves. Both the directions and the questions should be understood before an answer is undertaken. If the directions call for an outline, that procedure should be followed. If the directions suggest a complete answer, that kind should be given. Questions should not be answered in outline form unless the directions specifically call for that form of answer. In the giving of answers, technical language should be used only when needed. If examples will make clear the points that are being made, they should be used.

The best way for a student to reduce fear of tests to a minimum is for him to give time and energy to daily preparation of his work, with frequent reviews. Otherwise, the individual is likely to cram at the last minute. Cramming of material that has not been studied consistently may enable the student to pass an examination immediately after the cramming process, but forgetting will set in very soon thereafter. The systematic review that the individual undergoes during the cramming is valuable for immediate recall, but he tries to cover too much material in too short a time and is usually upset by this. The result is added fear of tests and examinations.

The purpose of examinations is not to find out how little the student knows. Examinations are measuring devices for the purpose of discovering the ability of the individual to recall facts, to evaluate, and to organize and use information in a situation in which others are participating at the same time, as a basis for further study. Questions should be so constructed as to enable the test taker to do his best.

# Development of Interest in Continued Study

Earning success is very important as a factor in the development of interest in schoolwork. Boys and girls need help in selecting curriculums and subjects that can assure them a fair degree of success in school. When activity is accompanied by success, there is interest in the activity. Today there are so many influences competing for the attention and interest of a young person that he often raises the question, "How can I develop interest in school?"

The adolescent often finds radio and television, sports, social activities, and work opportunities much more exciting and interesting than what he is doing in school. If he then confronts the possibility of failure and has to work under the guidance of teachers who do not vitalize their subjects, the student has little motivation for the kind of study that will help him develop an interest in schoolwork.

A student needs to be encouraged to do something that he can do with some success. With this success will go the roots of interest that usually carry through to other subjects that are fundamental to his growth and development. Parents having high ambitions for their child sometimes refuse to accept the fact that the young person's mental capacity may be on a much lower level than parental ambition.

Cold logic on the part of parent or teacher will never encourage an adolescent to become interested in any school activity. To engage in the activity because it is good for him is a negative suggestion. He needs help that will get him into action. Every parent should encourage his child to elect those courses or subjects for which he is mentally and temperamentally fitted. Every teacher should try to present his subject in such a way that the members of the class will grow to like it, even though they have come to it with an attitude of dislike.

It is a fact that those students who are punctual and regular in attendance are more likely to be interested in schoolwork than are those who cut classes and are late, thus missing many ideas that are presented in class. However, very often the cutting is a result of the fact that the young person is attempting to earn success in a subject that is too difficult for him or in which he is not interested.

Sometimes adolescents feel that assignments are too long. If they must do other work, either at home or away from home, they are hard pressed for enough time to prepare their homework well enough to compete with the other members of the class. This leads to discouragement and a lack of interest in schoolwork. The school adjustment of such young people needs the cooperative help of teachers and parents. Either the afterschool work should be lessened or the student's school program should be lightened.

Sometimes during the regular recitation periods adolescents allow their thoughts to wander to things that are of interest to them but are not directly related to the lesson. They find it difficult to keep their minds on the work of the class and often wonder what they can do to keep from daydreaming. The mind tends to be carried to the things of personal interest at the moment, since in any discussion many such experiences may be called to the student's mind. He should learn to bring his thinking back to the subject under consideration as soon as possible. Teachers can be of real help in this by keeping all students interested in what is going on through motivated discussions. The alert teacher is quick to recognize whether or not his students are following the thinking on the topic under discussion at the moment. Teachers who keep the pupils motivated thereby help them break their habit of daydreaming, since they have something concrete and definite to which to direct their attention.

## Relation of Ability to Success in Learning

Each individual brings to his high school and college experiences certain definite abilities, which are the result of his inheritance and of his training up to that time. In the past most schools were organized mainly for the purpose of educating those young people who had the kind of ability that would enable them to work successfully with abstractions and book learning.

Since more and more adolescents are now attending high school, all school registers include some young people who do not have the capacity to master difficult book material. Hence we need to find ways of adjusting subject requirements to the mental capacity of less able students, so that they can profit in a practical and cultural way from the time and energy spent on schoolwork.

A young person gains little if he attends school for an education but receives nothing but one failure after another. It is an educational crime to allow an adolescent to remain in an academic high school for two years without passing a single subject. The parents who insist upon such a young person's staying in this school, and the school authorities who do nothing about having his course adjusted to the level of his mental ability to profit by instruction, are failing in their responsibility to youth.

A careful analysis of the abilities of every boy and girl should be made to the end that each one is given something to do in school that will allow him a reasonable degree of success. The spur to stay in school and to continue education in some field of activity is based upon the success factor, not upon the failure factor.

The introduction of many new subjects into secondary school curriculums has done much to meet this youth need. Among these are such subjects as music, art, home economics, commercial subjects, speech, and many others that have gradually found a place in the curriculum. These curricular changes make it possible to satisfy the different interests and abilities of adolescents.

## Effect of Part-time Work on School Success

A secondary school student can gain much experience through part-time work. It is true that if he has to work too hard or too long hours on the part-time job, he may not have sufficient time or energy left to give to his study. His schoolwork may suffer, and he may become discouraged and drop out of school. However, if the part-time worker is properly supervised and is helped to plan a study and work schedule for his use in completing his daily program of activities, he can develop effectively in both areas. This is especially true of the college student in his later teens.

A part-time job can be of value to an adolescent for one of or all the following reasons: the insight gained through vocational tryout experiences, the information that can be gained only from work on the job, the gaining of a better understanding of money, and a keener appreciation of an education as a steppingstone to vocational success. An allowance that is *earned* by a young person will be appreciated in a way that is not possible if money is handed to him every time he asks for it. The interesting report of Frank shows the thoughtful interest that may be given to the value of money when an adolescent uses his own energy to earn it. This practical-minded boy continued as a man to use to his advantage the training he had gained from his earlier experiences. Hence the authors report the story of his developing attitudes in some detail.

Frank was the younger of two brothers by slightly more than a year. The parents of these boys were as objective as they could be in their treatment of them, and both Frank and his brother were popular among friends and acquaintances of the family. Frank especially was very sociable and in his early years showed definite extrovert tendencies. He would approach people whom he did not know and ask them questions in such a way that he was never considered pert. He was very active and enjoyed being among people.

Since the parents allowed their sons a great deal of freedom of activity, Frank was well able to go places and do things on his own. For example, during one summer he visited the New York World's Fair alone almost daily, and not only investigated every exhibit very carefully but met a great many different types of people.

When the boys were about 16 and 17 years old, they took a trip through Canada in an old Ford, unaccompanied by their parents. They traveled about 3,000 miles and had many exciting experiences. Frank has always been interested in going places. It was this spirit of restlessness and desire for adventure that was responsible for an incident that might have had serious results.

During his senior year at high school he had an argument with one of his teachers. He was convinced that he had been treated unjustly. Consequently, one morning he went to school with his brother as usual and then, without reporting to the school authorities, returned home. He knew that neither his mother nor his father would be there. He packed a few clothes, took with him about $7 which he had earned, and left. He was gone forty-eight hours. According to his story, he hitchhiked a distance of about 1,000 miles. He claimed that he would have continued his trip but that he was followed and robbed in a city about 500 miles from home. By this time he was sleepy, hungry, and moneyless, so he decided to return home. In the meanwhile he had not communicated with his parents; but he had given some indication of his plans to a pal, who told the parents. Knowing that Frank was resourceful and able to take care of himself, his parents were not too much worried about possible danger to him. When he reached home, they welcomed him without comment, accepted his story at face value, and sent him back to school.

He had always been interested in the value of money, and as soon as he was old enough to do so, he began to work at jobs suitable to his age. In connection with a high school project he gave the following account of his work experiences:

During my seventeen years of existence, my working experiences have been many and varied.

Shortly after our family moved from a small town to a city (I was in the third grade at the time), I started selling magazines. Each night, rain or shine, snow or otherwise, I would go from door to door selling magazines. I can never remember making much money, but, from the small amount I did earn, I learned the value of money. Even yet, when I spend money, I think of how many houses I would have to go to to sell magazines enough for the prescribed amount of money. My next job along this line was a paper route. My first route was an afternoon edition, but when I became 12 years old I got a morning route. Getting up at five in the morning required going to bed early; a job that requires regular living is worth much more than its pecuniary returns.

My grandparents live in a small town, where they operate a general store, a feed mill, and a coal business. They also buy large quantities of maple sirup. My first selling experience, that is, in a store, was in my grandparents' general store, selling groceries, hardware, and clothing. Also at their place of business I learned to operate a feed mill, to run grinders and mixers. Here I learned, by contrast, the value of a white-collar job. I also learned something about the process of making maple sirup, a product which I have been retailing in this city from door to door for the past year.

Other relatives operate farms and I have had the opportunity of working on their farms. Learning many of the activities of a farmer has been quite interesting and healthful.

I have spent many days caddying and working in a parking lot. These contacts with people have proved invaluable. During Christmas vacation I have worked in a post office, helping to deliver mail. An experience such as this is interesting at first but after a few weeks becomes dull and boring.

My next job was helping a milkman deliver milk. The milkman has a rather hard job, with long hours starting at three in the morning. However, through this contact I learned the workings of a modern dairy.

I've been working this summer while attending summer school. I first got a job in an ice-cream bar, selling cones, sodas, and sundaes. It did not pay very well so I got a position as a salesman in a Western Auto Store. This is rather interesting, as we sell 10,000 different items.

The day summer school is over and until my college term starts, I expect to get a job as a coal passer on a ship on the Great Lakes.

All the different types of work in which I have been engaged have been of great importance in helping me to determine my future life-work.

Upon graduation from high school that summer, Frank entered a leading college, where he made a good record. At age 18, after a year in college, he was accepted by the Army. Frank earned several promotions in the Army. His interest in people, helped by his many work experiences, were of value to him in his assignments, as they required leadership ability. Upon his release from the Army, he returned to college and majored in business administration. After graduation, he went into wholesale selling, a field in which he earned considerable success. He was not completely satisfied with his job, however. To the regret of his employer, he left the company and treated himself to a three-month tour of Europe. During the past nine years he has continued in sales activities, moving from one line to another, always with the thought that he wants to be self-employed. At the time of this writing, he has not definitely established himself in a worthwhile vocational activity. He is constantly looking for the kind of business activity that will bring him the greatest monetary return.

School and college advisers have found that a part-time job tends to act as a stimulator of interest in schoolwork. Even a few hours of work a week during the school year, or vacation jobs that are not too strenuous, help a boy or girl recognize the value of an education in its relation to the work world.

An increasing number of colleges and high schools are introducing a cooperative program of work and study. According to this plan, a student spends part of each week or month in the school, where he learns the techniques of his work and also studies subjects such as related English and related mathematics. He then spends the remainder of the week or month at work, applying the principles that he has learned at school to his actual practice on the job. Many values can be derived from this combination of activities, even for young people who are preparing themselves for a professional career. Contact with other workers on the job helps the young person increase his maturity of attitude. Moreover, actually working at a project for the success of which he is responsible gives the teen-ager a better appreciation of his strengths and weaknesses than is gained through his achievement in school projects and tests.

Unfortunately, too many high school students are satisfied with a mere passing mark. To such students the attainment of a minimum passing grade of 65 or 70 per cent means that promotion to the next unit of learning has been earned. They do not recognize the fact that they have failed to master the subject completely. The student-worker realizes that his failure to complete satisfactorily that which he is assigned to do on the job can be traced to his failure to learn sufficiently well the related material needed for better performance. Hence he usually is stimulated to do a better job of studying while he is in school so that he may gain greater success in his vocational work.

In general, the adjustment of a teen-age person to his school experiences cannot be considered apart from his adjustment in his out-of-school life. It is true, however, that much of the success of an adolescent's school life can be traced to the suitability of his school curriculum, the attitudes of his teachers, and the kind and extent of the school guidance that is made available to him.

## School Personnel and the Development of Self-discipline

The adolescent brings with him to the secondary school certain habit patterns that were acquired during his earlier home and school experiences. These habits of control may break down as he or she strives to gain independence from adult authority and satisfy newly felt needs and wants. Any help that school people can give the adolescent in his management of his affairs greatly influences his achievement of success in his schoolwork and in his social activities.

One of the important functions of a teacher is to motivate his students to develop an attitude of personal responsibility for their behavior in the school, home, and community. Most younger and some older adolescents are still too immature to direct their actions in the light of their own and others' welfare, however. Hence school authorities establish certain rules and regulations that are to be obeyed. These pertain to such matters as school attendance, preparation of study assignments, proper conduct in and outside the school, and the like. The teacher or another school official then employs disciplinary measures to correct the behavior of recalcitrant students.

Various approaches to the development of self-discipline are effective. The rewarding of students for cooperative behavior by means of verbalized commendations, extraclass credits, and special privileges usually stimulates the young people concerned to want to continue the approved behavior. Also, those students who find it difficult to conform may try to mend their ways so that they, too, may receive commendations or other rewards.

An adolescent may have an interest unrelated to school achievement that becomes so strong that it interferes with the meeting of school responsibilities. The young person may become very much involved in out-of-school social activities; he may be passing through a stage of "puppy" love; he may have a strong desire to earn money. Even the generally cooperative student may have his "off days" when he resents having to conform to any authority, especially that of the school. Consequently, he engages in uncontrolled behavior of one kind or another. He "cuts" classes or arrives late for class; he fails to prepare study assignments or submits carelessly written papers; in class, he is inattentive or discourteous, or he displays an attitude of boredom and lack of self-control.

Secondary school people should not ignore a student's infraction of school rules. Misbehavior must be recognized and corrected. A teacher or other school official must administer a penalty that the student recognizes as suitable and just. Moreover, the attitude of the adult should be objective and calm. The offender probably is already in an emotionalized state. A show of emotionalism by the penalizer is likely to worsen rather than improve the situation.

School people need to keep in mind that their purpose in administering disciplinary procedures is not so much to punish a single nonconforming act as it is to help a young person to develop the habit of self-discipline. Hence teachers and counselors should not only recognize a student's behavior as undesirable but also attempt to discover the underlying cause or causes for the misbehavior and to help improve the situation or condition that is basic to the young person's lack of self-control. A serious behavior problem, for example, may have its roots in disturbed home conditions, poor physical health, inappropriate school placement, or another emotion-arousing situation. To the extent that the school can discover and, with the assistance of other agencies, treat these causes, it can help improve adolescent attitudes.

A well-organized society expects its citizens to take personal responsibility for conducting themselves in such a manner that all the members of the group, including themselves, may benefit from their membership in it. School people need to help young people understand and practice personal and social ideals. To this end, the members of the school staff encourage students to participate in school management. A student-teacher organization, with officers elected by the student body, exercises control over student activities. A student court deals with minor infractions of school regulations. In the classroom, the teacher and students together plan learning activities.

A school in which the democratic ideal is put into practice gives every student an opportunity to recognize his role in school affairs. He is thereby learning to control his own wants and interests so that he does not interfere with the rights of other people. Such training can do much to help an adolescent achieve a self-disciplined personality pattern.

## Questions and Problems for Discussion

1. What responsibilities should be assumed by the school to help adolescent peer-group adjustments?
2. Recall a fellow high school student who did not seem to be well adjusted. What was your attitude toward him at that time? How do you feel toward him now?
3. Which of your present attitudes, beliefs, and interests were developed during your high school days? Suggest forces that influenced them.
4. Name the factors that influenced you in the choice of your high school. Your high school course. Did you make wise choices?
5. Select two teachers whom you admired during your high school years and two whom you disliked. Explain the differences in your attitudes.
6. Which of the recreational activities in which you engaged during your high school years do you still continue?
7. Discuss the advantages and disadvantages of a coeducational high school. An all-boy or an all-girl high school.
8. Why should a student continue his high school program through to graduation?
9. To what extent should adolescents be influenced by their parents in the selection of school subjects?
10. What are the advantages of having a place for study that is free from distracting influences?
11. *Special Exercises:*
    a. Draw up a time schedule for study and follow it for a period of eight weeks. Report to your class on its value.
    b. Outline a school social program that may be of value to an adolescent isolate.
    c. List shortcomings of secondary schools and indicate what changes might be made to correct them.

*d.* Visit a counselor in a secondary school and report your findings concerning his principal functions.

## Selected References

Conant, James B.: *The American High School Today,* McGraw-Hill Book Company, New York, 1959.

Cook, L. A., and E. F. Cook: *A Sociological Approach to Education,* 3d ed., McGraw-Hill Book Company, New York, 1960.

Crow, Lester D., and Alice Crow: *Education in the Secondary School,* American Book Company, New York, 1961.

Crow, Lester D., and Alice Crow: *Mental Hygiene for Teachers: A Book of Readings,* The Macmillan Company, New York, 1963.

Crow, Lester D., and Alice Crow: *Readings in Guidance,* David McKay Company, Inc., New York, 1962.

Grinder, R. E.: *Studies in Adolescence: A Book of Readings in Adolescent Psychology,* The Macmillan Company, New York, 1963.

Hutson, D. W.: *The Guidance Function in Education,* Appleton-Century-Crofts, Inc., New York, 1958.

Powell, M.: *The Psychology of Adolescence,* The Bobbs-Merrill Company, Inc., Indianapolis, 1963.

Schneiders, A. A.: *Personality Development and Adjustment in Adolescence,* The Bruce Publishing Company, Milwaukee, 1960.

Stoops, E. (ed.): *Guidance Services: Organization and Administration,* McGraw Hill Book Company, New York, 1959.

Strang, R.: *The Adolescent Views Himself: A Psychology of Adolescence,* McGraw-Hill Book Company, New York, 1957.

Williamson, E. G.: *Counseling Adolescents,* McGraw-Hill Book Company, New York, 1950.

Wittenberg, R. M.: *Adolescence and Discipline,* Association Press, New York, 1959.

# Chapter Sixteen

## Vocational Adjustment of Adolescents

If representative men and women who have been active in their respective professions, businesses, or industries for twenty years or more are asked how they happened to engage in their particular occupational activity, many of them report that they fell into the work quite by accident. They may have obtained their first job through the efforts of friends or because there was a need for workers at the time when they were seeking work. Some, of course, chose a certain occupation because of a real interest in it and started early to prepare for the vocation of their choice.

## Vocational and Occupational Problems

When occupational opportunities are plentiful, it is relatively easy for a person of average or more-than-average ability, with good habits of work, to find for himself, through the trial-and-error method, a field in which he can earn advancement and job satisfaction. However, as occupational qualifications become more technical and rigid, haphazard methods of vocational selection become ineffectual, costly, and time-wasting.

### Selection of a Vocation

We are fast becoming a nation of specialists. Specialization cannot be developed overnight, nor can any individual expect to become a specialist without an aptitude for the work. Furthermore, occupational history indicates that at any one time there is likely to be an oversupply of specialists in one field and a lack in another. This condition is often brought about by the fact that young people are influenced by success stories of adults in a particular field. As a result, a young person might hope to achieve a similar success in that field, regardless of personal fitness for the work or available opportunities in the field.

Furthermore, a temporary shortage of workers in one form or another of occupational activity may so excite community leaders that they bring to bear undue pressure upon young people to enter that field. Such leaders apparently are unaware of the fact that by the time the adolescents have finished their training, the need for that type of work may have lessened or that too many may have been encouraged to train themselves, with a resulting oversupply of trained workers in the field. Consequently, men and women have failed to earn vocational success because they were misfits in one field and were unable, because of financial responsibilities, to prepare for another field of work.

Parents often are at fault when their sons and daughters do not make wise vocational choices. It may be that the parent, in his youth, wanted to enter a certain field but was prevented from doing so by his parents' interests, by his own lack of ability, or by financial limitations. The parent now wishes to see his personal ambitions realized through his child and persuades or compels the young person to enter a field for which the latter is unsuited and in which he has little interest. Again, it may be that a certain profession or form of business is a family tradition and that the young person is expected to follow that tradition, regardless of a specific aptitude for another type of activity. Too many sons and daughters, as adults, harbor deep resentments because they are unhappy in the vocational work that was forced upon them by their parents or relatives.

During the past three decades, many students in junior high school have been required to make tentative vocational choices. Now we know that attention needs to be given to the factor of vocational maturity before a decision for a vocational choice is required of growing boys. They should be in an exploratory, not a decision making, stage of vocational development. Donald Super and his coworkers in Middletown, New York, discovered some interesting facts about vocational choice that point to the need of reassessing the time for making a vocational choice. Their conclusions follow:

Vocational maturity in the ninth grade, as assessed by our measures, was defined by the findings as behavior in preparation for vocational choice, as planning and looking ahead. The lack of significant intercorrelation among the Consistency, Crystallization, Independence of Work Experience, and Wisdom indices led to the conclusion that, in grade nine, vocational maturity is not characterizable as goal-attainment, as the having of consistent, realistic, preferences, nor as having begun to make a place for one's self in the world of work.[1]

Periods of occupational undersupply and oversupply fluctuate from time to time. Engineering, teaching, medicine, nursing, law, commercial

[1] Donald E. Super and P. L. Overstreet, *The Vocational Maturity of Ninth Grade Boys*, Bureau of Publications, Teachers College, Columbia University, New York, 1960, p. 146.

work, and the like, have had their ups and downs. At present, and for the next ten years, there appears to be a need for engineers, scientists, mathematicians, technicians, teachers, physicians, dentists, nurses, advertising workers, personnel workers, purchasing agents, artists, musicians, architects, lawyers, librarians, newspapermen, programmers, social workers, secretarial workers, salesmen, construction workers, and governmental workers.

Information received from the U.S. Department of Labor reveals some significant changes that have taken place in selected occupational groups between 1910 and 1963. The data presented in Table 36 are, on a percentage distribution basis, indicative of trends in occupations.

*Table 36.* Experienced Civilian Labor Force by Selected Occupation Groups, 1910, 1957, 1962, and 1963

| OCCUPATION GROUP | 1910* | 1957 | 1962 | 1963 |
|---|---|---|---|---|
| Professional, technical, and kindred workers.. | 4.7 | 9.7 | 11.5 | 11.9 |
| Managers, officials, and proprietors, except farm.............................. | 6.6 | 10.0 | 10.5 | 10.6 |
| Clerical and kindred workers.............. | 5.3 | 13.9 | 14.8 | 14.9 |
| Craftsmen, foremen, and kindred workers.... | 11.6 | 13.3 | 12.8 | 12.9 |
| Total.............................. | 28.2 | 46.9 | 49.6 | 50.3 |

* Data for 1910 are derived from decennial census results and cover the "economically active population." This refers to gainful workers 10 years old and over, whereas the data for later years refers to persons 14 years and over in the experienced civilian labor force (all employed and unemployed workers with previous work experience).

SOURCE: U.S. Department of Labor, Bureau of Labor Statistics, Division of Employment and Unemployment, February, 1964.

Many young people are very much disturbed over the present vocational situation. They are torn between selecting a vocation that appears to offer exceptional financial and promotional rewards and preparing themselves for a vocation that may be more nearly related to their interests, that ensures relative permanency, and in which demand is greater than available supply. For example, teaching on all levels is now and probably will continue to be an open field for the next twenty years at least. Hence many young people are being encouraged to enter this profession. Yet some twenty years ago opportunities in the teaching field were scarce.

It can be understood easily that youth's uncertainty regarding vocational planning is increased by the fact that it is difficult to determine with any degree of certainty what the occupational opportunities may be ten, or even five, years from now. Parents, interested friends, newspaper and magazine writers, radio speakers, and vocational specialists

*Table 97.* Percentage Distributions of the Reasons Given by Boys and Girls for Their Occupational Choices

| REASONS | JR. H. S. BOYS 1930 | JR. H. S. BOYS 1961 | SR. H. S. BOYS 1930 | SR. H. S. BOYS 1961 | JR. H. S. GIRLS 1930 | JR. H. S. GIRLS 1961 | SR. H. S. GIRLS 1930 | SR. H. S. GIRLS 1961 |
|---|---|---|---|---|---|---|---|---|
| A. Self-advantages: | | | | | | | | |
| 1. Financial rewards | 19.9 | 14.1 | 13.0 | 15.9 | 12.7 | 5.7 | 9.6 | 7.1 |
| 2. Possibilities for advancement | 6.3 | 0.7 | 8.0 | 2.6 | 3.6 | 0.3 | 8.0 | 1.9 |
| 3. Promising future of the industry | 3.2 | 3.2 | 6.1 | 4.9 | 1.3 | 0.8 | 0.3 | 2.1 |
| 4. Easy work | 3.0 | 1.0 | 0.8 | 1.7 | 3.2 | 0.9 | 0.7 | 0.9 |
| 5. Affords steady employment | 2.2 | 1.4 | 3.0 | 2.3 | 1.4 | 0.7 | 2.1 | 2.2 |
| 6. Field not crowded | 2.3 | 0.9 | 5.3 | 1.7 | 0.8 | 0.6 | 3.4 | 3.3 |
| 7. Others, as health, social status, opportunity for travel, ease of learning | 14.2 | 4.8 | 10.0 | 7.4 | 9.8 | 6.5 | 6.6 | 9.0 |
| Subtotal | 51.1 | 26.1 | 46.2 | 36.4 | 32.4 | 15.5 | 30.7 | 26.5 |
| B. Expressing like for, or interest in, the occupation (unanalyzed) | 31.6 | 19.5 | 35.3 | 19.3 | 41.5 | 28.2 | 46.2 | 21.2 |
| C. Expressing like for, or interest in, some aspect of the work, as, "I like mathematics," or "I am fond of little children" | 1.3 | 29.1 | 1.3 | 20.2 | 2.1 | 32.6 | 2.1 | 28.6 |
| D. To help my family | 0.1 | 0.4 | 0.0 | 0.0 | 1.1 | 0.6 | 0.6 | 0.0 |
| E. Influence of parents or other members of family, through advice, dictation, or example | 3.3 | 8.0 | 2.4 | 4.3 | 3.1 | 5.5 | 2.6 | 3.0 |
| F. Having some qualifications for the work (general and specific mentions of capacity and experience) | 6.4 | 5.1 | 8.4 | 9.8 | 10.8 | 4.6 | 8.0 | 4.1 |
| G. The occupation is socially serviceable | 2.7 | 6.0 | 2.3 | 2.8 | 3.1 | 7.6 | 3.9 | 9.3 |
| H. Mention of source of knowledge of the occupation, as, "Learned about it from reading" | 1.4 | 1.2 | 1.6 | 0.9 | 4.0 | 2.1 | 2.4 | 1.3 |
| I. Restrictions or obstacles forcing the choice | 0.1 | 0.6 | 0.5 | 0.9 | 0.5 | 0.1 | 1.6 | 1.4 |
| J. Affording outlet for, or challenge to, one's powers | 1.5 | 3.5 | 1.5 | 3.7 | 1.1 | 3.6 | 1.5 | 4.0 |
| K. Having the opportunity to enter the vocation | 0.4 | 0.4 | 0.5 | 2.1 | 0.4 | 0.1 | 0.5 | 0.5 |
| Total | 99.9 | 99.9 | 100.0 | 100.4 | 100.1 | 100.5 | 100.1 | 99.9 |

SOURCE: P. W. Hutson, "Vocational Choices, 1930 and 1961," *Vocational Guidance Quarterly*, p. 221, Summer, 1962.

441

are generous with their advice. Unfortunately, these groups do not always agree in their predictions concerning future vocational needs. Hence young people are often hindered by such advice, rather than helped, in making their decisions. They can be helped, however, by making use of the excellent source book *Occupational Outlook*.

Recently, P. W. Hutson studied the reasons given by boys and girls for their occupational choices at different grade levels and at different times—1930 and 1961. The results of his study are presented in Table 37.

## Training and Placement

Even when a young person is guided toward the making of a desirable vocational choice, he is still faced by many problems. Training opportunities are becoming more extensive and better organized than they have been in the past, but there are still obstacles in the way of a young person's receiving adequate training for one or another particular kind of work. The cost of training, geographical availability of training facilities, traditional prerequisites for continued study, and a lack of trained teachers in certain fields make difficult the achievement of an ideal program of vocational preparation. Many a potentially good worker in a particular field has been lost because of the lack of availability of adequate education.

There is a growing educational trend toward combining work experience with school study. The inclusion of on-the-job experience or of internship long has been an accepted aspect of training for professions such as medicine, law, teaching, and nursing. Cooperative education, first organized on the college level, has been introduced into high schools, especially in connection with commercial curriculums. Further, an increase in the number of jobs available to adolescents has motivated many high school students either to withdraw from school in favor of a full-time job or to take part-time work during out-of-school hours while they are continuing their school studies.

Although the value of part-time work that is unrelated to actual school study in the selection of and preparation for an occupation is rated low by the boys who participated in the Hutson study, an adolescent is helped thereby to gain certain desirable work attitudes that later may be helpful to him. Unfortunately, an adolescent trained in his specific field finds that under normal business conditions it is very difficult to secure a satisfactory job without experience. Hence he resorts to more or less reliable newspaper advertisements, to commercial placement agencies, to the assistance of his friends, or to personal application without introduction, in his search for employment.

Fortunate is the young aspirant for a job whose school is equipped to place its graduates in desirable positions on the basis of training and proficiency. During a period of worker shortage, however, there is danger that a young person may disregard the placement efforts of his school and accept a job for the sake of financial reward rather than permanency of position in a stable and reputable organization.

## Job Relationships

The neophyte in the occupational world has many adjustments to make on the job. He must learn to adjust to his employers and supervisors, to his fellow workers, and to the requirements and conditions of the job itself. He must be able to distinguish between his just rights and his fair responsibilities as a worker. These adjustments are not always made easily, since during his school life he was both more dependent and more independent than he is on the job.

At school his teachers were accustomed to rate his achievement in terms of his ability, and usually they were willing to help him with his difficulties and to excuse his failings if he appeared to be sincere in his efforts to learn. On the job he sinks or swims as a result of his own ability and willingness to do efficient work. He cannot lean upon someone else for assistance. If his work is not acceptable, his supervisors, who cannot afford to spend too much time and effort upon his retraining, are likely to replace him by a more efficient worker.

On the other hand, the young worker is introduced to a kind of personal freedom and independence that he did not experience in his school life. He is relatively on his own. He is given work to do and is usually allowed freedom in doing it, provided the results are satisfactory. His afterwork hours are his own to do with as he pleases. There is no school assignment to interfere with his home or social activities. This apparent increase in personal freedom often tempts young people to leave school and seek employment before they have finished their education, especially when jobs are plentiful.

A young worker is likely to have difficulties in his relations with older and more experienced fellow workers. At school he had learned to adjust to his teachers and to fellow students of about his own age and school status. On the job he must face the possible condescension and "bossiness" of older workers. He may stimulate jealousies among the workers, especially if he is enthusiastic and competent. He is introduced to the ambitious employee, the dissatisfied worker, or the shirker. He may be drawn into employee gossip, or he may not choose his worker associates carefully and thus may become a member of the wrong crowd.

In his relations with his employer or his supervisor he may not be able to distinguish between just and fair work requirements and possible exploitation. His employer may be too lax or too rigid. If the worker is a girl, she is in danger of misinterpreting the friendliness of her employer or her supervisor, or may allow herself to be drawn into an undesirable relationship with a male employer or employee. There is a question in the mind of a young worker concerning the extent to which his or her social life should be interrelated with the work life.

## Vocational Problems Experienced by Adolescents

The vocational life of a teen-age boy or girl is fraught with problems of adjustment. Young people early become aware of these problems and seek advice and guidance. The following questions indicate the extent to which many adolescents are concerned about their work life and the kind of problems that they are already facing or that they are anticipating.

1. How can a boy or girl overcome family objections in choosing a career?

2. How can school advisers help boys and girls make their vocational choices?

3. What should influence one's selection of a career—prestige, power, or money?

4. How can a boy or girl find out whether or not he or she possesses the right characteristics for a certain kind of work?

5. What can I do if my employer discovers that I do not know as much about my work as he thinks I do?

6. Should a fellow accept a job that is not mentally stimulating?

7. Is it good to apply to agencies for positions? If so, what agencies are reliable?

8. How can one be helped to apply for a job?

9. How can one overcome a feeling of inferiority when meeting an employer for an interview?

10. How can one adjust oneself to a job quickly?

11. Do clothes play a large part in business success?

12. How can a girl tactfully decline invitations made by a man employer who is married?

13. Why should a supervisor be so anxious to please his boss that he makes the rest of the employees under him nervous?

14. How can a boy or girl be helped to make a good job adjustment?

15. Should young workers be treated the same as adults or should they be separated and treated as children?

16. What should be the attitude of an employee toward his employer?

17. How can an employee be pleasant when the boss is always complaining about something?

18. How can jealousy among employees be overcome?

**19.** What should be the attitude of a young worker toward his fellow workers?

**20.** How do labor unions help young workers?

These questions indicate the extent to which the experiences of their older friends and relatives and their own part-time employment influence the thinking of young people. They become very much concerned about the many possible problems for which they may need to find solutions as they attempt to realize their vocational ambitions.

No one can predict ahead of time how successful or contented a worker may be in any chosen field. Usually, if there is brought to the work a sincere interest in it, as well as adequate training for it, the probability of job satisfaction is much greater than is possible if the worker is in a field that is not of his own choosing and for which he has not received sufficient or thorough preparation.

In some instances, job inadequacy is recognized early enough so that definite means can be employed by the individuals concerned for the betterment of their vocational status. However, many persons do not completely recognize the fact that they are misfits until it is almost too late to do much about the matter.

No one's vocational problem is exactly like that of another. Hence no more can be done in the field of vocational guidance than to make an honest effort to help remedy some of the most commonly observed causes of vocational maladjustment. Wider opportunities for gaining occupational information, more extensive and better-equipped training facilities, and improved working conditions are goals worthy of attainment. Yet the unpredictable human factor cannot be discounted entirely but must be dealt with as objectively and intelligently as possible so that work experiences may be placed upon a stable foundation of unemotionalized service to society with a minimum of problem adjustment.

## Suggestions for Improving Vocational Life

Vocational choice and preparation, job placement, and job satisfaction combine into a complex life pattern, each phase of which must be broken down and analyzed in detail if young people are to achieve success in their lifework. Each step of the way must be considered carefully as a young person in his early teens is started toward adult job adjustment.

Much can be done in this field. Hence specific and detailed suggestions are presented here for the use of parents and advisers as they attempt the vocational guidance of adolescents. Many of the questions asked by young people are treated in detail, since vocational success or lack of success may have its roots in a decision or an overt response which at the time seemed of little significance.

Parents and employers can well check their own attitudes toward young people's vocational problems as they consider the suggestions presented below under the following headings:

1. Choosing a career
2. Training for a job
3. Helping an adolescent obtain a job
4. Adjustment on the job

### Choosing a Career

The fact that a young person may believe that his parents are interfering unduly with his vocational interests may constitute a serious problem of vocational adjustment for that person. It is true that most young people go through phases of occupational interest. Beginning in early childhood, a boy may in turn want to be a candy-shop owner, a fireman, a policeman, a baseball pitcher, a prize fighter, a big banker, a politician, a physician, or any other of a number of successful business, professional, or sports leaders. A girl at various stages of her childhood and adolescent development may insist that she is going to be a school teacher, a nurse, an actress, a model, a writer, a missionary, a nun, or a diplomat. As the boy or girl reads about or meets a successful member of any one of these vocations, his youthful tendency toward hero worship is stimulated and he sees himself winning the fame and honor that are being earned by his current idol.

## Extent of Parental Influence

Youthful enthusiasms are understandable, and most parents do not take them too seriously. Intelligent parents are able to recognize any special type of vocational interest that seems to persist in the young person. If they believe that he shows ability for that particular field, as well as interest in it, they encourage him toward definite preparation for it. However, parents must be able to distinguish between the temporary interests of their children and any deep-seated interest born of an incipient aptitude for the vocation.

Every parent probably has high hopes for the future success of his children. These hopes must have a practical basis of good common sense. No parent should consider a young person's future solely in terms of his own interests and ambitions. Nor should a parent for purely selfish reasons discourage a young person from following a reasonable vocational ambition. Rarely, however, does a parent recognize the selfishness of his reasons for denying to his child a desired freedom of vocational choice. Many a parent believes himself to be influenced in his judgment by praiseworthy and logical motives.

A parent should encourage his child in a vocation for which the parent at one time had wanted to prepare himself *only* if parent and child both recognize the fact that the latter gives evidence of ability for, and interest in, that field. An educator was heard to remark that he believes a study should be made of the number of lives that have been ruined by too much parental domination of young people's vocational choice.

The parent who attempts to dominate his child's vocational life is only a little worse than the parent who will assume no responsibility whatever for his son's or daughter's choice of lifework. A man or woman is failing in his responsibilities as a parent if he gives no advice or shows no interest in his child's future, is unwilling to make any personal sacrifice so that his child may prepare for a desirable field, or interferes with his child's education by forcing the young person to give up his studies and go to work in a dead-end job, except in a serious financial emergency.

Adolescent career planning should be a cooperative venture on the part of both parent and child and should include the utilization of all available sources of vocational information. Some excellent information may be obtained in the following ways, each of which will be discussed briefly:

1. Reading of books and pamphlets dealing with occupational opportunities and job analyses

2. Visits to business, industrial, and professional organizations

3. Investigation of training programs offered by colleges and specialized schools

4. Attendance at vocational conferences

5. Consultation with school counselors

Modern, well-equipped public libraries are likely to have available for the reader's use many good books dealing with vocational material. In many communities civic, business, and industrial leaders welcome inquiries about their organizations from interested young people and their parents. Rotary, Kiwanis, Lions, and Exchange clubs often conduct planned programs presenting occupational needs and offerings for the benefit of citizens. Other organizations such as the Knights of Columbus and the Ys, parent-teacher associations, and business and professional clubs usually are very helpful.

Detailed information concerning opportunities for education after high school is presented in the publications of the American Council on Education, the U.S. Department of Labor, and the U.S. Office of Education. The yearly catalogues of colleges also are helpful. After the parents and the adolescent, as a result of reference reading, have narrowed their selection to two or three possible choices, a visit to each of the selected colleges usually is wise. Through a tour of the campus and consultation with appropriate members of the faculty, the visitors can discover much about the suitability of the institution's offerings in terms of their interest. In addition, by meeting and talking with the potential candidate and his parents, the college authorities can discover to what extent the young person can be expected to profit from attendance at the college.

Many private and community-controlled organizations are attempting to help young people, parents, and school advisers in teen-age career planning. Some of these groups conduct periodic conference programs at which leaders in the field discuss with interested adolescents and adults the practical problems connected with vocational planning and adjustment. Assistance also can be obtained from trained high school counselors who, with the aid of a well-equipped library, are in a position to offer excellent vocational and educational advice.

Since the occupational activities of men, and in the modern world, of women as well, are so important in the complete pattern of an individual's entire adult life, planning and preparation for this phase of living should not be hasty or influenced by such factors as temporary expediency or immediate satisfaction. A long-range program should be mapped out cooperatively by parent and child and should include the following considerations:

1. Demonstrated abilities and interests
2. Occupational opportunities in the field of interest, not only at the present but also in the future
3. The amount and kind of training needed
4. The schools that are best equipped for this training and that are most accessible

## Guidance Functions of School Personnel

In every school there can be found individual teachers whose interest in all or some of their pupils impels them to become very much concerned about the vocational plans of their young people. Consequently, such teachers are often able to give excellent advice informally to individual pupils. However, if every boy and girl is to receive adequate vocational guidance, every school should plan a practical and inclusive program of guidance for all pupils. There are many vehicles available for the offering of such assistance to young people.

Fortunately, trained and experienced leaders in the field have organized in book form some of the programs and techniques that they have found through experience to be practical and successful. The suggestions to be found in such writings usually can be adapted to the needs of particular schools and are worthy of study and application.

Although vocational guidance is generally considered to be the responsibility of secondary schools and schools of higher learning, certain groundwork can be done on the elementary school level. The first six years of a child's school life are devoted primarily to the mastery of certain simple and fundamental skills and information and to the development of desirable appreciations and civic attitudes. However, included in the child's program of work and play are many experiences that offer a background of occupational awareness, which at this level is not definitely aimed at vocational guidance but which will be helpful to him as he gives serious thought on the secondary school level to his vocational planning.

Moreover, well-kept cumulative records of the progress of elementary school pupils and of any special interests or abilities will be of great value later. Elementary school advisers should be constantly on the alert to recognize those vocational interests of their young pupils that seem to show some degree of permanency. These advisers should also take into consideration the mental and temperamental characteristics of the children. Upon the basis of these factors elementary school graduates can be steered toward entrance into the high school that is best suited to meet their vocational needs and interests. For the child who does not yet give evidence of any specific aptitude a general high school course is recommended.

The vocational guidance service beyond the elementary school level should be broad in its scope but so specific in application as to serve every student in terms of his needs and interests. An adequate guidance program provides up-to-the-minute vocational information, helps individual students evaluate their interests and potentialities, accumulates pertinent data concerning each student, offers trained counseling service, arranges for appropriate vocational preparation, maintains a full- or part-time placement service, and attempts to follow up former students on the job to help in their job adjustments. In addition, the guidance staff engages in continued research concerning job opportunities, improved training, and similar areas of vocational interest.

A well-organized, fully staffed, and adequately implemented guidance program is expensive and, consequently, not always achievable. To the extent that the budget permits, every young person should be helped, through the use of testing programs, appropriate reading, radio, television, and motion-picture presentations, visits to business and industrial organizations, a course in occupational information, and group and individual conferences, to attain an intelligent understanding of his own specific strengths and weaknesses, his vocational interests, the fields in which he may be expected to make the best adjustment, and the advancement possibilities in that field.

## Career Planning for Girls

At one or another stage of adolescence most girls dream about a future career. The connotation of the term *career* differs with adolescent appreciation of life values. It is sometimes used to indicate that a girl should prepare herself for a gainful occupation in which she will engage until she marries. It may imply that a girl is definitely planning to devote the remainder of her life to the achieving of success in a given occupational field. Advisers of girls needs to be very tactful as they help their students plan for the future.

Every girl should be encouraged to prepare herself for the eventual career of wifehood and motherhood, no matter how she plans for the time that will intervene between her graduation and probable marriage. To that end, every girl should receive some training in home care, home nursing, care of children, home decoration and furnishing, planning and care of clothes, and household budgeting. No preparation for a career should be allowed to interfere with the training to be gained in courses that prepare a girl for the career of homemaking.

Besides the training in the care of the home, it is desirable that every girl receive some vocational training; and that, for a shorter or longer period in her late adolescence and early adulthood, she receive some experience in a gainful occupation. There are several reasons for this.

The girl may not marry so soon as she expects to, and may need to support herself during the interim. Also it is probable that a young woman who has had experience as a worker will be able to manage her household in a more businesslike way than can the girl who has had no such experience. Earning and spending her own money helps the girl better to appreciate the value of money; she is likely to budget her household expenses with a minimum of extravagance.

The husband may die or become incapacitated for work, and the wife may be forced to become the breadwinner of the family. If she has a vocation for which she has been trained and in which she has worked previous to her marriage, she probably will find it relatively easy to obtain gainful employment. An incapacitated father and an untrained mother can do little for their children.

As the years pass, the husband may become very much engrossed in his own business or profession and the adolescent children may turn to interests outside the home. Many a middle-aged wife and mother who is and has been a good home manager finds herself with a great deal of free time on her hands and no satisfactory means of filling this time. Some women turn to philanthropic activities, but these do not always satisfy. A bored woman may become an irritable member of the household. However, if she can resume the place that she once had in the business or professional world, she adds another interest, not only to her own life but also to the lives of the other members of her family, provided that the outside work does not interfere too much with her home responsibilities.

In a time of national worker shortage, such as is experienced during a war, married women who have been trained in certain specific fields are of incalculable value.

If becoming a career woman is interpreted as meaning that a woman will devote her life to a field of work in which she has exceptional power of achievement, the question of whether or not she should marry cannot be answered by a simple "yes" or "no." Usually a woman who can earn fame for herself in a given field such as writing, business, law, teaching, nursing, social service, or scientific research has inherent qualities that should be passed on to another generation, and possesses also the essence of fine comradeship to share with a husband. It would seem unfortunate that a woman who has so much to give should be denied the satisfactions that can come only through the experiencing of family life.

It is possible for a woman to continue her career and also to make an adequate adjustment to wifehood and motherhood. If the woman brings to her home relationships the same intelligent management that she exercises in her out-of-the-home work, she can do both and at the same time enjoy the love and respect of her family. There are times when the career woman will need to subordinate her career to the needs of the home. Her husband and children should not be sacrificed for her outside interests.

## Relationship between Vocational Interest and Job Success

Rarely does a person earn success in a vocation that has been forced upon him, although in an emergency an able person may find it possible to make a satisfactory adjustment in a field of work that is very far removed from his interest. During the depression of the 1930s, many men and women who were forced out of their chosen vocations were able to make an excellent temporary adjustment to types of work which, under ordinary circumstances, would have been most unsatisfying to them. The majority of these persons returned to their accustomed vocations as soon as this was possible. A few found opportunities for advancement in the new field and remained in it. Modern technology and automation is causing worker displacement. These displaced workers need to be willing to accept retraining for new, highly technical jobs, although the interest factor is not easy to maintain.

Other things being equal, a person achieves his greatest job satisfaction and job success in that field for which he is mentally and temperamentally fitted and for which he has received adequate training. It may happen that an unusually able person can achieve success in more than one field. He may start in one of these and, for one reason or another, shift to the other with little, if any, diminution of successful achievement. Usually this is not true for less able individuals.

A person who exhibits more than one interest may be encouraged to use one of these as his vocational interest and the other as an avocational interest or hobby. Later, the avocation may become the prime interest of the individual or he may gain a definite reputation in his avocational field, so that the avocation becomes the vocation.

### Training for a Job

Job success includes many complex elements. The personal qualities of the worker, the conditions under which he works, and the effectiveness of worker supervision represent significant factors of worker competence and contentment. Of primary importance, however, is the worker's trained ability to perform adequately whatever constitutes job requirements.

## Amount and Kind of Training Needed by the Young Worker

A person should receive the best training possible for the work in which he is planning to engage. This statement needs to be explained in order to make its meaning clear. There is a difference of opinion among vocational experts about which of the two following procedures is a better course to follow: (1) obtain a thorough training for *entrance* into the field, so that minimal job requirements can be met adequately, and later the finer details of the work or the more complicated procedures be mastered by the worker in the form of apprentice training, or (2) complete the entire training before the actual experience begins, so that the worker may be a master workman from the start.

As a matter of fact, these two theories are really one, with different emphases. The extent of preparatory training completed before a young person enters into the activity itself depends upon the ultimate ambition of the worker, his financial ability to continue his training beyond a certain point, or the needs of the work world.

To say that a young medical student should be allowed to practice medicine before he has mastered all the needed training in materia medica would be allowing him indirectly to commit professional suicide. After he has mastered certain fundamental knowledges and skills, he can be allowed to practice these under guidance as a kind of medical apprentice. If, after he has become a licensed physician, he wishes to specialize in any one field of medicine or surgery, this specialized study could very well—and probably should—come after he has had some experience as a general practitioner in medicine.

Again, a young person majors in commercial work in high school and is prepared for secretarial work or bookkeeping. Which is better—to continue on the college level his study of personnel management, office management, or accountancy, or to practice the skills that he has mastered and, concurrently or later, continue his studies toward higher levels of job requirements? No definite policy can be set down. However, if the boy or girl continues his education before he has had experience as a worker, he needs some practice on a part-time or an apprentice basis in order to obtain a complete picture of job requirements.

At present, educational and occupational leaders are cooperating with one another in a manner that in the past was almost unknown. School counselors are making a conscientious attempt to analyze job requirements and, through individual and group conferences with employers, to familiarize themselves in a practical way with the employer point of view. Hence, training is geared to prepare the trainees for intelligent workmanship when they enter the specific field for which they have been trained.

Through educator-employer cooperation, employers are learning more about the capacities and limitations of young workers and are enabled to evaluate more adequately performance possibilities of job applicants and to provide further training whenever it seems desirable. Executives of many large organizations consider training on the job so important that they maintain their own training classes and allow time from the regular workday for attendance at these classes.

The purpose of this training is twofold: (1) improvement of the techniques of the job in which the worker is at present engaged and (2) advanced training for outstanding workers, aimed at promotion in the organization. For example, a nationally known insurance company gives a great amount of attention to the wise selection of workers and their subsequent success on the job. Once a worker is hired, he is rarely discharged unless he gives evidence of complete inability to adjust to any one of the many departments of the organization. If the worker shows dislike of the particular job for which he was hired or unsatisfactory performance in it, he is given tryouts and specific training for other forms of work within the organization until that one is found in which the young person is best able to make an adjustment.

Some employers go a step further in this matter of advanced training for their employees. It is not uncommon for an unusually promising worker to be encouraged by his employer (even to the giving of financial aid) temporarily to discontinue his work with the organization in order to prepare himself for a position of greater responsibility in the same organization upon the completion of his advanced study.

It is extremely important that a young person be discouraged from entering a field for which he is only partially trained. Whatever his beginning responsibilities in a particular vocation may be, the candidate for that work should be thoroughly trained to meet those responsibilities.

One of the tragedies of worker shortage in industry is the fact that many young people are encouraged to leave school and undertake work for which they are in the process of being trained. As a consequence, employers complain bitterly about the inefficiency of their workers, yet do not dare to discharge these untrained young people lest there be no others available. Hence these job holders pile up for themselves much unsatisfactory work experience. When there is a decrease in the demand for workers, they are in the anomalous position of having experience (which usually is desirable) but insufficient training. They must compete with inexperienced but thoroughly trained young people. It is too early to prophesy which the employer in the future will stress—experience with limited training or adequate training with little or no experience.

## Specialized Training versus Liberal Education

In the past, training for work experience in such fields as art, music, commercial work, and mechanics was received for the most part either by way of private tutors, in specialized schools, or through apprenticeship under the supervision of master workers. There still are such agencies; many do an excellent job of intensive training. However, no matter what the field of specialization may be, the trainee needs more than skill competence. All forms of work are social in nature, in that the worker must associate with other persons. These include workers like himself, persons for whom the work is being done, and employers or supervisors whose function it is to evaluate critically both the work and the worker. Moreover, a worker does not work at his job for twenty-four hours of the day. Hence he needs training for living a rich and full life during his nonworking hours.

Recognizing the need for more than specialized training, many colleges and other schools of higher learning are including specialized training in their broad program of education. Hence, in one or another college of excellent standing, opportunities are available for specific training in music, art, teaching, journalism, home economics, interior decorating, accountancy, merchandising, mechanics, and the like. In these colleges, as the student pursues his specialized training, he may also gain cultural education through such subjects as philosophy, the languages, literature, social science, psychology, pure science, and mathematics. At one and the same time he is being educated to be a worker and to appreciate fundamental life values.

The modern tendency is to educate along broad, as well as special, lines. Therefore, whenever it is geographically and economically possible to do so, parents and advisers should encourage young people to continue their specialized training in schools or colleges that offer broad cultural education. Of course the young person must be assured of receiving as intensive training in his specialization in a school of this kind as he would in a specialized school. Unfortunately, since this movement is relatively new, some colleges are not yet prepared to offer as exhaustive specialized training as can be obtained in the old and thorough specialized schools. This is not an argument for a return to narrow specialization, but it is a plea for the improvement of course offerings and teaching personnel in the colleges.

### Helping an Adolescent Obtain a Job

The kind of job in which an adolescent starts his occupational life is very important. Here he will need to acquire a new set of attitudes and behavior patterns in order to meet the demands of a new situation. His whole work life may be influenced by the stimulations to which he is exposed in his first job. It is here that he first learns about worker responsibility and rights, employer-employee relations, and employee-employee relations.

If an adolescent's experiences in his first job are wholesome and satisfying, he is likely to develop desirable worker attitudes. If in his first job he is allowed to develop habits of carelessness, if the employer is too easy or too rigid, or if the morale among the workers is undesirable, the young entrant into work life, like the young entrant into school life, gets off to a bad start and may have difficulty later in making a wholesome adjustment to any type of job situation.

## Job Information

It is imperative that parents and advisers give careful consideration to a young person's first job placement and that they do all that they can to help him secure employment with a reputable employer. If this is done, the adolescent is given an opportunity to do work that lies within the limits of his capacity and training among workers who give evidence of wholesome worker morale. Too many times the first job is looked upon as an unimportant steppingstone to better things. What is overlooked is the fact that the young worker is very suggestible at this time and can be influenced by his work environment more easily than will be possible later.

The usual avenues for gaining information about job vacancies include:

1. Friends and acquaintances
2. Newspaper advertisements
3. Magazines and occupational periodicals
4. Commercial employment agencies
5. Government employment agencies
6. School employment agencies
7. Civil service and other examination techniques
8. Random shopping around

*Friends and Acquaintances.* One of the most commonly used methods of job placement is that of seeking the assistance of relatives, friends, or acquaintances. A man or a woman known to the family has a position in which he is earning success, or he himself is an employer of young people. Hence he appears to be an excellent medium for helping the adolescent obtain his first job. One advantage of using this technique is that the parent usually can be assured that working conditions in this organization will be desirable.

However, this method of obtaining job placement has several possible disadvantages. If the prospective employer is a relative or a friend of the young worker, the latter's employment may stimulate an attitude of antagonism toward him among the other workers. He may be regarded by them as the "boss's pet" or, still worse, as an agent placed among them in order to spy upon them. This attitude is intensified if the young person received the position in preference to another applicant, possibly better fitted for the work but not personally known to the employer. Many businessmen for this reason refuse to employ close friends or members of their own families. The best that they will do is to refer such a person to the organization of a business associate, where the personal element is not obvious.

Often, especially in times of worker shortage, an employer requests his employees to inform their friends of vacancies on the staff. The employer philosophy is that satisfactory workers are likely to have friends who would possess desirable personality and worker attitudes. For a qualified young person this is an excellent approach to a job. If his friend is a capable and well-liked member of the organization, the new employee's early job adjustments will be made easy for him. Many employees who are asked to help in the filling of vacancies refer the request to their former school and thus are assured of as careful job placement as that which they received.

If the situation is merely that of a friend's or a relative's attempting to help out an adolescent without sufficient knowledge of the young person's attitudes or job qualifications, the results may be unsatisfactory. The fact that one person has earned success in a given type of work or in a particular organization is no guarantee that another person will be equally satisfactory or satisfied.

A young person rarely should start his work life in the employ of a friend or relative. He should seek employment in an organization in which a friend or relative works only if he is thoroughly qualified to meet the responsibilities of the job for which he is applying. In general, an appeal for help in job placement to those who are near to the family should be the last rather than the first approach to be used.

*Newspaper Advertisements.* Reputable newspapers are accustomed to investigate help-wanted advertisements. Many firms are well-known organizations, and there need be no doubt of their honesty and sincerity. The young applicant will probably be interviewed by a member of the firm's personnel department. The only concern here will be whether or not the applicant is qualified for the vacant position. It would be in order for the adolescent in such instances to answer the advertisement unaccompanied by an adult.

If, however, the advertisement has the appearance of a "blind ad," if the advertiser is an individual rather than a well-known organization, or if the nature of the work is not definitely stated, an adult of experience should investigate the reliability of the advertisement before a young person is allowed to apply for the job. Under no circumstances should an adolescent go for an interview in this type of opening unaccompanied by an adult. Sometimes young people feel that to take a relative with them when they are applying for work may militate against their chances of obtaining the position. This is not true. A reputable businessman, more often than not, prefers to employ a young person whose parents or advisers are concerned about the kind of place in which he or she will work. This applies especially to girls but holds also for young boys.

*Magazines and Occupational Periodicals.* Advertisements that appear in the better journals usually are authentic. Many organizations of national reputation advertise in trade journals. Such firms can offer ambitious, well-qualified young people excellent opportunities for success and advancement. Parents need have no fears concerning the advisability of their sons' or daughters' responding to such advertisements. However, if the advertiser is not known to the parents, the procedures suggested above should be followed.

*Commercial Employment Agencies.* There are some well-known commercial employment agencies that have a reputation for intelligent and honest placement. Others are very undesirable. These agencies are business concerns and rightly expect to receive payment for services rendered. They are active in bringing the individual and the job together. For this they receive a flat bonus or a percentage of his earnings.

Reputable agencies want satisfied clients—both employer and employee. They make certain that the vacancy is desirable and that the applicant meets the qualifications set for the opening. This is particularly true of agencies that deal with placement in professional fields such as teaching and chemistry or other technical work.

Less reputable agencies place the emphasis upon turnover of business. Hence they may not investigate employers or they may send to them applicants who do not have the proper qualifications for the positions. Moreover, in times of worker shortage they are likely to use little discretion in placing young people; and in time of worker oversupply their attitude toward possible applicants is often discourteous and disheartening.

*Government Employment Agencies.* Government employment agencies operate on a nonfee basis and are sincere in bringing work opportunities and workers together. They are often understaffed, with a consequent inability to make as careful placements as they would like. These agencies have the opportunity of obtaining long-range and long-view knowledge of work opportunities and needs. If their personnel could be increased to the point at which they would have enough well-trained placement counselors available to make a thorough analysis of job requirements and worker qualifications, a fine job of placement could be done by them.

*School Employment Agencies.* The use of school employment agencies has one distinct advantage. The school knows its students. In making placements it can give careful attention to the individual's abilities and extent of training.

Sometimes employers are a little afraid to make use of a school placement service until the school gains a reputation for thorough training and intelligent placement. However, there are employers who, as a result of previous experience with graduates of a particular school, consult that school first for their employees. A very fine relationship is further established and strengthened as the school's vocational counselor follows up the performance of his graduates on the job.

Very often school counselors consult with the parents when the latter sign the employment certificate of their son or daughter. In this way the parent receives firsthand information from the school concerning the kind of work for which his child is fitted and the kind of firm to which he is being sent. Often the parent is encouraged to accompany the young person for his first interview, in spite of the fact that a school counselor does not send a young person to a job vacancy that he himself has not first investigated.

Perhaps the most satisfactory function of school employment agencies might be that of cooperation with the state employment service. Successful job placement rests in good part upon two factors—extensive information concerning job opportunities and intensive knowledge of the skill and personal qualifications of the applicants.

This is where the government placement agencies and the schools that train the potential workers, by pooling their resources, could help one another. A suggestion for an effective means of achieving this cooperation is to have associated with each school a member of the state employment service, who would bring to the school his knowledge of available vacancies and receive from the school advisers intimate and detailed information concerning available and qualified candidates. In this way the job and the potential worker could be brought together with a minimum of record keeping and overlapping of effort.

*Civil Service and Other Examination Techniques.* Doctors, lawyers, teachers in many communities, nurses, all civil service employees, and the like must pass qualifying examinations of one kind or another before they are eligible to engage in their chosen work. Many large business houses employ a similar technique, although in a less rigid and more informal way.

If the examination techniques now in use could be modified in such a way that attitudes and personality qualities could be evaluated for all candidates who are qualified to enter competition, better placement of young people in jobs for which they are suited might be brought about. As leaders in the field come to recognize the importance of the more subtle elements of job efficiency, examination techniques will be adjusted in such a way that those candidates for placement who are best fitted in both personality and demonstrated skill will be the first to be considered for job placement.

When appointment to a particular job is based upon an individual's place on a list that has been promulgated as a result of an examination open to all qualified candidates, a beginner in a desired field is assured of the fact that his appointment is not based upon personal prejudice of any kind. His likelihood of early job placement will be in direct relationship to his demonstrated possession of certain qualities rather than on such factors as favoritism and prejudices. Moreover, if the placement carries with it a definite salary schedule, regular salary increments, at least partial tenure, and advancement through further examination, he is able to begin his employment relieved of those tensions which are likely to accompany placement in jobs in which there is the possibility of insecurity based on factors outside the proficiency of his work.

## Job Application

The technique of applying for a job has become much more formalized and follows a much more regular routine than formerly was the practice. In the past the procedure was somewhat as follows: The young applicant learned about a job vacancy in one of several ways. He then presented himself at a specified place, at a definite time, with or without a letter of introduction, and was interviewed by the prospective employer. The interview usually was informal and followed whatever pattern a particular employer considered to be the most successful for obtaining desirable workers.

In many organizations the above technique is still used, but there is an increasing tendency to supplement the interview by other, more objective methods of discovering the qualifications of the applicant. Assuming that entrance into a given field is not by way of a formal examination system, the following practices are common to many organizations:

1. Letter of application.
2. The filling in of formal application blanks, questionnaires, or interest blanks
3. The presentation of substantiating data concerning kind and extent of training
4. Letters of recommendation or formal recommendation blanks
5. Personal interview
6. Practical demonstration of skill or knowledge

Parents and advisers should be thoroughly acquainted with these techniques.

*Letter of Application.* Most prospective employers prefer that the letter of application be written in longhand rather than typewritten. They seem to believe that they can gain certain information about the applicant from his style of handwriting and from the composition and general arrangement of the letter. This does not imply that employers believe that a character analysis can be obtained from handwriting. However, a letter written in longhand is more likely to represent the candidate's own efforts than might a typewritten letter.

The personal information presented in this letter should be accurate and should be stated as briefly as is consistent with the inclusion of all necessary data.[2] The reader should find in the letter adequate coverage of the following matters:

1. Source of the applicant's knowledge of the vacancy.
2. Address, sex, and age of the applicant.
3. Reasons for the writer's application.
4. Education and specific training qualifications.
5. Work experiences, if any. (This might well include any part-time work or school activity related to the kind of work being sought.)
6. A request for an interview or for information concerning the next step to be taken by the applicant.

The letter should be neatly and carefully written and free from blots, erasures, striking out of letters and words, and the like. Margins should be even and punctuation correct. Unimportant information or comments should be avoided, as well as undue emphasis upon any exceptional achievements of the candidate. The letter should be neither apologetic nor humble in tone.

A young person writing his first letter of application should ask his parents or his adviser to edit it. However, the letter should be the young person's own composition and should not be written for him by an adult. An alert employer or personnel worker can usually recognize the extent to which a young person has been aided in the writing of a letter. Even though this fact is not immediately recognized by the employer, a letter written by an adult may be so well phrased that too much will be expected of the supposed young writer.

It is unwise to claim abilities that one does not possess. The teacher who coaches his students for a standardized test, and the parent or adviser who writes a letter for a young job applicant will not always be present to do the thinking for that young person if the latter is given certain responsibilities on the basis of his performance on the test or in the letter of application. Employer disillusionment and worker discouragement are likely to follow any dishonesty in job application.

*The Filling in of Application Blanks.* In many ways filling in application blanks is simpler for the applicant than writing a letter of application. Some companies require the letter of application to be followed by the filling in of blanks by candidates whose letters seem to warrant further consideration. Other organizations invite young people to send for or to call personally for the application blank and to enter on it all pertinent information.

Young people should be discouraged from presenting any information that is not entirely correct. Age should not be falsified. In a time of

---

[2] For examples of letters, see Robert Calvert, Jr., and John E. Steele, *Planning Your Career*, McGraw-Hill Book Company, New York, 1963, pp. 51–56.

extreme worker shortage some employers tend to be careless in this matter unless they are called to account for disregard of state law. Since employment certificates and social security cards are required for placement on a job, any attempt to give incorrect information on an application blank in order to increase one's eligibility for a job may be checked and cause embarrassment.

Personal questions such as those which deal with nationality, race, or religious affiliations are forbidden by law in some states. However, in those states where this information can be called for, answers should be given honestly, even though this may mean that the applicant is thereby refused employment. The truth will become known eventually and may result in extremely unpleasant experiences.

If an interest blank or similar questionnaire is administered, the young applicant's responses should be made in terms of his actual attitudes and interests, rather than in terms of what he thinks he should say. He may have a mistaken idea concerning what is expected of him and so may say the wrong thing, or he may convey an impression of himself as an individual that will not be substantiated by his later behavior if he obtains the position.

Briefly, parents and advisers should make certain that young people give honest and accurate answers to all questions addressed to them. Of course young people should-be taught to be honest and sincere in all their relations with other people. Honesty in job seeking is emphasized here because of the number of questions relative to this point that are constantly asked by young job seekers.

*The Presentation of Substantiating Data.* Little need be said about the presentation of substantiating data. An increasing number of employers send directly to the school concerned for transcripts of the applicant's school record, including age, date of graduation or of leaving the school, rank in class, subject-matter strengths and weaknesses, personal characteristics, and interests. This is a desirable procedure.

The information presented by the applicant usually agrees with authoritative records. Occasionally there is evidence that a young applicant has not presented accurate data. In the matter of application for positions of trust and confidence with the government, intensive follow-up and investigation of all records, as well as a check on personality characteristics, are made by government investigators.

*Letters of Recommendation and Recommendation Blanks.* Young people often find it difficult to recognize the relative worthlessness of a letter of recommendation that they have solicited from a friend and have then presented personally to a prospective employer. They need to be educated toward an understanding of the purpose and value of letters of recommendation.

If a young person is asked to present such letters, he will, of course, solicit them from persons who, he has reason to believe, think well of him and will write flattering letters about him. The writer of such a letter is thereby confronted with the problem of giving a fair estimate of the applicant and at the same time of helping him obtain the job.

To be of value, letters of recommendation should be sent directly to the prospective employer and should be honest in statement. To suppress information that would give indication of an applicant's unsuitability for a job or to overemphasize the young person's desirable qualities will hinder rather than help the applicant's future success if he obtains the position. Moreover, personal prejudice should never show itself in a letter of recommendation.

Many businessmen and personnel managers have discarded the use of letters of recommendation and are substituting for them regular recommendation blanks containing specific questions referring to those particular attitudes and behavior habits which are essential to success in the position to be filled. Anyone called upon to answer a questionnaire of this type should give accurate responses that are detailed enough to present a true picture of the young person concerned. If the writer does not have sufficient data at his disposal to answer some of the questions accurately, he should not hesitate to admit this fact. In some schools a cumulative personal record is included in the files of the graduates. These can be consulted when the blanks are being completed.

*Personal Interview.* Rarely is an applicant hired without a personal interview. This is a grueling experience for many young people. Often the more desirable the candidate, the more likely he is to show nervousness or fear of the interview. The majority of interviewers are trained to recognize applicant potentialities that may not show themselves in the interview. There are, however, certain ways in which the young person can be helped to create a favorable impression upon the interviewer. Parents and advisers should prepare a candidate for an interview by emphasizing the importance of the following points:

1. *Careful Grooming.* The candidate should make sure that his hair is neatly combed, that his hands and fingernails are clean, and that his clothes and shoes are appropriate, spotless, and in good condition. He should make certain that his handkerchief is clean and that his gloves are free of holes. If the applicant is a girl, her use of cosmetics should be sparing and artistic.

2. *Punctuality.* The candidate should arrive at the place of the interview early, so that he has sufficient time to compose himself or to make last-minute adjustments in his clothes or grooming. He should never be late unless he has been unavoidably detained, as by a serious transportation delay. In such circumstances it would be desirable for the applicant,

if he could, to telephone to the interviewer, reporting the cause of the delay, and leaving it to him to decide whether or not the interview should be held as soon as possible or should be postponed. An interviewer who is kept waiting is not likely to be favorably disposed toward the applicant who is responsible for the delay.

3. *General Behavior.* The applicant's manner should be dignified, courteous, and controlled. There should be no gumchewing. There should be no indication of a hail-fellow-well-met attitude on the part of the applicant, neither should he look as though he were on the way to his own execution. His manner should be pleasant and cheerful, but reserved. If the interviewer indulges in witticisms as a means of putting an applicant at ease, the latter should not so presume upon the friendly attitude of the former as to return in kind. Instead, the applicant should indicate by his attitude that he understands and appreciates the interviewer's attempts to remove nervous tensions.

4. *Answers to Questions.* All questions asked by the interviewer should be answered by the applicant in a distinct, well-modulated voice, and in easy but not slangy phraseology. In general, the answers should be brief unless the interviewer encourages a detailed explanation of certain points. The applicant should not allow himself to be drawn into an argument; neither should he hesitate to admit his limitations. Sometimes an interviewer deliberately baits a candidate in order to discover whether or not the young person has any clear conception of his own qualifications.

In one instance in which the applicant waxed eloquent concerning his varied abilities, the prospective employer terminated the interview with this statement: "You have convinced me that the job for which you are applying is too simple for your consideration. You should have my job, but I am not yet ready to turn it over to you. Good day." Not all interviewers are so frank as this one. They do not hire the applicant, but refrain from giving him the reason for their decision.

Some interviewers have pet stunts that they ask the applicant to perform. The activity, such as walking a straight line, looking up information in a book at hand and discussing it, or any similar task apparently unrelated to the duties of the position, may be utilized for one or another reason. The interviewer may wish to discover the attitude of the applicant toward the request, or he may desire to observe the quickness with which the young person responds to such directions. No matter what the reason for the request may be, if the candidate can meet it, he should do so with dignity and dispatch; nor should he question the reason for the activity unless the interviewer encourages him to do so.

As an aid to an interviewee, Calvert and Steele have prepared a list of thirty-nine questions frequently asked by employers during an interview. Their list of questions follows:

QUESTIONS MOST FREQUENTLY ASKED BY EMPLOYERS DURING INTERVIEWS

1. What are your future vocational plans?
2. How do you spend your spare time? What are your hobbies?
3. In what type of position are you most interested?
4. Why do you think you might like to work for our company?
5. What courses did you like best? Least? Why?
6. Why did you choose your particular field of work?
7. What percentage of your college expenses did you earn? How?
8. How did you spend your vacations while in school?
9. What do you know about our company?
10. What qualifications do you have that make you feel that you will be successful in your field?
11. What are your ideas of salary?
12. How do you feel about your family?
13. If you were starting college all over again, what courses would you take?
14. Do you have a girl? (or a boy friend?) Is it serious?
15. How much money do you hope to earn at age thirty? thirty-five?
16. Do you think that your extracurricular activities were worth the time you devoted to them? Why?
17. Why do you think you would like this particular type of job?
18. Tell me about your home life during the time you were growing up.
19. Are you looking for a permanent or temporary job?
20. Do you prefer working with others or by yourself?
21. What kind of a boss do you prefer?
22. Are you primarily interested in making money or do you feel that service to your fellow men is a satisfactory accomplishment?
23. Do you live with your parents? Which of your parents has had the most profound influence on you?
24. How did previous employers treat you?
25. What have you learned from some of the jobs you have held?
26. Have you ever changed your major field of interest while in college? Why?
27. Do you feel you have done the best scholastic work of which you are capable?
28. Have you ever had any difficulty getting along with fellow students and faculty?
29. Which of your college years was the most difficult?
30. Do you like routine work?
31. What is your major weakness?
32. Do you demand attention?
33. Are you willing to go where a company sends you?
34. What job in our company would you choose if you were entirely free to do so?
35. Is it an effort for you to be

tolerant of persons with a background and interests different
from your own?
36. What types of people seem to
"rub you the wrong way"?
37. Would you prefer a large or a
small company? Why?

38. What are the disadvantages of
your chosen field?
39. What have you done that shows
initiative and willingness to
work? [3]

*Practical Demonstration of Skill or Knowledge.* In certain fields, the
formal examination referred to earlier takes care of the practical demonstration of skill or knowledge. Many employers are beginning to use the
practical demonstration informally as a part of the interview. The applicant is requested to bring with him certain samples of work that he has
completed during his training period, is given a letter to type, is requested
to carry on a simple piece of work related to the job for which he is
applying, or is asked questions that will give evidence of his knowledge
of certain definite facts or principles connected with this work.

To perform adequately in situations of this kind is difficult, unless the
young person has a great deal of emotional control and confidence in his
own skill. His fingers may seem to be all thumbs or he may feel that he
has not a thought in his head. If the young person has been well trained
and if he has been given sufficient opportunity to assume responsibility in
other areas, he will have gained thereby a degree of self-confidence that
will help him in a situation of this kind. Moreover, understanding interviewers are able to distinguish between actual lack of ability and errors
that are the normal accompaniment of a testing situation.

## Adjustment on the Job

The majority of the responsibilities of an employer to his beginning
workers are no different from his responsibilities to all his workers. Many
of these are required by law. An employer is responsible for:

1. Paying a fair wage for work well done.
2. Providing hygienic working conditions. (These should include
sufficient light and air, well-constructed furniture and machinery, safety
devices, adequate facilities and sufficient time for lunch, short rest periods,
sanitary lavatories, clothes lockers, drinking fountains, and the like.)
3. Administering constructive supervision.

In addition to the above, the employer has definite responsibilities
for the welfare of a young employee. The beginning worker should be
viewed as an apprentice who can be helped to become a valuable and
satisfied member of the organization. He should be encouraged to do his

[3] From Calvert and Steele, *op. cit.,* pp. 90–91. Reprinted by permission.

work well and at the same time to learn through his experience on the job. He should never be exploited because of his youth and inexperience.

## The Employer's Attitudes and Responsibilities

Many large business organizations have developed definite programs of employee orientation. In such programs considerable emphasis usually is placed on the special help that can be given to the employee. The employer is as interested in the new employee's getting started right as is the employee. The supervisor or foreman should display a friendly attitude in order that the new employee may feel at ease. Both the employee and the employer are interested in making good impressions on each other. The new employee should be instructed on all rules and regulations, services and opportunities, and the system of payment. Personal introductions also should be made to other members of the company with whom the new employee will be working.

The first job experiences of a young man or woman may affect his usefulness as a worker during his entire work life, no matter what type of work his may be. Attitudes toward work in general and toward his special work in particular, relations with his fellow workers, reactions to supervision, and degree of job satisfaction are usually developed during a young person's first work experience. These general principles hold, whether the work life is started in the research laboratory, the business office, the classroom, the shop, the department store, the law office, the hospital, or any other seat of occupational endeavor.

Courtesy, dignity, kindness, and objectivity should characterize the attitude of an employer toward an employee at all times. The worker should be regarded as an honest, capable member of the organization, who expects to do his best and to receive an adequate monetary reward for his efforts. Each needs the other. The employer could not run his organization without the services of his employee. His employee would not be able to earn a living in his chosen vocation unless there were an opportunity for him to do so in an organized field of activity.

The office of a business firm or any other organization is no place for employer temper tantrums, harsh and destructive criticism, or unjust suspicions or accusations. The employer has the right to demand of his workers an honest day's work for an honest day's pay. Lack of punctuality, careless work, or loafing on the job should not be tolerated. An employee whose work is unsatisfactory or whose attitude is uncooperative should be helped by the employer or a supervisor to make desirable improvements. If this appears to be impossible, the worker should be asked to leave the organization but should be informed definitely and specifically concerning the reasons for his discharge.

There should be no favorites in an organization. All workers should be treated with equal justice and fairness. Promotion or salary increases should follow a definite plan with which the workers are acquainted and with which they are in agreement. An employer should never become a party to gossip about other workers, nor should he use an employee as an agent to spy upon other workers. The employer should do all in his power to build up a fine worker morale and friendly relations between the workers and himself, as well as among the workers.

Employers are as eager to have satisfied and efficient workers as are the workers to be happy and proficient. To this end many employers have put into practice certain techniques for resolving any conflicts that may arise. For example, in teaching, there are grievance committees, and in industry there are unions that help protect employee interests. The employer, of course, can do much to prevent worker dissatisfaction from arising. An open-minded attitude in which the employer is willing to deal with all facts and do it promptly, based on a willingness to "hear out" any employee who has a grievance, goes far toward establishing and maintaining good worker-employer relations.

An employer's attitude toward his workers should be friendly but not too informal. He cannot afford to mix his business with his social life. No matter how much an employer admires an employee, he should in no way make this interest apparent in his relations with the worker. The relationships that should exist between an employer and an individual employee follow the same general principles that were suggested earlier concerning teacher-pupil relations. One person cannot be singled out for special attention if a satisfied worker staff is desired. Human jealousies and resentments operate in the vocational field as they do in the home, in the classroom, or in any social group.

Undesirable as any show of favoritism is between an employer and an employee of the same sex, it is dangerous if it is evidenced between two persons of opposite sex, especially if the employer is a man and the employee is a young girl. The latter is impressionable and may view too seriously any exceptionally friendly behavior of an employer. She may feel that she has to accept his attention in order to keep her job. At the same time, if she is an emotionally stable young woman, she cannot help developing an attitude of contempt for an employer of this type, especially if she knows that he is a married man. The "office wife" has become the subject of much idle jest, which is sometimes ribald. Many young girls, in facing a first job, are seriously bothered as they try to determine what the proper attitude should be toward a male employer. Situations of this kind need to be corrected by social pressure.

In large, reputable organizations this employer-employee or supervisor-employee relationship is well controlled by the management. While friendly relations among the entire staff are encouraged, any deviation from that which is consistent with high standards of behavior is not tolerated. All employers need to take seriously their responsibility of earning, by their controlled and dignified behavior, the respect of all their employees.

## Job Adjustment of the Young Worker

In general, a young person who has achieved a good home adjustment, who has enjoyed pleasant relationships with his teachers and schoolmates, and who is an active and cooperative member of other social groups has little to fear in the matter of his job adjustment. Attitudes of sincerity, trustworthiness, responsibility, industry, and social adaptability have become a fixed part of his behavior pattern. His own nature and the training that he has received in his home and in his school have developed in him the ability to adjust successfully to new situations, new responsibilities, and new people.

In spite of their own beliefs to the contrary—often vehemently expressed—that school habits of carelessness, indolence, tardiness, and ill humor will not show themselves on a job, young people who exhibit such characteristics during their school life do not suddenly, with their advance into the work world, become models of cooperation, carefulness, and punctuality. Preparation for successful job adjustment, then, has its beginnings in the first responses of a young child and continues as he learns to adjust satisfactorily in his home, school, and social life.

In any new situation there are always found certain factors that will need intelligent consideration on the part of even the best-equipped individual if he is to meet the situation satisfactorily. A young worker must bring to his first job an understanding of the problems that may confront him, as well as an appreciation of his rights and responsibilities as a worker.

It is strongly recommended that parents and advisers prepare a young person ahead of time concerning his proper attitudes and conduct on the job. It is the function of school advisers to acquaint their students with the types of job adjustments that must be made. It then becomes the responsibility of parents to watch the progress of their working son or daughter and to help him in every way possible toward the achievement of job adjustment and job satisfaction. A young worker may be on his own economically, but he still needs guidance and counsel. Some of the more general job-adjustment factors are given below and discussed briefly.

*Dress and Grooming.* The kind of clothes to be worn depends upon the type of work to be done. Neatness and appropriateness of dress are essential. Whether overalls or business suit for the boy, or slacks, suit, or dress for the girl, all buttons should be secure, no rips or tears should be visible, and the handy safety pin should be conspicuous by its absence. Linen should be clean—at least at the beginning of the day. Moreover, the careful worker is able to keep himself reasonably neat and clean, no matter what his work may be.

Boys should shave daily and should keep their hair combed and fingernails clean. Girls should use make-up sparingly, avoid abnormally long and highly colored fingernails, and refrain from the use of cheap costume jewelry. Girls also should keep their hair well groomed and becomingly and conveniently arranged. The office or the workroom is not the powder room. All grooming activities should be taken care of in dressing rooms.

Businessmen and businesswomen of America have an international reputation for their dignified attitudes and excellent grooming. The young worker should get into step immediately, lest he be embarrassed by comparison of himself with his fellow workers.

*Promptness and Punctuality.* A young worker who finds it difficult to arrive at his job on time is piling up trouble for himself. Unless he is trained to arrive early enough so that he can reach his place of business a little before he is due, his last-minute scrambling is certain to affect his efficiency for the day. To catch the last car or bus and then to sit on the edge of the seat, wondering whether or not he will be late, give rise to an emotional disturbance that is difficult to overcome.

Employers are appreciative of the worker who is always ready to start his work on time. They look with favor on the employee who is not a "clock watcher" but is willing in an emergency to stay a few minutes overtime. Furthermore, one means of earning promotion or salary advancement is to be prompt in the execution of a piece of work that needs to be finished at a specified time.

*Trustworthiness.* The highest compliment that an employer can pay an employee is the expressed recognition of the fact that the latter is *absolutely trustworthy.* Such a worker will carry out his duties conscientiously. He will refrain from gossiping with his fellow employees and other business associates, or with his friends and family, about his employer's affairs.

A trustworthy employee regards the interests of his employer as his own interests. He feels a personal responsibility for the welfare of the organization. If there is any policy or practice of the organization that displeases him, he takes his criticism directly to his immediate superior.

*Industry.* A young worker must learn early that success usually accompanies the attitude of doing a little more, rather than a little less, than is expected of him. Here again, habits of work developed in the home and the school show themselves in the work life. To try to get out of responsibility does not bring personal job satisfaction or promotion. A workman is worthy of his hire, but he is not entitled to more than he deserves. Malingering on the job or being satisfied with mediocre achievement is neither honest nor ultimately satisfying.

*Following Directions.* No one is perfect—not even employers. It is possible for an alert, well-trained young worker to recognize the fact that certain practices in his place of business could be very much improved. Many employers encourage their workers to offer suggestions for the improvement of working techniques. However, no matter how much an employee disapproves of existing practices, it is not his function to make changes without the approval of his employer or the supervisor. The employee's duty is to take directions cheerfully and to carry them out to the best of his ability. He should always be on the alert, however, to find ways of improving techniques and then to present these suggestions clearly and tactfully to his employer or the supervisor.

## Employee Attitudes

Dignity, respect, and cooperation should characterize the attitude of an employee toward his employer. The young worker should not fear his employer any more than he should fear his parents or his teachers. If the employer's attitude is desirable, this is not difficult. However, an employee must never presume upon the good nature of his employer, nor mistake friendliness for easygoing laxity. The young worker should accept praise for work well done as well as reproof for poor workmanship. In fact, the young person who has been trained to respect his elders will have little difficulty in his relations with his employers.

Girl employees need to be very careful in their attitude toward men employers and supervisors. They should allow no social relationships to develop. If an employer and a woman employee need to discuss together any matter of business, this should be done at the place of business, not at luncheon or dinner. There is no excuse for a girl's accepting social invitations from her male employer. The importance of keeping employer-employee relations objective and businesslike cannot be stressed too strongly.

An unduly critical attitude toward the employer is equally undesirable. No employer, just as no parent or teacher, can please a young person at all times. If the employer is reasonable in his requests, the young worker should meet these cheerfully, painstakingly, and promptly. Parents should make it their business to discover the attitude of their working child toward his employer. If the employer cannot earn the young person's respect, the parents of the latter should encourage a change of job, since it is almost impossible for a worker to be successful if there is not a desirable relationship between him and his supervisors.

Much that has been said previously concerning dignity and objectivity holds for a young person's relations with his fellow workers. Sometimes older workers regard an alert, ambitious young worker with suspicion. Hence it may be difficult for the new worker to find a place for himself in the group. He usually can break down group antagonism by assuming a modest attitude of cooperation. He should not attempt to force himself upon fellow workers but should wait until he is invited to join them. In a group of satisfied workers there are usually at least a few who are eager to welcome a young worker and to help him adjust to his new environment.

If a new employee assumes an attitude of aloofness or superiority in order to conceal his inner fear of the situation, he is likely to build up resentments against himself. The more natural a young person is in his behavior on the job, the easier it will be for him to become an accepted member of the organization. He should also realize that certain privileges come with length of service.

As in any group, the majority of the workers are likely to be well adjusted in their work and to exhibit a wholesome worker attitude. A few members may be uncooperative and critical of authority. The young worker needs to be on his guard against this small group of malcontents. At first they may seem to be more friendly toward him than the others, but this friendliness may have an ulterior purpose. He should join groups, but he should know what the objectives of a group are before he joins it.

Friendships among employees are likely to develop, but these friendships should not be allowed to interfere with the fulfillment of required duties. Business hours are work hours. There is no time in them for social visits among employees, discussion of personal matters, and gossiping.

The history of labor unions has been the story of worker struggle for worker rights. The rise of industrialism was accompanied by definite worker exploitation. Labor unions have done and can do an excellent job of protecting the rights of the working man or woman.

Most young workers have received their first knowledge of the activities of labor organizations in their own homes. In school, young people learn about the Industrial Revolution and the present status of labor unions. However, it is as they hear these organizations discussed in the family group that they develop favorable or unfavorable attitudes toward this or that labor group.

Fathers and mothers and older brothers and sisters must be objective and open-minded as they discuss such matters in the presence of adolescents. These adults must be careful that their biased attitudes do not make it difficult for the younger members of their family to achieve, as workers, a desirable adjustment to the demands of a labor organization with which they may be expected to affiliate.

## Questions and Problems for Discussion

1. To what extent is advice from other people concerning vocational choice helpful?
2. What preparation is needed for a job-placement interview?
3. What help should an adolescent be given in making his vocational choice?
4. What attitude should a worker on the job assume toward a new fellow worker?
5. Discuss the values of work experience for high school students.
6. How has technological development influenced job opportunities and vocational training? Give examples to illustrate your answer.
7. What factors account for the large number of adolescents who give vocational indecision as one of their chief worries?
8. What conflicts are faced by girls that are seldom experienced by boys in vocational selection? In on-the-job activities?
9. To what extent should a worker go out of his way to assist a maladjusted worker?
10. *Special Exercises:*
    a. Visit a place of employment in which at least fifteen people are employed. Observe such things as worker attitudes, working conditions, length of work week, sanitary conditions, tenure of workers, attitude of the employer, and the like. Report your findings.
    b. With two other classmates, prepare a list of vocational opportunities available in your college community and/or in your home community.
    c. After you study the suggestions on interviewing an employer, arrange to interview an employer for a position for which you are qualified.
    d. Write a letter of application for a job or position. Ask your instructor to evaluate it critically.

## Selected References

Calvert, Robert, Jr., and John E. Steele: *Planning Your Career*, McGraw-Hill Book Company, New York, 1963.

Clark, K. E.: *The Vocational Interests of Non-Professional Men*, The University of Minnesota Press, Minneapolis, 1961.

Crawford, A., et al.: *The Choice of an Occupation*, Yale University Press, New Haven, Conn., 1959.

Crow, Lester D., and Alice Crow: *Readings in Guidance*, David McKay Company, Inc., New York, 1962.

Forrester, G.: *Occupational Litera-*

*ture,* The H. W. Wilson Company, New York, 1958.

Greenleaf, W. J.: *Occupations and Careers,* McGraw-Hill Book Company, New York, 1955.

Harris, D. B.: "Work and the Adolescent: Transition to Maturity," *Teachers College Record,* vol. 63, pp. 146–153, November, 1961.

Hoppock, R.: *Occupational Information,* 2d ed., McGraw-Hill Book Company, New York, 1963.

Kitson, H. D.: *I Find My Vocation,* 4th ed., McGraw-Hill Book Company, New York, 1954.

*Occupational Outlook,* U.S. Department of Labor Statistics, 1963.

Powell, M., and V. Bloom: "Development of and Reasons for Vocational Choices of Adolescents through the High School Years," *Journal of Educational Research,* vol. 56, pp. 126–133, November, 1962.

Reiss, A. J., Jr., et al.: *Occupations and Social Status,* The Free Press of Glencoe, New York, 1961.

Rood, A.: *Job Strategy,* McGraw-Hill Book Company, New York, 1961.

Roe, Anne: "Early Determinants of Vocational Choice," *Journal of Counseling Psychology,* vol. 4, pp. 212–217, 1957.

Roe, Anne: *The Psychology of Occupations,* John Wiley & Sons, Inc., New York, 1956.

Super, Donald E., and J. O. Crites: *Appraising Vocational Fitness,* Harper & Row, Publishers, Incorporated, New York, 1962.

Super, Donald E., and P. L. Overstreet: *The Vocational Maturity of Ninth Grade Boys,* Bureau of Publications, Teachers College, Columbia University, New York, 1960.

*Vocational Guidance Quarterly,* current issues.

Williamson, E. G.: *Counseling Adolescents,* McGraw-Hill Book Company, New York, 1950.

# Chapter Seventeen

## Social
## Adjustment
## of Adolescents

An individual's so-called "social attitudes and behavior" permeate all his interpersonal and intergroup relations. At the same time, his degree of social awareness and adaptability is rooted in his total developmental pattern—physical, mental, and emotional. It could be argued that developmental progress also is basic in home, school, and vocational adjustments. Fundamentally this is so, but youthful experiences in these areas of human relationships appear to be more or less conditioned by particular situational factors. Social adjustment implies a relatively broad base of operations. A young person's social adjustment reflects the influence upon him of his experiences in the more specific adjustment areas, but goes beyond them as the adolescent attempts to respond to all the human interrelationships by which he constantly and consistently is stimulated.

The many aspects of social adjustment, interpreted in its widest form, have been included in appropriate areas of discussion throughout this book. Hence in this chapter attention is focused upon adolescents' informal relationships with one another, as together they participate in leisure-time and recreational activities. These activities represent youthful strivings for peer acceptance, adult approval, and eventual self-realization in an adult social world.

## Adolescent Problems of Social Relationships

Adolescents tend to believe that in their social relationships they have the right to behave according to adult standards. On such matters as relations between the sexes, recreational activities, speech, mode of dress, and attitude toward the government, religion, and community affairs they quickly recognize the attitude and behavior of their elders.

### Adult Influence upon Adolescent Urges and Interests

Since the adolescent rarely does things by halves, not only does he tend to mold his conduct in terms of the examples that are set before him by his older associates but he goes a step further and throws himself enthusiastically into whatever activity he finds exciting or affords immediate satisfaction. He seldom either considers or recognizes the fact that the results may be disastrous. He often is stirred by a desire to reform the world. He takes seriously the social ills that are called to his attention. He has an urge to improve the sorry state of affairs in the world. Fortunately, he is therefore capable of being influenced by the ideals of his elders as they attempt to guide his behavior into socially desirable channels.

Teen-age boys and girls want to go outside the home to engage in various kinds of social activities and games. They want the independence that matches their increasing strength and maturity. They want to be permitted to make greater use of their enlarged reasoning powers. The denial of these desires often makes them discontented and restless. As we know, the struggle between adolescent urges seeking expression, and attempts at their direction by adults who themselves seem to lack control of their own behavior, leads to bewilderment and sometimes to defiance of social customs and mores.

*Importance of Adult Example.* Young people are taught to be honest and sincere in their relations with others, yet they see deceit and dishonesty in adult relationships. They are told to be tolerant, but they are surrounded by racial, religious, and class bigotry and intolerance. They are given suggestions for appropriate dress and grooming, but their elders may follow the latest fads. They are admonished to be neat and clean, but they see older people often careless about their own appearance. They are taught the value of controlled behavior and proper speech, but they are stimulated by emotional outbursts and sarcastic and sometimes violent or vulgar speech. Decent and honorable relations between the sexes are stressed by parents and other social leaders. Yet not only are the newspapers filled with reports of illicit sexual relations, but adolescents' associates among older men and women often stimulate them with examples of such behavior.

"Do as I say but not as I do" is an attitude that is responsible for many of the problems that arise in the life of teen-age boys and girls as they seek to adjust to their social relationships. "Don't smoke, don't drink, don't go to nightclubs and roadhouses. Don't stay out late, don't be late for appointments, don't choose the wrong companions, don't spend too much time at motion-picture houses. Don't! Don't! Don't!" On all sides the young person is warned of the dire results of his conduct if he does not follow these admonitions.

Many adults who thus attempt to direct the conduct of young people go blithely along in their own behavior practices, giving satisfaction to their immediate urges, prejudices, and desires, with no regard for the effect of their conduct upon the lives of others. Unfortunately, some adults who show a divergence between their own conduct and what they tell others to do are civic, educational, or social leaders whose behavior has a tremendous influence upon those with whom they come in contact.

Such situations make it very difficult for those adults who attempt to practice and teach desirable social attitudes to exert the influence that they should over young people. Their striving to do what is right and proper, as well as to teach what is right and proper, causes them to be less appealing and less exciting than those adults who are not sincere and honest in their social living. Young people respond to the glamorous. They too want to be interesting. Hence they seem to think that they must choose between virtuous but dull and less virtuous but fascinating individuals as patterns for their behavior.

## Adolescent Questions Concerning Social Relationships

The questions asked by young people concerning their social relations are many and varied, and reflect every possible phase of social-group living. They are keenly interested in their own attitudes toward their associates and in the attitudes of other people toward them. They want to know how to make and keep friends. Such matters as correct dress and grooming, ways of acquiring an attractive personality, and desirable behavior in public are very important to them.

The questions presented below typify young people's concern about the many problems that they encounter as they struggle toward adult adjustment in social relations.

1. In what kind of social activities should adolescents engage?
2. Why does the school not furnish more afterschool social activities?
3. What games should be played at parties when both girls and boys are present?
4. At what age would it be permissible for a girl to go to a formal dance without a chaperon?
5. Where should young people go for their social activities?
6. Should a boy decide where to go on a date or should he leave that to the girl?
7. What can a girl say when she does not want to go to undesirable places but wants to keep from appearing snobbish?
8. How can young people be helped to meet other young people?
9. What should a girl do if a strange boy starts a conversation with her?
10. Is it necessary to break old friendships when new ones are made?
11. How can a boy or girl develop social ease?

12. How can a boy overcome bashfulness in the presence of girls?

13. Should a girl accept a cocktail at a party in order to be sociable?

14. How can a boy or girl become popular?

15. Is it true that a boy who is popular with girls is not liked by other boys?

16. What is wrong if a girl is popular with the group but is not dated by boys?

17. Why are some girls popular with boys but not with girls?

18. Should one always be candid in expressing his opinions?

19. How important are friendships that are made during adolescence?

20. Why do some people take advantage of others?

21. How can one keep from doing things on impulse that are later regretted?

22. Parents and teachers are always talking about the right kind of companions. How can one know which people are the right kind?

23. What should be one's attitude toward his friends?

24. Why are we encouraged to form friendships with members of our own sex?

25. Are most girls very changeable in their likes and dislikes of boys?

26. Should a girl associate with another girl who is six years older than herself?

27. Should boys and girls ever go "Dutch"?

28. Should matters concerning sex be discussed between a boy and girl?

29. How can one tell if another really loves him or her?

30. How can one judge the character of the boys with whom one associates?

31. What is puppy love?

32. What is a good way to refuse an invitation more than once without offending the person who extends the invitation?

33. How can a girl encourage a certain boy to date her?

34. Should a boy ever ask a girl who is much taller than he is to dance with him?

35. Is necking or petting wrong?

36. Does a boy respect a girl more if she does not pet?

37. How can one differentiate between love and infatuation?

38. If a boy and girl expect to marry, should they make dates with other girls and boys?

39. After a boy or girl marries, who should come first—the mate or the parents?

40. Should a girl marry for security if she is not in love?

## Social Adjustment Linked to Home and School

A young person's social adjustment is not a thing apart, but is closely linked with his adjustment to his home and school relationships. It usually follows that a boy or girl who experiences a normal and well-integrated home and school life carries over into all his other associations a similar wholesomeness of attitude and control of behavior. Moreover, the cause of an adolescent's social maladjustment often can be traced to a home environment in which the teen-ager has had little or no opportunity to experience cooperative group living.

For example, 17-year-old Arthur is an only child. Since his early childhood both of his parents have worked outside the home. He always has been a lonely boy; his parents never have given him companionship, nor have they shown any concern about his social activities. In fact, his mother's attitude always has been that friends are not important. She repeatedly has told Arthur that if a person studies and becomes successful, "friends will come to you."

Although Arthur is an intelligent boy who does well in his studies, he is shy and retiring in the presence of young people. Hence his schoolmates do not include him in their social activities; in fact, they avoid him whenever they can. He became very much interested in one of the girls in the school, but she refused to socialize with him. Apparently he came to believe that she did not like him because he was not the gay, talkative type of boy who always has something funny to say.

Impelled by the need for group acceptance, Arthur now is trying to play the role of a sophisticated party boy, thereby making matters worse rather than improving the situation. His behavior is out of place and his schoolmates are coming to dislike him intensely. They resent his attempts to force his way into their groups and to impress them with "big talk" about all the places he has visited and all the important things he has done, such as reading books of college level and conducting scientific experiments. Arthur's difficulty stems from parentally induced self-centeredness, with a consequent nonunderstanding of the meaning of group cooperation.

## Need to Avoid Maladjustment

Although maladjustment cannot be labeled as completely home, school, vocational, or social, it usually is true that, unless early home or school difficulties can be adjusted, the uncontrolled behavior of the young person progresses (or rather, regresses) into actual delinquency or mental illness and becomes a serious social problem. Poverty, parental ignorance or indifference, and physical or mental disability are contributing factors in the setting up of a pattern of social inadequacy. The problems of social adjustment that are common to all normal young people who are growing up in normal environments become intensified if the young person has developed abnormal characteristics and is living in an unhygienic environment.

Fortunately, the majority of young people bring to the solution of their problems of social living a background of healthy attitudes and behavior practices. In spite of the fact that even normal adolescents are consistent in their desire for independence of behavior in their social relationships, they are equally consistent in seeking sympathetic advice concerning problems that may arise in their social life. They seldom spurn help that is given in the spirit of understanding and fair-mindedness by adults who, through their own experiences during adolescence, have learned to evaluate objectively the sincerity and earnestness with which young people come to them for assistance.

## Suggestions for Improving Social Relationships

In the past much of the social life of the members of a family centered around the home itself or the homes of friends and acquaintances. The associates of the younger members of the family usually were the sons and daughters of family friends. Playmates as children, companions as adolescents, these relationships often continued as adult friendships. In the days before the arrival of motion pictures, automobiles, and nightclubs, the parental task of guiding adolescent social activities was relatively simple. In fact, the whole social pattern was very much simpler than that which exists at present.

Today social offerings for adults as well as for adolescents are legion. The entire recreational program, especially in large cities, is so wide and varied that one can start in the morning, keep on the go until the early hours of the next day, and continue this program for seven days in the week without exhausting all the available possibilities for amusement or recreation. Motion pictures, nightclubs, dramatic productions, concerts, dances, sports, hikes, professional and school games, exhibitions, and organized recreational programs are at the disposal of young people —many of them at little or no cost.

### Roles of Adults and Adolescents Differ

Although social offerings may be attended by both adults and adolescents, it is no longer considered *comme il faut* for adults and adolescents to engage in activities together. Parents are expected to go their way and to allow their adolescent children to follow their own interests. Chaperonage is outmoded. Adolescent freedom in social activity is the order of the day. Hence whatever is done by parents and other adults in the way of guiding such activity must be done for the most part by remote control.

Many adults and adolescents need and welcome assistance aimed at fitting young people for satisfactory and satisfying relations with their associates during out-of-work or out-of-school hours. Some suggestions are presented here under the following headings:

1. Community responsibility for the social activities of teen-age youth
2. The gaining of social ease and popularity
3. Friends and companions
4. Adolescent relations with the opposite sex

The topics discussed will be considered from the point of view of young people. The implications of these suggestions are aimed at parents and other adults who are concerned with the development among teen-agers of wholesome social attitudes and behavior patterns.

### Community Responsibility for the Social Activities of Teen-age Youth

Adolescents want to participate in varied forms of social and recreational activity unhampered by too close adult supervision. They are willing to accept the sincerely offered but nondirecting cooperation of their elders. They resent what to them appears to be adult-imposed restriction of freedom to select and to participate in leisure-time activities that reflect their own felt needs and interests.

Parents, school people, and other adults concerned with the welfare of youth often experience considerable difficulty in determining the fine line that should exist between too rigid adult direction of adolescents' social life and cooperative guidance of their leisure-time activities. For young people to be granted complete permissiveness in the management of their social life would militate against their own well-being; for older people always to demand submission to adult-planned and adult-organized recreational and social programs might well drive young people to attempt to satisfy their socially pointed urges and interests through self-initiated, unwholesome practices.

## Adolescent Recreational Interests

Young people have many and varied leisure-time interests that range from large-group recreational and entertainment projects to small-group or individual participation in relaxing and/or intriguing types of performance or appreciation. Within the limits of personal capacity, background training, and environmental availability adolescents enjoy active or passive participation in one or more kinds of sports or games; they like dancing, parties, picnics, and various other forms of socializing entertainment; they participate enthusiastically in musical or dramatic activities such as glee clubs, bands or orchestras, operettas, plays, pageants, puppetry, and dramatic stunts; they often display deep appreciation of classical or semiclassical musical programs, dramatic presentations, and the pictorial arts.

Alone or with a small group having similar interests an adolescent may devote much of his free time to a special hobby such as photography, collecting, construction of radios, model airplanes, or boats, sewing or knitting, and leatherwork and other crafts. Some young people gain great satisfaction from their association with writing, reading, or discussion groups, and from attendance at lectures, forums, or debates. Not all adolescent interests are centered in themselves, however. They often take great pride in their community-service activities. Girls volunteer as aides in children's wards of community hospitals; boys enter enthusiastically into neighborhood clean-up projects. Both boys and girls take part in community-sponsored fund-raising campaigns and similar activities. On occasions youthful enthusiasm is so great that careful adult handling is needed lest adolescent community participation arouse attitudes of disapproval and resentment, rather than approving cooperation, among older community members.

## Community Recreational Facilities for Adolescents

Available space for leisure-time activities can be found in school buildings, churches, and other community centers. Too many school buildings are not used sufficiently during afterschool hours. Facilities should be made available for younger adolescents in the afternoon and for older boys and girls in the evening. The entire building for one or two evenings a week, or certain sections of the building every evening, could be reserved for the use of adults.

Any boy or girl who seeks wholesome recreation and who wants to be with others of his own age should be encouraged to participate in the activities that are organized by youth under the guiding supervision of able adult leadership. In the long run young people can gain much more enjoyment from such participation than they now think can be obtained in many of the commercially controlled places of amusement that they tend to frequent. These include bars and grills, roadhouses, cellar clubs, and public dance halls. Many young people complain that unless they patronize these undesirable places, the only activity left is attendance at motion pictures or remaining at home to watch television.

For community-sponsored facilities to compete with the glamour that is attached to some of the less wholesome commercial recreational centers, the former must be well organized and democratic. The following suggestions might serve as guides:

1. Provision for various informal leisure-time activities for adolescent boys and girls

2. Development of leadership on the part of youth for planning and carrying out their own programs

3. Combined cooperation of groups, such as social, economic, racial, and others in the community

4. Encouragement of community support for youth programs

5. Indirect supervision by paid and volunteer adult leaders, not more than two leaders to fifty young people.

### The Gaining of Social Ease and Popularity

The community-sponsored centers described in the foregoing section afford excellent opportunities for young people to meet others of their kind. However, the entire social life of a young person cannot be confined to his activities in one of these centers. Even getting young people to a center may be difficult. Hence parents, advisers, and other social leaders must be on the alert constantly for opportunities to assist young people in developing desirable associations with others.

## The Role of Parents in Adolescent Friendships

The old saying, "God gave us our relatives, but thank God we can choose our friends," seems to imply that the selecting of friends and associates is a very simple matter. Many adolescents do not find this to be a fact. Although they may be surrounded by many people of their own age and older, they may encounter difficulties as they attempt to become active members of a social group. In spite of an assumed aggressiveness of attitude, most young people are shy and find it difficult to make the initial advances toward other persons unless the path is smoothed for them.

Parents can keep open house. Adolescent boys and girls should be encouraged to bring other young people into the home, which should always be neat and clean even though it may be simple. More than that, mothers should plan to have cookies, fruit, or other simple foods at hand for a group of hungry boys who drop in, or should make it possible for a girl and her crowd to mix up a batch of fudge or some other concoction. If a boy or girl knows that, unannounced, he may bring a group of pals into the house on the way home from school or at any other time, he thereby gains a social confidence that is reflected in the attitude of other young people toward him.

Parents can help also by encouraging their adolescent children to plan parties or other get-togethers. Mothers should help in the arrangements for a party and in suggesting names of boys and girls to be invited. Parents can learn a great deal about their children's attitudes toward their schoolmates and coworkers as they listen to adolescent conversation. If the remarks of a young person in the home seem to indicate that he desires to become a member of a certain group, an interesting party arranged by the parent and the adolescent to which one or more members of the group are invited may help him to gain his wish. If the party is well planned and enjoyed by the guests, it may serve as an entering wedge into the desired group for the young host or hostess.

The mother of a high school senior was talking with her daughter's adviser in the latter's office concerning the girl's college plans. During the interview this mother greeted by name at least a dozen other seniors who happened to be in the office. Here is a mother who need not worry about her daughter's ability to meet people, since she herself has done an excellent job of cooperation in this respect. In sharp contrast with this mother is the one who knows little, if anything, about her son's or daughter's associates. The excuse given for this indifference may be, "You know how it is. I am so busy that I can't be bothered about the boys and girls he runs around with." Unfortunately, a parent of this kind may be compelled later to take time to be bothered if the boy or the girl forms undesirable associations as a result of lack of parental help in meeting the right kind of young people.

It is unfortunate that in too many families the mother is compelled by circumstances to engage in work outside the home. This lack of parental supervision of a growing adolescent may lead to undesirable consequences. Helping a young person to form wholesome peer friendships is not a responsibility of parents only. School people, religious leaders, and employers also can provide socializing experiences for young people.

## Role of the School in Adolescent Friendships

Merely to enroll a young adolescent in a school or class group is not enough. Active assistance should be given these entrants to become acquainted with other members of their group. For a young person to sit in a class for an entire term and not know the names of more than a few of his classmates, or for a graduating senior not to recognize the faces of the majority of the graduating group (even though it is a large class), is a sad commentary on the efficacy of the school's social leadership. Neither high schools nor colleges are doing enough along these lines, even though they are becoming increasingly aware of the social needs of their students.

Many schools are encouraging the organization of numerous and varied clubs that will give boys and girls of similar interests an opportunity to become acquainted with one another. More extensive programs, such as dances, athletic meets, dramatic presentations, musical programs, and picnics, afford opportunities for individual students to meet all the other students. The use of name tags on such occasions is an excellent method of helping boys and girls to become acquainted. A few high schools and colleges have extended this program of acquainting young people with one another by inviting prospective entrants to parties planned and conducted by the regular students of the school that they are about to join. In this way these young people are made to feel that upon entrance to the school they will be coming into a group of friends.

## The Role of the Church

Churches also are doing more for the social life of their young members. The religious and ethical values of church attendance should not be minimized, but the functions of adult church leaders must include that of providing for their young people one or more desirable outlets for their natural urge to be with people and make friends. In what better environment can this be done than through church affiliations? Young people's service groups and discussion groups led by adolescents are two of the means that are effective.

## The Role of Other Persons or Groups

More and more large business houses and industrial plants that employ many young people plan definite programs of social activity for their employees. Department parties to celebrate a birthday, engagement, or marriage of one of the group are encouraged. Periodic picnics, dances, and other forms of social activities are included in the companies' social programs.

Insofar as possible, boys and girls should be discouraged from "picking up" casual acquaintances on streetcars and buses or in places of amusement. In some states, hitchhiking is forbidden by law. The automobile is an excellent mode of transportation but a dangerous means of carrying on adolescent social activities. Occasionally, associations made in this way are wholesome, but as a general practice they should be avoided. The boy or girl who is provided with adequate opportunities for meeting young people in the home, church, place of work, or youth center is not tempted to seek his associates among unselected or unorganized groups.

The fact must be faced that at one time many of a person's present associates were strangers to him. An individual is unable to predict with what persons he will be associated intimately ten years hence. Social living and the social experiences developed in wholesome settings during the formative years will enable a young person later in life to make social adjustments to new situations and new people.

## Development of Social Ease

Unless during childhood a boy or girl has had a great deal of experience in meeting people, he may have difficulty in developing social grace and ease as he is introduced into social situations that are different from the relatively restricted home, school, and neighborhood environment. There are several reasons for his apparent or felt awkwardness. One of these may be that during his childhood he was not expected to take the initiative in starting or carrying on a conversation, especially in the presence of elders. In fact, he may have been warned constantly that "children should be seen and not heard."

An adolescent may find himself in the company of adults or older adolescents where he may wish to demonstrate his developing maturity by taking an active part in the conversation or discussion; yet he may be afraid of saying the wrong thing, thus betraying the fact that he is still immature. Young people are cruel to one another, often unconsciously so. The older or more sophisticated members of a group cannot always resist the temptation of making game of their younger associates. By seeming to be amused by, or tolerant of, opinions expressed in public by younger brothers or sisters or by younger friends, they are thereby bolstering their own morale and acquiring greater social poise.

Furthermore, adolescent physical development often is irregular. The boy or girl feels that he is all hands and feet. He tends to trip over rugs or furniture or he drops things at the wrong moment. The more eager he is to appear to be at ease, the more uncontrolled the management of his body may seem to become. The young teen-ager grows out of his clothes quickly and, rightly or wrongly, believes that people are recognizing the fact that his suit or his coat is too small for him.

Parents should provide clothes which are attractive and of the right size, even though they may be simple and inexpensive. It must be admitted that the keeping of a growing adolescent in clothes of the right size is difficult. A mother, known to the authors, believed in buying well-made and durable suits, dresses, and coats for her boy and girl. Since these were expensive, the young people were expected to wear them for a long time. The clothes were bought large enough for the adolescents to grow into, and then were worn after they had been outgrown. These young people were not impressed by the good quality of the material, but they were extremely conscious of the fact that their clothes did not fit them for at least two-thirds of the time during which they were worn. Moreover, the boy and girl were constantly admonished to be very careful of their clothes because of the high price paid for them. Here is an excellent basis for self-consciousness.

## Importance of Participating in Social Groups

A youth's desire to be an active rather than a passive member of a social group, his growing awareness of his physical characteristics, and the fact that he is being thrown into new and different social groups are the bases of youthful desire for help in gaining social ease. Most young people, unless too many embarrassing situations have caused them to shun participation in social activities, like people and want to be with them. "Practice makes perfect" applies to the development of social grace and poise in the same way that it applies to the development of any other skill. If a teen-age boy or girl is to acquire social ease, he must be given many opportunities for participation in social activities.

Active participation by young people in many social situations planned or encouraged by parents and advisers should be accompanied by informal guidance in the simple rudiments of good social practices. Adolescents need to be taught proper forms of introductions, ways of starting a conversation, control of voice, desirable eating manners, and the like. Many of these social forms are learned by young people as they imitate their elders. However, they may not always be stimulated by desirable adult behavior in such matters. Direct, as well as indirect, teaching is needed. This does not mean that the finishing school of the past should be revived, but it does mean that in every school there should be programs for training in good manners.

Through reading and discussion, high school students should familiarize themselves with the simple rules that underlie participation in social activities. This knowledge should then be applied in a tactful way through participation in many social activities in the school.

It is through projects of this kind that young people can be taught to meet social situations with ease and enjoyment. If the emphasis is laid upon service to others, a young person tends to forget himself as he attempts to put another person at ease. The plan of having upper-class students arrange social programs for younger students, and of having younger students with the help of their older schoolmates conduct similar programs for younger children, offers adolescents fine opportunities for developing a mature attitude toward their social relationships.

## Need to Make a Good First Impression

Girls and boys often find themselves ill at ease and tongue-tied in the presence of members of the opposite sex. This is usually caused by a natural desire to make a good impression. The boy tends to brag about his accomplishments. The girl may affect an artificial, sophisticated manner. Little is gained by attempting to be what one is not. Adults who are simple and unaffected in manner, who are careful of their vocabulary, and who practice good taste in their conversation with their friends and associates present excellent models for young people to follow.

There is no one, adult or adolescent, who does not find himself occasionally in a difficult social situation, with an accompaniment of nervousness or anxiety concerning the reactions toward him of other members of the group. Young people should be told frankly that adults have these experiences, and that if one does not know what to do or say, the best procedure is to remain quiet. A good listener is a most desirable adjunct of any group. As one gains social poise, one realizes that he does not have to be constantly active vocally, or in any other way, in order to be popular. This is a lesson that should be learned early by young people.

## Achieving Popularity

Poise, dignity, social ease, and consideration for others, rather than too free spending, elaborate dressing, loud talking, or aggressive behavior, are the secrets of popularity. Much of the enjoyment of school or business life is dependent upon a young person's relations with his fellows. The well-adjusted young person possesses a few good friends and many acquaintances among the group. If he is willing to cooperate with others in group projects, he is welcomed by all the members. When he is called upon to do something for the group, he accepts the responsibility cheerfully and does his best to fulfill the obligation. He is not jealous of the success of others, but is proud of the honor that another's achievement brings to the group.

The secret of popularity is the willingness to do for or to share with others. The members of any group appreciate the person who is interested in them, especially if he demonstrates the ability to make constructive contributions to their activities. However, any group, formal or informal, soon loses patience with any member who shows by his actions that he is interested only in those benefits of membership that can contribute to his own welfare or prestige.

A young person may have developed, through unwise guidance, a spirit of selfishness and self-centeredness that is disliked by others. It is difficult for adolescents to overlook selfish attitudes. Whether a boy or girl is engaged in gainful employment or is still a student, whether he is economically privileged or underprivileged, or whether he is physically attractive or unattractive, his chances for popularity among his associates depend upon his ability to subordinate his own interests and desires to those of the group and upon his habits of fair play and good sportsmanship.

These desirable behavior patterns do not suddenly materialize with the coming of adolescent interest in social participation. They are the result of a gradual habit formation which is encouraged in the young person by parents, teachers, and other adults.

### Friends and Companions

Young people are very much concerned about their friendships with other boys and girls. Their questions are specific and indicate the emotional disturbance that can arise as a result of unpleasant experiences in the realm of friendship. Their adolescent son's or daughter's choice of friends and companions is often a source of worry to parents. The boy or girl who finds it difficult to gain friends, the young person who selects undesirable friends, or the adolescent who seems to form violent friendships of short duration gives a parent many anxious moments.

## Importance of Adolescent Friendships

Friendships are important, not only during adolescence but also throughout adult life. The friendships formed during the teen-age years not only may be the beginning of pleasant lifelong associations, but also may afford opportunities for practice in the art of making and keeping friends, which will help in the formation of later adult friendships. For these reasons, parents and other adults need to be tactful and patient in their attempts at encouraging young people toward the development of wholesome attitudes in their social relations.

Adolescent boys and girls need friends among adults and young people of both sexes. Their questions indicate their interest in the fundamentals of maintaining friendly relations with any person, regardless of age or sex. Still more are they concerned about their relations with persons of their own sex and age. Most important of all, it would seem, is the relationship that should exist between members of opposite sexes. Because of that emphasis, the many phases of boy-girl relationships will be discussed under a separate heading. Further discussion of the present topic will be limited to a general consideration of the fundamentals of successful friendship and of friendship between members of the same sex.

## Significance of Friendship Attitudes

Young people often confuse the meaning of the term *friend* with that of *acquaintance* or *companion*. Adults who have experienced lifelong friendships do not always understand an adolescent's attitude toward his associates. During adolescence so-called "friendships" may be easily made and just as easily broken. The difficulty here lies not in the temporary nature of these relationships but in the terms used to describe them. Parents need to teach young people by their own conduct toward their associates and by their tactful suggestions that there are differences to be found in the degree of an individual's friendly relations with people.

Teen-agers should learn early to feel and exhibit a friendly attitude toward those with whom they associate. They should be helped to develop a uniformly courteous and cooperative manner in their dealings with other people of all ages. They should be slow to take offense at others' behavior, rather than suspicious of the good intentions of those with whom they come in contact, "butcher, baker, or candlestick maker," salesperson, delivery boy, car conductor, fellow student or fellow worker, teacher or supervisor, or family or personal friend.

Sharp retorts, unwarranted criticism, sulking, insistence upon one's rights or upon special privileges will not gain friends or companions. A habitually friendly attitude will achieve for a young person a host of acquaintances with whom he can enjoy work or recreational activity.

## The Need to Have Many Friends

Adults should encourage teen-age boys and girls to form many acquaintanceships. However, young people should be helped to realize that it is not wise to expect too much from these acquaintances or to confide in them too freely. The relationship should be based upon community of interest and congeniality of taste, yet it should leave all the individuals concerned free from obligations except those that are dictated by the rules of courtesy, respect for others, and cooperation.

Even these temporary associations may influence a young person's attitudes and behavior unduly during his formative years. Hence it is important that parents watch carefully the neighborhood and school groups with whom their sons and daughters may associate.

Much more significant, however, are the friendships of a young person, his attitude toward the meaning of friendship, and his own responsibilities for its success. A true friend is a person whom one can trust, in whom one can confide, and to whom one can take his joys and sorrows with the certainty that these will be understood and appreciated by the friend.

## Bases of True Friendship

Friendship is based upon personality qualities that lie deep beneath the surface. Economic status, prestige, personal attractiveness, and national or religious background are relatively unimportant as the bases of friendship. Very often parents and other adults fail to recognize this fact. They may disapprove of a friendship between two wholesome, democratic adolescents because they, the adults, are evaluating the relationship in terms of superficial standards. No parent or adviser should object to a friendship between two young people for any reason except antisocial characteristics exhibited by one that might influence the other toward socially unacceptable behavior.

As is true in any other human relationship, there are certain basic rights and responsibilities that must be known and adhered to strictly if a friendship is to survive. An adolescent has the right to expect his friends to help him when such help is needed, unless some social and ethical right would be violated by their doing so. For example, a high school or college student should not be expected to give his friend help during an examination or to work out study assignments that his friend would later submit to his instructor as his own work.

A person should not gossip about his friend; neither should he withhold incriminating knowledge of his friend's wrongdoing, especially if an innocent person is accused of the act. The culprit should first be encouraged by his friend to confess the wrongdoing. If this plea is not successful, it is the friend's duty to take the matter to the proper authorities. This is a difficult test of friendship, but it is the only honest course to take.

## Loyalty Important to Friendship

Friends should be loyal to one another, they should guard confidences given to one by the other, and they should share their pleasures and other activities insofar as this will not interfere with any obligations. Neither friend should make all the decisions about places to go, activities to participate in, and the like. Most of us are more or less self-centered, but in friendship there must be a mutual give-and-take. A friendship cannot thrive on selfishness, oversensitivity, jealousy, carelessness in keeping appointments, or too great demands upon the time and interest of either friend.

Too many so-called "friendships" among adolescents are no more than the temporary domination of one young person struggling for self-assertion over a weaker or younger companion who is passing through a hero-worshiping stage. Too great an admiration for any associate whose behavior is socially unacceptable may be dangerous to a suggestible young adolescent. However, the opposite also is true. Often a young person who is tempted to be careless in his home, work, or social responsibilities can be "reformed" by his adolescent friends who have developed more constructive practices. Hence parents need to watch carefully the friendships that their sons and daughters are forming and to evaluate the extent to which such friendships are desirable.

## Value of Friendships with Members of the Same Sex

The expression "He is a woman's man" or "She is a man's woman" may seem to the person concerned to be a tribute to his popularity with members of the opposite sex. As a matter of fact, such a comment usually is an indication of the unpopularity of the person with members of his own sex and thus is far from flattering. The person who is not generally liked and admired by members of his own sex lacks certain fundamental personality characteristics. One's own sex is able to penetrate below surface veneer and recognize wholesome qualities or basic insincerities that may not be apparent to members of the opposite sex.

Men know men and women know women because they know themselves. They are able to evaluate the behavior of a member of their own sex in terms of their own urges, interests, and behavior patterns. A boy who is respected by upstanding boys and a girl who is admired by wholesome girls need cause parents and advisers little concern regarding their social adjustment.

For a boy to be a boy's boy and a girl to be a girl's girl indicates that the individual is a fine, cooperative, trustworthy type of person. However, the adolescent who tends to devote all his time and energy to the formation of friendships within his own sex is not completely adjusted. As an adult he will need to work and associate with members of the other sex. During adolescence he must learn to meet the challenge of developing intelligent and controlled behavior with members of both sexes. Hence young people should be encouraged to form friendships with a few fine members of both sexes; but every young person should have at least one close and wholesome, but unselfish, friendship with a member of the same sex.

It is with this other adolescent that the boy or the girl can be himself to a degree that often is not otherwise possible, even with members of his own family. The friendship satisfies the urge for security in the affection of another, which may transcend the desire for security in the affection of the family. Parents should encourage such friendships, but must assure themselves that the friendship is wholesome, that there are no homosexual tendencies, and that the relationship is an addition to, not a substitute for, friendship with members of the oposite sex.

## Value of Similarity of Ages

During adolescence a friendship between two boys or between two girls who are too widely separated in age is not completely satisfying. The older boy's or girl's philosophy of life, physical and emotional development, attitude toward the opposite sex, and whole experiential pattern go beyond those of the younger teen-ager, unless the younger person is exceptionally mature.

One of the strongest arguments against too-rapid school progress of a mentally superior young person is found here. Although the bright younger student may be able to surpass the study achievement of his classmates, his emotional and social progress may lag behind theirs. Although they may admire his mental prowess, he cannot compete with, or even fully appreciate, their recreational and social interests and activities. He lacks the social ease and the good judgment in social affairs that are the outgrowth of such experiences. The older adolescents, either consciously or unconsciously, exclude him from their social plans. He is, however, too mature mentally to find recreational satisfaction in the company of his own age group, who are mentally younger than he is. Hence he may be forced to rely upon his academic superiority in order to satisfy his ego.

Parents and school leaders are beginning to realize the importance to a young person of his forming friendships with his peers. Consequently, the educational philosophy of encouraging an adolescent toward rapid school progress, which was very popular two decades ago, is now meeting criticism. Parents are refusing to allow their bright children to be advanced beyond their normal age levels unless this can be done in the company of a sufficient number of like young persons, among whom a normal social and emotional development is possible.

### Adolescent Relations with the Opposite Sex

In Chapter 9 relations with the opposite sex were discussed in some detail. At this point we shall consider only a relatively few of the problems experienced by boys and girls as together they participate in leisure-time and recreational activities. The degree of seriousness to an adolescent of the problems associated with social relationships with the other sex is dependent in good part upon the extent to which he was encouraged as a child to engage in parent- or school-sponsored sex-mixed group activities.

## Appropriateness of Boys and Girls Going "Dutch"

During adolescence pairing off does not necessarily mean that the boy or girl is contemplating an early marriage with the other. It is, rather, a matter of enjoying each other's company and of sharing social activities together. If each pays his own way, the girl is relieved of her feeling of obligation to the boy and is free to extend invitations as well as to await them.

Moreover, our present economic system is such that the girl is as likely as the boy to have the money to pay her way. If she does this occasionally, she avoids the accusation of being a "gold digger." There are perhaps more reasons for the extension of the practice of going "Dutch" than for the elimination of it. It tends to place friendships at these early ages on a firmer basis.

## Discussion of Sex Matters

If a boy and girl spend most of their hours together in the company of other young people, sex matters do not have serious significance. However, if they are alone too much, they may run out of topics of conversation unless they have many wholesome interests in common. Consequently, they may be tempted to turn to this subject, which is definitely tied up with their emotions.

There is great danger in encouraging the discussion of sex matters among young people. Too often the discussion may change from the scientific level to the personal. Since human emotions are strong, it may be difficult for the adolescents to avoid carrying over a discussion of the subject into active expression of sex behavior. The emotions are treacherous. It is almost impossible to keep any consideration of them on an objective and purely intellectual plane. Especially is this true concerning emotions arising out of sex urges. Usually it is better, therefore, to confine such topics to the classroom for scientific discussion until the two young persons become engaged. During that period these considerations become of vital and immediate importance to them.

## Detection of Sincere Affection

Love, or the attitude of affection, is something that is conveyed by actions rather than by words. When deep affection for another is felt, strong verbal or written expressions of this affection are not usually too important, although they are helpful. In an individual's behavior there is evidence of the love that is unmistakable.

A girl may be stirred emotionally by a boy's well-turned love phrases. A boy may "fall for" a girl's expressed attitude of "How wonderful you are!" Too often a less articulate but much more sincere young person is considered dull or uninteresting, since he does not seem to flatter one's ego. Young people should remember that fluency in amorous speech is usually the result of much practice and may, as a consequence, be lacking in sincerity. Consideration for one's interest and desires, understanding of one's personal problems, and sacrifices of personal desires for the loved one speak much more loudly than words.

Actually, a boy or girl in his teens should not be too greatly concerned about the depth of another's "love" for him. Young people should learn to live together and to work and play together without becoming too deeply involved in love affairs. Mothers need to watch their own attitudes in the matter of their daughter's relations with boys. Since a mother usually looks forward to a desirable marriage for her daughter, she may regard these teen-age boy-and-girl friendships too seriously, thereby encouraging the girl to view each current boy as a possible mate.

Sometimes, however, parents are tempted to be a little too casual about their adolescent children's social activities. The lack of restraining parental influence may play havoc with immature sex-stimulated urges, resulting in embarrassing or tragic consequences.

## Significance of Puppy Love

As the emotional life of a boy or girl develops through adolescence, he experiences an increasing interest in the opposite sex and in the love life. Stimulated by reading romantic novels, by viewing love stories on the screen, and by observing the love activities of his older associates, he is encouraged to experience these emotions for himself. He wants to love. Who shall be the object of his love is not especially important. A famous screen star, a sports leader, a seatmate at school, or a teacher or supervisor may become the object of the adolescent's secret or expressed adoration.

Any attention given him by the loved one is interpreted as an indication of a similar attitude toward him. The young person is in love with love itself and, because of his emotionalized state, is unable to evaluate correctly his own behavior or the behavior of the other person. Flirtations are engaged in as a kind of release of the emotions within him. If the flirtatious behavior is responded to either seriously or as a game, the young person may become so stirred that he loses intelligent control of himself and, as a result, may suffer great unhappiness or disappointment.

Girls are much more likely to be serious in their first love experiences than boys, since the latter know that during adolescence they are much too young to become serious about any one girl. A teen-age girl, for example, may become emotionally involved with a married man, especially if he is not living with his wife. No matter what his own marital situation may be, a decent and honorable man will not attempt to win the affection of a young girl. Any other kind of man is not worthy of a girl's attention.

A girl who has been guided toward an appreciation of moral ideals, and who has achieved a respect and fellow feeling for members of her own sex, could not engage in promiscuous relations with another woman's husband. A girl of this type would hold the marriage relation sacred. Any beginnings of an emotional regard on the part of a girl for a married man or for a man much older than herself should be diverted toward interest in wholesome young men who are free to marry and who are nearer her own age and interest level.

## Attitudes toward Dating Procedures

Correct attitude toward invitations has to do with manners rather than with psychological factors of boy-girl relations. However, uncertainty about how one should extend and accept or refuse an invitation may cause a young person some emotional disturbance. As is true in all matters dealing with courtesy in our relations with others, guidance is needed here so that young people may approach this phase of their social relations with confidence.

Parental example is the most potent teaching technique. If adults are motivated by ideals of consideration for others when they extend or accept or refuse invitations, young people will be guided by this same principle. Formal invitations are very little used nowadays by young people. A telephone call, a short note, or an invitation by word of mouth is the accepted procedure.

A boy may be awkward or embarrassed as he extends his first invitation to a girl. His shyness may cause him to be almost too casual about it. A sensible girl can usually detect the boy's underlying sincerity or lack of sincerity. Her acceptance or refusal of the invitation should be influenced by her own attitude toward the boy, her own program of activities, or her interest in the activity to which she is being invited. In all cases, the girl's response to the invitation should be given promptly and courteously, with an indication that she appreciates being invited.

If a girl refuses a boy's invitation, the latter is justified in inviting another girl; but he should not develop the habit of going the rounds and asking them all until he finds one who will accept. In the first place, a boy should be warned by too many refusals on the part of his girl acquaintances that there is something wrong with him. It may be his grooming, the choice of amusement to which he is inviting the girl, or his behavior toward a girl who does accept. Moreover, no girl likes to feel that she is just one of any number of girls who would serve as well as she for a companion. A girl wishes to feel that the boy has a special interest in her, and that she can be proud of him when she is with him.

In the same way, a girl should not be a "hound" for dates. She should not be so eager to engage in social activities that she will accept any invitations that come to her. This attitude does not point the way toward popularity. For a girl to have a date every night may be enviable, but a boy too wants to feel that he is someone special, not just any boy who can give a girl a good time.

## Problem of Accepting or Refusing an Invitation

A girl sometimes hesitates to refuse an invitation, even though she would prefer not to accept it, lest she lose the friendship of the boy. This is especially true if she is forced to refuse two invitations in succession. Probably, if her reasons for the refusal are legitimate, she can convince the boy of her sincerity. A friendship lost because of supersensitivity on the part of the boy under such circumstances need cause a girl no regret.

Once the invitation is extended and accepted, neither the boy nor the girl should allow any other more interesting invitation or activity to interfere with the keeping of the engagement. The "date" should be kept punctually unless either person has to withdraw because of serious illness or some other mishap.

A girl may refuse to accept a boy as her partner for a particular dance, but she may not dance with any other boy during that dance number. The same rule extends to participation in any group activity. With the consent of her parents, a girl may invite a boy to attend a party given at her home, but she should not use this method to take him away from another girl in whom he seems to be interested or to force herself upon him if he previously has given evidence of lack of interest in her.

Parental influence in such matters as invitations extended and accepted or refused is much greater than may be thought. Young people are not always free in their choice of the other young people with whom they would like to associate. There are many limiting factors—parental attitude, nationality, religion, tallness in girls and shortness in boys, financial ability to entertain as one would like to do, or to dress as one feels that he should. In general, young people who enjoy simple pleasures experience no difficulty in finding things to do together, especially if parents are willing to cooperate.

## Questions and Problems for Discussion

1. To what extent do you now associate with your former high school friends? Explain differences in attitude, if any, toward them.
2. What considerations affect your selection of friends today that were less significant during your earlier teen-age years?
3. What social adjustments are experienced by a new member as he is admitted to an organization or club?
4. Show how the socializing process can function, with benefit to all concerned, at the time of new admissions into high school. Into college.
5. Present differences between the play and recreational activities of 12-year-old girls and 16-year-old girls. Between 12-year-old boys and 16-year-old boys.
6. *Special Exercises:*
   a. Describe an experience that you have had in attempting to join an organized group, all the members of which were strangers to you.
   b. Describe an unhappy social experience you have had. Indicate what you did to meet the situation.
   c. Observe the behavior displayed by an adolescent as he strives for attention or for leadership in an informal group setting such as a meeting of a school club, a community agency, a fraternity, or another formal or informal group setting. Report your observations.

## Selected References

Chandler, B. J., et al.: *Education in Urban Society,* Dodd, Mead & Company, Inc., New York, 1962.

Coleman, J. S.: *The Adolescent: The Social Life of the Teenager and Its Impact on Education,* The Free Press of Glencoe, New York, 1961.

Conant, J. B.: *Slums and Suburbs: A Commentary on Schools in the Metropolitan Area,* McGraw-Hill Book Company, New York, 1961.

Cook, L., and E. Cook: *School Problems in Human Relations,* McGraw-Hill Book Company, New York, 1957.

Doll, E. A.: *The Measurement of Social Competence,* Educational Test Bureau, The University of Minnesota Press, Minneapolis, 1953.

Havighurst, R. J., et al.: *Growing up in River City*, John Wiley & Sons, Inc., New York, 1962.

Herriott, R. E.: "Some Social Determinants of Educational Aspiration," *Harvard Educational Review*, vol. 33, pp. 157–177, Spring, 1963.

Jennings, Helen H.: *Leadership and Isolation*, David McKay Company, Inc., New York, 1950.

Johnstone, J. W. C., and K. Johasson: *The Social Life of the Teenager and Its Impact on Education*, The Free Press of Glencoe, New York, 1962.

Miles, M. B.: *Learning to Work in Groups*, Bureau of Publications, Columbia University, New York, 1959.

Riessman, F.: *The Culturally Deprived Child and His Education*, Harper & Row, Publishers, Incorporated, New York, 1962.

# Appendix

## Recommended Films

Many of the topics in this book lend themselves well to supplementation by audio-visual learning aids. In general, the films listed here apply to specific areas of adolescence. A few, however, apply equally well to other areas of interest. Hence it is recommended that the films be previewed by the instructor before class showing in order that attention may be directed to the significant phases of life adjustment that are presented in them. All the films included in the list are 16-millimeter.

The addresses of producers and distributors are appended to the film list.

## Part One. Adolescent Experiences

*Chapter 1. Significance of Adolescence*

*Age of Turmoil* (McGraw-Hill, 20 min). Presents incisive and frequently amusing sketches of half a dozen boys and girls in their early teens.

*Farewell to Childhood* (IFB, 20 min). Concerns a normal teen-ager who is full of the swift emotions typical of adolescents.

*Meaning of Adolescence* (McGraw-Hill, 16 min). Interprets adolescent development in twentieth-century culture.

*Meeting the Needs of Adolescents* (McGraw-Hill, 19 min). Emphasizes the experiences of a brother and sister, aged 14 and 17 respectively, that make for satisfactory growth.

*Chapter 2. Biological and Cultural Heritage*

*Heredity and Environment* (Coronet, 11 min). Presents a sound understanding of the influences that shape our lives.

*Heredity and Prenatal Development* (McGraw-Hill, 21 min). Step-by-step picturization of growth, subdivision, and union of male and female sex cells.

*Human Reproduction* (McGraw-Hill, 20 min). Presents factual information concerning human reproduction and the process of normal human birth.

*Chapter 3. Approaches to the Study of Adolescence*

*Learning to Understand Children. Part I: A Diagnostic Approach* (McGraw-Hill, 21 min). Presents in detail the diagnostic techniques used by a teacher to discover the causes of the social maladjustment of Ada Adams, one of her pupils.

*Learning to Understand Children. Part II: A Remedial Program* (McGraw-Hill, 23 min). Gives a continuation of the story of Ada Adams; describes the remedial techniques employed by the teacher to assist Ada in her adjustment.

*Using Analytical Tools* (McGraw-Hill, 14 min). Portrays the analytical tools for counseling as a school counselor prepares for an interview with a student.

# Part Two. Adolescent Development

*Chapter 4. Physical and Physiological Growth*

*Human Growth* (Brown, 19 min). Concerns human growth and development from mating through pregnancy and birth, and through childhood and adolescence to adulthood.

*Physical Aspects of Puberty* (McGraw-Hill, 19 min). Gives greater practical meaning to the age of puberty.

*Chapter 5. Maturing Mental Abilities*

*Controlling Behavior through Reinforcement* (McGraw-Hill, 16 min). Shows, through the use of pigeons, that by reinforcing an organism on different schedules, both the speed and the distribution of work can be controlled within a given time.

*Development of Individual Differences* (McGraw-Hill, 13 min). Illustrates through a comparison of two brothers and another family how family resemblances in behavior are handed on from generation to generation.

*Learning Discrimination and Skills* (McGraw Hill, 10 min). Demonstrates that the learning of a skill involves discrimination between stimuli and application of this discrimination in the making of selected responses.

*Perception* (McGraw-Hill, 17 min). Presents the theory that human perception is not merely a sensing of stimuli, but a set of extremely elaborate processes through which individuals organize sensory impressions.

*Chapter 6. Changing Emotional Patterns*

*Act Your Age* (Coronet, 13 min). Shows how a principal deals with a high school boy who has carved his name on a desk.

*Children's Emotions* (McGraw-Hill, 22 min). The major emotions of childhood—fear, anger, jealousy, curiosity, and joy—are described, and methods of dealing with them are explained.

*Control Your Emotions* (Coronet, 13 min). Interprets emotional control in varying situations.

*Emotional Health* (McGraw-Hill, 20 min). Shows college students that emotional upsets are common, and demonstrates the importance of professional counseling and some basic techniques of psychiatric treatment.

*Endocrine Glands—How They Affect You* (McGraw-Hill, 15 min). Shows the location and function of each endocrine gland.

*Overcoming Fear* (Coronet, 13 min). Shows the value of courage in meeting problems in everyday living.

*Overcoming Worry* (Coronet, 11 min). Demonstrates that worry can be overcome.

*Self-conscious Guy* (Coronet, 11 min). Reveals how a self-conscious boy developed poise and self-assurance.

*Shy Guy* (Coronet, 13 min). Demonstrates the value of friendliness as a means of improving a shy adolescent's social adjustment.

*Shyness* (CanNFB, 23 min). Concerns abnormal shyness in children and how it can be dealt with.

*Snap Out of It* (Coronet, 13 min). Suggests how emotional balance can be developed if a high school boy works hard for an A and gets only a B.

*The Other Fellow's Feelings* (YAF, 8 min). Concerns the problem of teasing or ridicule that is prolonged to the point where it really hurts.

*Toward Emotional Maturity* (McGraw-Hill, 11 min). Concerns ways in which Sally, an 18-year-old student, makes decisions in troublesome situations.

*Understanding Your Emotions* (Coronet, 13 min). Reveals that emotions have many effects on the body, on both voluntary and involuntary behavior.

Chapter 7. *Personal and Social Aspects of Personality Development*

*Developing Character* (Coronet, 11 min). Indicates the significance of good character and how it can be achieved.

*Developing Self-reliance* (Coronet, 11 min). Shows how dependence grows and how necessary self-reliance is to all successful endeavor.

*Developing Responsibility* (Coronet, 11 min). Teaches lessons in responsibility through the story of a boy and a dog.

*Individual Differences* (McGraw-Hill, 23 min). Concerns two approaches used by a teacher in meeting the problems of pupils.

*Improve Your Personality* (Coronet, 11 min). Gives a frank discussion of personality to help students understand themselves better.

*Social Development* (CF, 26 min). Offers an analysis of social behavior at different age levels and the reasons underlying the changes in behavior patterns.

*The Teens* (McGraw-Hill, 26 min). Shows the normal behavior of three teen-agers in the everyday life of an urban middle-class family.

# Part Three. Adolescent Behavior Motivations

Chapter 8. *Importance of Interests and Attitudes*

*Attitudes and Health* (Coronet, 11 min). Emphasizes how wrong attitudes prevent the individual from doing his best.

*How to Develop Interest* (Coronet, 11 min). Concerns the encouragement of students to develop new interests in their studies and community activities.

*Picture in Your Mind* (IFF, 16 min). Shows causes of prejudice, accompanied by a plea for better understanding on the part of the viewer of his own attitudes toward people different from himself.

*Prejudice* (RFA, 60 min). Promotes personal examination of prejudices and stimulates discussion of intercultural relations.

*Who's Right* (McGraw-Hill, 18 min). Concerns a quarrel between two people who have been married for a short time.

Chapter 9. *Sex Behavior of Adolescents*

*Are You Ready for Marriage* (Coronet, 16 min). A marriage counselor presents practical criteria for engagement and marriage adjustments.

*Choosing Your Marriage Partner* (Coronet, 13 min). A counselor helps a boy to decide which of two girls he should marry.

*Courtship to Courthouse* (McGraw-Hill, 12 min). Concerns the problem of an increasing divorce rate.

*Going Steady* (Coronet, 11 min). Deals with problems met by teen-agers when they consider going steady.

*Marriage Is a Partnership* (Coronet, 16 min). Attempts to establish a positive approach to the realities of marriage.

*Marriage Series* (McGraw-Hill)

*Choosing for Happiness* (14 min). Presents the problems faced by the girl in the matter of choosing a mate.

*It Takes All Kinds* (20 min). Depicts various young people in similar tense situations involving mate selection.

*Marriage Today* (22 min). Portrays the efforts of two couples to achieve marital adjustment in spite of anticipated personality conflicts.

*This Charming Couple* (19 min). Places emphasis upon the fallacy of the belief that "romantic love" is the sole or primary basis for marital success.

*Who's Boss* (16 min). Shows the struggle of two young people (both of whom were successful in their business careers) to adjust to their marriage.

*In Time of Trouble* (14 min). Presents the story of a couple whose happy marriage is jeopardized by a lack of understanding of each other's needs. The advisability of seeking outside help is stressed.

*Jealousy* (16 min). Stresses the importance of continuous self-appraisal, and indicates that a basic change of attitude is often necessary to combat jealousy.

*Meaning of Engagement* (Coronet, 13 min). Concerns the importance of the engagement period in preparation for a successful marriage.

*Social-Sex Attitudes in Adolescence* (McGraw-Hill, 22 min). Illustrates the various experiences through which adolescents pass, such as crushes, steady dating, and final mate selection.

*Chapter 11. Conflicts and Behavior Disorders*

*Activity for Schizophrenia* (Castle, 23 min). Presents the modern concepts of activity as applied to the distinctive needs of schizophrenic patients.

*Breakdown* (McGraw-Hill, 40 min). Presents the treatment given to a young woman who developed a schizoid personality and had a breakdown.

*Feeling of Hostility* (IFB, 37 min). Analyzes the causes of a young woman's inner maladjustments, and her final readjustment through her occupational activities.

*Feelings of Depression* (McGraw-Hill, 30 min). Concerns the factors that precipitated a businessman's depression, tracing the important influences from childhood.

*Schizophrenia: Catatonic Type* (McGraw-Hill, 12 min). Shows the characteristics of stuporous catatonia.

*Schizophrenia: Hebephrenic Type* (McGraw-Hill, 13 min). Shows the chief manifestations of hebephrenic schizophrenia.

*Schizophrenia: Simple Type Deteriorated* (McGraw-Hill, 11 min). Shows characteristics of a chronic simple schizophrenia.

*Over-Dependency* (McGraw-Hill, 32 min). Shows how Jim, a young commercial artist, uses illness as an escape from responsibility.

*Chapter* 12. *Behavior Delinquencies*

*A Criminal Is Born* (TFC, 21 min). Shows the case history of three boys who develop criminal tendencies due to inadequate home life.

*Boy in Court* (NatPro, 12 min). Presents in detail the procedures used by the juvenile court in dealing with a delinquent boy.

*Children of the City* (IFB, 30 min). An English film showing how a Scottish town handles the adolescent problem.

*Children on Trial* (IFB, 62 min). Presents in detail the experiences in approved schools of three juvenile delinquents who finally make a satisfactory adjustment.

*Crime Lab* (RKO-Pathé, 14 min). Surveys the techniques in modern crime detection.

*New Prisons—New Men* (McGraw-Hill, 11 min). Shows the treatment of convicts at Southern Michigan State Prison.

*Who's Delinquent?* (McGraw-Hill, 16 min). Tells how a newspaper digs into the causes of local juvenile delinquency, and the program that comes out of it.

*The Quiet One* (Athena, 67 min). Presents the experiences of a mentally disturbed boy, first in a disrupted home and later in a school for delinquent boys where he is rehabilitated.

*The Story of a Teen-Age Drug Addict* (McGraw-Hill, 22 min). Presents the story of a teen-age drug addict, with the purpose of alerting community groups to the dangers of drug addition among adolescents.

*Three Steps to Start* (McGraw-Hill, 26 min). Shows how the resources of an entire town were enlisted to help meet the problem of delinquency.

*Chapter* 13. *Significant Life Values*

*High Wall* (McGraw-Hill, 32 min). Portrays intergroup conflict between two groups of teen-age boys, and traces the reasons for the conflict to parental attitudes.

*How Honest Are You?* (Coronet, 13 min). Gives the viewer an opportunity to draw certain conclusions concerning his own honesty.

*How to Say No (Moral Maturity)* (Coronet, 11 min). Concerns how to say "no" and keep your friends.

*Make Your Own Decisions* (Coronet, 11 min). Presents a series of five questions that illustrate the alternatives that exist in every situation, and shows how each contributes to making a self-reliant and mature individual. It portrays the fact that the ability to make decisions is prerequisite to mature, successful living.

*Right or Wrong* (Coronet, 11 min). Presents the making of moral decisions in connection with the breaking of a warehouse window by a gang of high school boys.

*Teaching Teen Agers about Alcohol* (McGraw-Hill, 16 min). Presents one teacher's successful approach to a better understanding of the problems of teaching students about alcohol.

*Understanding Your Ideals* (Coronet, 13 min). Emphasizes the importance of ideals to well-being and happiness.

# Part Four. Adolescent Adjustments

*Chapter 14. Home Adjustment of Adolescents*

*Family Circles* (CanNFB, 31 min). Shows the extension of the boundaries of the family circle into other agencies of the community.

*Family Life* (Coronet, 11 min). Creates an awareness of the happiness to be gained from a well-managed home.

*Family Teamwork* (Frith, 18 min). Gives a portrayal of family cooperation and adjustment in a home of high middle-class socioeconomic status.

*Friendship Begins at Home* (Coronet, 16 min). States as vividly and emphatically as possible the value of friendships in the home.

*You and Your Parents* (Coronet, 14 min). Describes the process of growing away from parents as a natural and normal one.

*Discipline During Adolescence* (McGraw-Hill, 16 min). Illustrates the results of too little and too much parental control in a typical family.

*Chapter 15. School Adjustment of Adolescents*

*College: Your Challenge* (Coronet, 11 min). Presents the benefits of college, both academic and nonacademic.

*High School: Your Challenge* (Coronet, 14 min). Emphasizes the importance of a good high school education and the advantages of taking part in extracurricular activities.

*Making the Most of School* (Coronet, 11 min). Reveals the value of school beyond day-by-day assignments.

*Problem of Pupil Adjustment. Part I. The Dropout: A Case Study* (McGraw-Hill, 20 min). The story of Martin, who quit high school after his freshman year. Suggests that a life adjustment program in the school may help him and other dropouts.

*Problem of Pupil Adjustment. Part II. The Stay-in: A School Study* (McGraw-Hill, 19 min). Shows what can be done to meet the dropout problem.

*School Spirit and Sportsmanship* (Coronet, 11 min). Stresses the idea that actions of individuals reflect upon the spirit of the entire school.

*Chapter 16. Vocational Adjustment of Adolescents*

*Aptitudes and Occupations* (Coronet, 16 min). Helps the student understand aptitudes and how to apply knowledge of them toward an intelligent choice of vocation.

*Better Use of Leisure Time* (Coronet, 11 min). Serves as a guide to developing an attitude toward and constructing a program of leisure-time activities.

*Careers for Girls* (MOT, 18 min). Presents types of work open to women, with emphasis on those that are related to girls' everyday interests.

*Choosing Your Occupation* (Coronet, 11 min). Includes self-appraisal, occupational possibilities, preparation requirements, and guidance facilities needed.

*Employment Interview* (McGraw-Hill, 11 min). Shows what can happen when a well-planned interviewing system is conducted by competent personnel officials.

*How Much Cooperation* (McGraw-Hill, 8 min). Shows what can happen when a supervisor asks special cooperation and overtime work of his staff.

*How to Investigate Vocations* (Coronet, 11 min). Motivates students to investigate vocations and determine the kind of work for which they are best suited.

*How to Keep a Job* (Coronet, 11 min). Shows the personality bases conducive to occupational success.

*Personal Qualities for Job Success* (Coronet, 11 min). Emphasizes the value of initiative, good personal appearance, businesslike work habits, and the ability to get along with others.

*Personality Conflict* (McGraw-Hill, 7 min). Shows what happens when two conflicting personalities must work together.

*The Bright Young Newcomer* (McGraw-Hill, 8 min). Shows the need for the proper channeling of grievances.

*Chapter 17. Social Adjustment of Adolescents*

*Alice Adams, Money Sequence* (NYU, 15 min). Concerns the effect on a girl of being poorer than her friends.

*Date Etiquette* (Coronet, 11 min). Shows how to be socially comfortable during the various steps in dating.

*Dating: Do's and Don't's* (Coronet, 13 min). Raises important questions regarding dating and suggests partial answers as guides for discussion.

*Feeling Left Out* (Coronet, 14 min). Concerns a potential isolate and how he developed social maturity.

*Developing Friendships* (Coronet, 11 min). Explores the differences in individual capacities for friendliness, and helps young people understand the meaning of friendship.

*Social Courtesy* (Coronet, 11 min). Shows that getting along in social groups requires a natural, easy form of behavior that makes use of courtesy.

*What to Do on a Date* (Coronet, 11 min). Illustrates the wide range of diversions available to high school students who want to make dating an entertaining, enjoyable, and constructive social custom.

*Social Acceptability* (McGraw-Hill, 20 min). Illustrates, through the story of a high school girl, the correlation between social acceptability and the successful adjustment and happiness of the average adolescent.

*Social Development* (McGraw-Hill, 16 min). Shows how behavior patterns change as a child grows.

# Directory of Sources

Anti-Def—Anti-Defamation League of B'nai B'rith (Films distributed by McGraw-Hill.)

Athena—Athena Films, Inc., 165 W. 46th St., New York 19.

Brown—E. C. Brown Trust, 220 S.W. Alder St., Portland 4, Oreg.

CanNFB—National Film Board of Canada. (Films distributed by McGraw-Hill.)

Castle—United World-Films, 1445 Park Ave., New York 29.

CF—Crawley Films. (Films distributed by McGraw-Hill.)

Coronet—Coronet Instructional Films, 65 E. South Water St., Chicago 1.

Frith—Frith Films, 840 Seward St., Hollywood 38, Calif.

IFB—International Film Bureau, Suite 1500, 6 N. Michigan Ave., Chicago 2.

IFF—International Film Foundation, Inc., 1600 Broadway, New York 19.

Io—State University of Iowa, Bureau of Audio-Visual Instruction, Extension Division, Iowa City, Iowa.

McGraw-Hill—McGraw-Hill Book Company, Text-Film Department, 330 W. 42d St., New York 36.

MOT—March of Time Films, 369 Lexington Ave., New York 17.

NatPro—National Probation and Parole Association, 1790 Broadway, New York 19.

NYU—New York University Film Library, 26 Washington Pl., New York 3.

RFA—Religious Film Association, Inc., 45 Astor Pl., New York 3.

RKO-Pathé. (Films distributed by McGraw-Hill.)

TFC—Teaching Film Custodians, Inc., 25 W. 43d St., New York 36.

YAF—Young America Films, Inc., 18 E. 41st St., New York 19.

# Name Index

# Subject Index